The Dramatized
Old Testament

The Dramatized
Old Testament

Volume 1: Genesis to Esther

New International Version

Edited by Michael Perry

Baker Books

A Division of Baker Book House Co
Grand Rapids, Michigan 49516

Library of Congress Cataloging-in-Publication Data

Bible. O.T. English. New International. 1994.
    The dramatized Old Testament: New International Version/Edited by Michael Perry.
        p. cm.
    Includes indexes.
    ISBN 0-8010-7136-4 (v. 1)
    1. Bible. O.T.—Liturgical use. I. Perry, Michael, 1942– II. Title.
BS895.N37   1993
221.5'208—dc 20   94-5701

Printed in the United States of America

To Helen and Simon
for whom may the Book live
as it has for me.

Contents

verse 27—"With boughs in hand, join in the festal procession / up to the horns of the altar"—which, in some traditions, we blindly *sing* as though the psalm were homogeneous. It does not take much imagination to see that what we are dealing with is the script of a drama or the libretto of an opera, set in the context of a magnificent act of worship. Here the intending (and noble?) worshiper approaches the door of the temple and asks to enter to give thanks for God's deliverance. The ministers/priests tell him righteousness is a prerequisite of an approach to God. And the drama progressed from there. Permeating the drama are the resonant choruses of the Hebrew liturgy:

Leader	Let Israel say:
All	His love endures forever.
Leader	Let the house of Aaron say:
All	His love endures forever.
Leader	Let those who fear the LORD say:
All	His love endures forever!

Finally, the worshiper is admitted ("Blessed is he who comes in the name of the Lord"), and the celebration begins ("With boughs in hand . . ."). As long as we consider the Old Testament dour and prosaic, its exciting suggestions for our own worship practice will be missed.

Barriers Broken

Much of my life's work has been in the interests of a clearer presentation of the facts of the faith in worship. Centrally within this context, *The Dramatized Old Testament* brings the text of Scripture to life. Using *The Dramatized Old Testament* means involving people in recalling and recounting their salvation history. The experience is memorable and challenging.

Those who listen to *The Dramatized Old Testament* are drawn into the presentation. As the story moves from voice to voice it is very difficult for attention to wander. Useful in all forms of church worship, *The Dramatized Old Testament* is especially an ideal focus for the "word" aspect of all-age (so-called family) worship. Even young children, who naturally grow restive during a long and uneventful reading, find their interest and imagination caught up in the narrative as the Scriptures are presented in dramatized form.

We confidently commend this book to churches, youth groups, schools, study groups, and all who work in the area of education. It may be that producers and presenters of religious programs for radio and television will also find inspiration here. We happily anticipate that *The Dramatized Old Testament* will enrich our worship by granting us a clearer vision of God and a surer knowledge of the revelation of the eternal purpose for our world in Jesus Christ.

Michael Perry

Preface to NIV

The New International Version is a completely new translation of the Holy Bible made by over a hundred scholars working directly from the best available Hebrew, Aramaic and Greek texts. It had its beginning in 1965 when, after several years of exploratory study by committees from the Christian Reformed Church and the National Association of Evangelicals, a group of scholars met at Palos Heights, Illinois, and concurred in the need for a new translation of the Bible in contemporary English. This group, though not made up of official church representatives, was transdenominational. Its conclusion was endorsed by a large number of leaders from many denominations who met in Chicago in 1966.

Responsibility for the new version was delegated by the Palos Heights group to a self-governing body of fifteen, the Committee on Bible Translation, composed for the most part of biblical scholars from colleges, universities, and seminaries. In 1967 the New York Bible Society (now the International Bible Society) generously undertook the financial sponsorship of the project—a sponsorship that made it possible to enlist the help of many distinguished scholars. The fact that participants from the United States, Great Britain, Canada, Australia and New Zealand worked together gave the project its international scope. That they were from many denominations—including Anglican, Assemblies of God, Baptist, Brethren, Christian Reformed, Church of Christ, Evangelical Free, Lutheran, Mennonite, Methodist, Nazarene, Presbyterian, Wesleyan and other churches—helped to safeguard the translation from sectarian bias.

How it was made helps to give the New International Version its distinctiveness. The translation of each book was assigned to a team of scholars. Next, one of the Intermediate Editorial Committees revised the initial translation, with constant reference to the Hebrew, Aramaic or Greek. Their work then went to one of the General Editorial Committees, which checked it in detail and made another thorough revision. This revision in turn was carefully reviewed by the Committee on Bible Translation, which made further changes and then released the final version for publication. In this way the entire Bible underwent three revisions, during each of which the translation was examined for its faithfulness to the original languages and for its English style.

All this involved many thousands of hours of research and discussion regarding the meaning of the texts and the precise way of putting them into English. It may well be that no other translation has been made by a more thorough process of review and revision from committee to committee than this one.

From the beginning of the project, the Committee on Bible Translation held to certain goals for the New International Version: that it would be an accurate translation and one that would have clarity and literary quality and so prove suitable for public and private reading, teaching, preaching, memorizing and liturgical use. The Committee also sought to preserve some measure of continuity with the long tradition of translating the Scriptures into English.

In working toward these goals, the translators were united in their commitment to the authority and infallibility of the Bible as God's Word in written form. They believe that it contains the divine answer to the deepest needs of humanity, that it sheds unique light on our path in a dark work, and that it sets forth the way to our eternal well-being.

The first concern of the translators has been the accuracy of the translation and its fidelity to the thought of the biblical writers. They have weighed the significance of the lexical and grammatical details of the Hebrew, Aramaic and Greek texts. At the same time, they have striven for more than a word-for-word translation. Because thought patterns and syntax differ from language to language, faithful communication of the meaning of the writers of the Bible demands frequent modifications in sentence structure and constant regard for the contextual meanings of words.

A sensitive feeling for style does not always accompany scholarship. Accordingly the Committee on Bible Translation submitted the developing version to a number of stylistic consultants. Two of them read every book of both the Old and New Testaments twice—once before and once after the last major revision—and made invaluable suggestions. Samples of the translation were tested for clarity and ease of reading by various kinds of people—young and old, highly educated and less well educated, ministers and laymen.

Concern for clear and natural English—that the New International Version should be idiomatic but not idiosyncratic, contemporary but not dated—motivated the translators and consultants. At the same time, they tried to reflect the differing styles of the biblical writers. In view of the international use of English, the translators sought to avoid obvious Americanisms on the one hand and obvious Anglicisms on the other. A British edition reflects the comparatively few differences of significant idiom and of spelling.

As for the traditional pronouns "thou," "thee" and "thine" in reference to the Deity, the translators judged that to use these archaisms (along with the verb forms such as "doest," "wouldest" and "hadst") would violate accuracy in translation. Neither Hebrew, Aramaic nor Greek uses special pronouns for the persons of the Godhead. A present-day translation is not enhanced by forms that in the time of the King James Version were used in everyday speech, whether referring to God or man.

For the Old Testament the standard Hebrew text, the Masoretic Text as published in the latest editions of *Biblia Hebraica,* was used throughout. The Dead Sea Scrolls contain material bearing on an earlier stage of the Hebrew text. They were consulted, as were the Samaritan Pentateuch and the ancient scribal traditions relating to textual changes. Sometimes a variant Hebrew reading in the margin of the Masoretic Text was followed instead of the text itself. Such instances, being variants within the Masoretic tradition, are not specified by footnotes. In rare cases, words in the consonantal text were divided differently from the way they appear in the Masoretic Text. Footnotes indicate this. The translators also consulted the more important early versions—the Septuagint; Aquila, Symmachus and Theodotion; the Vulgate; the Syriac Peshitta; the Targums; and for the Psalms the *Juxta Hebraica* of Jerome. Readings from these versions were occasionally followed where the Masoretic Text seemed doubtful and where accepted principles of textual criticism showed that one or more of these textual witnesses appeared to provide the correct reading. Such instances are footnoted. Sometimes vowel letters and vowel signs did not, in the judgment of the translators, represent the correct vowels for the original consonantal text. Accordingly some words were read with a different set of vowels. These instances are usually not indicated by footnotes.

The Greek text used in translating the New Testament was an eclectic one. No other piece of ancient literature has such an abundance of manuscript witnesses as does the New Testament. Where existing manuscripts differ, the translators made their choice of readings according to accepted principles of New Testament textual criticism. Footnotes call attention to places where there was uncertainty about what the original text was. The best current printed texts of the Greek New Testament were used.

There is a sense in which the work of translation is never wholly finished. This applies to all great literature and uniquely so to the Bible. In 1973 the New Testament in the New International Version was published. Since then, suggestions for corrections and revisions have been received from various sources. The Committee on Bible Translation carefully considered the suggestions and adopted a number of them. These were incorporated in the first printing of the entire Bible in 1978. Additional revisions were made by the Committee on Bible Translation in 1983 and appear in printings after that date.

As in other ancient documents, the precise meaning of the biblical texts is sometimes uncertain. This is more often the case with the Hebrew and Aramaic texts than with the Greek text. Although archaeological and linguistic discoveries in this century aid in understanding difficult passages, some uncertainties remain. The more significant of these have been called to the reader's attention in the footnotes.

In regard to the divine name *YHWH*, commonly referred to as the *Tetragrammaton,* the translators adopted the device used in most English versions of rendering that name as "LORD" in capital letters to distinguish it from Adonai, another Hebrew word rendered "Lord," for which small letters are used. Wherever the two names stand together in the Old Testament as a compound name of God, they are rendered "Sovereign LORD."

Because for most readers today the phrases "the Lord of hosts" and "God of hosts" have little meaning, this version renders them "the Lord Almighty" and "God Almighty." These renderings convey the sense of the Hebrew, namely, "he who is sovereign over all the 'hosts' (powers) in heaven and on earth, especially over the 'hosts' (armies) of Israel." For readers unacquainted with Hebrew this does not make clear the distinction between Sabaoth ("hosts" or Almighty") and Shaddai (which can also be translated "Almighty"), but the latter occurs infrequently and is always footnoted. When Adonai and YHWH Sabaoth occur together, they are rendered "the Lord, the Lord Almighty."

As for other proper nouns, the familiar spellings of the King James Version are generally retained. Names traditionally spelled with "ch," except where it is final, are usually spelled in this translation with "k" or "c," since the biblical languages do not have the sound that "ch" frequently indicates in English—for example, in *chant*. For well-known names such as Zechariah, however, the traditional spelling has been retained. Variation in the spelling of names in the original languages has usually not been indicated. Where a person or place has two or more different names in the Hebrew, Aramaic or Greek texts, the more familiar one has generally been used, with footnotes where needed.

To achieve clarity the translators sometimes supplied words not in the original texts but required by the context. If there was uncertainty about such materiel, it is enclosed in brackets. Also for the sake of clarity or style, nouns, including some proper nouns, are sometimes substituted for pronouns, and vice versa. And though the Hebrew writers often shifted back and forth between first, second and third personal pronouns without change of antecedent, this translation often makes them uniform, in accordance with English style and without the use of footnotes.

Poetical passages are printed as poetry, that is, with indentation of lines and with separate stanzas. These are generally designed to reflect the structure of Hebrew poetry. This poetry is normally characterized by parallelism in balanced lines. Most of the poetry in the Bible is in the Old Testament, and scholars differ regarding the scansion of Hebrew lines. The translators determined the stanza divisions for the most part by analysis of the subject matter. The stanzas therefore serve as poetic paragraphs.

As an aid to the reader, italicized sectional headings are inserted in most of the books. They are not to be regarded as part of the NIV text, are not for oral reading, and are not intended to dictate the interpretation of the sections they head.

The footnotes in this version are of several kinds, most of which need no explanation. Those giving alternative translations begin with "Or" and generally introduce the alternative with the last word preceding it in the text, except when it is a single-word alternative; in poetry quoted in a footnote a slant mark indicates a line division. Footnotes introduced by "Or" do not have uniform significance. In some cases two possible translations were considered to have about equal validity. In other cases, though the translators were convinced that the translation in the text was correct, they judged that another interpretation was possible and of sufficient importance to be represented in a footnote.

In the New Testament, footnotes that refer to uncertainty regarding the original text are introduced by "Some manuscripts" or similar expressions. In the Old Testament, evidence for the reading chosen is given first and evidence for the alternative is added after a semicolon (for example: Septuagint; Hebrew *father*). In such notes the term "Hebrew" refers to the Masoretic Text.

It should be noted that minerals, flora and fauna, architectural details, articles of clothing and jewelry, musical instruments, and other articles cannot always be identified with precision. Also measures of capacity in the biblical period are particularly uncertain (see the table of weights and measures following the text).

Like all translations of the Bible, made as they are by imperfect man, this one undoubtedly falls short of its goals. Yet we are grateful to God for the extent to which he has enabled us to realize these goals and for the strength he has given us and our colleagues to complete our task. We offer this version of the Bible to him in whose name and for whose glory it has been made. We pray that it will lead many into a better understanding of the Holy Scriptures and a fuller knowledge of Jesus Christ the incarnate Word, of whom the Scriptures so faithfully testify.

The Committee on Bible Translation

June 1978
(Revised August 1983)

Names of the translators and editors may be secured
from the International Bible Society,
translation sponsors of the New International Version,
P.O. Box 62970, Colorado Springs, Colorado 80962-2970

Acknowledgments

As editor of *The Dramatized Old Testament* I gladly acknowledge the skills of the teams of experts who prepared the outstanding and now celebrated New International Version of the Bible. I have appreciated the advice of the Reverend Kathleen Bowe upon the translation of my Liturgical Psalms, of the Reverend Robert Backhouse on all aspects of dramatization and typesetting and of Miss Janet Henderson on matters of copyright. My thanks go to my typist, Ann, my secretary, Bunty, and my daughter, Helen, for their conscientious work on copy, proofs, and indexes. I am grateful to church leaders and other authorities for their kind commendations and encouragement. I am indebted to the friendly staff at Baker Book House. I know that all who have cooperated in its production will find great satisfaction in the enthusiasm with which I am confident *The Dramatized Old Testament* will be received.

M.A.P.

Using *The Dramatized Old Testament*

Welcome to a new and powerful resource! If you are a minister, teacher, or leader, you will want to know how you can use this book to the greatest effect.

Realism

In designing *The Dramatized Old Testament* we have tried to be realistic about the pressure upon ministers, teachers, and leaders: on the whole they require a book that can be used spontaneously and without great forethought, preparation, or rehearsal. We suggest that each organization using *The Dramatized Old Testament* eventually needs five copies because, on average, there are five characters to a script. Then, at a moment's notice, willing readers can be given a copy each and invited to fill a character part. All characters are listed at the foot of each reading.

Superfluous "he said"s and the like are already excised from the text (with the permission of the copyright holders). While appropriate in prose, they are intrusive—sometimes even humorous—in drama. Usually in *The Dramatized Old Testament* they are left in at the beginning of the piece, in order to establish the character, and then omitted thereafter. Further phrases that for similar reasons might be thought to make performance stilted are enclosed in bold square brackets: [and]. But such phrases or sentences should not be omitted without considering the particular implications. To omit them may well enliven the drama, but it will require the cast to compensate for the omission. This can either be done visually, by turning to one of the other characters, or aurally, by a change of voice. The best solution will depend on the local circumstances, the initiative of the leader, and the availability of the participants. Therefore, a rule of thumb might be—only when consultation or rehearsal is possible, omit phrases in bold square brackets.

The proprietors of the NIV text have required the insertion of additional square brackets (not bold) to show where explanatory text has been added. Please distinguish between this and the phrases suitable for omission. Also, to aid in effective dramatic reading, words have been italicized for emphasis occasionally that do not appear in italics in the NIV. Please note that, unless they designate foreign words, all italics in the text have been added by us.

Shortening an Episode

Bold square brackets have a different function when they enclose one or more paragraphs: they indicate where the reading may sensibly be shortened. Unless a sermon, service, talk, or discussion requires use of these longer sections, they are best left out in the interests of lively presentation and greater impact upon an audience.

Local Reproduction

Applications for reproduction of material from *The Dramatized Old Testament* in the world outside North America may be addressed to Hope Publishing Company, Carol Stream, Illinois 60188 (phone 708-665-3200, FAX 708-665-2552, WATS 800-323-1049). For further information see the copyright page.

Audibility

Use of *The Dramatized Old Testament* has a positive effect on the attention that a reading is given by a congregation, class, youth group, or study group. It also makes the content of the reading more memorable—not least to those who have participated. Much depends on audibility; so care needs to be taken in larger buildings. In church, or in a school assembly hall, a stage holding a minimum of five people can be used to advantage. Where appropriate, a microphone with a wide field that will pick up all the speakers should be used; or separate microphones might be considered. This sort of preparation will enable the minister/leader to involve people whose voices are less clear and not so strong.

Casting

It is obviously important that a strong voice should be cast for any key character, such as the **Narrator.** In a church service, this part can most usefully be given to the person who would have taken the Scripture reading if it had not been dramatized, thus ensuring that no one feels usurped by what should be a welcome development in worship. It is worth noting that more male than female characters speak in the Bible. However, when using *The Dramatized Old Testament*, a good balance can still be obtained by employing female voices for narration, for the frequent anonymous **Persons**, and in the teaching passages that divide into **Voice 1, Voice 2.** Here it is good to have a contrast between the speakers.

Where **Voices 1–3** or **Persons 1–3** are used, participants should stand together in a group. Where **the Lord** or **God** speaks as a prophetic utterance and not in direct conversation, it is best for the reader to stand apart from the rest—even to be unseen.

Actions

There will be occasions—both formal and informal—when participants can add actions to a presentation from *The Dramatized Old Testament*. Then, prior agreement over what is to be done is a safeguard against unintended humorous accidents! A rehearsal will be necessary unless the actors are very confident and experienced. At the rehearsal it is sensible to have someone watching who is able to assess the drama's impact on the proposed audience, and for the cast to listen and respond to that person's objective criticism. When actions are used in the context of large gatherings, visibility and audibility (especially when the speaker turns away from the audience) are of utmost importance. In seminar and class work, or in small groups, carefully prepared actions will add a startlingly fresh dynamic.

Genesis

The Beginning

Genesis 1:1–2:4

Narrator

In the beginning God created the heavens and the earth. Now the earth was formless and empty, darkness was over the surface of the deep, and the Spirit of God was hovering over the waters. And God said:

God
(voice only) Let there be light.

Narrator

And there was light. God saw that the light was good, and he separated the light from the darkness. God called the light—

God (voice) Day.

Narrator And the darkness he called—

God (voice) Night.

Narrator

And there was evening, and there was morning—the first day. (PAUSE) And God said:

God (voice) Let there be an expanse between the waters to separate water from water.

Narrator

So God made the expanse and separated the water under the expanse from the water above it. And it was so. God called the expanse—

God (voice) Sky.

Narrator

And there was evening, and there was morning—the second day. (PAUSE) And God said:

God (voice) Let the water under the sky be gathered to one place, and let dry ground appear.

Narrator And it was so. God called the dry ground—

God (voice) Land.

Narrator And the gathered waters he called—

God (voice) Seas.

Narrator And God saw that it was good. Then God said:

God (voice) Let the land produce vegetation: seed-bearing plants and trees on the land that bear fruit with seed in it, according to their various kinds.

Narrator

And it was so. The land produced vegetation: plants bearing seed according to their kinds and trees bearing fruit with seed in it according to their kinds. And God saw that it was good. And there was evening, and there was morning—the third day. (PAUSE) And God said:

19

God (voice)	Let there be lights in the expanse of the sky to separate the day from the night, and let them serve as signs to mark seasons and days and years, and let them be lights in the expanse of the sky to give light on the earth.
Narrator	And it was so. God made two great lights—the greater light to govern the day and the lesser light to govern the night. He also made the stars. God set them in the expanse of the sky to give light on the earth, to govern the day and the night, and to separate light from darkness. And God saw that it was good. And there was evening, and there was morning—the fourth day. (PAUSE) And God said:
God (voice)	Let the water teem with living creatures, and let birds fly above the earth across the expanse of the sky.
Narrator	So God created the great creatures of the sea and every living and moving thing with which the water teems, according to their kinds, and every winged bird according to its kind. And God saw that it was good. God blessed them:
God (voice)	Be fruitful and increase in number and fill the water in the seas, and let the birds increase on the earth.
Narrator	And there was evening, and there was morning—the fifth day. (PAUSE) And God said:
God (voice)	Let the land produce living creatures according to their kinds: livestock, creatures that move along the ground, and wild animals, each according to its kind.
Narrator	And it was so. God made the wild animals according to their kinds, the livestock according to their kinds, and all the creatures that move along the ground according to their kinds. And God saw that it was good. (PAUSE) Then God said:
God (voice)	Let us make man in our image, in our likeness, and let them rule over the fish of the sea and the birds of the air, over the livestock, over all the earth, and over all the creatures that move along the ground.
Narrator	So God created man in his own image, in the image of God he created him; male and female he created them. God blessed them:
God (voice)	Be fruitful and increase in number; fill the earth and subdue it. Rule over the fish of the sea and the birds of the air and over every living creature that moves on the ground.
Narrator	Then God said:
God (voice)	I give you every seed-bearing plant on the face of the whole earth and every tree that has fruit with seed in it. They will be yours for food. And to all the beasts of the earth and all the birds of the air and all the creatures that move on the ground—everything that has the breath of life in it—I give every green plant for food.

20

Narrator	And it was so.

God saw all that he had made, and it was very good. And there was evening, and there was morning—the sixth day.

Thus the heavens and the earth were completed in all their vast array.

By the seventh day God had finished the work he had been doing; so on the seventh day he rested from all his work. And God blessed the seventh day and made it holy, because on it he rested from all the work of creating that he had done.

This is the account of the heavens and the earth when they were created.

Cast: **Narrator, God** (voice only)

Adam and Eve

Genesis 2:4–24 [25]

Narrator 1 When the LORD God made the earth and the heavens—and no shrub of the field had yet appeared on the earth and no plant of the field had yet sprung up, for the LORD God had not sent rain on the earth and there was no man to work the ground, but streams came up from the earth and watered the whole surface of the ground—

Narrator 2 The LORD God formed the man from the dust of the ground and breathed into his nostrils the breath of life, and the man became a living being.

Narrator 1 Now the LORD God had planted a garden in the east, in Eden; and there he put the man he had formed. And the LORD God made all kinds of trees grow out of the ground—trees that were pleasing to the eye and good for food. In the middle of the garden were the tree of life and the tree of the knowledge of good and evil.

Narrator 2 A river watering the garden flowed from Eden; from there it was separated into four headwaters. The name of the first is the Pishon; it winds through the entire land of Havilah, where there is gold.

Narrator 1 (The gold of that land is good; aromatic resin and onyx are also there.)

Narrator 2 The name of the second river is the Gihon; it winds through the entire land of Cush. The name of the third river is the Tigris; it runs along the east side of Asshur. And the fourth river is the Euphrates.

Narrator 1 The LORD God took the man and put him in the Garden of Eden to work it and take care of it. And the LORD God commanded the man:

God
(voice only) You are free to eat from any tree in the garden; but you must not eat from the tree of the knowledge of good and evil, for when you eat of it you will surely die. (PAUSE)

21

Narrator 1	The LORD God said:
God (voice, musing)	It is not good for the man to be alone. I will make a helper suitable for him.
Narrator 1	Now the LORD God had formed out of the ground all the beasts of the field and all the birds of the air. He brought them to the man to see what he would name them; and whatever the man called each living creature, that was its name. (PAUSE) So the man gave names to all the livestock, the birds of the air and all the beasts of the field.
	But for Adam no suitable helper was found.
Narrator 2	So the LORD God caused the man to fall into a deep sleep; and while he was sleeping, he took one of the man's ribs and closed up the place with flesh. Then the LORD God made a woman from the rib he had taken out of the man, and he brought her to the man. The man said:

Man	This is now bone of my bones
	    and flesh of my flesh;
	she shall be called "woman,"
	    for she was taken out of man.

Narrator 2	For this reason a man will leave his father and mother and be united to his wife, and they will become one flesh.
[Narrator 1	The man and his wife were both naked, and they felt no shame.]

Cast: **Narrator 1**, **Narrator 2** (can be the same as Narrator 1), **God** (voice only), **Man**

The Fall of Man

Genesis 3:1–19 [20–24]

Narrator	Now the serpent was more crafty than any of the wild animals the LORD God had made. He said to the woman:
Serpent	Did God *really* say, "You must not eat from any tree in the garden"?
Narrator	The woman said to the serpent:
Woman	We may eat fruit from the trees in the garden, but God did say, "You must not eat fruit from the tree that is in the middle of the garden, and you must not touch it, or you will die."
Serpent	You will not surely die. For God knows that when you eat of it your eyes will be opened, and you will be like God, knowing good and evil.
Narrator	When the woman saw that the fruit of the tree was good for food and pleasing to the eye, and also desirable for gaining wisdom, she took some and ate it. She also gave some to her husband, who was with her, and he ate it. Then the eyes of both of them were opened, and they realized they

were naked; so they sewed fig leaves together and made coverings for themselves.

Then the man and his wife heard the sound of the LORD God as he was walking in the garden in the cool of the day, and they hid from the LORD God among the trees of the garden. But the LORD God called to the man:

God   Where are you?

Man   I heard you in the garden, and I was afraid because I was naked; so I hid.

God
(to Man)   Who told you that you were naked? Have you eaten from the tree that I commanded you not to eat from?

Man   The woman you put here with me—she gave me some fruit from the tree, and I ate it.

Narrator   Then the LORD God said to the woman:

God (to
Woman)   What is this you have done?

Woman   The serpent deceived me, and I ate.

Narrator   So the LORD God said to the serpent:

God (to
Serpent)   Because you have done this,
    Cursed are you above all the livestock
      and all the wild animals!
    You will crawl on your belly
      and you will eat dust
      all the days of your life.
    And I will put enmity
      between you and the woman,
      and between your offspring and hers;
    he will crush your head,
      and you will strike his heel.

[Narrator   To the woman [God] said:**]**

God (to
Woman)   I will greatly increase your pains in childbearing;
    with pain you will give birth to children.
Your desire will be for your husband,
    and he will rule over you.

[Narrator   To Adam [God] said:**]**

God (to Man)   Because you listened to your wife and ate from the tree about which I commanded you, "You must not eat of it,"
Cursed is the ground because of you;
    through painful toil you will eat of it
    all the days of your life.

It will produce thorns and thistles for you,
   and you will eat the plants of the field.
By the sweat of your brow
   you will eat your food
until you return to the ground,
   since from it you were taken;
for dust you are
   and to dust you will return.

[Narrator   Adam named his wife Eve, because she would become the mother of all the living.

The Lord God made garments of skin for Adam and his wife and clothed them. (PAUSE) And the Lord God said:

God   The man has now become like one of us, knowing good and evil. He must not be allowed to reach out his hand and take also from the tree of life and eat, and live forever.

Narrator   So the Lord God banished him from the Garden of Eden to work the ground from which he had been taken. After he drove the man out, he placed on the east side of the Garden of Eden cherubim and a flaming sword flashing back and forth to guard the way to the tree of life.**]**

Cast: **Narrator, Serpent, Woman, God, Man.** (Please note the possibility of shortening this reading.)

Cain and Abel

Genesis 4:1–16

Narrator   Adam lay with his wife Eve, and she became pregnant and gave birth to Cain. **[She said:]**

Eve   With the help of the Lord I have brought forth a man.

Narrator   Later she gave birth to his brother Abel.

Now Abel kept flocks, and Cain worked the soil. In the course of time Cain brought some of the fruits of the soil as an offering to the Lord. But Abel brought fat portions from some of the firstborn of his flock. The Lord looked with favor on Abel and his offering, but on Cain and his offering he did not look with favor. So Cain was very angry, and his face was downcast. (PAUSE) Then the Lord said to Cain:

The Lord
(voice only) Why are you angry? Why is your face downcast? If you do what is right, will you not be accepted? But if you do not do what is right, sin is crouching at your door; it desires to have you, but you must master it.

Narrator   Now Cain said to his brother Abel:

Cain   Let's go out to the field.

Narrator	And while they were in the field, Cain attacked his brother Abel and killed him. (PAUSE)
Narrator	Then the Lord said to Cain:
The Lord (voice)	Where is your brother Abel?
Cain	I don't know. Am I my brother's keeper?
The Lord (voice)	What have you done? Listen! Your brother's blood cries out to me from the ground. Now you are under a curse and driven from the ground, which opened its mouth to receive your brother's blood from your hand. When you work the ground, it will no longer yield its crops for you. You will be a restless wanderer on the earth.
Cain (protesting)	My punishment is more than I can bear. Today you are driving me from the land, and I will be hidden from your presence; I will be a restless wanderer on the earth, and whoever finds me will kill me.
The Lord (voice)	Not so; if anyone kills Cain, he will suffer vengeance seven times over.
Narrator	Then the Lord put a mark on Cain so that no one who found him would kill him. So Cain went out from the Lord's presence and lived in the land of Nod, east of Eden.

Cast: **Narrator, Eve, the Lord** (voice only), **Cain**

The Descendants of Cain

Genesis 4:17–26

Narrator	Cain lay with his wife, and she became pregnant and gave birth to Enoch. Cain was then building a city, and he named it after his son Enoch. To Enoch was born Irad, and Irad was the father of Mehujael, and Mehujael was the father of Methushael, and Methushael was the father of Lamech.
	Lamech married two women, one named Adah and the other Zillah. Adah gave birth to Jabal; he was the father of those who live in tents and raise livestock. His brother's name was Jubal; he was the father of all who play the harp and flute. Zillah also had a son, Tubal-Cain, who forged all kinds of tools out of bronze and iron. Tubal-Cain's sister was Naamah.
	Lamech said to his wives:

Lamech	Adah and Zillah, listen to me;
	    wives of Lamech, hear my words.
	I have killed a man for wounding me,
	    a young man for injuring me.

> If Cain is avenged seven times,
>> then Lamech seventy-seven times.

Narrator   Adam lay with his wife again, and she gave birth to a son and named him Seth [saying:]

Eve   God has granted me another child in place of Abel, since Cain killed him.

Narrator   Seth also had a son, and he named him Enosh.

At that time men began to call on the name of the LORD.

Cast: **Narrator, Lamech, Eve**

The Wickedness of Mankind

Genesis 6:1–8

Narrator   When men began to increase in number on the earth and daughters were born to them, the sons of God saw that the daughters of men were beautiful, and they married any of them they chose. Then the LORD said:

The Lord
(voice only)   My Spirit will not contend with man forever, for he is mortal; his days will be a hundred and twenty years.

Narrator   The Nephilim were on the earth in those days—and also afterward—when the sons of God went to the daughters of men and had children by them. They were the heroes of old, men of renown.

The LORD saw how great man's wickedness on the earth had become, and that every inclination of the thoughts of his heart was only evil all the time. The LORD was grieved that he had made man on the earth, and his heart was filled with pain. [So the LORD said:]

The Lord
(bitterly)   I will wipe mankind, whom I have created, from the face of the earth—men and animals, and creatures that move along the ground, and birds of the air—for I am grieved that I have made them.

Narrator   But Noah found favor in the eyes of the LORD.

Cast: **Narrator, the Lord** (voice only)

The Flood

Genesis 6:9–7:16

Narrator 1   This is the account of Noah.

Noah was a righteous man, blameless among the people of his time, and he walked with God. Noah had three sons: Shem, Ham and Japheth.

Now the earth was corrupt in God's sight and was full of violence. God saw how corrupt the earth had become, for all the people on earth had corrupted their ways. So God said to Noah:

God
(voice only)   I am going to put an end to all people, for the earth is filled with violence because of them. I am surely going to destroy both them and the earth. So make yourself an ark of cypress wood; make rooms in it and coat it with pitch inside and out. This is how you are to build it: The ark is to be 450 feet long, 75 feet wide and 45 feet high. Make a roof for it and finish the ark to within 18 inches of the top. Put a door in the side of the ark and make lower, middle and upper decks. I am going to bring floodwaters on the earth to destroy all life under the heavens, every creature that has the breath of life in it. Everything on earth will perish. But I will establish my covenant with you, and you will enter the ark—you and your sons and your wife and your sons' wives with you. You are to bring into the ark two of all living creatures, male and female, to keep them alive with you. Two of every kind of bird, of every kind of animal and of every kind of creature that moves along the ground will come to you to be kept alive. You are to take every kind of food that is to be eaten and store it away as food for you and for them.

Narrator 2   Noah did everything just as God commanded him. (PAUSE) The LORD then said to Noah:

God (voice)   Go into the ark, you and your whole family, because I have found you righteous in this generation. Take with you seven of every kind of clean animal, a male and its mate, and two of every kind of unclean animal, a male and its mate, and also seven of every kind of bird, male and female, to keep their various kinds alive throughout the earth. Seven days from now I will send rain on the earth for forty days and forty nights, and I will wipe from the face of the earth every living creature I have made.

Narrator 1   And Noah did all that the LORD commanded him.

Noah was six hundred years old when the floodwaters came on the earth. And Noah and his sons and his wife and his sons' wives entered the ark to escape the waters of the flood. Pairs of clean and unclean animals, of birds and of all creatures that move along the ground, male and female, came to Noah and entered the ark, as God had commanded Noah. And after the seven days the floodwaters came on the earth.

Narrator 2   In the six hundredth year of Noah's life, on the seventeenth day of the second month—on that day all the springs of the great deep burst forth, and the floodgates of the heavens were opened. And rain fell on the earth forty days and forty nights.

On that very day Noah and his sons, Shem, Ham and Japheth, together with his wife and the wives of his three sons, entered the ark. They had with them every wild animal according to its kind, all livestock according to their kinds, every creature that moves along the ground according to its kind and every bird according to its kind, everything with wings.

Pairs of all creatures that have the breath of life in them came to Noah and entered the ark. The animals going in were male and female of every living thing, as God had commanded Noah. Then the LORD shut him in.

Cast: **Narrator 1, God** (voice only), **Narrator 2**

The End of the Flood

Genesis 7:17–8:19

Narrator 1 For forty days the flood kept coming on the earth, and as the waters increased they lifted the ark high above the earth. The waters rose and increased greatly on the earth, and the ark floated on the surface of the water. They rose greatly on the earth, and all the high mountains under the entire heavens were covered. The waters rose and covered the mountains to a depth of more than twenty feet. Every living thing that moved on the earth perished—birds, livestock, wild animals, all the creatures that swarm over the earth, and all mankind. Everything on dry land that had the breath of life in its nostrils died. Every living thing on the face of the earth was wiped out; men and animals and the creatures that move along the ground and the birds of the air were wiped from the earth. Only Noah was left, and those with him in the ark.

The waters flooded the earth for a hundred and fifty days.

Narrator 2 But God remembered Noah and all the wild animals and the livestock that were with him in the ark, and he sent a wind over the earth, and the waters receded. Now the springs of the deep and the floodgates of the heavens had been closed, and the rain had stopped falling from the sky. The water receded steadily from the earth. At the end of the hundred and fifty days the water had gone down, and on the seventeenth day of the seventh month the ark came to rest on the mountains of Ararat. The waters continued to recede until the tenth month, and on the first day of the tenth month the tops of the mountains became visible.

Narrator 1 After forty days Noah opened the window he had made in the ark and sent out a raven, and it kept flying back and forth until the water had dried up from the earth. Then he sent out a dove to see if the water had receded from the surface of the ground. But the dove could find no place to set its feet because there was water over all the surface of the earth; so it returned to Noah in the ark. He reached out his hand and took the dove and brought it back to himself in the ark. He waited seven more days and again sent out the dove from the ark. When the dove returned to him in the evening, there in its beak was a freshly plucked olive leaf! Then Noah knew that the water had receded from the earth. He waited seven more days and sent the dove out again, but this time it did not return to him.

Narrator 2	By the first day of the first month of Noah's six hundred and first year, the water had dried up from the earth. Noah then removed the covering from the ark and saw that the surface of the ground was dry. By the twenty-seventh day of the second month the earth was completely dry. Then God said to Noah:
God (voice only)	Come out of the ark, you and your wife and your sons and their wives. Bring out every kind of living creature that is with you—the birds, the animals, and all the creatures that move along the ground—so they can multiply on the earth and be fruitful and increase in number upon it.
Narrator 2	So Noah came out, together with his sons and his wife and his sons' wives. All the animals and all the creatures that move along the ground and all the birds—everything that moves on the earth—came out of the ark, one kind after another.

Cast: **Narrator 1, Narrator 2, God** (voice only)

God's Covenant with Noah

Genesis 8:20–9:17

Narrator	Noah built an altar to the LORD and, taking some of all the clean animals and clean birds, he sacrificed burnt offerings on it. The LORD smelled the pleasing aroma and said in his heart:
God (voice only—to himself)	Never again will I curse the ground because of man, even though every inclination of his heart is evil from childhood. And never again will I destroy all living creatures, as I have done.

> As long as the earth endures,
> seedtime and harvest,
> cold and heat,
> summer and winter,
> day and night
> will never cease.

Narrator	Then God blessed Noah and his sons:
God (voice—to Noah)	Be fruitful and increase in number and fill the earth. The fear and dread of you will fall upon all the beasts of the earth and all the birds of the air, upon every creature that moves along the ground, and upon all the fish of the sea; they are given into your hands. Everything that lives and moves will be food for you. Just as I gave you the green plants, I now give you everything.

29

But you must not eat meat that has its lifeblood still in it. And for your lifeblood I will surely demand an accounting. I will demand an accounting from every animal. And from each man, too, I will demand an accounting for the life of his fellow man.

Whoever sheds the blood of man,
  by man shall his blood be shed;
for in the image of God
  has God made man.

As for you, be fruitful and increase in number; multiply on the earth and increase upon it.

Narrator   Then God said to Noah and to his sons with him:

God (voice)   I now establish my covenant with you and with your descendants after you and with every living creature that was with you—the birds, the livestock and all the wild animals, all those that came out of the ark with you—every living creature on earth. I establish my covenant with you: Never again will all life be cut off by the waters of a flood; never again will there be a flood to destroy the earth.

This is the sign of the covenant I am making between me and you and every living creature with you, a covenant for all generations to come: I have set my rainbow in the clouds, and it will be the sign of the covenant between me and the earth. Whenever I bring clouds over the earth and the rainbow appears in the clouds, I will remember my covenant between me and you and all living creatures of every kind. Never again will the waters become a flood to destroy all life. Whenever the rainbow appears in the clouds, I will see it and remember the everlasting covenant between God and all living creatures of every kind on the earth.

This is the sign of the covenant I have established between me and all life on the earth.

Cast: **Narrator, God** (voice only)

The Tower of Babel

Genesis 11:1–9

Narrator   Now the whole world had one language and a common speech. As men moved eastward, they found a plain in Shinar and settled there. They said to each other:

Persons 1 and 2   Come!

Person 1   Let's make bricks—

Person 2   And bake them thoroughly.

Narrator	They used brick instead of stone, and tar for mortar. Then they said:
Person 1	Come, let us build ourselves a city, with a tower that reaches to the heavens, so that we may make a name for ourselves—
Person 2	And not be scattered over the face of the whole earth.
Narrator	But the LORD came down to see the city and the tower that the men were building. The LORD said:
The Lord (to himself)	If as one people speaking the same language they have begun to do this, then nothing they plan to do will be impossible for them. Come, let us go down and confuse their language so they will not understand each other.
Narrator	So the LORD scattered them from there over all the earth, and they stopped building the city. That is why it was called Babel—because there the LORD confused the language of the whole world. From there the LORD scattered them over the face of the whole earth.

Cast: **Narrator, Person 1, Person 2, the Lord**

The Call of Abram, Abram in Egypt

Genesis 12:1–20

Narrator 1	The LORD . . . said to Abram:
The Lord (voice only)	Leave your country, your people and your father's household and go to the land I will show you.

> I will make you into a great nation
>   and I will bless you;
> I will make your name great,
>   and you will be a blessing.
> I will bless those who bless you,
>   and whoever curses you I will curse;
> and all peoples on earth
>   will be blessed through you.

Narrator 1	So Abram left, as the LORD had told him; and Lot went with him. Abram was seventy-five years old when he set out from Haran. He took his wife Sarai, his nephew Lot, all the possessions they had accumulated and the people they had acquired in Haran, and they set out for the land of Canaan, and they arrived there.
Narrator 2	[Then] Abram traveled through the land as far as the site of the great tree of Moreh at Shechem. At that time the Canaanites were in the land. The LORD appeared to Abram [and said:]

The Lord
(voice)   To your offspring I will give this land.

Narrator 2   So he built an altar there to the Lord, who had appeared to him.

From there he went on toward the hills east of Bethel and pitched his tent, with Bethel on the west and Ai on the east. There he built an altar to the Lord and called on the name of the Lord. Then Abram set out and continued toward the Negev.

Narrator 3   Now there was a famine in the land, and Abram went down to Egypt to live there for a while because the famine was severe. As he was about to enter Egypt, he said to his wife Sarai:

Abram   I know what a beautiful woman you are. When the Egyptians see you, they will say, "This is his wife." Then they will kill me but will let you live. Say you are my sister, so that I will be treated well for your sake and my life will be spared because of you.

Narrator 3   When Abram came to Egypt, the Egyptians saw that she was a very beautiful woman. And when Pharaoh's officials saw her, they praised her to Pharaoh, and she was taken into his palace. He treated Abram well for her sake, and Abram acquired sheep and cattle, male and female donkeys, menservants and maidservants, and camels.

But the Lord inflicted serious diseases on Pharaoh and his household because of Abram's wife Sarai. So Pharaoh summoned Abram [and asked him]:

Pharaoh   What have you done to me? Why didn't you tell me she was your wife? Why did you say, "She is my sister," so that I took her to be my wife? Now then, here is your wife. Take her and go!

Narrator 3   Then Pharaoh gave orders about Abram to his men, and they sent him on his way, with his wife and everything he had.

Cast: **Narrator 1, the Lord** (voice only), **Narrator 2, Narrator 3, Abram, Pharaoh**

Abram and Lot Separate

Genesis 13:1–18

Narrator 1   So Abram went up from Egypt to the Negev, with his wife and everything he had, and Lot went with him. Abram had become very wealthy in livestock and in silver and gold.

From the Negev he went from place to place until he came to Bethel, to the place between Bethel and Ai where his tent had been earlier and where he had first built an altar. There Abram called on the name of the Lord.

Narrator 2   Now Lot, who was moving about with Abram, also had flocks and herds and tents. But the land could not support them while they stayed together, for their possessions were so great that they were not able to stay together. And quarreling arose between Abram's herdsmen and the herdsmen of Lot.

Narrator 1 The Canaanites and Perizzites were also living in the land at that time.

So Abram said to Lot:

Abram Let's not have any quarreling between you and me, or between your herdsmen and mine, for we are brothers. Is not the whole land before you? Let's part company. If you go to the left, I'll go to the right; if you go to the right, I'll go to the left.

Narrator 2 Lot looked up and saw that the whole plain of the Jordan was well watered, like the garden of the LORD, like the land of Egypt, toward Zoar. (This was before the LORD destroyed Sodom and Gomorrah.) So Lot chose for himself the whole plain of the Jordan and set out toward the east.

Narrator 1 The two men parted company:

Narrator 2 Abram lived in the land of Canaan, while Lot lived among the cities of the plain and pitched his tents near Sodom. Now the men of Sodom were wicked and were sinning greatly against the LORD.

Narrator 1 The LORD said to Abram after Lot had parted from him:

The Lord
(voice only) Lift up your eyes from where you are and look north and south, east and west. All the land that you see I will give to you and your offspring forever. I will make your offspring like the dust of the earth, so that if anyone could count the dust, then your offspring could be counted. Go, walk through the length and breadth of the land, for I am giving it to you.

Narrator 1 So Abram moved his tents and went to live near the great trees of Mamre at Hebron, where he built an altar to the LORD.

Cast: **Narrator 1, Narrator 2, Abram, the Lord** (voice only)

Melchizedek Blesses Abram

Genesis 14:17–24

Narrator After Abram returned from defeating Kedorlaomer and the kings allied with him, the king of Sodom came out to meet him in the Valley of Shaveh (that is, the King's Valley).

Then Melchizedek king of Salem brought out bread and wine. He was priest of God Most High, and he blessed Abram, saying:

Melchizedek Blessed be Abram by God Most High,
    Creator of heaven and earth.
And blessed be God Most High,
    who delivered your enemies into your hand.

Narrator	Then Abram gave him a tenth of everything. (PAUSE) The king of Sodom said to Abram:
King (to Abram)	Give me the people and keep the goods for yourself.
[Narrator	But Abram said to the king of Sodom:]
Abram (to King)	I have raised my hand to the LORD, God Most High, Creator of heaven and earth, and have taken an oath that I will accept nothing belonging to you, not even a thread or the thong of a sandal, so that you will never be able to say, "I made Abram rich." I will accept nothing but what my men have eaten and the share that belongs to the men who went with me—to Aner, Eshcol and Mamre. Let them have their share.

Cast: **Narrator, Melchizedek, King, Abram**

God's Covenant with Abram

From Genesis 15:1–18

Narrator	After this, the word of the LORD came to Abram in a vision:
The Lord (voice only)	Do not be afraid, Abram. I am your shield, your very great reward.
Abram	O Sovereign LORD, what can you give me since I remain childless [and the one who will inherit my estate is Eliezer of Damascus? You have given me no children; so a servant in my household will be my heir. . . .
The Lord (voice)	This man will not be your heir, but a son coming from your own body will be your heir.
Narrator	[The LORD] took him outside.
The Lord (voice)	Look up at the heavens and count the stars—if indeed you can count them. So shall your offspring be.
Narrator	Abram believed the LORD, and he credited it to him as righteousness. [The LORD] also said to him:
The Lord (voice)	I am the LORD, who brought you out of Ur of the Chaldeans to give you this land to take possession of it.
Abram	O Sovereign LORD, how can I know that I will gain possession of it?

The Lord (voice)	Bring me a heifer, a goat and a ram, each three years old, along with a dove and a young pigeon.
Narrator	Abram brought all these to him, cut them in two and arranged the halves opposite each other. . . .
	When the sun had set and darkness had fallen, a smoking firepot with a blazing torch appeared and passed between the pieces. On that day the LORD made a covenant with Abram:
The Lord (voice)	To your descendants I give this land, from the river of Egypt to the great river, the Euphrates. . . .

Cast: **Narrator, the Lord** (voice only), **Abram**

The Three Visitors

Genesis 18:1–15

Narrator	The LORD appeared to Abraham near the great trees of Mamre while he was sitting at the entrance to his tent in the heat of the day. Abraham looked up and saw three men standing nearby. When he saw them, he hurried from the entrance of his tent to meet them and bowed low to the ground. [He said:]
Abraham	If I have found favor in your eyes, my lord, do not pass your servant by. Let a little water be brought, and then you may all wash your feet and rest under this tree. Let me get you something to eat, so you can be refreshed and then go on your way—now that you have come to your servant.
[Narrator	They answered:]
Man 1	Very well.
Man 2	Do as you say.
Narrator	So Abraham hurried into the tent to Sarah. [He said:]
Abraham	Quick, get three seahs of fine flour and knead it and bake some bread.
Narrator	Then he ran to the herd and selected a choice, tender calf and gave it to a servant, who hurried to prepare it. He then brought some curds and milk and the calf that had been prepared, and set these before them. While they ate, he stood near them under a tree. [They asked him:]
Man 2	Where is your wife Sarah?
Abraham	There, in the tent.
[Narrator	Then the LORD said:]

The Lord	I will surely return to you about this time next year, and Sarah your wife will have a son.
Narrator	Now Sarah was listening at the entrance to the tent, which was behind him. Abraham and Sarah were already old and well advanced in years, and Sarah was past the age of childbearing. So Sarah laughed to herself as she thought:
Sarah (laughing to herself)	After I am worn out and my master is old, will I now have this pleasure?
[Narrator	Then the Lord said to Abraham:]
The Lord	Why did Sarah laugh and say, "Will I really have a child, now that I am old?" Is anything too hard for the Lord? I will return to you at the appointed time next year and Sarah will have a son.
[Narrator	Sarah was afraid, so she lied and said:]
Sarah	I did not laugh.
The Lord (slowly)	Yes, you *did* laugh.

Cast: **Narrator, Abraham, Man 1, Man 2, the Lord** (Men 1 and 2 and the Lord can be the same), **Sarah**

Abraham Pleads for Sodom

Genesis 18:16–33

Narrator	When the men got up to leave, they looked down toward Sodom, and Abraham walked along with them to see them on their way. Then the Lord said:
The Lord (voice only— thinking)	Shall I hide from Abraham what I am about to do? Abraham will surely become a great and powerful nation, and all nations on earth will be blessed through him. For I have chosen him, so that he will direct his children and his household after him to keep the way of the Lord by doing what is right and just, so that the Lord will bring about for Abraham what he has promised him.
[Narrator	Then the Lord said [to Abraham]:]
The Lord (voice)	The outcry against Sodom and Gomorrah is so great and their sin so grievous that I will go down and see if what they have done is as bad as the outcry that has reached me. If not, I will know.
Narrator	The men turned away and went toward Sodom, but Abraham remained standing before the Lord. Then Abraham approached him [and said:]

Abraham	Will you sweep away the righteous with the wicked? What if there are fifty righteous people in the city? Will you really sweep it away and not spare the place for the sake of the fifty righteous people in it? Far be it from you to do such a thing—to kill the righteous with the wicked, treating the righteous and the wicked alike. Far be it from you! Will not the Judge of all the earth do right?
The Lord (voice)	If I find fifty righteous people in the city of Sodom, I will spare the whole place for their sake. (PAUSE)
Abraham	Now that I have been so bold as to speak to the Lord, though I am nothing but dust and ashes, what if the number of the righteous is five less than fifty? Will you destroy the whole city because of five people?
The Lord (voice)	If I find forty-five there, I will not destroy it.
Abraham	What if only forty are found there?
The Lord (voice)	For the sake of forty, I will not do it. (PAUSE)
Abraham	May the Lord not be angry, but let me speak. What if only thirty can be found there?
The Lord (voice)	I will not do it if I find thirty there. (PAUSE)
Abraham	Now that I have been so bold as to speak to the Lord, what if only twenty can be found there?
The Lord (voice)	For the sake of twenty, I will not destroy it. (PAUSE)
Abraham	May the Lord not be angry, but let me speak just once more. What if only ten can be found there?
The Lord (voice)	For the sake of ten, I will not destroy it. (PAUSE)
Narrator	When the LORD had finished speaking with Abraham, he left, and Abraham returned home.

Cast: **Narrator, the Lord** (voice only), **Abraham**

The Sinfulness of Sodom

Genesis 19:1–11

Narrator	. . . two angels arrived at Sodom in the evening, and Lot was sitting in the gateway of the city. When he saw them, he got up to meet them and bowed down with his face to the ground.

Lot	My lords, please turn aside to your servant's house. You can wash your feet and spend the night and then go on your way early in the morning.
[Narrator	They answered:]
Angel	No, we will spend the night in the square.
Narrator	But he insisted so strongly that they did go with him and entered his house. He prepared a meal for them, baking bread without yeast, and they ate. (PAUSE) Before they had gone to bed, all the men from every part of the city of Sodom—both young and old—surrounded the house. They called to Lot:
Man 1 (calling)	Where are the men who came to you tonight?
Man 2 (calling)	Bring them out to us so that we can have sex with them.
Narrator	Lot went outside to meet them and shut the door behind him [and said:]
Lot	No, my friends. Don't do this wicked thing. Look, I have two daughters who have never slept with a man. Let me bring them out to you, and you can do what you like with them. But don't do anything to these men, for they have come under the protection of my roof.
Man 1	Get out of our way.
Man 2	This fellow came here as an alien, and now he wants to play the judge!
Man 1	We'll treat *you* worse than them.
Narrator	They kept bringing pressure on Lot and moved forward to break down the door.
	But the men inside reached out and pulled Lot back into the house and shut the door. Then they struck the men who were at the door of the house, young and old, with blindness so that they could not find the door.

Cast: **Narrator, Lot, Angel, Man 1, Man 2**

Lot Leaves Sodom, and Sodom and Gomorrah Are Destroyed

Genesis 19:12–29

Narrator	The two [angels who had come to Sodom] said to Lot:
Angel 1	Do you have anyone else here—sons-in-law, sons or daughters, or anyone else in the city who belongs to you? Get them out of here, because we are going to destroy this place.

Angel 2	The outcry to the Lord against its people is so great that he has sent us to destroy it.
Narrator	So Lot went out and spoke to his sons-in-law, who were pledged to marry his daughters.
Lot	Hurry and get out of this place, because the Lord is about to destroy the city!
Narrator	But his sons-in-law thought he was joking. (PAUSE) With the coming of dawn, the angels urged Lot:
Angels 1 and 2	Hurry!
Angel 1	Take your wife and your two daughters who are here, or you will be swept away when the city is punished.
Narrator	When he hesitated, the men grasped his hand and the hands of his wife and of his two daughters and led them safely out of the city, for the Lord was merciful to them. As soon as they had brought them out, one of them said:
Angel 2	Flee for your lives! Don't look back, and don't stop anywhere in the plain! Flee to the mountains or you will be swept away!
Lot	No, my lords, please! Your servant has found favor in your eyes, and you have shown great kindness to me in sparing my life. But I can't flee to the mountains; this disaster will overtake me, and I'll die. Look, here is a town near enough to run to, and it is small. Let me flee to it—it is very small, isn't it? Then my life will be spared.
Angel 1	Very well, I will grant this request too; I will not overthrow the town you speak of. But flee there quickly, because I cannot do anything until you reach it.
Narrator	(That is why the town was called Zoar [which means small].) (PAUSE) By the time Lot reached Zoar, the sun had risen over the land. Then the Lord rained down burning sulfur on Sodom and Gomorrah—from the Lord out of the heavens. Thus he overthrew those cities and the entire plain, including all those living in the cities—and also the vegetation in the land. But Lot's wife looked back, and she became a pillar of salt. (PAUSE) Early the next morning Abraham got up and returned to the place where he had stood before the Lord. He looked down toward Sodom and Gomorrah, toward all the land of the plain, and he saw dense smoke rising from the land, like smoke from a furnace. So when God destroyed the cities of the plain, he remembered Abraham, and he brought Lot out of the catastrophe that overthrew the cities where Lot had lived.

Cast: **Narrator, Angel 1, Angel 2** (can be the same as Angel 1), **Lot**

Lot and His Daughters

Genesis 19:30–38

Narrator	Lot and his two daughters left Zoar and settled in the mountains, for he was afraid to stay in Zoar. He and his two daughters lived in a cave. One day the older daughter said to the younger:
Older daughter	Our father is old, and there is no man around here to lie with us, as is the custom all over the earth. Let's get our father to drink wine and then lie with him and preserve our family line through our father.
Narrator	That night they got their father to drink wine, and the older daughter went in and lay with him. He was not aware of it when she lay down or when she got up.
	The next day the older daughter said to the younger:
Older daughter	Last night I lay with my father. Let's get him to drink wine again tonight, and you go in and lie with him so we can preserve our family line through our father.
Narrator	So they got their father to drink wine that night also, and the younger daughter went and lay with him. Again he was not aware of it when she lay down or when she got up.
	So both of Lot's daughters became pregnant by their father. The older daughter had a son, and she named him Moab; he is the father of the Moabites of today. The younger daughter also had a son, and she named him Ben-Ammi; he is the father of the Ammonites of today.

Cast: **Narrator, Older daughter**

Abraham and Abimelech

Genesis 20:1–18

Narrator	Abraham moved on . . . into the region of the Negev and lived between Kadesh and Shur. For a while he stayed in Gerar, and there Abraham said of his wife Sarah:
Abraham	She is my *sister*.
Narrator	Then Abimelech king of Gerar sent for Sarah and took her.
	But God came to Abimelech in a dream one night and said to him:
God (voice only)	You are as good as dead because of the woman you have taken; she is a married woman.

Narrator	Now Abimelech had not gone near her, so he said:
Abimelech	Lord, will you destroy an innocent nation? Did he not say to me, "She is my sister," and didn't she also say, "He is my brother"? I have done this with a clear conscience and clean hands.
[Narrator	Then God said to him in the dream:]
God (voice only)	Yes, I know you did this with a clear conscience, and so I have kept you from sinning against me. That is why I did not let you touch her. Now return the man's wife, for he is a prophet, and he will pray for you and you will live. But if you do not return her, you may be sure that you and all yours will die.
Narrator	Early the next morning Abimelech summoned all his officials, and when he told them all that had happened, they were very much afraid. Then Abimelech called Abraham in [and said:]
Abimelech	What have you done to us? How have I wronged you that you have brought such great guilt upon me and my kingdom? You have done things to me that should not be done. What was your reason for doing this?
[Narrator	Abraham replied:
Abraham	I said to myself, "There is surely no fear of God in this place, and they will kill me because of my wife." Besides, she really is my sister, the daughter of my father though not of my mother; and she became my wife. And when God had me wander from my father's household, I said to her, "This is how you can show your love to me: Everywhere we go, say of me 'He is my brother.'"
Narrator	Then Abimelech brought sheep and cattle and male and female slaves and gave them to Abraham, and he returned Sarah his wife to him. [And Abimelech said:]
Abimelech (to Abraham)	My land is before you; live wherever you like.
Narrator	To Sarah he said:
Abimelech	I am giving your brother a thousand shekels of silver. This is to cover the offense against you before all who are with you; you are completely vindicated.
Narrator	Then Abraham prayed to God, and God healed Abimelech, his wife and his slave girls so they could have children again, for the LORD had closed up every womb in Abimelech's household because of Abraham's wife Sarah.

Cast: **Narrator, Abraham, God** (voice only), **Abimelech**

41

The Birth of Isaac

Genesis 21:1–8

Narrator | The LORD was gracious to Sarah as he had said, and the LORD did for Sarah what he had promised. Sarah became pregnant and bore a son to Abraham in his old age, at the very time God had promised him. Abraham gave the name Isaac to the son Sarah bore him. When his son Isaac was eight days old, Abraham circumcised him, as God commanded him. Abraham was a hundred years old when his son Isaac was born to him. Sarah said:

Sarah | God has brought me laughter, and everyone who hears about this will laugh with me.

[Narrator | And she added:]

Sarah | Who would have said to Abraham that Sarah would nurse children? Yet I have borne him a son in his old age.

Narrator | The child grew and was weaned, and on the day Isaac was weaned Abraham held a great feast.

Cast: **Narrator, Sarah**

Hagar and Ishmael Sent Away

Genesis 21:9–21

Narrator | Sarah saw that the son whom Hagar the Egyptian had borne to Abraham was mocking, and she said to Abraham:

Sarah | Get rid of that slave woman and her son, for that slave woman's son will never share in the inheritance with my son Isaac.

Narrator | The matter distressed Abraham greatly because it concerned his son. But God said to him:

God
(voice only) | Do not be so distressed about the boy and your maidservant. Listen to whatever Sarah tells you, because it is through Isaac that your offspring will be reckoned. I will make the son of the maidservant into a nation also, because he is your offspring.

Narrator | Early the next morning Abraham took some food and a skin of water and gave them to Hagar. He set them on her shoulders and then sent her off with the boy. She went on her way and wandered in the desert of Beersheba.

When the water in the skin was gone, she put the boy under one of the bushes. Then she went off and sat down nearby, about a bowshot away [for she thought:]

Hagar
(thinking)   I cannot watch the boy die.

Narrator   And as she sat there nearby, she began to sob.

God heard the boy crying, and the angel of God called to Hagar from heaven:

Angel   What is the matter, Hagar? Do not be afraid; God has heard the boy crying as he lies there. Lift the boy up and take him by the hand, for I will make him into a great nation.

Narrator   Then God opened her eyes and she saw a well of water. So she went and filled the skin with water and gave the boy a drink.

God was with the boy as he grew up. He lived in the desert and became an archer. While he was living in the Desert of Paran, his mother got a wife for him from Egypt.

Cast: **Narrator, Sarah, God** (voice only), **Hagar, Angel**

The Treaty at Beersheba

Genesis 21:22–34

Narrator   Abimelech and Phicol the commander of his forces said to Abraham:

Abimelech   God is with you in everything you do. Now swear to me here before God that you will not deal falsely with me or my children or my descendants. Show to me and the country where you are living as an alien the same kindness I have shown to you.

[Narrator   Abraham said:]

Abraham   I swear it.

Narrator   Then Abraham complained to Abimelech about a well of water that Abimelech's servants had seized. [But Abimelech said:]

Abimelech   I don't know who has done this. You did not tell me, and I heard about it only today.

Narrator   So Abraham brought sheep and cattle and gave them to Abimelech, and the two men made a treaty. Abraham set apart seven ewe lambs from the flock [and Abimelech asked Abraham:]

Abimelech   What is the meaning of these seven ewe lambs you have set apart by themselves?

Abraham   Accept these seven lambs from my hand as a witness that I dug this well.

Narrator   So that place was called Beersheba, because the two men swore an oath there.

After the treaty had been made at Beersheba, Abimelech and Phicol the commander of his forces returned to the land of the Philistines. Abraham planted a tamarisk tree in Beersheba, and there he called upon the name of the Lord, the Eternal God. And Abraham stayed in the land of the Philistines for a long time.

Cast: **Narrator, Abimelech, Abraham**

Abraham Tested

Genesis 22:1–18

Narrator God tested Abraham. He said to him:

God
(voice only) Abraham!

[Narrator He replied:]

Abraham Here I am.

God
(voice) Take your son, your only son, Isaac, whom you love, and go to the region of Moriah. Sacrifice him there as a burnt offering on one of the mountains I will tell you about.

Narrator Early the next morning Abraham got up and saddled his donkey. He took with him two of his servants and his son Isaac. When he had cut enough wood for the burnt offering, he set out for the place God had told him about. On the third day Abraham looked up and saw the place in the distance. He said to his servants:

Abraham Stay here with the donkey while I and the boy go over there. We will worship and then we will come back to you.

Narrator Abraham took the wood for the burnt offering and placed it on his son Isaac, and he himself carried the fire and the knife. As the two of them went on together, Isaac spoke up and said to his father Abraham:

Isaac Father?

Abraham Yes, my son?

Isaac The fire and wood are here, but where is the *lamb* for the burnt offering?

Abraham God himself will provide the lamb for the burnt offering, my son.

Narrator And the two of them went on together. (PAUSE)

When they reached the place God had told him about, Abraham built an altar there and arranged the wood on it. He bound his son Isaac and laid him on the altar, on top of the wood. Then he reached out his hand and took the knife to slay his son. But the angel of the Lord called out to him from heaven:

God (voice)	Abraham! Abraham!
Abraham	Here I am.
God (voice)	Do not lay a hand on the boy. Do not do anything to him. Now I know that you fear God, because you have not withheld from me your son, your only son.
Narrator	Abraham looked up and there in a thicket he saw a ram caught by its horns. He went over and took the ram and sacrificed it as a burnt offering instead of his son. So Abraham called that place The LORD Will Provide. And to this day it is said:
Persons 1 and 2	On the mountain of the LORD it will be provided.
Narrator	The angel of the LORD called to Abraham from heaven a second time and said:
God (voice)	I swear by myself, declares the LORD, that because you have done this and have not withheld your son, your only son, I will surely bless you and make your descendants as numerous as the stars in the sky and as the sand on the seashore. Your descendants will take possession of the cities of their enemies, and through your offspring all nations on earth will be blessed, because you have obeyed me.

Cast: **Narrator, God** (voice only), **Abraham, Isaac, Persons 1 and 2** (can be the same as Abraham and Isaac)

The Death of Sarah

Genesis 23:1–20

Narrator	Sarah lived to be a hundred and twenty-seven years old. She died at Kiriath Arba (that is, Hebron) in the land of Canaan, and Abraham went to mourn for Sarah and to weep over her.
	Then Abraham rose from beside his dead wife and spoke to the Hittites.
Abraham	I am an alien and a stranger among you. Sell me some property for a burial site here so I can bury my dead.
[Narrator	The Hittites replied to Abraham:]
Hittite 1	Sir, listen to us. You are a mighty prince among us.
Hittite 2	Bury your dead in the choicest of our tombs.
Hittite 1	None of us will refuse you his tomb for burying your dead.
Narrator	Then Abraham rose and bowed down before the people of the land, the Hittites.

Abraham	If you are willing to let me bury my dead, then listen to me and intercede with Ephron son of Zohar on my behalf so he will sell me the cave of Machpelah, which belongs to him and is at the end of his field. Ask him to sell it to me for the full price as a burial site among you.
Narrator	Ephron the Hittite was sitting among his people and he replied to Abraham in the hearing of all the Hittites who had come to the gate of his city:
Ephron	No, my lord. Listen to me; I give you the field, and I give you the cave that is in it. I give it to you in the presence of my people. Bury your dead.
Narrator	Again Abraham bowed down before the people of the land [and he said to Ephron in their hearing:]
Abraham (to Ephron)	*Listen* to me, if you will. I will pay the price of the field. Accept it from me so I can bury my dead there.
Ephron (to Abraham)	Listen to *me*, my lord; the land is worth four hundred shekels of silver, but what is that between me and you? Bury your dead.
Narrator	Abraham agreed to Ephron's terms and weighed out for him the price he had named in the hearing of the Hittites: four hundred shekels of silver, according to the weight current among the merchants.
	So Ephron's field in Machpelah near Mamre—both the field and the cave in it, and all the trees within the borders of the field—was deeded to Abraham as his property in the presence of all the Hittites who had come to the gate of the city. (PAUSE) Afterward Abraham buried his wife Sarah in the cave in the field of Machpelah near Mamre (which is at Hebron) in the land of Canaan. So the field and the cave in it were deeded to Abraham by the Hittites as a burial site.

Cast: **Narrator, Abraham, Hittite 1, Hittite 2, Ephron**

Isaac and Rebekah

From Genesis 24:1–27 [28–53]

Narrator	Abraham was now old and well advanced in years, and the LORD had blessed him in every way. He said to the chief servant in his household, the one in charge of all that he had:
Abraham	Put your hand under my thigh. I want you to swear by the LORD, the God of heaven and the God of earth, that you will not get a wife for my son from the daughters of the Canaanites, among whom I am living, but will go to my country and my own relatives and get a wife for my son Isaac.
[Narrator	The servant asked him:]

Servant	What if the woman is unwilling to come back with me to this land? Shall I then take your son back to the country you came from?
Abraham	Make sure that you do not take my son back there. The LORD, the God of heaven, who brought me out of my father's household and my native land and who spoke to me and promised me on oath, saying, "To your offspring I will give this land"—he will send his angel before you so that you can get a wife for my son from there. If the woman is unwilling to come back with you, then you will be released from this oath of mine. Only do not take my son back there.
Narrator	So the servant put his hand under the thigh of his master Abraham and swore an oath to him concerning this matter. (PAUSE)
	Then the servant took ten of his master's camels and left, taking with him all kinds of good things from his master. He set out for Aram Naharaim and made his way to the town of Nahor. He had the camels kneel down near the well outside the town; it was toward evening, the time the women go out to draw water. [Then he prayed:]
Servant (praying)	O LORD, God of my master Abraham, give me success today, and show kindness to my master Abraham. See, I am standing beside this spring, and the daughters of the townspeople are coming out to draw water. May it be that when I say to a girl, "Please let down your jar that I may have a drink," and she says, "Drink, and I'll water your camels too"—let her be the one you have chosen for your servant Isaac. By this I will know that you have shown kindness to my master.
Narrator	Before he had finished praying, Rebekah came out with her jar on her shoulder. She was the daughter of Bethuel son of Milcah, who was the wife of Abraham's brother Nahor. The girl was very beautiful, a virgin; no man had ever lain with her. She went down to the spring, filled her jar and came up again. The servant hurried to meet her and said:
Servant	Please give me a little water from your jar.
Rebekah	Drink, my lord.
Narrator	She . . . quickly lowered the jar to her hands and gave him a drink. (PAUSE) After she had given him a drink, she said:
Rebekah	I'll draw water for your camels too, until they have finished drinking.
Narrator	So she quickly emptied her jar into the trough, ran back to the well to draw more water, and drew enough for all his camels. Without saying a word, the man watched her closely to learn whether or not the LORD had made his journey successful. (PAUSE)
	When the camels had finished drinking, the man took out a gold nose ring weighing a beka and two gold bracelets weighing ten shekels.

47

Servant

(to Rebekah) Whose daughter are you? Please tell me, is there room in your father's house for us to spend the night?

Rebekah I am the daughter of Bethuel, the son that Milcah bore to Nahor. We have plenty of straw and fodder, as well as room for you to spend the night.

Narrator Then the man bowed down and worshiped the LORD—

Servant Praise be to the LORD, the God of my master Abraham, who has not abandoned his kindness and faithfulness to my master. As for me, the LORD has led me on the journey to the house of my master's relatives.

[Narrator The girl ran and told her mother's household about these things. Now Rebekah had a brother named Laban, and he hurried out to the man at the spring. As soon as he had seen the nose ring, and the bracelets on his sister's arms, and had heard Rebekah tell what the man said to her, he went out to the man and found him standing by the camels near the spring.

Laban Come, you who are blessed by the LORD. Why are you standing out here? I have prepared the house and a place for the camels.

Narrator So the man went to the house, and the camels were unloaded. Straw and fodder were brought for the camels, and water for him and his men to wash their feet. Then food was set before him [but he said:]

Servant I will not eat until I have told you what I have to say.

Laban Then tell us.

Servant I am Abraham's servant. The LORD has blessed my master abundantly, and he has become wealthy. He has given him sheep and cattle, silver and gold, menservants and maidservants, and camels and donkeys. My master's wife Sarah has borne him a son in her old age, and he has given him everything he owns. And my master made me swear an oath, and said, "You must not get a wife for my son from the daughters of the Canaanites, in whose land I live, but go to my father's family and to my own clan, and get a wife for my son."

Then I asked my master, "What if the woman will not come back with me?"

He replied, "The LORD, before whom I have walked, will send his angel with you and make your journey a success, so that you can get a wife for my son from my own clan and from my father's family. . . ." Now if you will show kindness and faithfulness to my master, tell me; and if not, tell me, so I may know which way to turn.

Laban This is from the LORD; *we* can say nothing to you one way or the other.

Bethuel Here is Rebekah; take her and go, and let her become the wife of your master's son, as the LORD has directed.

Narrator   When Abraham's servant heard what they said, he bowed down to the ground before the LORD. Then the servant brought out gold and silver jewelry and articles of clothing and gave them to Rebekah; he also gave costly gifts to her brother and to her mother.]

Cast: **Narrator, Abraham, Servant, Rebekah, [Laban, Bethuel** (can be the same as Laban)]

Rebekah and Isaac Meet

Genesis 24:54–67

Narrator   [Abraham's servant] and the men who were with him ate and drank and spent the night [in Bethuel's household]. . . . When they got up the next morning, he said:

Servant   Send me on my way to my master.

Narrator   But [Rebekah's] brother and her mother replied:

Brother   Let the girl remain with us ten days or so . . .

Mother   then you may go.

Narrator   But he said to them:

Servant   Do not detain me, now that the LORD has granted success to my journey. Send me on my way so I may go to my master.

Narrator   Then they said:

Brother   Let's call the girl and ask her about it.

Narrator   So they called Rebekah [and asked her:]

Mother   Will you go with this man?

Rebekah   I will go.

Narrator   So they sent their sister Rebekah on her way, along with her nurse and Abraham's servant and his men. And they blessed Rebekah [and said to her:]

Brother   Our sister, may you increase
            to thousands upon thousands;

Mother   May your offspring possess
          the gates of their enemies.

Narrator   Then Rebekah and her maids got ready and mounted their camels and went back with the man. So the servant took Rebekah and left. (PAUSE)

            Now Isaac had come from Beer Lahai Roi, for he was living in the Negev. He went out to the field one evening to meditate, and as he looked up, he saw camels approaching. Rebekah also looked up and saw Isaac. She got down from her camel and asked the servant:

Rebekah	Who is that man in the field coming to meet us?
Servant	He is my master.
Narrator	So she took her veil and covered herself. (PAUSE)
	Then the servant told Isaac all he had done. Isaac brought her into the tent of his mother Sarah, and he married Rebekah. So she became his wife, and he loved her; and Isaac was comforted after his mother's death.

Cast: **Narrator, Servant, Brother, Mother, Rebekah**

Jacob and Esau

Genesis 25:19–34

Narrator	This is the account of Abraham's son Isaac.
	Abraham became the father of Isaac, and Isaac was forty years old when he married Rebekah daughter of Bethuel the Aramean from Paddan Aram and sister of Laban the Aramean.
	Isaac prayed to the Lord on behalf of his wife, because she was barren. The Lord answered his prayer, and his wife Rebekah became pregnant. The babies jostled each other within her, and she said:
Rebekah	Why is this happening to me?
Narrator	So she went to inquire of the Lord. (PAUSE) The Lord said to her:

The Lord (voice only)	Two nations are in your womb,
	     and two peoples from within you will be separated;
	 one people will be stronger than the other,
	     and the older will serve the younger.

Narrator	When the time came for her to give birth, there were twin boys in her womb. The first to come out was red, and his whole body was like a hairy garment; so they named him Esau. After this, his brother came out, with his hand grasping Esau's heel; so he was named Jacob. Isaac was sixty years old when Rebekah gave birth to them. (PAUSE)
	The boys grew up, and Esau became a skillful hunter, a man of the open country, while Jacob was a quiet man, staying among the tents. Isaac, who had a taste for wild game, loved Esau, but Rebekah loved Jacob.
	Once when Jacob was cooking some stew, Esau came in from the open country, famished. He said to Jacob:
Esau	Quick, let me have some of that red stew! I'm famished!
Narrator	(That is why he was also called Edom.)
	Jacob replied:

50

Jacob	First sell me your birthright.
Esau (hastily)	Look, I am about to *die*. What good is the birthright to me?
Narrator	But Jacob said:
Jacob	Swear to me first.
Narrator	So he swore an oath to him, selling his birthright to Jacob.
	Then Jacob gave Esau some bread and some lentil stew. He ate and drank, and then got up and left. (PAUSE)
	So Esau despised his birthright.

Cast: **Narrator, Rebekah, the Lord** (voice only), **Esau, Jacob**

Isaac and Abimelech

Genesis 26:1–25

Narrator	There was a famine in the land—besides the earlier famine of Abraham's time—and Isaac went to Abimelech king of the Philistines in Gerar. The LORD appeared to Isaac [and said:]
The Lord	Do not go down to Egypt; live in the land where I tell you to live. Stay in this land for a while, and I will be with you and will bless you. For to you and your descendants I will give all these lands and will confirm the oath I swore to your father Abraham. I will make your descendants as numerous as the stars in the sky and will give them all these lands, and through your offspring all nations on earth will be blessed, because Abraham obeyed me and kept my requirements, my commands, my decrees and my laws.
Narrator	So Isaac stayed in Gerar. When the men of that place asked him about his wife, he said, "She is my sister," because he was afraid to say, "She is my wife." He thought, "The men of this place might kill me on account of Rebekah, because she is beautiful."
	When Isaac had been there a long time, Abimelech king of the Philistines looked down from a window and saw Isaac caressing his wife Rebekah. So Abimelech summoned Isaac [and said:]
Abimelech	She is really your *wife*! Why did you say, "She is my sister"?
[Narrator	Isaac answered him:]
Isaac	Because I thought I might lose my life on account of her.
Abimelech	What is this you have done to us? One of the men might well have slept with your wife, and you would have brought guilt upon us.
Narrator	So Abimelech gave orders to all the people:

51

Abimelech	Anyone who molests this man or his wife shall surely be put to death.
Narrator	Isaac planted crops in that land and the same year reaped a hundredfold, because the Lord blessed him. The man became rich, and his wealth continued to grow until he became very wealthy. He had so many flocks and herds and servants that the Philistines envied him. So all the wells that his father's servants had dug in the time of his father Abraham, the Philistines stopped up, filling them with earth. (PAUSE) Then Abimelech said to Isaac:
Abimelech	Move away from us; you have become too powerful for us.
Narrator	So Isaac moved away from there and encamped in the Valley of Gerar and settled there. Isaac reopened the wells that had been dug in the time of his father Abraham, which the Philistines had stopped up after Abraham died, and he gave them the same names his father had given them. (PAUSE)
	Isaac's servants dug in the valley and discovered a well of fresh water there. But the herdsmen of Gerar quarreled with Isaac's herdsmen [and said:]
Herdsman 1	The water is ours!
Herdsman 2	The water is ours!
Narrator	So he named the well Esek, because they disputed with him. Then they dug another well, but they quarreled over that one also; so he named it Sitnah. He moved on from there and dug another well, and no one quarreled over it. He named it Rehoboth [saying:]
Isaac	Now the Lord has given us room and we will flourish in the land.
Narrator	From there he went up to Beersheba. That night the Lord appeared to him.
The Lord	I am the God of your father Abraham. Do not be afraid, for I am with you; I will bless you and will increase the number of your descendants for the sake of my servant Abraham.
Narrator	Isaac built an altar there and called on the name of the Lord. There he pitched his tent, and there his servants dug a well.

Cast: **Narrator, the Lord, Abimelech, Isaac, Herdsman 1, Herdsman 2**

The Agreement between Isaac and Abimelech

Genesis 26:26–33

Narrator	Abimelech had come to [Isaac] from Gerar, with Ahuzzath his personal adviser and Phicol the commander of his forces. Isaac asked them:

Isaac	Why have you come to me, since you were hostile to me and sent me away?
Abimelech	We saw clearly that the Lord was with you; so we said, "There ought to be a sworn agreement between us"—between us and you.
Phicol	Let us make a treaty with you that you will do us no harm . . .
Adviser	Just as we did not molest you but always treated you well and sent you away in peace.
Phicol	And now you are blessed by the Lord.
Narrator	Isaac then made a feast for them, and they ate and drank. Early the next morning the men swore an oath to each other. Then Isaac sent them on their way, and they left him in peace.
	That day Isaac's servants came and told him about the well they had dug:
Servant	We've found water!
Narrator	He called it Shibah, and to this day the name of the town has been Beer-sheba.

Cast: **Narrator, Isaac, Abimelech, Phicol, Adviser, Servant**

Jacob Gets Isaac's Blessing

Genesis 27:1–41

Narrator	When Isaac was old and his eyes were so weak that he could no longer see, he called for Esau his older son:
Isaac	My son.
Esau	Here I am.
Isaac	I am now an old man and don't know the day of my death. Now then, get your weapons—your quiver and bow—and go out to the open country to hunt some wild game for me. Prepare me the kind of tasty food I like and bring it to me to eat, so that I may give you my blessing before I die.
Narrator	Now Rebekah was listening as Isaac spoke to his son Esau. When Esau left for the open country to hunt game and bring it back, Rebekah said to her son Jacob:
Rebekah	Look, I overheard your father say to your brother Esau, "Bring me some game and prepare me some tasty food to eat, so that I may give you my blessing in the presence of the Lord before I die." Now, my son, listen carefully and do what I tell you: Go out to the flock and bring me two choice young goats, so I can prepare some tasty food for your father, just the way he likes it. Then take it to your father to eat, so that he may give you his blessing before he dies.

53

[Narrator	Jacob said to Rebekah his mother:]
Jacob	But my brother Esau is a hairy man, and I'm a man with smooth skin. What if my father touches me? I would appear to be tricking him and would bring down a curse on myself rather than a blessing.
Rebekah	My son, let the curse fall on me. Just do what I say; go and get them for me.
Narrator	So he went and got them and brought them to his mother, and she prepared some tasty food, just the way his father liked it. Then Rebekah took the best clothes of Esau her older son, which she had in the house, and put them on her younger son Jacob. She also covered his hands and the smooth part of his neck with the goatskins. Then she handed to her son Jacob the tasty food and the bread she had made. (PAUSE) He went to his father.
Jacob	My father.
Isaac	Yes, my son. Who is it?
Jacob	I am Esau your firstborn. I have done as you told me. Please sit up and eat some of my game so that you may give me your blessing.
Isaac	How did you find it so quickly, my son?
Jacob	The LORD your God gave me success.
Isaac	Come near so I can touch you, my son, to know whether you really are my son Esau or not.
Narrator	Jacob went close to his father Isaac, who touched him.
Isaac (hesitating)	The voice is the voice of Jacob, but the hands are the hands of Esau.
Narrator	He did not recognize him, for his hands were hairy like those of his brother Esau; so he blessed him.
Isaac	Are you really my son Esau?
Jacob	I am.
Isaac	My son, bring me some of your game to eat, so that I may give you my blessing.
Narrator	Jacob brought it to him and he ate; and he brought some wine and he drank. [Then his father Isaac said to him:]
Isaac (to Jacob)	Come here, my son, and kiss me.
Narrator	So he went to him and kissed him. When Isaac caught the smell of his clothes, he blessed him:

Isaac	Ah, the smell of my son
	  is like the smell of a field
	    that the LORD has blessed.
	May God give you of heaven's dew

> and of earth's richness—
> an abundance of grain and new wine.
> May nations serve you
> and peoples bow down to you.
> Be lord over your brothers,
> and may the sons of your mother bow down to you.
> May those who curse you be cursed
> and those who bless you be blessed. (PAUSE)

Narrator After Isaac finished blessing him and Jacob had scarcely left his father's presence, his brother Esau came in from hunting. He too prepared some tasty food and brought it to his father.

Esau My father, sit up and eat some of my game, so that you may give me your blessing.

Isaac Who are *you*?

Esau I am your son, your firstborn, Esau.

Narrator Isaac trembled violently [and said:]

Isaac
(shocked) Who was it, then, that hunted game and brought it to me? I ate it just before you came and I blessed him—and indeed he *will* be blessed!

Narrator When Esau heard his father's words, he burst out with a loud and bitter cry:

Esau Bless me—me too, my father!

Isaac Your brother came deceitfully and took your blessing.

Esau Isn't he rightly named Jacob? He has deceived me these two times: He took my birthright, and now he's taken my blessing! Haven't you reserved any blessing for me?

Isaac I have made him lord over you and have made all his relatives his servants, and I have sustained him with grain and new wine. So what can I possibly do for you, my son?

Esau Do you have only one blessing, my father? Bless me too, my father!

Narrator Then Esau wept aloud. [His father Isaac answered him:]

Isaac Your dwelling will be
> away from the earth's richness,
> away from the dew of heaven above.
> You will live by the sword
> and you will serve your brother.
> But when you grow restless,
> you will throw his yoke
> from off your neck.

Narrator Esau held a grudge against Jacob because of the blessing his father had given him. [He said to himself:]

Esau

(to himself)   The days of mourning for my father are near; then I will kill my brother Jacob.

Cast: **Narrator, Isaac, Esau, Rebekah, Jacob**

Isaac Sends Jacob to Laban

Genesis 27:46–28:9

Narrator   Rebekah said to Isaac:

Rebekah   I'm disgusted with living, because of these Hittite women. If Jacob takes a wife from among the women of this land, from Hittite women like these, my life will not be worth living.

Narrator   So Isaac called for Jacob and blessed him and commanded him:

Isaac   Do not marry a Canaanite woman. Go at once to Paddan Aram, to the house of your mother's father Bethuel. Take a wife for yourself there, from among the daughters of Laban, your mother's brother. May God Almighty bless you and make you fruitful and increase your numbers until you become a community of peoples. May he give you and your descendants the blessing given to Abraham, so that you may take possession of the land where you now live as an alien, the land God gave to Abraham.

Narrator   Then Isaac sent Jacob on his way, and he went to Paddan Aram, to Laban son of Bethuel the Aramean, the brother of Rebekah, who was the mother of Jacob and Esau.

Now Esau learned that Isaac had blessed Jacob and had sent him to Paddan Aram to take a wife from there, and that when he blessed him he commanded him, "Do not marry a Canaanite woman," and that Jacob had obeyed his father and mother and had gone to Paddan Aram. Esau then realized how displeasing the Canaanite women were to his father Isaac; so he went to Ishmael and married Mahalath, the sister of Nebaioth and daughter of Ishmael son of Abraham, in addition to the wives he already had.

Cast: **Narrator, Rebekah, Isaac**

Jacob's Dream at Bethel

Genesis 28:10–22

Narrator   Jacob left Beersheba and set out for Haran. When he reached a certain place, he stopped for the night because the sun had set. Taking one of the stones there, he put it under his head and lay down to sleep. He had a dream in which he saw a stairway resting on the earth, with its top reaching to heaven, and the angels of God were ascending and descending on it. There above it stood the Lord, and he said:

The Lord	I am the Lord, the God of your father Abraham and the God of Isaac. I will give you and your descendants the land on which you are lying. Your descendants will be like the dust of the earth, and you will spread out to the west and to the east, to the north and to the south. All peoples on earth will be blessed through you and your offspring. I am with you and will watch over you wherever you go, and I will bring you back to this land. I will not leave you until I have done what I have promised you.
Narrator	When Jacob awoke from his sleep, he thought:
Jacob (startled)	Surely the Lord is in this place, and I was not aware of it.
Narrator	He was afraid [and said:]
Jacob (afraid)	How awesome is this place! This is none other than the house of God; this is the gate of heaven.
Narrator	Early the next morning Jacob took the stone he had placed under his head and set it up as a pillar and poured oil on top of it. He called that place Bethel, though the city used to be called Luz. (PAUSE) Then Jacob made a vow:
Jacob	If God will be with me and will watch over me on this journey I am taking and will give me food to eat and clothes to wear so that I return safely to my father's house, then the Lord will be my God and this stone that I have set up as a pillar will be God's house, and of all that you give me I will give you a tenth.

Cast: **Narrator, the Lord, Jacob**

Jacob Arrives in Paddan Aram

Genesis 29:1–30

Narrator	Jacob continued on his journey and came to the land of the eastern peoples. There he saw a well in the field, with three flocks of sheep lying near it because the flocks were watered from that well. The stone over the mouth of the well was large. When all the flocks were gathered there, the shepherds would roll the stone away from the well's mouth and water the sheep. Then they would return the stone to its place over the mouth of the well. Jacob asked the shepherds:
Jacob	My brothers, where are you from?
Shepherds 1 and 2	We're from Haran.
Jacob	Do you know Laban, Nahor's grandson?

Shepherd 1	Yes, we know him.
Jacob	Is he well?
Shepherd 2	Yes, he is.
Shepherd 1	Here comes his daughter Rachel with the sheep.
Jacob	Look, the sun is still high; it is not time for the flocks to be gathered. Water the sheep and take them back to pasture.
Shepherd 2	We can't, until all the flocks are gathered and the stone has been rolled away from the mouth of the well.
Shepherd 1	Then we will water the sheep.
Narrator	While he was still talking with them, Rachel came with her father's sheep, for she was a shepherdess. When Jacob saw Rachel daughter of Laban, his mother's brother, and Laban's sheep, he went over and rolled the stone away from the mouth of the well and watered his uncle's sheep. (PAUSE) Then Jacob kissed Rachel and began to weep aloud. He had told Rachel that he was a relative of her father and a son of Rebekah. So she ran and told her father. (PAUSE)
	As soon as Laban heard the news about Jacob, his sister's son, he hurried to meet him. He embraced him and kissed him and brought him to his home, and there Jacob told him all these things. [Then Laban said to him:]
Laban	You are my own flesh and blood. (PAUSE)
Narrator	After Jacob had stayed with him for a whole month, Laban said to him:
Laban	Just because you are a relative of mine, should you work for me for nothing? Tell me what your wages should be.
Narrator	Now Laban had two daughters; the name of the older was Leah, and the name of the younger was Rachel. Leah had weak eyes, but Rachel was lovely in form, and beautiful. Jacob was in love with Rachel.
Jacob (to Laban)	I'll work for you seven years in return for your younger daughter Rachel.
Laban	It's better that I give her to you than to some other man. Stay here with me.
Narrator	So Jacob served seven years to get Rachel, but they seemed like only a few days to him because of his love for her. [Then Jacob said to Laban:]
Jacob	Give me my wife. My time is completed, and I want to lie with her.
Narrator	So Laban brought together all the people of the place and gave a feast. But when evening came, he took his daughter Leah and gave her to Jacob, and Jacob lay with her. And Laban gave his servant girl Zilpah to his daughter as her maidservant.
	When morning came, there was Leah! [So Jacob said to Laban:]

Jacob	What is this you have done to me? I served you for Rachel, didn't I? Why have you deceived me?
Laban	It is not our custom here to give the younger daughter in marriage before the older one. Finish this daughter's bridal week; then we will give you the younger one also, in return for another seven years of work.
Narrator	And Jacob did so. He finished the week with Leah, and then Laban gave him his daughter Rachel to be his wife. Laban gave his servant girl Bilhah to his daughter Rachel as her maidservant. Jacob lay with Rachel also, and he loved Rachel more than Leah. And he worked for Laban another seven years.

Cast: **Narrator, Jacob, Shepherd 1, Shepherd 2** (can be the same as Shepherd 1), **Laban**

Jacob's Children

Genesis 29:31–30:24

Narrator	When the LORD saw that Leah was not loved, he opened her womb, but Rachel was barren. Leah became pregnant and gave birth to a son. She named him Reuben [for she said:]
Leah	It is because the LORD has seen my misery. Surely my husband will love me now.
Narrator	She conceived again, and when she gave birth to a son she said:
Leah	Because the LORD heard that I am not loved, he gave me this one too.
Narrator	So she named him Simeon. Again she conceived, and . . . she gave birth to a son. [She said:]
Leah	Now at last my husband will become attached to me, because I have borne him three sons.
Narrator	So he was named Levi.
	She conceived again, and . . . she gave birth to a son. [She said:]
Leah	This time I will praise the LORD.
Narrator	So she named him Judah. Then she stopped having children. (PAUSE)
	When Rachel saw that she was not bearing Jacob any children, she became jealous of her sister. [So she said to Jacob:]
Rachel (to Jacob)	Give me children, or I'll die!
Narrator	Jacob became angry with her and said:
Jacob	Am I in the place of God, who has kept you from having children?

Rachel	Here is Bilhah, my maidservant. Sleep with her so that she can bear children for me and that through her I too can build a family.
Narrator	So she gave him her servant Bilhah as a wife. Jacob slept with her, and she became pregnant and bore him a son. [Then Rachel said:]
Rachel (to herself)	God has vindicated me; he has listened to my plea and given me a son.
Narrator	Because of this she named him Dan.
	Rachel's servant Bilhah conceived again and bore Jacob a second son. [Then Rachel said:]
Rachel (to herself)	I have had a great struggle with my sister, and I have won.
Narrator	So she named him Naphtali.
	When Leah saw that she had stopped having children, she took her maidservant Zilpah and gave her to Jacob as a wife. Leah's servant Zilpah bore Jacob a son. [Then Leah said:]
Leah (to herself)	What good fortune!
Narrator	So she named him Gad.
	Leah's servant Zilpah bore Jacob a second son. [Then Leah said:]
Leah (to herself)	How happy I am! The women will call me happy.
Narrator	So she named him Asher.
	During wheat harvest, Reuben went out into the fields and found some mandrake plants, which he brought to his mother Leah. [Rachel said to Leah:]
Rachel (to Leah)	Please give me some of your son's mandrakes.
Leah	Wasn't it enough that you took away my husband? Will you take my son's mandrakes too?
Rachel	Very well, he can sleep with you tonight in return for your son's mandrakes.
Narrator	So when Jacob came in from the fields that evening, Leah went out to meet him.
Leah	You must sleep with me. I have hired you with my son's mandrakes.
Narrator	So he slept with her that night.
	God listened to Leah, and she became pregnant and bore Jacob a fifth son. [Then Leah said:]

Leah (to herself)	God has rewarded me for giving my maidservant to my husband.
Narrator	So she named him Issachar.
	Leah conceived again and bore Jacob a sixth son. [Then Leah said:]
Leah (to herself)	God has presented me with a precious gift. This time my husband will treat me with honor, because I have borne him six sons.
Narrator	So she named him Zebulun.
	Some time later she gave birth to a daughter and named her Dinah.
	Then God remembered Rachel; he listened to her and opened her womb. She became pregnant and gave birth to a son and said:
Rachel	God has taken away my disgrace.
Narrator	She named him Joseph [and said:]
Rachel	May the LORD add to me another son.

Cast: **Narrator, Leah, Rachel, Jacob**

Jacob's Flocks Increase

Genesis 30:25–43

Narrator 1	After Rachel gave birth to Joseph, Jacob said to Laban:
Jacob	Send me on my way so I can go back to my own homeland. Give me my wives and children, for whom I have served you, and I will be on my way. You know how much work I've done for you.
[Narrator 2	But Laban said to him:]
Laban (to Jacob)	If I have found favor in your eyes, please stay. I have learned by divination that the LORD has blessed me because of you. Name your wages, and I will pay them.
Jacob	You know how I have worked for you and how your livestock has fared under my care. The little you had before I came has increased greatly, and the LORD has blessed you wherever I have been. But now, when may I do something for my own household?
Laban	What shall I give you?
Jacob	Don't give me anything. But if you will do this one thing for me, I will go on tending your flocks and watching over them: Let me go through all your flocks today and remove from them every speckled or spotted sheep, every dark-colored lamb and every spotted or speckled goat. They will be my wages. And my honesty will testify for me in the future, when-

ever you check on the wages you have paid me. Any goat in my possession that is not speckled or spotted, or any lamb that is not dark-colored, will be considered stolen.

Laban Agreed. Let it be as you have said.

Narrator 2 That same day he removed all the male goats that were streaked or spotted, and all the speckled or spotted female goats (all that had white on them) and all the dark-colored lambs, and he placed them in the care of his sons. Then he put a three-day journey between himself and Jacob, while Jacob continued to tend the rest of Laban's flocks.

Narrator 1 Jacob, however, took fresh-cut branches from poplar, almond and plane trees and made white stripes on them by peeling the bark and exposing the white inner wood of the branches. Then he placed the peeled branches in all the watering troughs, so that they would be directly in front of the flocks when they came to drink. When the flocks were in heat and came to drink, they mated in front of the branches. And they bore young that were streaked or speckled or spotted. (PAUSE) Jacob set apart the young of the flock by themselves, but made the rest face the streaked and dark-colored animals that belonged to Laban.

Narrator 2 Thus he made separate flocks for himself and did not put them with Laban's animals.

Narrator 1 Whenever the stronger females were in heat, Jacob would place the branches in the troughs in front of the animals so they would mate near the branches, but if the animals were weak, he would not place them there.

Narrator 2 So the weak animals went to Laban and the strong ones to Jacob.

Narrator 1 In this way the man grew exceedingly prosperous and came to own large flocks, and maidservants and menservants, and camels and donkeys.

Cast: **Narrator 1, Jacob, Narrator 2** (can be the same as Narrator 1), **Laban**

Jacob Flees from Laban

From Genesis 31:1–21

Narrator Jacob heard that Laban's sons were saying:

Son 1 Jacob has taken everything our father owned—

Son 2 And has gained all this wealth from what belonged to our father.

Narrator And Jacob noticed that Laban's attitude toward him was not what it had been. Then the LORD said to Jacob:

The Lord
(voice only) Go back to the land of your fathers and to your relatives, and I will be with you.

Narrator	So Jacob sent word to Rachel and Leah to come out to the fields where his flocks were.
Jacob	I see that your father's attitude toward me is not what it was before, but the God of my father has been with me. You know that I've worked for your father with all my strength, yet your father has cheated me by changing my wages ten times. However, God has not allowed him to harm me. If he said, "The speckled ones will be your wages," then all the flocks gave birth to speckled young; and if he said, "The streaked ones will be your wages," then all the flocks bore streaked young. So God has taken away your father's livestock and has given them to me. . . .
[Narrator	Then Rachel and Leah replied:]
Rachel	Do we still have any share in the inheritance of our father's estate?
Leah	Does he not regard us as foreigners? Not only has he sold us, but he has used up what was paid for us.
Rachel	Surely all the wealth that God took away from our father belongs to us and our children. So do whatever God has told you.
Narrator	Then Jacob put his children and his wives on camels, and he drove all his livestock ahead of him, along with all the goods he had accumulated in Paddan Aram, to go to his father Isaac in the land of Canaan. (PAUSE)
	When Laban had gone to shear his sheep, Rachel stole her father's household gods. Moreover, Jacob deceived Laban the Aramean by not telling him he was running away. So he fled with all he had, and crossing the River, he headed for the hill country of Gilead.

Cast: **Narrator, Son 1, Son 2, the Lord** (voice only), **Jacob, Rachel, Leah**

Laban Pursues Jacob

From Genesis 31:22–55

Narrator	On the third day Laban was told that Jacob had fled. Taking his relatives with him, he pursued Jacob for seven days and caught up with him in the hill country of Gilead. Then God came to Laban the Aramean in a dream at night:
God (voice only)	Be careful not to say anything to Jacob, either good or bad.
Narrator	Jacob had pitched his tent in the hill country of Gilead when Laban overtook him, and Laban and his relatives camped there too. (PAUSE) [Then Laban said to Jacob:]
Laban (to Jacob)	What have you done? You've deceived me, and you've carried off my daughters like captives in war. Why did you run off secretly and deceive

me? Why didn't you tell me, so I could send you away with joy and singing to the music of tambourines and harps? You didn't even let me kiss my grandchildren and my daughters good-by. You have done a foolish thing. I have the power to harm you; but last night the God of your father said to me, "Be careful not to say anything to Jacob, either good or bad." Now you have gone off because you longed to return to your father's house. But why did you steal my gods?

[Narrator   Jacob answered Laban:]

Jacob
(to Laban)   I was afraid, because I thought you would take your daughters away from me by force. But if you find anyone who has your gods, he shall not live. In the presence of our relatives, see for yourself whether there is anything of yours here with me; and if so, take it.

Narrator   Now Jacob did not know that Rachel had stolen the gods.

So Laban went into Jacob's tent and into Leah's tent and into the tent of the two maidservants, but he found nothing. After he came out of Leah's tent, he entered Rachel's tent. Now Rachel had taken the household gods and put them inside her camel's saddle and was sitting on them. Laban searched through everything in the tent but found nothing. . . .

Jacob
(angrily)   What is my crime? What sin have I committed that you hunt me down? Now that you have searched through all my goods, what have you found that belongs to your household? Put it here in front of your relatives and mine, and let them judge between the two of us.

I have been with you for twenty years now. Your sheep and goats have not miscarried, nor have I eaten rams from your flocks. I did not bring you animals torn by wild beasts; I bore the loss myself. And you demanded payment from me for whatever was stolen by day or night. This was my situation: The heat consumed me in the daytime and the cold at night, and sleep fled from my eyes. It was like this for the twenty years I was in your household. I worked for you fourteen years for your two daughters and six years for your flocks, and you changed my wages ten times. If the God of my father, the God of Abraham and the Fear of Isaac, had not been with me, you would surely have sent me away empty-handed. But God has seen my hardship and the toil of my hands, and last night he rebuked you.

Laban   The women are my daughters, the children are my children, and the flocks are my flocks. All you see is mine. Yet what can I do today about these daughters of mine, or about the children they have borne? Come now, let's make a covenant, you and I, and let it serve as a witness between us.

Narrator   So Jacob took a stone and set it up as a pillar. He said to his relatives:

Jacob   Gather some stones.

Narrator	So they took stones and piled them in a heap, and they ate there by the heap. Laban called it Jegar Sahadutha, and Jacob called it Galeed. [Laban said:]
Laban (to Jacob)	This heap is a witness between you and me today.
Narrator	That is why it was called Galeed. It was also called Mizpah, because he said:
Laban	May the LORD keep watch between you and me when we are away from each other. If you mistreat my daughters or if you take any wives besides my daughters, even though no one is with us, remember that God is a witness between you and me. Here is this heap, and here is this pillar I have set up between you and me. This heap is a witness, and this pillar is a witness, that I will not go past this heap to your side to harm you and that you will not go past this heap and pillar to my side to harm me. May the God of Abraham and the God of Nahor, the God of their father, judge between us.
Narrator	So Jacob took an oath in the name of the Fear of his father Isaac. He offered a sacrifice there in the hill country and invited his relatives to a meal. After they had eaten, they spent the night there. (PAUSE) Early the next morning Laban kissed his grandchildren and his daughters and blessed them. Then he left and returned home.

Cast: **Narrator, God** (voice only), **Laban, Jacob**

Jacob Prepares to Meet Esau

Genesis 32:[1–2], 3–21

[Narrator	Jacob . . . went on his way, and the angels of God met him. . . . Jacob saw them.
Jacob	This is the camp of God!
Narrator	So he named that place Mahanaim.]
Narrator	Jacob sent messengers ahead of him to his brother Esau in the land of Seir, the country of Edom.
Jacob (to Messengers)	This is what you are to say to my master Esau: "Your servant Jacob says, I have been staying with Laban and have remained there till now. I have cattle and donkeys, sheep and goats, menservants and maidservants. Now I am sending this message to my lord, that I may find favor in your eyes."
Narrator	[When] the messengers returned to Jacob [they said:]

65

Messenger 1	We went to your brother Esau, and now he is coming to meet you.
Messenger 2	And four hundred men are with him.
Narrator	In great fear and distress Jacob divided the people who were with him into two groups, and the flocks and herds and camels as well. [He thought:]
Jacob (thinking)	If Esau comes and attacks one group, the group that is left may escape.
[Narrator	Then Jacob prayed:]
Jacob (praying)	O God of my father Abraham, God of my father Isaac, O LORD, who said to me, "Go back to your country and your relatives, and I will make you prosper," I am unworthy of all the kindness and faithfulness you have shown your servant. I had only my staff when I crossed this Jordan, but now I have become two groups. Save me, I pray, from the hand of my brother Esau, for I am afraid he will come and attack me, and also the mothers with their children. But you have said, "I will surely make you prosper and will make your descendants like the sand of the sea, which cannot be counted."
Narrator	He spent the night there, and from what he had with him he selected a gift for his brother Esau: two hundred female goats and twenty male goats, two hundred ewes and twenty rams, thirty female camels with their young, forty cows and ten bulls, and twenty female donkeys and ten male donkeys. He put them in the care of his servants, each herd by itself, and said to his servants:
Jacob	Go ahead of me, and keep some space between the herds.
Narrator	He instructed the one in the lead:
Jacob	When my brother Esau meets you and asks, "To whom do you belong, and where are you going, and who owns all these animals in front of you?" then you are to say, "They belong to your servant Jacob. They are a gift sent to my lord Esau, and he is coming behind us."
Narrator	He also instructed the second, the third and all the others who followed the herds:
Jacob	You are to say the same thing to Esau when you meet him. And be sure to say, "Your servant Jacob is coming behind us."
Narrator	[Jacob was thinking:]
Jacob (thinking)	I will pacify him with these gifts I am sending on ahead; later, when I see him, perhaps he will receive me.
Narrator	So Jacob's gifts went on ahead of him, but he himself spent the night in the camp.

Cast: **Narrator, Jacob, Messenger 1, Messenger 2** (can be the same as Messenger 1)

Jacob Wrestles with God

Genesis 32:22–30

Narrator   [That night] Jacob got up and took his two wives, his two maidservants and his eleven sons and crossed the ford of the Jabbok. After he had sent them across the stream, he sent over all his possessions. So Jacob was left alone. (PAUSE) And a man wrestled with him till daybreak. When the man saw that he could not overpower him, he touched the socket of Jacob's hip so that his hip was wrenched as he wrestled with the man. Then the man said:

Man   Let me go, for it is daybreak.

Jacob   I will not let you go unless you bless me.

Man   What is your name?

Jacob   Jacob.

Man   Your name will no longer be Jacob, but Israel, because you have struggled with God and with men and have overcome.

Jacob   Please tell me your name.

Man   Why do you ask my name?

Narrator   Then he blessed him there. (PAUSE)

     So Jacob called the place Peniel, saying:

Jacob (amazed,
to audience)   It is because I saw God face to face, and yet my life was spared.

Cast: **Narrator, Man, Jacob**

Jacob Returns to Bethel

Genesis 35:1–15

Narrator   God said to Jacob:

God
(voice only)   Go up to Bethel and settle there, and build an altar there to God, who appeared to you when you were fleeing from your brother Esau.

Narrator   So Jacob said to his household and to all who were with him:

Jacob   Get rid of the foreign gods you have with you, and purify yourselves and change your clothes. Then come, let us go up to Bethel, where I will build an altar to God, who answered me in the day of my distress and who has been with me wherever I have gone.

Narrator	So they gave Jacob all the foreign gods they had and the rings in their ears, and Jacob buried them under the oak at Shechem. (PAUSE) Then they set out, and the terror of God fell upon the towns all around them so that no one pursued them.
	Jacob and all the people with him came to Luz (that is, Bethel) in the land of Canaan. There he built an altar, and he called the place El Bethel, because it was there that God revealed himself to him when he was fleeing from his brother.
	Now Deborah, Rebekah's nurse, died and was buried under the oak below Bethel. So it was named Allon Bacuth.
	After Jacob returned from Paddan Aram, God appeared to him again and blessed him:
God (voice)	Your name is Jacob, but you will no longer be called Jacob; your name will be Israel.
[Narrator	So he named him Israel. And God said to him:]
God (voice)	I am God Almighty; be fruitful and increase in number. A nation and a community of nations will come from you, and kings will come from your body. The land I gave to Abraham and Isaac I also give to you, and I will give this land to your descendants after you.
Narrator	Then God went up from him at the place where he had talked with him.
	Jacob set up a stone pillar at the place where God had talked with him, and he poured out a drink offering on it; he also poured oil on it. (PAUSE) Jacob called the place where God had talked with him Bethel.

Cast: **Narrator**, **God** (voice only), **Jacob**

The Death of Rachel

Genesis 35:16–21

Narrator	[Jacob and his family] moved on from Bethel. While they were still some distance from Ephrath, Rachel began to give birth and had great difficulty. And as she was having great difficulty in childbirth, the midwife said to her:
Midwife	Don't be afraid, for you have another son.
Narrator	As she breathed her last—for she was dying—she named her son Ben-Oni. But his father named him Benjamin.

68

So Rachel died and was buried on the way to Ephrath (that is, Bethlehem). Over her tomb Jacob set up a pillar, and to this day that pillar marks Rachel's tomb.

[Israel moved on again and pitched his tent beyond Migdal Eder.]

Cast: **Narrator, Midwife**

Joseph's Dreams

Genesis 37:1–36

Narrator   Jacob lived in the land where his father had stayed, the land of Canaan.

This is the account of Jacob.

Joseph, a young man of seventeen, was tending the flocks with his brothers, the sons of Bilhah and the sons of Zilpah, his father's wives, and he brought their father a bad report about them.

Now Israel loved Joseph more than any of his other sons, because he had been born to him in his old age; and he made a richly ornamented robe for him. When his brothers saw that their father loved him more than any of them, they hated him and could not speak a kind word to him. (PAUSE)

Joseph had a dream, and when he told it to his brothers, they hated him all the more.

Joseph
(to brothers)   Listen to this dream I had: We were binding sheaves of grain out in the field when suddenly my sheaf rose and stood upright, while your sheaves gathered around mine and bowed down to it.

Brother 1   Do you intend to reign over us?

Brother 2   Will you actually rule us?

Narrator   And they hated him all the more because of his dream and what he had said.

Then he had another dream, and he told it to his brothers:

Joseph   Listen, I had another dream, and this time the sun and moon and eleven stars were bowing down to me.

Narrator   When he told his father as well as his brothers, his father rebuked him:

Jacob   What is this dream you had? Will your mother and I and your brothers actually come and bow down to the ground before you?

Narrator   His brothers were jealous of him, but his father kept the matter in mind. (PAUSE)

Now his brothers had gone to graze their father's flocks near Shechem, and Israel said to Joseph:

Jacob As you know, your brothers are grazing the flocks near Shechem. Come, I am going to send you to them.

Joseph Very well.

Jacob Go and see if all is well with your brothers and with the flocks, and bring word back to me.

Narrator Then he sent him off from the Valley of Hebron.

When Joseph arrived at Shechem, a man found him wandering around in the fields.

Man What are you looking for?

Joseph I'm looking for my brothers. Can you tell me where they are grazing their flocks?

Man They have moved on from here. I heard them say, "Let's go to Dothan."

Narrator So Joseph went after his brothers and found them near Dothan. But they saw him in the distance, and before he reached them, they plotted to kill him.

Brother 1 (to Brothers 2–4) Here comes that dreamer!

Brother 2 Come now, let's kill him and throw him into one of these cisterns.

Brother 3 And say that a ferocious animal devoured him.

Brother 4 *Then* we'll see what comes of his dreams.

Narrator When Reuben heard this, he tried to rescue him from their hands.

Reuben Let's not take his life. Don't shed any blood. Throw him into this cistern here in the desert, but don't lay a hand on him.

Narrator Reuben said this to rescue him from them and take him back to his father.

So when Joseph came to his brothers, they stripped him of his robe—the richly ornamented robe he was wearing—and they took him and threw him into the cistern. Now the cistern was empty; there was no water in it. (PAUSE)

As they sat down to eat their meal, they looked up and saw a caravan of Ishmaelites coming from Gilead. Their camels were loaded with spices, balm and myrrh, and they were on their way to take them down to Egypt.

Judah said to his brothers:

Judah What will we gain if we kill our brother and cover up his blood? Come, let's sell him to the Ishmaelites and not lay our hands on him; after all, he is our brother, our own flesh and blood.

Narrator	His brothers agreed.
	So when the Midianite merchants came by, his brothers pulled Joseph up out of the cistern and sold him for twenty shekels of silver to the Ishmaelites, who took him to Egypt.
	When Reuben returned to the cistern and saw that Joseph was not there, he tore his clothes. He went back to his brothers.
Reuben	The boy isn't there! Where can I turn now?
Narrator	Then they got Joseph's robe, slaughtered a goat and dipped the robe in the blood. They took the ornamented robe back to their father.
Brother 3	We found this. Examine it to see whether it is your son's robe.
Narrator	He recognized it:
Jacob (grieving)	It is my son's robe! Some ferocious animal has devoured him. Joseph has surely been torn to pieces.
Narrator	Then Jacob tore his clothes, put on sackcloth and mourned for his son many days. All his sons and daughters came to comfort him, but he refused to be comforted.
Jacob	No, in mourning will I go down to the grave to my son.
Narrator	So his father wept for him. (PAUSE)
	Meanwhile, the Midianites sold Joseph in Egypt to Potiphar, one of Pharaoh's officials, the captain of the guard.

Cast: **Narrator, Joseph, Brother 1, Brother 2, Jacob, Brother 3** (can be the same as Man or as Brother 2), **Brother 4, Reuben** (can be the same as Brother 1), **Judah** (can be the same as Brother 4)

Joseph and Potiphar's Wife

Genesis 39:1–23

Narrator	Now Joseph had been taken down to Egypt. Potiphar, an Egyptian who was one of Pharaoh's officials, the captain of the guard, bought him from the Ishmaelites who had taken him there.
	The LORD was with Joseph and he prospered, and he lived in the house of his Egyptian master. When his master saw that the LORD was with him and that the LORD gave him success in everything he did, Joseph found favor in his eyes and became his attendant. Potiphar put him in charge of his household, and he entrusted to his care everything he owned. From the time he put him in charge of his household and of all that he owned, the LORD blessed the household of the Egyptian because of Joseph. The blessing of the LORD was on everything Potiphar had, both in the house and in the field. So he left in Joseph's care everything he had; with Joseph

in charge, he did not concern himself with anything except the food he ate.

Now Joseph was well-built and handsome, and after a while his master's wife took notice of Joseph [and said:]

Wife	Come to bed with me!
[Narrator	But he refused.]
Joseph	With me in charge, my master does not concern himself with anything in the house; everything he owns he has entrusted to my care. No one is greater in this house than I am. My master has withheld nothing from me except you, because you are his wife. How then could I do such a wicked thing and sin against God?
Narrator	And though she spoke to Joseph day after day, he refused to go to bed with her or even be with her.
	One day he went into the house to attend to his duties, and none of the household servants was inside. She caught him by his cloak—
Wife	Come to bed with me!
Narrator	But he left his cloak in her hand and ran out of the house.
	When she saw that he had left his cloak in her hand and had run out of the house, she called her household servants.
Wife	Look, this Hebrew has been brought to us to make sport of us! He came in here to sleep with me, but I screamed. When he heard me scream for help, he left his cloak beside me and ran out of the house.
Narrator	She kept his cloak beside her until his master came home. Then she told him this story:
Wife	That Hebrew slave you brought us came to me to make sport of me. But as soon as I screamed for help, he left his cloak beside me and ran out of the house.
Narrator	When his master heard the story his wife told him, saying, "This is how your slave treated me," he burned with anger. Joseph's master took him and put him in prison, the place where the king's prisoners were confined.
	But while Joseph was there in the prison, the LORD was with him; he showed him kindness and granted him favor in the eyes of the prison warden. So the warden put Joseph in charge of all those held in the prison, and he was made responsible for all that was done there. The warden paid no attention to anything under Joseph's care, because the LORD was with Joseph and gave him success in whatever he did.

Cast: **Narrator, Wife, Joseph**

The Cupbearer and the Baker

Genesis 40:1–23

Narrator	[Some time later,] the cupbearer and the baker of the king of Egypt offended their master, the king of Egypt. Pharaoh was angry with his two officials, the chief cupbearer and the chief baker, and put them in custody in the house of the captain of the guard, in the same prison where Joseph was confined. (PAUSE) The captain of the guard assigned them to Joseph, and he attended them.
	After they had been in custody for some time, each of the two men—the cupbearer and the baker of the king of Egypt, who were being held in prison—had a dream the same night, and each dream had a meaning of its own. (PAUSE)
	When Joseph came to them the next morning, he saw that they were dejected. So he asked Pharaoh's officials who were in custody with him in his master's house:
Joseph	Why are your faces so sad today?
[Narrator	They answered:]
Baker	We both had dreams—
Cupbearer	But there is no one to interpret them.
[Narrator	Then Joseph said to them:]
Joseph	Do not interpretations belong to God? Tell me your dreams.
Narrator	So the chief cupbearer told Joseph his dream:
Cupbearer	In my dream I saw a vine in front of me, and on the vine were three branches. As soon as it budded, it blossomed, and its clusters ripened into grapes. Pharaoh's cup was in my hand, and I took the grapes, squeezed them into Pharaoh's cup and put the cup in his hand.
Joseph	This is what it means. The three branches are three days. Within three days Pharaoh will lift up your head and restore you to your position, and you will put Pharaoh's cup in his hand, just as you used to do when you were his cupbearer. But when all goes well with you, remember me and show me kindness; mention me to Pharaoh and get me out of this prison. For I was forcibly carried off from the land of the Hebrews, and even here I have done nothing to deserve being put in a dungeon.
Narrator	When the chief baker saw that Joseph had given a favorable interpretation, he said to Joseph:
Baker	I too had a dream: On my head were three baskets of bread. In the top basket were all kinds of baked goods for Pharaoh, but the birds were eating them out of the basket on my head.

Joseph	This is what it means. The three baskets are three days. Within three days Pharaoh will lift off your head and hang you on a tree. And the birds will eat away your flesh.
Narrator	Now the third day was Pharaoh's birthday, and he gave a feast for all his officials. He lifted up the heads of the chief cupbearer and the chief baker in the presence of his officials: He restored the chief cupbearer to his position, so that he once again put the cup into Pharaoh's hand, but he hanged the chief baker, just as Joseph had said to them in his interpretation.
	The chief cupbearer, however, did not remember Joseph; he forgot him.

Cast: **Narrator, Joseph, Baker, Cupbearer**

Pharaoh's Dreams

Genesis 41:1–44

Narrator	[When two full years had passed,] Pharaoh had a dream: He was standing by the Nile, when out of the river there came up seven cows, sleek and fat, and they grazed among the reeds. After them, seven other cows, ugly and gaunt, came up out of the Nile and stood beside those on the riverbank. And the cows that were ugly and gaunt ate up the seven sleek, fat cows. Then Pharaoh woke up.
	He fell asleep again and had a second dream: Seven heads of grain, healthy and good, were growing on a single stalk. After them, seven other heads of grain sprouted—thin and scorched by the east wind. The thin heads of grain swallowed up the seven healthy, full heads. Then Pharaoh woke up; it had been a dream.
	In the morning his mind was troubled, so he sent for all the magicians and wise men of Egypt. Pharaoh told them his dreams, but no one could interpret them for him.
	Then the chief cupbearer said to Pharaoh:
Cupbearer	Today I am reminded of my shortcomings. Pharaoh was once angry with his servants, and he imprisoned me and the chief baker in the house of the captain of the guard. Each of us had a dream the same night, and each dream had a meaning of its own. (PAUSE) Now a young Hebrew was there with us, a servant of the captain of the guard. We told him our dreams, and he interpreted them for us, giving each man the interpretation of his dream. And things turned out exactly as he interpreted them to us: I was restored to my position, and the other man was hanged.
Narrator	So Pharaoh sent for Joseph, and he was quickly brought from the dungeon. When he had shaved and changed his clothes, he came before Pharaoh. Pharaoh said to Joseph:

74

Pharaoh
  (to Joseph)   I had a dream, and no one can interpret it. But I have heard it said of you that when you hear a dream you can interpret it.

Joseph
  (to Pharaoh)   *I* cannot do it, but *God* will give Pharaoh the answer he desires.

Pharaoh   In my dream I was standing on the bank of the Nile, when out of the river there came up seven cows, fat and sleek, and they grazed among the reeds. After them, seven other cows came up—scrawny and very ugly and lean. I had never seen such ugly cows in all the land of Egypt. The lean, ugly cows ate up the seven fat cows that came up first. But even after they ate them, no one could tell that they had done so; they looked just as ugly as before. Then I woke up.

In my dreams I also saw seven heads of grain, full and good, growing on a single stalk. After them, seven other heads sprouted—withered and thin and scorched by the east wind. The thin heads of grain swallowed up the seven good heads. I told this to the magicians, but none could explain it to me.

Joseph   The dreams of Pharaoh are one and the same. God has revealed to Pharaoh what he is about to do. The seven good cows are seven years, and the seven good heads of grain are seven years; it is one and the same dream. The seven lean, ugly cows that came up afterward are seven years, and so are the seven worthless heads of grain scorched by the east wind: They are seven years of famine.

It is just as I said to Pharaoh: God has shown Pharaoh what he is about to do. Seven years of great abundance are coming throughout the land of Egypt, but seven years of famine will follow them. Then all the abundance in Egypt will be forgotten, and the famine will ravage the land. The abundance in the land will not be remembered, because the famine that follows it will be so severe. The reason the dream was given to Pharaoh in two forms is that the matter has been firmly decided by God, and God will do it soon.

And now let Pharaoh look for a discerning and wise man and put him in charge of the land of Egypt. Let Pharaoh appoint commissioners over the land to take a fifth of the harvest of Egypt during the seven years of abundance. They should collect all the food of these good years that are coming and store up the grain under the authority of Pharaoh, to be kept in the cities for food. This food should be held in reserve for the country, to be used during the seven years of famine that will come upon Egypt, so that the country may not be ruined by the famine.

Narrator   The plan seemed good to Pharaoh and to all his officials. So Pharaoh asked them:

Pharaoh
  (to
  audience)   Can we find *anyone* like this man, one in whom is the spirit of God?

[Narrator   Then Pharaoh said to Joseph:**]**

75

Pharaoh	Since God has made all this known to you, there is no one so discerning and wise as you. You shall be in charge of my palace, and all my people are to submit to your orders. Only with respect to the throne will I be greater than you. I hereby put you in charge of the whole land of Egypt.
Narrator	Then Pharaoh took his signet ring from his finger and put it on Joseph's finger. He dressed him in robes of fine linen and put a gold chain around his neck. He had him ride in a chariot as his second-in-command, and men shouted before him:
Guard	Make way!
Narrator	Thus [Pharaoh] put him in charge of the whole land of Egypt. [Then Pharaoh said to Joseph:]
Pharaoh	I am Pharaoh, but without your word no one will lift hand or foot in all Egypt.

Cast: **Narrator, Cupbearer, Pharaoh, Joseph, Guard**

Joseph's Brothers Go to Egypt

Genesis 41:46–42:24

Narrator	Joseph was thirty years old when he entered the service of Pharaoh king of Egypt. And Joseph went out from Pharaoh's presence and traveled throughout Egypt. During the seven years of abundance the land produced plentifully. Joseph collected all the food produced in those seven years of abundance in Egypt and stored it in the cities. In each city he put the food grown in the fields surrounding it. Joseph stored up huge quantities of grain, like the sand of the sea; it was so much that he stopped keeping records because it was beyond measure. (PAUSE) Before the years of famine came, two sons were born to Joseph by Asenath daughter of Potiphera, priest of On. Joseph named his firstborn Manasseh:
Joseph	It is because God has made me forget all my trouble and all my father's household.
Narrator	The second son he named Ephraim:
Joseph	It is because God has made me fruitful in the land of my suffering.
Narrator	The seven years of abundance in Egypt came to an end, and the seven years of famine began, just as Joseph had said. There was famine in all the other lands, but in the whole land of Egypt there was food. When all Egypt began to feel the famine, the people cried to Pharaoh for food. Then Pharaoh told all the Egyptians:

76

Pharaoh	Go to Joseph and do what he tells you.
Narrator	When the famine had spread over the whole country, Joseph opened the storehouses and sold grain to the Egyptians, for the famine was severe throughout Egypt. And all the countries came to Egypt to buy grain from Joseph, because the famine was severe in all the world.
	When Jacob learned that there was grain in Egypt, he said to his sons:
Jacob	Why do you just keep looking at each other? I have heard that there is grain in Egypt. Go down there and buy some for us, so that we may live and not die.
Narrator	Then ten of Joseph's brothers went down to buy grain from Egypt. But Jacob did not send Benjamin, Joseph's brother, with the others, because he was afraid that harm might come to him. So Israel's sons were among those who went to buy grain, for the famine was in the land of Canaan also.
	Now Joseph was the governor of the land, the one who sold grain to all its people. So when Joseph's brothers arrived, they bowed down to him with their faces to the ground. As soon as Joseph saw his brothers, he recognized them, but he pretended to be a stranger [and spoke harshly to them:]
Joseph (harshly)	Where do you come from?
Brother 1	From the land of Canaan, to buy food.
Narrator	Although Joseph recognized his brothers, they did not recognize him. Then he remembered his dreams about them [and said to them:]
Joseph	You are spies! You have come to see where our land is unprotected.
Brothers (protesting)	No, my lord.
Brother 1	Your servants have come to buy food.
Reuben	We are all the sons of one man.
Brother 3	Your servants are honest men, not spies.
Joseph	No! You have come to see where our land is unprotected.
Brother 1	Your servants *were* twelve brothers—
Reuben	The sons of one man, who lives in the land of Canaan.
Brother 3	The youngest is now with our father, and one is no more.
Joseph	It is just as I told you: You are spies! And this is how you will be tested: As surely as Pharaoh lives, you will not leave this place unless your youngest brother comes here. Send one of your number to get your brother; the rest of you will be kept in prison, so that your words may be tested to see if you are telling the truth. If you are not, then as surely as Pharaoh lives, you are spies!

77

Narrator	And he put them all in custody for three days. On the third day, Joseph said to them:
Joseph	Do this and you will live, for I fear God: If you are honest men, let one of your brothers stay here in prison, while the rest of you go and take grain back for your starving households. But you must bring your youngest brother to me, so that your words may be verified and that you may not die.
Narrator	This they proceeded to do. They said to one another:
Brother 1	Surely we are being punished because of our brother. We saw how distressed he was when he pleaded with us for his life, but we would not listen; that's why this distress has come upon us.
Reuben	Didn't I tell you not to sin against the boy? But you wouldn't listen!
Brother 3	Now we must give an accounting for his blood.
Narrator	They did not realize that Joseph could understand them, since he was using an interpreter.
	He turned away from them and began to weep, but then turned back and spoke to them again. He had Simeon taken from them and bound before their eyes.

Cast: **Narrator, Joseph, Pharaoh, Jacob, Brother 1, Reuben, Brother 3** (can be the same as Reuben)

Joseph's Brothers Return to Canaan

Genesis 42:25–38

Narrator	Joseph gave orders to fill their bags with grain, to put each man's silver back in his sack, and to give them provisions for their journey. After this was done for them, they loaded their grain on their donkeys and left.
	At the place where they stopped for the night one of them opened his sack to get feed for his donkey, and he saw his silver in the mouth of his sack. [He said to his brothers.]
Brother 1	My silver has been returned. Here it is in my sack.
Narrator	Their hearts sank and they turned to each other trembling:
Reuben	What is this that God has done to us?
Narrator	When they came to their father Jacob in the land of Canaan, they told him all that had happened to them.
Brother 1	The man who is lord over the land spoke harshly to us and treated us as though we were spying on the land.

Brother 2	But we said to him, "We are honest men; we are not spies. We were twelve brothers, sons of one father. One is no more, and the youngest is now with our father in Canaan."
Brother 3	Then the man who is lord over the land said to us, "This is how I will know whether you are honest men: Leave one of your brothers here with me, and take food for your starving households and go.
Brother 2	"But bring your youngest brother to me so I will know that you are not spies but honest men. Then I will give your brother back to you, and you can trade in the land."
Narrator	As they were emptying their sacks, there in each man's sack was his pouch of silver! When they and their father saw the money pouches, they were frightened. [Their father Jacob said to them:]
Jacob	You have deprived me of my children. Joseph is no more and Simeon is no more, and now you want to take Benjamin. Everything is against me!
[Narrator	Then Reuben said to his father:]
Reuben	You may put both of my sons to death if I do not bring him back to you. Entrust him to my care, and I will bring him back.
Jacob	My son will not go down there with you; his brother is dead and he is the only one left. If harm comes to him on the journey you are taking, you will bring my gray head down to the grave in sorrow.

Cast: **Narrator, Brother 1, Reuben, Brother 2, Brother 3** (Brothers 1–3 can be the same), **Jacob**

The Second Journey to Egypt

Genesis 43:1–34

Narrator	Now the famine was still severe in the land. So when they had eaten all the grain they had brought from Egypt, their father said to them:
Jacob	Go back and buy us a little more food.
Narrator	But Judah said to him:
Judah	The man warned us solemnly, "You will not see my face again unless your brother is with you." If you will send our brother along with us, we will go down and buy food for you. But if you will not send him, we will not go down, because the man said to us, "You will not see my face again unless your brother is with you."
Jacob	Why did you bring this trouble on me by telling the man you had another brother?
Brother 1	The man questioned us closely about ourselves and our family.
Brother 2 (imitating Joseph)	"Is your father still living?" "Do you have another brother?"

Brother 3	We simply answered his questions.
Brother 4	How were we to know he would say, "Bring your brother down here"?
Judah (to Jacob)	Send the boy along with me and we will go at once, so that we and you and our children may live and not die. I myself will guarantee his safety; you can hold me personally responsible for him. If I do not bring him back to you and set him here before you, I will bear the blame before you all my life. As it is, if we had not delayed, we could have gone and returned twice.
Jacob	If it must be, then do this: Put some of the best products of the land in your bags and take them down to the man as a gift—a little balm and a little honey, some spices and myrrh, some pistachio nuts and almonds. Take double the amount of silver with you, for you must return the silver that was put back into the mouths of your sacks. Perhaps it was a mistake. Take your brother also and go back to the man at once. And may God Almighty grant you mercy before the man so that he will let your other brother and Benjamin come back with you. As for me, if I am bereaved, I am bereaved. (PAUSE)
Narrator	So the men took the gifts and double the amount of silver, and Benjamin also. They hurried down to Egypt and presented themselves to Joseph. When Joseph saw Benjamin with them, he said to the steward of his house:
Joseph (to Steward)	Take these men to my house, slaughter an animal and prepare dinner; they are to eat with me at noon.
Narrator	The man did as Joseph told him and took the men to Joseph's house. Now the men were frightened when they were taken to his house. [They thought:]
Brother 1 (to Brothers 2–4)	We were brought here because of the silver that was put back into our sacks the first time.
Brother 2	He wants to attack us and overpower us and seize us as slaves and take our donkeys.
Narrator	So they went up to Joseph's steward and spoke to him at the entrance to the house.
Brother 1	Please, sir, we came down here the first time to buy food.
Brother 2	But at the place where we stopped for the night we opened our sacks and each of us found his silver—the exact weight—in the mouth of his sack.
Brother 3	So we have brought it back with us.
Brother 4	We have also brought additional silver with us to buy food.
Brother 2	We don't know who put our silver in our sacks.

Steward	It's all right. Don't be afraid. Your God, the God of your father, has given you treasure in your sacks; I *received* your silver.
Narrator	Then he brought Simeon out to them. (PAUSE)
	The steward took the men into Joseph's house, gave them water to wash their feet and provided fodder for their donkeys. They prepared their gifts for Joseph's arrival at noon, because they had heard that they were to eat there.
	When Joseph came home, they presented to him the gifts they had brought into the house, and they bowed down before him to the ground. He asked them how they were, and then he said:
Joseph	How is your aged father you told me about? Is he still living?
Brother 1	Your servant our father is still alive and well.
Narrator	And they bowed low to pay him honor.
	He looked about and saw his brother Benjamin, his own mother's son.
Joseph (to Brothers)	Is this your youngest brother, the one you told me about? God be gracious to you, my son.
Narrator	Deeply moved at the sight of his brother, Joseph hurried out and looked for a place to weep. He went into his private room and wept there. (PAUSE)
	After he had washed his face, he came out and, controlling himself, said:
Joseph	Serve the food.
Narrator	They served him by himself, the brothers by themselves, and the Egyptians who ate with him by themselves, because Egyptians could not eat with Hebrews, for that is detestable to Egyptians. The men had been seated before him in the order of their ages, from the firstborn to the youngest; and they looked at each other in astonishment. When portions were served to them from Joseph's table, Benjamin's portion was five times as much as anyone else's. So they feasted and drank freely with him.

Cast: **Narrator, Jacob, Judah, Brother 1** (can be the same as Judah), **Brother 2, Brother 3, Brother 4** (Brothers 1–4 can be the same), **Joseph, Steward**

A Silver Cup in a Sack

From Genesis 44 and 45

Narrator	Joseph gave these instructions to the steward of his house:
Joseph	Fill the men's sacks with as much food as they can carry, and put each man's silver in the mouth of his sack. Then put my cup, the silver one,

in the mouth of the youngest one's sack, along with the silver for his grain.

Narrator   And he did as Joseph said.

As morning dawned, the men were sent on their way with their donkeys. They had not gone far from the city when Joseph said to his steward:

Joseph   Go after those men at once, and when you catch up with them, say to them, "Why have you repaid good with evil? Isn't this the cup my master drinks from and also uses for divination? This is a wicked thing you have done."

Narrator   When he caught up with them, he repeated these words to them. But they said to him:

Brother 1   Why does my lord say such things?

Brother 2   Far be it from your servants to do anything like that!

Brother 3   We even brought back to you from the land of Canaan the silver we found inside the mouths of our sacks. So why would we steal silver or gold from your master's house?

Brother 4   If any of your servants is found to have it, he will die; and the rest of us will become my lord's slaves.

Steward   Very well, then, let it be as you say. Whoever is found to have it will become my slave; the rest of you will be free from blame.

Narrator   Each of them quickly lowered his sack to the ground and opened it. Then the steward proceeded to search, beginning with the oldest and ending with the youngest. And the cup was found in Benjamin's sack. At this, they tore their clothes. Then they all loaded their donkeys and returned to the city. (PAUSE)

Joseph was still in the house when Judah and his brothers came in, and they threw themselves to the ground before him. [Joseph said to them:]

Joseph   What is this you have done? Don't you know that a man like me can find things out by divination?

[Narrator   Judah replied:]

Judah
(to Joseph)   What can we say to my lord? What can we say? How can we prove our innocence? God has uncovered your servants' guilt. We are now my lord's slaves—we ourselves and the one who was found to have the cup.

Joseph   Far be it from me to do such a thing! Only the man who was found to have the cup will become my slave. The rest of you, go back to your father in peace.

Narrator   Then Judah went up to him.

Judah   Please, my lord, let your servant speak a word to my lord. [Do not be angry with your servant, though you are equal to Pharaoh himself. My lord asked his servants, "Do you have a father or a brother?" And we answered, "We have an aged father, and there is a young son born to him in his old age. His brother is dead, and he is the only one of his mother's sons left, and his father loves him."

Then you said to your servants, "Bring him down to me so I can see him for myself." And we said to my lord, "The boy cannot leave his father; if he leaves him, his father will die." But you told your servants, "Unless your youngest brother comes down with you, you will not see my face again." When we went back to your servant my father, we told him what my lord had said.

Then our father said, "Go back and buy a little more food." But we said, "We cannot go down. Only if our youngest brother is with us will we go. We cannot see the man's face unless our youngest brother is with us." Your servant my father said to us, "You know that my wife bore me two sons. One of them went away from me, and I said, 'He has surely been torn to pieces.' And I have not seen him since. If you take this one from me too and harm comes to him, you will bring my gray head down to the grave in misery."

So now,] if the boy is not with us when I go back to your servant my father and if my father, whose life is closely bound up with the boy's life, sees that the boy isn't there, he will die. Your servants will bring the gray head of our father down to the grave in sorrow. Your servant guaranteed the boy's safety to my father. I said, "If I do not bring him back to you, I will bear the blame before you, my father, all my life!"

Now then, please let your servant remain here as my lord's slave in place of the boy, and let the boy return with his brothers. How can I go back to my father if the boy is not with me? No! Do not let me see the misery that would come upon my father.

Narrator	Then Joseph could no longer control himself before all his attendants.
Joseph (crying out)	Have everyone leave my presence!
Narrator	So there was no one with Joseph when he made himself known to his brothers. And he wept so loudly that the Egyptians heard him, and Pharaoh's household heard about it. [Joseph said to his brothers:]
Joseph	I am Joseph! Is my father still living?
Narrator	But his brothers were not able to answer him, because they were terrified at his presence. [Then Joseph said to his brothers:]
Joseph	Come close to me. (PAUSE)
[Narrator	When they had done so, he said:]
Joseph (confiden- tially)	I am your brother Joseph, the one you sold into Egypt! And now, do not be distressed and do not be angry with yourselves for selling me

here, because it was to save lives that God sent me ahead of you. For two years now there has been famine in the land, and for the next five years there will not be plowing and reaping. But God sent me ahead of you to preserve for you a remnant on earth and to save your lives by a great deliverance.

So then, it was not you who sent me here, but God. He made me father to Pharaoh, lord of his entire household and ruler of all Egypt. Now hurry back to my father and say to him, "This is what your son Joseph says: God has made me lord of all Egypt. Come down to me; don't delay. You shall live in the region of Goshen and be near me—you, your children and grandchildren, your flocks and herds, and all you have. I will provide for you there, because five years of famine are still to come. Otherwise you and your household and all who belong to you will become destitute."

You can see for yourselves, and so can my brother Benjamin, that it is really I who am speaking to you. Tell my father about all the honor accorded me in Egypt and about everything you have seen. And bring my father down here quickly.

Narrator Then he threw his arms around his brother Benjamin and wept, and Benjamin embraced him, weeping. And he kissed all his brothers and wept over them. Afterward his brothers talked with him. . . . (PAUSE)

So they went up out of Egypt and came to their father Jacob in the land of Canaan. [They told him:]

Brother 1 Joseph is still alive!

Brother 2 In fact, he is ruler of all Egypt.

Cast: **Narrator, Joseph, Brother 1, Brother 2, Brother 3, Brother 4** (Brothers 1–4 can be the same), **Steward, Judah** (can be the same as Brother 4)

Jacob Goes to Egypt

Genesis 46:1–7, 28–30

Narrator Israel set out with all that was his, and when he reached Beersheba, he offered sacrifices to the God of his father Isaac.

And God spoke to Israel in a vision at night:

God (voice only) Jacob! Jacob!

Jacob Here I am.

God (voice) I am God, the God of your father. Do not be afraid to go down to Egypt, for I will make you into a great nation there. I will go down to Egypt with you, and I will surely bring you back again. And Joseph's own hand will close your eyes.

Narrator   Then Jacob left Beersheba, and Israel's sons took their father Jacob and their children and their wives in the carts that Pharaoh had sent to transport him. They also took with them their livestock and the possessions they had acquired in Canaan, and Jacob and all his offspring went to Egypt. He took with him to Egypt his sons and grandsons and his daughters and granddaughters—all his offspring. . . . (PAUSE)

Now Jacob sent Judah ahead of him to Joseph to get directions to Goshen. When they arrived in the region of Goshen, Joseph had his chariot made ready and went to Goshen to meet his father Israel. (PAUSE) As soon as Joseph appeared before him, he threw his arms around his father and wept for a long time. [Israel said to Joseph:]

Jacob   Now I am ready to die, since I have seen for myself that you are still alive.

Cast: **Narrator, God, Jacob**

Jacob and His Family in Egypt

Genesis 46:31–47:12

Narrator   Joseph said to his brothers and to his father's household:

Joseph   I will go up and speak to Pharaoh and will say to him, "My brothers and my father's household, who were living in the land of Canaan, have come to me. The men are shepherds; they tend livestock, and they have brought along their flocks and herds and everything they own." When Pharaoh calls you in and asks, "What is your occupation?" you should answer, "Your servants have tended livestock from our boyhood on, just as our fathers did." Then you will be allowed to settle in the region of Goshen, for all shepherds are detestable to the Egyptians.

Narrator   Joseph went and told Pharaoh:

Joseph
(to Pharaoh)   My father and brothers, with their flocks and herds and everything they own, have come from the land of Canaan and are now in Goshen.

Narrator   He chose five of his brothers and presented them before Pharaoh. Pharaoh asked the brothers:

Pharaoh   What is your occupation?

Brother 1   Your servants are shepherds, just as our fathers were.

Brother 2   We have come to live here awhile, because the famine is severe in Canaan and your servants' flocks have no pasture. So now, please let your servants settle in Goshen.

[Narrator   Pharaoh said to Joseph:]

85

Pharaoh	Your father and your brothers have come to you, and the land of Egypt is before you; settle your father and your brothers in the best part of the land. Let them live in Goshen. And if you know of any among them with special ability, put them in charge of my own livestock.
Narrator	Then Joseph brought his father Jacob in and presented him before Pharaoh. After Jacob blessed Pharaoh, Pharaoh asked him:
Pharaoh	How old are you?
Jacob	The years of my pilgrimage are a hundred and thirty. My years have been few and difficult, and they do not equal the years of the pilgrimage of my fathers.
Narrator	Then Jacob blessed Pharaoh and went out from his presence.
	So Joseph settled his father and his brothers in Egypt and gave them property in the best part of the land, the district of Rameses, as Pharaoh directed. Joseph also provided his father and his brothers and all his father's household with food, according to the number of their children.

Cast: **Narrator, Joseph, Pharaoh, Brother 1, Brother 2** (can be the same as Brother 1), **Jacob**

Joseph and the Famine

Genesis 47:13–26

Narrator	There was no food . . . in the whole region because the famine was severe; both Egypt and Canaan wasted away because of the famine. Joseph collected all the money that was to be found in Egypt and Canaan in payment for the grain they were buying, and he brought it to Pharaoh's palace. When the money of the people of Egypt and Canaan was gone, all Egypt came to Joseph and said:
Egyptian 1	Give us food.
Egyptian 2	Why should we die before your eyes?
Egyptian 3	Our money is used up.
[Narrator	Joseph answered:]
Joseph	Then bring your livestock. I will sell you food in exchange for your livestock, since your money is gone.
Narrator	So they brought their livestock to Joseph, and he gave them food in exchange for their horses, their sheep and goats, their cattle and donkeys. And he brought them through that year with food in exchange for all their livestock.
	When that year was over, they came to him the following year [and said:]

Egyptian 1	We cannot hide from our lord the fact that since our money is gone and our livestock belongs to you—
Egyptian 2	There is nothing left for our lord except our bodies and our land.
Egyptian 3	Why should we perish before your eyes—we and our land as well?
Egyptian 2	Buy us and our land in exchange for food.
Egyptian 3	We with our land will be in bondage to Pharaoh.
Egyptian 1	Give us seed so that we may live and not die, and that the land may not become desolate.
Narrator	So Joseph bought all the land in Egypt for Pharaoh. The Egyptians, one and all, sold their fields, because the famine was too severe for them. The land became Pharaoh's, and Joseph reduced the people to servitude, from one end of Egypt to the other. However, he did not buy the land of the priests, because they received a regular allotment from Pharaoh and had food enough from the allotment Pharaoh gave them. That is why they did not sell their land. Joseph said to the people:
Joseph	Now that I have bought you and your land today for Pharaoh, here is seed for you so you can plant the ground. But when the crop comes in, give a fifth of it to Pharaoh. The other four-fifths you may keep as seed for the fields and as food for yourselves and your households and your children.
Egyptian 1	You have saved our lives.
Egyptian 2	May we find favor in the eyes of our lord.
Egyptian 3	We will be in bondage to Pharaoh.
Narrator	So Joseph established it as a law concerning land in Egypt—still in force today—that a fifth of the produce belongs to Pharaoh. It was only the land of the priests that did not become Pharaoh's.

Cast: **Narrator, Egyptian 1, Egyptian 2, Egyptian 3,** Joseph

Jacob's Last Request and Blessing

Genesis 47:27–48:16 [17–22]

Narrator	The Israelites settled in Egypt in the region of Goshen. They acquired property there and were fruitful and increased greatly in number.
	Jacob lived in Egypt seventeen years, and the years of his life were a hundred and forty-seven. When the time drew near for [Jacob] to die, he called for his son Joseph [and said to him:]
Jacob	If I have found favor in your eyes, put your hand under my thigh and promise that you will show me kindness and faithfulness. Do not bury

	me in Egypt, but when I rest with my fathers, carry me out of Egypt and bury me where they are buried.
[**Narrator**	Joseph answered:]
Joseph	I will do as you say.
Jacob	Swear to me.
Narrator	Then Joseph swore to him, and [Jacob] worshiped as he leaned on the top of his staff. (PAUSE)
	Some time later Joseph was told:
Servant 1	Your father is ill.
Narrator	So he took his two sons Manasseh and Ephraim along with him. (PAUSE) When Jacob was told—
Servant 2	Your son Joseph has come to you—
Narrator	[Jacob] rallied his strength and sat up on the bed. [He] said to Joseph:
Jacob (to Joseph)	God Almighty appeared to me at Luz in the land of Canaan, and there he blessed me and said to me, "I am going to make you fruitful and will increase your numbers. I will make you a community of peoples, and I will give this land as an everlasting possession to your descendants after you."
	Now then, your two sons born to you in Egypt before I came to you here will be reckoned as mine; Ephraim and Manasseh will be mine, just as Reuben and Simeon are mine. Any children born to you after them will be yours; in the territory they inherit they will be reckoned under the names of their brothers. As I was returning from Paddan, to my sorrow Rachel died in the land of Canaan while we were still on the way, a little distance from Ephrath. So I buried her there beside the road to Ephrath.
Narrator	(That is, Bethlehem.) (PAUSE) When [Jacob] saw the sons of Joseph, he asked:
Jacob	Who are these?
Joseph	They are the sons God has given me here.
Jacob	Bring them to me so I may bless them.
Narrator	Now [Jacob's] eyes were failing because of old age, and he could hardly see. So Joseph brought his sons close to him, and his father kissed them and embraced them. [Jacob] said to Joseph:
Jacob (to Joseph)	I never expected to see your face again, and now God has allowed me to see your children too.
Narrator	Then Joseph removed them from [Jacob's] knees and bowed down with his face to the ground. And Joseph took both of them, Ephraim on his right toward [Jacob's] left hand and Manasseh on his left toward [Jacob's]

right hand, and brought them close to him. But [Jacob] reached out his right hand and put it on Ephraim's head, though he was the younger, and crossing his arms, he put his left hand on Manasseh's head, even though Manasseh was the firstborn.

Then he blessed Joseph:

Jacob	May the God before whom my fathers
	    Abraham and Isaac walked,
	the God who has been my shepherd
	    all my life to this day,
	the Angel who has delivered me from all harm
	    —may he bless these boys.
	May they be called by my name
	    and the names of my fathers Abraham and Isaac,
	and may they increase greatly
	    upon the earth.

[Narrator	When Joseph saw his father placing his right hand on Ephraim's head he was displeased; so he took hold of his father's hand to move it from Ephraim's head to Manasseh's head. Joseph said to him:
Joseph	No, my father, this one is the firstborn; put your right hand on his head.
Narrator	But his father refused:
Jacob	I know, my son, I know. He too will become a people, and he too will become great. Nevertheless, his younger brother will be greater than he, and his descendants will become a group of nations.
Narrator	He blessed them that day:
Jacob	In your name will [Jacob] pronounce this blessing: "May God make you like Ephraim and Manasseh."
Narrator	So he put Ephraim ahead of Manasseh. (PAUSE) Then [Jacob] said to Joseph:
Jacob	I am about to die, but God will be with you and take you back to the land of your fathers. And to you, as one who is over your brothers, I give the ridge of land I took from the Amorites with my sword and my bow.]

Cast: **Narrator, Jacob, Joseph, Servant 1, Servant 2.** ("Israel" has been identified as Jacob in the text above to avoid dramatic confusion.)

The Death and Burial of Jacob

Genesis 49:29–50:14

Narrator	[Jacob gave his sons] these instructions:

89

Jacob	I am about to be gathered to my people. Bury me with my fathers in the cave in the field of Ephron the Hittite, the cave in the field of Machpelah, near Mamre in Canaan, which Abraham bought as a burial place from Ephron the Hittite, along with the field. There Abraham and his wife Sarah were buried, there Isaac and his wife Rebekah were buried, and there I buried Leah. The field and the cave in it were bought from the Hittites.
Narrator	When Jacob had finished giving instructions to his sons, he drew his feet up into the bed, breathed his last and was gathered to his people.
	Joseph threw himself upon his father and wept over him and kissed him. (PAUSE) Then Joseph directed the physicians in his service to embalm his father Israel. So the physicians embalmed him, taking a full forty days, for that was the time required for embalming. And the Egyptians mourned for him seventy days.
	When the days of mourning had passed, Joseph said to Pharaoh's court:
Joseph	If I have found favor in your eyes, speak to Pharaoh for me. Tell him, "My father made me swear an oath and said, 'I am about to die; bury me in the tomb I dug for myself in the land of Canaan.' Now let me go up and bury my father; then I will return."
Pharaoh	Go up and bury your father, as he made you swear to do.
Narrator	So Joseph went up to bury his father. All Pharaoh's officials accompanied him—the dignitaries of his court and all the dignitaries of Egypt—besides all the members of Joseph's household and his brothers and those belonging to his father's household. Only their children and their flocks and herds were left in Goshen. Chariots and horsemen also went up with him. It was a very large company.
	When they reached the threshing floor of Atad, near the Jordan, they lamented loudly and bitterly; and there Joseph observed a seven-day period of mourning for his father. When the Canaanites who lived there saw the mourning at the threshing floor of Atad, they said:
Canaanite	The Egyptians are holding a solemn ceremony of mourning.
Narrator	That is why that place near the Jordan is called Abel Mizraim.
	So Jacob's sons did as he had commanded them: They carried him to the land of Canaan and buried him in the cave in the field of Machpelah, near Mamre, which Abraham had bought as a burial place from Ephron the Hittite, along with the field. After burying his father, Joseph returned to Egypt, together with his brothers and all the others who had gone with him to bury his father.

Cast: **Narrator, Jacob, Joseph, Pharaoh, Canaanite**

Joseph's Reassurance and His Death

Genesis 50:15–21 [24–26]

Narrator	When Joseph's brothers saw that their father was dead, they said:
Brother 1	What if Joseph holds a grudge against us—
Brother 2	And pays us back for all the wrongs we did to him?
Narrator	So they sent word to Joseph:
Brother 2	Your father left these instructions before he died: "This is what you are to say to Joseph: I ask you to forgive your brothers the sins and the wrongs they committed in treating you so badly."
Brother 1	Now please forgive the sins of the servants of the God of your father.
Narrator	When their message came to him, Joseph wept.
	His brothers then came and threw themselves down before him.
Brother 1	We are your slaves.
[Narrator	But Joseph said to them:]
Joseph	Don't be afraid. Am I in the place of God? You intended to harm me, but God intended it for good to accomplish what is now being done, the saving of many lives. So then, don't be afraid. I will provide for you and your children.
Narrator	And he reassured them and spoke kindly to them. (PAUSE) [Joseph stayed in Egypt, along with all his father's family. He lived a hundred and ten years and saw the third generation of Ephraim's children. Also the children of Makir son of Manasseh were placed at birth on Joseph's knees.
	Then Joseph said to his brothers:
Joseph	I am about to die. But God will surely come to your aid and take you up out of this land to the land he promised on oath to Abraham, Isaac and Jacob.
Narrator	And Joseph made the sons of Israel swear an oath [and said:]
Joseph	God will surely come to your aid, and then you must carry my bones up from this place.
Narrator	So Joseph died at the age of a hundred and ten. And after they embalmed him, he was placed in a coffin in Egypt.]

Cast: **Narrator, Brother 1, Brother 2** (can be the same as Brother 1), **Joseph**

Exodus

The Israelites Oppressed

Exodus 1:1–22

Narrator These are the names of the sons of Israel who went to Egypt with Jacob, each with his family: Reuben, Simeon, Levi and Judah; Issachar, Zebulun and Benjamin; Dan and Naphtali; Gad and Asher. The descendants of Jacob numbered seventy in all; Joseph was already in Egypt.

Now Joseph and all his brothers and all that generation died, but the Israelites were fruitful and multiplied greatly and became exceedingly numerous, so that the land was filled with them. (PAUSE)

Then a new king, who did not know about Joseph, came to power in Egypt. [He said to his people:]

Pharaoh Look, the Israelites have become much too numerous for us. Come, we must deal shrewdly with them or they will become even more numerous and, if war breaks out, will join our enemies, fight against us and leave the country.

Narrator So they put slave masters over them to oppress them with forced labor, and they built Pithom and Rameses as store cities for Pharaoh. But the more they were oppressed, the more they multiplied and spread; so the Egyptians came to dread the Israelites and worked them ruthlessly. They made their lives bitter with hard labor in brick and mortar and with all kinds of work in the fields; in all their hard labor the Egyptians used them ruthlessly.

The king of Egypt said to the Hebrew midwives, whose names were Shiphrah and Puah:

Pharaoh
(brutally) When you help the Hebrew women in childbirth and observe them on the delivery stool, if it is a boy, kill him; but if it is a girl, let her live.

Narrator The midwives, however, feared God and did not do what the king of Egypt had told them to do; they let the boys live. Then the king of Egypt summoned the midwives [and asked them:]

Pharaoh Why have you done this? Why have you let the boys live?

[Narrator The midwives answered Pharaoh:]

Midwife 1 Hebrew women are not like Egyptian women.

Midwife 2 They are vigorous and give birth before the midwives arrive. (PAUSE)

Narrator	So God was kind to the midwives and the people increased and became even more numerous. And because the midwives feared God, he gave them families of their own.

Then Pharaoh gave this order to all his people:

Pharaoh	Every boy that is born you must throw into the Nile, but let every girl live.

Cast: **Narrator, Pharaoh, Midwife 1, Midwife 2**

The Birth of Moses

Exodus 2:1–10

Narrator 1	A man of the house of Levi married a Levite woman, and she became pregnant and gave birth to a son. When she saw that he was a fine child, she hid him for three months. But when she could hide him no longer, she got a papyrus basket for him and coated it with tar and pitch. Then she placed the child in it and put it among the reeds along the bank of the Nile. His sister stood at a distance to see what would happen to him.
Narrator 2	Then Pharaoh's daughter went down to the Nile to bathe, and her attendants were walking along the river bank. She saw the basket among the reeds and sent her slave girl to get it. She opened it and saw the baby. He was crying, and she felt sorry for him.
Princess	This is one of the Hebrew babies.
Narrator 1	Then his sister asked Pharaoh's daughter:
Moses' sister	Shall I go and get one of the Hebrew women to nurse the baby for you?
Princess	Yes, go.
Narrator 2	And the girl went and got the baby's [*own*] mother. (PAUSE) Pharaoh's daughter said to her:
Princess	Take this baby and nurse him for me, and I will pay you.
Narrator 1	So the woman took the baby and nursed him. (PAUSE)
Narrator 2	When the child grew older, she took him to Pharaoh's daughter and he became her son. She named him Moses [saying:]
Princess	I drew him out of the water.

Cast: **Narrator 1, Narrator 2, Princess, Moses' sister**

93

Moses Flees to Midian

Exodus 2:11–25

Narrator	One day, after Moses had grown up, he went out to where his own people were and watched them at their hard labor. He saw an Egyptian beating a Hebrew, one of his own people. Glancing this way and that and seeing no one, he killed the Egyptian and hid him in the sand. The next day he went out and saw two Hebrews fighting. He asked the one in the wrong:
Moses	Why are you hitting your fellow Hebrew?
[Narrator	The man said:]
Hebrew	Who made you ruler and judge over us? Are you thinking of killing me as you killed the Egyptian?
Narrator	Then Moses was afraid [and thought:]
Moses (thinking)	What I did must have become known.
Narrator	When Pharaoh heard of this, he tried to kill Moses, but Moses fled from Pharaoh and went to live in Midian, where he sat down by a well. (PAUSE) Now a priest of Midian had seven daughters, and they came to draw water and fill the troughs to water their father's flock. Some shepherds came along and drove them away, but Moses got up and came to their rescue and watered their flock.
	When the girls returned to Reuel their father, he asked them:
Reuel	Why have you returned so early today?
Daughter	An Egyptian rescued us from the shepherds. He even drew water for us and watered the flock.
Reuel	And where is he? Why did you leave him? Invite him to have something to eat.
Narrator	Moses agreed to stay with the man, who gave his daughter Zipporah to Moses in marriage. Zipporah gave birth to a son, and Moses named him Gershom, saying:
Moses	I have become an alien in a foreign land. (PAUSE)
Narrator	During that long period, the king of Egypt died. The Israelites groaned in their slavery and cried out, and their cry for help because of their slavery went up to God. God heard their groaning and he remembered his covenant with Abraham, with Isaac and with Jacob. So God looked on the Israelites and was concerned about them.

Cast: **Narrator, Moses, Hebrew, Reuel, Daughter**

Moses and the Burning Bush (i)

Exodus 3:1–15

Narrator Moses was tending the flock of Jethro his father-in-law, the priest of Midian, and he led the flock to the far side of the desert and came to Horeb, the mountain of God. There the angel of the LORD appeared to him in flames of fire from within a bush. Moses saw that though the bush was on fire it did not burn up.

Moses
(thinking) I will go over and see this strange sight—why the bush does not burn up.

Narrator When the LORD saw that he had gone over to look, God called to him from within the bush:

God
(voice only) Moses! Moses!

Moses Here I am.

God
(voice) Do not come any closer. Take off your sandals, for the place where you are standing is holy ground. (PAUSE) I am the God of your father, the God of Abraham, the God of Isaac and the God of Jacob.

Narrator At this, Moses hid his face, because he was afraid to look at God.

God
(voice) I have indeed seen the misery of my people in Egypt. I have heard them crying out because of their slave drivers, and I am concerned about their suffering. So I have come down to rescue them from the hand of the Egyptians and to bring them up out of that land into a good and spacious land, a land flowing with milk and honey—the home of the Canaanites, Hittites, Amorites, Perizzites, Hivites and Jebusites. And now the cry of the Israelites has reached me, and I have seen the way the Egyptians are oppressing them. So now, go. I am sending you to Pharaoh to bring my people the Israelites out of Egypt.

Moses Who am I, that I should go to Pharaoh and bring the Israelites out of Egypt?

God
(voice) I will be with you. And this will be the sign to you that it is I who have sent you: When you have brought the people out of Egypt, you will worship God on this mountain.

Moses Suppose I go to the Israelites and say to them, "The God of your fathers has sent me to you," and they ask me, "What is his name?" Then what shall I tell them?

[Narrator God said to Moses:]

God (voice,
  slowly)   I AM WHO I AM. This is what you are to say to the Israelites: I AM has sent me to you.

[Narrator   God also said to Moses:**]**

God
  (voice)   Say to the Israelites, "The LORD, the God of your fathers—the God of Abraham, the God of Isaac and the God of Jacob—has sent me to you." (PAUSE) This is my name forever, the name by which I am to be remembered from generation to generation.

Cast: **Narrator, Moses, God** (voice only). (See also extended version below.)

Moses and the Burning Bush (ii)

From Exodus 3:1–14; 4:1–17

Narrator   Moses was tending the flock of Jethro his father-in-law, the priest of Midian, and he led the flock to the far side of the desert and came to Horeb, the mountain of God. There the angel of the LORD appeared to him in flames of fire from within a bush. Moses saw that though the bush was on fire it did not burn up.

Moses
  (thinking)   I will go over and see this strange sight—why the bush does not burn up.

Narrator   When the LORD saw that he had gone over to look, God called to him from within the bush:

God
  (voice only) Moses! Moses!

Moses
  (calling)   Here I am.

God
  (voice)   Do not come any closer. Take off your sandals, for the place where you are standing is holy ground. (PAUSE) I am the God of your father, the God of Abraham, the God of Isaac and the God of Jacob.

Narrator   At this, Moses hid his face, because he was afraid to look at God.

God
  (voice)   I have indeed seen the misery of my people in Egypt. . . . So now, go. I am sending you to Pharaoh to bring my people the Israelites out of Egypt.

Moses   Who am I, that I should go to Pharaoh and bring the Israelites out of Egypt?

God
  (voice)   I will be with you. And this will be the sign to you that it is I who have sent you: When you have brought the people out of Egypt, you will worship God on this mountain.

Moses Suppose I go to the Israelites and say to them, "The God of your fathers has sent me to you," and they ask me, "What is his name?" Then what shall I tell them?

God
(voice) I AM WHO I AM. This is what you are to say to the Israelites: "I AM has sent me to you.". . .

Moses What if they do not believe me or listen to me and say, "The LORD did not appear to you"?

God
(voice) What is that in your hand?

Moses A staff.

God
(voice) Throw it on the ground.

Narrator Moses threw it on the ground (PAUSE) and it became a snake, and he ran from it.

God
(voice) Reach out your hand and take it by the tail.

Narrator So Moses reached out and took hold of the snake and it turned back into a staff in his hand.

God
(voice) This is so that they may believe that the LORD, the God of their fathers—the God of Abraham, the God of Isaac and the God of Jacob—has appeared to you. (PAUSE)

Put your hand inside your cloak.

Narrator So Moses put his hand into his cloak, and when he took it out, it was leprous, like snow.

God
(voice) Now put it back into your cloak.

Narrator So Moses put his hand back into his cloak, and when he took it out, it was restored, like the rest of his flesh.

God
(voice) If they do not believe you or pay attention to the first miraculous sign, they may believe the second. But if they do not believe these two signs or listen to you, take some water from the Nile and pour it on the dry ground. The water you take from the river will become blood on the ground.

Moses O Lord, I have never been eloquent, neither in the past nor since you have spoken to your servant. I am slow of speech and tongue.

God
(voice) Who gave man his mouth? Who makes him deaf or mute? Who gives him sight or makes him blind? Is it not I, the LORD? Now go; I will help you speak and will teach you what to say.

Moses
(weakly) O Lord, please send someone else to do it.

Narrator Then the LORD's anger burned against Moses:

God (voice,
angrily) What about your brother, Aaron the Levite? I know he can speak well. He is already on his way to meet you, and his heart will be glad when he sees you. You shall speak to him and put words in his mouth; I will help both of you speak and will teach you what to do. He will speak to the people for you, and it will be as if he were your mouth and as if you were God to him. But take this staff in your hand so you can perform miraculous signs with it.

Cast: **Narrator, Moses, God** (voice only). (See also shorter version above.)

Moses Returns to Egypt

Exodus 4:18–23, 29–31

Narrator Moses went back to Jethro his father-in-law [and said to him:]

Moses Let me go back to my own people in Egypt to see if any of them are still alive.

Jethro Go, and I wish you well.

Narrator Now the LORD had said to Moses in Midian:

The Lord
(voice only) Go back to Egypt, for all the men who wanted to kill you are dead.

Narrator So Moses took his wife and sons, put them on a donkey and started back to Egypt. And he took the staff of God in his hand. (PAUSE) [The LORD said to Moses:]

The Lord
(voice) When you return to Egypt, see that you perform before Pharaoh all the wonders I have given you the power to do. But I will harden his heart so that he will not let the people go. Then say to Pharaoh, "This is what the LORD says: Israel is my firstborn son, and I told you, 'Let my son go, so he may worship me.' But you refused to let him go; so I will kill your firstborn son." . . .

Narrator Moses and Aaron brought together all the elders of the Israelites, and Aaron told them everything the LORD had said to Moses. He also performed the signs before the people, and they believed. And when they heard that the LORD was concerned about them and had seen their misery, they bowed down and worshiped.

Cast: **Narrator, Moses, Jethro, the Lord** (voice only)

Bricks without Straw

Exodus 5:1–21

Narrator	Moses and Aaron went to Pharaoh and said:
Moses	This is what the LORD, the God of Israel, says: "Let my people go—
Aaron	"So that they may hold a festival to me in the desert."
Pharaoh (demanding)	Who is the LORD, that I should obey him and let Israel go? I do not know the LORD and I will not let Israel go.
Moses	The God of the Hebrews has met with us.
Aaron	Now let us take a three-day journey into the desert to offer sacrifices to the LORD our God, or he may strike us with plagues or with the sword.
Pharaoh (angrily)	Moses and Aaron, why are you taking the people away from their labor? Get back to your work! Look, the people of the land are now numerous, and you are stopping them from working.
Narrator	That same day Pharaoh gave this order to the slave drivers and foremen in charge of the people:
Pharaoh (meanly)	You are no longer to supply the people with straw for making bricks; let them go and gather their own straw. But require them to make the same number of bricks as before; don't reduce the quota. They are lazy; that is why they are crying out, "Let us go and sacrifice to our God." Make the work harder for the men so that they keep working and pay no attention to lies.
Narrator	Then the slave drivers and the foremen went out and said to the people:
Slave driver 1	This is what Pharaoh says: "I will not give you any more straw.
Slave driver 2	"Go and get your own straw wherever you can find it, but your work will not be reduced at all."
Narrator	So the people scattered all over Egypt to gather stubble to use for straw. The slave drivers kept pressing them, saying: "Complete the work required of you for each day, just as when you had straw." The Israelite foremen appointed by Pharaoh's slave drivers were beaten:
Slave driver 1	Why didn't you meet your quota of bricks yesterday or today, as before?
Narrator	Then the Israelite foremen went and appealed to Pharaoh:
Foreman 1	Why have you treated your servants this way?
Foreman 2	Your servants are given no straw, yet we are told, "Make bricks!"
Foreman 1	Your servants are being beaten—

99

Foreman 2	But the fault is with your own people.
[Narrator	Pharaoh said:]
Pharaoh	Lazy, that's what you are—lazy! That is why you keep saying, "Let us go and sacrifice to the LORD." Now get to work. You will not be given any straw, yet you must produce your full quota of bricks.
Narrator	The Israelite foremen realized they were in trouble when they were told, "You are not to reduce the number of bricks required of you for each day." When they left Pharaoh, they found Moses and Aaron waiting to meet them, and they said:
Foreman 1	May the LORD look upon you and judge you!
Foreman 2	You have made us a stench to Pharaoh and his officials and have put a sword in their hand to kill us.

Cast: **Narrator, Moses, Aaron** (can be the same as Moses), **Pharaoh, Slave driver 1, Slave driver 2** (can be the same as Slave driver 1), **Foreman 1, Foreman 2** (can be the same as Foreman 1)

God Promises Deliverance

Exodus 5:22–6:13

Narrator	Moses returned to the LORD:
Moses	O Lord, why have you brought trouble upon this people? Is this why you sent me? Ever since I went to Pharaoh to speak in your name, he has brought trouble upon this people, and you have not rescued your people at all.
[Narrator	Then the LORD said to Moses:]
The Lord (voice only)	Now you will see what I will do to Pharaoh: Because of my mighty hand he will let them go; because of my mighty hand he will *drive* them out of his country. (PAUSE)
	I am the LORD. I appeared to Abraham, to Isaac and to Jacob as God Almighty, but by my name the LORD I did not make myself known to them. I also established my covenant with them to give them the land of Canaan, where they lived as aliens. Moreover, I have heard the groaning of the Israelites, whom the Egyptians are enslaving, and I have remembered my covenant.
	Therefore, say to the Israelites: "I am the LORD, and I will bring you out from under the yoke of the Egyptians. I will free you from being slaves to them, and I will redeem you with an outstretched arm and with mighty acts of judgment. I will take you as my own people, and I will be your God. Then you will know that I am the LORD your God, who brought you out from under the yoke of the Egyptians. And I will bring you to the

	land I swore with uplifted hand to give to Abraham, to Isaac and to Jacob. I will give it to you as a possession. I am the LORD."
Narrator	Moses reported this to the Israelites, but they did not listen to him because of their discouragement and cruel bondage. Then the LORD said to Moses:
The Lord (voice)	Go, tell Pharaoh king of Egypt to let the Israelites go out of his country.
Moses	If the Israelites will not listen to me, why would Pharaoh listen to me, since I speak with faltering lips?
Narrator	Now the LORD spoke to Moses and Aaron about the Israelites and Pharaoh king of Egypt, and he commanded them to bring the Israelites out of Egypt.

Cast: **Narrator, Moses, the Lord** (voice only)

Aaron to Speak for Moses

Exodus 6:28–7:13

Narrator	When the LORD spoke to Moses in Egypt, he said to him:
The Lord (voice only)	I am the LORD. Tell Pharaoh king of Egypt everything I tell you.
Narrator	But Moses said to the LORD:
Moses	Since I speak with faltering lips, why would Pharaoh listen to me?
The Lord (voice)	See, I have made you like God to Pharaoh, and your brother Aaron will be your prophet. You are to say everything I command you, and your brother Aaron is to tell Pharaoh to let the Israelites go out of his country. But I will harden Pharaoh's heart, and though I multiply my miraculous signs and wonders in Egypt, he will not listen to you. Then I will lay my hand on Egypt and with mighty acts of judgment I will bring out my divisions, my people the Israelites. And the Egyptians will know that I am the LORD when I stretch out my hand against Egypt and bring the Israelites out of it.
Narrator	Moses and Aaron did just as the LORD commanded them. Moses was eighty years old and Aaron eighty-three when they spoke to Pharaoh.
	The LORD said to Moses and Aaron:
The Lord (voice)	When Pharaoh says to you, "Perform a miracle," then say to Aaron, "Take your staff and throw it down before Pharaoh," and it will become a snake.
Narrator	So Moses and Aaron went to Pharaoh and did just as the LORD commanded. Aaron threw his staff down in front of Pharaoh and his officials, and it became a snake. Pharaoh then summoned wise men and sor-

101

cerers, and the Egyptian magicians also did the same things by their secret arts: Each one threw down his staff and it became a snake. But Aaron's staff swallowed up their staffs. Yet Pharaoh's heart became hard and he would not listen to them, just as the LORD had said.

Cast: **Narrator, the Lord** (voice only), **Moses**

The Plague of Blood

Exodus 7:14–25

Narrator   The LORD said to Moses:

The Lord
(voice only)   Pharaoh's heart is unyielding; he refuses to let the people go. Go to Pharaoh in the morning as he goes out to the water. Wait on the bank of the Nile to meet him, and take in your hand the staff that was changed into a snake. Then say to him, "The LORD, the God of the Hebrews, has sent me to say to you: Let my people go, so that they may worship me in the desert. But until now you have not listened. This is what the LORD says: By this you will know that I am the LORD: With the staff that is in my hand I will strike the water of the Nile, and it will be changed into blood. The fish in the Nile will die, and the river will stink; the Egyptians will not be able to drink its water."

[Narrator   The LORD said to Moses:]

The Lord
(voice)   Tell Aaron, "Take your staff and stretch out your hand over the waters of Egypt—over the streams and canals, over the ponds and all the reservoirs"—and they will turn to blood. Blood will be everywhere in Egypt, even in the wooden buckets and stone jars.

Narrator   Moses and Aaron did just as the LORD had commanded. He raised his staff in the presence of Pharaoh and his officials and struck the water of the Nile, and all the water was changed into blood. The fish in the Nile died, and the river smelled so bad that the Egyptians could not drink its water. Blood was everywhere in Egypt.

But the Egyptian magicians did the same things by their secret arts, and Pharaoh's heart became hard; he would not listen to Moses and Aaron, just as the LORD had said. Instead, he turned and went into his palace, and did not take even this to heart. And all the Egyptians dug along the Nile to get drinking water, because they could not drink the water of the river.

Seven days passed after the LORD struck the Nile.

Cast: **Narrator, the Lord** (voice only)

The Plague of Frogs

Exodus 8:1–15

Narrator   The Lord said to Moses:

The Lord
(voice only)   Go to Pharaoh and say to him, "This is what the Lord says: Let my people go, so that they may worship me. If you refuse to let them go, I will plague your whole country with frogs. The Nile will teem with frogs. They will come up into your palace and your bedroom and onto your bed, into the houses of your officials and on your people, and into your ovens and kneading troughs. The frogs will go up on you and your people and all your officials."

[Narrator   Then the Lord said to Moses:]

The Lord
(voice)   Tell Aaron, "Stretch out your hand with your staff over the streams and canals and ponds, and make frogs come up on the land of Egypt."

Narrator   So Aaron stretched out his hand over the waters of Egypt, and the frogs came up and covered the land. But the magicians did the same things by their secret arts; they also made frogs come up on the land of Egypt.

Pharaoh summoned Moses and Aaron:

Pharaoh   Pray to the Lord to take the frogs away from me and my people, and I will let your people go to offer sacrifices to the Lord.

Moses
(to Pharaoh)   I leave to you the honor of setting the time for me to pray for you and your officials and your people that you and your houses may be rid of the frogs, except for those that remain in the Nile.

Pharaoh   Tomorrow.

Moses   It will be as you say, so that you may know there is no one like the Lord our God. The frogs will leave you and your houses, your officials and your people; they will remain only in the Nile.

Narrator   After Moses and Aaron left Pharaoh, Moses cried out to the Lord about the frogs he had brought on Pharaoh. And the Lord did what Moses asked. The frogs died in the houses, in the courtyards and in the fields. They were piled into heaps, and the land reeked of them. But when Pharaoh saw that there was relief, he hardened his heart and would not listen to Moses and Aaron, just as the Lord had said.

Cast: **Narrator, the Lord** (voice only), **Pharaoh, Moses**

The Plague of Gnats

Exodus 8:16–19

Narrator The Lord said to Moses:

The Lord
(voice only) Tell Aaron, "Stretch out your staff and strike the dust of the ground," and throughout the land of Egypt the dust will become gnats.

Narrator They did this, and when Aaron stretched out his hand with the staff and struck the dust of the ground, gnats came upon men and animals. All the dust throughout the land of Egypt became gnats. But when the magicians tried to produce gnats by their secret arts, they could not. And the gnats were on men and animals. The magicians said to Pharaoh:

Magician This is the finger of God.

Narrator But Pharaoh's heart was hard and he would not listen, just as the Lord had said.

Cast: **Narrator, the Lord** (voice only), **Magician**

The Plague of Flies

Exodus 8:20–32

Narrator The Lord said to Moses:

The Lord
(voice only) Get up early in the morning and confront Pharaoh as he goes to the water and say to him, "This is what the Lord says: Let my people go, so that they may worship me. If you do not let my people go, I will send swarms of flies on you and your officials, on your people and into your houses. The houses of the Egyptians will be full of flies, and even the ground where they are.

"But on that day I will deal differently with the land of Goshen, where my people live; no swarms of flies will be there, so that you will know that I, the Lord, am in this land. I will make a distinction between my people and your people. This miraculous sign will occur tomorrow."

Narrator And the Lord did this. Dense swarms of flies poured into Pharaoh's palace and into the houses of his officials, and throughout Egypt the land was ruined by the flies.

Then Pharaoh summoned Moses and Aaron:

Pharaoh Go, sacrifice to your God here in the land.

Moses	That would not be right. The sacrifices we offer the LORD our God would be detestable to the Egyptians. And if we offer sacrifices that are detestable in their eyes, will they not stone us? We must take a three-day journey into the desert to offer sacrifices to the LORD our God, as he commands us.
Pharaoh	I will let you go to offer sacrifices to the LORD your God in the desert, but you must not go very far. Now pray for me.
Moses	As soon as I leave you, I will pray to the LORD, and tomorrow the flies will leave Pharaoh and his officials and his people. Only be sure that Pharaoh does not act deceitfully again by not letting the people go to offer sacrifices to the LORD.
Narrator	Then Moses left Pharaoh and prayed to the LORD, and the LORD did what Moses asked: The flies left Pharaoh and his officials and his people; not a fly remained. But this time also Pharaoh hardened his heart and would not let the people go.

Cast: **Narrator, the Lord** (voice only), **Pharaoh, Moses**

The Plague on Livestock

Exodus 9:1–7

Narrator	The LORD said to Moses:
The Lord (voice only)	Go to Pharaoh and say to him, "This is what the LORD, the God of the Hebrews, says: 'Let my people go, so that they may worship me.' If you refuse to let them go and continue to hold them back, the hand of the LORD will bring a terrible plague on your livestock in the field—on your horses and donkeys and camels and on your cattle and sheep and goats. But the LORD will make a distinction between the livestock of Israel and that of Egypt, so that no animal belonging to the Israelites will die."
Narrator	The LORD set a time and said:
The Lord (voice)	Tomorrow the LORD will do this in the land.
Narrator	And the next day the LORD did it: All the livestock of the Egyptians died, but not one animal belonging to the Israelites died. Pharaoh sent men to investigate and found that not even one of the animals of the Israelites had died. Yet his heart was unyielding and he would not let the people go.

Cast: **Narrator, the Lord** (voice only)

105

The Plague of Boils

Exodus 9:8–12

Narrator   The LORD said to Moses and Aaron:

The Lord
(voice only)   Take handfuls of soot from a furnace and have Moses toss it into the air in the presence of Pharaoh. It will become fine dust over the whole land of Egypt, and festering boils will break out on men and animals throughout the land.

Narrator   So they took soot from a furnace and stood before Pharaoh. Moses tossed it into the air, and festering boils broke out on men and animals. The magicians could not stand before Moses because of the boils that were on them and on all the Egyptians. But the LORD hardened Pharaoh's heart and he would not listen to Moses and Aaron, just as the LORD had said to Moses.

Cast: **Narrator, the Lord** (voice only)

The Plague of Hail

Exodus 9:13–35

Narrator   The LORD said to Moses:

The Lord
(voice only)   Get up early in the morning, confront Pharaoh and say to him, "This is what the LORD, the God of the Hebrews, says: Let my people go, so that they may worship me, or this time I will send the full force of my plagues against you and against your officials and your people, so you may know that there is no one like me in all the earth. For by now I could have stretched out my hand and struck you and your people with a plague that would have wiped you off the earth. But I have raised you up for this very purpose, that I might show you my power and that my name might be proclaimed in all the earth. You still set yourself against my people and will not let them go. Therefore, at this time tomorrow I will send the worst hailstorm that has ever fallen on Egypt, from the day it was founded till now. Give an order now to bring your livestock and everything you have in the field to a place of shelter, because the hail will fall on every man and animal that has not been brought in and is still out in the field, and they will die."

Narrator   Those officials of Pharaoh who feared the word of the LORD hurried to bring their slaves and their livestock inside. But those who ignored the word of the LORD left their slaves and livestock in the field. Then the LORD said to Moses:

The Lord	
(voice)	Stretch out your hand toward the sky so that hail will fall all over Egypt—on men and animals and on everything growing in the fields of Egypt.
Narrator	When Moses stretched out his staff toward the sky, the LORD sent thunder and hail, and lightning flashed down to the ground. So the LORD rained hail on the land of Egypt; hail fell and lightning flashed back and forth. It was the worst storm in all the land of Egypt since it had become a nation. Throughout Egypt hail struck everything in the fields—both men and animals; it beat down everything growing in the fields and stripped every tree. The only place it did not hail was the land of Goshen, where the Israelites were. Then Pharaoh summoned Moses and Aaron.
Pharaoh	This time I have sinned. The LORD is in the right, and I and my people are in the wrong. Pray to the LORD, for we have had enough thunder and hail. I will let you go; you don't have to stay any longer.
Moses	When I have gone out of the city, I will spread out my hands in prayer to the LORD. The thunder will stop and there will be no more hail, so you may know that the earth is the LORD's. But I know that you and your officials still do not fear the LORD God.
Narrator	(The flax and barley were destroyed, since the barley had headed and the flax was in bloom. The wheat and spelt, however, were not destroyed, because they ripen later.) Then Moses left Pharaoh and went out of the city. He spread out his hands toward the LORD; the thunder and hail stopped, and the rain no longer poured down on the land. When Pharaoh saw that the rain and hail and thunder had stopped, he sinned again: He and his officials hardened their hearts. So Pharaoh's heart was hard and he would not let the Israelites go, just as the LORD had said through Moses.

Cast: **Narrator, the Lord** (voice only), **Pharaoh, Moses**

The Plague of Locusts

Exodus 10:1–20

Narrator	The LORD said to Moses:
The Lord	
(voice only)	Go to Pharaoh, for I have hardened his heart and the hearts of his officials so that I may perform these miraculous signs of mine among them that you may tell your children and grandchildren how I dealt harshly with the Egyptians and how I performed my signs among them, and that you may know that I am the LORD.

Narrator	So Moses and Aaron went to Pharaoh [and said to him:]
Moses	This is what the LORD, the God of the Hebrews, says: "How long will you refuse to humble yourself before me? Let my people go, so that they may worship me. If you refuse to let them go, I will bring locusts into your country tomorrow.
Aaron	"They will cover the face of the ground so that it cannot be seen. They will devour what little you have left after the hail, including every tree that is growing in your fields. They will fill your houses and those of all your officials and all the Egyptians—something neither your fathers nor your forefathers have ever seen from the day they settled in this land till now."
Narrator	Then Moses turned and left Pharaoh.

Pharaoh's officials said to him: |
Official 1	How long will this man be a snare to us?
Official 2	Let the people go, so that they may worship the LORD their God.
Official 1	Do you not yet realize that Egypt is ruined?
Narrator	Then Moses and Aaron were brought back to Pharaoh.
Pharaoh	Go, worship the LORD your God. (PAUSE) But just who will be going?
Moses	We will go with our young and old, with our sons and daughters, and with our flocks and herds, because we are to celebrate a festival to the LORD.
Pharaoh	The LORD be with you—if I let you go, along with your women and children! Clearly you are bent on evil. No! Have only the *men* go; and worship the LORD, since that's what you have been asking for.
Narrator	Then Moses and Aaron were driven out of Pharaoh's presence.

[And the LORD said to Moses:] |
| **The Lord**
(voice) | Stretch out your hand over Egypt so that locusts will swarm over the land and devour everything growing in the fields, everything left by the hail. |
| **Narrator** | So Moses stretched out his staff over Egypt, and the LORD made an east wind blow across the land all that day and all that night. By morning the wind had brought the locusts; they invaded all Egypt and settled down in every area of the country in great numbers. Never before had there been such a plague of locusts, nor will there ever be again. They covered all the ground until it was black. They devoured all that was left after the hail—everything growing in the fields and the fruit on the trees. Nothing green remained on tree or plant in all the land of Egypt.

Pharaoh quickly summoned Moses and Aaron: |

Pharaoh	I have sinned against the Lord your God and against you. Now forgive my sin once more and pray to the Lord your God to take this deadly plague away from me.
Narrator	Moses then left Pharaoh and prayed to the Lord. And the Lord changed the wind to a very strong west wind, which caught up the locusts and carried them into the Red Sea. Not a locust was left anywhere in Egypt. (PAUSE)
(slowly)	But the Lord hardened Pharaoh's heart, and he would not let the Israelites go.

Cast: **Narrator, the Lord** (voice only), **Moses, Aaron** (can be the same as Moses), **Official 1, Official 2, Pharaoh**

The Plague of Darkness

Exodus 10:21–29

Narrator	The Lord said to Moses:
The Lord (voice only)	Stretch out your hand toward the sky so that darkness will spread over Egypt—darkness that can be felt.
Narrator	So Moses stretched out his hand toward the sky, and total darkness covered all Egypt for three days. No one could see anyone else or leave his place for three days. Yet all the Israelites had light in the places where they lived. Then Pharaoh summoned Moses [and said:]
Pharaoh	Go, worship the Lord. Even your women and children may go with you; only leave your flocks and herds behind.
[Narrator	But Moses said:]
Moses	You must allow us to have sacrifices and burnt offerings to present to the Lord our God. Our livestock too must go with us; not a hoof is to be left behind. We have to use some of them in worshiping the Lord our God, and until we get there we will not know what we are to use to worship the Lord.
Narrator	But the Lord hardened Pharaoh's heart, and he was not willing to let them go.
Pharaoh	Get out of my sight! Make sure you do not appear before me again! The day you see my face you will die.
Moses (with emphasis)	Just as you say. I will never appear before you again.

Cast: **Narrator, the Lord** (voice only), **Pharaoh, Moses.** (This overlaps the next reading.)

109

Moses Announces the Plague on the Firstborn

Exodus [10:24–29], 11:4–8

[Narrator	Pharaoh summoned Moses and said:
Pharaoh	Go, worship the Lord. Even your women and children may go with you; only leave your flocks and herds behind.
[Narrator	But Moses said:]
Moses	You must allow us to have sacrifices and burnt offerings to present to the Lord our God. Our livestock too must go with us; not a hoof is to be left behind. We have to use some of them in worshiping the Lord our God, and until we get there we will not know what we are to use to worship the Lord.
Narrator	But the Lord hardened Pharaoh's heart, and he was not willing to let them go.
Pharaoh	Get out of my sight! Make sure you do not appear before me again! The day you see my face you will die.
Moses	Just as you say. I will never appear before you again.] . . .
	This is what the Lord says:
The Lord (voice only)	About midnight I will go throughout Egypt. Every firstborn son in Egypt will die, from the firstborn son of Pharaoh, who sits on the throne, to the firstborn son of the slave girl, who is at her hand mill, and all the firstborn of the cattle as well. There will be loud wailing throughout Egypt—worse than there has ever been or ever will be again. But among the Israelites not a dog will bark at any man or animal.
Moses	Then you will know that the Lord makes a distinction between Egypt and Israel. All these officials of yours will come to me, bowing down before me and saying, "Go, you and all the people who follow you!" After that I will leave.
Narrator	Then Moses, hot with anger, left Pharaoh.

Cast: **Narrator, Pharaoh, Moses, the Lord** (voice only, or can be the same as Moses). (This overlaps the previous reading.)

The Plague on the Firstborn

Exodus 11:1–10

Narrator	The Lord had said to Moses:
The Lord (voice only)	I will bring one more plague on Pharaoh and on Egypt. After that, he will let you go from here, and when he does, he will drive you out completely.

Tell the people that men and women alike are to ask their neighbors for articles of silver and gold.

Narrator   (The LORD made the Egyptians favorably disposed toward the people, and Moses himself was highly regarded in Egypt by Pharaoh's officials and by the people.)

So Moses said:

Moses   This is what the LORD says: "About midnight I will go throughout Egypt. Every firstborn son in Egypt will die, from the firstborn son of Pharaoh, who sits on the throne, to the firstborn son of the slave girl, who is at her hand mill, and all the firstborn of the cattle as well. There will be loud wailing throughout Egypt—worse than there has ever been or ever will be again. But among the Israelites not a dog will bark at any man or animal." Then you will know that the LORD makes a distinction between Egypt and Israel. (ANGRILY) All these officials of yours will come to me, bowing down before me and saying, "Go, you and all the people who follow you!" After that I will leave.

Narrator   Then Moses, hot with anger, left Pharaoh. (PAUSE)

The LORD had said to Moses:

The Lord
   (voice)   Pharaoh will refuse to listen to you—so that my wonders may be multiplied in Egypt.

Narrator   Moses and Aaron performed all these wonders before Pharaoh, but the LORD hardened Pharaoh's heart, and he would not let the Israelites go out of his country.

Cast: **Narrator, the Lord** (voice only), **Moses.** (This overlaps the previous reading.)

The Passover

Exodus 12:21–36

Narrator   Moses summoned all the elders of Israel:

Moses   Go at once and select the animals for your families and slaughter the Passover lamb. Take a bunch of hyssop, dip it into the blood in the basin and put some of the blood on the top and on both sides of the doorframe. Not one of you shall go out the door of his house until morning. When the LORD goes through the land to strike down the Egyptians, he will see the blood on the top and sides of the doorframe and will pass over that doorway, and he will not permit the destroyer to enter your houses and strike you down.

Obey these instructions as a lasting ordinance for you and your descendants. When you enter the land that the LORD will give you as he promised, observe this ceremony. And when your children ask you,

"What does this ceremony mean to you?" then tell them, "It is the Passover sacrifice to the LORD, who passed over the houses of the Israelites in Egypt and spared our homes when he struck down the Egyptians."

Narrator	Then the people bowed down and worshiped. The Israelites did just what the LORD commanded Moses and Aaron. (PAUSE)

At midnight the LORD struck down all the firstborn in Egypt, from the firstborn of Pharaoh, who sat on the throne, to the firstborn of the prisoner, who was in the dungeon, and the firstborn of all the livestock as well. Pharaoh and all his officials and all the Egyptians got up during the night, and there was loud wailing in Egypt, for there was not a house without someone dead.

During the night Pharaoh summoned Moses and Aaron:

Pharaoh	Up! Leave my people, you and the Israelites! Go, worship the LORD as you have requested. Take your flocks and herds, as you have said, and go. And also bless me.
Narrator	The Egyptians urged the people to hurry and leave the country.
Egyptian	For otherwise we will all die!
Narrator	So the people took their dough before the yeast was added, and carried it on their shoulders in kneading troughs wrapped in clothing. The Israelites did as Moses instructed and asked the Egyptians for articles of silver and gold and for clothing. The LORD had made the Egyptians favorably disposed toward the people, and they gave them what they asked for; so they plundered the Egyptians.

Cast: **Narrator, Moses, Pharaoh, Egyptian**

Crossing the Sea

Exodus 13:17–14:9

Narrator	When Pharaoh let the people go, God did not lead them on the road through the Philistine country, though that was shorter. For God said:
The Lord (voice only)	If they face war, they might change their minds and return to Egypt.
Narrator	So God led the people around by the desert road toward the Red Sea. The Israelites went up out of Egypt armed for battle.

Moses took the bones of Joseph with him because Joseph had made the sons of Israel swear an oath. He had said:

Joseph	God will surely come to your aid, and then you must carry my bones up with you from this place.
Narrator	After leaving Succoth they camped at Etham on the edge of the desert. By day the LORD went ahead of them in a pillar of cloud to guide them

112

on their way and by night in a pillar of fire to give them light, so that they could travel by day or night. Neither the pillar of cloud by day nor the pillar of fire by night left its place in front of the people.

Then the LORD said to Moses:

The Lord
(voice)

Tell the Israelites to turn back and encamp near Pi Hahiroth, between Migdol and the sea. They are to encamp by the sea, directly opposite Baal Zephon. Pharaoh will think, "The Israelites are wandering around the land in confusion, hemmed in by the desert." And I will harden Pharaoh's heart, and he will pursue them. But I will gain glory for myself through Pharaoh and all his army, and the Egyptians will know that I am the LORD.

Narrator

So the Israelites did this.

When the king of Egypt was told that the people had fled, Pharaoh and his officials changed their minds about them and said:

Pharaoh

What have we done?

Official 1

We have let the Israelites go—

Official 2

And have lost their services!

Narrator

So he had his chariot made ready and took his army with him. He took six hundred of the best chariots, along with all the other chariots of Egypt, with officers over all of them. The LORD hardened the heart of Pharaoh king of Egypt, so that he pursued the Israelites, who were marching out boldly. The Egyptians—all Pharaoh's horses and chariots, horsemen and troops—pursued the Israelites and overtook them as they camped by the sea near Pi Hahiroth, opposite Baal Zephon.

Cast: **Narrator, the Lord** (voice only), **Joseph** (preferably unseen, can be the same as Narrator), **Pharaoh, Official 1, Official 2** (can be the same as Official 1)

The Lord Defeats the Egyptians

Exodus 14:10–18 [19–20], 21–29

Narrator

As Pharaoh approached, the Israelites looked up, and there were the Egyptians, marching after them. They were terrified and cried out to the LORD. They said to Moses:

Israelite 1

Was it because there were no graves in Egypt that you brought us to the desert to die? What have you done to us by bringing us out of Egypt?

Israelite 2

Didn't we say to you in Egypt, "Leave us alone; let us serve the Egyptians"?

Israelite 3

It would have been better for us to serve the Egyptians than to die in the desert!

[Narrator

Moses answered the people:**]**

Moses (firmly)	Do not be afraid. Stand firm and you will see the deliverance the LORD will bring you today. The Egyptians you see today you will never see again. The LORD will fight for you; you need only to be still.
Narrator	Then the LORD said to Moses:
The Lord (voice only)	Why are you crying out to me? Tell the Israelites to move on. Raise your staff and stretch out your hand over the sea to divide the water so that the Israelites can go through the sea on dry ground. I will harden the hearts of the Egyptians so that they will go in after them. And I will gain glory through Pharaoh and all his army, through his chariots and his horsemen. The Egyptians will know that I am the LORD when I gain glory through Pharaoh, his chariots and his horsemen.
[Narrator	Then the angel of God, who had been traveling in front of Israel's army, withdrew and went behind them. The pillar of cloud also moved from in front and stood behind them, coming between the armies of Egypt and Israel. Throughout the night the cloud brought darkness to the one side and light to the other side; so neither went near the other all night long.]
Narrator	Then Moses stretched out his hand over the sea, and all that night the LORD drove the sea back with a strong east wind and turned it into dry land. The waters were divided, and the Israelites went through the sea on dry ground, with a wall of water on their right and on their left.
	The Egyptians pursued them, and all Pharaoh's horses and chariots and horsemen followed them into the sea. During the last watch of the night the LORD looked down from the pillar of fire and cloud at the Egyptian army and threw it into confusion. He made the wheels of their chariots come off so that they had difficulty driving. And the Egyptians said:
Egyptian 1	Let's get away from the Israelites!
Egyptian 2	The LORD is fighting for them against Egypt.
Narrator	Then the LORD said to Moses:
The Lord (voice)	Stretch out your hand over the sea so that the waters may flow back over the Egyptians and their chariots and horsemen.
Narrator	Moses stretched out his hand over the sea, and at daybreak the sea went back to its place. The Egyptians were fleeing toward it, and the LORD swept them into the sea. The water flowed back and covered the chariots and horsemen—the entire army of Pharaoh that had followed the Israelites into the sea. Not one of them survived.
	But the Israelites went through the sea on dry ground, with a wall of water on their right and on their left.

Cast: **Narrator, Israelite 1, Israelite 2, Israelite 3** (Israelites 1–3 can be the same), **Moses, the Lord** (voice only), **Egyptian 1, Egyptian 2** (can be the same as Egyptian 1)

114

The Waters of Marah and Elim

Exodus 15:22–27

Narrator Moses led Israel from the Red Sea and they went into the Desert of Shur. For three days they traveled in the desert without finding water. When they came to Marah, they could not drink its water because it was bitter.

Commentator (That is why the place is called Marah.)

Narrator So the people grumbled against Moses:

Israelite What are we to drink?

Narrator Then Moses cried out to the LORD, and the LORD showed him a piece of wood. He threw it into the water, and the water became sweet. (PAUSE)

There the LORD made a decree and a law for them, and there he tested them.

The Lord
(voice only) If you listen carefully to the voice of the LORD your God and do what is right in his eyes, if you pay attention to his commands and keep all his decrees, I will not bring on you any of the diseases I brought on the Egyptians, for I am the LORD who heals you.

Narrator Then they came to Elim, where there were twelve springs and seventy palm trees, and they camped there near the water.

Cast: **Narrator, Commentator, Israelite, the Lord** (voice only)

Manna and Quail

Exodus 16:1–35

Narrator The whole Israelite community set out from Elim and came to the Desert of Sin, which is between Elim and Sinai, on the fifteenth day of the second month after they had come out of Egypt. In the desert the whole community grumbled against Moses and Aaron.

Israelite 1 If only we had died by the LORD's hand in Egypt!

Israelite 2 There we sat around pots of meat and ate all the food we wanted.

Israelite 1 But you have brought us out into this desert to starve this entire assembly to death.

Narrator Then the LORD said to Moses:

The Lord
(voice only) I will rain down bread from heaven for you. The people are to go out each day and gather enough for that day. In this way I will test them and see whether they will follow my instructions. On the sixth day they are

115

to prepare what they bring in, and that is to be twice as much as they gather on the other days.

Narrator　So Moses and Aaron said to all the Israelites:

Aaron　In the evening you will know that it was the Lord who brought you out of Egypt, and in the morning you will see the glory of the Lord, because he has heard your grumbling against him. Who are we, that you should grumble against us?

Moses　You will know that it was the Lord when he gives you meat to eat in the evening and all the bread you want in the morning, because he has heard your grumbling against him. Who are we? You are not grumbling against us, but against the Lord.

[Narrator　Then Moses told Aaron:]

Moses
(to Aaron)　Say to the entire Israelite community, "Come before the Lord, for he has heard your grumbling."

Narrator　While Aaron was speaking to the whole Israelite community, they looked toward the desert, and there was the glory of the Lord appearing in the cloud.

The Lord said to Moses:

The Lord
(voice)　I have heard the grumbling of the Israelites. Tell them, "At twilight you will eat meat, and in the morning you will be filled with bread. Then you will know that I am the Lord your God."

Narrator　That evening quail came and covered the camp, and in the morning there was a layer of dew around the camp. When the dew was gone, thin flakes like frost on the ground appeared on the desert floor. When the Israelites saw it, they said to each other:

Israelites 1
and 2　What is it?

Narrator　For they did not know what it was. Moses said to them:

Moses　It is the bread the Lord has given you to eat. This is what the Lord has commanded: "Each one is to gather as much as he needs. Take an omer for each person you have in your tent."

Narrator　The Israelites did as they were told; some gathered much, some little. And when they measured it by the omer, he who gathered much did not have too much, and he who gathered little did not have too little. Each one gathered as much as he needed.

[Then Moses said to them:]

Moses　No one is to keep any of it until morning.

Narrator	However, some of them paid no attention to Moses; they kept part of it until morning, but it was full of maggots and began to smell. So Moses was angry with them.
	Each morning everyone gathered as much as he needed, and when the sun grew hot, it melted away. On the sixth day, they gathered twice as much—two omers for each person—and the leaders of the community came and reported this to Moses. He said to them:
Moses	This is what the LORD commanded: "Tomorrow is to be a day of rest, a holy Sabbath to the LORD. So bake what you want to bake and boil what you want to boil. Save whatever is left and keep it until morning."
Narrator	So they saved it until morning, as Moses commanded, and it did not stink or get maggots in it.
Moses	Eat it today, because today is a Sabbath to the LORD. You will not find any of it on the ground today. Six days you are to gather it, but on the seventh day, the Sabbath, there will not be any.
Narrator	Nevertheless, some of the people went out on the seventh day to gather it, but they found none. Then the LORD said to Moses:
The Lord (voice)	How long will you refuse to keep my commands and my instructions? Bear in mind that the LORD has given you the Sabbath; that is why on the sixth day he gives you bread for two days. Everyone is to stay where he is on the seventh day; no one is to go out.
Narrator	So the people rested on the seventh day.
	The people of Israel called the bread manna. It was white like coriander seed and tasted like wafers made with honey. Moses said:
Moses	This is what the LORD has commanded: "Take an omer of manna and keep it for the generations to come, so they can see the bread I gave you to eat in the desert when I brought you out of Egypt."
[Narrator	So Moses said to Aaron:]
Moses (to Aaron)	Take a jar and put an omer of manna in it. Then place it before the LORD to be kept for the generations to come.
Narrator	As the LORD commanded Moses, Aaron put the manna in front of the Testimony, that it might be kept. The Israelites ate manna forty years, until they came to a land that was settled; they ate manna until they reached the border of Canaan.

Cast: **Narrator, Israelite 1, Israelite 2** (can be the same as Israelite 1), **the Lord** (voice only), **Aaron, Moses**

Water from the Rock

Exodus 17:1–7

Narrator	The whole Israelite community set out from the Desert of Sin, traveling from place to place as the LORD commanded. They camped at Rephidim, but there was no water for the people to drink. So they quarreled with Moses and said:
Israelite 1	Give us water to drink.
[Narrator	Moses replied:]
Moses	Why do you quarrel with me? Why do you put the LORD to the test?
Narrator	But the people were thirsty for water there, and they grumbled against Moses:
Israelite 2	Why did you bring us up out of Egypt to make us and our children and livestock die of thirst?
Narrator	Then Moses cried out to the LORD:
Moses	What am I to do with these people? They are almost ready to stone me.
[Narrator	The LORD answered Moses:]
The Lord (voice only)	Walk on ahead of the people. Take with you some of the elders of Israel and take in your hand the staff with which you struck the Nile, and go. I will stand there before you by the rock at Horeb. Strike the rock, and water will come out of it for the people to drink.
Narrator	So Moses did this in the sight of the elders of Israel. And he called the place Massah and Meribah because the Israelites quarreled and because they tested the LORD saying:
Israelite 1	Is the LORD among us or not?

Cast: **Narrator, Israelite 1, Moses, Israelite 2** (can be the same as Israelite 1), **the Lord** (voice only)

The Amalekites Defeated

Exodus 17:8–16

Narrator	The Amalekites came and attacked the Israelites at Rephidim. Moses said to Joshua:
Moses	Choose some of our men and go out to fight the Amalekites. Tomorrow I will stand on top of the hill with the staff of God in my hands.
Narrator	So Joshua fought the Amalekites as Moses had ordered, and Moses, Aaron and Hur went to the top of the hill. As long as Moses held up his hands, the Israelites were winning, but whenever he lowered his hands, the

Amalekites were winning. When Moses' hands grew tired, they took a stone and put it under him and he sat on it. Aaron and Hur held his hands up—one on one side, one on the other—so that his hands remained steady till sunset. So Joshua overcame the Amalekite army with the sword. (PAUSE) Then the LORD said to Moses:

The Lord
(voice only) Write this on a scroll as something to be remembered and make sure that Joshua hears it, because I will completely blot out the memory of Amalek from under heaven.

Narrator Moses built an altar and called it:

Moses The LORD is my Banner.

Narrator For hands were lifted up to the throne of the LORD.

Moses The LORD will be at war against the Amalekites from generation to generation.

Cast: **Narrator, Moses, the Lord** (voice only)

Jethro Visits Moses

Exodus 18:1–12

Narrator Jethro, the priest of Midian and father-in-law of Moses, heard of everything God had done for Moses and for his people Israel, and how the LORD had brought Israel out of Egypt.

After Moses had sent away his wife Zipporah, his father-in-law Jethro received her and her two sons. One son was named Gershom, for Moses said:

Moses I have become an alien in a foreign land.

Narrator And the other was named Eliezer, for he said:

Moses My father's God was my helper; he saved me from the sword of Pharaoh.

Narrator Jethro, Moses' father-in-law, together with Moses' sons and wife, came to him in the desert, where he was camped near the mountain of God. Jethro had sent word to him:

Jethro I, your father-in-law Jethro, am coming to you with your wife and her two sons.

Narrator So Moses went out to meet his father-in-law and bowed down and kissed him. They greeted each other and then went into the tent. Moses told his father-in-law about everything the LORD had done to Pharaoh and the Egyptians for Israel's sake and about all the hardships they had met along the way and how the LORD had saved them.

119

Jethro was delighted to hear about all the good things the LORD had done for Israel in rescuing them from the hand of the Egyptians.

Jethro   Praise be to the LORD, who rescued you from the hand of the Egyptians and of Pharaoh, and who rescued the people from the hand of the Egyptians. Now I know that the LORD is greater than all other gods, for he did this to those who had treated Israel arrogantly.

Narrator   Then Jethro, Moses' father-in-law, brought a burnt offering and other sacrifices to God, and Aaron came with all the elders of Israel to eat bread with Moses' father-in-law in the presence of God.

Cast: **Narrator, Moses, Jethro**

The Appointment of Judges

Exodus 18:13–26

Narrator   Moses took his seat to serve as judge for the people, and they stood around him from morning till evening. When his father-in-law saw all that Moses was doing for the people, he said:

Jethro   What is this you are doing for the people? Why do you alone sit as judge, while all these people stand around you from morning till evening?

Narrator   Moses answered him:

Moses   Because the people come to me to seek God's will. Whenever they have a dispute, it is brought to me, and I decide between the parties and inform them of God's decrees and laws.

[Narrator   Moses' father-in-law replied:]

Jethro   What you are doing is not good. You and these people who come to you will only wear yourselves out. The work is too heavy for you; you cannot handle it alone. Listen now to me and I will give you some advice, and may God be with you. You must be the people's representative before God and bring their disputes to him. Teach them the decrees and laws, and show them the way to live and the duties they are to perform. But select capable men from all the people—men who fear God, trustworthy men who hate dishonest gain—and appoint them as officials over thousands, hundreds, fifties and tens. Have them serve as judges for the people at all times, but have them bring every difficult case to you; the simple cases they can decide themselves. That will make your load lighter, because they will share it with you. If you do this and God so commands, you will be able to stand the strain, and all these people will go home satisfied.

Narrator   Moses listened to his father-in-law and did everything he said. He chose capable men from all Israel and made them leaders of the people, officials over thousands, hundreds, fifties and tens. They served as judges for the people at all times. The difficult cases they brought to Moses, but the simple ones they decided themselves.

Cast: **Narrator, Jethro, Moses**

At Mount Sinai

Exodus 19:2–13

Narrator   After [the people of Israel] set out from Rephidim, they entered the Desert of Sinai, and Israel camped there in the desert in front of the mountain.

Then Moses went up to God, and the LORD called to him from the mountain:

The Lord
(voice only)   This is what you are to say to the house of Jacob and what you are to tell the people of Israel: "You yourselves have seen what I did to Egypt, and how I carried you on eagles' wings and brought you to myself. Now if you obey me fully and keep my covenant, then out of all nations you will be my treasured possession. Although the whole earth is mine, you will be for me a kingdom of priests and a holy nation." These are the words you are to speak to the Israelites.

Narrator   So Moses went back and summoned the elders of the people and set before them all the words the LORD had commanded him to speak. The people all responded together:

Person(s)   We will do everything the LORD has said.

Narrator   So Moses brought their answer back to the LORD. (PAUSE)

The LORD said to Moses:

The Lord
(voice)   I am going to come to you in a dense cloud, so that the people will hear me speaking with you and will always put their trust in you.

Narrator   Then Moses told the LORD what the people had said. And the LORD said to Moses:

The Lord
(voice)   Go to the people and consecrate them today and tomorrow. Have them wash their clothes and be ready by the third day, because on that day the LORD will come down on Mount Sinai in the sight of all the people. Put limits for the people around the mountain and tell them, "Be careful that you do not go up the mountain or touch the foot of it. Whoever touches the mountain shall surely be put to death. He shall surely be stoned or shot with arrows; not a hand is to be laid on him. Whether man or animal, he shall not be permitted to live." Only when the ram's horn sounds a long blast may they go up to the mountain.

Cast: **Narrator, the Lord** (voice only), **Person(s)** (two or more)

The Ten Commandments

From Exodus 19:14–20:21

Narrator   After Moses had gone down the mountain to the people, he consecrated them, and they washed their clothes. . . . (PAUSE)

On the morning of the third day there was thunder and lightning, with a thick cloud over the mountain, and a very loud trumpet blast. Everyone in the camp trembled. Then Moses led the people out of the camp to meet with God, and they stood at the foot of the mountain. Mount Sinai was covered with smoke, because the LORD descended on it in fire. The smoke billowed up from it like smoke from a furnace, the whole mountain trembled violently, and the sound of the trumpet grew louder and louder. Then Moses spoke and the voice of God answered him.

The LORD descended to the top of Mount Sinai and called Moses to the top of the mountain. So Moses went up and the LORD said to him:

The Lord
(voice only) Go down and warn the people so they do not force their way through to see the LORD and many of them perish. Even the priests, who approach the LORD, must consecrate themselves, or the LORD will break out against them.

[Narrator   Moses said to the LORD:]

Moses   The people cannot come up Mount Sinai, because you yourself warned us, "Put limits around the mountain and set it apart as holy."

The Lord
(voice)   Go down and bring Aaron up with you. But the priests and the people must not force their way through to come up to the LORD, or he will break out against them.

Narrator   So Moses went down to the people and told them. (PAUSE)

And God spoke all these words:

The Lord
(voice)   I am the LORD your God, who brought you out of Egypt, out of the land of slavery.

You shall have no other gods before me.

You shall not make for yourself an idol in the form of anything in heaven above or on the earth beneath or in the waters below. You shall not bow down to them or worship them; for I, the LORD your God, am a jealous God, punishing the children for the sin of the fathers to the third and fourth generation of those who hate me, but showing love to a thousand ⌊generations⌋ of those who love me and keep my commandments.

You shall not misuse the name of the LORD your God, for the LORD will not hold anyone guiltless who misuses his name.

Remember the Sabbath day by keeping it holy. Six days you shall labor and do all your work, but the seventh day is a Sabbath to the Lord your God. On it you shall not do any work, neither you, nor your son or daughter, nor your manservant or maidservant, nor your animals, nor the alien within your gates. For in six days the Lord made the heavens and the earth, the sea, and all that is in them, but he rested on the seventh day. Therefore the Lord blessed the Sabbath day and made it holy.

Honor your father and your mother, so that you may live long in the land the Lord your God is giving you.

You shall not murder.

You shall not commit adultery.

You shall not steal.

You shall not give false testimony against your neighbor.

You shall not covet your neighbor's house. You shall not covet your neighbor's wife, or his manservant or maidservant, his ox or donkey, or anything that belongs to your neighbor.

Narrator When the people saw the thunder and lightning and heard the trumpet and saw the mountain in smoke, they trembled with fear. They stayed at a distance and said to Moses:

Israelite 1 Speak to us yourself and we will listen.

Israelite 2 But do not have God speak to us or we will die.

[Narrator Moses said to the people:]

Moses Do not be afraid. God has come to test you, so that the fear of God will be with you to keep you from sinning.

Narrator The people remained at a distance, while Moses approached the thick darkness where God was.

Cast: **Narrator, the Lord** (voice only), **Moses, Israelite 1, Israelite 2** (can be the same as Israelite 1)

The Covenant Confirmed

Exodus 24:1–11

Narrator [The Lord] said to Moses:

The Lord
(voice only) Come up to the Lord, you and Aaron, Nadab and Abihu, and seventy of the elders of Israel. You are to worship at a distance, but Moses alone is to approach the Lord; the others must not come near. And the people may not come up with him.

123

Narrator	When Moses went and told the people all the LORD's words and laws, they responded with one voice:
Israelite(s)	Everything the LORD has said we will do.
Narrator	Moses then wrote down everything the LORD had said.
	He got up early the next morning and built an altar at the foot of the mountain and set up twelve stone pillars representing the twelve tribes of Israel. Then he sent young Israelite men, and they offered burnt offerings and sacrificed young bulls as fellowship offerings to the LORD. Moses took half of the blood and put it in bowls, and the other half he sprinkled on the altar. Then he took the Book of the Covenant and read it to the people. They responded:
Israelite(s)	We will do everything the LORD has said; we will obey.
Narrator	Moses then took the blood, sprinkled it on the people [and said:]
Moses	This is the blood of the covenant that the LORD has made with you in accordance with all these words.
Narrator	Moses and Aaron, Nadab and Abihu, and the seventy elders of Israel went up and saw the God of Israel. Under his feet was something like a pavement made of sapphire, clear as the sky itself. But God did not raise his hand against these leaders of the Israelites; they saw God, and they ate and drank.

Cast: **Narrator, the Lord** (voice only), **Israelite(s)** (three or more), **Moses**

Moses on Mount Sinai

Exodus 24:12–18

Narrator	The LORD said to Moses:
The Lord (voice only)	Come up to me on the mountain and stay here, and I will give you the tablets of stone, with the law and commands I have written for their instruction.
Narrator	Then Moses set out with Joshua his aide, and Moses went up on the mountain of God. He said to the elders:
Moses	Wait here for us until we come back to you. Aaron and Hur are with you, and anyone involved in a dispute can go to them.
Narrator	When Moses went up on the mountain, the cloud covered it, and the glory of the LORD settled on Mount Sinai. For six days the cloud covered the mountain, and on the seventh day the LORD called to Moses from within the cloud. To the Israelites the glory of the LORD looked like a consuming fire on top of the mountain. Then Moses entered the cloud as he

went on up the mountain. And he stayed on the mountain forty days and forty nights.

Cast: **Narrator, the Lord** (voice only), **Moses**

The Sabbath

Exodus 31:12–18

Narrator   The LORD said to Moses:

The Lord
(voice only)   Say to the Israelites, "You must observe my Sabbaths. This will be a sign between me and you for the generations to come, so you may know that I am the LORD, who makes you holy.

"Observe the Sabbath, because it is holy to you. Anyone who desecrates it must be put to death; whoever does any work on that day must be cut off from his people. For six days, work is to be done, but the seventh day is a Sabbath of rest, holy to the LORD. Whoever does any work on the Sabbath day must be put to death. The Israelites are to observe the Sabbath, celebrating it for the generations to come as a lasting covenant. It will be a sign between me and the Israelites forever, for in six days the LORD made the heavens and the earth, and on the seventh day he abstained from work and rested."

Narrator   When the LORD finished speaking to Moses on Mount Sinai, he gave him the two tablets of the Testimony, the tablets of stone inscribed by the finger of God.

Cast: **Narrator, the Lord** (voice only)

The Golden Calf

Exodus 32:1–20

Narrator   When the people saw that Moses was so long in coming down from the mountain, they gathered around Aaron.

Israelite 1   Come, make us gods who will go before us.

Israelite 2   As for this fellow Moses who brought us up out of Egypt, we don't know what has happened to him.

[Narrator   Aaron answered them:]

Aaron
(wearily)   Take off the gold earrings that your wives, your sons and your daughters are wearing, and bring them to me.

125

Narrator	So all the people took off their earrings and brought them to Aaron. He took what they handed him and made it into an idol cast in the shape of a calf, fashioning it with a tool. (PAUSE) Then they said:
Israelites 1 and 2	O Israel—
Israelite 1	These are your gods . . .
Israelite 2	Who brought you up out of Egypt.
Narrator	When Aaron saw this, he built an altar in front of the calf and announced:
Aaron	Tomorrow there will be a festival to the LORD.
Narrator	So the next day the people rose early and sacrificed burnt offerings and presented fellowship offerings. Afterward they sat down to eat and drink and got up to indulge in revelry. Then the LORD said to Moses:
The Lord (voice only— to Moses)	Go down, because your people, whom you brought up out of Egypt, have become corrupt. They have been quick to turn away from what I commanded them and have made themselves an idol cast in the shape of a calf. They have bowed down to it and sacrificed to it and have said, "These are your gods, O Israel, who brought you up out of Egypt."
	I have seen these people, and they are a stiff-necked people. Now leave me alone so that my anger may burn against them and that I may destroy them. Then I will make you into a great nation.
Narrator	But Moses sought the favor of the LORD his God.
Moses	O LORD, why should your anger burn against your people, whom you brought out of Egypt with great power and a mighty hand? Why should the Egyptians say, "It was with evil intent that he brought them out, to kill them in the mountains and to wipe them off the face of the earth"? Turn from your fierce anger; relent and do not bring disaster on your people. Remember your servants Abraham, Isaac and Israel, to whom you swore by your own self: "I will make your descendants as numerous as the stars in the sky and I will give your descendants all this land I promised them, and it will be their inheritance forever."
Narrator	Then the LORD relented and did not bring on his people the disaster he had threatened.
	Moses turned and went down the mountain with the two tablets of the Testimony in his hands. They were inscribed on both sides, front and back. The tablets were the work of God; the writing was the writing of God, engraved on the tablets.
	When Joshua heard the noise of the people shouting, he said to Moses:
Joshua (to Moses)	There is the sound of war in the camp.

Moses	It is not the sound of victory,
	it is not the sound of defeat;
	it is the sound of singing that I hear.

Narrator   When Moses approached the camp and saw the calf and the dancing, his anger burned and he threw the tablets out of his hands, breaking them to pieces at the foot of the mountain. And he took the calf they had made and burned it in the fire; then he ground it to powder, scattered it on the water and made the Israelites drink it.

Cast: **Narrator, Israelite 1, Israelite 2** (can be the same as Israelite 1), **Aaron, the Lord** (voice only), **Moses, Joshua**

The Lord Orders Israel to Leave Mount Sinai

Exodus 33:1–6 [7–11]

Narrator   The LORD said to Moses:

The Lord
(voice only)   Leave this place, you and the people you brought up out of Egypt, and go up to the land I promised on oath to Abraham, Isaac and Jacob, saying, "I will give it to your descendants." I will send an angel before you and drive out the Canaanites, Amorites, Hittites, Perizzites, Hivites and Jebusites. Go up to the land flowing with milk and honey. But I will not go with you, because you are a stiff-necked people and I might destroy you on the way.

Narrator   When the people heard these distressing words, they began to mourn and no one put on any ornaments. For the LORD had said to Moses:

The Lord
(voice)   Tell the Israelites, "You are a stiff-necked people. If I were to go with you even for a moment, I might destroy you. Now take off your ornaments and I will decide what to do with you."

Narrator   So the Israelites stripped off their ornaments at Mount Horeb.

[Now Moses used to take a tent and pitch it outside the camp some distance away, calling it the "tent of meeting." Anyone inquiring of the LORD would go to the tent of meeting outside the camp. And whenever Moses went out to the tent, all the people rose and stood at the entrances to their tents, watching Moses until he entered the tent. As Moses went into the tent, the pillar of cloud would come down and stay at the entrance, while the LORD spoke with Moses. Whenever the people saw the pillar of cloud standing at the entrance to the tent, they all stood and worshiped, each at the entrance to his tent. The LORD would speak to Moses face to face, as a man speaks with his friend. Then Moses would return to the camp, but his young aide Joshua son of Nun did not leave the tent.]

Cast: **Narrator, the Lord** (voice only)

127

Moses and the Glory of the Lord

Exodus 33:12–23

Narrator Moses said to the LORD:

Moses You have been telling me, "Lead these people," but you have not let me know whom you will send with me. You have said, "I know you by name and you have found favor with me." If you are pleased with me, teach me your ways so I may know you and continue to find favor with you. Remember that this nation is your people.

The Lord
(voice only) My Presence will go with you, and I will give you rest.

Moses If your Presence does not go with us, do not send us up from here. How will anyone know that you are pleased with me and with your people unless you go with us? What else will distinguish me and your people from all the other people on the face of the earth?

The Lord
(voice) I will do the very thing you have asked, because I am pleased with you and I know you by name.

Moses Now show me your glory.

The Lord
(voice) I will cause all my goodness to pass in front of you, and I will proclaim my name, the LORD, in your presence. I will have mercy on whom I will have mercy, and I will have compassion on whom I will have compassion. But you cannot see my face, for no one may see me and live.

There is a place near me where you may stand on a rock. When my glory passes by, I will put you in a cleft in the rock and cover you with my hand until I have passed by. Then I will remove my hand and you will see my back; but my face must not be seen.

Cast: **Narrator, Moses, the Lord** (voice only)

The New Stone Tablets

Exodus 34:1–9

Narrator The LORD said to Moses:

The Lord
(voice only) Chisel out two stone tablets like the first ones, and I will write on them the words that were on the first tablets, which you broke. Be ready in the morning, and then come up on Mount Sinai. Present yourself to me there on top of the mountain. No one is to come with you or be seen anywhere on the mountain; not even the flocks and herds may graze in front of the mountain.

Narrator	So Moses chiseled out two stone tablets like the first ones and went up Mount Sinai early in the morning, as the LORD had commanded him; and he carried the two stone tablets in his hands. Then the LORD came down in the cloud and stood there with him and proclaimed his name, the LORD. And he passed in front of Moses, proclaiming:
The Lord (voice)	The LORD, the LORD, the compassionate and gracious God, slow to anger, abounding in love and faithfulness, maintaining love to thousands, and forgiving wickedness, rebellion and sin. Yet he does not leave the guilty unpunished; he punishes the children and their children for the sin of the fathers to the third and fourth generation.
Narrator	Moses bowed to the ground at once and worshiped:
Moses	O Lord, if I have found favor in your eyes, then let the Lord go with us. Although this is a stiff-necked people, forgive our wickedness and our sin, and take us as your inheritance.

Cast: **Narrator, the Lord** (voice only), **Moses**

Leviticus

The Ordination of Aaron and His Sons

From Leviticus 8:1–36

Narrator 1   The LORD said to Moses:

The Lord
(voice only)   Bring Aaron and his sons, their garments, the anointing oil, the bull for the sin offering, the two rams and the basket containing bread made without yeast, and gather the entire assembly at the entrance to the Tent of Meeting.

Narrator 2   Moses did as the LORD commanded him, and the assembly gathered at the entrance to the Tent of Meeting. Moses said to the assembly:

Moses   This is what the LORD has commanded to be done.

Narrator 1   Then Moses brought Aaron and his sons forward and washed them with water. He put the tunic on Aaron, tied the sash around him, clothed him with the robe and put the ephod on him. He also tied the ephod to him by its skillfully woven waistband; so it was fastened on him. He placed the breastpiece on him and put the Urim and Thummim in the breastpiece. Then he placed the turban on Aaron's head and set the gold plate, the sacred diadem, on the front of it, as the LORD commanded Moses.

Narrator 2   Then Moses took the anointing oil and anointed the tabernacle and everything in it, and so consecrated them. He sprinkled some of the oil on the altar seven times, anointing the altar and all its utensils and the basin with its stand, to consecrate them. He poured some of the anointing oil on Aaron's head and anointed him to consecrate him.

Narrator 1   Then he brought Aaron's sons forward, put tunics on them, tied sashes around them and put headbands on them, as the LORD commanded Moses.

Narrator 2   He then presented the bull for the sin offering, and Aaron and his sons laid their hands on its head.

Narrator 1   Moses slaughtered the bull and took some of the blood, and with his finger he put it on all the horns of the altar to purify the altar. He poured out the rest of the blood at the base of the altar. So he consecrated it to make atonement for it. . . .

Narrator 2   He then presented the ram for the burnt offering, and Aaron and his sons laid their hands on its head. Then Moses slaughtered the ram and sprinkled the blood against the altar on all sides. He . . . burned the whole ram on the altar as a burnt offering, a pleasing aroma, an offering made to the LORD by fire, as the LORD commanded Moses.

Narrator 1	He then presented the other ram, the ram for the ordination, and Aaron and his sons laid their hands on its head.
Narrator 2	Moses slaughtered the ram and took some of its blood and put it on the lobe of Aaron's right ear, on the thumb of his right hand and on the big toe of his right foot.
Narrator 1	Moses also brought Aaron's sons forward and put some of the blood on the lobes of their right ears, on the thumbs of their right hands and on the big toes of their right feet. Then he sprinkled blood against the altar on all sides. . . .
Narrator 2	Then Moses took some of the anointing oil and some of the blood from the altar and sprinkled them on Aaron and his garments and on his sons and their garments. So he consecrated Aaron and his garments and his sons and their garments.
Narrator 1	Moses then said to Aaron and his sons:
Moses	. . . Do not leave the entrance to the Tent of Meeting for seven days, until the days of your ordination are completed, for your ordination will last seven days. What has been done today was commanded by the LORD to make atonement for you. You must stay at the entrance to the Tent of Meeting day and night for seven days and do what the LORD requires, so you will not die; for that is what I have been commanded.
Narrator 1	So Aaron and his sons did everything the LORD commanded through Moses.

Cast: **Narrator 1, the Lord** (voice only), **Narrator 2, Moses**

The Priests Begin Their Ministry

From Leviticus 9:2–24

Narrator	[Moses] said to Aaron:
Moses	Take a bull calf for your sin offering and a ram for your burnt offering, both without defect, and present them before the LORD. Then say to the Israelites: "Take a male goat for a sin offering, a calf and a lamb—both a year old and without defect—for a burnt offering, and an ox and a ram for a fellowship offering to sacrifice before the LORD, together with a grain offering mixed with oil. For today the LORD will appear to you."
Narrator	They took the things Moses commanded to the front of the Tent of Meeting, and the entire assembly came near and stood before the LORD. Then Moses said:
Moses (to audience)	This is what the LORD has commanded you to do, so that the glory of the LORD may appear to you.

131

Narrator	Moses said to Aaron:
Moses	Come to the altar and sacrifice your sin offering and your burnt offering and make atonement for yourself and the people; sacrifice the offering that is for the people and make atonement for them, as the LORD has commanded.
Narrator	So Aaron came to the altar and slaughtered the calf as a sin offering for himself. His sons brought the blood to him, and he dipped his finger into the blood and put it on the horns of the altar; the rest of the blood he poured out at the base of the altar. . . .
	Then Aaron lifted his hands toward the people and blessed them. And having sacrificed the sin offering, the burnt offering and the fellowship offering, he stepped down.
	Moses and Aaron then went into the Tent of Meeting. When they came out, they blessed the people; and the glory of the LORD appeared to all the people. Fire came out from the presence of the LORD and consumed the burnt offering and the fat portions on the altar. And when all the people saw it, they shouted for joy and fell facedown.

Cast: **Narrator, Moses**

Various Laws

From Leviticus 19:1–37

Reader 1	The LORD said to Moses, "Speak to the entire assembly of Israel and say to them:
Readers 1 and 2	"Be holy because I, the LORD your God, am holy.
Reader 2	"Each of you must respect his mother and father, and you must observe my Sabbaths.
Readers 1 and 2	"I am the LORD your God.
Reader 3	"Do not turn to idols or make gods of cast metal for yourselves.
Readers 1 and 2	"I am the LORD your God. . . .
Reader 1	"When you reap the harvest of your land, do not reap to the very edges of your field or gather the gleanings of your harvest. Do not go over your vineyard a second time or pick up the grapes that have fallen. Leave them for the poor and the alien.
Readers 1 and 2	"I am the LORD your God.

Reader 2	"Do not steal. Do not lie. Do not deceive one another. Do not swear falsely by my name and so profane the name of your God.
Readers 1 and 2	"I am the LORD.
Reader 3	"Do not defraud your neighbor or rob him. Do not hold back the wages of a hired man overnight. Do not curse the deaf or put a stumbling block in front of the blind, but fear your God.
Readers 1 and 2	"I am the LORD.
Reader 1	"Do not pervert justice; do not show partiality to the poor or favoritism to the great, but judge your neighbor fairly. Do not go about spreading slander among your people. Do not do anything that endangers your neighbor's life.
Readers 1 and 2	"I am the LORD.
Reader 2	"Do not hate your brother in your heart. Rebuke your neighbor frankly so you will not share in his guilt. Do not seek revenge or bear a grudge against one of your people, but love your neighbor as yourself.
Readers 1 and 2	"I am the LORD. . . .
Reader 3	"Do not turn to mediums or seek out spiritists, for you will be defiled by them.
Readers 1 and 2	"I am the LORD your God.
Reader 2	"Rise in the presence of the aged, show respect for the elderly and revere your God.
Readers 1 and 2	"I am the LORD.
Reader 3	"When an alien lives with you in your land, do not mistreat him. The alien living with you must be treated as one of your native-born. Love him as yourself, for you were aliens in Egypt.
Readers 1 and 2	"I am the LORD your God.
Reader 1	"Do not use dishonest standards when measuring length, weight or quantity. Use honest scales and honest weights, an honest ephah and an honest hin.

133

Readers 1
and 2   "I am the LORD your God, who brought you out of Egypt.

                   Keep all my decrees and all my laws and follow them. I am the LORD."

Cast: **Reader 1, Reader 2, Reader 3**

The Feast of Weeks

From Leviticus 23:15–22; Deuteronomy 14:22–29; 16:9–12

Leviticus   From the day after the Sabbath, the day you brought the sheaf of the wave offering, count off seven full weeks. Count off fifty days up to the day after the seventh Sabbath, and then present an offering of new grain to the LORD. From wherever you live, bring two loaves made of two-tenths of an ephah of fine flour, baked with yeast, as a wave offering of firstfruits to the LORD. . . . On that same day you are to proclaim a sacred assembly and do no regular work. This is to be a lasting ordinance for the generations to come, wherever you live.

Deuteronomy   Be sure to set aside a tenth of all that your fields produce each year. Eat the tithe of your grain, new wine and oil, and the firstborn of your herds and flocks in the presence of the LORD your God at the place he will choose as a dwelling for his Name, so that you may learn to revere the LORD your God always. . . . And do not neglect the Levites living in your towns, for they have no allotment or inheritance of their own.

                   At the end of every three years, bring all the tithes of that year's produce and store it in your towns, so that the Levites (who have no allotment or inheritance of their own) and the aliens, the fatherless and the widows who live in your towns may come and eat and be satisfied, and so that the LORD your God may bless you in all the work of your hands. . . .

Leviticus   When you reap the harvest of your land, do not reap to the very edges of your field or gather the gleanings of your harvest. Leave them for the poor and the alien. I am the LORD your God.

Deuteronomy   Count off seven weeks from the time you begin to put the sickle to the standing grain. Then celebrate the Feast of Weeks to the LORD your God by giving a freewill offering in proportion to the blessings the LORD your God has given you. And rejoice before the LORD your God at the place he will choose as a dwelling for his Name—you, your sons and daughters, your menservants and maidservants, the Levites in your towns, and the aliens, the fatherless and the widows living among you. Remember that you were slaves in Egypt, and follow carefully these decrees.

Cast: **Leviticus, Deuteronomy**

Numbers

In the Wilderness

From Numbers 10:33–11:32

Narrator   [The Israeliltes] set out from the mountain of the LORD and traveled for three days. The ark of the covenant of the LORD went before them during those three days to find them a place to rest. The cloud of the LORD was over them by day when they set out from the camp.

Whenever the ark set out, Moses said:

Moses   Rise up, O LORD!
May your enemies be scattered;
may your foes flee before you.

Narrator   Whenever it came to rest, he said:

Moses   Return, O LORD,
to the countless thousands of Israel.

Narrator   Now the people complained about their hardships in the hearing of the LORD. [When he heard them his anger was aroused. Then fire from the LORD burned among them and consumed some of the outskirts of the camp. When the people cried out to Moses, he prayed to the LORD and the fire died down. So that place was called Taberah, because fire from the LORD had burned among them.]

The [foreigners] with them began to crave other food, and again the Israelites started wailing and said:

Israelite 1   If only we had meat to eat!

Israelite 2   We remember the fish we ate in Egypt at no cost—also the cucumbers, melons, leeks, onions and garlic.

Israelite 1   But now we have lost our appetite—

Israelite 2   We never see anything but this manna!

Narrator   The manna was like coriander seed and looked like resin. The people went around gathering it, and then ground it in a handmill or crushed it in a mortar. They cooked it in a pot or made it into cakes. And it tasted like something made with olive oil. . . . (PAUSE)

Moses heard the people of every family wailing, each at the entrance to his tent. The LORD became exceedingly angry, and Moses was troubled.

Moses
(praying)   [LORD,] why have you brought this trouble on your servant? What have I done to displease you that you put the burden of all these people on me? Did I conceive all these people? Did I give them birth? Why do you

tell me to carry them in my arms, as a nurse carries an infant, to the land you promised on oath to their forefathers? Where can I get meat for all these people? They keep wailing to me, "Give us meat to eat!" I cannot carry all these people by myself; the burden is too heavy for me. If this is how you are going to treat me, put me to death right now—if I have found favor in your eyes—and do not let me face my own ruin.

[Narrator   The LORD said to Moses:]

The Lord
(voice)   Bring me seventy of Israel's elders who are known to you as leaders and officials among the people. Have them come to the Tent of Meeting, that they may stand there with you. I will come down and speak with you there, and I will take of the Spirit that is on you and put the Spirit on them. They will help you carry the burden of the people so that you will not have to carry it alone.

Tell the people: "Consecrate yourselves in preparation for tomorrow, when you will eat meat. The LORD heard you when you wailed, 'If only we had meat to eat! We were better off in Egypt!' Now the LORD will give you meat, and you will eat it. . . ."

Moses   Here I am among six hundred thousand men on foot, and you say, "I will give them meat to eat for a whole month!" Would they have enough if flocks and herds were slaughtered for them? Would they have enough if all the fish in the sea were caught for them?

The Lord
(voice)   Is the LORD's arm too short? You will now see whether or not what I say will come true for you.

Narrator   So Moses went out and told the people what the LORD had said. He brought together seventy of their elders and had them stand around the Tent. Then the LORD came down in the cloud and spoke with him, and he took of the Spirit that was on him and put the Spirit on the seventy elders. When the Spirit rested on them, they prophesied, but they did not do so again.

However, two men, whose names were Eldad and Medad, had remained in the camp. They were listed among the elders, but did not go out to the Tent. Yet the Spirit also rested on them, and they prophesied in the camp. A young man ran and told Moses:

Young man   Eldad and Medad are prophesying in the camp.

Narrator   Joshua son of Nun, who had been Moses' aide since youth, spoke up and said:

Joshua
(to Moses)   Moses, my lord, stop them!

Moses
(to Joshua)   Are you jealous for my sake? I wish that all the LORD's people were prophets and that the LORD would put his Spirit on them!

Narrator	Then Moses and the elders of Israel returned to the camp.
	Now a wind went out from the LORD and drove quail in from the sea. It brought them down all around the camp to about three feet above the ground, as far as a day's walk in any direction. All that day and night and all the next day the people went out and gathered quail. No one gathered less than ten homers. Then they spread them out all around the camp.

Cast: **Narrator, Moses, Israelite 1, Israelite 2** (can be the same as Israelite 1), **the Lord** (voice only), **Young man, Joshua**

Miriam and Aaron Oppose Moses

Numbers 12:1–16

Narrator	Miriam and Aaron began to talk against Moses because of his Cushite wife, for he had married a Cushite.
Miriam	Has the LORD spoken only through Moses?
Aaron	Hasn't he also spoken through *us*?
Narrator	And the LORD heard this. (PAUSE)
	(Now Moses was a very humble man, more humble than anyone else on the face of the earth.)
	At once the LORD said to Moses, Aaron and Miriam:
The Lord (voice only)	Come out to the Tent of Meeting, all three of you.
Narrator	So the three of them came out. Then the LORD came down in a pillar of cloud; he stood at the entrance to the Tent and summoned Aaron and Miriam. When both of them stepped forward, he said:
The Lord (voice)	Listen to my words: When a prophet of the LORD is among you, I reveal myself to him in visions, I speak to him in dreams. But this is not true of my servant Moses; he is faithful in all my house. With him I speak face to face, clearly and not in riddles; he sees the form of the LORD. Why then were you not afraid to speak against my servant Moses?
Narrator	The anger of the LORD burned against them, and he left them.

137

When the cloud lifted from above the Tent, there stood Miriam—leprous, like snow. Aaron turned toward her and saw that she had leprosy; and he said to Moses:

Aaron   Please, my lord, do not hold against us the sin we have so foolishly committed. Do not let her be like a stillborn infant coming from its mother's womb with its flesh half eaten away.

[Narrator   So Moses cried out to the LORD:]

Moses   O God, please heal her!

Narrator   The LORD replied to Moses:

The Lord
(voice)   If her father had spit in her face, would she not have been in disgrace for seven days? Confine her outside the camp for seven days; after that she can be brought back.

Narrator   So Miriam was confined outside the camp for seven days, and the people did not move on till she was brought back.

After that, the people left Hazeroth and encamped in the Desert of Paran.

Cast: **Narrator, Miriam, Aaron, the Lord** (voice only), **Moses**

Exploring Canaan

From Numbers 13:1–33

Narrator   The LORD said to Moses:

The Lord
(voice only)   Send some men to explore the land of Canaan, which I am giving to the Israelites. From each ancestral tribe send one of its leaders.

Narrator   So at the LORD's command Moses sent them out from the Desert of Paran. All of them were leaders of the Israelites. . . .

Moses sent them to explore Canaan:

Moses   Go up through the Negev and on into the hill country. See what the land is like and whether the people who live there are strong or weak, few or many. What kind of land do they live in? Is it good or bad? What kind of towns do they live in? Are they unwalled or fortified? How is the soil? Is it fertile or poor? Are there trees on it or not? Do your best to bring back some of the fruit of the land.

Commentator   (It was the season for the first ripe grapes.)

Narrator   So they went up and explored the land from the Desert of Zin as far as Rehob, toward Lebo Hamath. They went up through the Negev and came to Hebron, where Ahiman, Sheshai and Talmai, the descendants of Anak, lived.

Commentator (Hebron had been built seven years before Zoan in Egypt.)

Narrator When they reached the Valley of Eshcol, they cut off a branch bearing a single cluster of grapes. Two of them carried it on a pole between them, along with some pomegranates and figs.

Commentator That place was called the Valley of Eshcol because of the cluster of grapes the Israelites cut off there.

Narrator At the end of forty days they returned from exploring the land.

They came back to Moses and Aaron and the whole Israelite community at Kadesh in the Desert of Paran. There they reported to them and to the whole assembly and showed them the fruit of the land. They gave Moses this account:

Spy 1 We went into the land to which you sent us, and it does flow with milk and honey!

Spy 2 Here is its fruit.

Spy 3 But the people who live there are powerful, and the cities are fortified and very large.

Spy 1 We even saw descendants of Anak there.

Spy 2 The Amalekites live in the Negev—

Spy 3 The Hittites, Jebusites and Amorites live in the hill country—

Spy 1 And the Canaanites live near the sea and along the Jordan.

Narrator Then Caleb silenced the people before Moses and said:

Caleb We should go up and take possession of the land, for we can certainly do it.

Narrator But the men who had gone up with him said:

Spy 1 We can't attack those people—

Spy 2 They are stronger than we are.

Narrator And they spread among the Israelites a bad report about the land they had explored. They said:

Spy 2 The land we explored devours those living in it.

Spy 1 All the people we saw there are of great size.

Spy 3 We saw the Nephilim there.

Commentator (The descendants of Anak come from the Nephilim.)

Spy 2 We seemed like grasshoppers in our own eyes—

Spy 1 And we looked the same to them.

Cast: **Narrator, the Lord** (voice only), **Moses, Commentator, Spy 1, Spy 2, Spy 3, Caleb**

The People Rebel

Numbers 14:1–10

Narrator	[That night all] the people of the community raised their voices and wept aloud. All the Israelites grumbled against Moses and Aaron, and the whole assembly said to them:
Person 1	If only we had died in Egypt!
Person 2	Or in this desert!
Person 3	Why is the LORD bringing us to this land only to let us fall by the sword?
Person 1	Our wives and children will be taken as plunder.
Person 2	Wouldn't it be better for us to go back to Egypt?
[Narrator	And they said to each other:]
Person 3	We should choose a leader and go back to Egypt.
Narrator	Then Moses and Aaron fell facedown in front of the whole Israelite assembly gathered there. Joshua son of Nun and Caleb son of Jephunneh, who were among those who had explored the land, tore their clothes and said to the entire Israelite assembly:
Joshua	The land we passed through and explored is exceedingly good.
Caleb	If the LORD is pleased with us, he will lead us into that land, a land flowing with milk and honey, and will give it to us.
Joshua	Only do not rebel against the LORD. And do not be afraid of the people of the land, because we will swallow them up.
Caleb	Their protection is gone, but the LORD is with us. Do not be afraid of them.
Narrator	But the whole assembly talked about stoning them. Then the glory of the LORD appeared at the Tent of Meeting to all the Israelites.

Cast: **Narrator, Person 1, Person 2, Person 3, Joshua, Caleb**

Moses Prays for the People

Numbers 14:11–25

Narrator	The LORD said to Moses:
The Lord (voice only)	How long will these people treat me with contempt? How long will they refuse to believe in me, in spite of all the miraculous signs I have performed among them? I will strike them down with a plague and destroy them, but I will make you into a nation greater and stronger than they.

Narrator	Moses said to the LORD:

| Moses | Then the Egyptians will hear about it! By your power you brought these people up from among them. And they will tell the inhabitants of this land about it. They have already heard that you, O LORD, are with these people and that you, O LORD, have been seen face to face, that your cloud stays over them, and that you go before them in a pillar of cloud by day and a pillar of fire by night. If you put these people to death all at one time, the nations who have heard this report about you will say, "The LORD was not able to bring these people into the land he promised them on oath; so he slaughtered them in the desert." |

Now may the LORD's strength be displayed, just as you have declared: "The LORD is slow to anger, abounding in love and forgiving sin and rebellion. Yet he does not leave the guilty unpunished; he punishes the children for the sin of the fathers to the third and fourth generation." In accordance with your great love, forgive the sin of these people, just as you have pardoned them from the time they left Egypt until now.

[Narrator	The LORD replied:]
The Lord (voice)	I have forgiven them, as you asked. Nevertheless, as surely as I live and as surely as the glory of the LORD fills the whole earth, not one of the men who saw my glory and the miraculous signs I performed in Egypt and in the desert but who disobeyed me and tested me ten times—not one of them will ever see the land I promised on oath to their forefathers. No one who has treated me with contempt will ever see it. But because my servant Caleb has a different spirit and follows me wholeheartedly, I will bring him into the land he went to, and his descendants will inherit it. Since the Amalekites and Canaanites are living in the valleys, turn back tomorrow and set out toward the desert along the route to the Red Sea.

Cast: **Narrator, the Lord** (voice only), **Moses**

The Lord Punishes the People for Rebelling

Numbers 14:26–38

Narrator	The LORD said to Moses and Aaron:
The Lord (voice only)	How long will this wicked community grumble against me? I have heard the complaints of these grumbling Israelites. So tell them, "As surely as I live, declares the LORD, I will do to you the very things I heard you say: In this desert your bodies will fall—every one of you twenty years old or more who was counted in the census and who has grumbled against me. Not one of you will enter the land I swore with uplifted hand to

make your home, except Caleb son of Jephunneh and Joshua son of Nun. As for your children that you said would be taken as plunder, I will bring them in to enjoy the land you have rejected. But you—your bodies will fall in this desert. Your children will be shepherds here for forty years, suffering for your unfaithfulness, until the last of your bodies lies in the desert. For forty years—one year for each of the forty days you explored the land—you will suffer for your sins and know what it is like to have me against you." I, the LORD, have spoken, and I will surely do these things to this whole wicked community, which has banded together against me. They will meet their end in this desert; here they will die.

Narrator   So the men Moses had sent to explore the land, who returned and made the whole community grumble against him by spreading a bad report about it—these men responsible for spreading the bad report about the land were struck down and died of a plague before the LORD. Of the men who went to explore the land, only Joshua son of Nun and Caleb son of Jephunneh survived.

Cast: **Narrator, the Lord** (voice only)

The First Attempt to Invade the Land

Numbers 14:39–45

Narrator   When Moses reported [what the LORD had said] to all the Israelites, they mourned bitterly. Early the next morning they went up toward the high hill country.

Israelite 1   We have sinned.

Israelite 2   We will go up to the place the LORD promised.

Narrator   But Moses said:

Moses   Why are you disobeying the LORD's command? This will not succeed! Do not go up, because the LORD is not with you. You will be defeated by your enemies, for the Amalekites and Canaanites will face you there. Because you have turned away from the LORD, he will not be with you and you will fall by the sword.

Narrator   Nevertheless, in their presumption they went up toward the high hill country, though neither Moses nor the ark of the LORD's covenant moved from the camp. Then the Amalekites and Canaanites who lived in that hill country came down and attacked them and beat them down all the way to Hormah.

Cast: **Narrator, Israelite 1, Israelite 2** (can be the same as Israelite 1), **Moses**

Korah, Dathan and Abiram

Numbers 16:1–22

Narrator	Korah son of Izhar, the son of Kohath, the son of Levi, and certain Reuben-ites—Dathan and Abiram, sons of Eliab, and On son of Peleth—became insolent and rose up against Moses. With them were 250 Israelite men, well-known community leaders who had been appointed members of the council. They came as a group to oppose Moses and Aaron:
Rebel 1	You have gone too far!
Rebel 2	The whole community is holy, every one of them, and the LORD is with them.
Rebel 3	Why then do you set yourselves above the LORD's assembly?
Narrator	When Moses heard this, he fell facedown. Then he said to Korah and all his followers:
Moses	In the morning the LORD will show who belongs to him and who is holy, and he will have that person come near him. The man he chooses he will cause to come near him. You, Korah, and all your followers are to do this: Take censers and tomorrow put fire and incense in them before the LORD. The man the LORD chooses will be the one who is holy. You Levites have gone too far!
Narrator	Moses also said to Korah:
Moses	Now listen, you Levites! Isn't it enough for you that the God of Israel has separated you from the rest of the Israelite community and brought you near himself to do the work at the LORD's tabernacle and to stand before the community and minister to them? He has brought you and all your fellow Levites near himself, but now you are trying to get the priesthood too. It is against the LORD that you and all your followers have banded together. Who is Aaron that you should grumble against him?
Narrator	Then Moses summoned Dathan and Abiram, the sons of Eliab. But they said:
Rebel 1	We will not come! Isn't it enough that you have brought us up out of a land flowing with milk and honey to kill us in the desert?
Rebel 3	And now you also want to lord it over us?
Rebel 1	Moreover, you haven't brought us into a land flowing with milk and honey or given us an inheritance of fields and vineyards. Will you gouge out the eyes of these men?
Rebels 1 and 3	No, we will not come!
Narrator	Then Moses became very angry and said to the LORD:

Moses	Do not accept their offering. I have not taken so much as a donkey from them, nor have I wronged any of them.
Narrator	Moses said to Korah:
Moses	You and all your followers are to appear before the LORD tomorrow—you and they and Aaron. Each man is to take his censer and put incense in it—250 censers in all—and present it before the LORD. You and Aaron are to present your censers also.
Narrator	So each man took his censer, put fire and incense in it, and stood with Moses and Aaron at the entrance to the Tent of Meeting. When Korah had gathered all his followers in opposition to them at the entrance to the Tent of Meeting, the glory of the LORD appeared to the entire assembly. The LORD said to Moses and Aaron:
The Lord (voice only)	Separate yourselves from this assembly so I can put an end to them at once.
Narrator	But Moses and Aaron fell facedown and cried out:
Moses	O God, God of the spirits of all mankind, will you be angry with the entire assembly when only one man sins?

Cast: **Narrator, Rebel 1, Rebel 2, Rebel 3, Moses, the Lord** (voice only)

The Lord's Judgment

Numbers 16:23–35, 41–48

Narrator	The LORD said to Moses:
The Lord (voice only)	Say to the assembly, "Move away from the tents of Korah, Dathan and Abiram."
Narrator	Moses got up and went to Dathan and Abiram, and the elders of Israel followed him. He warned the assembly:
Moses	Move back from the tents of these wicked men! Do not touch anything belonging to them, or you will be swept away because of all their sins.
Narrator	So they moved away from the tents of Korah, Dathan and Abiram. Dathan and Abiram had come out and were standing with their wives, children and little ones at the entrances to their tents. [Then Moses said:]
Moses	This is how you will know that the LORD has sent me to do all these things and that it was not my idea: If these men die a natural death and experience only what usually happens to men, then the LORD has not sent me. But if the LORD brings about something totally new, and the earth opens its mouth and swallows them, with everything that belongs to

them, and they go down alive into the grave, then you will know that these men have treated the LORD with contempt.

Narrator As soon as he finished saying all this, the ground under them split apart and the earth opened its mouth and swallowed them, with their households and all Korah's men and all their possessions. They went down alive into the grave, with everything they owned; the earth closed over them, and they perished and were gone from the community. At their cries, all the Israelites around them fled [shouting:]

Israelite The earth is going to swallow us too!

Narrator And fire came out from the LORD and consumed the 250 men who were offering the incense. . . .

The next day the whole Israelite community grumbled against Moses and Aaron.

Israelite You have killed the LORD's people.

Narrator But when the assembly gathered in opposition to Moses and Aaron and turned toward the Tent of Meeting, suddenly the cloud covered it and the glory of the LORD appeared. Then Moses and Aaron went to the front of the Tent of Meeting, and the LORD said to Moses:

The Lord
(voice) Get away from this assembly so I can put an end to them at once.

Narrator And they fell facedown. Then Moses said to Aaron:

Moses Take your censer and put incense in it, along with fire from the altar, and hurry to the assembly to make atonement for them. Wrath has come out from the LORD; the plague has started.

Narrator So Aaron did as Moses said, and ran into the midst of the assembly. The plague had already started among the people, but Aaron offered the incense and made atonement for them. He stood between the living and the dead, and the plague stopped.

Cast: **Narrator, the Lord** (voice only), **Moses, Israelite**

The Budding of Aaron's Staff

Numbers 17:1–18:7

Narrator The LORD said to Moses:

The Lord
(voice only) Speak to the Israelites and get twelve staffs from them, one from the leader of each of their ancestral tribes. Write the name of each man on his staff. On the staff of Levi write Aaron's name, for there must be one staff for the head of each ancestral tribe. Place them in the Tent of Meeting in front of the Testimony, where I meet with you. The staff belonging to

the man I choose will sprout, and I will rid myself of this constant grumbling against you by the Israelites.

Narrator   So Moses spoke to the Israelites, and their leaders gave him twelve staffs, one for the leader of each of their ancestral tribes, and Aaron's staff was among them. Moses placed the staffs before the LORD in the Tent of the Testimony.

The next day Moses entered the Tent of the Testimony and saw that Aaron's staff, which represented the house of Levi, had not only sprouted but had budded, blossomed and produced almonds. Then Moses brought out all the staffs from the LORD's presence to all the Israelites. They looked at them, and each man took his own staff. The LORD said to Moses:

The Lord
(voice)   Put back Aaron's staff in front of the Testimony, to be kept as a sign to the rebellious. This will put an end to their grumbling against me, so that they will not die.

Narrator   Moses did just as the LORD commanded him. The Israelites said to Moses:

Israelite 1   We will die!

Israelite 2   We are lost, we are all lost!

Israelite 1   Anyone who even comes near the tabernacle of the LORD will die.

Israelite 2   Are we all going to die?

Narrator   The LORD said to Aaron:

The Lord
(voice)   You, your sons and your father's family are to bear the responsibility for offenses against the sanctuary, and you and your sons alone are to bear the responsibility for offenses against the priesthood. Bring your fellow Levites from your ancestral tribe to join you and assist you when you and your sons minister before the Tent of the Testimony. They are to be responsible to you and are to perform all the duties of the Tent, but they must not go near the furnishings of the sanctuary or the altar, or both they and you will die. They are to join you and be responsible for the care of the Tent of Meeting—all the work at the Tent—and no one else may come near where you are.

You are to be responsible for the care of the sanctuary and the altar, so that wrath will not fall on the Israelites again. I myself have selected your fellow Levites from among the Israelites as a gift to you, dedicated to the LORD to do the work at the Tent of Meeting. But only you and your sons may serve as priests in connection with everything at the altar and inside the curtain. I am giving you the service of the priesthood as a gift. Anyone else who comes near the sanctuary must be put to death.

Cast: **Narrator, the Lord** (voice only), **Israelite 1, Israelite 2** (can be the same as Israelite 1)

Water from the Rock

Numbers 20:1–13

Narrator	In the first month the whole Israelite community arrived at the Desert of Zin, and they stayed at Kadesh. There Miriam died and was buried.
	Now there was no water for the community, and the people gathered in opposition to Moses and Aaron. They quarreled with Moses:
Israelite 1	If only we had died when our brothers fell dead before the LORD!
Israelite 2	Why did you bring the LORD's community into this desert, that we and our livestock should die here?
Israelite 3	Why did you bring us up out of Egypt to this terrible place?
Israelite 1	It has no grain or figs, grapevines or pomegranates.
Israelite 2	And there is no water to drink!
Narrator	Moses and Aaron went from the assembly to the entrance to the Tent of Meeting and fell facedown, and the glory of the LORD appeared to them. [The LORD said to Moses:]
The Lord (voice only)	Take the staff, and you and your brother Aaron gather the assembly together. Speak to that rock before their eyes and it will pour out its water. You will bring water out of the rock for the community so they and their livestock can drink.
Narrator	So Moses took the staff from the LORD's presence, just as he commanded him. He and Aaron gathered the assembly together in front of the rock and Moses said to them:
Moses (angrily)	Listen, you rebels, must we bring you water out of this rock?
Narrator	Then Moses raised his arm and struck the rock twice with his staff. Water gushed out, and the community and their livestock drank. (PAUSE) But the LORD said to Moses and Aaron:
The Lord (voice)	Because you did not trust in me enough to honor me as holy in the sight of the Israelites, you will not bring this community into the land I give them.
Narrator	These were the waters of Meribah, where the Israelites quarreled with the LORD and where he showed himself holy among them.

Cast: **Narrator, Israelite 1, Israelite 2, Israelite 3** (can be the same as Israelite 1, or Israelites 1–3 can be the same), **the Lord** (voice only), **Moses**

Edom Denies Israel Passage

Numbers 20:14–21

Narrator	Moses sent messengers from Kadesh to the king of Edom, saying: "This is what your brother Israel says:"
Israelite 1	You know about all the hardships that have come upon us.
Israelite 2	Our forefathers went down into Egypt, and we lived there many years. The Egyptians mistreated us and our fathers, but when we cried out to the LORD, he heard our cry and sent an angel and brought us out of Egypt.
Israelite 1	Now we are here at Kadesh, a town on the edge of your territory.
Israelite 2	Please let us pass through your country.
Israelite 1	We will not go through any field or vineyard, or drink water from any well.
Israelite 2	We will travel along the king's highway and not turn to the right or to the left until we have passed through your territory.
Narrator	But Edom answered:
Edomite 1	You may not pass through here—
Edomite 2	If you try, we will march out and attack you with the sword.
Narrator	The Israelites replied:
Israelite 1	We will go along the main road, and if we or our livestock drink any of your water, we will pay for it.
Israelite 2	We only want to pass through on foot—nothing else.
[Narrator	Again they answered:]
Edomites 1 and 2	You may *not* pass through.
Narrator	Then Edom came out against them with a large and powerful army. Since Edom refused to let them go through their territory, Israel turned away from them.

Cast: **Narrator, Israelite 1, Israelite 2, Edomite 1, Edomite 2**

The Death of Aaron

Numbers 20:22–29

Narrator	The whole Israelite community set out from Kadesh and came to Mount Hor. At Mount Hor, near the border of Edom, the LORD said to Moses and Aaron:

The Lord

(voice only)   Aaron will be gathered to his people. He will not enter the land I give the Israelites, because both of you rebelled against my command at the waters of Meribah. Get Aaron and his son Eleazar and take them up Mount Hor. Remove Aaron's garments and put them on his son Eleazar, for Aaron will be gathered to his people; he will die there.

Narrator   Moses did as the LORD commanded: They went up Mount Hor in the sight of the whole community. Moses removed Aaron's garments and put them on his son Eleazar. And Aaron died there on top of the mountain. Then Moses and Eleazar came down from the mountain, and when the whole community learned that Aaron had died, the entire house of Israel mourned for him thirty days.

Cast: **Narrator, the Lord** (voice only)

The Bronze Snake

Numbers 21:4–9

Narrator   [The Israelites] traveled from Mount Hor along the route to the Red Sea, to go around Edom. But the people grew impatient on the way; they spoke against God and against Moses:

Israelite 1   Why have you brought us up out of Egypt to die in the desert?

Israelite 2   There is no bread! There is no water!

Israelite 1   And we detest this miserable food!

Narrator   Then the LORD sent venomous snakes among them; they bit the people and many Israelites died. The people came to Moses:

Israelite 2   We sinned when we spoke against the LORD and against you.

Israelite 1   Pray that the LORD will take the snakes away from us.

Narrator   So Moses prayed for the people. (PAUSE) The LORD said to Moses:

The Lord

(voice only)   Make a snake and put it up on a pole; anyone who is bitten can look at it and live.

Narrator   So Moses made a bronze snake and put it up on a pole. Then when anyone was bitten by a snake and looked at the bronze snake, he lived.

Cast: **Narrator, Israelite 1, Israelite 2, the Lord** (voice only)

The Journey to Moab

Numbers 21:10–20

Narrator	The Israelites moved on and camped at Oboth. Then they set out from Oboth and camped in Iye Abarim, in the desert that faces Moab toward the sunrise. From there they moved on and camped in the Zered Valley. They set out from there and camped alongside the Arnon, which is in the desert extending into Amorite territory. The Arnon is the border of Moab, between Moab and the Amorites. That is why the Book of the Wars of the LORD says:

Reader	. . . Waheb in Suphah and the ravines,
	      the Arnon and the slopes of the ravines
	that lead to the site of Ar
	      and lie along the border of Moab.

Narrator	From there they continued on to Beer, the well where the LORD said to Moses:
The Lord (voice only)	Gather the people together and I will give them water.
Narrator	Then Israel sang this song:

Singer(s)	Spring up, O well!
	      Sing about it,
	about the well that the princes dug,
	      that the nobles of the people sank—
	      the nobles with scepters and staffs.

Narrator	Then they went from the desert to Mattanah, from Mattanah to Nahaliel, from Nahaliel to Bamoth, and from Bamoth to the valley in Moab where the top of Pisgah overlooks the wasteland.

Cast: **Narrator, Reader, the Lord** (voice only), **Singer(s)**

Defeat of Sihon and Og

Numbers 21:21–35

Narrator	Israel sent messengers to say to Sihon king of the Amorites:
Israelite 1	Let us pass through your country.
Israelite 2	We will not turn aside into any field or vineyard—
Israelite 1	Or drink water from any well.
Israelite 2	We will travel along the king's highway until we have passed through your territory.

Narrator	But Sihon would not let Israel pass through his territory. He mustered his entire army and marched out into the desert against Israel. When he reached Jahaz, he fought with Israel. Israel, however, put him to the sword and took over his land from the Arnon to the Jabbok, but only as far as the Ammonites, because their border was fortified. Israel captured all the cities of the Amorites and occupied them, including Heshbon and all its surrounding settlements. Heshbon was the city of Sihon king of the Amorites, who had fought against the former king of Moab and had taken from him all his land as far as the Arnon. (PAUSE) That is why the poets say:
Poets 1 and 2	Come to Heshbon and let it be rebuilt; let Sihon's city be restored.
Poet 1	Fire went out from Heshbon, a blaze from the city of Sihon.
Poet 2	It consumed Ar of Moab, the citizens of Arnon's heights.
Poet 1	Woe to you, O Moab!
Poet 2	You are destroyed, O people of Chemosh!

Poet 1	He has given up his sons as fugitives
	    and his daughters as captives
	    to Sihon king of the Amorites.

Poet 2	But we have overthrown them;
	    Heshbon is destroyed all the way to Dibon.
	 We have demolished them as far as Nophah,
	    which extends to Medeba.

Narrator	So Israel settled in the land of the Amorites.
	After Moses had sent spies to Jazer, the Israelites captured its surrounding settlements and drove out the Amorites who were there. Then they turned and went up along the road toward Bashan, and Og king of Bashan and his whole army marched out to meet them in battle at Edrei. The LORD said to Moses:
The Lord (voice only)	Do not be afraid of him, for I have handed him over to you, with his whole army and his land. Do to him what you did to Sihon king of the Amorites, who reigned in Heshbon.
Narrator	So they struck him down, together with his sons and his whole army, leaving them no survivors. And they took possession of his land.

Cast: **Narrator, Israelite 1, Israelite 2, Poet 1, Poet 2** (can be the same as Poet 1), **the Lord** (voice only)

Balak Summons Balaam

Numbers 22:1–21

Narrator	The Israelites traveled to the plains of Moab and camped along the Jordan across from Jericho.
	Now Balak son of Zippor saw all that Israel had done to the Amorites, and Moab was terrified because there were so many people. Indeed, Moab was filled with dread because of the Israelites. The Moabites said to the elders of Midian:
Moabite	This horde is going to lick up everything around us, as an ox licks up the grass of the field.
Narrator	So Balak son of Zippor, who was king of Moab at that time, sent messengers to summon Balaam son of Beor, who was at Pethor, near the River, in his native land. Balak said:
Balak	A people has come out of Egypt; they cover the face of the land and have settled next to me. Now come and put a curse on these people, because they are too powerful for me. Perhaps then I will be able to defeat them and drive them out of the country. For I know that those you bless are blessed, and those you curse are cursed.
Narrator	The elders of Moab and Midian left, taking with them the fee for divination. When they came to Balaam, they told him what Balak had said. Balaam said to them:
Balaam	Spend the night here, and I will bring you back the answer the Lord gives me.
Narrator	So the Moabite princes stayed with him. (PAUSE)
	God came to Balaam and asked:
God (voice only)	Who are these men with you?
Narrator	Balaam said to God:
Balaam	Balak son of Zippor, king of Moab, sent me this message: "A people that has come out of Egypt covers the face of the land. Now come and put a curse on them for me. Perhaps then I will be able to fight them and drive them away."
God (voice)	Do not go with them. You must not put a curse on those people, because they are blessed.
Narrator	The next morning Balaam got up and said to Balak's princes:
Balaam	Go back to your own country, for the Lord has refused to let me go with you.

Narrator	So the Moabite princes returned to Balak and said: "Balaam refused to come with us."
	Then Balak sent other princes, more numerous and more distinguished than the first. They came to Balaam and said: "This is what Balak son of Zippor says":
Balak	Do not let anything keep you from coming to me, because I will reward you handsomely and do whatever you say. Come and put a curse on these people for me.
[Narrator	But Balaam answered them:]
Balaam	Even if Balak gave me his palace filled with silver and gold, I could not do anything great or small to go beyond the command of the LORD my God. Now stay here tonight as the others did, and I will find out what else the LORD will tell me.
Narrator	That night God came to Balaam and said:
God (voice)	Since these men have come to summon you, go with them, but do only what I tell you.
Narrator	Balaam got up in the morning, saddled his donkey and went with the princes of Moab.

Cast: **Narrator, Moabite, Balak, Balaam, God** (voice only)

Balaam's Donkey

Numbers 22:22–35

Narrator	God was very angry when [Balaam] went, and the angel of the LORD stood in the road to oppose him. Balaam was riding on his donkey, and his two servants were with him. When the donkey saw the angel of the LORD standing in the road with a drawn sword in his hand, she turned off the road into a field. Balaam beat her to get her back on the road.
	Then the angel of the LORD stood in a narrow path between two vineyards, with walls on both sides. When the donkey saw the angel of the LORD, she pressed close to the wall, crushing Balaam's foot against it. So he beat her again.
	Then the angel of the LORD moved on ahead and stood in a narrow place where there was no room to turn, either to the right or to the left. When the donkey saw the angel of the LORD, she lay down under Balaam, and he was angry and beat her with his staff. Then the LORD opened the donkey's mouth, and she said to Balaam:
Donkey	What have I done to you to make you beat me these three times?
[Narrator	Balaam answered the donkey:]

153

Balaam	You have made a fool of me! If I had a sword in my hand, I would kill you right now.
[Narrator	The donkey said to Balaam:]
Donkey	Am I not your own donkey, which you have always ridden, to this day? Have I been in the habit of doing this to you?
Balaam	No.
Narrator	Then the LORD opened Balaam's eyes, and he saw the angel of the LORD standing in the road with his sword drawn. So he bowed low and fell facedown. [The angel of the LORD asked him:]
Angel	Why have you beaten your donkey these three times? I have come here to oppose you because your path is a reckless one before me. The donkey saw me and turned away from me these three times. If she had not turned away, I would certainly have killed you by now, but I would have spared her.
[Narrator	Balaam said to the angel of the LORD:]
Balaam	I have sinned. I did not realize you were standing in the road to oppose me. Now if you are displeased, I will go back.
[Narrator	The angel of the LORD said to Balaam:]
Angel	Go with the men, but speak only what I tell you.
Narrator	So Balaam went with the princes of Balak.

Cast: **Narrator, Donkey, Balaam, Angel**

Balaam and Balak

Numbers 22:36–38; 23:28–24:13

Narrator	When Balak heard that Balaam was coming, he went out to meet him at the Moabite town on the Arnon border, at the edge of his territory. Balak said to Balaam:
Balak	Did I not send you an urgent summons? Why didn't you come to me? Am I really not able to reward you?
Balaam	Well, I have come to you now. But can I say just anything? I must speak only what God puts in my mouth. . . .
Narrator	And Balak took Balaam to the top of Peor, overlooking the wasteland. Balaam said:
Balaam	Build me seven altars here, and prepare seven bulls and seven rams for me.
Narrator	Balak did as Balaam had said, and offered a bull and a ram on each altar.

154

Now when Balaam saw that it pleased the LORD to bless Israel, he did not resort to sorcery as at other times, but turned his face toward the desert. When Balaam looked out and saw Israel encamped tribe by tribe, the Spirit of God came upon him and he uttered his oracle:

Herald

The oracle of Balaam son of Beor,
the oracle of one whose eye sees clearly,
the oracle of one who hears the words of God,
who sees a vision from the Almighty,
who falls prostrate, and whose eyes are opened:

Balaam

How beautiful are your tents, O Jacob,
your dwelling places, O Israel!

Like valleys they spread out,
like gardens beside a river,
like aloes planted by the LORD,
like cedars beside the waters.
Water will flow from their buckets;
their seed will have abundant water.

Their king will be greater than Agag;
their kingdom will be exalted.

God brought them out of Egypt;
they have the strength of a wild ox.
They devour hostile nations
and break their bones in pieces;
with their arrows they pierce them.
Like a lion they crouch and lie down,
like a lioness—who dares to rouse them?

May those who bless you be blessed
and those who curse you be cursed!

Narrator

Then Balak's anger burned against Balaam. He struck his hands together [and said to him:]

Balak

I summoned you to *curse* my enemies, but you have blessed them these three times. Now leave at once and go home! I said I would reward you handsomely, but the LORD has kept you from being rewarded.

[Narrator

Balaam answered Balak:]

Balaam

Did I not tell the messengers you sent me, "Even if Balak gave me his palace filled with silver and gold, I could not do anything of my own accord, good or bad, to go beyond the command of the LORD—and I must say only what the LORD says"?

Cast: **Narrator, Balak, Balaam, Herald** (can be the same as Balaam)

Zelophehad's Daughters

Numbers 27:1–11

Narrator	The daughters of Zelophehad . . . stood before Moses, Eleazar the priest, the leaders and the whole assembly [and said:]
Daughter 1	Our father died in the desert.
Daughter 2	He was not among Korah's followers, who banded together against the LORD, but he died for his own sin and left no sons.
Daughter 1	Why should our father's name disappear from his clan because he had no son?
Daughter 2	Give us property among our father's relatives.
Narrator	So Moses brought their case before the LORD and the LORD said to him:
The Lord (voice only)	What Zelophehad's daughters are saying is right. You must certainly give them property as an inheritance among their father's relatives and turn their father's inheritance over to them.
	Say to the Israelites, "If a man dies and leaves no son, turn his inheritance over to his daughter. If he has no daughter, give his inheritance to his brothers. If he has no brothers, give his inheritance to his father's brothers. If his father had no brothers, give his inheritance to the nearest relative in his clan, that he may possess it. This is to be a legal requirement for the Israelites, as the LORD commanded Moses."

Cast: **Narrator, Daughter 1, Daughter 2, the Lord** (voice only)

Joshua to Succeed Moses

Numbers 27:12–23

Narrator	The LORD said to Moses:
The Lord (voice only)	Go up this mountain in the Abarim range and see the land I have given the Israelites. After you have seen it, you too will be gathered to your people, as your brother Aaron was, for when the community rebelled at the waters in the Desert of Zin, both of you disobeyed my command to honor me as holy before their eyes.
Narrator	(These were the waters of Meribah Kadesh, in the Desert of Zin.) (PAUSE)
	Moses said to the LORD:
Moses	May the LORD, the God of the spirits of all mankind, appoint a man over this community to go out and come in before them, one who will lead

156

them out and bring them in, so the Lord's people will not be like sheep without a shepherd.

Narrator   So the Lord said to Moses:

The Lord
(voice)   Take Joshua son of Nun, a man in whom is the spirit, and lay your hand on him. Have him stand before Eleazar the priest and the entire assembly and commission him in their presence. Give him some of your authority so the whole Israelite community will obey him. He is to stand before Eleazar the priest, who will obtain decisions for him by inquiring of the Urim before the Lord. At his command he and the entire community of the Israelites will go out, and at his command they will come in.

Narrator   Moses did as the Lord commanded him. He took Joshua and had him stand before Eleazar the priest and the whole assembly. Then he laid his hands on him and commissioned him, as the Lord instructed through Moses.

Cast: **Narrator, the Lord** (voice only), **Moses**

Deuteronomy

The Command to Leave Horeb

Deuteronomy 1:6–18

Moses speaks to the people

Moses (to audience)

The LORD our God said to us at Horeb:

The Lord (voice only)

You have stayed long enough at this mountain. Break camp, and advance into the hill country of the Amorites; go to all the neighboring peoples in the Arabah, in the mountains, in the western foothills, in the Negev and along the coast, to the land of the Canaanites and to Lebanon, as far as the great river, the Euphrates. See, I have given you this land. Go in and take possession of the land that the LORD swore he would give to your fathers—to Abraham, Isaac and Jacob—and to their descendants after them.

Moses (to audience)

At that time I said to you:

Younger Moses

You are too heavy a burden for me to carry alone. The LORD your God has increased your numbers so that today you are as many as the stars in the sky. May the LORD, the God of your fathers, increase you a thousand times and bless you as he has promised! But how can I bear your problems and your burdens and your disputes all by myself? Choose some wise, understanding and respected men from each of your tribes, and I will set them over you.

Moses (to audience)

You answered me, "What you propose to do is good."

So I took the leading men of your tribes, wise and respected men, and appointed them to have authority over you—as commanders of thousands, of hundreds, of fifties and of tens and as tribal officials. And I charged your judges at that time:

Younger Moses (to audience)

Hear the disputes between your brothers and judge fairly, whether the case is between brother Israelites or between one of them and an alien. Do not show partiality in judging; hear both small and great alike. Do not be afraid of any man, for judgment belongs to God. Bring me any case too hard for you, and I will hear it.

Moses (to audience)

And at that time I told you everything you were to do.

Cast: **Moses, the Lord** (voice only), **Younger Moses.** (Moses speaks to the audience as if to the people of Israel.)

Spies Sent Out

Deuteronomy 1:19–33

Moses speaks to the people

Moses (to audience)

Then, as the LORD our God commanded us, we set out from Horeb and went toward the hill country of the Amorites through all that vast and dreadful desert that you have seen, and so we reached Kadesh Barnea. Then I said to you:

Younger Moses

You have reached the hill country of the Amorites, which the LORD our God is giving us. See, the LORD your God has given you the land. Go up and take possession of it as the LORD, the God of your fathers, told you. Do not be afraid; do not be discouraged.

Moses (to audience)

Then all of you came to me and said:

Israelite 1

Let us send men ahead to spy out the land for us and bring back a report about the route we are to take and the towns we will come to.

Moses (to audience)

The idea seemed good to me; so I selected twelve of you, one man from each tribe. They left and went up into the hill country, and came to the Valley of Eshcol and explored it. Taking with them some of the fruit of the land, they brought it down to us and reported, "It is a good land that the LORD our God is giving us."

But you were unwilling to go up; you rebelled against the command of the LORD your God. You grumbled in your tents and said:

Israelite 2

The LORD hates us—

Israelite 3

So he brought us out of Egypt to deliver us into the hands of the Amorites to destroy us. Where can we go?

Israelite 2

Our brothers have made us lose heart. They say, "The people are stronger and taller than we are; the cities are large, with walls up to the sky."

Israelite 1

"We even saw the Anakites there."

Moses (to audience)

Then I said to you:

Younger Moses

Do not be terrified; do not be afraid of them. The LORD your God, who is going before you, will fight for you, as he did for you in Egypt, before your very eyes, and in the desert. There you saw how the LORD your God carried you, as a father carries his son, all the way you went until you reached this place.

Moses (to
audience)   In spite of this, you did not trust in the LORD your God, who went ahead
of you on your journey, in fire by night and in a cloud by day, to search
out places for you to camp and to show you the way you should go.

Cast: **Moses, Younger Moses, Israelite 1, Israelite 2, Israelite 3.** (Moses speaks to the audience as
if to the people of Israel.)

The Lord Punishes Israel

Deuteronomy 1:34–45

Moses speaks to the people

Moses (to
audience)   When the LORD heard what you said, he was angry [and solemnly swore:]

The Lord
(voice only)   Not a man of this evil generation shall see the good land I swore to give
your forefathers, except Caleb son of Jephunneh. He will see it, and I will
give him and his descendants the land he set his feet on, because he followed the LORD wholeheartedly.

Moses (to
audience)   Because of you the LORD became angry with me also [and said:]

The Lord
(voice)   *You* shall not enter it, either. But your assistant, Joshua son of Nun, will
enter it. Encourage him, because he will lead Israel to inherit it. And the
little ones that you said would be taken captive, your children who do
not yet know good from bad—they will enter the land. I will give it to
them and they will take possession of it. But as for you, turn around and
set out toward the desert along the route to the Red Sea.

Moses (to
audience)   Then you replied:

Israelite 1   We have sinned against the LORD.

Israelite 2   We will go up and fight, as the LORD our God commanded us.

Moses (to
audience)   So every one of you put on his weapons, thinking it easy to go up into
the hill country. But the LORD said to me:

The Lord
(voice)   Tell them, "Do not go up and fight, because I will not be with you. You
will be defeated by your enemies."

Moses (to
audience)   So I told you, but you would not listen. You rebelled against the LORD's
command and in your arrogance you marched up into the hill country.
The Amorites who lived in those hills came out against you; they chased

160

you like a swarm of bees and beat you down from Seir all the way to Hormah. You came back and wept before the LORD, but he paid no attention to your weeping and turned a deaf ear to you.

Cast: **Moses, the Lord** (voice only), **Israelite 1, Israelite 2.** (Moses speaks to the audience as if to the people of Israel.)

Wanderings in the Desert

From Deuteronomy 1:46–2:25

Moses speaks to the people

Moses (to audience)   You stayed in Kadesh many days—all the time you spent there.

Then we turned back and set out toward the desert along the route to the Red Sea, as the LORD had directed me. For a long time we made our way around the hill country of Seir.

Then the LORD said to me:

The Lord (voice only)   You have made your way around this hill country long enough; now turn north. Give the people these orders: "You are about to pass through the territory of your brothers the descendants of Esau, who live in Seir. They will be afraid of you, but be very careful. Do not provoke them to war, for I will not give you any of their land, not even enough to put your foot on. I have given Esau the hill country of Seir as his own. You are to pay them in silver for the food you eat and the water you drink."

Moses (to audience)   The LORD your God has blessed you in all the work of your hands. He has watched over your journey through this vast desert. These forty years the LORD your God has been with you, and you have not lacked anything. (PAUSE)

So we went on past our brothers the descendants of Esau, who live in Seir. We turned from the Arabah road, which comes up from Elath and Ezion Geber, and traveled along the desert road of Moab. Then the LORD said to me:

The Lord (voice)   Do not harass the Moabites or provoke them to war, for I will not give you any part of their land. I have given Ar to the descendants of Lot as a possession. . . .

Moses (to audience)   So we crossed the valley.

Thirty-eight years passed from the time we left Kadesh Barnea until we crossed the Zered Valley. By then, that entire generation of fighting men

161

had perished from the camp, as the LORD had sworn to them. The LORD's hand was against them until he had completely eliminated them from the camp.

Now when the last of these fighting men among the people had died, the LORD said to me:

The Lord
(voice)

Today you are to pass by the region of Moab at Ar. When you come to the Ammonites, do not harass them or provoke them to war, for I will not give you possession of any land belonging to the Ammonites. I have given it as a possession to the descendants of Lot. . . .

[Moses (to
audience)

After we had passed through Moab, the LORD said to us:]

The Lord
(voice)

Set out now and cross the Arnon Gorge. See, I have given into your hand Sihon the Amorite, king of Heshbon, and his country. Begin to take possession of it and engage him in battle. This very day I will begin to put the terror and fear of you on all the nations under heaven. They will hear reports of you and will tremble and be in anguish because of you.

Cast: **Moses, the Lord** (voice only). (Moses speaks to the audience as if to the people of Israel.)

Defeat of Sihon King of Heshbon and Og King of Bashan

From Deuteronomy 2:26–3:4

Moses speaks to the people

Moses (to
audience)

From the desert of Kedemoth I sent messengers to Sihon king of Heshbon offering peace and saying:

Messenger 1   Let us pass through your country.

Messenger 2   We will stay on the main road; we will not turn aside to the right or to the left.

Messenger 1   Sell us food to eat and water to drink for their price in silver.

Messenger 2   Only let us pass through on foot—as the descendants of Esau, who live in Seir, and the Moabites, who live in Ar, did for us—until we cross the Jordan into the land the LORD our God is giving us.

Moses (to
audience)

But Sihon king of Heshbon refused to let us pass through. For the LORD your God had made his spirit stubborn and his heart obstinate in order to give him into your hands, as he has now done.

The LORD said to me:

The Lord

(voice only) See, I have begun to deliver Sihon and his country over to you. Now begin to conquer and possess his land.

Moses (to

audience) When Sihon and all his army came out to meet us in battle at Jahaz, the LORD our God delivered him over to us and we struck him down, together with his sons and his whole army. From Aroer on the rim of the Arnon Gorge, and from the town in the gorge, even as far as Gilead, not one town was too strong for us. The LORD our God gave us all of them. . . .

Next we turned and went up along the road toward Bashan, and Og king of Bashan with his whole army marched out to meet us in battle at Edrei. [The LORD said to me:]

The Lord

(voice) Do not be afraid of him, for I have handed him over to you with his whole army and his land. Do to him what you did to Sihon king of the Amorites, who reigned in Heshbon.

Moses (to

audience) So the LORD our God also gave into our hands Og king of Bashan and all his army. At that time we took all his cities. There was not one of the sixty cities that we did not take from them—the whole region of Argob, Og's kingdom in Bashan.

Cast: **Moses, Messenger 1, Messenger 2** (can be the same as Messenger 1), **the Lord** (voice only). (Moses speaks to the audience as if to the people of Israel.)

Division of the Land

From Deuteronomy 3:12–29

Moses speaks to the people

Moses (to

audience) Of the land that we took over . . . I commanded you:

**Younger

Moses** The LORD your God has given you this land to take possession of it. But all your able-bodied men, armed for battle, must cross over ahead of your brother Israelites. However, your wives, your children and your livestock (I know you have much livestock) may stay in the towns I have given you, until the LORD gives rest to your brothers as he has to you, and they too have taken over the land that the LORD your God is giving them, across the Jordan. After that, each of you may go back to the possession I have given you.

Moses (to

audience) At that time I commanded Joshua:

Younger Moses	You have seen with your own eyes all that the LORD your God has done to these two kings. The LORD will do the same to all the kingdoms over there where you are going. Do not be afraid of them; the LORD your God himself will fight for you.
Moses (to audience)	At that time I pleaded with the LORD:
Younger Moses (praying)	O Sovereign LORD, you have begun to show to your servant your greatness and your strong hand. For what god is there in heaven or on earth who can do the deeds and mighty works you do? Let me go over and see the good land beyond the Jordan—that fine hill country and Lebanon.
Moses (to audience)	But because of you the LORD was angry with me and would not listen to me.
The Lord (voice only)	That is enough. Do not speak to me anymore about this matter. Go up to the top of Pisgah and look west and north and south and east. Look at the land with your own eyes, since you are not going to cross this Jordan. But commission Joshua, and encourage and strengthen him, for he will lead this people across and will cause them to inherit the land that you will see.
Moses (to audience)	So we stayed in the valley near Beth Peor.

Cast: **Moses, Younger Moses, the Lord** (voice only). (Moses speaks to the audience as if to the people of Israel.)

The Ten Commandments

Deuteronomy 5:1–22

Moses speaks to the people

Interpreter	Moses summoned all Israel and said:
Moses (to audience)	Hear, O Israel, the decrees and laws I declare in your hearing today. Learn them and be sure to follow them. The LORD our God made a covenant with us at Horeb. It was not with our fathers that the LORD made this covenant, but with us, with all of us who are alive here today. The LORD spoke to you face to face out of the fire on the mountain. (At that time I stood between the LORD and you to declare to you the word of the LORD, because you were afraid of the fire and did not go up the mountain.) [And he said:]

The Lord
(voice only) I am the LORD your God, who brought you out of Egypt, out of the land of slavery.

You shall have no other gods before me.

You shall not make for yourself an idol in the form of anything in heaven above or on the earth beneath or in the waters below. You shall not bow down to them or worship them; for I, the LORD your God, am a jealous God, punishing the children for the sin of the fathers to the third and fourth generation of those who hate me, but showing love to a thousand ⌊generations⌋ of those who love me and keep my commandments.

You shall not misuse the name of the LORD your God.

Interpreter For the LORD will not hold anyone guiltless who misuses his name.

The Lord
(voice) Observe the Sabbath day by keeping it holy—

Interpreter As the LORD your God has commanded you. Six days you shall labor and do all your work, but the seventh day is a Sabbath to the LORD your God. On it you shall not do any work, neither you, nor your son or daughter, nor your manservant or maidservant, nor your ox, your donkey or any of your animals, nor the alien within your gates, so that your manservant and maidservant may rest, as you do. Remember that you were slaves in Egypt and that the LORD your God brought you out of there with a mighty hand and an outstretched arm. Therefore the LORD your God has commanded you to observe the Sabbath day.

The Lord
(voice) Honor your father and your mother—

Interpreter As the LORD your God has commanded you, so that you may live long and that it may go well with you in the land the LORD your God is giving you.

The Lord
(voice) You shall not murder.

You shall not commit adultery.

You shall not steal.

You shall not give false testimony against your neighbor.

You shall not covet your neighbor's wife. You shall not set your desire on your neighbor's house or land, his manservant or maidservant, his ox or donkey, or anything that belongs to your neighbor.

Moses (to
audience) These are the commandments the LORD proclaimed in a loud voice to your whole assembly there on the mountain from out of the fire, the cloud and the deep darkness; and he added nothing more. (PAUSE) Then he wrote them on two stone tablets and gave them to me.

Cast: **Interpreter, Moses, the Lord** (voice only; can be the same as Interpreter, who states the Lord's words). (Moses speaks to the audience as if to the people of Israel.)

The People Are Afraid

Deuteronomy 5:23–33

Moses speaks to the people

Moses (to
audience)　When you heard the voice out of the darkness, while the mountain was ablaze with fire, all the leading men of your tribes and your elders came to me. [And you said:]

Leader 1　The LORD our God has shown us his glory and his majesty, and we have heard his voice from the fire.

Leader 2　Today we have seen that a man can live even if God speaks with him.

Leader 3　But now, why should we die?

Leader 2　This great fire will consume us, and we will die if we hear the voice of the LORD our God any longer.

Leader 1　For what mortal man has ever heard the voice of the living God speaking out of fire, as we have, and survived?

Leader 2　Go near and listen to all that the LORD our God says.

Leader 3　Then tell us whatever the LORD our God tells you. We will listen and obey.

Moses (to
audience)　The LORD heard you when you spoke to me and the LORD said to me:

The Lord
(voice only)　I have heard what this people said to you. Everything they said was good. Oh, that their hearts would be inclined to fear me and keep all my commands always, so that it might go well with them and their children forever!

Go, tell them to return to their tents. But you stay here with me so that I may give you all the commands, decrees and laws you are to teach them to follow in the land I am giving them to possess.

Moses (to
audience)　So be careful to do what the LORD your God has commanded you; do not turn aside to the right or to the left. Walk in all the way that the LORD your God has commanded you, so that you may live and prosper and prolong your days in the land that you will possess.

Cast: **Moses, Leader 1, Leader 2, Leader 3, the Lord** (voice only). (Moses speaks to the audience as if to the people of Israel.)

Love the Lord Your God

Deuteronomy 6:1–9

Moses speaks to the people

Moses (to audience)　These are the commands, decrees and laws the Lord your God directed me to teach you to observe in the land that you are crossing the Jordan to possess, so that you, your children and their children after them may fear the Lord your God as long as you live by keeping all his decrees and commands that I give you, and so that you may enjoy long life. Hear, O Israel, and be careful to obey so that it may go well with you and that you may increase greatly in a land flowing with milk and honey, just as the Lord, the God of your fathers, promised you.

Voice　Hear, O Israel: The Lord our God, the Lord is one. Love the Lord your God with all your heart and with all your soul and with all your strength.

Moses (to audience)　These commandments that I give you today are to be upon your hearts. Impress them on your children. Talk about them when you sit at home and when you walk along the road, when you lie down and when you get up. Tie them as symbols on your hands and bind them on your foreheads. Write them on the doorframes of your houses and on your gates.

Cast: **Moses, Voice.** (Moses speaks to the audience as if to the people of Israel.)

Passing on the Faith

Deuteronomy 6:10–25

Moses speaks to the people

Moses (to audience)　When the Lord your God brings you into the land he swore to your fathers, to Abraham, Isaac and Jacob, to give you—a land with large, flourishing cities you did not build, houses filled with all kinds of good things you did not provide, wells you did not dig, and vineyards and olive groves you did not plant—then when you eat and are satisfied, be careful that you do not forget the Lord, who brought you out of Egypt, out of the land of slavery.

Fear the Lord your God, serve him only and take your oaths in his name. Do not follow other gods, the gods of the peoples around you; for the Lord your God, who is among you, is a jealous God and his anger will burn against you, and he will destroy you from the face of the land. Do not test the Lord your God as you did at Massah. Be sure to keep the commands of the Lord your God and the stipulations and decrees he has given you. Do what is right and good in the Lord's sight, so that it may go well with you and you may go in and take over the good land that the LORD promised on oath to your forefathers, thrusting out all your enemies before you, as the LORD said.

In the future, when your son asks you:

Son   What is the meaning of the stipulations, decrees and laws the LORD our God has commanded you?

Moses (to audience)   Tell him:

Israelite   We were slaves of Pharaoh in Egypt, but the LORD brought us out of Egypt with a mighty hand. Before our eyes the LORD sent miraculous signs and wonders—great and terrible—upon Egypt and Pharaoh and his whole household. But he brought us out from there to bring us in and give us the land that he promised on oath to our forefathers. The LORD commanded us to obey all these decrees and to fear the LORD our God, so that we might always prosper and be kept alive, as is the case today. And if we are careful to obey all this law before the LORD our God, as he has commanded us, that will be our righteousness.

Cast: **Moses, Son, Israelite.** (Moses speaks to the audience as if to the people of Israel.)

Not Because of Israel's Righteousness

From Deuteronomy 9:1–29

Moses speaks to the people

Moses (to audience)   Hear, O Israel. You are now about to cross the Jordan to go in and dispossess nations greater and stronger than you, with large cities that have walls up to the sky. The people are strong and tall—Anakites! You know about them and have heard it said: "Who can stand up against the Anakites?" But be assured today that the LORD your God is the one who goes across ahead of you like a devouring fire. He will destroy them; he will subdue them before you. And you will drive them out and annihilate them quickly, as the LORD has promised you.

After the LORD your God has driven them out before you, do not say to yourself, "The LORD has brought me here to take possession of this land because of my righteousness." No, it is on account of the wickedness of these nations that the LORD is going to drive them out before you. It is not because of your righteousness or your integrity that you are going in to take possession of their land; but on account of the wickedness of these nations, the LORD your God will drive them out before you, to accomplish what he swore to your fathers, to Abraham, Isaac and Jacob. (PAUSE) Understand, then, that it is not because of your righteousness that the

LORD your God is giving you this good land to possess, for you are a stiff-necked people.

Remember this and never forget how you provoked the LORD your God to anger in the desert. From the day you left Egypt until you arrived here, you have been rebellious against the LORD. At Horeb you aroused the LORD's wrath so that he was angry enough to destroy you. When I went up on the mountain to receive the tablets of stone, the tablets of the covenant that the LORD had made with you, I stayed on the mountain forty days and forty nights; I ate no bread and drank no water. The LORD gave me two stone tablets inscribed by the finger of God. On them were all the commandments the LORD proclaimed to you on the mountain out of the fire, on the day of the assembly.

At the end of the forty days and forty nights, the LORD gave me the two stone tablets, the tablets of the covenant. Then the LORD told me:

The Lord
(voice only)   Go down from here at once, because your people whom you brought out of Egypt have become corrupt. They have turned away quickly from what I commanded them and have made a cast idol for themselves. . . .

Moses (to
audience)   So I turned and went down from the mountain while it was ablaze with fire. And the two tablets of the covenant were in my hands. When I looked, I saw that you had sinned against the LORD your God; you had made for yourselves an idol cast in the shape of a calf. You had turned aside quickly from the way that the LORD had commanded you. So I took the two tablets and threw them out of my hands, breaking them to pieces before your eyes.

Then once again I fell prostrate before the LORD for forty days and forty nights; I ate no bread and drank no water, because of all the sin you had committed, doing what was evil in the LORD's sight and so provoking him to anger. . . . I prayed to the LORD:

**Younger
Moses**   O Sovereign LORD, do not destroy your people, your own inheritance that you redeemed by your great power and brought out of Egypt with a mighty hand. Remember your servants Abraham, Isaac and Jacob. Overlook the stubbornness of this people, their wickedness and their sin. Otherwise, the country from which you brought us will say, "Because the LORD was not able to take them into the land he had promised them, and because he hated them, he brought them out to put them to death in the desert." But they are your people, your inheritance that you brought out by your great power and your outstretched arm.

Cast: **Moses, the Lord** (voice only), **Younger Moses.** (Moses speaks to the audience as if to the people of Israel.)

Tablets Like the First Ones

Deuteronomy 10:1–5

Moses speaks to the people

Moses (to
audience)   At that time the LORD said to me:

The Lord
(voice only)   Chisel out two stone tablets like the first ones and come up to me on the
mountain. Also make a wooden chest. I will write on the tablets the words
that were on the first tablets, which you broke. Then you are to put them
in the chest.

Moses (to
audience)   So I made the ark out of acacia wood and chiseled out two stone tablets
like the first ones, and I went up on the mountain with the two tablets
in my hands. The LORD wrote on these tablets what he had written before,
the Ten Commandments he had proclaimed to you on the mountain,
out of the fire, on the day of the assembly. And the LORD gave them to
me. Then I came back down the mountain and put the tablets in the ark
I had made, as the LORD commanded me, and they are there now.

Cast: **Moses, the Lord** (voice only). (Moses speaks to the audience as if to the people of Israel.)

Laws about Tithes

From Deuteronomy 14:22–29; 16:9–12; Leviticus 23:15–22

Leviticus   From the day after the Sabbath, the day you brought the sheaf of the
wave offering, count off seven full weeks. Count off fifty days up to the
day after the seventh Sabbath, and then present an offering of new grain
to the LORD. From wherever you live, bring two loaves made of two-tenths
of an ephah of fine flour, baked with yeast, as a wave offering of firstfruits
to the LORD. . . . On that same day you are to proclaim a sacred assembly
and do no regular work. This is to be a lasting ordinance for the generations to come, wherever you live.

Deuteronomy   Be sure to set aside a tenth of all that your fields produce each year. Eat
the tithe of your grain, new wine and oil, and the firstborn of your herds
and flocks in the presence of the LORD your God at the place he will choose
as a dwelling for his Name, so that you may learn to revere the LORD your
God always. . . . And do not neglect the Levites living in your towns, for
they have no allotment or inheritance of their own.

At the end of every three years, bring all the tithes of that year's produce
and store it in your towns, so that the Levites (who have no allotment
or inheritance of their own) and the aliens, the fatherless and the wid-

ows who live in your towns may come and eat and be satisfied, and so that the LORD your God may bless you in all the work of your hands. . . .

Leviticus When you reap the harvest of your land, do not reap to the very edges of your field or gather the gleanings of your harvest. Leave them for the poor and the alien. I am the LORD your God.

Deuteronomy Count off seven weeks from the time you begin to put the sickle to the standing grain. Then celebrate the Feast of Weeks to the LORD your God by giving a freewill offering in proportion to the blessings the LORD your God has given you. And rejoice before the LORD your God at the place he will choose as a dwelling for his Name—you, your sons and daughters, your menservants and maidservants, the Levites in your towns, and the aliens, the fatherless and the widows living among you. Remember that you were slaves in Egypt, and follow carefully these decrees.

Cast: **Leviticus, Deuteronomy**

Firstfruits and Tithes

Deuteronomy 26:1–15

Moses speaks to the people

Moses (to audience) When you have entered the land the LORD your God is giving you as an inheritance and have taken possession of it and settled in it, take some of the firstfruits of all that you produce from the soil of the land the LORD your God is giving you and put them in a basket. Then go to the place the LORD your God will choose as a dwelling for his Name and say to the priest in office at the time:

Worshiper I declare today to the LORD your God that I have come to the land the LORD swore to our forefathers to give us.

Moses (to audience) The priest shall take the basket from your hands and set it down in front of the altar of the LORD your God. Then you shall declare before the LORD your God:

Worshiper My father was a wandering Aramean, and he went down into Egypt with a few people and lived there and became a great nation, powerful and numerous. But the Egyptians mistreated us and made us suffer, putting us to hard labor. Then we cried out to the LORD, the God of our fathers, and the LORD heard our voice and saw our misery, toil and oppression. So the LORD brought us out of Egypt with a mighty hand and an outstretched arm, with great terror and with miraculous signs and wonders. He brought us to this place and gave us this land, a land flowing with milk and honey; and now I bring the firstfruits of the soil that you, O LORD, have given me.

Moses (to
  audience)   Place the basket before the Lord your God and bow down before him. And you and the Levites and the aliens among you shall rejoice in all the good things the Lord your God has given to you and your household.

When you have finished setting aside a tenth of all your produce in the third year, the year of the tithe, you shall give it to the Levite, the alien, the fatherless and the widow, so that they may eat in your towns and be satisfied. Then say to the Lord your God:

Worshiper   I have removed from my house the sacred portion and have given it to the Levite, the alien, the fatherless and the widow, according to all you commanded. I have not turned aside from your commands nor have I forgotten any of them. I have not eaten any of the sacred portion while I was in mourning, nor have I removed any of it while I was unclean, nor have I offered any of it to the dead. I have obeyed the Lord my God; I have done everything you commanded me. Look down from heaven, your holy dwelling place, and bless your people Israel and the land you have given us as you promised on oath to our forefathers, a land flowing with milk and honey.

Cast: **Moses, Worshiper.** (Moses speaks to the audience as if to the people of Israel.)

If You Break the Covenant

Deuteronomy 29:22–29

Moses speaks to the people

Moses (to
  audience)   Your children who follow you in later generations and foreigners who come from distant lands will see the calamities that have fallen on the land and the diseases with which the Lord has afflicted it. The whole land will be a burning waste of salt and sulfur—nothing planted, nothing sprouting, no vegetation growing on it. It will be like the destruction of Sodom and Gomorrah, Admah and Zeboiim, which the Lord overthrew in fierce anger. All the nations will ask:

Person 1   Why has the Lord done this to this land?

Person 2   Why this fierce, burning anger?

Moses (to
  audience)   And the answer will be:

Person 3   It is because this people abandoned the covenant of the Lord, the God of their fathers, the covenant he made with them when he brought them out of Egypt. They went off and worshiped other gods and bowed down to them, gods they did not know, gods he had not given them. Therefore the Lord's anger burned against this land, so that he brought on it all the curses written in this book. In furious anger and in great wrath the LORD uprooted them from their land and thrust them into another land, as it is now.

Moses (to audience)

The secret things belong to the LORD our God, but the things revealed belong to us and to our children forever, that we may follow all the words of this law.

Cast: **Moses, Person 1, Person 2, Person 3** (Moses speaks to the audience as if to the people of Israel.)

The Offer of Life or Death

Deuteronomy 30:9–20

Moses speaks to the people

Moses (to audience)

The LORD your God will make you most prosperous in all the work of your hands and in the fruit of your womb, the young of your livestock and the crops of your land. The LORD will again delight in you and make you prosperous, just as he delighted in your fathers, if you obey the LORD your God and keep his commands and decrees that are written in this Book of the Law and turn to the LORD your God with all your heart and with all your soul.

Now what I am commanding you today is not too difficult for you or beyond your reach. It is not up in heaven, so that you have to ask:

Person 1

Who will ascend into heaven to get it and proclaim it to us so we may obey it?

Moses (to audience)

Nor is it beyond the sea, so that you have to ask:

Person 2

Who will cross the sea to get it and proclaim it to us so we may obey it?

Moses (to audience)

No, the word is very near you; it is in your mouth and in your heart so you may obey it. (PAUSE)

See, I set before you today life and prosperity, death and destruction. For I command you today to love the LORD your God, to walk in his ways, and to keep his commands, decrees and laws; then you will live and increase, and the LORD your God will bless you in the land you are entering to possess.

But if your heart turns away and you are not obedient, and if you are drawn away to bow down to other gods and worship them, I declare to you this day that you will certainly be destroyed. You will not live long in the land you are crossing the Jordan to enter and possess.

This day I call heaven and earth as witnesses against you that I have set before you life and death, blessings and curses. Now choose life, so that you and your children may live and that you may love the LORD your

God, listen to his voice, and hold fast to him. For the LORD is your life, and he will give you many years in the land he swore to give to your fathers, Abraham, Isaac and Jacob.

Cast: **Moses, Person 1, Person 2.** (Moses speaks to the audience as if to the people of Israel.)

Joshua to Succeed Moses

Deuteronomy 31:1–8

Narrator Moses went out and spoke these words to all Israel:

Moses I am now a hundred and twenty years old and I am no longer able to lead you. The LORD has said to me, "You shall not cross the Jordan." The LORD your God himself will cross over ahead of you. He will destroy these nations before you, and you will take possession of their land. Joshua also will cross over ahead of you, as the LORD said. And the LORD will do to them what he did to Sihon and Og, the kings of the Amorites, whom he destroyed along with their land. The LORD will deliver them to you, and you must do to them all that I have commanded you. Be strong and courageous. Do not be afraid or terrified because of them, for the LORD your God goes with you; he will never leave you nor forsake you.

Narrator Then Moses summoned Joshua and said to him in the presence of all Israel:

Moses Be strong and courageous, for you must go with this people into the land that the LORD swore to their forefathers to give them, and you must divide it among them as their inheritance. The LORD himself goes before you and will be with you; he will never leave you nor forsake you. Do not be afraid; do not be discouraged.

Cast: **Narrator, Moses**

The Reading of the Law

Deuteronomy 31:9–13

Narrator So Moses wrote down this law and gave it to the priests, the sons of Levi, who carried the ark of the covenant of the LORD, and to all the elders of Israel. Then Moses commanded them:

Moses At the end of every seven years, in the year for canceling debts, during the Feast of Tabernacles, when all Israel comes to appear before the LORD your God at the place he will choose, you shall read this law before them in their hearing. Assemble the people—men, women and children, and the

174

aliens living in your towns—so they can listen and learn to fear the LORD your God and follow carefully all the words of this law. Their children, who do not know this law, must hear it and learn to fear the LORD your God as long as you live in the land you are crossing the Jordan to possess.

Cast: **Narrator, Moses**

Israel's Rebellion Predicted

From Deuteronomy 31:14–29

Narrator   The LORD said to Moses:

The Lord
(voice only)   Now the day of your death is near. Call Joshua and present yourselves at the Tent of Meeting, where I will commission him.

Narrator   So Moses and Joshua came and presented themselves at the Tent of Meeting.

Then the LORD appeared at the Tent in a pillar of cloud, and the cloud stood over the entrance to the Tent. And the LORD said to Moses:

The Lord
(voice)   You are going to rest with your fathers, and these people will soon prostitute themselves to the foreign gods of the land they are entering. They will forsake me and break the covenant I made with them. . . .

Narrator   The LORD gave this command to Joshua son of Nun:

The Lord
(voice)   Be strong and courageous, for you will bring the Israelites into the land I promised them on oath, and I myself will be with you.

Narrator   After Moses finished writing in a book the words of this law from beginning to end, he gave this command to the Levites who carried the ark of the covenant of the LORD:

Moses   Take this Book of the Law and place it beside the ark of the covenant of the LORD your God. There it will remain as a witness against you. For I know how rebellious and stiff-necked you are. If you have been rebellious against the LORD while I am still alive and with you, how much more will you rebel after I die! Assemble before me all the elders of your tribes and all your officials, so that I can speak these words in their hearing and call heaven and earth to testify against them. For I know that after my death you are sure to become utterly corrupt and to turn from the way I have commanded you. In days to come, disaster will fall upon you because you will do evil in the sight of the LORD and provoke him to anger by what your hands have made.

Cast: **Narrator, the Lord** (voice only), **Moses**

Moses' Final Instructions

Deuteronomy 32:45–52

Narrator   When Moses finished reciting all these words to all Israel, he said to them:

Moses   Take to heart all the words I have solemnly declared to you this day, so that you may command your children to obey carefully all the words of this law. They are not just idle words for you—they are your life. By them you will live long in the land you are crossing the Jordan to possess.

Narrator   On that same day the LORD told Moses:

The Lord
(voice only)   Go up into the Abarim Range to Mount Nebo in Moab, across from Jericho, and view Canaan, the land I am giving the Israelites as their own possession. There on the mountain that you have climbed you will die and be gathered to your people, just as your brother Aaron died on Mount Hor and was gathered to his people. This is because both of you broke faith with me in the presence of the Israelites at the waters of Meribah Kadesh in the Desert of Zin and because you did not uphold my holiness among the Israelites. Therefore, you will see the land only from a distance; you will not enter the land I am giving to the people of Israel.

Cast: **Narrator, Moses, the Lord** (voice only)

The Death of Moses

Deuteronomy 34:1–12

Narrator   Moses climbed Mount Nebo from the plains of Moab to the top of Pisgah, across from Jericho. There the LORD showed him the whole land— from Gilead to Dan, all of Naphtali, the territory of Ephraim and Manasseh, all the land of Judah as far as the western sea, the Negev and the whole region from the Valley of Jericho, the City of Palms, as far as Zoar. Then the LORD said to him:

The Lord
(voice only)   This is the land I promised on oath to Abraham, Isaac and Jacob when I said, "I will give it to your descendants." I have let you see it with your eyes, but you will not cross over into it.

Narrator   And Moses the servant of the LORD died there in Moab, as the LORD had said. He buried him in Moab, in the valley opposite Beth Peor, but to this day no one knows where his grave is. Moses was a hundred and twenty years old when he died, yet his eyes were not weak nor his strength gone. The Israelites grieved for Moses in the plains of Moab thirty days, until the time of weeping and mourning was over.

Now Joshua son of Nun was filled with the spirit of wisdom because Moses had laid his hands on him. So the Israelites listened to him and did what the LORD had commanded Moses.

Since then, no prophet has risen in Israel like Moses, whom the LORD knew face to face, who did all those miraculous signs and wonders the LORD sent him to do in Egypt—to Pharaoh and to all his officials and to his whole land. For no one has ever shown the mighty power or performed the awesome deeds that Moses did in the sight of all Israel.

Cast: **Narrator, the Lord** (voice only)

Joshua

The Lord Commands Joshua

Joshua 1:1–18

Narrator After the death of Moses the servant of the LORD, the LORD said to Joshua son of Nun, Moses' aide:

The Lord
(voice only) Moses my servant is dead. Now then, you and all these people, get ready to cross the Jordan River into the land I am about to give to them—to the Israelites. I will give you every place where you set your foot, as I promised Moses. Your territory will extend from the desert to Lebanon, and from the great river, the Euphrates—all the Hittite country—to the Great Sea on the west. No one will be able to stand up against you all the days of your life. As I was with Moses, so I will be with you; I will never leave you nor forsake you.

Be strong and courageous, because you will lead these people to inherit the land I swore to their forefathers to give them. Be strong and very courageous. Be careful to obey all the law my servant Moses gave you; do not turn from it to the right or to the left, that you may be successful wherever you go. Do not let this Book of the Law depart from your mouth; meditate on it day and night, so that you may be careful to do everything written in it. Then you will be prosperous and successful. Have I not commanded you? Be strong and courageous. Do not be terrified; do not be discouraged, for the LORD your God will be with you wherever you go.

Narrator So Joshua ordered the officers of the people:

Joshua Go through the camp and tell the people, "Get your supplies ready. Three days from now you will cross the Jordan here to go in and take possession of the land the LORD your God is giving you for your own."

Narrator But to the Reubenites, the Gadites and the half-tribe of Manasseh, Joshua said:

Joshua Remember the command that Moses the servant of the LORD gave you: "The LORD your God is giving you rest and has granted you this land." Your wives, your children and your livestock may stay in the land that Moses gave you east of the Jordan, but all your fighting men, fully armed, must cross over ahead of your brothers. You are to help your brothers until the LORD gives them rest, as he has done for you, and until they too have taken possession of the land that the LORD your God is giving them. After that, you may go back and occupy your own land, which Moses the servant of the LORD gave you east of the Jordan toward the sunrise.

Narrator Then they answered Joshua:

178

Person 1	Whatever you have commanded us we will do, and wherever you send us we will go.
Person 2	Just as we fully obeyed Moses, so we will obey you.
Person 1	Only may the LORD your God be with you as he was with Moses.
Person 2	Whoever rebels against your word and does not obey your words, whatever you may command them, will be put to death.
Person 1	Only be strong and courageous!

Cast: **Narrator, the Lord** (voice only), **Joshua, Person 1, Person 2** (can be the same as Person 1)

Rahab and the Spies

Joshua 2:1–24

Narrator	Joshua son of Nun secretly sent two spies from Shittim. He said:
Joshua	Go, look over the land, especially Jericho.
Narrator	So they went and entered the house of a prostitute named Rahab and stayed there. The king of Jericho was told:
Informant	Look! Some of the Israelites have come here tonight to spy out the land.
Narrator	So the king of Jericho sent this message to Rahab:
King of Jericho	Bring out the men who came to you and entered your house, because they have come to spy out the whole land.
Narrator	But the woman had taken the two men and hidden them. She said:
Rahab	Yes, the men came to me, but I did not know where they had come from. At dusk, when it was time to close the city gate, the men left. I don't know which way they went. Go after them quickly. You may catch up with them.
Narrator	(But she had taken them up to the roof and hidden them under the stalks of flax she had laid out on the roof.) So the men set out in pursuit of the spies on the road that leads to the fords of the Jordan, and as soon as the pursuers had gone out, the gate was shut.
	Before the spies lay down for the night, she went up on the roof [and said to them:]
Rahab	I know that the LORD has given this land to you and that a great fear of you has fallen on us, so that all who live in this country are melting in fear because of you. We have heard how the LORD dried up the water of the Red Sea for you when you came out of Egypt, and what you did to Sihon and Og, the two kings of the Amorites east of the Jordan, whom you completely destroyed. When we heard of it, our hearts melted and

179

everyone's courage failed because of you, for the LORD your God is God in heaven above and on the earth below. Now then, please swear to me by the LORD that you will show kindness to my family, because I have shown kindness to you. Give me a sure sign that you will spare the lives of my father and mother, my brothers and sisters, and all who belong to them, and that you will save us from death.

Narrator   The men assured her:

Spy 1   Our lives for your lives!

Spy 2   If you don't tell what we are doing, we will treat you kindly and faithfully when the LORD gives us the land.

Narrator   So she let them down by a rope through the window, for the house she lived in was part of the city wall. Now she had said to them:

Rahab   Go to the hills so the pursuers will not find you. Hide yourselves there three days until they return, and then go on your way.

[Narrator   The men said to her:]

Spy 1   This oath you made us swear will not be binding on us unless, when we enter the land, you have tied this scarlet cord in the window through which you let us down, and unless you have brought your father and mother, your brothers and all your family into your house.

Spy 2   If anyone goes outside your house into the street, his blood will be on his own head; we will not be responsible.

Spy 1   As for anyone who is in the house with you, his blood will be on our head if a hand is laid on him.

Spy 2   But if you tell what we are doing, we will be released from the oath you made us swear.

Rahab   Agreed. Let it be as you say.

Narrator   So she sent them away and they departed. And she tied the scarlet cord in the window.

When they left, they went into the hills and stayed there three days, until the pursuers had searched all along the road and returned without finding them. Then the two men started back. They went down out of the hills, forded the river and came to Joshua son of Nun and told him everything that had happened to them. They said to Joshua:

Spy 2   The LORD has surely given the whole land into our hands—

Spy 1   All the people are melting in fear because of us.

Cast: **Narrator, Joshua, Informant, King of Jericho, Rahab, Spy 1, Spy 2**

180

Crossing the Jordan

Joshua 3:1–17

Narrator	Early in the morning Joshua and all the Israelites set out from Shittim and went to the Jordan, where they camped before crossing over. After three days the officers went throughout the camp, giving orders to the people:
Officer 1	When you see the ark of the covenant of the LORD your God, and the priests, who are Levites, carrying it, you are to move out from your positions and follow it.
Officer 2	Then you will know which way to go, since you have never been this way before.
Officer 3	But keep a distance of about a thousand yards between you and the ark; do not go near it.
Narrator	Joshua told the people:
Joshua	Consecrate yourselves, for tomorrow the LORD will do amazing things among you.
Narrator	Joshua said to the priests:
Joshua	Take up the ark of the covenant and pass on ahead of the people.
Narrator	So they took it up and went ahead of them.
	And the LORD said to Joshua:
The Lord (voice only)	Today I will begin to exalt you in the eyes of all Israel, so they may know that I am with you as I was with Moses. Tell the priests who carry the ark of the covenant: "When you reach the edge of the Jordan's waters, go and stand in the river."
Narrator	Joshua said to the Israelites:
Joshua	Come here and listen to the words of the LORD your God. This is how you will know that the living God is among you and that he will certainly drive out before you the Canaanites, Hittites, Hivites, Perizzites, Girgashites, Amorites and Jebusites. See, the ark of the covenant of the Lord of all the earth will go into the Jordan ahead of you. Now then, choose twelve men from the tribes of Israel, one from each tribe. And as soon as the priests who carry the ark of the LORD—the Lord of all the earth—set foot in the Jordan, its waters flowing downstream will be cut off and stand up in a heap.
Narrator	So when the people broke camp to cross the Jordan, the priests carrying the ark of the covenant went ahead of them. Now the Jordan is at flood stage all during harvest. Yet as soon as the priests who carried the ark reached the Jordan and their feet touched the water's edge, the water from upstream stopped flowing. It piled up in a heap a great distance

away, at a town called Adam in the vicinity of Zarethan, while the water flowing down to the Sea of the Arabah (the Salt Sea) was completely cut off. So the people crossed over opposite Jericho. The priests who carried the ark of the covenant of the LORD stood firm on dry ground in the middle of the Jordan, while all Israel passed by until the whole nation had completed the crossing on dry ground.

Cast: **Narrator, Officer 1, Officer 2, Officer 3** (Officers 1–3 can be the same), **Joshua, the Lord** (voice only)

Memorial Stones Are Set Up

Joshua 4:1–5:1

Narrator 1   When the whole nation had finished crossing the Jordan, the LORD said to Joshua:

The Lord
(voice only)   Choose twelve men from among the people, one from each tribe, and tell them to take up twelve stones from the middle of the Jordan from right where the priests stood and to carry them over with you and put them down at the place where you stay tonight.

Narrator 2   So Joshua called together the twelve men he had appointed from the Israelites, one from each tribe, and said to them:

Joshua   Go over before the ark of the LORD your God into the middle of the Jordan. Each of you is to take up a stone on his shoulder, according to the number of the tribes of the Israelites, to serve as a sign among you. In the future, when your children ask you, "What do these stones mean?" tell them that the flow of the Jordan was cut off before the ark of the covenant of the LORD. When it crossed the Jordan, the waters of the Jordan were cut off. These stones are to be a memorial to the people of Israel forever.

Narrator 1   So the Israelites did as Joshua commanded them. They took twelve stones from the middle of the Jordan, according to the number of the tribes of the Israelites, as the LORD had told Joshua; and they carried them over with them to their camp, where they put them down. Joshua set up the twelve stones that had been in the middle of the Jordan at the spot where the priests who carried the ark of the covenant had stood.

Narrator 2   And they are there to this day.

Narrator 1   Now the priests who carried the ark remained standing in the middle of the Jordan until everything the LORD had commanded Joshua was done by the people, just as Moses had directed Joshua.

Narrator 2   The people hurried over, and as soon as all of them had crossed, the ark of the LORD and the priests came to the other side while the people watched. The men of Reuben, Gad and the half-tribe of Manasseh crossed over, armed, in front of the Israelites, as Moses had directed them. About forty thousand armed for battle crossed over before the LORD to the plains of Jericho for war.

Narrator 1 That day the LORD exalted Joshua in the sight of all Israel; and they revered him all the days of his life, just as they had revered Moses.

Narrator 2 Then the LORD said to Joshua:

The Lord
(voice) Command the priests carrying the ark of the Testimony to come up out of the Jordan.

Narrator 1 So Joshua commanded the priests:

Joshua Come up out of the Jordan.

Narrator 2 And the priests came up out of the river carrying the ark of the covenant of the LORD. No sooner had they set their feet on the dry ground than the waters of the Jordan returned to their place and ran at flood stage as before.

On the tenth day of the first month the people went up from the Jordan and camped at Gilgal on the eastern border of Jericho. And Joshua set up at Gilgal the twelve stones they had taken out of the Jordan. [He said to the Israelites:]

Joshua In the future when your descendants ask their fathers, "What do these stones mean?" tell them, "Israel crossed the Jordan on dry ground." For the LORD your God dried up the Jordan before you until you had crossed over. The LORD your God did to the Jordan just what he had done to the Red Sea when he dried it up before us until we had crossed over. He did this so that all the peoples of the earth might know that the hand of the LORD is powerful and so that you might always fear the LORD your God.

Narrator 1 Now when all the Amorite kings west of the Jordan and all the Canaanite kings along the coast heard how the LORD had dried up the Jordan before the Israelites until we had crossed over, their hearts melted and they no longer had the courage to face the Israelites.

Cast: **Narrator 1, the Lord** (voice only), **Narrator 2, Joshua**

Joshua and the Man with a Sword

Joshua 5:13–15

Narrator When Joshua was near Jericho, he looked up and saw a man standing in front of him with a drawn sword in his hand. Joshua went up to him [and asked:]

Joshua Are you for us or for our enemies?

[Narrator	He replied:]
Commander	Neither, but as commander of the army of the LORD I have now come.
Narrator	Then Joshua fell facedown to the ground in reverence, and asked him:
Joshua	What message does my Lord have for his servant?
[Narrator	The commander of the LORD's army replied:]
Commander	Take off your sandals, for the place where you are standing is holy.
Narrator	And Joshua did so.

Cast: **Narrator, Joshua, Commander**

Joshua at Jericho

From Joshua 5:13–6:20 (combined reading)

Narrator	When Joshua was near Jericho, he looked up and saw a man standing in front of him with a drawn sword in his hand. Joshua went up to him [and asked:]
Joshua	Are you for us or for our enemies?
[Narrator	He replied:]
Commander	Neither, but as commander of the army of the LORD I have now come.
Narrator	Then Joshua fell facedown to the ground in reverence [and asked him:]
Joshua	What message does my LORD have for his servant?
[Narrator	The commander of the LORD's army replied:]
Commander	Take off your sandals, for the place where you are standing is holy.
Narrator	And Joshua did so. (PAUSE)
	Now Jericho was tightly shut up because of the Israelites. No one went out and no one came in. Then the LORD said to Joshua:
The Lord (voice only)	See, I have delivered Jericho into your hands, along with its king and its fighting men. March around the city once with all the armed men. Do this for six days. Have seven priests carry trumpets of rams' horns in front of the ark. On the seventh day, march around the city seven times, with the priests blowing the trumpets. When you hear them sound a long blast on the trumpets, have all the people give a loud shout; then the wall of the city will collapse and the people will go up, every man straight in.
Narrator	So Joshua son of Nun called the priests and said to them:
Joshua	Take up the ark of the covenant of the LORD and have seven priests carry trumpets in front of it.

Narrator	And he ordered the people:
Joshua	Advance! March around the city, with the armed guard going ahead of the ark of the LORD.
Narrator	When Joshua had spoken to the people, the seven priests carrying the seven trumpets before the LORD went forward, blowing their trumpets, and the ark of the LORD's covenant followed them. . . . (PAUSE)
	Joshua got up early the next morning and the priests took up the ark of the LORD. The seven priests carrying the seven trumpets went forward, marching before the ark of the LORD and blowing the trumpets. The armed men went ahead of them and the rear guard followed the ark of the LORD, while the trumpets kept sounding. So on the second day they marched around the city once and returned to the camp. They did this for six days.
	On the seventh day, they got up at daybreak and marched around the city seven times in the same manner, except that on that day they circled the city seven times. The seventh time around, when the priests sounded the trumpet blast, Joshua commanded the people:
Joshua	Shout! For the LORD has given you the city! . . .
Narrator	When the trumpets sounded, the people shouted, and at the sound of the trumpet, when the people gave a loud shout, the wall collapsed; so every man charged straight in, and they took the city.

Cast: **Narrator, Joshua, Commander, the Lord** (voice only; can be the same as Commander). (See full readings in separate parts, pages 184 and 185–87.)

The Fall of Jericho

Joshua 6:1–20

Narrator 1	Now Jericho was tightly shut up because of the Israelites.
Narrator 2	No one went out and no one came in.
Narrator 1	Then the LORD said to Joshua:
The Lord (voice only)	See, I have delivered Jericho into your hands, along with its king and its fighting men. March around the city once with all the armed men. Do this for six days. Have seven priests carry trumpets of rams' horns in front of the ark. On the seventh day, march around the city seven times, with the priests blowing the trumpets. When you hear them sound a long blast on the trumpets, have all the people give a loud shout; then the wall of the city will collapse and the people will go up, every man straight in.
Narrator 2	So Joshua son of Nun called the priests and said to them:
Joshua	Take up the ark of the covenant of the LORD and have seven priests carry trumpets in front of it.

Narrator 1	And he ordered the people:
Joshua	Advance! March around the city, with the armed guard going ahead of the ark of the LORD.
Narrator 2	When Joshua had spoken to the people, the seven priests carrying the seven trumpets before the LORD went forward, blowing their trumpets, and the ark of the LORD's covenant followed them.
Narrator 1	The armed guard marched ahead of the priests who blew the trumpets, and the rear guard followed the ark. All this time the trumpets were sounding.
Narrator 2	But Joshua had commanded the people:
Joshua	Do not give a war cry, do not raise your voices, do not say a word until the day I tell you to shout. Then shout!
Narrator 1	So he had the ark of the LORD carried around the city, circling it once. Then the people returned to camp and spent the night there.
Narrator 2	Joshua got up early the next morning and the priests took up the ark of the LORD.
Narrator 1	The seven priests carrying the seven trumpets went forward—
Narrator 2	Marching before the ark of the LORD and blowing the trumpets.
Narrator 1	The armed men went ahead of them—
Narrator 2	And the rear guard followed the ark of the LORD—
Narrator 1	While the trumpets kept sounding.
Narrator 2	So on the second day they marched around the city once and returned to the camp. They did this for six days.
Narrator 1	On the seventh day, they got up at daybreak and marched around the city seven times in the same manner, except that on that day they circled the city seven times.
Narrator 2	The seventh time around, when the priests sounded the trumpet blast, Joshua commanded the people:
Joshua	Shout! For the LORD has given you the city! The city and all that is in it are to be devoted to the LORD. Only Rahab the prostitute and all who are with her in her house shall be spared, because she hid the spies we sent. But keep away from the devoted things, so that you will not bring about your own destruction by taking any of them. Otherwise you will make the camp of Israel liable to destruction and bring trouble on it. All the silver and gold and the articles of bronze and iron are sacred to the LORD and must go into his treasury.
Narrator 1	When the trumpets sounded—
Narrator 2	The people shouted, and at the sound of the trumpet, when the people gave a loud shout (PAUSE), the wall collapsed—

Narrator 1	So every man charged straight in—
Narrators **1 and 2**	And they took the city.

Cast: **Narrator 1, Narrator 2, the Lord** (voice only), **Joshua**

Rahab's Rescue from Jericho

Joshua 6:22–27

Narrator 1	Joshua said to the two men who had spied out the land:
Joshua	Go into the prostitute's house and bring her out and all who belong to her, in accordance with your oath to her.
Narrator 1	So the young men who had done the spying went in and brought out Rahab, her father and mother and brothers and all who belonged to her. They brought out her entire family and put them in a place outside the camp of Israel.
Narrator 2	Then they burned the whole city and everything in it, but they put the silver and gold and the articles of bronze and iron into the treasury of the Lord's house.
Narrator 1	But Joshua spared Rahab the prostitute, with her family and all who belonged to her, because she hid the men Joshua had sent as spies to Jericho—and she lives among the Israelites to this day.
Narrator 2	At that time Joshua pronounced this solemn oath:

Joshua	Cursed before the Lord is the man who undertakes to rebuild this city, Jericho:
	
	At the cost of his firstborn son
	   will he lay its foundations;
	at the cost of his youngest
	   will he set up its gates.

Narrators **1 and 2**	So the Lord was with Joshua, and his fame spread throughout the land.

Cast: **Narrator 1, Joshua, Narrator 2** (can be the same as Narrator 1)

Achan's Sin (i)

Joshua 7:1–15

Narrator 1	The Israelites acted unfaithfully in regard to the devoted things; Achan son of Carmi, the son of Zimri, the son of Zerah, of the tribe of Judah, took some of them. So the Lord's anger burned against Israel.

Narrator 2	Now Joshua sent men from Jericho to Ai, which is near Beth Aven to the east of Bethel, and told them:
Joshua	Go up and spy out the region.
Narrator 1	So the men went up and spied out Ai.
	When they returned to Joshua, they said:
Man 1	Not all the people will have to go up against Ai.
Man 2	Send two or three thousand men to take it—
Man 1	And do not weary all the people—
Man 2	For only a few men are there.
Narrator 1	So about three thousand men went up.
Narrator 2	But they were routed by the men of Ai, who killed about thirty-six of them. They chased the Israelites from the city gate as far as the stone quarries and struck them down on the slopes. At this the hearts of the people melted and became like water.
Narrator 1	Then Joshua tore his clothes and fell facedown to the ground before the ark of the Lord, remaining there till evening. The elders of Israel did the same, and sprinkled dust on their heads. And Joshua said:
Joshua	Ah, Sovereign Lord, why did you ever bring this people across the Jordan to deliver us into the hands of the Amorites to destroy us? If only we had been content to stay on the other side of the Jordan! O Lord, what can I say, now that Israel has been routed by its enemies? The Canaanites and the other people of the country will hear about this and they will surround us and wipe out our name from the earth. What then will you do for your own great name?
Narrator 2	The Lord said to Joshua:
The Lord (voice only)	Stand up! What are you doing down on your face? Israel has sinned; they have violated my covenant, which I commanded them to keep. They have taken some of the devoted things; they have stolen, they have lied, they have put them with their own possessions. That is why the Israelites cannot stand against their enemies; they turn their backs and run because they have made liable to destruction. I will not be with you anymore unless you destroy whatever among you is devoted to destruction.
	Go, consecrate the people. Tell them, "Consecrate yourselves in preparation for tomorrow; for this is what the Lord, the God of Israel, says: That which is devoted is among you, O Israel. You cannot stand against your enemies until you remove it.
	"In the morning, present yourselves tribe by tribe. The tribe that the Lord takes shall come forward clan by clan; the clan that the Lord takes shall come forward family by family; and the family that the Lord takes shall come forward man by man. He who is caught with the devoted things

shall be destroyed by fire, along with all that belongs to him. He has violated the covenant of the LORD and has done a disgraceful thing in Israel!"

Cast: **Narrator 1, Narrator 2, Joshua, Man 1, Man 2** (can be the same as Man 1), **the Lord** (voice only)

Achan's Sin (ii)

Joshua 7:16–26

Narrator 1   Early the next morning Joshua had Israel come forward by tribes, and Judah was taken.

Narrator 2   The clans of Judah came forward, and he took the Zerahites.

Narrator 1   He had the clan of the Zerahites come forward by families, and Zimri was taken.

Narrator 2   Joshua had his family come forward man by man, and Achan son of Carmi, the son of Zimri, the son of Zerah, of the tribe of Judah, was taken. (PAUSE) Then Joshua said to Achan:

Joshua   My son, give glory to the LORD, the God of Israel, and give him the praise. Tell me what you have done; do not hide it from me.

Narrator 2   Achan replied:

Achan   It is true! I have sinned against the LORD, the God of Israel. This is what I have done: When I saw in the plunder a beautiful robe from Babylonia, two hundred shekels of silver and a wedge of gold weighing fifty shekels, I coveted them and took them. They are hidden in the ground inside my tent, with the silver underneath.

Narrator 1   So Joshua sent messengers, and they ran to the tent, and there it was, hidden in his tent, with the silver underneath. They took the things from the tent, brought them to Joshua and all the Israelites and spread them out before the LORD.

Narrator 2   Then Joshua, together with all Israel, took Achan son of Zerah, the silver, the robe, the gold wedge, his sons and daughters, his cattle, donkeys and sheep, his tent and all that he had, to the Valley of Achor. Joshua said:

Joshua   Why have you brought this trouble on us? The LORD will bring trouble on you today.

Narrator 1   Then all Israel stoned him.

Narrator 2   And after they had stoned the rest, they burned them.

Narrator 1   Over Achan they heaped up a large pile of rocks—

Narrator 2   Which remains to this day. (PAUSE)

Narrators
1 and 2   Then the L<small>ORD</small> turned from his fierce anger.

Narrator 2   Therefore that place has been called the Valley of Achor ever since.

Cast: **Narrator 1, Narrator 2, Joshua, Achan**

Ai Destroyed

Joshua 8:1–23

Narrators
1 and 2   The L<small>ORD</small> said to Joshua:

The Lord
(voice only)   Do not be afraid; do not be discouraged. Take the whole army with you, and go up and attack Ai. For I have delivered into your hands the king of Ai, his people, his city and his land. You shall do to Ai and its king as you did to Jericho and its king, except that you may carry off their plunder and livestock for yourselves. Set an ambush behind the city.

Narrator 1   So Joshua and the whole army moved out to attack Ai.

Narrator 2   He chose thirty thousand of his best fighting men and sent them out at night with these orders:

Joshua   Listen carefully. You are to set an ambush behind the city. Don't go very far from it. All of you be on the alert. I and all those with me will advance on the city, and when the men come out against us, as they did before, we will flee from them. They will pursue us until we have lured them away from the city, for they will say, "They are running away from us as they did before." So when we flee from them, you are to rise up from ambush and take the city. The L<small>ORD</small> your God will give it into your hand. When you have taken the city, set it on fire. Do what the L<small>ORD</small> has commanded. See to it; you have my orders.

Narrator 1   Then Joshua sent them off, and they went to the place of ambush and lay in wait between Bethel and Ai, to the west of Ai—but Joshua spent that night with the people.

Narrator 2   Early the next morning Joshua mustered his men, and he and the leaders of Israel marched before them to Ai.

Narrator 1   The entire force that was with him marched up and approached the city and arrived in front of it. They set up camp north of Ai, with the valley between them and the city. Joshua had taken about five thousand men and set them in ambush between Bethel and Ai, to the west of the city. They had the soldiers take up their positions—all those in the camp to the north of the city and the ambush to the west of it. That night Joshua went into the valley. (PAUSE)

Narrator 2	When the king of Ai saw this, he and all the men of the city hurried out early in the morning to meet Israel in battle at a certain place overlooking the Arabah. But he did not know that an ambush had been set against him behind the city.
Narrator 1	Joshua and all Israel let themselves be driven back before them, and they fled toward the desert.
Narrator 2	All the men of Ai were called to pursue them, and they pursued Joshua and were lured away from the city.
Narrator 1	Not a man remained in Ai or Bethel who did not go after Israel. They left the city open and went in pursuit of Israel.
Narrator 2	Then the LORD said to Joshua:
The Lord (voice)	Hold out toward Ai the javelin that is in your hand, for into your hand I will deliver the city.
Narrator 1	So Joshua held out his javelin toward Ai. As soon as he did this, the men in the ambush rose quickly from their position and rushed forward. They entered the city and captured it and quickly set it on fire.
Narrator 2	The men of Ai looked back and saw the smoke of the city rising against the sky, but they had no chance to escape in any direction, for the Israelites who had been fleeing toward the desert had turned back against their pursuers.
Narrator 1	For when Joshua and all Israel saw that the ambush had taken the city and that smoke was going up from the city, they turned around and attacked the men of Ai.
Narrator 2	The men of the ambush also came out of the city against them, so that they were caught in the middle, with Israelites on both sides. Israel cut them down, leaving them neither survivors nor fugitives. But they took the king of Ai alive and brought him to Joshua.

Cast: **Narrator 1, Narrator 2** (can be the same as Narrator 1), **the Lord** (voice only), **Joshua**

The Gibeonite Deception

Joshua 9:1–27

Narrator	When all the kings west of the Jordan heard about these things—those in the hill country, in the western foothills, and along the entire coast of the Great Sea as far as Lebanon (the kings of the Hittites, Amorites, Canaanites, Perizzites, Hivites and Jebusites)—they came together to make war against Joshua and Israel.
	However, when the people of Gibeon heard what Joshua had done to Jericho and Ai, they resorted to a ruse: They went as a delegation whose

donkeys were loaded with worn-out sacks and old wineskins, cracked and mended. The men put worn and patched sandals on their feet and wore old clothes. All the bread of their food supply was dry and moldy. Then they went to Joshua in the camp at Gilgal and said to him and the men of Israel:

Gibeonite 1   We have come from a distant country.

Gibeonite 2   Make a treaty with us.

Narrator   The men of Israel said to the Hivites:

Israelite 1
(suspicious-
ly)   But perhaps you live near us.

Israelite 2   How then can we make a treaty with you?

Narrator   They said to Joshua:

**Gibeonites
1 and 2**   We are your servants.

Narrator   But Joshua asked:

Joshua   Who are you and where do you come from?

Gibeonite 1   Your servants have come from a very distant country because of the fame of the Lord your God.

Gibeonite 2   For we have heard reports of him: all that he did in Egypt, and all that he did to the two kings of the Amorites east of the Jordan—Sihon king of Heshbon, and Og king of Bashan, who reigned in Ashtaroth.

Gibeonite 1   And our elders and all those living in our country said to us, "Take provisions for your journey; go and meet them and say to them, 'We are your servants; make a treaty with us.'"

Gibeonite 2   This bread of ours was warm when we packed it at home on the day we left to come to you. But now see how dry and moldy it is.

Gibeonite 1   And these wineskins that we filled were new, but see how cracked they are. And our clothes and sandals are worn out by the very long journey.

Narrator   The men of Israel sampled their provisions but did not inquire of the Lord. Then Joshua made a treaty of peace with them to let them live, and the leaders of the assembly ratified it by oath.

Three days after they made the treaty with the Gibeonites, the Israelites heard that they were neighbors, living near them. (PAUSE) So the Israelites set out and on the third day came to their cities: Gibeon, Kephirah, Beeroth and Kiriath Jearim. But the Israelites did not attack them, because the leaders of the assembly had sworn an oath to them by the Lord, the God of Israel.

The whole assembly grumbled against the leaders, but all the leaders answered:

Israelite 1	We have given them our oath by the Lord, the God of Israel, and we cannot touch them now.
Israelite 2	This is what we will do to them: We will let them live, so that wrath will not fall on us for breaking the oath we swore to them.
Israelite 1	Let them live, but let them be woodcutters and water carriers for the entire community.
Narrator	So the leaders' promise to them was kept.
	Then Joshua summoned the Gibeonites and said:
Joshua	Why did you deceive us by saying, "We live a long way from you," while actually you live near us? You are now under a curse: You will never cease to serve as woodcutters and water carriers for the house of my God.
Narrator	They answered Joshua:
Gibeonite 1	Your servants were clearly told how the Lord your God had commanded his servant Moses to give you the whole land and to wipe out all its inhabitants from before you.
Gibeonite 2	So we feared for our lives because of you, and that is why we did this. We are now in your hands. Do to us whatever seems good and right to you.
Narrator	So Joshua saved them from the Israelites, and they did not kill them. That day he made the Gibeonites woodcutters and water carriers for the community and for the altar of the Lord at the place the Lord would choose. And that is what they are to this day.

Cast: **Narrator, Gibeonite 1, Gibeonite 2, Israelite 1, Israelite 2, Joshua**

The Sun Stands Still

Joshua 10:1–15

Narrator	Adoni-Zedek king of Jerusalem heard that Joshua had taken Ai and totally destroyed it, doing to Ai and its king as he had done to Jericho and its king, and that the people of Gibeon had made a treaty of peace with Israel and were living near them. He and his people were very much alarmed at this, because Gibeon was an important city, like one of the royal cities; it was larger than Ai, and all its men were good fighters. So Adoni-Zedek king of Jerusalem appealed to Hoham king of Hebron, Piram king of Jarmuth, Japhia king of Lachish and Debir king of Eglon.
Adoni-Zedek	Come up and help me attack Gibeon, because it has made peace with Joshua and the Israelites.
Narrator	Then the five kings of the Amorites—the kings of Jerusalem, Hebron, Jarmuth, Lachish and Eglon—joined forces. They moved up with all their troops and took up positions against Gibeon and attacked it.

	The Gibeonites then sent word to Joshua in the camp at Gilgal:
Gibeonite 1	Do not abandon your servants.
Gibeonite 2	Come up to us quickly and save us!
Gibeonites 1 and 2	Help us—
Gibeonite 1	Because all the Amorite kings from the hill country have joined forces against us.
Narrator	So Joshua marched up from Gilgal with his entire army, including all the best fighting men. The LORD said to Joshua:
The Lord (voice only)	Do not be afraid of them; I have given them into your hand. Not one of them will be able to withstand you.
Narrator	After an all-night march from Gilgal, Joshua took them by surprise. The LORD threw them into confusion before Israel, who defeated them in a great victory at Gibeon. Israel pursued them along the road going up to Beth Horon and cut them down all the way to Azekah and Makkedah. As they fled before Israel on the road down from Beth Horon to Azekah, the LORD hurled large hailstones down on them from the sky, and more of them died from the hailstones than were killed by the swords of the Israelites.

On the day the LORD gave the Amorites over to Israel, Joshua said to the LORD in the presence of Israel: |
| **Joshua** | O sun, stand still over Gibeon,
　O moon, over the Valley of Aijalon.
So the sun stood still,
　and the moon stopped,
　　till the nation avenged itself on its enemies,
as it is written in the Book of Jashar. |
| **Narrator** | The sun stopped in the middle of the sky and delayed going down about a full day. There has never been a day like it before or since, a day when the LORD listened to a man. Surely the LORD was fighting for Israel!

Then Joshua returned with all Israel to the camp at Gilgal. |

Cast: **Narrator**, **Adoni-Zedek**, **Gibeonite 1**, **Gibeonite 2**, **the Lord** (voice only), **Joshua**

Five Amorite Kings Killed

Joshua 10:16–27

Narrator	The five [Amorite] kings had fled and hidden in the cave at Makkedah. When Joshua was told that the five kings had been found hiding in the cave at Makkedah, he said:

194

Joshua	Roll large rocks up to the mouth of the cave, and post some men there to guard it. But don't stop! Pursue your enemies, attack them from the rear and don't let them reach their cities, for the LORD your God has given them into your hand.
Narrator	So Joshua and the Israelites destroyed them completely—almost to a man—but the few who were left reached their fortified cities. The whole army then returned safely to Joshua in the camp at Makkedah, and no one uttered a word against the Israelites.
	Joshua said:
Joshua	Open the mouth of the cave and bring those five kings out to me.
Narrator	So they brought the five kings out of the cave—the kings of Jerusalem, Hebron, Jarmuth, Lachish and Eglon. When they had brought these kings to Joshua, he summoned all the men of Israel and said to the army commanders who had come with him:
Joshua	Come here and put your feet on the necks of these kings.
Narrator	So they came forward and placed their feet on their necks. Joshua said to them:
Joshua	Do not be afraid; do not be discouraged. Be strong and courageous. This is what the LORD will do to all the enemies you are going to fight.
Narrator	Then Joshua struck and killed the kings and hung them on five trees, and they were left hanging on the trees until evening.
	At sunset Joshua gave the order and they took them down from the trees and threw them into the cave where they had been hiding. At the mouth of the cave they placed large rocks, which are there to this day.

Cast: **Narrator, Joshua**

Allotment for Ephraim and Manasseh

Joshua 17:14–18

Narrator	The people of Joseph said to Joshua:
Person 1	Why have you given us only one allotment and one portion for an inheritance?
Person 2	We are a numerous people and the LORD has blessed us abundantly.
Narrator	Joshua answered:
Joshua	If you are so numerous, and if the hill country of Ephraim is too small for you, go up into the forest and clear land for yourselves there in the land of the Perizzites and Rephaites.
Narrator	The people of Joseph replied:

195

Person 2	The hill country is not enough for us—
Person 1	And all the Canaanites who live in the plain have iron chariots, both those in Beth Shan and its settlements and those in the Valley of Jezreel.
Narrator	But Joshua said to the house of Joseph—to Ephraim and Manasseh:
Joshua	You are numerous and very powerful. You will have not only one allotment but the forested hill country as well. Clear it, and its farthest limits will be yours; though the Canaanites have iron chariots and though they are strong, you can drive them out.

Cast: **Narrator, Person 1, Person 2, Joshua**

Israel Takes Possession of the Land

Joshua 21:43–22:9

Narrator	The LORD gave Israel all the land he had sworn to give their forefathers, and they took possession of it and settled there. The LORD gave them rest on every side, just as he had sworn to their forefathers. Not one of their enemies withstood them; the LORD handed all their enemies over to them. Not one of all the LORD's good promises to the house of Israel failed; every one was fulfilled. Then Joshua summoned the Reubenites, the Gadites and the half-tribe of Manasseh:
Joshua	You have done all that Moses the servant of the LORD commanded, and you have obeyed me in everything I commanded. For a long time now— to this very day—you have not deserted your brothers but have carried out the mission the LORD your God gave you. Now that the LORD your God has given your brothers rest as he promised, return to your homes in the land that Moses the servant of the LORD gave you on the other side of the Jordan. But be very careful to keep the commandment and the law that Moses the servant of the LORD gave you: to love the LORD your God, to walk in all his ways, to obey his commands, to hold fast to him and to serve him with all your heart and all your soul.
Narrator	Then Joshua blessed them and sent them away, and they went to their homes. (PAUSE) (To the half-tribe of Manasseh Moses had given land in Bashan, and to the other half of the tribe Joshua gave land on the west side of the Jordan with their brothers.) When Joshua sent them home, he blessed them, saying:
Joshua	Return to your homes with your great wealth—with large herds of livestock, with silver, gold, bronze and iron, and a great quantity of clothing—and divide with your brothers the plunder from your enemies.
Narrator	So the Reubenites, the Gadites and the half-tribe of Manasseh left the Israelites at Shiloh in Canaan to return to Gilead, their own land, which

they had acquired in accordance with the command of the LORD through Moses.

Cast: **Narrator, Joshua**

The Altar by the Jordan

From Joshua 22:10–33

Narrator   When they came to Geliloth near the Jordan in the land of Canaan, the Reubenites, the Gadites and the half-tribe of Manasseh built an imposing altar there by the Jordan. And when the Israelites heard that they had built the altar on the border of Canaan at Geliloth near the Jordan on the Israelite side, the whole assembly of Israel gathered at Shiloh to go to war against them.

So the Israelites sent Phinehas son of Eleazar, the priest, to the land of Gilead—to Reuben, Gad and the half-tribe of Manasseh. With him they sent ten of the chief men, one for each of the tribes of Israel, each the head of a family division among the Israelite clans.

When they went to Gilead—to Reuben, Gad and the half-tribe of Manasseh—they said to them:

Chief 1   The whole assembly of the LORD says:

Chiefs 1–3   How could you break faith with the God of Israel like this?

Chief 2   How could you turn away from the LORD and build yourselves an altar in rebellion against him now?

Chief 1   Was not the sin of Peor enough for us?

Chief 2   Up to this very day we have not cleansed ourselves from that sin, even though a plague fell on the community of the LORD!

Chief 3   And are you now turning away from the LORD?

Chief 2   If you rebel against the LORD today, tomorrow he will be angry with the whole community of Israel. If the land you possess is defiled, come over to the LORD's land, where the LORD's tabernacle stands, and share the land with us.

Chief 1   But do not rebel against the LORD or against us by building an altar for yourselves, other than the altar of the LORD our God.

Chief 3   When Achan son of Zerah acted unfaithfully regarding the devoted things, did not wrath come upon the whole community of Israel? He was not the only one who died for his sin.

Narrator   Then Reuben, Gad and the half-tribe of Manasseh replied to the heads of the clans of Israel:

Person 1	The Mighty One, God, the LORD!
Persons 2 and 3	The Mighty One, God, the LORD!
Person 1	He knows!
Person 2	And let *Israel* know!
Person 3	If this has been in rebellion or disobedience to the LORD, do not spare us this day.
Person 1	If we have built our own altar to turn away from the LORD and to offer burnt offerings and grain offerings, or to sacrifice fellowship offerings on it, may the LORD himself call us to account.
Person 3	No! We did it for fear that some day your descendants might say to ours, "What do you have to do with the LORD, the God of Israel?". . .
Narrator	When Phinehas the priest and the leaders of the community—the heads of the clans of the Israelites—heard what Reuben, Gad and Manasseh had to say, they were pleased. . . .
	Then Phinehas son of Eleazar, the priest, and the leaders returned to Canaan from their meeting with the Reubenites and Gadites in Gilead and reported to the Israelites. They were glad to hear the report and praised God. And they talked no more about going to war against them to devastate the country where the Reubenites and the Gadites lived.

Cast: **Narrator, Chief 1, Chief 2, Chief 3** (Chiefs 1–3 can be the same), **Person 1, Person 2** (can be the same as Person 1), **Person 3**

Joshua Speaks to the People at Shechem

Joshua 24:14–25

[[Narrator	Joshua said to all the people:]]
Joshua	Fear the LORD and serve him with all faithfulness. Throw away the gods your forefathers worshiped beyond the River and in Egypt, and serve the LORD. But if serving the LORD seems undesirable to you, then choose for yourselves this day whom you will serve, whether the gods your forefathers served beyond the River, or the gods of the Amorites, in whose land you are living. But as for me and my household, we will serve the LORD.
[Narrator	Then the people answered:]
Person 1	Far be it from us to forsake the LORD to serve other gods!
Person 2	It was the LORD our God himself who brought us and our fathers up out of Egypt, from that land of slavery—
Person 3	And performed those great signs before our eyes.

198

Person 2	He protected us on our entire journey and among all the nations through which we traveled.
Person 3	And the LORD drove out before us all the nations, including the Amorites, who lived in the land.
Person 1	We too will serve the LORD, because he is our God.
[Narrator	Joshua said to the people:]
Joshua	You are not able to serve the LORD. He is a holy God; he is a jealous God. He will not forgive your rebellion and your sins. If you forsake the LORD and serve foreign gods, he will turn and bring disaster on you and make an end of you, after he has been good to you.
[Narrator	But the people said to Joshua:]
Person 1	No!
Persons 2 and 3	We *will* serve the LORD.
Narrator	Then Joshua said:
Joshua (firmly)	You are witnesses against yourselves that you have chosen to serve the LORD.
Persons 1 and 2	Yes, we are witnesses.
Joshua (demanding)	Now then, throw away the foreign gods that are among you and yield your hearts to the LORD, the God of Israel.
[Narrator	And the people said to Joshua:]
Person 1	We will serve the LORD our God—
Person 2	And obey him.
Narrator	On that day Joshua made a covenant for the people, and there at Shechem he drew up for them decrees and laws.

Cast: **Narrator, Joshua, Person 1, Person 2, Person 3** (Persons 1–3 can be the same)

Judges

Israel Fights the Remaining Canaanites

Judges 1:1–7

Narrator   After the death of Joshua, the Israelites asked the Lord:

Person 1   Who will be the first to go up and fight for us against the Canaanites?

[Narrator   The Lord answered:]

The Lord
(voice only)   Judah is to go; I have given the land into their hands.

Narrator   Then the men of Judah said to the Simeonites their brothers:

Person 2   Come up with us into the territory allotted to us, to fight against the Canaanites.

Person 3   We in turn will go with you into yours.

Narrator   So the Simeonites went with them.

When Judah attacked, the Lord gave the Canaanites and Perizzites into their hands and they struck down ten thousand men at Bezek. It was there that they found Adoni-Bezek and fought against him, putting to rout the Canaanites and Perizzites. Adoni-Bezek fled, but they chased him and caught him, and cut off his thumbs and big toes. (PAUSE) Then Adoni-Bezek said:

Adoni-Bezek   Seventy kings with their thumbs and big toes cut off have picked up scraps under my table. Now God has paid me back for what I did to them.

Narrator   They brought him to Jerusalem, and he died there.

Cast: **Narrator**, **Person 1**, the Lord (voice only), **Person 2**, **Person 3** (can be the same as Person 2), **Adoni-Bezek**

Deborah and Barak

Judges 4:1–5:3

Narrator 1   After Ehud died, the Israelites once again did evil in the eyes of the Lord. So the Lord sold them into the hands of Jabin, a king of Canaan, who reigned in Hazor. The commander of his army was Sisera, who lived in Harosheth Haggoyim. Because he had nine hundred iron chariots and had cruelly oppressed the Israelites for twenty years, they cried to the Lord for help.

Narrator 2	Deborah, a prophetess, the wife of Lappidoth, was leading Israel at that time. She held court under the Palm of Deborah between Ramah and Bethel in the hill country of Ephraim, and the Israelites came to her to have their disputes decided. She sent for Barak son of Abinoam from Kedesh in Naphtali [and said to him:]
Deborah (to Barak)	The LORD, the God of Israel, commands you:
The Lord (voice only)	Go, take with you ten thousand men of Naphtali and Zebulun and lead the way to Mount Tabor. I will lure Sisera, the commander of Jabin's army, with his chariots and his troops to the Kishon River and give him into your hands.
[Narrator 1	Barak said to her:]
Barak (to Deborah)	If you go with me, I will go; but if you don't go with me, I won't go.
Deborah	Very well, I will go with you. But because of the way you are going about this, the honor will not be yours, for the LORD will hand Sisera over to a woman.
Narrator 1	So Deborah went with Barak to Kedesh, where he summoned Zebulun and Naphtali. (PAUSE) Ten thousand men followed him, and Deborah also went with him.
Narrator 2	Now Heber the Kenite had left the other Kenites, the descendants of Hobab, Moses' brother-in-law, and pitched his tent by the great tree in Zaanannim near Kedesh.
Narrator 1	When they told Sisera that Barak son of Abinoam had gone up to Mount Tabor, Sisera gathered together his nine hundred iron chariots and all the men with him, from Harosheth Haggoyim to the Kishon River. Then Deborah said to Barak:
Deborah	Go! This is the day the LORD has given Sisera into your hands. Has not the LORD gone ahead of you?
Narrator 1	So Barak went down Mount Tabor, followed by ten thousand men. At Barak's advance, the LORD routed Sisera and all his chariots and army by the sword, and Sisera abandoned his chariot and fled on foot. But Barak pursued the chariots and army as far as Harosheth Haggoyim. All the troops of Sisera fell by the sword; not a man was left.
Narrator 2	Sisera, however, fled on foot to the tent of Jael, the wife of Heber the Kenite, because there were friendly relations between Jabin king of Hazor and the clan of Heber the Kenite. Jael went out to meet Sisera and said to him:
Jael (to Sisera)	Come, my lord, come right in. Don't be afraid.
Narrator 2	So he entered her tent, and she put a covering over him.

Sisera	I'm thirsty. Please give me some water.
Narrator 2	She opened a skin of milk, gave him a drink, and covered him up.
Sisera (to Jael)	Stand in the doorway of the tent. If someone comes by and asks you, "Is anyone here?" say "No."
Narrator 2	But Jael, Heber's wife, picked up a tent peg and a hammer and went quietly to him while he lay fast asleep, exhausted. She drove the peg through his temple into the ground, and he died.
Narrator 1	Barak came by in pursuit of Sisera, and Jael went out to meet him:
Jael	Come, I will show you the man you're looking for.
Narrator 1	So he went in with her, and there lay Sisera with the tent peg through his temple—dead.
Narrator 2	On that day God subdued Jabin, the Canaanite king, before the Israelites. And the hand of the Israelites grew stronger and stronger against Jabin, the Canaanite king, until they destroyed him.
Narrator 1	On that day Deborah and Barak son of Abinoam sang this song:
Deborah	When the princes in Israel take the lead—
Barak	When the people willingly offer themselves—
Deborah and **Barak**	Praise the Lord!
Barak	Hear this, you kings! Listen, you rulers!
Deborah	I will sing to the Lord, I will sing; I will make music to the Lord, the God of Israel.

Cast: **Narrator 1**, **Narrator 2** (can be the same as Narrator 1), **Deborah**, **the Lord** (voice only), **Barak**, **Jael**, **Sisera**

Gideon

Judges 6:[1–10], 11–24

The people cry out to the Lord (Judges 6:1–10)

[Narrator	Again the Israelites did evil in the eyes of the Lord, and for seven years he gave them into the hands of the Midianites. Because the power of Midian was so oppressive, the Israelites prepared shelters for themselves in mountain clefts, caves and strongholds. (PAUSE) Whenever the Israelites planted their crops, the Midianites, Amalekites and other eastern peoples invaded the country. They camped on the land and ruined the crops all the way to Gaza and did not spare a living thing for Israel, neither sheep nor cattle nor donkeys. They came up with their livestock and their

tents like swarms of locusts. It was impossible to count the men and their camels; they invaded the land to ravage it. (PAUSE) Midian so impoverished the Israelites that they cried out to the LORD for help. When the Israelites cried to the LORD because of Midian, he sent them a prophet, who said:

The Lord
(voice only) This is what the LORD, the God of Israel, says: I brought you up out of Egypt, out of the land of slavery. I snatched you from the power of Egypt and from the hand of all your oppressors. I drove them from before you and gave you their land. I said to you, "I am the LORD your God; do not worship the gods of the Amorites, in whose land you live." But you have not listened to me.]

God calls Gideon (Judges 6:11–24)

Narrator The angel of the LORD came and sat down under the oak in Ophrah that belonged to Joash the Abiezrite, where his son Gideon was threshing wheat in a winepress to keep it from the Midianites. When the angel of the LORD appeared to Gideon, he said:

Angel The LORD is with you, mighty warrior.

Gideon But sir, if the LORD is with us, why has all this happened to us? Where are all his wonders that our fathers told us about when they said, "Did not the LORD bring us up out of Egypt?" But now the LORD has abandoned us and put us into the hand of Midian.

Narrator The LORD turned to him and said:

The Lord
(voice) Go in the strength you have and save Israel out of Midian's hand. Am I not sending you?

Gideon But Lord, how can I save Israel? My clan is the weakest in Manasseh, and I am the least in my family.

Narrator The LORD answered:

The Lord
(voice) I will be with you, and you will strike down all the Midianites together.

Gideon If now I have found favor in your eyes, give me a sign that it is really you talking to me. Please do not go away until I come back and bring my offering and set it before you.

Narrator And the LORD said:

Angel I will wait until you return.

Narrator Gideon went in, prepared a young goat, and from an ephah of flour he made bread without yeast. Putting the meat in a basket and its broth in a pot, he brought them out and offered them to him under the oak. (PAUSE) The angel of God said to him:

Angel	Take the meat and the unleavened bread, place them on this rock, and pour out the broth.
Narrator	And Gideon did so. (PAUSE) With the tip of the staff that was in his hand, the angel of the LORD touched the meat and the unleavened bread. Fire flared from the rock, consuming the meat and the bread. And the angel of the LORD disappeared. When Gideon realized that it was the angel of the LORD, he exclaimed:
Gideon	Ah, Sovereign LORD! I have seen the angel of the LORD face to face!
[Narrator	But the LORD said to him:]
The Lord (voice)	Peace! Do not be afraid. You are not going to die.
Narrator	So Gideon built an altar to the LORD there and called it:
Gideon	The LORD is Peace.
Narrator	To this day it stands in Ophrah of the Abiezrites.

Cast: **Narrator**, **the Lord** (voice only), **Angel** (can be the same as the Lord), **Gideon**

Gideon Tears Down the Altar

Judges 6:25–32

Narrator	[That same night] the LORD said to [Gideon:]
The Lord (voice only)	Take the second bull from your father's herd, the one seven years old. Tear down your father's altar to Baal and cut down the Asherah pole beside it. Then build a proper kind of altar to the LORD your God on the top of this height. Using the wood of the Asherah pole that you cut down, offer the second bull as a burnt offering.
Narrator	So Gideon took ten of his servants and did as the LORD told him. But because he was afraid of his family and the men of the town, he did it at night rather than in the daytime. (PAUSE) In the morning when the men of the town got up, there was Baal's altar, demolished, with the Asherah pole beside it cut down and the second bull sacrificed on the newly built altar! They asked each other:
Person 1	Who did this?
Narrator	When they carefully investigated, they were told:
Person 2	Gideon son of Joash did it.
Narrator	The men of the town demanded of Joash:
Person 2	Bring out your son.

204

Person 1	He must die, because he has broken down Baal's altar and cut down the Asherah pole beside it.
Narrator	But Joash replied to the hostile crowd around him:
Joash	Are *you* going to plead Baal's *cause*? Are you trying to *save* him? Whoever fights for him shall be put to death by morning! If Baal really *is* a god, he can defend *himself* when someone breaks down his altar.
Narrator	So that day they called Gideon "Jerub-Baal," saying, "Let Baal contend with him," because he broke down Baal's altar.

Cast: **Narrator, the Lord** (voice only), **Person 1, Person 2** (can be the same as Person 1), **Joash**

Gideon and the Fleece

Judges 6:33–40

Narrator	Now all the Midianites, Amalekites and other eastern peoples joined forces and crossed over the Jordan and camped in the Valley of Jezreel. Then the Spirit of the LORD came upon Gideon, and he blew a trumpet, summoning the Abiezrites to follow him. He sent messengers throughout Manasseh, calling them to arms, and also into Asher, Zebulun and Naphtali, so that they too went up to meet them. Gideon said to God:
Gideon	If you will save Israel by my hand as you have promised—look, I will place a wool fleece on the threshing floor. If there is dew only on the fleece and all the ground is dry, then I will know that you will save Israel by my hand, as you said.
Narrator	And that is what happened. Gideon rose early the next day; he squeezed the fleece and wrung out the dew—a bowlful of water. Then Gideon said to God:
Gideon	Do not be angry with me. Let me make just one more request. Allow me one more test with the fleece. This time make the fleece dry and the ground covered with dew.
Narrator	That night God did so. Only the fleece was dry; all the ground was covered with dew.

Cast: **Narrator, Gideon**

Gideon Chooses His Men

Judges 7:1–8

Narrator	Early in the morning, Jerub-Baal (that is, Gideon) and all his men camped at the spring of Harod. The camp of Midian was north of them in the valley near the hill of Moreh. The LORD said to Gideon:

The Lord
(voice only)   You have too many men for me to deliver Midian into their hands. In order that Israel may not boast against me that her own strength has saved her, announce now to the people, "Anyone who trembles with fear may turn back and leave Mount Gilead."

Narrator   So twenty-two thousand men left, while ten thousand remained. (PAUSE)

[But the LORD said to Gideon:]

The Lord
(voice)   There are still too many men. Take them down to the water, and I will sift them for you there. If I say, "This one shall go with you," he shall go; but if I say, "This one shall not go with you," he shall not go.

Narrator   So Gideon took the men down to the water. [There the LORD told him:]

The Lord
(voice)   Separate those who lap the water with their tongues like a dog from those who kneel down to drink.

Narrator   Three hundred men lapped with their hands to their mouths. All the rest got down on their knees to drink. [The LORD said to Gideon:]

The Lord
(voice)   With the three hundred men that lapped I will save you and give the Midianites into your hands. Let all the other men go, each to his own place.

Narrator   So Gideon sent the rest of the Israelites to their tents but kept the three hundred, who took over the provisions and trumpets of the others.

Now the camp of Midian lay below him in the valley.

Cast: **Narrator, the Lord** (voice only)

Gideon Defeats the Midianites

Judges 7:9–21

Narrator   [During that night] the LORD said to Gideon:

The Lord
(voice only)   Get up, go down against the camp, because I am going to give it into your hands. If you are afraid to attack, go down to the camp with your servant Purah and listen to what they are saying. Afterward, you will be encouraged to attack the camp.

Narrator   So he and Purah his servant went down to the outposts of the camp. The Midianites, the Amalekites and all the other eastern peoples had settled in the valley, thick as locusts. Their camels could no more be counted than the sand on the seashore. (PAUSE)

Gideon arrived just as a man was telling a friend his dream.

Man (to Friend)	I had a dream. A round loaf of barley bread came tumbling into the Midianite camp. It struck the tent with such force that the tent overturned and collapsed.
Narrator	His friend responded:
Friend (awestruck)	This can be nothing other than the sword of Gideon son of Joash, the Israelite. God has given the Midianites and the whole camp into his hands.
Narrator	When Gideon heard the dream and its interpretation, he worshiped God. He returned to the camp of Israel [and called out:]
Gideon (calling)	Get up! The LORD has given the Midianite camp into your hands.
Narrator	Dividing the three hundred men into three companies, he placed trumpets and empty jars in the hands of all of them, with torches inside.
Gideon	Watch me. Follow my lead. When I get to the edge of the camp, do exactly as I do. When I and all who are with me blow our trumpets, then from all around the camp blow yours and shout, "For the LORD and for Gideon."
Narrator	Gideon and the hundred men with him reached the edge of the camp at the beginning of the middle watch, just after they had changed the guard. They blew their trumpets and broke the jars that were in their hands. The three companies blew the trumpets and smashed the jars. Grasping the torches in their left hands and holding in their right hands the trumpets they were to blow, they shouted:
Gideon and **Soldiers 1** and **2** (shouting)	A sword for the LORD and for Gideon!
Narrator	While each man held his position around the camp, all the Midianites ran, crying out as they fled.

Cast: **Narrator**, **the Lord** (voice only), **Man**, **Friend**, **Gideon**, **Soldiers 1** and **2** (can be replaced by whole cast except for Narrator)

Zebah and Zalmunna

Judges 8:1–28

Narrator	Now the Ephraimites asked Gideon:
Man 1	Why have you treated us like this?
Man 2	Why didn't you call us when you went to fight Midian?
[Narrator	And they criticized him sharply. But he answered them:]

Gideon	What have I accomplished compared to you? Aren't the gleanings of Ephraim's grapes better than the full grape harvest of Abiezer? God gave Oreb and Zeeb, the Midianite leaders, into your hands. What was I able to do compared to you?
Narrator	At this, their resentment against him subsided.
	Gideon and his three hundred men, exhausted yet keeping up the pursuit, came to the Jordan and crossed it. He said to the men of Succoth:
Gideon	Give my troops some bread; they are worn out, and I am still pursuing Zebah and Zalmunna, the kings of Midian.
Narrator	But the officials of Succoth said:
Official 1	Do you already have the hands of Zebah and Zalmunna in your possession?
Official 2	Why should we give bread to your troops?
Narrator	Then Gideon replied:
Gideon	Just for that, when the LORD has given Zebah and Zalmunna into my hand, I will tear your flesh with desert thorns and briers.
Narrator	From there he went up to Peniel and made the same request of them, but they answered as the men of Succoth had. So he said to the men of Peniel:
Gideon	When I return in triumph, I will tear down this tower.
Narrator	Now Zebah and Zalmunna were in Karkor with a force of about fifteen thousand men, all that were left of the armies of the eastern peoples; a hundred and twenty thousand swordsmen had fallen. (PAUSE) Gideon went up by the route of the nomads east of Nobah and Jogbehah and fell upon the unsuspecting army. Zebah and Zalmunna, the two kings of Midian, fled, but he pursued them and captured them, routing their entire army.
	Gideon son of Joash then returned from the battle by the Pass of Heres. He caught a young man of Succoth and questioned him, and the young man wrote down for him the names of the seventy-seven officials of Succoth, the elders of the town. Then Gideon came and said to the men of Succoth:
Gideon	Here are Zebah and Zalmunna, about whom you taunted me by saying, "Do you already have the hands of Zebah and Zalmunna in your possession? Why should we give bread to your exhausted men?"
Narrator	He took the elders of the town and taught the men of Succoth a lesson by punishing them with desert thorns and briers. He also pulled down the tower of Peniel and killed the men of the town.
	Then he asked Zebah and Zalmunna:
Gideon	What kind of men did you kill at Tabor?
[Narrator	They answered:]

Zebah	Men like you—
Zalmunna	Each one with the bearing of a prince.
Gideon (bitterly)	Those were my brothers, the sons of my own mother. As surely as the LORD lives, if you had spared their lives, I would not kill you.
Narrator	Turning to Jether, his oldest son, he said:
Gideon	Kill them!
Narrator	But Jether did not draw his sword, because he was only a boy and was afraid. [Zebah and Zalmunna said:]
Zebah (to Gideon)	Come, do it yourself.
Zalmunna	"As is the man, so is his strength."
Narrator	So Gideon stepped forward and killed them, and took the ornaments off their camels' necks. (PAUSE) The Israelites said to Gideon:
Person 1	Rule over us—you, your son and your grandson.
Person 2	Because you have saved us out of the hand of Midian.
Narrator	But Gideon told them:
Gideon	I will not rule over you, nor will my son rule over you. The LORD will rule over you. (PAUSE)
[Narrator	And he said:]
Gideon	I do have one request, that each of you give me an earring from your share of the plunder.
Narrator	(It was the custom of the Ishmaelites to wear gold earrings.) [They answered:]
Person 1	We'll be glad to give them.
Narrator	So they spread out a garment, and each man threw a ring from his plunder onto it. The weight of the gold rings he asked for came to seventeen hundred shekels, not counting the ornaments, the pendants and the purple garments worn by the kings of Midian or the chains that were on their camels' necks. Gideon made the gold into an ephod, which he placed in Ophrah, his town. All Israel prostituted themselves by worshiping it there, and it became a snare to Gideon and his family. Thus Midian was subdued before the Israelites and did not raise its head again. During Gideon's lifetime, the land enjoyed peace forty years.

Cast: **Narrator, Man 1, Man 2** (can be the same as Man 1), **Gideon, Official 1, Official 2** (can be the same as Official 1), **Zebah, Zalmunna, Person 1, Person 2** (can be the same as Person 1)

Abimelech (i)

Judges 9:1–21

Narrator	Abimelech son of Jerub-Baal went to his mother's brothers in Shechem and said to them and to all his mother's clan:
Abimelech	Ask all the citizens of Shechem, "Which is better for you: to have all seventy of Jerub-Baal's sons rule over you, or just one man?" Remember, I am your flesh and blood.
Narrator	When the brothers repeated all this to the citizens of Shechem, they were inclined to follow Abimelech, for they said:
Citizen	He is our brother.
Narrator	They gave him seventy shekels of silver from the temple of Baal-Berith, and Abimelech used it to hire reckless adventurers, who became his followers. He went to his father's home in Ophrah and on one stone murdered his seventy brothers, the sons of Jerub-Baal. But Jotham, the youngest son of Jerub-Baal, escaped by hiding. Then all the citizens of Shechem and Beth Millo gathered beside the great tree at the pillar in Shechem to crown Abimelech king.
	When Jotham was told about this, he climbed up on the top of Mount Gerizim and shouted to them:
Jotham	Listen to me, citizens of Shechem, so that God may listen to you. One day the trees went out to anoint a king for themselves. They said to the olive tree:
Tree(s)	Be our king.
Jotham	But the olive tree answered:
Olive tree	Should I give up my oil, by which both gods and men are honored, to hold sway over the trees?
Jotham	Next, the trees said to the fig tree:
Tree(s)	Come and be our king.
Jotham	But the fig tree replied:
Fig tree	Should I give up my fruit, so good and sweet, to hold sway over the trees?
Jotham	Then the trees said to the vine:
Tree(s)	Come and be our king.
Jotham	But the vine answered:
Vine	Should I give up my wine, which cheers both gods and men, to hold sway over the trees?
Jotham	Finally all the trees said to the thornbush:

210

Tree(s)	Come and be our king.
Jotham	The thornbush said to the trees:
Thornbush	If you really want to anoint me king over you, come and take refuge in my shade; but if not, then let fire come out of the thornbush and consume the cedars of Lebanon!
Jotham	Now if you have acted honorably and in good faith when you made Abimelech king, and if you have been fair to Jerub-Baal and his family, [and if you have treated him as he deserves—and to think that my father fought for you, risked his life to rescue you from the hand of Midian (but today you have revolted against my father's family, murdered his seventy sons on a single stone, and made Abimelech, the son of his slave girl, king over the citizens of Shechem because he is your brother)—if then you have acted honorably and in good faith toward Jerub-Baal and his family today,] may Abimelech be your joy, and may you be his, too! But if you have not, let fire come out from Abimelech and consume you, citizens of Shechem and Beth Millo, and let fire come out from you, citizens of Shechem and Beth Millo, and consume Abimelech!
Narrator	Then Jotham fled, escaping to Beer, and he lived there because he was afraid of his brother Abimelech.

Cast: **Narrator, Abimelech, Citizen, Jotham, Tree(s), Olive tree, Fig tree, Vine, Thornbush**

Abimelech (ii)

Judges 9:22–41

Narrator	After Abimelech had governed Israel three years, God sent an evil spirit between Abimelech and the citizens of Shechem, who acted treacherously against Abimelech. God did this in order that the crime against Jerub-Baal's seventy sons, the shedding of their blood, might be avenged on their brother Abimelech and on the citizens of Shechem, who had helped him murder his brothers. In opposition to him these citizens of Shechem set men on the hilltops to ambush and rob everyone who passed by, and this was reported to Abimelech.
	Now Gaal son of Ebed moved with his brothers into Shechem, and its citizens put their confidence in him. After they had gone out into the fields and gathered the grapes and trodden them, they held a festival in the temple of their god. While they were eating and drinking, they cursed Abimelech. Then Gaal son of Ebed said:
Gaal	Who is Abimelech, and who is Shechem, that we should be subject to him? Isn't he Jerub-Baal's son, and isn't Zebul his deputy? Serve the men of Hamor, Shechem's father! Why should we serve Abimelech? If only

	this people were under my command! Then I would get rid of him. I would say to Abimelech, "Call out your whole army!"
Narrator	When Zebul the governor of the city heard what Gaal son of Ebed said, he was very angry. Under cover he sent messengers to Abimelech, saying:
Zebul	Gaal son of Ebed and his brothers have come to Shechem and are stirring up the city against you. Now then, during the night you and your men should come and lie in wait in the fields. In the morning at sunrise, advance against the city. When Gaal and his men come out against you, do whatever your hand finds to do.
Narrator	So Abimelech and all his troops set out by night and took up concealed positions near Shechem in four companies. Now Gaal son of Ebed had gone out and was standing at the entrance to the city gate just as Abimelech and his soldiers came out from their hiding place. When Gaal saw them, he said to Zebul:
Gaal (stage whisper to Zebul)	Look, people are coming down from the tops of the mountains!
Zebul (wearily)	You mistake the shadows of the mountains for men.
Gaal	Look, people *are* coming down from the center of the land, and a company is coming from the direction of the soothsayers' tree.
Zebul (alarmed)	Where is your big talk now, you who said, "Who is Abimelech that we should be subject to him?" Aren't these the men you ridiculed? Go out and fight them!
Narrator	So Gaal led out the citizens of Shechem and fought Abimelech. Abimelech chased him, and many fell wounded in the flight—all the way to the entrance to the gate. Abimelech stayed in Arumah, and Zebul drove Gaal and his brothers out of Shechem.

Cast: **Narrator, Gaal, Zebul**

Jephthah

Judges 10:10–11:11

Narrator	The Israelites cried out to the LORD:
Israelite 1	We have sinned against you—
Israelite 2	Forsaking our God and serving the Baals.
Narrator	The LORD replied:

The Lord

(voice only) When the Egyptians, the Amorites, the Ammonites, the Philistines, the Sidonians, the Amalekites and the Maonites oppressed you and you cried to me for help, did I not save you from their hands? But you have forsaken me and served other gods, so I will no longer save you. Go and cry out to the gods you have chosen. Let them save you when you are in trouble!

Narrator But the Israelites said to the LORD:

Israelite 1 We have sinned—

Israelite 2 Do with us whatever you think best, but please rescue us now.

Narrator Then they got rid of the foreign gods among them and served the LORD. And he could bear Israel's misery no longer.

When the Ammonites were called to arms and camped in Gilead, the Israelites assembled and camped at Mizpah. The leaders of the people of Gilead said to each other:

Israelite 1 Whoever will launch the attack against the Ammonites will be the head of all those living in Gilead.

Narrator Jephthah the Gileadite was a mighty warrior. His father was Gilead; his mother was a prostitute. Gilead's wife also bore him sons, and when they were grown up, they drove Jephthah away.

Israelite 2 You are not going to get any inheritance in our family, because you are the son of another woman.

Narrator So Jephthah fled from his brothers and settled in the land of Tob, where a group of adventurers gathered around him and followed him.

Some time later, when the Ammonites made war on Israel, the elders of Gilead went to get Jephthah from the land of Tob. [They said:]

Israelite 1 Come, be our commander—

Israelite 2 So we can fight the Ammonites.

Narrator Jephthah said to them:

Jephthah Didn't you hate me and drive me from my father's house? Why do you come to me now, when you're in trouble?

Narrator The elders of Gilead said to him:

Israelite 1 Nevertheless, we are turning to you now.

Israelite 2 Come with us to fight the Ammonites and you will be our head over all who live in Gilead.

Jephthah Suppose you take me back to fight the Ammonites and the LORD gives them to me—will I really be your head? . . .

Israelites 1	
and **2**	The L<small>ORD</small> is our witness; we will certainly do as you say.
Narrator	So Jephthah went with the elders of Gilead, and the people made him head and commander over them. And he repeated all his words before the L<small>ORD</small> in Mizpah.

Cast: **Narrator, Israelite 1, Israelite 2, the Lord** (voice only), **Jephthah**

Jephthah Defeats Ammon

From Judges 11:12–33

Narrator	Jephthah sent messengers to the Ammonite king with the question:
Messenger	What do you have against us that you have attacked our country?
Narrator	The king of the Ammonites answered Jephthah's messengers:
King	When Israel came up out of Egypt, they took away my land from the Arnon to the Jabbok, all the way to the Jordan. Now give it back peaceably.
Narrator	Jephthah sent back messengers to the Ammonite king, saying:
Jephthah	This is what Jephthah says: Israel did not take the land of Moab or the land of the Ammonites. . . . For three hundred years Israel occupied Heshbon, Aroer, the surrounding settlements and all the towns along the Arnon. Why didn't you retake them during that time? I have not wronged you, but you are doing me wrong by waging war against me. Let the L<small>ORD</small>, the Judge, decide the dispute this day between the Israelites and the Ammonites.
Narrator	The king of Ammon, however, paid no attention to the message Jephthah sent him. (PAUSE)
	Then the Spirit of the L<small>ORD</small> came upon Jephthah. He crossed Gilead and Manasseh, passed through Mizpah of Gilead, and from there he advanced against the Ammonites. And Jephthah made a vow to the L<small>ORD</small>:
Jephthah	If you give the Ammonites into my hands, whatever comes out of the door of my house to meet me when I return in triumph from the Ammonites will be the L<small>ORD</small>'s, and I will sacrifice it as a burnt offering.
Narrator	Then Jephthah went over to fight the Ammonites, and the L<small>ORD</small> gave them into his hands. He devastated twenty towns from Aroer to the vicinity of Minnith, as far as Abel Keramim. Thus Israel subdued Ammon.

Cast: **Narrator, Messenger, King, Jephthah**

Jephthah and Ephraim

Judges 12:1–7

Narrator	The men of Ephraim called out their forces, crossed over to Zaphon and said to Jephthah:
Ephraimite 1	Why did you go to fight the Ammonites without calling us to go with you?
Ephraimite 2	We're going to burn down your house over your head.
Narrator	Jephthah answered:
Jephthah	I and my people were engaged in a great struggle with the Ammonites, and although I called, you didn't save me out of their hands. When I saw that you wouldn't help, I took my life in my hands and crossed over to fight the Ammonites, and the LORD gave me the victory over them. Now why have you come up today to fight me?
Narrator	Jephthah then called together the men of Gilead and fought against Ephraim.
Commentator	The Gileadites struck them down because the Ephraimites had said, "You Gileadites are renegades from Ephraim and Manasseh."
Narrator	The Gileadites captured the fords of the Jordan leading to Ephraim, and whenever a survivor of Ephraim said:
Ephraimite 2	Let me cross over.
Narrator	The men of Gilead asked him:
Gileadite	Are you an Ephraimite?
Narrator	If he replied:
Ephraimite 2	No.
Narrator	They said:
Gileadite	All right, say "Shibboleth."
Narrator	If he said:
Ephraimite 2	Sibboleth,
Narrator	. . . because he could not pronounce the word correctly, they seized him and killed him at the fords of the Jordan. Forty-two thousand Ephraimites were killed at that time.
	Jephthah led Israel six years. Then Jephthah the Gileadite died, and was buried in a town in Gilead.

Cast: **Narrator, Ephraimite 1, Ephraimite 2, Jephthah, Commentator** (can be the same as Narrator), **Gileadite**

The Birth of Samson

Judges 13:1–25

Narrator	The Israelites did evil in the eyes of the LORD, so the LORD delivered them into the hands of the Philistines for forty years.
	A certain man of Zorah, named Manoah, from the clan of the Danites, had a wife who was sterile and remained childless. The angel of the LORD appeared to her and said:
Angel	You are sterile and childless, but you are going to conceive and have a son. Now see to it that you drink no wine or other fermented drink and that you do not eat anything unclean, because you will conceive and give birth to a son. No razor may be used on his head, because the boy is to be a Nazirite, set apart to God from birth, and he will begin the deliverance of Israel from the hands of the Philistines.
Narrator	Then the woman went to her husband and told him:
Wife	A man of God came to me. He looked like an angel of God, very awesome. I didn't ask him where he came from, and he didn't tell me his name. But he said to me, "You will conceive and give birth to a son. Now then, drink no wine or other fermented drink and do not eat anything unclean, because the boy will be a Nazirite of God from birth until the day of his death."
Narrator	Then Manoah prayed to the LORD:
Manoah	O Lord, I beg you, let the man of God you sent to us come again to teach us how to bring up the boy who is to be born.
Narrator	God heard Manoah, and the angel of God came again to the woman while she was out in the field; but her husband Manoah was not with her. The woman hurried to tell her husband:
Wife	He's here! The man who appeared to me the other day!
Narrator	Manoah got up and followed his wife. [When he came to the man, he said:]
Manoah	Are you the one who talked to my wife?
Angel	I am.
[Narrator	So Manoah asked him:]
Manoah	When your words are fulfilled, what is to be the rule for the boy's life and work?
Narrator	The angel of the LORD answered:
Angel	Your wife must do all that I have told her. She must not eat anything that comes from the grapevine, nor drink any wine or other fermented drink

216

	nor eat anything unclean. She must do everything I have commanded her.
Narrator	Manoah said to the angel of the LORD:
Manoah	We would like you to stay until we prepare a young goat for you.
Angel	Even though you detain me, I will not eat any of your food. But if you prepare a burnt offering, offer it to the LORD.
Narrator	(Manoah did not realize that it was the angel of the LORD.)
	Then Manoah inquired of the angel of the LORD:
Manoah	What is your name, so that we may honor you when your word comes true?
Angel	Why do you ask my name? It is beyond understanding.
Narrator	Then Manoah took a young goat, together with the grain offering, and sacrificed it on a rock to the LORD. And the LORD did an amazing thing while Manoah and his wife watched: (PAUSE) As the flame blazed up from the altar toward heaven, the angel of the LORD ascended in the flame. Seeing this, Manoah and his wife fell with their faces to the ground. When the angel of the LORD did not show himself again to Manoah and his wife, Manoah realized that it was the angel of the LORD.
Manoah (to Wife)	We are doomed to die! We have seen God!
Wife	If the LORD had meant to kill us, he would not have accepted a burnt offering and grain offering from our hands, nor shown us all these things or now told us this.
Narrator	The woman gave birth to a boy and named him Samson. He grew and the LORD blessed him, and the Spirit of the LORD began to stir him while he was in Mahaneh Dan, between Zorah and Eshtaol.

Cast: **Narrator, Angel, Wife, Manoah**

Samson's Marriage

Judges 14:1–20

Narrator	Samson went down to Timnah and saw there a young Philistine woman. When he returned, he said to his father and mother:
Samson	I have seen a Philistine woman in Timnah; now get her for me as my wife.
[Narrator	His father and mother replied:]
Mother	Isn't there an acceptable woman among your relatives or among all our people?

Father	Must you go to the uncircumcised Philistines to get a wife?
Narrator	But Samson said to his father:
Samson	Get her for me. She's the right one for me.
Narrator	(His parents did not know that this was from the Lord, who was seeking an occasion to confront the Philistines; for at that time they were ruling over Israel.) (PAUSE) Samson went down to Timnah together with his father and mother. As they approached the vineyards of Timnah, suddenly a young lion came roaring toward him. The Spirit of the Lord came upon him in power so that he tore the lion apart with his bare hands as he might have torn a young goat. But he told neither his father nor his mother what he had done. Then he went down and talked with the woman, and he liked her.
	Some time later, when he went back to marry her, he turned aside to look at the lion's carcass. In it was a swarm of bees and some honey, which he scooped out with his hands and ate as he went along. When he rejoined his parents, he gave them some, and they too ate it. But he did not tell them that he had taken the honey from the lion's carcass.
	Now his father went down to see the woman. And Samson made a feast there, as was customary for bridegrooms. When he appeared, he was given thirty companions.
Samson	Let me tell you a riddle. If you can give me the answer within the seven days of the feast, I will give you thirty linen garments and thirty sets of clothes. If you can't tell me the answer, you must give me thirty linen garments and thirty sets of clothes.
Man 1	Tell us your riddle.
Man 2	Let's hear it.
Samson (slowly)	Out of the eater, something to eat; out of the strong, something sweet.
Narrator	For three days they could not give the answer.
	On the fourth day, they said to Samson's wife:
Man 1	Coax your husband into explaining the riddle for us, or we will burn you and your father's household to death.
Man 2	Did you invite us here to rob us?
Narrator	Then Samson's wife threw herself on him, sobbing:
Wife	You hate me! You don't really love me. You've given my people a riddle, but you haven't told me the answer.
Samson	I haven't even explained it to my father or mother, so why should I explain it to you?

Narrator	She cried the whole seven days of the feast. So on the seventh day he finally told her, because she continued to press him. She in turn explained the riddle to her people.
	Before sunset on the seventh day the men of the town said to him:
Man 1	What is sweeter than honey?
Man 2	What is stronger than a lion?
Narrator	Samson said to them:
Samson (rhyming)	If you had not plowed with my heifer, you would not have solved my riddle.
Narrator	Then the Spirit of the LORD came upon him in power. He went down to Ashkelon, struck down thirty of their men, stripped them of their belongings and gave their clothes to those who had explained the riddle. Burning with anger, he went up to his father's house. And Samson's wife was given to the friend who had attended him at his wedding.

Cast: **Narrator, Samson, Mother, Father, Man 1, Man 2, Wife**

Samson's Vengeance on the Philistines

Judges 15:1–8

Narrator	At the time of wheat harvest, Samson took a young goat and went to visit his wife. He said:
Samson	I'm going to my wife's room.
Narrator	But her father would not let him go in.
Father	I was so sure you thoroughly hated her, that I gave her to your friend. Isn't her younger sister more attractive? Take her instead.
Samson (angrily)	This time I have a right to get even with the Philistines; I will really harm them.
Narrator	So he went out and caught three hundred foxes and tied them tail to tail in pairs. He then fastened a torch to every pair of tails, lit the torches and let the foxes loose in the standing grain of the Philistines. He burned up the shocks and standing grain, together with the vineyards and olive groves. The Philistines asked:
Person 1	Who did this?
Narrator	[They were told:]
Person 2	Samson, the Timnite's son-in-law, because his wife was given to his friend.

Narrator	So the Philistines went up and burned her and her father to death. Samson said to them:
Samson	Since you've acted like this, I won't stop until I get my revenge on you.
Narrator	He attacked them viciously and slaughtered many of them. Then he went down and stayed in a cave in the rock of Etam.

Cast: **Narrator, Samson, Father, Person 1, Person 2**

Samson Defeats the Philistines

Judges 15:9–16:3

Narrator	The Philistines went up and camped in Judah, spreading out near Lehi. The men of Judah asked:
Man 1	Why have you come to fight us?
Narrator	They answered:
Philistine	We have come to take Samson prisoner, to do to him as he did to us.
Narrator	Then three thousand men from Judah went down to the cave in the rock of Etam and said to Samson:
Man 1	Don't you realize that the Philistines are rulers over us?
Man 2	What have you done to us?
Samson	I merely did to them what they did to me.
Man 2	We've come to tie you up and hand you over to the Philistines.
Samson	Swear to me that you won't kill me yourselves.
Men 1 and 2	Agreed.
Man 1	We will only tie you up and hand you over to them. We will not kill you.
Narrator	So they bound him with two new ropes and led him up from the rock. (PAUSE) As he approached Lehi, the Philistines came toward him shouting. The Spirit of the LORD came upon him in power. The ropes on his arms became like charred flax, and the bindings dropped from his hands. Finding a fresh jawbone of a donkey, he grabbed it and struck down a thousand men. (PAUSE)
Samson	With a donkey's jawbone I have made donkeys of them. With a donkey's jawbone I have killed a thousand men.
Narrator	When he finished speaking, he threw away the jawbone; and the place was called Ramath Lehi.

	Because he was very thirsty, he cried out to the LORD:
Samson	You have given your servant this great victory. Must I now die of thirst and fall into the hands of the uncircumcised?
Narrator	Then God opened up the hollow place in Lehi, and water came out of it. When Samson drank, his strength returned and he revived. So the spring was called En Hakkore, and it is still there in Lehi.
	Samson led Israel for twenty years in the days of the Philistines. (PAUSE)
	One day Samson went to Gaza, where he saw a prostitute. He went in to spend the night with her. The people of Gaza were told:
Person 1	Samson is here!
Narrator	So they surrounded the place and lay in wait for him all night at the city gate. They made no move during the night, saying:
Person 2	At dawn we'll kill him.
Narrator	But Samson lay there only until the middle of the night. Then he got up and took hold of the doors of the city gate, together with the two posts, and tore them loose, bar and all. He lifted them to his shoulders and carried them to the top of the hill that faces Hebron.

Cast: **Narrator, Man 1, Philistine, Man 2, Samson, Person 1, Person 2**

Samson and Delilah

Judges 16:4–22

Narrator	[Samson] fell in love with a woman in the Valley of Sorek whose name was Delilah. The rulers of the Philistines went to her and said:
Philistine 1	See if you can lure him into showing you the secret of his great strength and how we can overpower him—
Philistine 2	So we may tie him up and subdue him.
Philistine 3	Each one of us will give you eleven hundred shekels of silver.
Narrator	So Delilah said to Samson:
Delilah	Tell me the secret of your great strength and how you can be tied up and subdued.
Samson	If anyone ties me with seven fresh thongs that have not been dried, I'll become as weak as any other man.
Narrator	Then the rulers of the Philistines brought her seven fresh thongs that had not been dried, and she tied him with them. With men hidden in the room, she called to him:
Delilah	Samson, the Philistines are upon you!

Narrator	But he snapped the thongs as easily as a piece of string snaps when it comes close to a flame. So the secret of his strength was not discovered. (PAUSE) [Then Delilah said to Samson:]
Delilah	You have made a fool of me; you lied to me. Come now, tell me how you can be tied.
Samson	If anyone ties me securely with new ropes that have never been used, I'll become as weak as any other man.
Narrator	So Delilah took new ropes and tied him with them. Then, with men hidden in the room, she called to him:
Delilah	Samson, the Philistines are upon you!
Narrator	But he snapped the ropes off his arms as if they were threads. (PAUSE) [Delilah then said to Samson:]
Delilah	Until now, you have been making a fool of me and lying to me. Tell me how you can be tied.
Samson	If you weave the seven braids of my head into the fabric ˎon the loomˌ and tighten it with the pin, I'll become as weak as any other man.
Narrator	So while he was sleeping, Delilah took the seven braids of his head, wove them into the fabric and tightened it with the pin. Again she called to him:
Delilah	Samson, the Philistines are upon you!
Narrator	He awoke from his sleep and pulled up the pin and the loom, with the fabric. (PAUSE) [Then she said to him:]
Delilah	How can you say, "I love you," when you won't confide in me? This is the third time you have made a fool of me and haven't told me the secret of your great strength.
Narrator	With such nagging she prodded him day after day until he was tired to death. So he told her everything.
Samson	No razor has ever been used on my head, because I have been a Nazirite set apart to God since birth. If my head were shaved, my strength would leave me, and I would become as weak as any other man.
Narrator	When Delilah saw that he had told her everything, she sent word to the rulers of the Philistines:
Delilah (aside)	Come back once more; he has told me everything.
Narrator	So the rulers of the Philistines returned with the silver in their hands. Having put him to sleep on her lap, she called a man to shave off the

seven braids of his hair, and so began to subdue him. And his strength left him. Then she called:

Delilah   Samson, the Philistines are upon you!

Narrator   He awoke from his sleep and thought:

Samson
(sleepily)   I'll go out as before and shake myself free.

Narrator
(slowly)   But he did not know that the LORD had left him.

Then the Philistines seized him, gouged out his eyes and took him down to Gaza. Binding him with bronze shackles, they set him to grinding in the prison. But the hair on his head began to grow again after it had been shaved.

Cast: **Narrator, Philistine 1, Philistine 2, Philistine 3** (can be the same as Philistine 1, or Philistines 1–3 can be the same), **Delilah, Samson**

The Death of Samson

Judges 16:23–30 [31]

Narrator   The rulers of the Philistines assembled to offer a great sacrifice to Dagon their god and to celebrate, saying:

Philistine 1   Our god has delivered Samson, our enemy, into our hands.

Narrator   When the people saw him, they praised their god, saying:

Philistine 2   Our god has delivered our enemy
        into our hands,
    the one who laid waste our land
        and multiplied our slain.

Narrator   While they were in high spirits, they shouted:

Philistine 3   Bring out Samson to entertain us.

Narrator   So they called Samson out of the prison, and he performed for them.

When they stood him among the pillars, Samson said to the servant who held his hand:

Samson   Put me where I can feel the pillars that support the temple, so that I may lean against them.

Narrator   Now the temple was crowded with men and women; all the rulers of the Philistines were there, and on the roof were about three thousand men and women watching Samson perform. (PAUSE) Then Samson prayed to the LORD:

223

Samson	O Sovereign LORD, remember me. O God, please strengthen me just once more, and let me with one blow get revenge on the Philistines for my two eyes.
Narrator	Then Samson reached toward the two central pillars on which the temple stood. Bracing himself against them, his right hand on the one and his left hand on the other, Samson said:
Samson	Let me die with the Philistines!
Narrator	Then he pushed with all his might, and down came the temple on the rulers and all the people in it. Thus he killed many more when he died than while he lived.
	[Then his brothers and his father's whole family went down to get him. They brought him back and buried him between Zorah and Eshtaol in the tomb of Manoah his father. He had led Israel twenty years.]

Cast: **Narrator, Philistine 1, Philistine 2, Philistine 3** (Philistines 1–3 can be the same), **Samson**

Micah's Idols

Judges 17:1–13

Narrator	Now a man named Micah from the hill country of Ephraim said to his mother:
Micah	The eleven hundred shekels of silver that were taken from you and about which I heard you utter a curse—I have that silver with me; I took it.
[Narrator	Then his mother said:]
Mother	The LORD bless you, my son!
Narrator	When he returned the eleven hundred shekels of silver to his mother, she said:
Mother (to audience)	I solemnly consecrate my silver to the LORD for my son to make a carved image and a cast idol.
(to Micah)	I will give it back to you.
Narrator	So he returned the silver to his mother, and she took two hundred shekels of silver and gave them to a silversmith, who made them into the image and the idol. And they were put in Micah's house.
	Now this man Micah had a shrine, and he made an ephod and some idols and installed one of his sons as his priest. In those days Israel had no king; everyone did as he saw fit. (PAUSE)
	A young Levite from Bethlehem in Judah, who had been living within the clan of Judah, left that town in search of some other place to stay.

On his way he came to Micah's house in the hill country of Ephraim. Micah asked him:

Micah
(to Levite)   Where are you from?

Levite   I'm a Levite from Bethlehem in Judah, and I'm looking for a place to stay.

Narrator   Then Micah said to him:

Micah   Live with me and be my father and priest, and I'll give you ten shekels of silver a year, your clothes and your food.

Narrator   So the Levite agreed to live with him, and the young man was to him like one of his sons. Then Micah installed the Levite, and the young man became his priest and lived in his house. [And Micah said:]

Micah
(to
audience)   Now I know that the LORD will be good to me, since this Levite has become my priest.

Cast: **Narrator, Micah, Mother, Levite**

Danites Settle in Laish

Judges 18:1–31

Narrator   In those days Israel had no king.

And in those days the tribe of the Danites was seeking a place of their own where they might settle, because they had not yet come into an inheritance among the tribes of Israel. So the Danites sent five warriors from Zorah and Eshtaol to spy out the land and explore it. These men represented all their clans. They told them, "Go, explore the land."

The men entered the hill country of Ephraim and came to the house of Micah, where they spent the night. When they were near Micah's house, they recognized the voice of the young Levite; so they turned in there and asked him:

Man 1   Who brought you here?

Man 2   What are you doing in this place? Why are you here?

Narrator   He told them what Micah had done for him, and said:

Levite   He has hired me and I am his priest.

Narrator   Then they said to him:

Man 3   Please inquire of God to learn whether our journey will be successful.

[Narrator   The priest answered them:]

Levite	Go in peace. Your journey has the LORD's approval.
Narrator	So the five men left and came to Laish, where they saw that the people were living in safety, like the Sidonians, unsuspecting and secure. And since their land lacked nothing, they were prosperous. Also, they lived a long way from the Sidonians and had no relationship with anyone else.
	When they returned to Zorah and Eshtaol, their brothers asked them, "How did you find things?" They answered:
Man 1	Come on, let's attack them!
Man 2	We have seen that the land is very good.
Man 3	Aren't you going to do something?
Man 1	Don't hesitate to go there and take it over.
Man 3	When you get there, you will find an unsuspecting people—
Man 2	And a spacious land that God has put into your hands.
Man 1	A land that lacks nothing whatever.
Narrator	Then six hundred men from the clan of the Danites, armed for battle, set out from Zorah and Eshtaol. On their way they set up camp near Kiriath Jearim in Judah. This is why the place west of Kiriath Jearim is called Mahaneh Dan to this day. From there they went on to the hill country of Ephraim and came to Micah's house.
	Then the five men who had spied out the land of Laish said to their brothers:
Man 1	Do you know that one of these houses has an ephod [and] other household gods?
Man 2	A carved image and a cast idol!
Man 3	Now you know what to do.
Narrator	So they turned in there and went to the house of the young Levite at Micah's place and greeted him. The six hundred Danites, armed for battle, stood at the entrance to the gate. The five men who had spied out the land went inside and took the carved image, the ephod, the other household gods and the cast idol while the priest and the six hundred armed men stood at the entrance to the gate. (PAUSE)
	When these men went into Micah's house and took the carved image, the ephod, the other household gods and the cast idol, the priest said to them:
Levite	What are you doing?
Man 1	Be quiet!
Man 2	Don't say a word.
Man 3	Come with us, and be our father and priest.

Man 1	Isn't it better that you serve a tribe and clan in Israel as priest rather than just one man's household?
Narrator	Then the priest was glad. He took the ephod, the other household gods and the carved image and went along with the people. (PAUSE) Putting their little children, their livestock and their possessions in front of them, they turned away and left.
	When they had gone some distance from Micah's house, the men who lived near Micah were called together and overtook the Danites. As they shouted after them, the Danites turned and said to Micah:
Man 1	What's the matter with you that you called out your men to fight?
Micah	You took the gods I made, and my priest, and went away. What else do I have? How can you ask, "What's the matter with you?"
Narrator	The Danites answered:
Man 1	Don't argue with us, or some hot-tempered men will attack you.
Man 3	And you and your family will lose your lives.
Narrator	So the Danites went their way, and Micah, seeing that they were too strong for him, turned around and went back home.
	Then they took what Micah had made, and his priest, and went on to Laish, against a peaceful and unsuspecting people. They attacked them with the sword and burned down their city. There was no one to rescue them because they lived a long way from Sidon and had no relationship with anyone else. The city was in a valley near Beth Rehob.
	The Danites rebuilt the city and settled there. They named it Dan after their forefather Dan, who was born to Israel—though the city used to be called Laish. There the Danites set up for themselves the idols, and Jonathan son of Gershom, the son of Moses, and his sons were priests for the tribe of Dan until the time of the captivity of the land. They continued to use the idols Micah had made, all the time the house of God was in Shiloh.

Cast: **Narrator, Man 1, Man 2, Levite, Man 3, Micah**

A Levite and His Concubine (i)

Judges 19:1–21

Narrator	In those days Israel had no king. Now a Levite who lived in a remote area in the hill country of Ephraim took a concubine from Bethlehem in Judah. But she was unfaithful to him. She left him and went back to her father's house in Bethlehem, Judah. After she had been there four months, her husband went to her to persuade her to return. He had with him his servant and two donkeys. She took him into her father's house, and when

227

her father saw him, he gladly welcomed him. His father-in-law, the girl's father, prevailed upon him to stay; so he remained with him three days, eating and drinking, and sleeping there.

On the fourth day they got up early and he prepared to leave, but the girl's father said to his son-in-law:

Father   Refresh yourself with something to eat; then you can go.

Narrator   So the two of them sat down to eat and drink together. Afterward the girl's father said:

Father   Please stay tonight and enjoy yourself.

Narrator   And when the man got up to go, his father-in-law persuaded him, so he stayed there that night. On the morning of the fifth day, when he rose to go, the girl's father said:

Father   Refresh yourself. Wait till afternoon!

Narrator   So the two of them ate together. (PAUSE)

Then when the man, with his concubine and his servant, got up to leave, his father-in-law, the girl's father, said:

Father   Now look, it's almost evening. Spend the night here; the day is nearly over. Stay and enjoy yourself. Early tomorrow morning you can get up and be on your way home.

Narrator   But, unwilling to stay another night, the man left and went toward Jebus—

Commen-
tator   (That is, Jerusalem—)

Narrator   With his two saddled donkeys and his concubine.

When they were near Jebus and the day was almost gone, the servant said to his master:

Servant   Come, let's stop at this city of the Jebusites and spend the night.

Levite   No. We won't go into an alien city, whose people are not Israelites. We will go on to Gibeah. (PAUSE) Come, let's try to reach Gibeah or Ramah and spend the night in one of those places.

Narrator   So they went on, and the sun set as they neared Gibeah in Benjamin. There they stopped to spend the night. They went and sat in the city square, but no one took them into his home for the night.

That evening an old man from the hill country of Ephraim, who was living in Gibeah came in from his work in the fields.

[Commen-
tator   The men of the place were Benjamites.]

Narrator   When he looked and saw the traveler in the city square, the old man asked:

Old man	Where are you going? Where did you come from?
Levite	We are on our way from Bethlehem in Judah to a remote area in the hill country of Ephraim where I live. I have been to Bethlehem in Judah and now I am going to the house of the LORD. No one has taken me into his house. We have both straw and fodder for our donkeys and bread and wine for ourselves your servants—me, your maidservant, and the young man with us. We don't need anything.
Old man	You are welcome at my house. Let me supply whatever you need. Only don't spend the night in the square.
Narrator	So he took him into his house and fed his donkeys. After they had washed their feet, they had something to eat and drink.

Cast: **Narrator, Father, Commentator, Servant, Levite, Old man**

A Levite and His Concubine (ii)

Judges 19:22–30

Narrator	While [the old man and his guests] were enjoying themselves, some of the wicked men of the city surrounded the house. Pounding on the door, they shouted to the old man who owned the house:
Man 1	Bring out the man who came to your house—
Man 2	So we can have sex with him.
Narrator	The owner of the house went outside and said to them:
Old man	No, my friends, don't be so vile. Since this man is my guest, don't do this disgraceful thing. Look, here is my virgin daughter, and his concubine. I will bring them out to you now, and you can use them and do to them whatever you wish. But to this man, don't do such a disgraceful thing.
Narrator	But the men would not listen to him. So the man took his concubine and sent her outside to them, and they raped her and abused her throughout the night, and at dawn they let her go. (PAUSE) At daybreak the woman went back to the house where her master was staying, fell down at the door and lay there until daylight.
	When her master got up in the morning and opened the door of the house and stepped out to continue on his way, there lay his concubine, fallen in the doorway of the house, with her hands on the threshold. He said to her:
Levite	Get up; let's go.
Narrator	But there was no answer. Then the man put her on his donkey and set out for home.

229

When he reached home, he took a knife and cut up his concubine, limb by limb, into twelve parts and sent them into all the areas of Israel. Everyone who saw it said:

Person 1   Such a thing has never been seen or done.

Person 2   Not since the day the Israelites came up out of Egypt.

Person 1   Think about it! Consider it! Tell us what to do!

Cast: **Narrator, Man 1, Man 2, Old man, Levite, Person 1, Person 2**

Israel Prepares for War

Judges 20:1–17

Narrator   All the Israelites from Dan to Beersheba and from the land of Gilead came out as one man and assembled before the LORD in Mizpah. The leaders of all the people of the tribes of Israel took their places in the assembly of the people of God, four hundred thousand soldiers armed with swords. (The Benjamites heard that the Israelites had gone up to Mizpah.) [Then the Israelites said:]

Person 1   Tell us how this awful thing happened.

Narrator   So the Levite, the husband of the murdered woman, said:

Levite   I and my concubine came to Gibeah in Benjamin to spend the night. During the night the men of Gibeah came after me and surrounded the house, intending to kill me. They raped my concubine, and she died. I took my concubine, cut her into pieces and sent one piece to each region of Israel's inheritance, because they committed this lewd and disgraceful act in Israel. Now, all you Israelites, speak up and give your verdict.

Narrator   All the people rose as one man, saying:

Person 1   None of us will go home.

Person 2   No, not one of us will return to his house.

Person 1   But now this is what we'll do to Gibeah:

Person 2   We'll go up against it as the lot directs.

Person 1   We'll take ten men out of every hundred from all the tribes of Israel, and a hundred from a thousand, and a thousand from ten thousand, to get provisions for the army.

Person 2   Then, when the army arrives at Gibeah in Benjamin, it can give them what they deserve for all this vileness done in Israel.

Narrator   So all the men of Israel got together and united as one man against the city.

The tribes of Israel sent men throughout the tribe of Benjamin, saying:

Messenger 1   What about this awful crime that was committed among you?

Messenger 2   Now surrender those wicked men of Gibeah so that we may put them to death and purge the evil from Israel.

Narrator   But the Benjamites would not listen to their fellow Israelites. From their towns they came together at Gibeah to fight against the Israelites. At once the Benjamites mobilized twenty-six thousand swordsmen from their towns, in addition to seven hundred chosen men from those living in Gibeah. Among all these soldiers there were seven hundred chosen men who were left-handed, each of whom could sling a stone at a hair and not miss.

Israel, apart from Benjamin, mustered four hundred thousand swordsmen, all of them fighting men.

Cast: **Narrator, Person 1, Levite, Person 2, Messenger 1, Messenger 2** (can be the same as Messenger 1)

Israelites Fight the Benjamites

Judges 20:18–36

Narrator   The Israelites went up to Bethel and inquired of God.

Person 1   Who of us shall go first to fight against the Benjamites?

Narrator   The LORD replied:

The Lord
(voice only)   Judah shall go first.

Narrator   The next morning the Israelites got up and pitched camp near Gibeah. The men of Israel went out to fight the Benjamites and took up battle positions against them at Gibeah. The Benjamites came out of Gibeah and cut down twenty-two thousand Israelites on the battlefield that day. But the men of Israel encouraged one another and again took up their positions where they had stationed themselves the first day. The Israelites went up and wept before the LORD until evening, and they inquired of the LORD.

Person 2   Shall we go up again to battle against the Benjamites, our brothers?

[Narrator   The LORD answered:]

The Lord
(voice)   Go up against them.

Narrator   Then the Israelites drew near to Benjamin the second day. This time, when the Benjamites came out from Gibeah to oppose them, they cut down another eighteen thousand Israelites, all of them armed with swords.

Then the Israelites, all the people, went up to Bethel, and there they sat weeping before the LORD. They fasted that day until evening and presented burnt offerings and fellowship offerings to the LORD. And the Israelites inquired of the LORD. [(In those days the ark of the covenant of God was there, with Phinehas son of Eleazar, the son of Aaron, ministering before it.)]

Person 1 Shall we go up again to battle with Benjamin our brother?

Person 2 Or not?

[Narrator The LORD responded:]

The Lord
(voice) Go, for tomorrow I will give them into your hands.

Narrator Then Israel set an ambush around Gibeah. They went up against the Benjamites on the third day and took up positions against Gibeah as they had done before. The Benjamites came out to meet them and were drawn away from the city. They began to inflict casualties on the Israelites as before, so that about thirty men fell in the open field and on the roads—the one leading to Bethel and the other to Gibeah.

While the Benjamites were saying:

**Benjamites
1 and 2** We are defeating them as before.

Narrator The Israelites were saying:

Person 1 Let's retreat and draw them away from the city to the roads.

Narrator All the men of Israel moved from their places and took up positions at Baal Tamar, and the Israelite ambush charged out of its place on the west of Gibeah. Then ten thousand of Israel's finest men made a frontal attack on Gibeah. The fighting was so heavy that the Benjamites did not realize how near disaster was. The LORD defeated Benjamin before Israel, and on that day the Israelites struck down 25,100 Benjamites, all armed with swords. Then the Benjamites saw that they were beaten.

Now the men of Israel had given way before Benjamin, because they relied on the ambush they had set near Gibeah.

Cast: **Narrator, Person 1, the Lord** (voice only), **Person 2** (can be the same as Person 1), **Benjamite 1, Benjamite 2** (can be the same as Benjamite 1)

Wives for the Benjamites

Judges 21:1–25

Narrator The men of Israel had taken an oath at Mizpah:

Person 1 Not one of us will give his daughter in marriage to a Benjamite.

Narrator	The people went to Bethel, where they sat before God until evening, raising their voices and weeping bitterly.
Person 1	O LORD, the God of Israel, why has this happened to Israel?
Person 2	Why should one tribe be missing from Israel today?
Narrator	Early the next day the people built an altar and presented burnt offerings and fellowship offerings. Then the Israelites asked:
Person 3	Who from all the tribes of Israel has failed to assemble before the LORD?
Narrator	For they had taken a solemn oath that anyone who failed to assemble before the LORD at Mizpah should certainly be put to death.
	Now the Israelites grieved for their brothers, the Benjamites.
Person 1	Today one tribe is cut off from Israel.
Person 2	How can we provide wives for those who are left, since we have taken an oath by the LORD not to give them any of our daughters in marriage?
Person 3	Which one of the tribes of Israel failed to assemble before the LORD at Mizpah?
Narrator	They discovered that no one from Jabesh Gilead had come to the camp for the assembly. For when they counted the people, they found that none of the people of Jabesh Gilead were there.
	So the assembly sent twelve thousand fighting men with instructions to go to Jabesh Gilead and put to the sword those living there, including the women and children.
Person 3	This is what you are to do. Kill every male and every woman who is not a virgin.
Narrator	They found among the people living in Jabesh Gilead four hundred young women who had never slept with a man, and they took them to the camp at Shiloh in Canaan.
	Then the whole assembly sent an offer of peace to the Benjamites at the rock of Rimmon. So the Benjamites returned at that time and were given the women of Jabesh Gilead who had been spared. But there were not enough for all of them.
	The people grieved for Benjamin, because the LORD had made a gap in the tribes of Israel. And the elders of the assembly said:
Person 1	With the women of Benjamin destroyed, how shall we provide wives for the men who are left?
Person 2	The Benjamite survivors must have heirs, so that a tribe of Israel will not be wiped out.
Person 1	We can't give them our daughters as wives, since we Israelites have taken this oath: "Cursed be anyone who gives a wife to a Benjamite."

Person 3	But look, there is the annual festival of the Lord in Shiloh, to the north of Bethel, and east of the road that goes from Bethel to Shechem, and to the south of Lebonah.
Narrator	So they instructed the Benjamites, saying:
Person 2	Go and hide in the vineyards and watch. When the girls of Shiloh come out to join in the dancing, then rush from the vineyards and each of you seize a wife from the girls of Shiloh and go to the land of Benjamin.
Person 3	When their fathers or brothers complain to us, we will say to them, "Do us a kindness by helping them, because we did not get wives for them during the war, and you are innocent, since you did not give your daughters to them."
Narrator	So that is what the Benjamites did. While the girls were dancing, each man caught one and carried her off to be his wife. Then they returned to their inheritance and rebuilt the towns and settled in them.
	At that time the Israelites left that place and went home to their tribes and clans, each to his own inheritance.
	In those days Israel had no king; everyone did as he saw fit.

Cast: **Narrator, Person 1, Person 2, Person 3** (Persons 1–3 can be the same)

Ruth

Naomi and Ruth

Ruth 1:6–22

Narrator	When [Naomi] heard in Moab that the LORD had come to the aid of his people by providing food for them, [she] and her daughters-in-law prepared to return home from there. With her two daughters-in-law she left the place where she had been living and set out on the road that would take them back to the land of Judah. Then Naomi said to her two daughters-in-law:
Naomi	Go back, each of you, to your mother's home. May the LORD show kindness to you, as you have shown to your dead and to me. May the LORD grant that each of you will find rest in the home of another husband.
Narrator	Then she kissed them and they wept aloud [and said to her:]
Ruth and **Orpah**	We *will* go back with you to your people.
Naomi	Return *home*, my daughters. Why would you come with me? Am I going to have any more sons, who could become your husbands? Return home, my daughters; I am too old to have another husband. Even if I thought there was still hope for me—even if I had a husband tonight and then gave birth to sons—would you wait until they grew up? Would you remain unmarried for them? No, my daughters. It is more bitter for me than for you, because the LORD's hand has gone out against me!
Narrator	At this they wept again. Then Orpah kissed her mother-in-law good-by, but Ruth clung to her.
Naomi (to Ruth)	Look, your sister-in-law is going back to her people and her gods. Go back with her.
Ruth	Don't urge me to leave you or to turn back from you. Where you go I will go, and where you stay I will stay. Your people will be my people and your God my God. Where you die I will die, and there I will be buried. May the LORD deal with me, be it ever so severely, if anything but death separates you and me.
Narrator	When Naomi realized that Ruth was determined to go with her, she stopped urging her. (PAUSE)
	So the two women went on until they came to Bethlehem. When they arrived in Bethlehem, the whole town was stirred because of them [and the women exclaimed:]
Women	Can this be Naomi?

Naomi	Don't call me Naomi. Call me Mara, because the Almighty has made my life very bitter. I went away full, but the LORD has brought me back empty. Why call me Naomi? The LORD has afflicted me; the Almighty has brought misfortune upon me.
Narrator	So Naomi returned from Moab accompanied by Ruth the Moabitess, her daughter-in-law, arriving in Bethlehem as the barley harvest was beginning.

Cast: **Narrator, Naomi, Ruth, Orpah** (can be the same as Ruth), **Women** (two or more)

Ruth Meets Boaz

Ruth 2:1–23

Narrator	Naomi had a relative on her husband's side, from the clan of Elimelech, a man of standing, whose name was Boaz.
	And Ruth the Moabitess said to Naomi:
Ruth	Let me go to the fields and pick up the leftover grain behind anyone in whose eyes I find favor.
Naomi	Go ahead, my daughter.
Narrator	So she went out and began to glean in the fields behind the harvesters. As it turned out, she found herself working in a field belonging to Boaz, who was from the clan of Elimelech.
	Just then Boaz arrived from Bethlehem and greeted the harvesters:
Boaz	The LORD be with you!
Men 1 and **2**	The LORD bless you!
Narrator	Boaz asked the foreman of his harvesters:
Boaz	Whose young woman is that?
Man 2	She is the Moabitess who came back from Moab with Naomi. She said, "Please let me glean and gather among the sheaves behind the harvesters." She went into the field and has worked steadily from morning till now, except for a short rest in the shelter.
Narrator	So Boaz said to Ruth:
Boaz (to Ruth)	My daughter, listen to me. Don't go and glean in another field and don't go away from here. Stay here with my servant girls. Watch the field where the men are harvesting, and follow along after the girls. I have told the men not to touch you. And whenever you are thirsty, go and get a drink from the water jars the men have filled.
Narrator	At this, she bowed down with her face to the ground. [She exclaimed:]

236

Ruth (amazed)	Why have I found such favor in your eyes that you notice me—a foreigner?
Boaz	I've been told all about what you have done for your mother-in-law since the death of your husband—how you left your father and mother and your homeland and came to live with a people you did not know before. May the Lord repay you for what you have done. May you be richly rewarded by the Lord, the God of Israel, under whose wings you have come to take refuge.
Ruth	May I continue to find favor in your eyes, my lord. You have given me comfort and have spoken kindly to your servant—though I do not have the standing of one of your servant girls.
Narrator	At mealtime Boaz said to her:
Boaz	Come over here. Have some bread and dip it in the wine vinegar.
Narrator	When she sat down with the harvesters, he offered her some roasted grain. She ate all she wanted and had some left over. As she got up to glean, Boaz gave orders to his men:
Boaz	Even if she gathers among the sheaves, don't embarrass her. Rather, pull out some stalks for her from the bundles and leave them for her to pick up, and don't rebuke her.
Narrator	So Ruth gleaned in the field until evening. Then she threshed the barley she had gathered, and it amounted to about an ephah. She carried it back to town, and her mother-in-law saw how much she had gathered. Ruth also brought out and gave her what she had left over after she had eaten enough. Her mother-in-law asked her:
Naomi	Where did you glean today? Where did you work? Blessed be the man who took notice of you!
Narrator	Then Ruth told her mother-in-law about the one at whose place she had been working.
Ruth	The name of the man I worked with today is Boaz.
Naomi (exclaiming)	The Lord bless him! He has not stopped showing his kindness to the living and the dead. That man is our close relative; he is one of our kinsman-redeemers.
[Narrator	Then Ruth the Moabitess said:]
Ruth	He even said to me, "Stay with my workers until they finish harvesting all my grain."
Naomi	It will be good for you, my daughter, to go with *his* girls, because in someone else's field you might be harmed.
Narrator	So Ruth stayed close to the servant girls of Boaz to glean until the barley and wheat harvests were finished. And she lived with her mother-in-law.

Cast: **Narrator, Ruth, Naomi, Boaz, Man 1, Man 2**

Ruth and Boaz at the Threshing Floor

Ruth 3:1–18

Narrator   One day Naomi her mother-in-law said to [Ruth:]

Naomi   My daughter, should I not try to find a home for you, where you will be well provided for? Is not Boaz, with whose servant girls you have been, a kinsman of ours? Tonight he will be winnowing barley on the threshing floor. Wash and perfume yourself, and put on your best clothes. Then go down to the threshing floor, but don't let him know you are there until he has finished eating and drinking. When he lies down, note the place where he is lying. Then go and uncover his feet and lie down. He will tell you what to do.

[Narrator   Ruth answered:]

Ruth   I will do whatever you say.

Narrator   So she went down to the threshing floor and did everything her mother-in-law told her to do.

When Boaz had finished eating and drinking and was in good spirits, he went over to lie down at the far end of the grain pile. Ruth approached quietly, uncovered his feet and lay down. In the middle of the night something startled the man, and he turned and discovered a woman lying at his feet.

Boaz
(whispering) Who are you?

Ruth
(whispering) I am your servant Ruth. Spread the corner of your garment over me, since you are a kinsman-redeemer.

Boaz   The LORD bless you, my daughter. This kindness is greater than that which you showed earlier: You have not run after the younger men, whether rich or poor. And now, my daughter, don't be afraid. I will do for you all you ask. All my fellow townsmen know that you are a woman of noble character. Although it is true that I am near of kin, there is a kinsman-redeemer nearer than I. Stay here for the night, and in the morning if he wants to redeem, good; let him redeem. But if he is not willing, as surely as the LORD lives I will do it. Lie here until morning.

Narrator   So she lay at his feet until morning, but got up before anyone could be recognized [and he said:]

Boaz   Don't let it be known that a woman came to the threshing floor.

Bring me the shawl you are wearing and hold it out.

Narrator   When she did so, he poured into it six measures of barley and put it on her. Then he went back to town.

When Ruth came to her mother-in-law, Naomi asked:

238

Naomi	How did it go, my daughter?
Narrator	Then she told her everything Boaz had done for her and added:
Ruth	He gave me these six measures of barley, saying, "Don't go back to your mother-in-law empty-handed."
Naomi	Wait, my daughter, until you find out what happens. For the man will not rest until the matter is settled today.

Cast: **Narrator, Naomi, Ruth, Boaz**

Boaz Marries Ruth

Ruth 4:1–22

Narrator	Boaz went up to the town gate and sat there. When the kinsman-redeemer he had mentioned came along, Boaz said:
Boaz	Come over here, my friend, and sit down.
Narrator	So he went over and sat down. Boaz took ten of the elders of the town and said:
Boaz	Sit here.
Narrator	They did so. Then he said to the kinsman-redeemer:
Boaz	Naomi, who has come back from Moab, is selling the piece of land that belonged to our brother Elimelech. I thought I should bring the matter to your attention and suggest that you buy it in the presence of these seated here and in the presence of the elders of my people. If you will redeem it, do so. But if you will not, tell me, so I will know. For no one has the right to do it except you, and I am next in line.
Man	I will redeem it.
Boaz	On the day you buy the land from Naomi and from Ruth the Moabitess, you acquire the dead man's widow, in order to maintain the name of the dead with his property.
[Narrator	At this, the kinsman-redeemer said:]
Man	Then I cannot redeem it because I might endanger my own estate. You redeem it yourself. I cannot do it.
Narrator	(Now in earlier times in Israel, for the redemption and transfer of property to become final, one party took off his sandal and gave it to the other. This was the method of legalizing transactions in Israel.) So the kinsman-redeemer said to Boaz:
Man	Buy it yourself.

Narrator	And he removed his sandal. Then Boaz announced to the elders and all the people:
Boaz	Today you are witnesses that I have bought from Naomi all the property of Elimelech, Kilion and Mahlon. I have also acquired Ruth the Moabitess, Mahlon's widow, as my wife, in order to maintain the name of the dead with his property, so that his name will not disappear from among his family or from the town records. Today you are witnesses! (PAUSE) Then the elders and all those at the gate said:
Elder 1	We are witnesses.
Elder 2	May the LORD make the woman who is coming into your home like Rachel and Leah, who together built up the house of Israel.
Elder 3	May you have standing in Ephrathah and be famous in Bethlehem.
Elder 1	Through the offspring the LORD gives you by this young woman, may your family be like that of Perez, whom Tamar bore to Judah.
Narrator	So Boaz took Ruth and she became his wife. Then he went to her, and the LORD enabled her to conceive, and she gave birth to a son. The women said to Naomi:
Woman 1	Praise be to the LORD, who this day has not left you without a kinsman-redeemer.
Woman 2	May he become famous throughout Israel!
Woman 1	He will renew your life and sustain you in your old age.
Woman 2	For your daughter-in-law, who loves you and who is better to you than seven sons, has given him birth.
Narrator	Then Naomi took the child, laid him in her lap and cared for him. The women living there said:
Women 1 and 2	Naomi has a son.
Narrator	And they named him Obed. He was the father of Jesse, the father of David. This, then, is the family line of Perez: Perez was the father of Hezron, Hezron the father of Ram, Ram the father of Amminadab, Amminadab the father of Nahshon, Nahshon the father of Salmon, Salmon the father of Boaz, Boaz the father of Obed, Obed the father of Jesse, and Jesse the father of David.

Cast: **Narrator**, **Boaz**, **Man**, **Elder 1**, **Elder 2** (can be the same as Elder 1), **Elder 3**, **Woman 1**, **Woman 2**

1 Samuel

The Birth of Samuel

From 1 Samuel 1:1–20

Narrator   There was a certain man from Ramathaim, a Zuphite from the hill country of Ephraim, whose name was Elkanah son of Jeroham, the son of Elihu, the son of Tohu, the son of Zuph, an Ephraimite. . . .

Year after year this man went up from his town to worship and sacrifice to the LORD Almighty at Shiloh, where Hophni and Phinehas, the two sons of Eli, were priests of the LORD. Whenever the day came for Elkanah to sacrifice, he would give portions of the meat to his wife Peninnah and to all her sons and daughters. But to Hannah he gave a double portion because he loved her, and the LORD had closed her womb. And because the LORD had closed her womb, her rival kept provoking her in order to irritate her. This went on year after year. Whenever Hannah went up to the house of the LORD, her rival provoked her till she wept and would not eat. Elkanah her husband would say to her:

Elkanah   Hannah, why are you weeping? Why don't you eat? Why are you downhearted? Don't I mean more to you than ten sons?

Narrator   Once when they had finished eating and drinking in Shiloh, Hannah stood up. Now Eli the priest was sitting on a chair by the doorpost of the LORD's temple. In bitterness of soul Hannah wept much and prayed to the LORD. And she made a vow:

Hannah
(praying)   O LORD Almighty, if you will only look upon your servant's misery and remember me, and not forget your servant but give her a son, then I will give him to the LORD for all the days of his life, and no razor will ever be used on his head.

Narrator   As she kept on praying to the LORD, Eli observed her mouth. Hannah was praying in her heart, and her lips were moving but her voice was not heard. Eli thought she was drunk:

Eli (severely)   How long will you keep on getting drunk? Get rid of your wine.

Hannah
(sadly)   Not so, my lord. I am a woman who is deeply troubled. I have not been drinking wine or beer; I was pouring out my soul to the LORD. Do not take your servant for a wicked woman; I have been praying here out of my great anguish and grief.

Eli (with
compassion)   Go in peace, and may the God of Israel grant you what you have asked of him.

Hannah
(pleased)   May your servant find favor in your eyes.

Narrator	Then she went her way and ate something, and her face was no longer downcast.
	Early the next morning they arose and worshiped before the LORD and then went back to their home at Ramah. Elkanah lay with Hannah his wife, and the LORD remembered her. So in the course of time Hannah conceived and gave birth to a son. She named him
Hannah (slowly)	Samuel.
Narrator	Saying,
Hannah	Because I asked the LORD for him.

Cast: **Narrator, Elkanah, Hannah, Eli**

Hannah Dedicates Samuel

1 Samuel 1:21–2:11

Narrator	When the man Elkanah went up with all his family to offer the annual sacrifice to the LORD and to fulfill his vow, Hannah did not go. [She said to her husband,]
Hannah (to Elkanah)	After the boy is weaned, I will take him and present him before the LORD, and he will live there always.
[Narrator	Elkanah her husband told her,]
Elkanah (to Hannah)	Do what seems best to you. Stay here until you have weaned him; only may the LORD make good his word.
Narrator	So the woman stayed at home and nursed her son until she had weaned him.
	After he was weaned, she took the boy with her, young as he was, along with a three-year-old bull, an ephah of flour and a skin of wine, and brought him to the house of the LORD at Shiloh. When they had slaughtered the bull, they brought the boy to Eli [and she said to him,]
Hannah	As surely as you live, my lord, I am the woman who stood here beside you praying to the LORD. I prayed for this child, and the LORD has granted me what I asked of him. So now I give him to the LORD. For his whole life he will be given over to the LORD.
Narrator	And he worshiped the LORD there. [Then Hannah prayed and said:]
Hannah (praying)	My heart rejoices in the LORD; in the LORD my horn is lifted high. My mouth boasts over my enemies, for I delight in your deliverance.

There is no one holy like the LORD;
    there is no one besides you;
there is no Rock like our God.

Do not keep talking so proudly
    or let your mouth speak such arrogance,
for the LORD is a God who knows,
    and by him deeds are weighed.

The bows of the warriors are broken,
    but those who stumbled are armed with strength.
Those who were full hire themselves out for food,
    but those who were hungry hunger no more.
She who was barren has borne seven children,
    but she who has had many sons pines away.

The LORD brings death and makes alive;
    he brings down to the grave and raises up.
The LORD sends poverty and wealth;
    he humbles and he exalts.
He raises the poor from the dust
    and lifts the needy from the ash heap;
he seats them with princes
    and has them inherit a throne of honor.

For the foundations of the earth are the LORD's;
    upon them he has set the world.
He will guard the feet of his saints,
    but the wicked will be silenced in darkness.

It is not by strength that one prevails;
    those who oppose the LORD will be shattered.
He will thunder against them from heaven;
    the LORD will judge the ends of the earth.

He will give strength to his king
    and exalt the horn of his anointed.

Narrator   Then Elkanah went home to Ramah, but the boy ministered before the LORD under Eli the priest.

Cast: **Narrator, Hannah, Elkanah**

Eli's Wicked Sons

1 Samuel 2:12–26

Narrator   Eli's sons were wicked men; they had no regard for the LORD. Now it was the practice of the priests with the people that whenever anyone offered a sacrifice and while the meat was being boiled, the servant of the priest would come with a three-pronged fork in his hand. He would plunge it into the pan or kettle or caldron or pot, and the priest would take for him-

243

	self whatever the fork brought up. This is how they treated all the Israelites who came to Shiloh. But even before the fat was burned, the servant of the priest would come and say to the man who was sacrificing:
Servant	Give the priest some meat to roast; he won't accept boiled meat from you, but only raw.
Narrator	If the man said to him:
Man	Let the fat be burned up first, and then take whatever you want,
Narrator	The servant would then answer,
Servant	No, hand it over now; if you don't, I'll take it by force.
Narrator	This sin of the young men was very great in the LORD's sight, for they were treating the LORD's offering with contempt.
	But Samuel was ministering before the LORD—a boy wearing a linen ephod. Each year his mother made him a little robe and took it to him when she went up with her husband to offer the annual sacrifice. Eli would bless Elkanah and his wife:
Eli	May the LORD give you children by this woman to take the place of the one she prayed for and gave to the LORD.
Narrator	Then they would go home. And the LORD was gracious to Hannah; she conceived and gave birth to three sons and two daughters. Meanwhile, the boy Samuel grew up in the presence of the LORD.
	Now Eli, who was very old, heard about everything his sons were doing to all Israel and how they slept with the women who served at the entrance to the Tent of Meeting. So he said to them:
Eli	Why do you do such things? I hear from all the people about these wicked deeds of yours. No, my sons; it is not a good report that I hear spreading among the LORD's people. If a man sins against another man, God may mediate for him; but if a man sins against the LORD, who will intercede for him?
Narrator	His sons, however, did not listen to their father's rebuke, for it was the LORD's will to put them to death.
	And the boy Samuel continued to grow in stature and in favor with the LORD and with men.

Cast: **Narrator, Servant, Man, Eli**

The Lord Calls Samuel

1 Samuel 3:1–10

Narrator	The boy Samuel ministered before the LORD under Eli. In those days the word of the LORD was rare; there were not many visions.

One night Eli, whose eyes were becoming so weak that he could barely see, was lying down in his usual place. The lamp of God had not yet gone out, and Samuel was lying down in the temple of the LORD, where the ark of God was. Then the LORD called Samuel. Samuel answered:

Samuel   Here I am.

Narrator   And he ran to Eli [and said:]

Samuel
(to Eli)   Here I am; you called me.

[Narrator   But Eli said:]

Eli   *I* did not call; go back and lie down.

Narrator   So he went and lay down. Again the LORD called:

The Lord
(voice only)   Samuel!

Narrator   And Samuel got up and went to Eli [and said:]

Samuel   Here I am; you called me.

Eli   My son, I did *not* call; go back and lie down.

Narrator   Now Samuel did not yet know the LORD: The word of the LORD had not yet been revealed to him.

The LORD called Samuel a third time, and Samuel got up and went to Eli [and said:]

Samuel   Here I am; you called me.

Narrator   Then Eli realized that the LORD was calling the boy. So Eli told Samuel:

Eli   Go and lie down, and if he calls you, say, "Speak, LORD, for your servant is listening."

Narrator   So Samuel went and lay down in his place. (PAUSE) The LORD came and stood there, calling as at the other times:

The Lord
(voice)   Samuel! Samuel!

Narrator   Then Samuel said:

Samuel   Speak, for your servant is listening.

Cast: **Narrator, Samuel** (as a boy), **Eli, the Lord** (voice only)

The Lord's Message to Eli

1 Samuel 3:11–4:1a

Narrator   And the LORD said to Samuel:

The Lord

(voice only)   See, I am about to do something in Israel that will make the ears of everyone who hears of it tingle. At that time I will carry out against Eli everything I spoke against his family—from beginning to end. For I told him that I would judge his family forever because of the sin he knew about; his sons made themselves contemptible, and he failed to restrain them. Therefore, I swore to the house of Eli, "The guilt of Eli's house will never be atoned for by sacrifice or offering."

Narrator   Samuel lay down until morning and then opened the doors of the house of the LORD. He was afraid to tell Eli the vision, but Eli called him:

Eli   Samuel, my son.

Samuel   Here I am.

Eli   What was it he said to you? Do not hide it from me. May God deal with you, be it ever so severely, if you hide from me anything he told you.

Narrator   So Samuel told him everything, hiding nothing from him. [Then Eli said:]

Eli (sadly)   He is the LORD; let him do what is good in his eyes.

Narrator   The LORD was with Samuel as he grew up, and he let none of his words fall to the ground. And all Israel from Dan to Beersheba recognized that Samuel was attested as a prophet of the LORD. The LORD continued to appear at Shiloh, and there he revealed himself to Samuel through his word.

And Samuel's word came to all Israel.

Cast: **Narrator, the Lord, Eli, Samuel** (as a boy)

The Philistines Capture the Ark

1 Samuel 4:1b–11

Narrator   The Israelites went out to fight against the Philistines. The Israelites camped at Ebenezer, and the Philistines at Aphek. The Philistines deployed their forces to meet Israel, and as the battle spread, Israel was defeated by the Philistines, who killed about four thousand of them on the battlefield. When the soldiers returned to camp, the elders of Israel asked:

Elder 1   Why did the LORD bring defeat upon us today before the Philistines?

Elder 2   Let us bring the ark of the LORD's covenant from Shiloh, so that it may go with us and save us from the hand of our enemies. (PAUSE)

Narrator   So the people sent men to Shiloh, and they brought back the ark of the covenant of the LORD Almighty, who is enthroned between the cherubim. And Eli's two sons, Hophni and Phinehas, were there with the ark of the covenant of God.

When the ark of the LORD's covenant came into the camp, all Israel raised such a great shout that the ground shook. Hearing the uproar, the Philistines asked:

Philistine 1   What's all this shouting in the Hebrew camp?

Narrator   When they learned that the ark of the LORD had come into the camp, the Philistines were afraid.

Philistine 1   A god has come into the camp.

Philistine 2   We're in trouble!

Philistine 3   Nothing like this has happened before.

Philistine 1   Woe to us!

Philistine 2   Who will deliver us from the hand of these mighty gods?

Philistine 3   They are the gods who struck the Egyptians with all kinds of plagues in the desert.

Philistine 2   Be strong, Philistines!

Philistine 1   Be men, or you will be subject to the Hebrews, as they have been to you. Be men, and fight!

Narrator   So the Philistines fought, and the Israelites were defeated and every man fled to his tent. The slaughter was very great; Israel lost thirty thousand foot soldiers. The ark of God was captured, and Eli's two sons, Hophni and Phinehas, died.

Cast: **Narrator**, **Elder 1**, **Elder 2** (can be the same as Elder 1), **Philistine 1**, **Philistine 2**, **Philistine 3**

Death of Eli

1 Samuel 4:12–22

Narrator   [That same day] a Benjamite ran from the battle line and went to Shiloh, his clothes torn and dust on his head. When he arrived, there was Eli sitting on his chair by the side of the road, watching, because his heart feared for the ark of God. When the man entered the town and told what had happened, the whole town sent up a cry. Eli heard the outcry [and asked:]

Eli   What is the meaning of this uproar?

Narrator   The man hurried over to Eli, who was ninety-eight years old and whose eyes were set so that he could not see. [He told Eli:]

Man   I have just come from the battle line; I fled from it this very day.

247

Eli	What happened, my son?
Narrator	The man who brought the news replied:
Man	Israel fled before the Philistines, and the army has suffered heavy losses. Also your two sons, Hophni and Phinehas, are dead, and the ark of God has been captured.
Narrator	When he mentioned the ark of God, Eli fell backward off his chair by the side of the gate. His neck was broken and he died, for he was an old man and heavy. He had led Israel forty years.
	His daughter-in-law, the wife of Phinehas, was pregnant and near the time of delivery. When she heard the news that the ark of God had been captured and that her father-in-law and her husband were dead, she went into labor and gave birth, but was overcome by her labor pains. As she was dying, the women attending her said:
Woman 1	Don't despair.
Woman 2	You have given birth to a son.
Narrator	But she did not respond or pay any attention.
	She named the boy Ichabod [saying:]
Wife	The glory has departed from Israel—
Narrator	Because of the capture of the ark of God and the deaths of her father-in-law and her husband. [She said:]
Wife	The glory has departed from Israel, for the ark of God has been captured.

Cast: **Narrator, Eli, Man, Woman 1, Woman 2** (can be the same as Woman 1), **Wife**

The Ark Returned to Israel

1 Samuel 6:1–16

Narrator	When the ark of the Lord had been in Philistine territory seven months, the Philistines called for the priests and the diviners [and said:]
Person 1	What shall we do with the ark of the Lord?
Person 2	Tell us how we should send it back to its place.
Priest	If you return the ark of the god of Israel, do not send it away empty.
Diviner	But by all means send a guilt offering to him. Then you will be healed, and you will know why his hand has not been lifted from you.
Person 1	What guilt offering should we send to him?
Diviner	Five gold tumors and five gold rats, according to the number of the Philistine rulers, because the same plague has struck both you and your rulers.

Priest	Make models of the tumors and of the rats that are destroying the country, and pay honor to Israel's god. Perhaps he will lift his hand from you and your gods and your land. Why do you harden your hearts as the Egyptians and Pharaoh did? When he treated them harshly, did they not send the Israelites out so they could go on their way?
Diviner	Now then, get a new cart ready, with two cows that have calved and have never been yoked. Hitch the cows to the cart, but take their calves away and pen them up.
Priest	Take the ark of the LORD and put it on the cart, and in a chest beside it put the gold objects you are sending back to him as a guilt offering.
Diviner	Send it on its way, but keep watching it. If it goes up to its own territory, toward Beth Shemesh, then the LORD has brought this great disaster on us. But if it does not, then we will know that it was not his hand that struck us and that it happened to us by chance.
Narrator	So they did this. They took two such cows and hitched them to the cart and penned up their calves. They placed the ark of the LORD on the cart and along with it the chest containing the gold rats and the models of the tumors. Then the cows went straight up toward Beth Shemesh, keeping on the road and lowing all the way; they did not turn to the right or to the left. The rulers of the Philistines followed them as far as the border of Beth Shemesh. (PAUSE)
	Now the people of Beth Shemesh were harvesting their wheat in the valley, and when they looked up and saw the ark, they rejoiced at the sight. The cart came to the field of Joshua of Beth Shemesh, and there it stopped beside a large rock. The people chopped up the wood of the cart and sacrificed the cows as a burnt offering to the LORD. The Levites took down the ark of the LORD, together with the chest containing the gold objects, and placed them on the large rock. On that day the people of Beth Shemesh offered burnt offerings and made sacrifices to the LORD. The five rulers of the Philistines saw all this and then returned that same day to Ekron.

Cast: **Narrator, Person 1, Person 2** (can be the same as Person 1), **Priest, Diviner**

The Ark at Kiriath Jearim

1 Samuel 6:18b–7:1

Narrator	The large rock, on which they set the ark of the LORD, is a witness to this day in the field of Joshua of Beth Shemesh.
	But God struck down some of the men of Beth Shemesh, putting seventy of them to death because they had looked into the ark of the LORD. The people mourned because of the heavy blow the LORD had dealt them, and the men of Beth Shemesh asked:

Man 1	Who can stand in the presence of the LORD, this holy God?
Man 2	To whom will the ark go up from here?
Narrator	Then they sent messengers to the people of Kiriath Jearim [saying:]
Messenger 1	The Philistines have returned the ark of the LORD.
Messenger 2	Come down and take it up to your place.
Narrator	So the men of Kiriath Jearim came and took up the ark of the LORD. They took it to Abinadab's house on the hill and consecrated Eleazar his son to guard the ark of the LORD.

Cast: **Narrator**, **Man 1**, **Man 2** (can be the same as Man 1), **Messenger 1**, **Messenger 2** (can be the same as Messenger 1)

Samuel Subdues the Philistines at Mizpah

1 Samuel 7:2–14

Narrator	It was a long time, twenty years in all, that the ark remained at Kiriath Jearim, and all the people of Israel mourned and sought after the LORD. And Samuel said to the whole house of Israel:
Samuel	If you are returning to the LORD with all your hearts, then rid yourselves of the foreign gods and the Ashtoreths and commit yourselves to the LORD and serve him only, and he will deliver you out of the hand of the Philistines.
Narrator	So the Israelites put away their Baals and Ashtoreths, and served the LORD only. Then Samuel said:
Samuel	Assemble all Israel at Mizpah and I will intercede with the LORD for you.
Narrator	When they had assembled at Mizpah, they drew water and poured it out before the LORD. On that day they fasted and there they confessed:
Israelite	We have sinned against the LORD.
Narrator	And Samuel was leader of Israel at Mizpah.
	When the Philistines heard that Israel had assembled at Mizpah, the rulers of the Philistines came up to attack them. And when the Israelites heard of it, they were afraid because of the Philistines. They said to Samuel:
Israelite	Do not stop crying out to the LORD our God for us, that he may rescue us from the hand of the Philistines.
Narrator	Then Samuel took a suckling lamb and offered it up as a whole burnt offering to the LORD. He cried out to the LORD on Israel's behalf, and the LORD answered him.

While Samuel was sacrificing the burnt offering, the Philistines drew near to engage Israel in battle. But that day the LORD thundered with loud thunder against the Philistines and threw them into such a panic that they were routed before the Israelites. The men of Israel rushed out of Mizpah and pursued the Philistines, slaughtering them along the way to a point below Beth Car.

Then Samuel took a stone and set it up between Mizpah and Shen. He named it Ebenezer, saying:

Samuel   Thus far has the LORD helped us.

Narrator   So the Philistines were subdued and did not invade Israelite territory again.

Throughout Samuel's lifetime, the hand of the LORD was against the Philistines. The towns from Ekron to Gath that the Philistines had captured from Israel were restored to her, and Israel delivered the neighboring territory from the power of the Philistines. And there was peace between Israel and the Amorites.

Cast: **Narrator, Samuel, Israelite**

Israel Asks for a King

1 Samuel 7:15–8:22

Narrator   Samuel continued as judge over Israel all the days of his life. From year to year he went on a circuit from Bethel to Gilgal to Mizpah, judging Israel in all those places. But he always went back to Ramah, where his home was, and there he also judged Israel. And he built an altar there to the LORD.

When Samuel grew old, he appointed his sons as judges for Israel. The name of his firstborn was Joel and the name of his second was Abijah, and they served at Beersheba. But his sons did not walk in his ways. They turned aside after dishonest gain and accepted bribes and perverted justice.

So all the elders of Israel gathered together and came to Samuel at Ramah. They said to him:

Leader   You are old, and your sons do not walk in your ways; now appoint a king to lead us, such as all the other nations have. . . .

Narrator   This displeased Samuel; so he prayed to the LORD. And the LORD told him:

The Lord
(voice only)   Listen to all that the people are saying to you; it is not you they have rejected, but they have rejected me as their king. As they have done from the day I brought them up out of Egypt until this day, forsaking me and serving other gods, so they are doing to you. Now listen to them; but

251

	warn them solemnly and let them know what the king who will reign over them will do.
Narrator	Samuel told all the words of the Lord to the people who were asking him for a king.
Samuel	This is what the king who will reign over you will do: He will take your sons and make them serve with his chariots and horses, and they will run in front of his chariots. Some he will assign to be commanders of thousands and commanders of fifties, and others to plow his ground and reap his harvest, and still others to make weapons of war and equipment for his chariots. He will take your daughters to be perfumers and cooks and bakers. He will take the best of your fields and vineyards and olive groves and give them to his attendants. He will take a tenth of your grain and of your vintage and give it to his officials and attendants. Your menservants and maidservants and the best of your cattle and donkeys he will take for his own use. He will take a tenth of your flocks, and you yourselves will become his slaves. When that day comes, you will cry out for relief from the king you have chosen, and the Lord will not answer you in that day.
Narrator	But the people refused to listen to Samuel.
Person 1	No!
Person 2	We want a king over us.
Person 1	Then we will be like all the other nations.
Person 2	With a king to lead us and to go out before us and fight our battles.
Narrator	When Samuel heard all that the people said, he repeated it before the Lord.
The Lord (voice)	Listen to them and give them a king.
Narrator	Then Samuel said to the men of Israel,
Samuel	Everyone go back to his town.

Cast: **Narrator, Leader, the Lord** (voice only), **Samuel, Person 1, Person 2** (can be the same as Leader, or both Person 1 and Person 2 can be the same as Leader)

Samuel Anoints Saul

1 Samuel 9:1–10:1

Narrator	There was a Benjamite, a man of standing, whose name was Kish son of Abiel, the son of Zeror, the son of Becorath, the son of Aphiah of Benjamin. He had a son named Saul, an impressive young man without equal among the Israelites—a head taller than any of the others.

	Now the donkeys belonging to Saul's father Kish were lost, and Kish said to his son Saul:
Kish	Take one of the servants with you and go and look for the donkeys.
Narrator	So he passed through the hill country of Ephraim and through the area around Shalisha, but they did not find them. They went on into the district of Shaalim, but the donkeys were not there. Then he passed through the territory of Benjamin, but they did not find them.
	When they reached the district of Zuph, Saul said to the servant who was with him:
Saul	Come, let's go back, or my father will stop thinking about the donkeys and start worrying about us.
[Narrator	But the servant replied:]
Servant (respectfully)	Look, in this town there is a man of God; he is highly respected, and everything he says comes true. Let's go there now. Perhaps he will tell us what way to take.
Narrator	Saul said to his servant:
Saul	If we go, what can we give the man? The food in our sacks is gone. We have no gift to take to the man of God. What do we have? . . .
Servant	Look, I have a quarter of a shekel of silver. I will give it to the man of God so that he will tell us what way to take.
[Narrator	(Formerly in Israel, if a man went to inquire of God, he would say, "Come, let us go to the seer," because the prophet of today used to be called a seer.)]
Saul	Good. Come, let's go.
Narrator	So they set out for the town where the man of God was.
	As they were going up the hill to the town, they met some girls coming out to draw water, and they asked them:
Servant	Is the seer here?
Girls 1 and 2	He is.
Girl 1	He's ahead of you.
Girl 2	Hurry now; he has just come to our town today, for the people have a sacrifice at the high place.
Girl 1	As soon as you enter the town, you will find him before he goes up to the high place to eat.
Girl 2	The people will not begin eating until he comes, because he must bless the sacrifice; afterward, those who are invited will eat.
Girl 1	Go up now; you should find him about this time.

Narrator	They went up to the town, and as they were entering it, there was Samuel, coming toward them on his way up to the high place.
	Now the day before Saul came, the LORD had revealed this to Samuel:
The Lord (voice only)	About this time tomorrow I will send you a man from the land of Benjamin. Anoint him leader over my people Israel; he will deliver my people from the hand of the Philistines. I have looked upon my people, for their cry has reached me.
Narrator	When Samuel caught sight of Saul, the LORD said to him:
The Lord (voice)	This is the man I spoke to you about; he will govern my people.
Narrator	Saul approached Samuel in the gateway and asked:
Saul	Would you please tell me where the seer's house is?
Samuel	I *am* the seer. Go up ahead of me to the high place, for today you are to eat with me, and in the morning I will let you go and will tell you all that is in your heart. As for the donkeys you lost three days ago, do not worry about them; they have been found. And to whom is all the desire of Israel turned, if not to you and all your father's family?
Saul	But am I not a Benjamite, from the smallest tribe of Israel, and is not my clan the least of all the clans of the tribe of Benjamin? Why do you say such a thing to me?
Narrator	Then Samuel brought Saul and his servant into the hall and seated them at the head of those who were invited—about thirty in number. Samuel said to the cook:
Samuel	Bring the piece of meat I gave you, the one I told you to lay aside.
Narrator	So the cook took up the leg with what was on it and set it in front of Saul.
Samuel	Here is what has been kept for you. Eat, because it was set aside for you for this occasion, from the time I said, "I have invited guests."
Narrator	And Saul dined with Samuel that day.
	After they came down from the high place to the town, Samuel talked with Saul on the roof of his house. They rose about daybreak and Samuel called to Saul on the roof:
Samuel	Get ready, and I will send you on your way.
Narrator	When Saul got ready, he and Samuel went outside together. As they were going down to the edge of the town, Samuel said to Saul:
Samuel	Tell the servant to go on ahead of us . . . but you stay here awhile, so that I may give you a message from God.
Narrator	Then Samuel took a flask of oil and poured it on Saul's head and kissed him [saying:]

Samuel
(to Saul)   Has not the LORD anointed you leader over his inheritance?

Cast: **Narrator, Kish, Saul** (younger than his father, Kish), **Servant, Girl 1, Girl 2, the Lord** (voice only), **Samuel**

Samuel and Saul

1 Samuel 10:1–2, 9–16

Narrator   Samuel took a flask of oil and poured it on Saul's head and kissed him, saying:

Samuel   Has not the LORD anointed you leader over his inheritance? When you leave me today, you will meet two men near Rachel's tomb, at Zelzah on the border of Benjamin. They will say to you, "The donkeys you set out to look for have been found. And now your father has stopped thinking about them and is worried about you. He is asking, 'What shall I do about my son?'" . . .

Narrator   As Saul turned to leave Samuel, God changed Saul's heart, and all these signs were fulfilled that day. When they arrived at Gibeah, a procession of prophets met him; the Spirit of God came upon him in power, and he joined in their prophesying. When all those who had formerly known him saw him prophesying with the prophets, they asked each other:

Person 1   What is this that has happened to the son of Kish?

Person 2   Is Saul also among the prophets?

Narrator   A man who lived there answered:

Man   And who is their father?

Narrator   So it became a saying, "Is Saul also among the prophets?" (PAUSE) After Saul stopped prophesying, he went to the high place.

Now Saul's uncle asked him and his servant:

Uncle   Where have you been?

Saul   Looking for the donkeys. But when we saw they were not to be found, we went to Samuel.

Uncle   Tell me what Samuel said to you.

Saul   He assured us that the donkeys had been found.

Narrator   But he did not tell his uncle what Samuel had said about the kingship.

Cast: **Narrator, Samuel, Person 1, Person 2, Man** (can be the same as Person 1), **Uncle, Saul**

Saul Made King

1 Samuel 10:17–27

Narrator   Samuel summoned the people of Israel to the Lord at Mizpah:

Samuel   This is what the Lord, the God of Israel, says:

The Lord
(voice only)   I brought Israel up out of Egypt, and I delivered you from the power of Egypt and all the kingdoms that oppressed you.

Samuel   But you have now rejected your God, who saves you out of all your calamities and distresses. And you have said:

Person 1   No, set a king over us.

Samuel   So now present yourselves before the Lord by your tribes and clans.

Narrator   When Samuel brought all the tribes of Israel near, the tribe of Benjamin was chosen. Then he brought forward the tribe of Benjamin, clan by clan, and Matri's clan was chosen. Finally Saul son of Kish was chosen. But when they looked for him, he was not to be found. So they inquired further of the Lord:

Person 2   Has the man come here yet?

[Narrator   And the Lord said:]

The Lord
(voice)   Yes, he has hidden himself among the baggage.

Narrator   They ran and brought him out, and as he stood among the people he was a head taller than any of the others. Samuel said to all the people:

Samuel   Do you see the man the Lord has chosen? There is no one like him among all the people.

[Narrator   Then the people shouted:]

Persons 1
and 2   Long live the king!

Narrator   Samuel explained to the people the regulations of the kingship. He wrote them down on a scroll and deposited it before the Lord. Then Samuel dismissed the people, each to his own home.

Saul also went to his home in Gibeah, accompanied by valiant men whose hearts God had touched. But some troublemakers said:

Person 2   How can this fellow save us?

Narrator   They despised him and brought him no gifts. But Saul kept silent.

Cast: **Narrator, Samuel, the Lord** (voice only; can be the same as Samuel), **Person 1, Person 2**

Saul Rescues the City of Jabesh

1 Samuel 11:1–15

Narrator	Nahash the Ammonite went up and besieged Jabesh Gilead. And all the men of Jabesh said to him:
Man 1	Make a treaty with us.
Man 2	And we will be subject to you.
Narrator	But Nahash the Ammonite replied:
Nahash	I will make a treaty with you only on the condition that I gouge out the right eye of every one of you and so bring disgrace on all Israel.
Narrator	The elders of Jabesh said to him:
Elder 1	Give us seven days so we can send messengers throughout Israel.
Elder 2	If no one comes to rescue us, we will surrender to you.
Narrator	When the messengers came to Gibeah of Saul and reported these terms to the people, they all wept aloud. Just then Saul was returning from the fields, behind his oxen, and he asked:
Saul	What is wrong with the people? Why are they weeping?
Narrator	Then they repeated to him what the men of Jabesh had said.
	When Saul heard their words, the Spirit of God came upon him in power, and he burned with anger. He took a pair of oxen, cut them into pieces, and sent the pieces by messengers throughout Israel, proclaiming:
Saul	This is what will be done to the oxen of anyone who does not follow Saul and Samuel.
Narrator	Then the terror of the LORD fell on the people, and they turned out as one man. When Saul mustered them at Bezek, the men of Israel numbered three hundred thousand and the men of Judah thirty thousand.
	They told the messengers who had come:
Saul	Say to the men of Jabesh Gilead, "By the time the sun is hot tomorrow, you will be delivered."
Narrator	When the messengers went and reported this to the men of Jabesh, they were elated. They said to the Ammonites:
Person 1 (cunningly)	Tomorrow we will surrender to you.
Person 2 (cunningly)	And you can do to us whatever seems good to you.
Narrator	The next day Saul separated his men into three divisions; during the last watch of the night they broke into the camp of the Ammonites and

slaughtered them until the heat of the day. Those who survived were scattered, so that no two of them were left together.

The people then said to Samuel:

Person 1　Who was it that asked, "Shall Saul reign over us?"

Person 2　Bring these men to us and we will put them to death.

Saul　No one shall be put to death today, for this day the LORD has rescued Israel.

Narrator　Then Samuel said to the people:

Samuel　Come, let us go to Gilgal and there reaffirm the kingship.

Narrator　So all the people went to Gilgal and confirmed Saul as king in the presence of the LORD. There they sacrificed fellowship offerings before the LORD, and Saul and all the Israelites held a great celebration.

Cast: **Narrator, Man 1, Man 2, Nahash, Elder 1, Elder 2, Saul, Person 1, Person 2, Samuel.** (Man 1, Leader 1, Person 1 can be the same; Man 2, Leader 2, Person 2 can be the same.)

Samuel's Farewell Speech

1 Samuel 12:1–15

Narrator　Samuel said to all Israel:

Samuel　I have listened to everything you said to me and have set a king over you. Now you have a king as your leader. As for me, I am old and gray, and my sons are here with you. I have been your leader from my youth until this day. Here I stand. Testify against me in the presence of the LORD and his anointed. Whose ox have I taken? Whose donkey have I taken? Whom have I cheated? Whom have I oppressed? From whose hand have I accepted a bribe to make me shut my eyes? If I have done any of these, I will make it right.

Narrator　[They replied,]

Person 1　You have not cheated or oppressed us.

Person 2　You have not taken anything from anyone's hand.

Narrator　Samuel said to [them]:

Samuel　The LORD is witness against you, and also his anointed is witness this day, that you have not found anything in my hand.

Persons 1 and 2　He is witness.

Samuel　It is the LORD who appointed Moses and Aaron and brought your forefathers up out of Egypt. Now then, stand here, because I am going to confront you with evidence before the LORD as to all the righteous acts performed by the LORD for you and your fathers.

After Jacob entered Egypt, they cried to the LORD for help, and the LORD sent Moses and Aaron, who brought your forefathers out of Egypt and settled them in this place.

But they forgot the LORD their God; so he sold them into the hand of Sisera, the commander of the army of Hazor, and into the hands of the Philistines and the king of Moab, who fought against them. They cried out to the LORD and said:

Person 1   We have sinned; we have forsaken the LORD and served the Baals and the Ashtoreths.

Person 2   But now deliver us from the hands of our enemies, and we will serve you.

Samuel   Then the LORD sent Jerub-Baal, Barak, Jephthah and Samuel, and he delivered you from the hands of your enemies on every side, so that you lived securely.

But when you saw that Nahash king of the Ammonites was moving against you, you said to me:

**Persons 1
and 2**   No, we want a *king* to rule over us—

Samuel   Even though the LORD your God was your king.

Now here is the king you have chosen, the one you asked for; see, the LORD has set a king over you. If you fear the LORD and serve and obey him and do not rebel against his commands, and if both you and the king who reigns over you follow the LORD your God—good! But if you do not obey the LORD, and if you rebel against his commands, his hand will be against you, as it was against your fathers.

Cast: **Narrator, Samuel, Person 1, Person 2**

Samuel's Sign

1 Samuel 12:16–25

[Narrator   Samuel said:]

Samuel   Stand still and see this great thing the LORD is about to do before your eyes! Is it not wheat harvest now? I will call upon the LORD to send thunder and rain. And you will realize what an evil thing you did in the eyes of the LORD when you asked for a king.

Narrator   Then Samuel called upon the LORD, and that same day the LORD sent thunder and rain. So all the people stood in awe of the LORD and of Samuel.

259

	The people all said to Samuel:
Person 1	Pray to the LORD your God for your servants so that we will not die.
Person 2	For we have added to all our other sins the evil of asking for a king.
Samuel	Do not be afraid. You have done all this evil; yet do not turn away from the LORD, but serve the LORD with all your heart. Do not turn away after useless idols. They can do you no good, nor can they rescue you, because they are useless. For the sake of his great name the LORD will not reject his people, because the LORD was pleased to make you his own. As for me, far be it from me that I should sin against the LORD by failing to pray for you. And I will teach you the way that is good and right. But be sure to fear the LORD and serve him faithfully with all your heart; consider what great things he has done for you. Yet if you persist in doing evil, both you and your king will be swept away.

Cast: **Narrator, Samuel, Person 1, Person 2**

Samuel Rebukes Saul

1 Samuel 13:5–14

Narrator	The Philistines assembled to fight Israel, with three thousand chariots, six thousand charioteers, and soldiers as numerous as the sand on the seashore. They went up and camped at Micmash, east of Beth Aven. When the men of Israel saw that their situation was critical and that their army was hard pressed, they hid in caves and thickets, among the rocks, and in pits and cisterns. Some Hebrews even crossed the Jordan to the land of Gad and Gilead.
	Saul remained at Gilgal, and all the troops with him were quaking with fear. He waited seven days, the time set by Samuel; but Samuel did not come to Gilgal, and Saul's men began to scatter. So he said:
Saul	Bring me the burnt offering and the fellowship offerings.
Narrator	And Saul offered up the burnt offering. Just as he finished making the offering, Samuel arrived, and Saul went out to greet him.
Samuel	What have you done?
Saul	When I saw that the men were scattering, and that you did not come at the set time, and that the Philistines were assembling at Micmash, I thought, "Now the Philistines will come down against me at Gilgal, and I have not sought the LORD's favor." So I felt compelled to offer the burnt offering.
Samuel	You acted foolishly. You have not kept the command the LORD your God gave you; if you had, he would have established your kingdom over Israel for all time. But now your kingdom will not endure; the LORD has sought

out a man after his own heart and appointed him leader of his people, because you have not kept the LORD's command.

Cast: **Narrator, Saul, Samuel**

Jonathan Attacks the Philistines

1 Samuel 14:1–15

Narrator   One day Jonathan son of Saul said to the young man bearing his armor:

Jonathan   Come, let's go over to the Philistine outpost on the other side.

Narrator   But he did not tell his father.

Saul was staying on the outskirts of Gibeah under a pomegranate tree in Migron. With him were about six hundred men, among whom was Ahijah, who was wearing an ephod. He was a son of Ichabod's brother Ahitub son of Phinehas, the son of Eli, the LORD's priest in Shiloh. No one was aware that Jonathan had left. (PAUSE)

On each side of the pass that Jonathan intended to cross to reach the Philistine outpost was a cliff; one was called Bozez, and the other Seneh. One cliff stood to the north toward Micmash, the other to the south toward Geba.

Jonathan said to his young armor-bearer:

Jonathan   Come, let's go over to the outpost of those uncircumcised fellows. Perhaps the LORD will act in our behalf. Nothing can hinder the LORD from saving, whether by many or by few.

[Narrator   [His armor-bearer said]:]

Armor-bearer   Do all that you have in mind. Go ahead; I am with you heart and soul.

Jonathan   Come, then; we will cross over toward the men and let them see us. If they say to us, "Wait there until we come to you," we will stay where we are and not go up to them. But if they say, "Come up to us," we will climb up, because that will be our sign that the LORD has given them into our hands.

Narrator   So both of them showed themselves to the Philistine outpost. [The Philistines said:]

Philistine 2
   (taunting)   Look! The Hebrews are crawling out of the holes they were hiding in.

Narrator   The men of the outpost shouted to Jonathan and his armor-bearer:

Philistine 1   Come up to us and we'll teach you a lesson.

Narrator   So Jonathan said to his armor-bearer:

261

Jonathan (to Armor- bearer)	Climb up after me; the LORD has given them into the hand of Israel.
Narrator	Jonathan climbed up, using his hands and feet, with his armor-bearer right behind him. The Philistines fell before Jonathan, and his armor-bearer followed and killed behind him. (PAUSE) In that first attack Jonathan and his armor-bearer killed some twenty men in an area of about half an acre.
	Then panic struck the whole army—those in the camp and field, and those in the outposts and raiding parties—and the ground shook. It was a panic sent by God.

Cast: **Narrator, Jonathan, Armor-bearer, Philistine 1, Philistine 2** (can be the same as Philistine 1)

Israel Routs the Philistines

1 Samuel 14:16–23

Narrator	Saul's lookouts at Gibeah in Benjamin saw the army melting away in all directions. Then Saul said to the men who were with him:
Saul	Muster the forces and see who has left us.
Narrator	When they did, it was Jonathan and his armor-bearer who were not there. Saul said to Ahijah:
Saul	Bring the ark of God.
Narrator	(At that time it was with the Israelites.) While Saul was talking to the priest, the tumult in the Philistine camp increased more and more. So Saul said to the priest:
Saul	Withdraw your hand.
Narrator	Then Saul and all his men assembled and went to the battle. They found the Philistines in total confusion, striking each other with their swords. Those Hebrews who had previously been with the Philistines and had gone up with them to their camp went over to the Israelites who were with Saul and Jonathan. When all the Israelites who had hidden in the hill country of Ephraim heard that the Philistines were on the run, they joined the battle in hot pursuit. So the LORD rescued Israel that day, and the battle moved on beyond Beth Aven.

Cast: **Narrator, Saul**

Jonathan Eats Honey

1 Samuel 14:24–46

Narrator	Now the men of Israel were in distress that day, because Saul had bound the people under an oath, saying:

Saul	Cursed be any man who eats food before evening comes, before I have avenged myself on my enemies!
Narrator	So none of the troops tasted food.
	The entire army entered the woods, and there was honey on the ground. When they went into the woods, they saw the honey oozing out, yet no one put his hand to his mouth, because they feared the oath. But Jonathan had not heard that his father had bound the people with the oath, so he reached out the end of the staff that was in his hand and dipped it into the honeycomb. He raised his hand to his mouth, and his eyes brightened. Then one of the soldiers told him:
Soldier	Your father bound the army under a strict oath, saying, "Cursed be any man who eats food today!" That is why the men are faint.
Narrator	Jonathan said:
Jonathan	My father has made trouble for the country. See how my eyes brightened when I tasted a little of this honey. How much better it would have been if the men had eaten today some of the plunder they took from their enemies. Would not the slaughter of the Philistines have been even greater?
Narrator	That day, after the Israelites had struck down the Philistines from Micmash to Aijalon, they were exhausted. They pounced on the plunder and, taking sheep, cattle and calves, they butchered them on the ground and ate them, together with the blood. Then someone said to Saul:
Soldier	Look, the men are sinning against the Lord by eating meat that has blood in it.
Saul	You have broken faith. Roll a large stone over here at once.
[Narrator	Then he said:]
Saul	Go out among the men and tell them, "Each of you bring me your cattle and sheep, and slaughter them here and eat them. Do not sin against the Lord by eating meat with blood still in it."
Narrator	So everyone brought his ox that night and slaughtered it there. Then Saul built an altar to the Lord; it was the first time he had done this. (PAUSE)
	[Saul said:]
Saul	Let us go down after the Philistines by night and plunder them till dawn, and let us not leave one of them alive.
Soldier	Do whatever seems best to you.
Narrator	But the priest said:
Priest	Let us inquire of God here.
Narrator	So Saul asked God:

Saul	Shall I go down after the Philistines? Will you give them into Israel's hand?
Narrator	But God did not answer him that day. [Saul therefore said:]
Saul	Come here, all you who are leaders of the army, and let us find out what sin has been committed today. As surely as the LORD who rescues Israel lives, even if it lies with my son Jonathan, he must die.
Narrator	But not one of the men said a word.
	Saul then said to all the Israelites:
Saul	You stand over there; I and Jonathan my son will stand over here.
Man	Do what seems best to you.
Narrator	Then Saul prayed to the LORD, the God of Israel:
Saul	Give me the right answer.
Narrator	And Jonathan and Saul were taken by lot, and the men were cleared. [Saul said:]
Saul	Cast the lot between me and Jonathan my son.
Narrator	And Jonathan was taken.
	Then Saul said to Jonathan:
Saul (to Jonathan)	Tell me what you have done.
Narrator	So Jonathan told him:
Jonathan	I merely tasted a little honey with the end of my staff. And now must I *die*?
Saul	May God deal with me, be it ever so severely, if you do not die, Jonathan.
Person 1	Should Jonathan die—he who has brought about this great deliverance in Israel?
Person 1 and 2	Never!
Person 2	As surely as the LORD lives, not a hair of his head will fall to the ground.
Person 1	For he did this today with God's help.
Narrator	So the men rescued Jonathan, and he was not put to death.
	Then Saul stopped pursuing the Philistines, and they withdrew to their own land.

Cast: **Narrator, Saul, Soldier, Jonathan, Priest, Person 1** (can be the same as Priest), **Person 2** (can be the same as Soldier)

War against the Amalekites

1 Samuel 15:1–9

Narrator Samuel said to Saul:

Samuel I am the one the LORD sent to anoint you king over his people Israel; so listen now to the message from the LORD. This is what the LORD Almighty says: "I will punish the Amalekites for what they did to Israel when they waylaid them as they came up from Egypt. Now go, attack the Amalekites and totally destroy everything that belongs to them. Do not spare them; put to death men and women, children and infants, cattle and sheep, camels and donkeys."

Narrator So Saul summoned the men and mustered them at Telaim—two hundred thousand foot soldiers and ten thousand men from Judah. Saul went to the city of Amalek and set an ambush in the ravine. Then he said to the Kenites:

Saul Go away, leave the Amalekites so that I do not destroy you along with them; for you showed kindness to all the Israelites when they came up out of Egypt.

Narrator So the Kenites moved away from the Amalekites. (PAUSE)

Then Saul attacked the Amalekites all the way from Havilah to Shur, to the east of Egypt. He took Agag king of the Amalekites alive, and all his people he totally destroyed with the sword. But Saul and the army spared Agag and the best of the sheep and cattle, the fat calves and lambs—everything that was good. These they were unwilling to destroy completely, but everything that was despised and weak they totally destroyed.

Cast: **Narrator, Samuel, Saul**

The Lord Rejects Saul as King

1 Samuel 15:10–31, 34–35

Narrator The word of the LORD came to Samuel:

The Lord
(voice only) I am grieved that I have made Saul king, because he has turned away from me and has not carried out my instructions.

Narrator Samuel was troubled, and he cried out to the LORD all that night.

Early in the morning Samuel got up and went to meet Saul, but he was told:

Servant Saul has gone to Carmel. There he has set up a monument in his own honor and has turned and gone on down to Gilgal.

Narrator	When Samuel reached him, Saul said:
Saul	The Lord bless you! I have carried out the Lord's instructions.
[Narrator	But Samuel said:]
Samuel	What then is this bleating of sheep in my ears? What is this lowing of cattle that I hear?
Saul	The soldiers brought them from the Amalekites; they spared the best of the sheep and cattle to sacrifice to the Lord your God, but we totally destroyed the rest.
Samuel (inter-rupting)	Stop! Let me tell you what the Lord said to me last night.
Saul	Tell me.
Samuel	Although you were once small in your own eyes, did you not become the head of the tribes of Israel? The Lord anointed you king over Israel. And he sent you on a mission, saying, "Go and completely destroy those wicked people, the Amalekites; make war on them until you have wiped them out." Why did you not obey the Lord? Why did you pounce on the plunder and do evil in the eyes of the Lord?
Saul	But I did obey the Lord. I went on the mission the Lord assigned me. I completely destroyed the Amalekites and brought back Agag their king. The soldiers took sheep and cattle from the plunder, the best of what was devoted to God, in order to sacrifice them to the Lord your God at Gilgal.

Samuel	Does the Lord delight in burnt offerings and sacrifices
	    as much as in obeying the voice of the Lord?
	To obey is better than sacrifice,
	    and to heed is better than the fat of rams.
	For rebellion is like the sin of divination,
	    and arrogance like the evil of idolatry.
	Because you have rejected the word of the Lord,
	    he has rejected you as king.

Saul (contritely)	I have sinned. I violated the Lord's command and your instructions. I was afraid of the people and so I gave in to them. Now I beg you, forgive my sin and come back with me, so that I may worship the Lord.
Samuel	I will not go back with you. You have rejected the word of the Lord, and the Lord has rejected you as king over Israel!
Narrator	As Samuel turned to leave, Saul caught hold of the hem of his robe, and it tore. Samuel said to him:
Samuel (assertively)	The Lord has torn the kingdom of Israel from you today and has given it to one of your neighbors—to one better than you. He who is the Glory

	of Israel does not lie or change his mind; for he is not a man, that he should change his mind.
Saul	I have sinned. But please honor me before the elders of my people and before Israel; come back with me, so that I may worship the LORD your God.
Narrator	So Samuel went back with Saul, and Saul worshiped the LORD. . . .
	Then Samuel left for Ramah, but Saul went up to his home in Gibeah of Saul. Until the day Samuel died, he did not go to see Saul again, though Samuel mourned for him. And the LORD was grieved that he had made Saul king over Israel.

Cast: **Narrator, the Lord** (voice only), **Saul, Samuel, Servant**

Samuel Anoints David

1 Samuel 16:1–13

Narrator	The LORD said to Samuel:
The Lord (voice only)	How long will you mourn for Saul, since I have rejected him as king over Israel? Fill your horn with oil and be on your way; I am sending you to Jesse of Bethlehem. I have chosen one of his sons to be king.
[Narrator	But Samuel said:]
Samuel	How can I go? Saul will hear about it and kill me.
[Narrator	The LORD said:]
The Lord (voice)	Take a heifer with you and say, "I have come to sacrifice to the LORD." Invite Jesse to the sacrifice, and I will show you what to do. You are to anoint for me the one I indicate.
Narrator	Samuel did what the LORD said. When he arrived at Bethlehem, the elders of the town trembled when they met him. [They asked:]
Elder (trembling)	Do you come in peace?
Samuel	Yes, in peace; I have come to sacrifice to the LORD. Consecrate yourselves and come to the sacrifice with me.
Narrator	Then he consecrated Jesse and his sons and invited them to the sacrifice.
	When they arrived, Samuel saw Eliab and thought:
Samuel (to himself)	Surely the LORD's anointed stands here before the LORD.
[Narrator	But the LORD said to Samuel:]

The Lord (voice)	Do not consider his appearance or his height, for I have rejected him. The LORD does not look at the things man looks at. Man looks at the outward appearance, but the LORD looks at the heart.
Narrator	Then Jesse called Abinadab and had him pass in front of Samuel. But Samuel said:
Samuel	The LORD has not chosen this one either.
Narrator	Jesse then had Shammah pass by, but Samuel said:
Samuel	Nor has the LORD chosen this one.
Narrator	Jesse had seven of his sons pass before Samuel, but Samuel said to him:
Samuel	The LORD has not chosen these. (PAUSE) Are these all the sons you have?
Jesse	There is still the youngest, but he is tending the sheep.
Samuel	Send for him; we will not sit down until he arrives.
Narrator	So he sent and had him brought in. He was ruddy, with a fine appearance and handsome features. [Then the LORD said:]
The Lord (voice)	Rise and anoint him; he is the one.
Narrator	So Samuel took the horn of oil and anointed him in the presence of his brothers, and from that day on the Spirit of the LORD came upon David in power. Samuel then went to Ramah.

Cast: **Narrator, the Lord** (voice only), **Samuel, Elder, Jesse**

David in Saul's Service

1 Samuel 16:14–23

Narrator	The Spirit of the LORD had departed from Saul, and an evil spirit from the LORD tormented him. Saul's attendants said to him:
Attendant 1	See, an evil spirit from God is tormenting you.
Attendant 2	Let our lord command his servants here to search for someone who can play the harp. He will play when the evil spirit from God comes upon you, and you will feel better.
Narrator	So Saul said to his attendants:
Saul	Find someone who plays well and bring him to me.
Narrator	One of the servants answered:
Attendant 2	I have seen a son of Jesse of Bethlehem who knows how to play the harp.
Attendant 1	He is a brave man and a warrior. He speaks well and is a fine-looking man. And the LORD is with him.

Narrator	Then Saul sent messengers to Jesse and said:
Saul	Send me your son David, who is with the sheep.
Narrator	So Jesse took a donkey loaded with bread, a skin of wine and a young goat and sent them with his son David to Saul.
	David came to Saul and entered his service. Saul liked him very much, and David became one of his armor-bearers. Then Saul sent word to Jesse, saying:
Saul	Allow David to remain in my service, for I am pleased with him.
Narrator	Whenever the spirit from God came upon Saul, David would take his harp and play. Then relief would come to Saul; he would feel better, and the evil spirit would leave him.

Cast: **Narrator**, **Attendant 1**, **Attendant 2** (can be the same as Attendant 1), **Saul**

Goliath Challenges the Israelites

1 Samuel 17:1–11

Narrator	The Philistines gathered their forces for war and assembled at Socoh in Judah. They pitched camp at Ephes Dammim, between Socoh and Azekah. Saul and the Israelites assembled and camped in the Valley of Elah and drew up their battle line to meet the Philistines. The Philistines occupied one hill and the Israelites another, with the valley between them.
	A champion named Goliath, who was from Gath, came out of the Philistine camp. He was over nine feet tall. He had a bronze helmet on his head and wore a coat of scale armor of bronze weighing five thousand shekels; on his legs he wore bronze greaves, and a bronze javelin was slung on his back. His spear shaft was like a weaver's rod, and its iron point weighed six hundred shekels. His shield bearer went ahead of him.
	Goliath stood and shouted to the ranks of Israel:
Goliath	Why do you come out and line up for battle? Am I not a Philistine, and are you not the servants of Saul? Choose a man and have him come down to me. If he is able to fight and kill me, we will become your subjects; but if I overcome him and kill him, you will become our subjects and serve us.
	This day I defy the ranks of Israel! Give me a man and let us fight each other.
Narrator	On hearing the Philistine's words, Saul and all the Israelites were dismayed and terrified.

Cast: **Narrator, Goliath**

David in Saul's Camp

1 Samuel 17:12–40

Narrator David was the son of an Ephrathite named Jesse, who was from Bethlehem in Judah. Jesse had eight sons, and in Saul's time he was old and well advanced in years. Jesse's three oldest sons had followed Saul to the war: The firstborn was Eliab; the second, Abinadab; and the third, Shammah. David was the youngest. The three oldest followed Saul, but David went back and forth from Saul to tend his father's sheep at Bethlehem.

For forty days the Philistine came forward every morning and evening and took his stand.

Now Jesse said to his son David:

Jesse Take this ephah of roasted grain and these ten loaves of bread for your brothers and hurry to their camp. Take along these ten cheeses to the commander of their unit. See how your brothers are and bring back some assurance from them. They are with Saul and all the men of Israel in the Valley of Elah, fighting against the Philistines.

Narrator Early in the morning David left the flock with a shepherd, loaded up and set out, as Jesse had directed. He reached the camp as the army was going out to its battle positions, shouting the war cry. Israel and the Philistines were drawing up their lines facing each other. David left his things with the keeper of supplies, ran to the battle lines and greeted his brothers. As he was talking with them, Goliath, the Philistine champion from Gath, stepped out from his lines and shouted his usual defiance, and David heard it. When the Israelites saw the man, they all ran from him in great fear. (PAUSE) Now the Israelites had been saying:

Man 1 Do you see how this man keeps coming out?

Man 2 He comes out to defy Israel. . . .

Narrator David asked the men standing near him:

David What will be done for the man who kills this Philistine and removes this disgrace from Israel? Who is this uncircumcised Philistine that he should defy the armies of the living God?

Man 1 [The king will give great wealth to the man who kills him.

Man 2 He will also give him his daughter in marriage and will exempt his father's family from taxes in Israel.]

Man 1 This is what will be done for the man who kills him.

Narrator When Eliab, David's oldest brother, heard him speaking with the men, he burned with anger at him and asked:

Eliab Why have you come down here? And with whom did you leave those few sheep in the desert? I know how conceited you are and how wicked your heart is; you came down only to watch the battle.

David	*Now* what have I done? Can't I even *speak*?
Narrator	He then turned away to someone else and brought up the same matter, and the men answered him as before. What David said was overheard and reported to Saul, and Saul sent for him. David said to Saul:
David	Let no one lose heart on account of this Philistine; your servant will go and fight him.
Saul	*You* are not able to go out against this Philistine and fight him; you are only a *boy*, and he has been a fighting man from his youth.
David	Your servant has been keeping his father's sheep. When a lion or a bear came and carried off a sheep from the flock, I went after it, struck it and rescued the sheep from its mouth. When it turned on me, I seized it by its hair, struck it and killed it. Your servant has killed both the lion and the bear; this uncircumcised Philistine will be like one of them, because he has defied the armies of the living God. The LORD who delivered me from the paw of the lion and the paw of the bear will deliver me from the hand of this Philistine.
Saul	Go, and the LORD be with you.
Narrator	Then Saul dressed David in his own tunic. He put a coat of armor on him and a bronze helmet on his head. David fastened on his sword over the tunic and tried walking around, because he was not used to them.
David	I cannot go in these, because I am not used to them.
Narrator	So he took them off. (PAUSE) Then he took his staff in his hand, chose five smooth stones from the stream, put them in the pouch of his shepherd's bag and, with his sling in his hand, approached the Philistine.

Cast: **Narrator, Jesse,** Man 1, Man 2, **David,** Eliab (can be the same as Man 2), **Saul**

David Defeats Goliath

1 Samuel 17:[40], 41–50

Narrator	[[David] took his staff in his hand, chose five smooth stones from the stream, put them in the pouch of his shepherd's bag and, with his sling in his hand, approached the Philistine.]
	Meanwhile, the Philistine, with his shield bearer in front of him, kept coming closer to David. He looked David over and saw that he was only a boy, ruddy and handsome, and he despised him. He said to David:
Goliath	Am I a dog, that you come at me with sticks?
Narrator	And the Philistine cursed David by his gods.
Goliath	Come here, and I'll give your flesh to the birds of the air and the beasts of the field!

271

Narrator	David said to the Philistine:
David	You come against me with sword and spear and javelin, but I come against you in the name of the LORD Almighty, the God of the armies of Israel, whom you have defied. This day the LORD will hand you over to me, and I'll strike you down and cut off your head. Today I will give the carcasses of the Philistine army to the birds of the air and the beasts of the earth, and the whole world will know that there is a God in Israel. All those gathered here will know that it is not by sword or spear that the LORD saves; for the battle is the LORD's, and he will give all of you into our hands.
Narrator	As the Philistine moved closer to attack him, David ran quickly toward the battle line to meet him. Reaching into his bag and taking out a stone, he slung it and struck the Philistine on the forehead. The stone sank into his forehead, and he fell facedown on the ground.
	So David triumphed over the Philistine with a sling and a stone; without a sword in his hand he struck down the Philistine and killed him.

Cast: **Narrator, Goliath, David.** (Please note: This reading overlaps with the previous one.)

David Presented to Saul

1 Samuel 17:55–18:5

Narrator	As Saul watched David going out to meet the Philistine, he said to Abner, commander of the army:
Saul	Abner, whose son is that young man?
[Narrator	Abner replied:]
Abner	As surely as you live, O king, I don't know.
Saul	Find out whose son this young man is.
Narrator	As soon as David returned from killing the Philistine, Abner took him and brought him before Saul, with David still holding the Philistine's head. [Saul asked him:]
Saul	Whose son are you, young man?
[Narrator	David said:]
David	I am the son of your servant Jesse of Bethlehem.
Narrator	After David had finished talking with Saul, Jonathan became one in spirit with David, and he loved him as himself. From that day Saul kept David with him and did not let him return to his father's house. And Jonathan made a covenant with David because he loved him as himself. Jonathan took off the robe he was wearing and gave it to David, along with his tunic, and even his sword, his bow and his belt.

Whatever Saul sent him to do, David did it so successfully that Saul gave him a high rank in the army. This pleased all the people, and Saul's officers as well.

Cast: **Narrator, Saul, Abner, David**

Saul's Jealousy of David

1 Samuel 18:6–16

Narrator When the men were returning home after David had killed the Philistine, the women came out from all the towns of Israel to meet King Saul with singing and dancing, with joyful songs and with tambourines and lutes. As they danced, they sang:

Women 1 and 2 Saul has slain his thousands,
and David his tens of thousands.

Narrator Saul was very angry; this refrain galled him.

Saul They have credited David with tens of thousands, but me with only thousands. What more can he get but the kingdom?

Narrator And from that time on Saul kept a jealous eye on David. (PAUSE)

The next day an evil spirit from God came forcefully upon Saul. He was prophesying in his house, while David was playing the harp, as he usually did. Saul had a spear in his hand and he hurled it [saying to himself:]

Saul (angrily, to himself) I'll pin David to the wall.

Narrator But David eluded him twice. (PAUSE)

Saul was afraid of David, because the LORD was with David but had left Saul. So he sent David away from him and gave him command over a thousand men, and David led the troops in their campaigns. In everything he did he had great success, because the LORD was with him. When Saul saw how successful he was, he was afraid of him. But all Israel and Judah loved David, because he led them in their campaigns.

Cast: **Narrator, Woman 1, Woman 2** (can be the same as Woman 1), **Saul**

David Marries Saul's Daughter

From 1 Samuel 18:17–30

Narrator Saul said to David:

Saul Here is my older daughter Merab. I will give her to you in marriage; only serve me bravely and fight the battles of the LORD.

273

Narrator	For Saul said to himself:
Saul	I will not raise a hand against him. Let the Philistines do that!
Narrator	But David said to Saul:
David	Who am I, and what is my family or my father's clan in Israel, that I should become the king's son-in-law?
Narrator	So when the time came for Merab, Saul's daughter, to be given to David, she was given in marriage to Adriel of Meholah.
	Now Saul's daughter Michal was in love with David, and when they told Saul about it, he was pleased.
Saul (to himself)	I will give her to him, so that she may be a snare to him and so that the hand of the Philistines may be against him.
Narrator	So Saul said to David:
Saul	Now you have a second opportunity to become my son-in-law.
Narrator	Then Saul ordered his attendants:
Saul	Speak to David privately and say, "Look, the king is pleased with you, and his attendants all like you; now become his son-in-law."
Narrator	They repeated these words to David. But David said:
David	Do you think it is a small matter to become the king's son-in-law? I'm only a poor man and little known.
Narrator	When Saul's servants told him what David had said, Saul replied:
Saul	Say to David, "The king wants no other price for the bride than a hundred Philistine foreskins, to take revenge on his enemies."
Narrator	Saul's plan was to have David fall by the hands of the Philistines.
	When the attendants told David these things, he was pleased to become the king's son-in-law. So before the allotted time elapsed, David and his men went out and killed two hundred Philistines. He brought their foreskins and presented the full number to the king so that he might become the king's son-in-law. Then Saul gave him his daughter Michal in marriage. (PAUSE)
	When Saul realized that the LORD was with David and that his daughter Michal loved David, Saul became still more afraid of him, and he remained his enemy the rest of his days.
	The Philistine commanders continued to go out to battle, and as often as they did, David met with more success than the rest of Saul's officers, and his name became well known.

Cast: **Narrator, Saul, David**

Saul Tries to Kill David

1 Samuel 19:1–18

Narrator	Saul told his son Jonathan and all the attendants to kill David. But Jonathan was very fond of David and warned him:
Jonathan	My father Saul is looking for a chance to kill you. Be on your guard tomorrow morning; go into hiding and stay there. I will go out and stand with my father in the field where you are. I'll speak to him about you and will tell you what I find out.
Narrator	Jonathan spoke well of David to Saul his father:
Jonathan	Let not the king do wrong to his servant David; he has not wronged you, and what he has done has benefited you greatly. He took his life in his hands when he killed the Philistine. The LORD won a great victory for all Israel, and you saw it and were glad. Why then would you do wrong to an innocent man like David by killing him for no reason?
Narrator	Saul listened to Jonathan and took this oath:
Saul	As surely as the LORD lives, David will not be put to death.
Narrator	So Jonathan called David and told him the whole conversation. He brought him to Saul, and David was with Saul as before.
	Once more war broke out, and David went out and fought the Philistines. He struck them with such force that they fled before him.
	But an evil spirit from the LORD came upon Saul as he was sitting in his house with his spear in his hand. While David was playing the harp, Saul tried to pin him to the wall with his spear, but David eluded him as Saul drove the spear into the wall. That night David made good his escape.
	Saul sent men to David's house to watch it and to kill him in the morning. But Michal, David's wife, warned him:
Michal	If you don't run for your life tonight, tomorrow you'll be killed.
Narrator	So Michal let David down through a window, and he fled and escaped. Then Michal took an idol and laid it on the bed, covering it with a garment and putting some goats' hair at the head. (PAUSE) When Saul sent the men to capture David, Michal said:
Michal	He is ill.
Narrator	Then Saul sent the men back to see David and told them:
Saul	Bring him up to me in his bed so that I may kill him.
Narrator	But when the men entered, there was the idol in the bed, and at the head was some goats' hair. Saul said to Michal:
Saul	Why did you deceive me like this and send my enemy away so that he escaped?

275

Narrator	Michal told him:
Michal	He said to me, "Let me get away. Why should I kill you?"
Narrator	When David had fled and made his escape, he went to Samuel at Ramah and told him all that Saul had done to him. Then he and Samuel went to Naioth and stayed there.

Cast: **Narrator, Jonathan, Saul, Michal**

Jonathan Helps David (i)

1 Samuel 20:1–17

Narrator	David fled from Naioth at Ramah and went to Jonathan [and asked:]
David	What have I done? What is my crime? How have I wronged your father, that he is trying to take my life?
Narrator	[Jonathan replied:]
Jonathan	Never! You are not going to die! Look, my father doesn't do anything, great or small, without confiding in me. Why would he hide this from me? It's not so!
Narrator	But David took an oath [and said:]
David	Your father knows very well that I have found favor in your eyes, and he has said to himself, "Jonathan must not know this or he will be grieved." Yet as surely as the LORD lives and as you live, there is only a step between me and death.
[Narrator	Jonathan said to David:]
Jonathan	Whatever you want me to do, I'll do for you.
David	Look, tomorrow is the New Moon festival, and I am supposed to dine with the king; but let me go and hide in the field until the evening of the day after tomorrow. If your father misses me at all, tell him, "David earnestly asked my permission to hurry to Bethlehem, his hometown, because an annual sacrifice is being made there for his whole clan." If he says, "Very well," then your servant is safe. But if he loses his temper, you can be sure that he is determined to harm me. As for you, show kindness to your servant, for you have brought him into a covenant with you before the LORD. If I am guilty, then kill me yourself! Why hand me over to your father?
Jonathan	Never! If I had the least inkling that my father was determined to harm you, wouldn't I tell you? (PAUSE)
David	Who will tell me if your father answers you harshly?
Jonathan	Come, let's go out into the field.

276

Narrator	So they went there together. (PAUSE) [Then Jonathan said to David:]
Jonathan	By the LORD, the God of Israel, I will surely sound out my father by this time the day after tomorrow! If he is favorably disposed toward you, will I not send you word and let you know? But if my father is inclined to harm you, may the LORD deal with me, be it ever so severely, if I do not let you know and send you away safely. May the LORD be with you as he has been with my father. But show me unfailing kindness like that of the LORD as long as I live, so that I may not be killed, and do not ever cut off your kindness from my family—not even when the LORD has cut off every one of David's enemies from the face of the earth.
Narrator	So Jonathan made a covenant with the house of David.
Jonathan	May the LORD call David's enemies to account.
Narrator	And Jonathan had David reaffirm his oath out of love for him, because he loved him as he loved himself.

Cast: **Narrator, David, Jonathan**

Jonathan Helps David (ii)

1 Samuel 20:18–24

Narrator	Jonathan said to David:
Jonathan	Tomorrow is the New Moon festival. You will be missed, because your seat will be empty. The day after tomorrow, toward evening, go to the place where you hid when this trouble began, and wait by the stone Ezel. I will shoot three arrows to the side of it, as though I were shooting at a target. Then I will send a boy and say:
Voice	Go, find the arrows.
Jonathan	If I say to him:
Voice	Look, the arrows are on this side of you; bring them here.
Jonathan	Then come, because, as surely as the LORD lives, you are safe; there is no danger. But if I say to the boy:
Voice	Look, the arrows are beyond you.
Jonathan	Then you must go, because the LORD has sent you away. And about the matter you and I discussed—remember, the LORD is witness between you and me forever.
Narrator	So David hid in the field, and when the New Moon festival came, the king sat down to eat.

Cast: **Narrator, Jonathan, Voice**

Jonathan Helps David (iii)

1 Samuel 20:24–34

Narrator	David hid in the field, and when the New Moon festival came, the king sat down to eat. He sat in his customary place by the wall, opposite Jonathan, and Abner sat next to Saul, but David's place was empty. Saul said nothing that day [for he thought:]
Saul (thinking)	Something must have happened to David to make him ceremonially unclean—surely he is unclean.
Narrator	But the next day, the second day of the month, David's place was empty again. [Then Saul said to his son Jonathan:]
Saul (to Jonathan)	Why hasn't the son of Jesse come to the meal, either yesterday or today?
[Narrator	Jonathan answered:]
Jonathan	David earnestly asked me for permission to go to Bethlehem. He said, "Let me go, because our family is observing a sacrifice in the town and my brother has ordered me to be there. If I have found favor in your eyes, let me get away to see my brothers." That is why he has not come to the king's table.
Narrator	Saul's anger flared up at Jonathan:
Saul (angrily)	You son of a perverse and rebellious woman! Don't I know that you have sided with the son of Jesse to your own shame and to the shame of the mother who bore you? As long as the son of Jesse lives on this earth, neither you nor your kingdom will be established. Now send and bring him to me, for he must die!
Jonathan	Why should he be put to death? What has he done?
Narrator	But Saul hurled his spear at him to kill him. Then Jonathan knew that his father intended to kill David.
	Jonathan got up from the table in fierce anger; on that second day of the month he did not eat, because he was grieved at his father's shameful treatment of David.

Cast: **Narrator, Saul, Jonathan**

Jonathan Helps David (iv)

1 Samuel 20:35–42

Narrator	[In the morning] Jonathan went out to the field for his meeting with David. He had a small boy with him [and he said to the boy:]

Jonathan	Run and find the arrows I shoot.
Narrator	As the boy ran, he shot an arrow beyond him. When the boy came to the place where Jonathan's arrow had fallen, Jonathan called out after him:
Jonathan	Isn't the arrow beyond you?
[Narrator	Then he shouted:]
Jonathan (shouting)	Hurry! Go quickly! Don't stop!
Narrator	The boy picked up the arrow and returned to his master. (The boy knew nothing of all this; only Jonathan and David knew.) Then Jonathan gave his weapons to the boy:
Jonathan	Go, carry them back to town.
Narrator	After the boy had gone, David got up from the south side ⌐of the stone⌐ and bowed down before Jonathan three times, with his face to the ground. Then they kissed each other and wept together—but David wept the most. Jonathan said to David:
Jonathan	Go in peace, for we have sworn friendship with each other in the name of the LORD, saying, "The LORD is witness between you and me, and between your descendants and my descendants forever."
Narrator	Then David left, and Jonathan went back to the town.

Cast: **Narrator, Jonathan**

David at Nob

From 1 Samuel 21:1–11 [12–15]

Narrator	David went to Nob, to Ahimelech the priest. Ahimelech trembled when he met him:
Ahimelech (to David, trembling)	Why are you alone? Why is no one with you?
Narrator	David answered Ahimelech the priest:
David (to Ahimelech)	The king charged me with a certain matter and said to me, "No one is to know anything about your mission and your instructions." As for my men, I have told them to meet me at a certain place. Now then, what do you have on hand? Give me five loaves of bread, or whatever you can find.
[Narrator	But the priest answered David:]

Ahimelech	I don't have any ordinary bread on hand; however, there is some consecrated bread here. . . .
Narrator	So the priest gave him the consecrated bread, since there was no bread there except the bread of the Presence that had been removed from before the LORD and replaced by hot bread on the day it was taken away. . . . (PAUSE) [David asked Ahimelech:]
David	Don't you have a spear or a sword here? I haven't brought my sword or any other weapon, because the king's business was urgent.
Ahimelech	The sword of Goliath the Philistine, whom you killed in the Valley of Elah, is here; it is wrapped in a cloth behind the ephod. If you want it, take it; there is no sword here but that one.
David	There is none like it; give it to me. (PAUSE)
Narrator	That day David fled from Saul and went to Achish king of Gath. But the servants of Achish said to him:
Servant 1	Isn't this David, the king of the land?
Servant 2	Isn't he the one they sing about in their dances:
	"Saul has slain his thousands, and David his tens of thousands"?
[Narrator	David took these words to heart and was very much afraid of Achish king of Gath. So he pretended to be insane in their presence; and while he was in their hands he acted like a madman, making marks on the doors of the gate and letting saliva run down his beard. Achish said to his servants:
Achish	Look at the man! He is insane! Why bring him to me? Am I so short of madmen that you have to bring this fellow here to carry on like this in front of me? Must this man come into my house?]

Cast: **Narrator, Ahimelech, David, Servant 1, Servant 2** (can be the same as Servant 1), **Achish**

Saul Kills the Priests of Nob

1 Samuel 22:1–23

Narrator	David left Gath and escaped to the cave of Adullam. When his brothers and his father's household heard about it, they went down to him there. All those who were in distress or in debt or discontented gathered around him, and he became their leader. About four hundred men were with him.
	From there David went to Mizpah in Moab and said to the king of Moab:
David	Would you let my father and mother come and stay with you until I learn what God will do for me?

Narrator	So he left them with the king of Moab, and they stayed with him as long as David was in the stronghold. But the prophet Gad said to David:
Prophet	Do not stay in the stronghold. Go into the land of Judah.
Narrator	So David left and went to the forest of Hereth. (PAUSE)
	Now Saul heard that David and his men had been discovered. And Saul, spear in hand, was seated under the tamarisk tree on the hill at Gibeah, with all his officials standing around him. Saul said to them:
Saul	Listen, men of Benjamin! Will the son of Jesse give all of you fields and vineyards? Will he make all of you commanders of thousands and commanders of hundreds? Is that why you have all conspired against me? No one tells me when my son makes a covenant with the son of Jesse. None of you is concerned about me or tells me that my son has incited my servant to lie in wait for me, as he does today.
Narrator	But Doeg the Edomite, who was standing with Saul's officials, said:
Doeg	I saw the son of Jesse come to Ahimelech son of Ahitub at Nob. Ahimelech inquired of the Lord for him; he also gave him provisions and the sword of Goliath the Philistine.
Narrator	Then the king sent for the priest Ahimelech son of Ahitub and his father's whole family, who were the priests at Nob, and they all came to the king. Saul said:
Saul	Listen now, son of Ahitub.
Ahimelech	Yes, my lord.
Saul	Why have you conspired against me, you and the son of Jesse, giving him bread and a sword and inquiring of God for him, so that he has rebelled against me and lies in wait for me, as he does today?
Ahimelech	Who of all your servants is as loyal as David, the king's son-in-law, captain of your bodyguard and highly respected in your household? Was that day the first time I inquired of God for him? Of course not! Let not the king accuse your servant or any of his father's family, for your servant knows nothing at all about this whole affair.
Saul (angrily)	You will surely die, Ahimelech, you and your father's whole family.
Narrator	Then the king ordered the guards at his side:
Saul	Turn and kill the priests of the Lord, because they too have sided with David. They knew he was fleeing, yet they did not tell me.
Narrator	But the king's officials were not willing to raise a hand to strike the priests of the Lord. The king then ordered Doeg:
Saul	You turn and strike down the priests.
Narrator	So Doeg the Edomite turned and struck them down. That day he killed eighty-five men who wore the linen ephod. He also put to the sword Nob,

281

the town of the priests, with its men and women, its children and infants, and its cattle, donkeys and sheep.

But Abiathar, a son of Ahimelech son of Ahitub, escaped and fled to join David. He told David that Saul had killed the priests of the LORD. Then David said to Abiathar:

David That day, when Doeg the Edomite was there, I knew he would be sure to tell Saul. I am responsible for the death of your father's whole family. Stay with me; don't be afraid; the man who is seeking your life is seeking mine also. You will be safe with me.

Cast: **Narrator, David, Prophet, Saul, Doeg, Ahimelech**

David Saves Keilah

1 Samuel 23:1–13

Narrator When David was told:

Man 1 Look, the Philistines are fighting against Keilah and are looting the threshing floors.

Narrator He inquired of the LORD, saying:

David Shall I go and attack these Philistines?

[Narrator The LORD answered him:**]**

The Lord
(voice only) Go, attack the Philistines and save Keilah.

Narrator But David's men said to him:

Man 1 Here in Judah we are afraid.

Man 2 How much more, then, if we go to Keilah against the Philistine forces!

Narrator Once again David inquired of the LORD, and the LORD answered him:

The Lord
(voice) Go down to Keilah, for I am going to give the Philistines into your hand.

Narrator So David and his men went to Keilah, fought the Philistines and carried off their livestock. He inflicted heavy losses on the Philistines and saved the people of Keilah. (Now Abiathar son of Ahimelech had brought the ephod down with him when he fled to David at Keilah.)

Saul was told that David had gone to Keilah, and he said:

Saul (with cunning voice) God has handed him over to me, for David has imprisoned himself by entering a town with gates and bars.

Narrator	And Saul called up all his forces for battle, to go down to Keilah to besiege David and his men. (PAUSE) When David learned that Saul was plotting against him, he said to Abiathar the priest:
David	Bring the ephod.
[Narrator	David prayed:]
David (praying)	O LORD, God of Israel, your servant has heard definitely that Saul plans to come to Keilah and destroy the town on account of me. Will the citizens of Keilah surrender me to him? Will Saul come down, as your servant has heard? O LORD, God of Israel, tell your servant.
Narrator	And the LORD said:
The Lord (voice)	He will.
Narrator	Again David asked:
David (praying)	Will the citizens of Keilah surrender me and my men to Saul?
The Lord (voice)	They will.
Narrator	So David and his men, about six hundred in number, left Keilah and kept moving from place to place. When Saul was told that David had escaped from Keilah, he did not go there.

Cast: **Narrator, Man 1, David, the Lord** (voice only), **Man 2** (can be the same as Man 1), **Saul**

Saul Pursues David

1 Samuel 23:14–29

Narrator	David stayed in the desert strongholds and in the hills of the Desert of Ziph. Day after day Saul searched for him, but God did not give David into his hands.
	While David was at Horesh in the Desert of Ziph, he learned that Saul had come out to take his life. And Saul's son Jonathan went to David at Horesh and helped him find strength in God.
Jonathan	Don't be afraid. My father Saul will not lay a hand on you. You will be king over Israel, and I will be second to you. Even my father Saul knows this.
Narrator	The two of them made a covenant before the LORD. Then Jonathan went home, but David remained at Horesh. (PAUSE) The Ziphites went up to Saul at Gibeah:

Person 1	Is not David hiding among us in the strongholds at Horesh, on the hill of Hakilah, south of Jeshimon?
Person 2	Now, O king, come down whenever it pleases you to do so, and we will be responsible for handing him over to the king.
[Narrator	Saul replied:]
Saul	The LORD bless you for your concern for me. Go and make further preparation. Find out where David usually goes and who has seen him there. They tell me he is very crafty. Find out about all the hiding places he uses and come back to me with definite information. Then I will go with you; if he is in the area, I will track him down among all the clans of Judah.
Narrator	So they set out and went to Ziph ahead of Saul. Now David and his men were in the Desert of Maon, in the Arabah south of Jeshimon. Saul and his men began the search, and when David was told about it, he went down to the rock and stayed in the Desert of Maon. When Saul heard this, he went into the Desert of Maon in pursuit of David.
	Saul was going along one side of the mountain, and David and his men were on the other side, hurrying to get away from Saul. As Saul and his forces were closing in on David and his men to capture them, a messenger came to Saul:
Messenger	Come quickly! The Philistines are raiding the land.
Narrator	Then Saul broke off his pursuit of David and went to meet the Philistines. That is why they call this place Sela Hammahlekoth. And David went up from there and lived in the strongholds of En Gedi.

Cast: **Narrator, Jonathan, Person 1, Person 2, Saul, Messenger**

David Spares Saul's Life

1 Samuel 24:1–22

Narrator	After Saul returned from pursuing the Philistines, he was told:
Man	David is in the Desert of En Gedi.
Narrator	So Saul took three thousand chosen men from all Israel and set out to look for David and his men near the Crags of the Wild Goats.
	He came to the sheep pens along the way; a cave was there, and Saul went in to relieve himself. David and his men were far back in the cave. The men said:
Man (loud whisper)	This is the day the LORD spoke of when he said to you, "I will give your enemy into your hands for you to deal with as you wish."
Narrator	Then David crept up unnoticed and cut off a corner of Saul's robe.

Afterward, David was conscience-stricken for having cut off a corner of his robe. He said to his men:

David   The LORD forbid that I should do such a thing to my master, the LORD's anointed, or lift my hand against him; for he is the anointed of the LORD.

Narrator   With these words David rebuked his men and did not allow them to attack Saul. And Saul left the cave and went his way. (PAUSE) Then David went out of the cave and called out to Saul:

David
(calling)   My lord the king!

Narrator   When Saul looked behind him, David bowed down and prostrated himself with his face to the ground. [He said to Saul:]

David
(to Saul)   Why do you listen when men say, "David is bent on harming you"? This day you have seen with your own eyes how the LORD delivered you into my hands in the cave. Some urged me to kill you, but I spared you; I said, "I will not lift my hand against my master, because he is the LORD's anointed." See, my father, look at this piece of your robe in my hand! I cut off the corner of your robe but did not kill you. Now understand and recognize that I am not guilty of wrongdoing or rebellion. I have not wronged you, but you are hunting me down to take my life. May the LORD judge between you and me. And may the LORD avenge the wrongs you have done to me, but my hand will not touch you. As the old saying goes, "From evildoers come evil deeds," so my hand will not touch you.

Against whom has the king of Israel come out? Whom are you pursuing? A dead dog? A flea? May the LORD be our judge and decide between us. May he consider my cause and uphold it; may he vindicate me by delivering me from your hand. . . .

Saul   Is that your voice, David my son?

Narrator   And he wept aloud.

Saul   You are more righteous than I. You have treated me well, but I have treated you badly. You have just now told me of the good you did to me; the LORD delivered me into your hands, but you did not kill me. When a man finds his enemy, does he let him get away unharmed? May the LORD reward you well for the way you treated me today. I know that you will surely be king and that the kingdom of Israel will be established in your hands. Now swear to me by the LORD that you will not cut off my descendants or wipe out my name from my father's family.

Narrator   So David gave his oath to Saul. Then Saul returned home, but David and his men went up to the stronghold.

Cast: **Narrator, Man, David, Saul** (at the back of the audience)

David, Nabal, and Abigail

1 Samuel 25:1–42

Narrator	[Samuel died, and all Israel assembled and mourned for him; and they buried him at his home in Ramah.] David moved down into the Desert of Maon. A certain man in Maon, who had property there at Carmel, was very wealthy. He had a thousand goats and three thousand sheep, which he was shearing in Carmel. His name was Nabal and his wife's name was Abigail. She was an intelligent and beautiful woman, but her husband, a Calebite, was surly and mean in his dealings.
	While David was in the desert, he heard that Nabal was shearing sheep. So he sent ten young men:
David	Go up to Nabal at Carmel and greet him in my name. Say to him: "Long life to you! Good health to you and your household! And good health to all that is yours!
	"Now I hear that it is sheep-shearing time. When your shepherds were with us, we did not mistreat them, and the whole time they were at Carmel nothing of theirs was missing. Ask your own servants and they will tell you. Therefore be favorable toward my young men, since we come at a festive time. Please give your servants and your son David whatever you can find for them."
Narrator	When David's men arrived, they gave Nabal this message in David's name. Then they waited. Nabal answered David's servants:
Nabal	Who is this David? Who is this son of Jesse? Many servants are breaking away from their masters these days. Why should I take my bread and water, and the meat I have slaughtered for my shearers, and give it to men coming from who knows where?
Narrator	David's men turned around and went back. When they arrived, they reported every word. David said to his men:
David (angrily)	Put on your swords!
Narrator	So they put on their swords, and David put on his. About four hundred men went up with David, while two hundred stayed with the supplies.
	One of the servants told Nabal's wife Abigail:
Servant	David sent messengers from the desert to give our master his greetings, but he hurled insults at them. Yet these men were very good to us. They did not mistreat us, and the whole time we were out in the fields near them nothing was missing. Night and day they were a wall around us all the time we were herding our sheep near them. Now think it over and see what you can do, because disaster is hanging over our master and his whole household. He is such a wicked man that no one can talk to him.

Narrator	Abigail lost no time. She took two hundred loaves of bread, two skins of wine, five dressed sheep, five seahs of roasted grain, a hundred cakes of raisins and two hundred cakes of pressed figs, and loaded them on donkeys. Then she told her servants:
Abigail	Go on ahead; I'll follow you.
Narrator	But she did not tell her husband Nabal.
	As she came riding her donkey into a mountain ravine, there were David and his men descending toward her, and she met them. David had just said:
David (musing)	It's been useless—all my watching over this fellow's property in the desert so that nothing of his was missing. He has paid me back evil for good. May God deal with David, be it ever so severely, if by morning I leave alive one male of all who belong to him!
Narrator	When Abigail saw David, she quickly got off her donkey and bowed down before David with her face to the ground. She fell at his feet:
Abigail (to David)	My lord, let the blame be on me alone. Please let your servant speak to you; hear what your servant has to say. May my Lord pay no attention to that wicked man Nabal. He is just like his name—his name is Fool, and folly goes with him. But as for me, your servant, I did not see the men my master sent.
	Now since the Lord has kept you, my master, from bloodshed and from avenging yourself with your own hands, as surely as the Lord lives and as you live, may your enemies and all who intend to harm my master be like Nabal. And let this gift, which your servant has brought to my master, be given to the men who follow you. Please forgive your servant's offense, for the Lord will certainly make a lasting dynasty for my master, because he fights the Lord's battles. Let no wrongdoing be found in you as long as you live. Even though someone is pursuing you to take your life, the life of my master will be bound securely in the bundle of the living by the Lord your God. But the lives of your enemies he will hurl away as from the pocket of a sling. When the Lord has done for my master every good thing he promised concerning him and has appointed him leader over Israel, my master will not have on his conscience the staggering burden of needless bloodshed or of having avenged himself. And when the Lord has brought my master success, remember your servant.
[Narrator	David said to Abigail:]
David (to Abigail)	Praise be to the Lord, the God of Israel, who has sent you today to meet me. May you be blessed for your good judgment and for keeping me from bloodshed this day and from avenging myself with my own hands. Otherwise, as surely as the Lord, the God of Israel, lives, who has kept me

from harming you, if you had not come quickly to meet me, not one male belonging to Nabal would have been left alive by daybreak.

Narrator   Then David accepted from her hand what she had brought him.

David
(to Abigail)   Go home in peace. I have heard your words and granted your request.

Narrator   When Abigail went to Nabal, he was in the house holding a banquet like that of a king. He was in high spirits and very drunk. So she told him nothing until daybreak. Then in the morning, when Nabal was sober, his wife told him all these things, and his heart failed him and he became like a stone. About ten days later, the LORD struck Nabal and he died.
(LONG PAUSE)

[When David heard that Nabal was dead, he said:

David   Praise be to the LORD, who has upheld my cause against Nabal for treating me with contempt. He has kept his servant from doing wrong and has brought Nabal's wrongdoing down on his own head.]

Narrator   Then David sent word to Abigail, asking her to become his wife. His servants went to Carmel and said to Abigail:

Servant   David has sent us to you to take you to become his wife.

Narrator   She bowed down with her face to the ground:

Abigail   Here is your maidservant, ready to serve you and wash the feet of my master's servants.

Narrator   Abigail quickly got on a donkey and, attended by her five maids, went with David's messengers and became his wife.

Cast: **Narrator, David, Nabal, Servant, Abigail**

David Again Spares Saul's Life

1 Samuel 26:1–25

Narrator   The Ziphites went to Saul at Gibeah:

Ziphite   Is not David hiding on the hill of Hakilah, which faces Jeshimon?

Narrator   So Saul went down to the Desert of Ziph, with his three thousand chosen men of Israel, to search there for David. Saul made his camp beside the road on the hill of Hakilah facing Jeshimon, but David stayed in the desert. When he saw that Saul had followed him there, he sent out scouts and learned that Saul had definitely arrived.

Then David set out and went to the place where Saul had camped. He saw where Saul and Abner son of Ner, the commander of the army, had lain down. Saul was lying inside the camp, with the army encamped

	around him. (PAUSE) David then asked Ahimelech the Hittite and Abishai son of Zeruiah, Joab's brother:
David	Who will go down into the camp with me to Saul?
Abishai	I'll go with you.
Narrator	So David and Abishai went to the army by night, and there was Saul, lying asleep inside the camp with his spear stuck in the ground near his head. Abner and the soldiers were lying around him. Abishai said to David:
Abishai	Today God has delivered your enemy into your hands. Now let me pin him to the ground with one thrust of my spear; I won't strike him twice.
[Narrator	But David said to Abishai:]
David	Don't destroy him! Who can lay a hand on the LORD's anointed and be guiltless? As surely as the LORD lives, the LORD himself will strike him; either his time will come and he will die, or he will go into battle and perish. But the LORD forbid that I should lay a hand on the LORD's anointed. Now get the spear and water jug that are near his head, and let's go.
Narrator	So David took the spear and water jug near Saul's head, and they left. No one saw or knew about it, nor did anyone wake up. They were all sleeping, because the LORD had put them into a deep sleep.
	Then David crossed over to the other side and stood on top of the hill some distance away; there was a wide space between them. He called out to the army and to Abner son of Ner:
David (calling)	Aren't you going to answer me, Abner?
Abner (calling)	Who are you who calls to the king?
David (calling)	You're a man, aren't you? And who is like you in Israel? Why didn't you guard your lord the king? Someone came to destroy your lord the king. What you have done is not good. As surely as the LORD lives, you and your men deserve to die, because you did not guard your master, the LORD's anointed. Look around you. Where are the king's spear and water jug that were near his head?
Narrator	Saul recognized David's voice and said:
Saul (calling)	Is that your voice, David my son?
David (calling)	Yes it is, my lord the king. (PAUSE)
	Why is my lord pursuing his servant? What have I done, and what wrong am I guilty of? (PAUSE) Now let my lord the king listen to his servant's words. If the LORD has incited you against me, then may he accept an offering. If, however, men have done it, may they be cursed before the LORD! They have now driven me from my share in the LORD's inheritance and have said, "Go, serve other gods." Now do not let my blood fall to

	the ground far from the presence of the LORD. The king of Israel has come out to look for a flea—as one hunts a partridge in the mountains.
Saul (calling)	I have sinned. Come back, David my son. Because you considered my life precious today, I will not try to harm you again. Surely I have acted like a fool and have erred greatly.
David (calling)	Here is the king's spear. Let one of your young men come over and get it. The LORD rewards every man for his righteousness and faithfulness. The LORD delivered you into my hands today, but I would not lay a hand on the LORD's anointed. As surely as I valued your life today, so may the LORD value my life and deliver me from all trouble.
Saul	May you be blessed, my son David; you will do great things and surely triumph.
Narrator	So David went on his way, and Saul returned home.

Cast: **Narrator, Ziphite, David, Abishai, Abner** (at the back of the audience), **Saul** (at the back of the audience)

David among the Philistines

1 Samuel 27:1–28:2

Narrator	David thought to himself:
David (thinking)	One of these days I will be destroyed by the hand of Saul. The best thing I can do is to escape to the land of the Philistines. Then Saul will give up searching for me anywhere in Israel, and I will slip out of his hand.
Narrator	So David and the six hundred men with him left and went over to Achish son of Maoch king of Gath. David and his men settled in Gath with Achish. Each man had his family with him, and David had his two wives: Ahinoam of Jezreel and Abigail of Carmel, the widow of Nabal. When Saul was told that David had fled to Gath, he no longer searched for him. Then David said to Achish:
David	If I have found favor in your eyes, let a place be assigned to me in one of the country towns, that I may live there. Why should your servant live in the royal city with you?
Narrator	So on that day Achish gave him Ziklag, and it has belonged to the kings of Judah ever since. David lived in Philistine territory a year and four months. (PAUSE) Now David and his men went up and raided the Geshurites, the Girzites and the Amalekites. (From ancient times these peoples had lived in the land extending to Shur and Egypt.) Whenever David attacked an area, he did not leave a man or woman alive, but took sheep and cattle, don-

	keys and camels, and clothes. Then he returned to Achish. When Achish asked:
Achish	Where did you go raiding today?
Narrator	David would say:
David	Against the Negev of Judah
Narrator	Or
David	Against the Negev of Jerahmeel
Narrator	Or
David	Against the Negev of the Kenites.
Narrator	He did not leave a man or woman alive to be brought to Gath, for he thought:
David	They might inform on us and say, "This is what David did."
Narrator	And such was his practice as long as he lived in Philistine territory. (PAUSE) Achish trusted David [and said to himself:]
Achish (craftily, to himself)	He has become so odious to his people, the Israelites, that he will be my servant forever.
Narrator	In those days the Philistines gathered their forces to fight against Israel. [Achish said to David:]
Achish (to David)	You must understand that you and your men will accompany me in the army.
David	Then you will see for yourself what your servant can do.
Achish	Very well, I will make you my bodyguard for life.

Cast: **Narrator, David, Achish**

Saul and the Witch of Endor

1 Samuel 28:3–25

Narrator	Now Samuel was dead, and all Israel had mourned for him and buried him in his own town of Ramah. Saul had expelled the mediums and spiritists from the land.
	The Philistines assembled and came and set up camp at Shunem, while Saul gathered all the Israelites and set up camp at Gilboa. When Saul saw the Philistine army, he was afraid; terror filled his heart. He inquired of

the LORD, but the LORD did not answer him by dreams or Urim or prophets. Saul then said to his attendants:

Saul   Find me a woman who is a medium, so I may go and inquire of her.

Narrator   [They said:]

Attendant   There *is* one in Endor.

Narrator   So Saul disguised himself, putting on other clothes, and at night he and two men went to the woman.

Saul   Consult a spirit for me, and bring up for me the one I name.

[Narrator   But the woman said to him:]

Woman   Surely you know what Saul has done. He has cut off the mediums and spiritists from the land. Why have you set a trap for my life to bring about my death?

Narrator   Saul swore to her by the LORD:

Saul (slowly)   As surely as the LORD lives, you will not be punished for this.

Woman   Whom shall I bring up for you?

Saul   Bring up Samuel.

Narrator   When the woman saw Samuel, she cried out at the top of her voice:

Woman   Why have you deceived me? You are Saul!

[Narrator   The king said to her:]

Saul   Don't be afraid. What do you see?

Woman   I see a spirit coming up out of the ground.

Saul   What does he look like?

Woman   An old man wearing a robe is coming up.

Narrator   Then Saul knew it was Samuel, and he bowed down and prostrated himself with his face to the ground. [Samuel said to Saul:]

Samuel
(voice only)   Why have you disturbed me by bringing me up?

Saul   I am in great distress. The Philistines are fighting against me, and God has turned away from me. He no longer answers me, either by prophets or by dreams. So I have called on you to tell me what to do.

Samuel
(voice)   Why do you consult me, now that the LORD has turned away from you and become your enemy? The LORD has done what he predicted through me. The LORD has torn the kingdom out of your hands and given it to one of your neighbors—to David. Because you did not obey the LORD or carry out his fierce wrath against the Amalekites, the LORD has done this to you today. The LORD will hand over both Israel and you to the

Philistines, and tomorrow you and your sons will be with me. The LORD will also hand over the army of Israel to the Philistines.

Narrator   Immediately Saul fell full length on the ground, filled with fear because of Samuel's words. His strength was gone, for he had eaten nothing all that day and night. The woman came to Saul and saw that he was greatly shaken.

Woman   Look, your maidservant has obeyed you. I took my life in my hands and did what you told me to do. Now please listen to your servant and let me give you some food so you may eat and have the strength to go on your way.

[Narrator   He refused and said:**]**

Saul   I will not eat.

Narrator   But his men joined the woman in urging him, and he listened to them. He got up from the ground and sat on the couch.

The woman had a fattened calf at the house, which she butchered at once. She took some flour, kneaded it and baked bread without yeast. Then she set it before Saul and his men, and they ate. That same night they got up and left.

Cast: **Narrator, Saul, Attendant, Woman, Samuel** (voice only, or can be Woman with voice disguised as Samuel)

Achish Sends David Back to Ziklag

1 Samuel 29:1–11

Narrator   The Philistines gathered all their forces at Aphek, and Israel camped by the spring in Jezreel. As the Philistine rulers marched with their units of hundreds and thousands, David and his men were marching at the rear with Achish. The commanders of the Philistines asked:

Philistine 1   What about these Hebrews?

Narrator   Achish replied:

Achish   Is this not David, who was an officer of Saul king of Israel? He has already been with me for over a year, and from the day he left Saul until now, I have found no fault in him.

Narrator   But the Philistine commanders were angry with him:

Philistine 1
(angrily)   Send the man back, that he may return to the place you assigned him.

Philistine 2   He must not go with us into battle, or he will turn against us during the fighting.

Philistine 1	How better could he regain his master's favor than by taking the heads of our own men?
Philistine 2	Isn't this the David they sang about in their dances:
	"Saul has slain his thousands, and David his tens of thousands"?
Narrator	So Achish called David:
Achish	As surely as the LORD lives, you have been reliable, and I would be pleased to have you serve with me in the army. From the day you came to me until now, I have found no fault in you, but the rulers don't approve of you. Turn back and go in peace; do nothing to displease the Philistine rulers.
David	But what have I done? What have you found against your servant from the day I came to you until now? Why can't I go and fight against the enemies of my LORD the king?
Achish	I know that you have been as pleasing in my eyes as an angel of God; nevertheless, the Philistine commanders have said, "He must not go up with us into battle." Now get up early, along with your master's servants who have come with you, and leave in the morning as soon as it is light.
Narrator	So David and his men got up early in the morning to go back to the land of the Philistines, and the Philistines went up to Jezreel.

Cast: **Narrator, Philistine 1, Achish, Philistine 2, David**

David Destroys the Amalekites

1 Samuel 30:1–30

Narrator	David and his men reached Ziklag on the third day. Now the Amalekites had raided the Negev and Ziklag. They had attacked Ziklag and burned it, and had taken captive the women and all who were in it, both young and old. They killed none of them, but carried them off as they went on their way.
	When David and his men came to Ziklag, they found it destroyed by fire and their wives and sons and daughters taken captive. So David and his men wept aloud until they had no strength left to weep. David's two wives had been captured—Ahinoam of Jezreel and Abigail, the widow of Nabal of Carmel. (PAUSE) David was greatly distressed because the men were talking of stoning him; each one was bitter in spirit because of his sons and daughters. But David found strength in the LORD his God. (PAUSE) Then David said to Abiathar the priest, the son of Ahimelech:
David	Bring me the ephod.
Narrator	Abiathar brought it to him, and David inquired of the LORD:

David	Shall I pursue this raiding party? Will I overtake them?
The Lord (voice only)	Pursue them. You will certainly overtake them and succeed in the rescue.
Narrator	David and the six hundred men with him came to the Besor Ravine, where some stayed behind, for two hundred men were too exhausted to cross the ravine. But David and four hundred men continued the pursuit.
	They found an Egyptian in a field and brought him to David. They gave him water to drink and food to eat—part of a cake of pressed figs and two cakes of raisins. He ate and was revived, for he had not eaten any food or drunk any water for three days and three nights. David asked him:
David	To whom do you belong, and where do you come from?
[Narrator	He said:]
Egyptian	I am an Egyptian, the slave of an Amalekite. My master abandoned me when I became ill three days ago. We raided the Negev of the Kerethites and the territory belonging to Judah and the Negev of Caleb. And we burned Ziklag.
David	Can you lead me down to this raiding party?
Egyptian	Swear to me before God that you will not kill me or hand me over to my master, and I will take you down to them.
Narrator	He led David down, and there they were, scattered over the countryside, eating, drinking and reveling because of the great amount of plunder they had taken from the land of the Philistines and from Judah. David fought them from dusk until the evening of the next day, and none of them got away, except four hundred young men who rode off on camels and fled. David recovered everything the Amalekites had taken, including his two wives. Nothing was missing: young or old, boy or girl, plunder or anything else they had taken. David brought everything back. He took all the flocks and herds, and his men drove them ahead of the other livestock, saying:
Men 1 and **2**	This is David's plunder.
Narrator	Then David came to the two hundred men who had been too exhausted to follow him and who were left behind at the Besor Ravine. They came out to meet David and the people with him. As David and his men approached, he greeted them. But all the evil men and troublemakers among David's followers said:
Man 1	Because they did not go out with us, we will not share with them the plunder we recovered.
Man 2	However, each man may take his wife and children and go.
David	No, my brothers, you must not do that with what the LORD has given us. He has protected us and handed over to us the forces that came against

	us. Who will listen to what you say? The share of the man who stayed with the supplies is to be the same as that of him who went down to the battle. All will share alike.
Narrator	David made this a statute and ordinance for Israel from that day to this.
	When David arrived in Ziklag, he sent some of the plunder to the elders of Judah, who were his friends, saying:
David	Here is a present for you from the plunder of the LORD's enemies.
Narrator	He sent it to those who were in Bethel, Ramoth Negev and Jattir; to those in Aroer, Siphmoth, Eshtemoa and Racal; to those in the towns of the Jerahmeelites and the Kenites; to those in Hormah, Bor Ashan, Athach and Hebron; and to those in all the other places where David and his men had roamed.

Cast: **Narrator, David, the Lord** (voice only), **Egyptian, Man 1, Man 2**

Saul Takes His Life

1 Samuel 31:1–6

Narrator	The Philistines fought against Israel; the Israelites fled before them, and many fell slain on Mount Gilboa. The Philistines pressed hard after Saul and his sons, and they killed his sons Jonathan, Abinadab and Malki-Shua. The fighting grew fierce around Saul, and when the archers overtook him, they wounded him critically. Saul said to his armor-bearer:
Saul	Draw your sword and run me through, or these uncircumcised fellows will come and run me through and abuse me.
Narrator	But his armor-bearer was terrified and would not do it; so Saul took his own sword and fell on it. When the armor-bearer saw that Saul was dead, he too fell on his sword and died with him. So Saul and his three sons and his armor-bearer and all his men died together that same day.

Cast: **Narrator, Saul**

2 Samuel

David Hears of Saul's Death

2 Samuel 1:1–16

Narrator	After the death of Saul, David returned from defeating the Amalekites and stayed in Ziklag two days. On the third day a man arrived from Saul's camp, with his clothes torn and with dust on his head. When he came to David, he fell to the ground to pay him honor.
David	Where have you come from?
Young man	I have escaped from the Israelite camp.
David	What happened? Tell me.
Young man	The men fled from the battle. Many of them fell and died. And Saul and his son Jonathan are dead.
Narrator	Then David said to the young man who brought him the report:
David (alarmed)	How do you know that Saul and his son Jonathan are dead?
Young man	I happened to be on Mount Gilboa, and there was Saul, leaning on his spear, with the chariots and riders almost upon him. When he turned around and saw me, he called out to me, and I said, "What can I do?" He asked me, "Who are you?" "An Amalekite," I answered. Then he said to me, "Stand over me and kill me! I am in the throes of death, but I'm still alive." So I stood over him and killed him, because I knew that after he had fallen he could not survive. And I took the crown that was on his head and the band on his arm and have brought them here to my lord.
Narrator	Then David and all the men with him took hold of their clothes and tore them. They mourned and wept and fasted till evening for Saul and his son Jonathan, and for the army of the Lord and the house of Israel, because they had fallen by the sword. [David said to the young man who brought him the report:]
David	Where are you from?
Young man	I am the son of an alien, an Amalekite.
David (angrily)	Why were you not afraid to lift your hand to destroy the Lord's anointed?
Narrator	Then David called one of his men [and said:]
David	Go, strike him down!

| Narrator | So he struck him down, and he died. |
| David | Your blood be on your own head. Your own mouth testified against you when you said, "I killed the LORD's anointed." |

Cast: **Narrator, David, Young man**

David Laments for Saul and Jonathan

2 Samuel 1:17–27

Narrator	David took up this lament concerning Saul and his son Jonathan, and ordered that the men of Judah be taught this lament of the bow—
Commentator	(It is written in the Book of Jashar):
David	Your glory, O Israel, lies slain on your heights.
Person 1	How the mighty have fallen!
David	Tell it not in Gath—
Person 2	Proclaim it not in the streets of Ashkelon—
David	Lest the daughters of the Philistines be glad—
Person 1	Lest the daughters of the uncircumcised rejoice.
David	O mountains of Gilboa, may you have neither dew nor rain—
Person 2	Nor fields that yield offerings ⌞of grain⌟.
David	For there the shield of the mighty was defiled—
Person 1	The shield of Saul—no longer rubbed with oil.
David	From the blood of the slain—
Person 2	From the flesh of the mighty—
David	The bow of Jonathan did not turn back—
Person 1	The sword of Saul did not return unsatisfied.
David	Saul and Jonathan— in life they were loved and gracious—
Person 2	And in death they were not parted.
David	They were swifter than eagles—
Person 1	They were stronger than lions.
David	O daughters of Israel, weep for Saul—
Person 1	Who clothed you in scarlet and finery—

298

Person 2	Who adorned your garments with ornaments of gold.
David	How the mighty have fallen in battle!
Person 1	Jonathan lies slain on your heights. (PAUSE)

David	I grieve for you, Jonathan my brother;
	     you were very dear to me.
	 Your love for me was wonderful,
	     more wonderful than that of women.

Person 2	How the mighty have fallen! The weapons of war have perished!

Cast: **Narrator, Commentator** (can be the same as Narrator), **David, Person 1, Person 2**. The words of David are arranged responsively for dramatic purposes.

David Anointed King over Judah

2 Samuel 2:1–7

Narrator	In the course of time, David inquired of the LORD:
David	Shall I go up to one of the towns of Judah?
Narrator	The LORD said:
The Lord (voice only)	Go up.
David	Where shall I go?
The Lord (voice)	To Hebron.
Narrator	So David went up there with his two wives, Ahinoam of Jezreel and Abigail, the widow of Nabal of Carmel. David also took the men who were with him, each with his family, and they settled in Hebron and its towns. Then the men of Judah came to Hebron and there they anointed David king over the house of Judah. (PAUSE)
	When David was told that it was the men of Jabesh Gilead who had buried Saul, he sent messengers to the men of Jabesh Gilead to say to them:
David	The LORD bless you for showing this kindness to Saul your master by burying him. May the LORD now show you kindness and faithfulness, and I too will show you the same favor because you have done this. Now then, be strong and brave, for Saul your master is dead, and the house of Judah has anointed me king over them.

Cast: **Narrator, David, the Lord** (voice only)

War between the Houses of David and Saul

2 Samuel 2:12–3:1

Narrator	Abner son of Ner, together with the men of Ish-Bosheth son of Saul, left Mahanaim and went to Gibeon. Joab son of Zeruiah and David's men went out and met them at the pool of Gibeon. One group sat down on one side of the pool and one group on the other side. Then Abner said to Joab:
Abner	Let's have some of the young men get up and fight hand to hand in front of us.
[Narrator	Joab said:]
Joab	All right, let them do it.
Narrator	So they stood up and were counted off—twelve men for Benjamin and Ish-Bosheth son of Saul, and twelve for David. Then each man grabbed his opponent by the head and thrust his dagger into his opponent's side, and they fell down together. So that place in Gibeon was called Helkath Hazzurim.
	The battle that day was very fierce, and Abner and the men of Israel were defeated by David's men.
	The three sons of Zeruiah were there: Joab, Abishai and Asahel. Now Asahel was as fleet-footed as a wild gazelle. He chased Abner, turning neither to the right nor to the left as he pursued him. Abner looked behind him.
Abner (calling)	Is that you, Asahel?
Asahel (calling)	It is.
Abner	Turn aside to the right or to the left; take on one of the *young* men and strip *him* of his weapons.
Narrator	But Asahel would not stop chasing him. [Again Abner warned Asahel:]
Abner	Stop chasing me! Why should I strike you down? How could I look your brother Joab in the face?
Narrator	But Asahel refused to give up the pursuit; so Abner thrust the butt of his spear into Asahel's stomach, and the spear came out through his back. He fell there and died on the spot. And every man stopped when he came to the place where Asahel had fallen and died.
	But Joab and Abishai pursued Abner, and as the sun was setting, they came to the hill of Ammah, near Giah on the way to the wasteland of Gibeon. Then the men of Benjamin rallied behind Abner. They formed themselves into a group and took their stand on top of a hill. Abner called out to Joab:

Abner

(calling)   Must the sword devour forever? Don't you realize that this will end in bitterness? How long before you order your men to stop pursuing their brothers?

Joab

(calling)   As surely as God lives, if you had not spoken, the men would have continued the pursuit of their brothers until morning.

Narrator   So Joab blew the trumpet, and all the men came to a halt; they no longer pursued Israel, nor did they fight anymore.

All that night Abner and his men marched through the Arabah. They crossed the Jordan, continued through the whole Bithron and came to Mahanaim.

Then Joab returned from pursuing Abner and assembled all his men. Besides Asahel, nineteen of David's men were found missing. But David's men had killed three hundred and sixty Benjamites who were with Abner. They took Asahel and buried him in his father's tomb at Bethlehem. Then Joab and his men marched all night and arrived at Hebron by daybreak. (PAUSE) The war between the house of Saul and the house of David lasted a long time. David grew stronger and stronger, while the house of Saul grew weaker and weaker.

Cast: **Narrator, Abner, Joab, Asahel.** (Note: During the course of this narrative, distances between speakers change.)

Abner Goes Over to David

From 2 Samuel 3:6–21

Narrator   During the war between the house of Saul and the house of David, Abner had been strengthening his own position in the house of Saul. Now Saul had had a concubine named Rizpah daughter of Aiah. And Ish-Bosheth said to Abner:

Ish-Bosheth   Why did you sleep with my father's concubine?

Narrator   Abner was very angry because of what Ish-Bosheth said and he answered:

Abner

(angrily)   Am I a dog's head—on Judah's side? This very day I am loyal to the house of your father Saul and to his family and friends. I haven't handed you over to David. Yet now you accuse me of an offense involving this woman! May God deal with Abner, be it ever so severely, if I do not do for David what the LORD promised him on oath and transfer the kingdom from the house of Saul and establish David's throne over Israel and Judah from Dan to Beersheba.

301

Narrator	Ish-Bosheth did not dare to say another word to Abner, because he was afraid of him. (PAUSE) Then Abner sent messengers on his behalf to say to David:
Abner	Whose land is it? Make an agreement with me, and I will help you bring all Israel over to you.
David	Good. I will make an agreement with you. But I demand one thing of you: Do not come into my presence unless you bring Michal daughter of Saul when you come to see me. . . .
Narrator	Abner conferred with the elders of Israel and said:
Abner	For some time you have wanted to make David your king. Now do it! For the LORD promised David:
The Lord (voice only)	By my servant David I will rescue my people Israel from the hand of the Philistines and from the hand of all their enemies. . . .
Narrator	When Abner, who had twenty men with him, came to David at Hebron, David prepared a feast for him and his men. Then Abner said to David:
Abner	Let me go at once and assemble all Israel for my LORD the king, so that they may make a compact with you, and that you may rule over all that your heart desires.
Narrator	So David sent Abner away, and he went in peace.

Cast: **Narrator, Ish-Bosheth, Abner, David, the Lord** (voice only)

Joab Murders Abner

2 Samuel 3:22–30

Narrator	[Just then] David's men and Joab returned from a raid and brought with them a great deal of plunder. But Abner was no longer with David in Hebron, because David had sent him away, and he had gone in peace. When Joab and all the soldiers with him arrived, he was told that Abner son of Ner had come to the king and that the king had sent him away and that he had gone in peace. So Joab went to the king and said:
Joab	What have you done? Look, Abner came to you. Why did you let him go? Now he is gone! You know Abner son of Ner; he came to deceive you and observe your movements and find out everything you are doing.
Narrator	Joab then left David and sent messengers after Abner, and they brought him back from the well of Sirah. But David did not know it. Now when Abner returned to Hebron, Joab took him aside into the gateway, as though to speak with him privately. And there, to avenge the blood of his brother Asahel, Joab stabbed him in the stomach, and he died. (PAUSE) Later, when David heard about this, he said:

David	I and my kingdom are forever innocent before the LORD concerning the blood of Abner son of Ner. May his blood fall upon the head of Joab and upon all his father's house! May Joab's house never be without someone who has a running sore or leprosy or who leans on a crutch or who falls by the sword or who lacks food.
Narrator	(Joab and his brother Abishai murdered Abner because he had killed their brother Asahel in the battle at Gibeon.)

Cast: **Narrator, Joab, David**

Abner Is Buried

2 Samuel 3:31–39

Narrator	David said to Joab and all the people with him:
David	Tear your clothes and put on sackcloth and walk in mourning in front of Abner.
Narrator	King David himself walked behind the bier. They buried Abner in Hebron, and the king wept aloud at Abner's tomb. All the people wept also. The king sang this lament for Abner:

David	Should Abner have died as the lawless die?
	   Your hands were not bound,
	   your feet were not fettered.
	You fell as one falls before wicked men.

Narrator	And all the people wept over him again. Then they all came and urged David to eat something while it was still day; but David took an oath, saying:
David	May God deal with me, be it ever so severely, if I taste bread or anything else before the sun sets!
Narrator	All the people took note and were pleased; indeed, everything the king did pleased them. So on that day all the people and all Israel knew that the king had no part in the murder of Abner son of Ner. Then the king said to his men:
David	Do you not realize that a prince and a great man has fallen in Israel this day? And today, though I am the anointed king, I am weak, and these sons of Zeruiah are too strong for me. May the LORD repay the evildoer according to his evil deeds!

Cast: **Narrator, David**

Ish-Bosheth Is Murdered

2 Samuel 4:1–12

Narrator When Ish-Bosheth son of Saul heard that Abner had died in Hebron, he lost courage, and all Israel became alarmed. Now Saul's son had two men who were leaders of raiding bands. One was named Baanah and the other Recab; they were sons of Rimmon the Beerothite from the tribe of Benjamin.

**Commenta-
tor** Beeroth is considered part of Benjamin, because the people of Beeroth fled to Gittaim and have lived there as aliens to this day.

(Jonathan son of Saul had a son who was lame in both feet. He was five years old when the news about Saul and Jonathan came from Jezreel. His nurse picked him up and fled, but as she hurried to leave, he fell and became crippled. His name was Mephibosheth.)

Narrator Now Recab and Baanah, the sons of Rimmon the Beerothite, set out for the house of Ish-Bosheth, and they arrived there in the heat of the day while he was taking his noonday rest. They went into the inner part of the house as if to get some wheat, and they stabbed him in the stomach. Then Recab and his brother Baanah slipped away.

They had gone into the house while he was lying on the bed in his bedroom. After they stabbed and killed him, they cut off his head. Taking it with them, they traveled all night by way of the Arabah. They brought the head of Ish-Bosheth to David at Hebron and said to the king:

Recab Here is the head of Ish-Bosheth son of Saul, your enemy, who tried to take your life.

Baanah This day the Lord has avenged my lord the king against Saul and his off-spring.

Narrator David answered Recab and his brother Baanah, the sons of Rimmon the Beerothite:

David As surely as the Lord lives, who has delivered me out of all trouble, when a man told me, "Saul is dead," and thought he was bringing good news, I seized him and put him to death in Ziklag. That was the reward I gave him for his news! How much more—when wicked men have killed an innocent man in his own house and on his own bed—should I not now demand his blood from your hand and rid the earth of you!

Narrator So David gave an order to his men, and they killed them. They cut off their hands and feet and hung the bodies by the pool in Hebron. But they took the head of Ish-Bosheth and buried it in Abner's tomb at Hebron.

Cast: **Narrator, Commentator, Recab, Baanah, David**

David Becomes King over Israel and Judah

2 Samuel 5:1–12

Narrator 1	All the tribes of Israel came to David at Hebron and said:
Person 1	We are your own flesh and blood.
Person 2	In the past, while Saul was king over us, you were the one who led Israel on their military campaigns.
Person 1	And the LORD said to you, "You will shepherd my people Israel, and you will become their ruler."
Narrator 2	When all the elders of Israel had come to King David at Hebron, the king made a compact with them at Hebron before the LORD, and they anointed David king over Israel.
	David was thirty years old when he became king, and he reigned forty years. In Hebron he reigned over Judah seven years and six months, and in Jerusalem he reigned over all Israel and Judah thirty-three years.
Narrator 1	The king and his men marched to Jerusalem to attack the Jebusites, who lived there. The Jebusites said to David:
Jebusite 1	You will not get in here—
Jebusite 2	Even the blind and the lame can ward you off.
[Narrator 2	They thought:]
Jebusite 1	David cannot get in here.
Narrator 2	Nevertheless, David captured the fortress of Zion, the City of David.
Narrator 1	On that day, David said:
David	Anyone who conquers the Jebusites will have to use the water shaft to reach those "lame and blind" who are David's enemies.
Narrator 1	That is why they say:
Jebusites 1 and 2	The "blind and lame" will not enter the palace.
Narrator 2	David then took up residence in the fortress and called it the City of David. He built up the area around it, from the supporting terraces inward. And he became more and more powerful, because the LORD God Almighty was with him.
Narrator 1	Now Hiram king of Tyre sent messengers to David, along with cedar logs and carpenters and stonemasons, and they built a palace for David. And David knew that the LORD had established him as king over Israel and had exalted his kingdom for the sake of his people Israel.

Cast: **Narrator 1, Person 1, Person 2** (can be the same as Person 1), **Narrator 2** (can be the same as Narrator 1), **Jebusite 1, Jebusite 2** (can the the same as Jebusite 1), **David**

David Defeats the Philistines

2 Samuel 5:17–25

Narrator	When the Philistines heard that David had been anointed king over Israel, they went up in full force to search for him, but David heard about it and went down to the stronghold. Now the Philistines had come and spread out in the Valley of Rephaim; so David inquired of the LORD:
David	Shall I go and attack the Philistines? Will you hand them over to me?
[Narrator	The LORD answered him:]
The Lord (voice only)	Go, for I will surely hand the Philistines over to you.
Narrator	So David went to Baal Perazim, and there he defeated them. [He said:]
David (victoriously)	As waters break out, the LORD has broken out against my enemies before me.
Narrator	So that place was called Baal Perazim. The Philistines abandoned their idols there, and David and his men carried them off. Once more the Philistines came up and spread out in the Valley of Rephaim; so David inquired of the LORD, and he answered:
The Lord (voice)	Do not go straight up, but circle around behind them and attack them in front of the balsam trees. As soon as you hear the sound of marching in the tops of the balsam trees, move quickly, because that will mean the LORD has gone out in front of you to strike the Philistine army.
Narrator	So David did as the LORD commanded him, and he struck down the Philistines all the way from Gibeon to Gezer.

Cast: **Narrator, David, the Lord** (voice only)

The Ark Is Brought to Jerusalem

2 Samuel 6:1–23

Narrator 1	David again brought together out of Israel chosen men, thirty thousand in all. He and all his men set out from Baalah of Judah to bring up from there the ark of God, which is called by the Name, the name of the LORD Almighty, who is enthroned between the cherubim that are on the ark.
Narrator 2	They set the ark of God on a new cart and brought it from the house of Abinadab, which was on the hill. Uzzah and Ahio, sons of Abinadab, were guiding the new cart with the ark of God on it, and Ahio was walking in front of it.

Narrator 1	David and the whole house of Israel were celebrating with all their might before the LORD, with songs and with harps, lyres, tambourines, sistrums and cymbals.
Narrator 2	When they came to the threshing floor of Nacon, Uzzah reached out and took hold of the ark of God, because the oxen stumbled.
Narrator 1	The LORD's anger burned against Uzzah because of his irreverent act; therefore God struck him down and he died there beside the ark of God.
Narrator 2	Then David was angry because the LORD's wrath had broken out against Uzzah, and to this day that place is called Perez Uzzah.
Narrator 1	David was afraid of the LORD that day and said:
David	How can the ark of the LORD ever come to me?
Narrator 1	He was not willing to take the ark of the LORD to be with him in the City of David. Instead, he took it aside to the house of Obed-Edom the Gittite. The ark of the LORD remained in the house of Obed-Edom the Gittite for three months, and the LORD blessed him and his entire household. (PAUSE)
Narrator 2	Now King David was told:
Person	The LORD has blessed the household of Obed-Edom and everything he has, because of the ark of God.
Narrator 2	So David went down and brought up the ark of God from the house of Obed-Edom to the City of David with rejoicing.
Narrator 1	When those who were carrying the ark of the LORD had taken six steps, he sacrificed a bull and a fattened calf.
Narrator 2	David, wearing a linen ephod, danced before the LORD with all his might, while he and the entire house of Israel brought up the ark of the LORD with shouts and the sound of trumpets.
Narrator 1	As the ark of the LORD was entering the City of David, Michal daughter of Saul watched from a window. And when she saw King David leaping and dancing before the LORD, she despised him in her heart.
Narrator 2	They brought the ark of the LORD and set it in its place inside the tent that David had pitched for it, and David sacrificed burnt offerings and fellowship offerings before the LORD. After he had finished sacrificing the burnt offerings and fellowship offerings, he blessed the people in the name of the LORD Almighty. Then he gave a loaf of bread, a cake of dates and a cake of raisins to each person in the whole crowd of Israelites, both men and women. And all the people went to their homes.
Narrator 1	When David returned home to bless his household, Michal daughter of Saul came out to meet him and said:
Michal	How the king of Israel has distinguished himself today, disrobing in the sight of the slave girls of his servants as any vulgar fellow would!

Narrator 1	David said to Michal:
David	It was before the LORD, who chose me rather than your father or anyone from his house when he appointed me ruler over the LORD's people Israel—I will celebrate before the LORD. I will become even more undignified than this, and I will be humiliated in my own eyes. But by these slave girls you spoke of, I will be held in honor.
Narrator 2	And Michal daughter of Saul had no children to the day of her death.

Cast: **Narrator 1, Narrator 2, David, Person, Michal**

God's Promise to David

2 Samuel 7:1–17

Narrator	After the king was settled in his palace and the LORD had given him rest from all his enemies around him, he said to Nathan the prophet:
David	Here I am, living in a palace of cedar, while the ark of God remains in a tent.
Narrator	Nathan replied to the king:
Nathan	Whatever you have in mind, go ahead and do it, for the LORD is with you.
Narrator (slowly)	That night the word of the LORD came to Nathan, saying:
The Lord (voice only)	Go and tell my servant David, "This is what the LORD says: Are you the one to build me a house to dwell in? I have not dwelt in a house from the day I brought the Israelites up out of Egypt to this day. I have been moving from place to place with a tent as my dwelling. Wherever I have moved with all the Israelites, did I ever say to any of their rulers whom I commanded to shepherd my people Israel, 'Why have you not built me a house of cedar?'
	"Now then, tell my servant David, 'This is what the LORD Almighty says: I took you from the pasture and from following the flock to be ruler over my people Israel. I have been with you wherever you have gone, and I have cut off all your enemies from before you. Now I will make your name great, like the names of the greatest men of the earth. And I will provide a place for my people Israel and will plant them so that they can have a home of their own and no longer be disturbed. Wicked people will not oppress them anymore, as they did at the beginning and have done ever since the time I appointed leaders over my people Israel. I will also give you rest from all your enemies.
	"The LORD declares to you that the LORD himself will establish a house for you: When your days are over and you rest with your fathers, I will raise up your offspring to succeed you, who will come from your own

body, and I will establish his kingdom. He is the one who will build a house for my Name, and I will establish the throne of his kingdom forever. I will be his father, and he will be my son. When he does wrong, I will punish him with the rod of men, with floggings inflicted by men. But my love will never be taken away from him, as I took it away from Saul, whom I removed from before you. Your house and your kingdom will endure forever before me; your throne will be established forever.'"

Narrator	Nathan reported to David all the words of this entire revelation.

Cast: **Narrator, David, Nathan, the Lord** (voice only)

David and Mephibosheth

2 Samuel 9:1–13

Narrator	David asked:
David	Is there anyone still left of the house of Saul to whom I can show kindness for Jonathan's sake?
Narrator	Now there was a servant of Saul's household named Ziba. They called him to appear before David, and the king said to him:
David	Are you Ziba?
[Narrator	[He replied:]]
Ziba	Your servant.
David	Is there no one still left of the house of Saul to whom I can show God's kindness?
Ziba	There is still a son of Jonathan; he is crippled in both feet.
David	Where is he?
Ziba	He is at the house of Makir son of Ammiel in Lo Debar.
Narrator	So King David had him brought from Lo Debar, from the house of Makir son of Ammiel. (PAUSE) When Mephibosheth son of Jonathan, the son of Saul, came to David, he bowed down to pay him honor. David said:
David	Mephibosheth!
Mephibosheth	Your servant.
David	Don't be afraid, for I will surely show you kindness for the sake of your father Jonathan. I will restore to you all the land that belonged to your grandfather Saul, and you will always eat at my table.
Narrator	Mephibosheth bowed down and said:
Mephibosheth	What is your servant, that you should notice a dead dog like me?

Narrator	Then the king summoned Ziba, Saul's servant, and said to him:
David	I have given your master's grandson everything that belonged to Saul and his family. You and your sons and your servants are to farm the land for him and bring in the crops, so that your master's grandson may be provided for. And Mephibosheth, grandson of your master, will always eat at my table.
Narrator	(Now Ziba had fifteen sons and twenty servants.) Then Ziba said to the king:
Ziba	Your servant will do whatever my lord the king commands his servant to do.
Narrator	So Mephibosheth ate at David's table like one of the king's sons.
	Mephibosheth had a young son named Mica, and all the members of Ziba's household were servants of Mephibosheth. And Mephibosheth lived in Jerusalem, because he always ate at the king's table, and he was crippled in both feet.

Cast: **Narrator, David, Ziba, Mephibosheth**

David Defeats the Ammonites

2 Samuel 10:1–14 [15–19]

Narrator	In the course of time, the king of the Ammonites died, and his son Hanun succeeded him as king. David thought:
David	I will show kindness to Hanun son of Nahash, just as his father showed kindness to me.
Narrator	So David sent a delegation to express his sympathy to Hanun concerning his father. (PAUSE) When David's men came to the land of the Ammonites, the Ammonite nobles said to Hanun their lord:
Ammonite	Do you think David is honoring your father by sending men to you to express sympathy? Hasn't David sent them to you to explore the city and spy it out and overthrow it?
Narrator	So Hanun seized David's men, shaved off half of each man's beard, cut off their garments in the middle at the buttocks, and sent them away.
	When David was told about this, he sent messengers to meet the men, for they were greatly humiliated. The king said:
David	Stay at Jericho till your beards have grown, and then come back.
Narrator	When the Ammonites realized that they had become a stench in David's nostrils, they hired twenty thousand Aramean foot soldiers from Beth Rehob and Zobah, as well as the king of Maacah with a thousand men, and also twelve thousand men from Tob.

On hearing this, David sent Joab out with the entire army of fighting men. The Ammonites came out and drew up in battle formation at the entrance to their city gate, while the Arameans of Zobah and Rehob and the men of Tob and Maacah were by themselves in the open country.

Joab saw that there were battle lines in front of him and behind him; so he selected some of the best troops in Israel and deployed them against the Arameans. He put the rest of the men under the command of Abishai his brother and deployed them against the Ammonites. [Joab said:]

Joab   If the Arameans are too strong for me, then you are to come to my rescue; but if the Ammonites are too strong for you, then I will come to rescue you. Be strong and let us fight bravely for our people and the cities of our God. The LORD will do what is good in his sight.

Narrator   Then Joab and the troops with him advanced to fight the Arameans, and they fled before him. When the Ammonites saw that the Arameans were fleeing, they fled before Abishai and went inside the city. So Joab returned from fighting the Ammonites and came to Jerusalem.

[After the Arameans saw that they had been routed by Israel, they regrouped. Hadadezer had Arameans brought from beyond the River; they went to Helam, with Shobach the commander of Hadadezer's army leading them.

When David was told of this, he gathered all Israel, crossed the Jordan and went to Helam. The Arameans formed their battle lines to meet David and fought against him. But they fled before Israel, and David killed seven hundred of their charioteers and forty thousand of their foot soldiers. He also struck down Shobach the commander of their army, and he died there. When all the kings who were vassals of Hadadezer saw that they had been defeated by Israel, they made peace with the Israelites and became subject to them.

So the Arameans were afraid to help the Ammonites anymore.]

Cast: **Narrator, David, Ammonite, Joab**

David and Bathsheba

From 2 Samuel 11:1–27

Narrator   In the spring, at the time when kings go off to war, David sent Joab out with the king's men and the whole Israelite army. They destroyed the Ammonites and besieged Rabbah. But David remained in Jerusalem. (PAUSE)

One evening David got up from his bed and walked around on the roof of the palace. From the roof he saw a woman bathing. The woman was very beautiful, and David sent someone to find out about her. The man said:

Servant	Isn't this Bathsheba, the daughter of Eliam and the wife of Uriah the Hittite?
Narrator	Then David sent messengers to get her. She came to him, and he slept with her. . . . Then she went back home. The woman conceived and sent word to David:
Bathsheba	I am pregnant.
Narrator	So David sent this word to Joab:
David	Send me Uriah the Hittite.
Narrator	And Joab sent him to David. (PAUSE) When Uriah came to him, David asked him how Joab was, how the soldiers were and how the war was going. Then David said to Uriah:
David	Go down to your house and wash your feet.
Narrator	So Uriah left the palace, and a gift from the king was sent after him. But Uriah slept at the entrance to the palace with all his master's servants and did not go down to his house. David was told:
Servant (anxiously)	Uriah did not go home.
David (to Uriah)	Haven't you just come from a distance? Why didn't you go home?
[Narrator	Uriah said to David:]
Uriah	The ark and Israel and Judah are staying in tents, and my master Joab and my lord's men are camped in the open fields. How could I go to my house to eat and drink and lie with my wife? As surely as you live, I will not do such a thing!
David	Stay here one more day, and tomorrow I will send you back.
Narrator	So Uriah remained in Jerusalem that day and the next. At David's invitation, he ate and drank with him, and David made him drunk. But in the evening Uriah went out to sleep on his mat among his master's servants; he did not go home.
	In the morning David wrote a letter to Joab and sent it with Uriah. In it he wrote:
David	Put Uriah in the front line where the fighting is fiercest. Then withdraw from him so he will be struck down and die.
Narrator	So while Joab had the city under siege, he put Uriah at a place where he knew the strongest defenders were. When the men of the city came out and fought against Joab, some of the men in David's army fell; moreover, Uriah the Hittite died. (PAUSE)
	Joab sent David a full account of the battle. He instructed the messenger:

Joab	When you have finished giving the king this account of the battle, the king's anger may flare up, and he may ask you, "Why did you get so close to the city to fight? Didn't you know they would shoot arrows from the wall? Who killed Abimelech son of Jerub-Besheth? Didn't a woman throw an upper millstone on him from the wall, so that he died in Thebez? Why did you get so close to the wall?" If he asks you this, then say to him, "Also, your servant Uriah the Hittite is dead."
Narrator	The messenger set out, and when he arrived he told David everything Joab had sent him to say.
Messenger (to David)	The men overpowered us and came out against us in the open, but we drove them back to the entrance to the city gate. Then the archers shot arrows at your servants from the wall, and some of the king's men died. (PAUSE) Moreover, your servant Uriah the Hittite is dead.
[Narrator	David told the messenger:]
David	Say this to Joab: "Don't let this upset you; the sword devours one as well as another. Press the attack against the city and destroy it." Say this to encourage Joab. (PAUSE)
Narrator	When Uriah's wife heard that her husband was dead, she mourned for him. After the time of mourning was over, David had her brought to his house, and she became his wife and bore him a son.
(deliberately)	But the thing David had done displeased the LORD.

Cast: **Narrator, Servant, Bathsheba, David, Joab, Messenger**

Nathan Rebukes David

2 Samuel 12:1–15

Narrator	The LORD sent Nathan to David. When he came to him, he said:
Nathan	There were two men in a certain town, one rich and the other poor. The rich man had a very large number of sheep and cattle, but the poor man had nothing except one little ewe lamb he had bought. He raised it, and it grew up with him and his children. It shared his food, drank from his cup and even slept in his arms. It was like a daughter to him.
	Now a traveler came to the rich man, but the rich man refrained from taking one of his own sheep or cattle to prepare a meal for the traveler who had come to him. Instead, he took the ewe lamb that belonged to the poor man and prepared it for the one who had come to him.
Narrator	David burned with anger against the man [and said to Nathan:]

David
(angrily,
to Nathan)   As surely as the LORD lives, the man who did this deserves to die! He must pay for that lamb four times over, because he did such a thing and had no pity.

Nathan
(pointedly)   You are the man! This is what the LORD, the God of Israel, says: "I anointed you king over Israel, and I delivered you from the hand of Saul. I gave your master's house to you, and your master's wives into your arms. I gave you the house of Israel and Judah. And if all this had been too little, I would have given you even more. Why did you despise the word of the LORD by doing what is evil in his eyes? You struck down Uriah the Hittite with the sword and took his wife to be your own. You killed him with the sword of the Ammonites. Now, therefore, the sword will never depart from your house, because you despised me and took the wife of Uriah the Hittite to be your own."

This is what the LORD says: "Out of your own household I am going to bring calamity upon you. Before your very eyes I will take your wives and give them to one who is close to you, and he will lie with your wives in broad daylight. You did it in secret, but I will do this thing in broad daylight before all Israel."

David (sadly)   I have sinned against the LORD.

Nathan   The LORD has taken away your sin. You are not going to die. But because by doing this you have made the enemies of the LORD show utter contempt, the son born to you will die.

Narrator   After Nathan had gone home, the LORD struck the child that Uriah's wife had borne to David, and he became ill.

Cast: **Narrator, Nathan, David**

David's Son Dies

From 2 Samuel 12:15–25

Narrator   After Nathan had gone home, the LORD struck the child that Uriah's wife had borne to David, and he became ill. David pleaded with God for the child. He fasted and went into his house and spent the nights lying on the ground. The elders of his household stood beside him to get him up from the ground, but he refused, and he would not eat any food with them. (PAUSE)

On the seventh day the child died. David's servants were afraid to tell him that the child was dead [for they thought:]

Servant 1 (to Servant 2)	While the child was still living, we spoke to David but he would not listen to us.
Servant 2	How can we tell him the child is dead?
Servant 1	He may do something desperate.
Narrator	David noticed that his servants were whispering among themselves and he realized the child was dead.
David	Is the child dead?
Servants 1 and 2	Yes, he *is* dead.
Narrator	Then David got up from the ground. After he had washed, put on lotions and changed his clothes, he went into the house of the LORD and worshiped. Then he went to his own house, and at his request they served him food, and he ate. His servants asked him:
Servant 2	Why are you acting this way?
Servant 1	While the child was alive, you fasted and wept—
Servant 2	But now that the child is dead, you get up and eat!
David	While the child was still alive, I fasted and wept. I thought, "Who knows? The LORD may be gracious to me and let the child live." But now that he is dead, why should I fast? Can I bring him back again? I will go to him, but he will not return to me.
Narrator	Then David comforted his wife Bathsheba, and he went to her and lay with her. She gave birth to a son, and they named him Solomon. The LORD loved him; and because the LORD loved him, he sent word through Nathan the prophet to name him Jedidiah.

Cast: **Narrator**, **Servant 1**, **Servant 2** (can be the same as Servant 1), **David**

David Captures Rabbah

2 Samuel 12:26–31

Narrator	Joab fought against Rabbah of the Ammonites and captured the royal citadel. Joab then sent messengers to David:
Joab	I have fought against Rabbah and taken its water supply. Now muster the rest of the troops and besiege the city and capture it. Otherwise I will take the city, and it will be named after me.
Narrator	So David mustered the entire army and went to Rabbah, and attacked and captured it. He took the crown from the head of their king—its weight was a talent of gold, and it was set with precious stones—and it was placed

on David's head. He took a great quantity of plunder from the city and brought out the people who were there, consigning them to labor with saws and with iron picks and axes, and he made them work at brickmaking. He did this to all the Ammonite towns. Then David and his entire army returned to Jerusalem.

Cast: **Narrator, Joab**

Amnon and Tamar

2 Samuel 13:1–22

Narrator	[In the course of time,] Amnon son of David fell in love with Tamar, the beautiful sister of Absalom son of David.
	Amnon became frustrated to the point of illness on account of his sister Tamar, for she was a virgin, and it seemed impossible for him to do anything to her.
	Now Amnon had a friend named Jonadab son of Shimeah, David's brother. Jonadab was a very shrewd man. He asked Amnon:
Jonadab	Why do you, the king's son, look so haggard morning after morning? Won't you tell me?
Amnon (to Jonadab)	I'm in love with Tamar, my brother Absalom's sister.
Jonadab	Go to bed and pretend to be ill. When your father comes to see you, say to him, "I would like my sister Tamar to come and give me something to eat. Let her prepare the food in my sight so I may watch her and then eat it from her hand."
Narrator	So Amnon lay down and pretended to be ill. When the king came to see him, Amnon said to him:
Amnon	I would like my sister Tamar to come and make some special bread in my sight, so I may eat from her hand.
Narrator	David sent word to Tamar at the palace:
David	Go to the house of your brother Amnon and prepare some food for him.
Narrator	So Tamar went to the house of her brother Amnon, who was lying down. She took some dough, kneaded it, made the bread in his sight and baked it. Then she took the pan and served him the bread, but he refused to eat.
Amnon	Send everyone out of here.
Narrator	So everyone left him. Then Amnon said to Tamar:
Amnon	Bring the food here into my bedroom so I may eat from your hand.
Narrator	And Tamar took the bread she had prepared and brought it to her brother Amnon in his bedroom. But when she took it to him to eat, he grabbed her:

Amnon
(roughly) Come to bed with me, my sister.

Tamar
(urgently) Don't, my brother! Don't force me. Such a thing should not be done in Israel! Don't do this wicked thing. What about me? Where could I get rid of my disgrace? And what about you? You would be like one of the wicked fools in Israel. Please speak to the king; he will not keep me from being married to you.

Narrator But he refused to listen to her, and since he was stronger than she, he raped her.

Then Amnon hated her with intense hatred. In fact, he hated her more than he had loved her. [Amnon said to her:]

Amnon
(to Tamar) Get up and get out!

Tamar
(to Amnon) No! Sending me away would be a greater wrong than what you have already done to me.

Narrator But he refused to listen to her. He called his personal servant:

Amnon Get this woman out of here and bolt the door after her.

Narrator So his servant put her out and bolted the door after her. She was wearing a richly ornamented robe, for this was the kind of garment the virgin daughters of the king wore. Tamar put ashes on her head and tore the ornamented robe she was wearing. She put her hand on her head and went away, weeping aloud as she went. [Her brother Absalom said to her:]

Absalom Has that Amnon, your brother, been with you? Be quiet now, my sister; he is your brother. Don't take this thing to heart.

Narrator And Tamar lived in her brother Absalom's house, a desolate woman. (PAUSE)

When King David heard all this, he was furious. Absalom never said a word to Amnon, either good or bad; he hated Amnon because he had disgraced his sister Tamar.

Cast: **Narrator, Jonadab, Amnon, David, Tamar, Absalom**

Absalom Kills Amnon

2 Samuel 13:23–39

Narrator [Two years later,] when Absalom's sheepshearers were at Baal Hazor near the border of Ephraim, he invited all the king's sons to come there. Absalom went to the king:

317

Absalom	Your servant has had shearers come. Will the king and his officials please join me?
[Narrator	The king replied:]
David	No, my son. All of us should not go; we would only be a burden to you.
Narrator	Although Absalom urged him, he still refused to go, but gave him his blessing. [Then Absalom said:]
Absalom	If not, please let my brother Amnon come with us.
David	Why should *he* go with you?
Narrator	But Absalom urged him, so he sent with him Amnon and the rest of the king's sons. (PAUSE) Absalom ordered his men:
Absalom	Listen! When Amnon is in high spirits from drinking wine and I say to you, "Strike Amnon down," then kill him. Don't be afraid. Have not *I* given you this order? Be strong and brave.
Narrator	So Absalom's men did to Amnon what Absalom had ordered. Then all the king's sons got up, mounted their mules and fled. (PAUSE) While they were on their way, the report came to David:
Messenger (breathless)	Absalom has struck down all the king's sons; not one of them is left.
Narrator	The king stood up, tore his clothes and lay down on the ground; and all his servants stood by with their clothes torn. But Jonadab son of Shimeah, David's brother, said:
Jonadab	My lord should not think that they killed *all* the princes; only Amnon is dead. This has been Absalom's expressed intention ever since the day Amnon raped his sister Tamar. My lord the king should not be concerned about the report that *all* the king's sons are dead. Only *Amnon* is dead.
Narrator	Meanwhile, Absalom had fled.
	Now the man standing watch looked up and saw many people on the road west of him, coming down the side of the hill. The watchman went and told the king:
Watchman (calling)	I see men in the direction of Horonaim, on the side of the hill.
Narrator	Jonadab said to the king:
Jonadab	See, the king's sons are here; it has happened just as your servant said.
Narrator	As he finished speaking, the king's sons came in, wailing loudly. The king, too, and all his servants wept very bitterly. (PAUSE)
	Absalom fled and went to Talmai son of Ammihud, the king of Geshur. But King David mourned for his son every day.

After Absalom fled and went to Geshur, he stayed there three years. And the spirit of the king longed to go to Absalom, for he was consoled concerning Amnon's death.

Cast: **Narrator, Absalom, David, Messenger, Jonadab, Watchman** (can be the same as Messenger)

Absalom Returns to Jerusalem

2 Samuel 14:1–24

Narrator   Joab son of Zeruiah knew that the king's heart longed for Absalom. So Joab sent someone to Tekoa and had a wise woman brought from there. [He said to her:]

Joab
(to Woman)   Pretend you are in mourning. Dress in mourning clothes, and don't use any cosmetic lotions. Act like a woman who has spent many days grieving for the dead. Then go to the king and speak these words to him.

Narrator   And Joab put the words in her mouth.

When the woman from Tekoa went to the king, she fell with her face to the ground to pay him honor, and she said:

Woman   Help me, O king!

[Narrator   The king asked her:]

David   What is troubling you?

Woman   I am indeed a widow; my husband is dead. I your servant had two sons. They got into a fight with each other in the field, and no one was there to separate them. One struck the other and killed him. Now the whole clan has risen up against your servant; they say, "Hand over the one who struck his brother down, so that we may put him to death for the life of his brother whom he killed; then we will get rid of the heir as well." They would put out the only burning coal I have left, leaving my husband neither name nor descendant on the face of the earth.

David   Go home, and I will issue an order in your behalf.

Woman   My lord the king, let the blame rest on me and on my father's family, and let the king and his throne be without guilt.

David   If anyone says anything to you, bring him to me, and he will not bother you again.

Woman   Then let the king invoke the Lord his God to prevent the avenger of blood from adding to the destruction, so that my son will not be destroyed.

David   As surely as the Lord lives, not one hair of your son's head will fall to the ground.

319

Woman	Let your servant speak a word to my lord the king.
David	Speak.
Woman	Why then have you devised a thing like this against the people of God? When the king says this, does he not convict himself, for the king has not brought back his banished son? Like water spilled on the ground, which cannot be recovered, so we must die. But God does not take away life; instead, he devises ways so that a banished person may not remain estranged from him.
	And now I have come to say this to my lord the king because the people have made me afraid. Your servant thought, "I will speak to the king; perhaps he will do what his servant asks. Perhaps the king will agree to deliver his servant from the hand of the man who is trying to cut off both me and my son from the inheritance God gave us." And now your servant says, "May the word of my lord the king bring me rest, for my lord the king is like an angel of God in discerning good and evil. May the LORD your God be with you."
David	Do not keep from me the answer to what I am going to ask you.
Woman	Let my lord the king speak.
David	Isn't the hand of Joab with you in all this? (PAUSE)
Woman	As surely as you live, my lord the king, no one can turn to the right or to the left from anything my lord the king says. Yes, it was your servant Joab who instructed me to do this and who put all these words into the mouth of your servant. Your servant Joab did this to change the present situation. My lord has wisdom like that of an angel of God—he knows everything that happens in the land.
Narrator	The king said to Joab:
David (to Joab)	Very well, I will do it. Go, bring back the young man Absalom.
Narrator	Joab fell with his face to the ground to pay him honor, and he blessed the king.
Joab	Today your servant knows that he has found favor in your eyes, my lord the king, because the king has granted his servant's request.
Narrator	Then Joab went to Geshur and brought Absalom back to Jerusalem. But the king said:
David	He must go to his own house; he must not see my face.
Narrator	So Absalom went to his own house and did not see the face of the king.

Cast: **Narrator, Joab, Woman, David**

Absalom Is Reconciled to David

2 Samuel 14:25–33

Narrator   In all Israel there was not a man so highly praised for his handsome appearance as Absalom. From the top of his head to the sole of his foot there was no blemish in him. Whenever he cut the hair of his head—he used to cut his hair from time to time when it became too heavy for him—he would weigh it, and its weight was two hundred shekels by the royal standard.

Three sons and a daughter were born to Absalom. The daughter's name was Tamar, and she became a beautiful woman.

Absalom lived two years in Jerusalem without seeing the king's face. Then Absalom sent for Joab in order to send him to the king, but Joab refused to come to him. So he sent a second time, but he refused to come. Then he said to his servants:

Absalom   Look, Joab's field is next to mine, and he has barley there. Go and set it on fire.

Narrator   So Absalom's servants set the field on fire. (PAUSE) Then Joab did go to Absalom's house and he said to him:

Joab   Why have your servants set my field on fire?

[Narrator   Absalom said to Joab:**]**

Absalom   Look, I sent word to you and said, "Come here so I can send you to the king to ask, 'Why have I come from Geshur? It would be better for me if I were still there!'" (PAUSE) Now then, I want to see the king's face, and if I am guilty of anything, let him put me to death.

Narrator   So Joab went to the king and told him this. Then the king summoned Absalom, and he came in and bowed down with his face to the ground before the king. And the king kissed Absalom.

Cast: **Narrator, Absalom, Joab**

Absalom's Conspiracy

2 Samuel 15:1–12

Narrator   [In the course of time,] Absalom provided himself with a chariot and horses and with fifty men to run ahead of him. He would get up early and stand by the side of the road leading to the city gate. Whenever anyone came with a complaint to be placed before the king for a decision, Absalom would call out to him:

Absalom   What town are you from?

Narrator	He would answer:
Man	Your servant is from one of the tribes of Israel.
Narrator	Then Absalom would say to him:
Absalom	Look, your claims are valid and proper, but there is no representative of the king to hear you.
Narrator	And Absalom would add:
Absalom	If only I were appointed judge in the land! Then everyone who has a complaint or case could come to me and I would see that he gets justice.
Narrator	Also, whenever anyone approached him to bow down before him, Absalom would reach out his hand, take hold of him and kiss him. Absalom behaved in this way toward all the Israelites who came to the king asking for justice, and so he stole the hearts of the men of Israel. (PAUSE) At the end of four years, Absalom said to the king:
Absalom	Let me go to Hebron and fulfill a vow I made to the LORD. While your servant was living at Geshur in Aram, I made this vow: "If the LORD takes me back to Jerusalem, I will worship the LORD in Hebron."
[Narrator	The king said to him:]
David	Go in peace.
Narrator	So he went to Hebron.
	Then Absalom sent secret messengers throughout the tribes of Israel:
Absalom	As soon as you hear the sound of the trumpets, then say, "Absalom is king in Hebron."
Narrator	Two hundred men from Jerusalem had accompanied Absalom. They had been invited as guests and went quite innocently, knowing nothing about the matter. While Absalom was offering sacrifices, he also sent for Ahithophel the Gilonite, David's counselor, to come from Giloh, his hometown. And so the conspiracy gained strength, and Absalom's following kept on increasing.

Cast: **Narrator, Absalom, Man, David**

David Flees (i)

2 Samuel 15:13–23

Narrator	A messenger came and told David:
Messenger	The hearts of the men of Israel are with Absalom.
Narrator	Then David said to all his officials who were with him in Jerusalem:

David	Come! We must flee, or none of us will escape from Absalom. We must leave immediately, or he will move quickly to overtake us and bring ruin upon us and put the city to the sword.
Narrator	The king's officials answered him:
Official	Your servants are ready to do whatever our lord the king chooses.
Narrator	The king set out, with his entire household following him; but he left ten concubines to take care of the palace. So the king set out, with all the people following him, and they halted at a place some distance away. All his men marched past him, along with all the Kerethites and Pelethites; and all the six hundred Gittites who had accompanied him from Gath marched before the king. The king said to Ittai the Gittite:
David	Why should *you* come along with us? Go back and stay with King Absalom. You are a foreigner, an exile from your homeland. You came only yesterday. And today shall I make you wander about with us, when I do not know where I am going? Go back, and take your countrymen. May kindness and faithfulness be with you.
[Narrator	But Ittai replied to the king:]
Ittai	As surely as the LORD lives, and as my lord the king lives, wherever my lord the king may be, whether it means life or death, there will your servant be.
David	Go ahead, march on.
Narrator	So Ittai the Gittite marched on with all his men and the families that were with him.
	The whole countryside wept aloud as all the people passed by. The king also crossed the Kidron Valley, and all the people moved on toward the desert.

Cast: **Narrator, Messenger, David, Official, Ittai**

David Flees (ii)

2 Samuel 15:23–37

Narrator	The whole countryside wept aloud as all the people passed by. The king also crossed the Kidron Valley, and all the people moved on toward the desert.
	Zadok was there, too, and all the Levites who were with him were carrying the ark of the covenant of God. They set down the ark of God, and Abiathar offered sacrifices until all the people had finished leaving the city. Then the king said to Zadok:
David	Take the ark of God back into the city. If I find favor in the LORD's eyes, he will bring me back and let me see it and his dwelling place again. But

	if he says, "I am not pleased with you," then I am ready; let him do to me whatever seems good to him.
[Narrator	The king also said to Zadok the priest:**]**
David	Aren't you a seer? Go back to the city in peace, with your son Ahimaaz and Jonathan son of Abiathar. You and Abiathar take your two sons with you. I will wait at the fords in the desert until word comes from you to inform me.
Narrator	So Zadok and Abiathar took the ark of God back to Jerusalem and stayed there.
	But David continued up the Mount of Olives, weeping as he went; his head was covered and he was barefoot. All the people with him covered their heads too and were weeping as they went up. Now David had been told, "Ahithophel is among the conspirators with Absalom." So David prayed:
David (praying)	O LORD, turn Ahithophel's counsel into foolishness.
Narrator	When David arrived at the summit, where people used to worship God, Hushai the Arkite was there to meet him, his robe torn and dust on his head. David said to him:
David	If you go with me, you will be a burden to me. But if you return to the city and say to Absalom, "I will be your servant, O king; I was your father's servant in the past, but now I will be your servant," then you can help me by frustrating Ahithophel's advice. Won't the priests Zadok and Abiathar be there with you? Tell them anything you hear in the king's palace. Their two sons, Ahimaaz son of Zadok and Jonathan son of Abiathar, are there with them. Send them to me with anything you hear.
Narrator	So David's friend Hushai arrived at Jerusalem as Absalom was entering the city.

Cast: **Narrator, David**

David and Ziba

2 Samuel 16:1–4

Narrator	When David had gone a short distance beyond the summit, there was Ziba, the steward of Mephibosheth, waiting to meet him. He had a string of donkeys saddled and loaded with two hundred loaves of bread, a hundred cakes of raisins, a hundred cakes of figs and a skin of wine. The king asked Ziba:
David	Why have you brought these?
[Narrator	Ziba answered:**]**
Ziba	The donkeys are for the king's household to ride on, the bread and fruit are for the men to eat, and the wine is to refresh those who become exhausted in the desert.

David	Where is your master's grandson?
Ziba	He is staying in Jerusalem, because he thinks, "Today the house of Israel will give me back my grandfather's kingdom."
David	All that belonged to Mephibosheth is now yours.
Ziba	I humbly bow. May I find favor in your eyes, my lord the king.

Cast: **Narrator, David, Ziba**

Shimei Curses David

2 Samuel 16:5–14

Narrator	As King David approached Bahurim, a man from the same clan as Saul's family came out from there. His name was Shimei son of Gera, and he cursed as he came out. He pelted David and all the king's officials with stones, though all the troops and the special guard were on David's right and left. As he cursed, Shimei said:
Shimei	Get out, get out, you man of blood, you scoundrel! The LORD has repaid you for all the blood you shed in the household of Saul, in whose place you have reigned. The LORD has handed the kingdom over to your son Absalom. You have come to ruin because you are a man of blood!
Narrator	Then Abishai son of Zeruiah said to the king:
Abishai	Why should this dead dog curse my lord the king? Let me go over and cut off his head.
[Narrator	But the king said:]
David (to Abishai)	What do you and I have in common, you sons of Zeruiah? If he is cursing because the LORD said to him, "Curse David," who can ask, "Why do you do this?"
Narrator	David then said to Abishai and all his officials:
David	My son, who is of my own flesh, is trying to take my life. How much more, then, this Benjamite! Leave him alone; let him curse, for the LORD has told him to. It may be that the LORD will see my distress and repay me with good for the cursing I am receiving today.
Narrator	So David and his men continued along the road while Shimei was going along the hillside opposite him, cursing as he went and throwing stones at him and showering him with dirt. The king and all the people with him arrived at their destination exhausted. And there he refreshed himself.

Cast: **Narrator, Shimei, Abishai, David**

The Advice of Hushai and Ahithophel

2 Samuel 16:15–23

Narrator [Meanwhile,] Absalom and all the men of Israel came to Jerusalem, and Ahithophel was with him. Then Hushai the Arkite, David's friend, went to Absalom.

Hushai Long live the king! Long live the king!

Narrator Absalom asked Hushai:

Absalom Is this the love you show your friend? Why didn't you go with your friend?

Hushai No, the one chosen by the LORD, by these people, and by all the men of Israel—his I will be, and I will remain with him. Furthermore, whom should I serve? Should I not serve the son? Just as I served your father, so I will serve you.

Narrator Absalom said to Ahithophel:

Absalom Give us your advice. What should we do?

Ahithophel
(to Absalom) Lie with your father's concubines whom he left to take care of the palace. Then all Israel will hear that you have made yourself a stench in your father's nostrils, and the hands of everyone with you will be strengthened.

Narrator So they pitched a tent for Absalom on the roof, and he lay with his father's concubines in the sight of all Israel. Now in those days the advice Ahithophel gave was like that of one who inquires of God. That was how both David and Absalom regarded all of Ahithophel's advice.

Cast: **Narrator, Hushai, Absalom, Ahithophel**

Hushai Misleads Absalom

2 Samuel 17:1–14

Narrator Ahithophel said to Absalom:

Ahithophel I would choose twelve thousand men and set out tonight in pursuit of David. I would attack him while he is weary and weak. I would strike him with terror, and then all the people with him will flee. I would strike down only the king and bring all the people back to you. The death of the man you seek will mean the return of all; all the people will be unharmed.

Narrator This plan seemed good to Absalom and to all the elders of Israel.

Absalom Summon also Hushai the Arkite, so we can hear what he has to say.

Narrator When Hushai came to him, Absalom said:

Absalom

(to Hushai)   Ahithophel has given this advice. Should we do what he says? If not, give us your opinion.

Hushai

(to Absalom) The advice Ahithophel has given is not good this time. You know your father and his men; they are fighters, and as fierce as a wild bear robbed of her cubs. Besides, your father is an experienced fighter; he will not spend the night with the troops. Even now, he is hidden in a cave or some other place. If he should attack your troops first, whoever hears about it will say, "There has been a slaughter among the troops who follow Absalom." Then even the bravest soldier, whose heart is like the heart of a lion, will melt with fear, for all Israel knows that your father is a fighter and that those with him are brave.

So I advise you: Let all Israel, from Dan to Beersheba—as numerous as the sand on the seashore—be gathered to you, with you yourself leading them into battle. Then we will attack him wherever he may be found, and we will fall on him as dew settles on the ground. Neither he nor any of his men will be left alive. If he withdraws into a city, then all Israel will bring ropes to that city, and we will drag it down to the valley until not even a piece of it can be found.

Narrator   Absalom and all the men of Israel said:

Absalom   The advice of Hushai the Arkite is better than that of Ahithophel.

Narrator   For the LORD had determined to frustrate the good advice of Ahithophel in order to bring disaster on Absalom.

Cast: **Narrator, Ahithophel, Absalom, Hushai**

David Is Warned and Escapes

2 Samuel 17:15–22 [23–29]

Narrator   Hushai told Zadok and Abiathar, the priests:

Hushai   Ahithophel has advised Absalom and the elders of Israel to do such and such, but I have advised them to do so and so. Now send a message immediately and tell David, "Do not spend the night at the fords in the desert; cross over without fail, or the king and all the people with him will be swallowed up."

Narrator   Jonathan and Ahimaaz were staying at En Rogel. A servant girl was to go and inform them, and they were to go and tell King David, for they could not risk being seen entering the city. But a young man saw them and told Absalom. So the two of them left quickly and went to the house of a man in Bahurim. He had a well in his courtyard, and they climbed down into it. His wife took a covering and spread it out over the opening of the well and scattered grain over it. No one knew anything about it. When Absalom's men came to the woman at the house, they asked:

Man   Where are Ahimaaz and Jonathan?

[Narrator   The woman answered them:]

Woman   They crossed over the brook.

Narrator   The men searched but found no one, so they returned to Jerusalem.

After the men had gone, the two climbed out of the well and went to inform King David. They said to him:

Jonathan   Set out and cross the river at once; Ahithophel has advised such and such against you.

Narrator   So David and all the people with him set out and crossed the Jordan. By daybreak, no one was left who had not crossed the Jordan.

[When Ahithophel saw that his advice had not been followed, he saddled his donkey and set out for his house in his hometown. He put his house in order and then hanged himself. So he died and was buried in his father's tomb.

David went to Mahanaim, and Absalom crossed the Jordan with all the men of Israel. Absalom had appointed Amasa over the army in place of Joab. Amasa was the son of a man named Jether, an Israelite who had married Abigail, the daughter of Nahash and sister of Zeruiah the mother of Joab. The Israelites and Absalom camped in the land of Gilead.

When David came to Mahanaim, Shobi son of Nahash from Rabbah of the Ammonites, and Makir son of Ammiel from Lo Debar, and Barzillai the Gileadite from Rogelim brought bedding and bowls and articles of pottery. They also brought wheat and barley, flour and roasted grain, beans and lentils, honey and curds, sheep, and cheese from cows' milk for David and his people to eat. For they said:

Person   The people have become hungry and tired and thirsty in the desert.]

Cast: **Narrator, Hushai, Man, Woman, Jonathan, Person**

Absalom's Death

2 Samuel 18:1–18

Narrator   David mustered the men who were with him and appointed over them commanders of thousands and commanders of hundreds. David sent the troops out—a third under the command of Joab, a third under Joab's brother Abishai son of Zeruiah, and a third under Ittai the Gittite. The king told the troops:

David   I myself will surely march out with you.

[Narrator	But the men said:]
Man 1	You must not go out.
Man 2	If we are forced to flee, they won't care about us.
Man 1	Even if half of us die, they won't care.
Man 2	But you are worth ten thousand of us.
Man 1	It would be better now for you to give us support from the city.
[Narrator	The king answered:]
David	I will do whatever seems best to you.
Narrator	So the king stood beside the gate while all the men marched out in units of hundreds and of thousands. The king commanded Joab, Abishai and Ittai:
David	Be gentle with the young man Absalom for my sake.
Narrator	And all the troops heard the king giving orders concerning Absalom to each of the commanders.
	The army marched into the field to fight Israel, and the battle took place in the forest of Ephraim. There the army of Israel was defeated by David's men, and the casualties that day were great—twenty thousand men. The battle spread out over the whole countryside, and the forest claimed more lives that day than the sword.
	Now Absalom happened to meet David's men. He was riding his mule, and as the mule went under the thick branches of a large oak, Absalom's head got caught in the tree. He was left hanging in midair, while the mule he was riding kept on going. When one of the men saw this, he told Joab:
Man 2	I just saw Absalom hanging in an oak tree.
Narrator	Joab said to the man who had told him this:
Joab	What! You saw him? Why didn't you strike him to the ground right there? Then I would have had to give you ten shekels of silver and a warrior's belt.
Man 2	Even if a thousand shekels were weighed out into my hands, I would not lift my hand against the king's son. In our hearing the king commanded you and Abishai and Ittai, "Protect the young man Absalom for my sake." And if I had put my life in jeopardy—and nothing is hidden from the king—you would have kept your distance from me.
Joab	I'm not going to wait like this for you.
Narrator	So he took three javelins in his hand and plunged them into Absalom's heart while Absalom was still alive in the oak tree. And ten of Joab's armor-bearers surrounded Absalom, struck him and killed him.

Then Joab sounded the trumpet, and the troops stopped pursuing Israel, for Joab halted them. They took Absalom, threw him into a big pit in the forest and piled up a large heap of rocks over him. Meanwhile, all the Israelites fled to their homes.

During his lifetime Absalom had taken a pillar and erected it in the King's Valley as a monument to himself, for he thought, "I have no son to carry on the memory of my name." He named the pillar after himself, and it is called Absalom's Monument to this day.

Cast: **Narrator, David, Man 1, Man 2** (can be the same as Man 1), **Joab**

David Mourns

2 Samuel 18:19–33

Narrator	Ahimaaz son of Zadok said:
Ahimaaz	Let me run and take the news to the king that the LORD has delivered him from the hand of his enemies.
[Narrator	[Joab told him]:**]**
Joab	You are not the one to take the news today. You may take the news another time, but you must not do so today, because the king's son is dead.
Narrator	Then Joab said to a Cushite:
Joab	Go, tell the king what you have seen.
Narrator	The Cushite bowed down before Joab and ran off. (PAUSE) Ahimaaz son of Zadok *again* said to Joab:
Ahimaaz	Come what may, please let me run behind the Cushite.
Joab	My son, why do you want to go? You don't have any news that will bring you a reward.
Ahimaaz	Come what may, I want to run.
Joab (impatiently)	Run!
Narrator	Then Ahimaaz ran by way of the plain and outran the Cushite.
	While David was sitting between the inner and outer gates, the watchman went up to the roof of the gateway by the wall. As he looked out, he saw a man running alone. The watchman called out to the king and reported it. The king said:
David	If he is alone, he must have good news.
Narrator	And the man came closer and closer.

Then the watchman saw another man running, and he called down to the gatekeeper:

Watchman
(calling)   Look, another man running alone!

[Narrator   The king said:]

David   He must be bringing good news, too.

Watchman
(calling)   It seems to me that the first one runs like Ahimaaz son of Zadok.

David   He's a good man. He comes with good news.

Narrator   Then Ahimaaz called out to the king:

Ahimaaz   All is well!

Narrator   He bowed down before the king with his face to the ground [and said:]

Ahimaaz   Praise be to the LORD your God! He has delivered up the men who lifted their hands against my lord the king.

David
(anxiously)   Is the young man Absalom safe?

Ahimaaz   I saw great confusion just as Joab was about to send the king's servant and me, your servant, but I don't know what it was.

David   Stand aside and wait here.

Narrator   So he stepped aside and stood there. Then the Cushite arrived:

Cushite   My lord the king, hear the good news! The LORD has delivered you today from all who rose up against you.

David   Is the young man Absalom safe?

Cushite   May the enemies of my lord the king and all who rise up to harm you be like that young man.

Narrator   The king was shaken. He went up to the room over the gateway and wept.

David   O my son Absalom! My son, my son Absalom! If only I had died instead of you—O Absalom, my son, my son!

Cast: **Narrator, Ahimaaz, Joab, David, Watchman, Cushite**

Joab Reprimands David

2 Samuel 19:1–8

Narrator   Joab was told:

Servant   The king is weeping and mourning for Absalom.

Narrator	And for the whole army the victory that day was turned into mourning, because on that day the troops heard it said, "The king is grieving for his son." The men stole into the city that day as men steal in who are ashamed when they flee from battle. The king covered his face and cried aloud:
David	O my son Absalom! O Absalom, my son, my son!
Narrator	Then Joab went into the house to the king [and said:]
Joab	Today you have humiliated all your men, who have just saved your life and the lives of your sons and daughters and the lives of your wives and concubines. You love those who hate you and hate those who love you. You have made it clear today that the commanders and their men mean nothing to you. I see that you would be pleased if Absalom were alive today and all of us were dead. Now go out and encourage your men. I swear by the LORD that if you don't go out, not a man will be left with you by nightfall. This will be worse for you than all the calamities that have come upon you from your youth till now.
Narrator	So the king got up and took his seat in the gateway. When the men were told:
Servant	The king is sitting in the gateway.
Narrator	They all came before him.
	Meanwhile, the Israelites had fled to their homes.

Cast: **Narrator, Servant, David, Joab**

David Returns to Jerusalem

2 Samuel 19:8b–18a

Narrator	The Israelites had fled to their homes. Throughout the tribes of Israel, the people were all arguing with each other:
Israelite 1	The king delivered us from the hand of our enemies—
Israelite 2	He is the one who rescued us from the hand of the Philistines.
Israelite 1	But now he has fled the country because of Absalom—
Israelite 2	And Absalom, whom we anointed to rule over us, has died in battle. So why do you say nothing about bringing the king back?
Narrator	King David sent this message to Zadok and Abiathar, the priests:
David	Ask the elders of Judah, "Why should you be the last to bring the king back to his palace, since what is being said throughout Israel has reached the king at his quarters? You are my brothers, my own flesh and blood. So why should you be the last to bring back the king?" And say to Amasa, "Are you not my own flesh and blood? May God deal with me, be it ever

	so severely, if from now on you are not the commander of my army in place of Joab."
Narrator	He won over the hearts of all the men of Judah as though they were one man. They sent word to the king:
Elder 1	Return—
Elders 1 and 2	You and all your men. (PAUSE)
Narrator	Then the king returned and went as far as the Jordan.
	Now the men of Judah had come to Gilgal to go out and meet the king and bring him across the Jordan. Shimei son of Gera, the Benjamite from Bahurim, hurried down with the men of Judah to meet King David. With him were a thousand Benjamites, along with Ziba, the steward of Saul's household, and his fifteen sons and twenty servants. They rushed to the Jordan, where the king was. They crossed at the ford to take the king's household over and to do whatever he wished.

Cast: **Narrator, Israelite 1, Israelite 2, David, Elder 1** (can be the same as Israelite 1), **Elder 2** (can be the same as Israelite 2)

David Shows Kindness

2 Samuel 19:18b–39

Narrator	Shimei son of Gera . . . fell prostrate before the king and said to him:
Shimei	May my lord not hold me guilty. Do not remember how your servant did wrong on the day my lord the king left Jerusalem. May the king put it out of his mind. For I your servant know that I have sinned, but today I have come here as the first of the whole house of Joseph to come down and meet my lord the king.
Narrator	Then Abishai son of Zeruiah said:
Abishai	Shouldn't Shimei be put to death for this? He cursed the Lord's anointed.
Narrator	David replied:
David	What do you and I have in common, you sons of Zeruiah? This day you have become my adversaries! Should *anyone* be put to death in Israel today? Do I not know that today I am king over Israel?
Narrator	So the king said to Shimei:
David	You shall not die.
Narrator	And the king promised him on oath.
	Mephibosheth, Saul's grandson, also went down to meet the king. He had not taken care of his feet or trimmed his mustache or washed his

clothes from the day the king left until the day he returned safely. When he came from Jerusalem to meet the king, the king asked him:

David Why didn't you go with me, Mephibosheth?

Mephibosheth My lord the king, since I your servant am lame, I said, "I will have my donkey saddled and will ride on it, so I can go with the king." But Ziba my servant betrayed me. And he has slandered your servant to my lord the king. My lord the king is like an angel of God; so do whatever pleases you. All my grandfather's descendants deserved nothing but death from my lord the king, but you gave your servant a place among those who sat at your table. So what right do I have to make any more appeals to the king?

David Why say more? I order you and Ziba to divide the fields.

[Narrator Mephibosheth said to the king:**]**

Mephibosheth Let him take everything, now that my lord the king has arrived home safely.

Narrator Barzillai the Gileadite also came down from Rogelim to cross the Jordan with the king and to send him on his way from there. Now Barzillai was a very old man, eighty years of age. He had provided for the king during his stay in Mahanaim, for he was a very wealthy man. The king said to Barzillai:

David Cross over with me and stay with me in Jerusalem, and I will provide for you.

Barzillai How many more years will I live, that I should go up to Jerusalem with the king? I am now eighty years old. Can I tell the difference between what is good and what is not? Can your servant taste what he eats and drinks? Can I still hear the voices of men and women singers? Why should your servant be an added burden to my lord the king? Your servant will cross over the Jordan with the king for a short distance, but why should the king reward me in this way? Let your servant return, that I may die in my own town near the tomb of my father and mother. But here is your servant Kimham. Let him cross over with my lord the king. Do for him whatever pleases you.

David Kimham shall cross over with me, and I will do for him whatever pleases you. And anything you desire from me I will do for you.

Narrator So all the people crossed the Jordan, and then the king crossed over. The king kissed Barzillai and gave him his blessing, and Barzillai returned to his home.

Cast: **Narrator, Shimei, Abishai, David, Mephibosheth, Barzillai**

Judah and Israel Argue over the King

2 Samuel 19:40–43

Narrator	When the king crossed over to Gilgal, Kimham crossed with him. All the troops of Judah and half the troops of Israel had taken the king over. Soon all the men of Israel were coming to the king and saying to him:
Israelite 1	Why did our brothers, the men of Judah, steal the king away—
Israelite 2	And bring him and his household across the Jordan, together with all his men?
Narrator	All the men of Judah answered the men of Israel:
Judaean 1 (indignant-ly)	We did this because the king is closely related to us.
Judaean 2	Why are you angry about it?
Judaean 1	Have we eaten any of the king's provisions?
Judaean 2	Have we taken anything for ourselves?
Narrator	Then the men of Israel answered the men of Judah:
Israelite 1	We have ten shares in the king!
Israelite 2	And besides, we have a greater claim on David than you have.
Israelite 1	So why do you treat us with contempt?
Israelite 2	Were we not the first to speak of bringing back our king?
Narrator	But the men of Judah responded even more harshly than the men of Israel.

Cast: **Narrator**, **Israelite 1**, **Israelite 2** (can be the same as Israelite 1), **Judaean 1**, **Judaean 2** (can be the same as Judaean 1)

Sheba Rebels against David

From 2 Samuel 20:1–26

Narrator	Now a troublemaker named Sheba son of Bicri, a Benjamite, happened to be there. He sounded the trumpet and shouted:
Sheba	We have no share in David, no part in Jesse's son! Every man to his tent, O Israel!
Narrator	So all the men of Israel deserted David to follow Sheba son of Bicri. But the men of Judah stayed by their king all the way from the Jordan to Jerusalem.

When David returned to his palace in Jerusalem, he took the ten concubines he had left to take care of the palace and put them in a house under guard. He provided for them, but did not lie with them. They were kept in confinement till the day of their death, living as widows. (PAUSE) Then the king said to Amasa:

David Summon the men of Judah to come to me within three days, and be here yourself.

Narrator But when Amasa went to summon Judah, he took longer than the time the king had set for him. David said to Abishai:

David Now Sheba son of Bicri will do us more harm than Absalom did. Take your master's men and pursue him, or he will find fortified cities and escape from us.

Narrator So Joab's men and the Kerethites and Pelethites and all the mighty warriors went out under the command of Abishai. They marched out from Jerusalem to pursue Sheba son of Bicri.

While they were at the great rock in Gibeon, Amasa came to meet them. Joab was wearing his military tunic, and strapped over it at his waist was a belt with a dagger in its sheath. As he stepped forward, it dropped out of its sheath. Joab said to Amasa:

Joab
(cunningly) How are you, my brother?

Narrator Then Joab took Amasa by the beard with his right hand to kiss him. Amasa was not on his guard against the dagger in Joab's hand, and Joab plunged it into his belly, and his intestines spilled out on the ground. Without being stabbed again, Amasa died. Then Joab and his brother Abishai pursued Sheba son of Bicri. . . .

Sheba passed through all the tribes of Israel to Abel Beth Maacah and through the entire region of the Berites, who gathered together and followed him. All the troops with Joab came and besieged Sheba in Abel Beth Maacah. They built a siege ramp up to the city, and it stood against the outer fortifications. While they were battering the wall to bring it down, a wise woman called from the city:

Woman Listen! Listen! Tell Joab to come here so I can speak to him.

Narrator He went toward her [and she asked:]

Woman Are you Joab?

Joab I am.

Woman Listen to what your servant has to say.

Joab I'm listening.

Woman Long ago they used to say, "Get your answer at Abel," and that settled it. We are the peaceful and faithful in Israel. You are trying to destroy a

336

city that is a mother in Israel. Why do you want to swallow up the LORD's inheritance?

Joab	Far be it from me! Far be it from me to swallow up or destroy! That is not the case. A man named Sheba son of Bicri, from the hill country of Ephraim, has lifted up his hand against the king, against David. Hand over this one man, and I'll withdraw from the city.
Woman	His head will be thrown to you from the wall.
Narrator	Then the woman went to all the people with her wise advice, and they cut off the head of Sheba son of Bicri and threw it to Joab. So he sounded the trumpet, and his men dispersed from the city, each returning to his home. And Joab went back to the king in Jerusalem.
	Joab was over Israel's entire army; Benaiah son of Jehoiada was over the Kerethites and Pelethites; Adoniram was in charge of forced labor; Jehoshaphat son of Ahilud was recorder; Sheva was secretary; Zadok and Abiathar were priests; and Ira the Jairite was David's priest.

Cast: **Narrator, Sheba, David, Joab, Woman**

The Gibeonites Avenged

2 Samuel 21:1–9

Narrator	During the reign of David, there was a famine for three successive years; so David sought the face of the LORD. **[**The LORD said:**]**
The Lord (voice only)	It is on account of Saul and his blood-stained house; it is because he put the Gibeonites to death.
Narrator	The king summoned the Gibeonites and spoke to them.
Commentator	(Now the Gibeonites were not a part of Israel but were survivors of the Amorites; the Israelites had sworn to ˻spare˼ them, but Saul in his zeal for Israel and Judah had tried to annihilate them.)
David	What shall I do for you? How shall I make amends so that you will bless the LORD's inheritance?
Gibeonite 1	We have no right to demand silver or gold from Saul or his family.
Gibeonite 2	Nor do we have the right to put anyone in Israel to death.
David	What do you want me to do for you?
Gibeonite 1	As for the man who destroyed us and plotted against us so that we have been decimated and have no place anywhere in Israel—
Gibeonite 2	Let seven of his male descendants be given to us to be killed and exposed before the LORD at Gibeah of Saul—the LORD's chosen one.

337

David	I will give them to you.
Narrator	The king spared Mephibosheth son of Jonathan, the son of Saul, because of the oath before the LORD between David and Jonathan son of Saul. But the king took Armoni and Mephibosheth, the two sons of Aiah's daughter Rizpah, whom she had borne to Saul, together with the five sons of Saul's daughter Merab, whom she had borne to Adriel son of Barzillai the Meholathite. He handed them over to the Gibeonites, who killed and exposed them on a hill before the LORD. All seven of them fell together; they were put to death during the first days of the harvest, just as the barley harvest was beginning.

Cast: **Narrator, the Lord** (voice only), **Commentator** (can be the same as the Lord), **David, Gibeonite 1, Gibeonite 2**

The Last Words of David

2 Samuel 23:1–7

Narrator	These are the last words of David:

David	The oracle of David son of Jesse,
	    the oracle of the man exalted by the Most High,
	the man anointed by the God of Jacob,
	    Israel's singer of songs:
	
	The Spirit of the LORD spoke through me;
	    his word was on my tongue.
	The God of Israel spoke,
	    the Rock of Israel said to me:

Voice of God	When one rules over men in righteousness,
	    when he rules in the fear of God,
	he is like the light of morning at sunrise
	    on a cloudless morning,
	like the brightness after rain
	    that brings the grass from the earth.

David	Is not my house right with God?
	    Has he not made with me an everlasting covenant,
	    arranged and secured in every part?
	Will he not bring to fruition my salvation
	    and grant me my every desire?
	But evil men are all to be cast aside like thorns,
	    which are not gathered with the hand.
	Whoever touches thorns
	    uses a tool of iron or the shaft of a spear;
	    they are burned up where they lie.

Cast: **Narrator, David, Voice of God**

David's Mighty Men

From 2 Samuel 23:8–17 [18–39]

Narrator 1	These are the names of David's mighty men:
	Josheb-Basshebeth, a Tahkemonite, was chief of the Three; he raised his spear against eight hundred men, whom he killed in one encounter.
Narrator 2	Next to him was Eleazar son of Dodai the Ahohite. As one of the three mighty men, he was with David when they taunted the Philistines gathered ˻at Pas Dammim˼ for battle. Then the men of Israel retreated, but he stood his ground and struck down the Philistines till his hand grew tired and froze to the sword. The Lord brought about a great victory that day. The troops returned to Eleazar, but only to strip the dead.
Narrator 1	Next to him was Shammah son of Agee the Hararite. When the Philistines banded together at a place where there was a field full of lentils, Israel's troops fled from them. But Shammah took his stand in the middle of the field. He defended it and struck the Philistines down, and the Lord brought about a great victory.
Narrator 2	During harvest time, three of the thirty chief men came down to David at the cave of Adullam, while a band of Philistines was encamped in the Valley of Rephaim. At that time David was in the stronghold, and the Philistine garrison was at Bethlehem. David longed for water:
David	Oh, that someone would get me a drink of water from the well near the gate of Bethlehem!
Narrator 1	So the three mighty men broke through the Philistine lines, drew water from the well near the gate of Bethlehem and carried it back to David. But he refused to drink it; instead, he poured it out before the Lord.
David	Far be it from me, O Lord, to do this! Is it not the blood of men who went at the risk of their lives?
Narrator 2	And David would not drink it.
Narrator 1	Such were the exploits of the three mighty men.
[Narrator 1	Abishai the brother of Joab son of Zeruiah was chief of the Three. He raised his spear against three hundred men, whom he killed, and so he became as famous as the Three. Was he not held in greater honor than the Three? He became their commander, even though he was not included among them.
Narrator 2	Benaiah son of Jehoiada was a valiant fighter from Kabzeel, who performed great exploits. He struck down two of Moab's best men. He also went down into a pit on a snowy day and killed a lion. And he struck down a huge Egyptian. Although the Egyptian had a spear in his hand, Benaiah went against him with a club. He snatched the spear from the Egyptian's hand and killed him with his own spear. Such were the exploits of Benaiah son of Jehoiada; he too was as famous as the three mighty men. He was held

339

in greater honor than any of the Thirty, but he was not included among the Three. And David put him in charge of his bodyguard. . . .

Narrator 1 There were thirty-seven in all.]

Cast: **Narrator 1, Narrator 2, David**

David Counts the Fighting Men

2 Samuel 24:1–25

Narrator The anger of the Lord burned against Israel, and he incited David against them [saying:]

The Lord
(voice only,
angrily) Go and take a census of Israel and Judah.

Narrator So the king said to Joab and the army commanders with him:

David Go throughout the tribes of Israel from Dan to Beersheba and enroll the fighting men, so that I may know how many there are.

Narrator But Joab replied to the king:

Joab May the Lord your God multiply the troops a hundred times over, and may the eyes of my lord the king see it. But why does my lord the king want to do such a thing?

Narrator The king's word, however, overruled Joab and the army commanders; so they left the presence of the king to enroll the fighting men of Israel. After crossing the Jordan, they camped near Aroer, south of the town in the gorge, and then went through Gad and on to Jazer. They went to Gilead and the region of Tahtim Hodshi, and on to Dan Jaan and around toward Sidon. Then they went toward the fortress of Tyre and all the towns of the Hivites and Canaanites. Finally, they went on to Beersheba in the Negev of Judah. (PAUSE) After they had gone through the entire land, they came back to Jerusalem at the end of nine months and twenty days.

Joab reported the number of the fighting men to the king: In Israel there were eight hundred thousand able-bodied men who could handle a sword, and in Judah five hundred thousand.

David was conscience-stricken after he had counted the fighting men, and he said to the Lord:

David I have sinned greatly in what I have done. Now, O Lord, I beg you, take away the guilt of your servant. I have done a very foolish thing.

Narrator Before David got up the next morning, the word of the Lord had come to Gad the prophet, David's seer:

The Lord (voice)	Go and tell David, "This is what the Lord says: I am giving you three options. Choose one of them for me to carry out against you."
Narrator	So Gad went to David and said to him:
Gad	Shall there come upon you three years of famine in your land? Or three months of fleeing from your enemies while they pursue you? Or three days of plague in your land? Now then, think it over and decide how I should answer the one who sent me.
David (hesitating)	I am in deep distress. Let us fall into the hands of the Lord, for his mercy is great; but do not let me fall into the hands of men.
Narrator	So the Lord sent a plague on Israel from that morning until the end of the time designated, and seventy thousand of the people from Dan to Beersheba died. When the angel stretched out his hand to destroy Jerusalem, the Lord was grieved because of the calamity and said to the angel who was afflicting the people:
The Lord (voice)	Enough! Withdraw your hand.
Narrator	The angel of the Lord was then at the threshing floor of Araunah the Jebusite. (PAUSE) When David saw the angel who was striking down the people, he said to the Lord:
David	I am the one who has sinned and done wrong. These are but sheep. What have they done? Let your hand fall upon me and my family.
Narrator	On that day Gad went to David [and said to him:]
Gad	Go up and build an altar to the Lord on the threshing floor of Araunah the Jebusite.
Narrator	So David went up, as the Lord had commanded through Gad. When Araunah looked and saw the king and his men coming toward him, he went out and bowed down before the king with his face to the ground. Araunah said:
Araunah	Why has my lord the king come to his servant?
David	To buy your threshing floor, so I can build an altar to the Lord, that the plague on the people may be stopped.
Araunah	Let my lord the king take whatever pleases him and offer it up. Here are oxen for the burnt offering, and here are threshing sledges and ox yokes for the wood. O king, Araunah gives all this to the king.
Narrator	Araunah also said to him:
Araunah	May the Lord your God accept you.

David No, I insist on paying you for it. I will not sacrifice to the LORD my God burnt offerings that cost me nothing.

Narrator So David bought the threshing floor and the oxen and paid fifty shekels of silver for them. David built an altar to the LORD there and sacrificed burnt offerings and fellowship offerings. (PAUSE) Then the LORD answered prayer in behalf of the land, and the plague on Israel was stopped.

Cast: **Narrator, the Lord** (voice only), **David, Joab, Gad, Araunah**

1 Kings

David Makes Solomon King

1 Kings 1:11–52

Narrator	Nathan asked Bathsheba, Solomon's mother:
Nathan	Have you not heard that Adonijah, the son of Haggith, has become king without our lord David's knowing it? Now then, let me advise you how you can save your own life and the life of your son Solomon. Go in to King David and say to him, "My lord the king, did you not swear to me your servant: 'Surely Solomon your son shall be king after me, and he will sit on my throne'? Why then has Adonijah become king?" While you are still there talking to the king, I will come in and confirm what you have said.
Narrator	So Bathsheba went to see the aged king in his room, where Abishag the Shunammite was attending him. Bathsheba bowed low and knelt before the king.
David	What is it you want?
Bathsheba	My lord, you yourself swore to me your servant by the Lord your God: "Solomon your son shall be king after me, and he will sit on my throne." But now *Adonijah* has become king, and you, my lord the king, do not know about it. He has sacrificed great numbers of cattle, fattened calves, and sheep, and has invited all the king's sons, Abiathar the priest and Joab the commander of the army, but he has not invited Solomon your servant. My lord the king, the eyes of all Israel are on you, to learn from you who will sit on the throne of my lord the king after him. Otherwise, as soon as my lord the king is laid to rest with his fathers, I and my son Solomon will be treated as criminals.
Narrator	While she was still speaking with the king, Nathan the prophet arrived. And they told the king:
Person 1	Nathan the prophet is here.
Narrator	So he went before the king and bowed with his face to the ground. [Nathan said:]
Nathan	Have you, my lord the king, declared that *Adonijah* shall be king after you, and that he will sit on your throne? Today he has gone down and sacrificed great numbers of cattle, fattened calves, and sheep. He has invited all the king's sons, the commanders of the army and Abiathar the priest. Right now they are eating and drinking with him and saying, "Long live King Adonijah!" But me your servant, and Zadok the priest, and Benaiah son of Jehoiada, and your servant Solomon he did not invite.

	Is this something my lord the king has done without letting his servants know who should sit on the throne of my lord the king after him?
David	Call in Bathsheba.
Narrator	So she came into the king's presence and stood before him. The king then took an oath:
David (to Bath- sheba)	As surely as the LORD lives, who has delivered me out of every trouble, I will surely carry out today what I swore to you by the LORD, the God of Israel: Solomon your son shall be king after me, and he will sit on my throne in my place.
Narrator	Then Bathsheba bowed low with her face to the ground . . . , kneeling before the king:
Bathsheba	May my lord King David live forever!
David	Call in Zadok the priest, Nathan the prophet and Benaiah son of Jehoiada.
Narrator	When they came before the king, he said to them:
David	Take your lord's servants with you and set Solomon my son on my own mule and take him down to Gihon. There have Zadok the priest and Nathan the prophet anoint him king over Israel. Blow the trumpet and shout, "Long live King Solomon!" Then you are to go up with him, and he is to come and sit on my throne and reign in my place. I have appointed him ruler over Israel and Judah.
Narrator	Benaiah son of Jehoiada answered the king:
Benaiah	Amen! May the LORD, the God of my lord the king, so declare it. As the LORD was with my lord the king, so may he be with Solomon to make his throne even greater than the throne of my lord King David!
Narrator	So Zadok the priest, Nathan the prophet, Benaiah son of Jehoiada, the Kerethites and the Pelethites went down and put Solomon on King David's mule and escorted him to Gihon. Zadok the priest took the horn of oil from the sacred tent and anointed Solomon. Then they sounded the trumpet and all the people shouted:
Persons 1 and 2	Long live King Solomon!
Narrator	And all the people went up after him, playing flutes and rejoicing greatly, so that the ground shook with the sound.
	Adonijah and all the guests who were with him heard it as they were finishing their feast. On hearing the sound of the trumpet, Joab asked:
Joab	What's the meaning of all the noise in the city?
Narrator	Even as he was speaking, Jonathan son of Abiathar the priest arrived. [Adonijah said:]

Adonijah   Come in. A worthy man like you must be bringing good news.

Jonathan   Not at all! Our lord King David has made Solomon king. The king has sent with him Zadok the priest, Nathan the prophet, Benaiah son of Jehoiada, the Kerethites and the Pelethites, and they have put him on the king's mule, and Zadok the priest and Nathan the prophet have anointed him king at Gihon. From there they have gone up cheering, and the city resounds with it. That's the noise you hear. Moreover, Solomon has taken his seat on the royal throne. Also, the royal officials have come to congratulate our lord King David, saying, "May your God make Solomon's name more famous than yours and his throne greater than yours!" And the king bowed in worship on his bed and said, "Praise be to the LORD, the God of Israel, who has allowed my eyes to see a successor on my throne today."

Narrator   At this, all Adonijah's guests rose in alarm and dispersed. But Adonijah, in fear of Solomon, went and took hold of the horns of the altar. [Then Solomon was told:]

Person 1
(to
Solomon)   Adonijah is afraid of King Solomon and is clinging to the horns of the altar.

Person 2
(to
Solomon)   He says, "Let King Solomon swear to me today that he will not put his servant to death with the sword."

[Narrator   Solomon replied:]

Solomon   If he shows himself to be a worthy man, not a hair of his head will fall to the ground; but if evil is found in him, he will die.

Cast: **Narrator, Nathan, David, Bathsheba, Person 1, Benaiah, Person 2, Joab, Adonijah, Jonathan, Solomon**

David's Charge to Solomon

From 1 Kings 2:1–12

Narrator   When the time drew near for David to die, he gave a charge to Solomon his son.

David   I am about to go the way of all the earth. So be strong, show yourself a man, and observe what the LORD your God requires: Walk in his ways, and keep his decrees and commands, his laws and requirements, as written in the Law of Moses, so that you may prosper in all you do and wherever you go, and that the LORD may keep his promise to me: "If your descendants watch how they live, and if they walk faithfully before me with all their heart and soul, you will never fail to have a man on the throne of Israel." . . .

Narrator	Then David rested with his fathers and was buried in the City of David. He had reigned forty years over Israel—seven years in Hebron and thirty-three in Jerusalem. So Solomon sat on the throne of his father David, and his rule was firmly established.

Cast: **Narrator, David**

The Death of Adonijah

1 Kings 2:13–25 (with introduction from 1 Kings 1:1–4)

Narrator	When King David was old and well advanced in years, he could not keep warm even when they put covers over him. So his servants said to him:
Servant	Let us look for a young virgin to attend the king and take care of him. She can lie beside him so that our lord the king may keep warm.
Narrator	Then they searched throughout Israel for a beautiful girl and found Abishag, a Shunammite, and brought her to the king. The girl was very beautiful; she took care of the king and waited on him, but the king had no intimate relations with her.
	Now Adonijah, the son of Haggith, went to Bathsheba, Solomon's mother. [Bathsheba asked him:]
Bathsheba	Do you come peacefully?
Adonijah	Yes, peacefully. I have something to say to you.
Bathsheba	You may say it.
Adonijah	As you know, the kingdom was mine. All Israel looked to me as their king. But things changed, and the kingdom has gone to my brother; for it has come to him from the LORD. Now I have one request to make of you. Do not refuse me.
Bathsheba	You may make it.
Adonijah	Please ask King Solomon—he will not refuse you—to give me Abishag the Shunammite as my wife.
Bathsheba	Very well. I will speak to the king for you.
Narrator	When Bathsheba went to King Solomon to speak to him for Adonijah, the king stood up to meet her, bowed down to her and sat down on his throne. He had a throne brought for the king's mother, and she sat down at his right hand.
Bathsheba	I have one small request to make of you. Do not refuse me.
Solomon	Make it, my mother; I will not refuse you.
Bathsheba	Let Abishag the Shunammite be given in marriage to your brother Adonijah.

Solomon	Why do you request Abishag the Shunammite for Adonijah? You might as well request the kingdom for him—after all, he is my older brother—yes, for him and for Abiathar the priest and Joab son of Zeruiah!
Narrator	Then King Solomon swore by the LORD:
Solomon	May God deal with me, be it ever so severely, if Adonijah does not pay with his life for this request! And now, as surely as the LORD lives—he who has established me securely on the throne of my father David and has founded a dynasty for me as he promised—Adonijah shall be put to death today!
Narrator	So King Solomon gave orders to Benaiah son of Jehoiada, and he struck down Adonijah and he died.

Cast: **Narrator, Servant, Bathsheba, Adonijah, Solomon**

Abiathar's Banishment and Joab's Death

1 Kings 2:26–35

Narrator	To Abiathar the priest the king said:
Solomon	Go back to your fields in Anathoth. You deserve to die, but I will not put you to death now, because you carried the ark of the Sovereign LORD before my father David and shared all my father's hardships.
Narrator	So Solomon removed Abiathar from the priesthood of the LORD, fulfilling the word the LORD had spoken at Shiloh about the house of Eli.
	When the news reached Joab, who had conspired with Adonijah though not with Absalom, he fled to the tent of the LORD and took hold of the horns of the altar. King Solomon was told that Joab had fled to the tent of the LORD and was beside the altar. Then Solomon ordered Benaiah son of Jehoiada:
Solomon	Go, strike him down!
Narrator	So Benaiah entered the tent of the LORD and said to Joab:
Benaiah	The king says, "Come out!"
[Narrator	But he answered:]
Joab	No, I will die here.
Narrator	Benaiah reported to the king:
Benaiah	This is how Joab answered me: ["I will die here."]
Narrator	Then the king commanded Benaiah:
Solomon	Do as he says. Strike him down and bury him, and so clear me and my father's house of the guilt of the innocent blood that Joab shed. The LORD will repay him for the blood he shed, because without the knowledge of my father David he attacked two men and killed them with the

sword. Both of them—Abner son of Ner, commander of Israel's army, and Amasa son of Jether, commander of Judah's army—were better men and more upright than he. May the guilt of their blood rest on the head of Joab and his descendants forever. But on David and his descendants, his house and his throne, may there be the LORD's peace forever.

Narrator   So Benaiah son of Jehoiada went up and struck down Joab and killed him, and he was buried on his own land in the desert. The king put Benaiah son of Jehoiada over the army in Joab's position and replaced Abiathar with Zadok the priest.

Cast: **Narrator, Solomon, Benaiah, Joab**

The Death of Shimei

1 Kings 2:36–46

Narrator   Then the king sent for Shimei and said to him:

Solomon   Build yourself a house in Jerusalem and live there, but do not go anywhere else. The day you leave and cross the Kidron Valley, you can be sure you will die; your blood will be on your own head.

[Narrator   Shimei answered the king:]

Shimei   What you say is good. Your servant will do as my lord the king has said.

Narrator   And Shimei stayed in Jerusalem for a long time. (PAUSE)

But three years later, two of Shimei's slaves ran off to Achish son of Maacah, king of Gath, and Shimei was told:

Person   Your slaves are in Gath.

Narrator   At this, he saddled his donkey and went to Achish at Gath in search of his slaves. So Shimei went away and brought the slaves back from Gath.

When Solomon was told that Shimei had gone from Jerusalem to Gath and had returned, the king summoned Shimei and said to him:

Solomon   Did I not make you swear by the LORD and warn you, "On the day you leave to go anywhere else, you can be sure you will die"? At that time you said to me, "What you say is good. I will obey." Why then did you not keep your oath to the LORD and obey the command I gave you? You know in your heart all the wrong you did to my father David. Now the LORD will repay you for your wrongdoing. But King Solomon will be blessed, and David's throne will remain secure before the LORD forever.

Narrator   Then the king gave the order to Benaiah son of Jehoiada, and he went out and struck Shimei down and killed him. The kingdom was now firmly established in Solomon's hands.

Cast: **Narrator, Solomon, Shimei, Person**

Solomon Asks for Wisdom

1 Kings 3:5–15a

Narrator At Gibeon the LORD appeared to Solomon during the night in a dream [and God said:]

The Lord
(voice only) Ask for whatever you want me to give you.

[Narrator Solomon answered:]

Solomon You have shown great kindness to your servant, my father David, because he was faithful to you and righteous and upright in heart. You have continued this great kindness to him and have given him a son to sit on his throne this very day.

Now, O LORD my God, you have made your servant king in place of my father David. But I am only a little child and do not know how to carry out my duties. Your servant is here among the people you have chosen, a great people, too numerous to count or number. So give your servant a discerning heart to govern your people and to distinguish between right and wrong. For who is able to govern this great people of yours?

Narrator The Lord was pleased that Solomon had asked for this.

The Lord
(voice) Since you have asked for this and not for long life or wealth for yourself, nor have asked for the death of your enemies but for discernment in administering justice, I will do what you have asked. I will give you a wise and discerning heart, so that there will never have been anyone like you, nor will there ever be. Moreover, I will give you what you have not asked for—both riches and honor—so that in your lifetime you will have no equal among kings. And if you walk in my ways and obey my statutes and commands as David your father did, I will give you a long life.

Narrator
(slowly) Then Solomon awoke—and he realized it had been a dream.

Cast: **Narrator, the Lord** (voice only), **Solomon**

A Wise Ruling

1 Kings 3:16–28

Narrator Two prostitutes came to the king and stood before him. [One of them said:]

Woman 1 My lord, this woman and I live in the same house. I had a baby while she was there with me. The third day after my child was born, this woman also had a baby. We were alone; there was no one in the house but the two of us.

During the night this woman's son died because she lay on him. So she got up in the middle of the night and took my son from my side while I your servant was asleep. She put him by her breast and put her dead son by my breast. The next morning, I got up to nurse my son—and he was dead! But when I looked at him closely in the morning light, I saw that it wasn't the son I had borne.

[Narrator   The other woman said:]

Woman 2   No! The living one is *my* son; the *dead* one is yours.

Narrator   But the first one insisted:

Woman 1   No! The dead one is *yours*; the living one is *mine*.

Narrator   And so they argued before the king. (PAUSE)

The king said:

Solomon   This one says, "My son is alive and your son is dead," while that one says, "No! Your son is dead and mine is alive."

Bring me a sword.

Narrator   So they brought a sword for the king. (PAUSE) He then gave an order:

Solomon   Cut the living child in two and give half to one and half to the other.

Narrator   The woman whose son was alive was filled with compassion for her son:

Woman 1
(distraught,
to Solomon)   Please, my lord, give her the living baby! Don't kill him!

[Narrator   But the other said:]

Woman 2
(callously)   Neither I nor you shall have him. Cut him in two! (PAUSE)

[Narrator   Then the king gave his ruling:]

Solomon
(solemnly)   Give the living baby to the first woman. Do not kill him; *she* is his mother.

Narrator   When all Israel heard the verdict the king had given, they held the king in awe, because they saw that he had wisdom from God to administer justice.

Cast: **Narrator, Woman 1, Woman 2, Solomon**

Preparations for Building the Temple

1 Kings 5:1–12

Narrator   When Hiram king of Tyre heard that Solomon had been anointed king to succeed his father David, he sent his envoys to Solomon, because he had always been on friendly terms with David. Solomon sent back this message to Hiram:

Solomon You know that because of the wars waged against my father David from all sides, he could not build a temple for the Name of the LORD his God until the LORD put his enemies under his feet. But now the LORD my God has given me rest on every side, and there is no adversary or disaster. I intend, therefore, to build a temple for the Name of the LORD my God, as the LORD told my father David, when he said:

The Lord
(voice only) Your son whom I will put on the throne in your place will build the temple for my Name.

Solomon So give orders that cedars of Lebanon be cut for me. My men will work with yours, and I will pay you for your men whatever wages you set. You know that we have no one so skilled in felling timber as the Sidonians.

Narrator When Hiram heard Solomon's message, he was greatly pleased:

Hiram Praise be to the LORD today, for he has given David a wise son to rule over this great nation.

Narrator So Hiram sent word to Solomon:

Hiram I have received the message you sent me and will do all you want in providing the cedar and pine logs. My men will haul them down from Lebanon to the sea, and I will float them in rafts by sea to the place you specify. There I will separate them and you can take them away. And you are to grant my wish by providing food for my royal household.

Narrator In this way Hiram kept Solomon supplied with all the cedar and pine logs he wanted, and Solomon gave Hiram twenty thousand cors of wheat as food for his household, in addition to twenty thousand baths of pressed olive oil. Solomon continued to do this for Hiram year after year. The LORD gave Solomon wisdom, just as he had promised him. There were peaceful relations between Hiram and Solomon, and the two of them made a treaty.

Cast: **Narrator, Solomon, the Lord** (voice only; can be the same as Solomon), **Hiram**

The Ark Brought to the Temple

From 1 Kings 8:1–13

Narrator 1 King Solomon summoned into his presence at Jerusalem the elders of Israel, all the heads of the tribes and the chiefs of the Israelite families, to bring up the ark of the LORD's covenant from Zion, the City of David. . . .

Narrator 2 When all the elders of Israel had arrived, the priests took up the ark, and they brought up the ark of the LORD and the Tent of Meeting and all the sacred furnishings in it.

Narrator 1   The priests and Levites carried them up, and King Solomon and the entire assembly of Israel that had gathered about him were before the ark. . . .

Narrator 2   The priests then brought the ark of the LORD's covenant to its place in the inner sanctuary of the temple, the Most Holy Place, and put it beneath the wings of the cherubim. The cherubim spread their wings over the place of the ark and overshadowed the ark and its carrying poles. . . .

Narrator 1   There was nothing in the ark except the two stone tablets that Moses had placed in it at Horeb, where the LORD made a covenant with the Israelites after they came out of Egypt.

Narrator 2   When the priests withdrew from the Holy Place, the cloud filled the temple of the LORD. And the priests could not perform their service because of the cloud, for the glory of the LORD filled his temple.

Narrator 1   Then Solomon said:

Solomon
(in prayer)   The LORD has said that he would dwell in a dark cloud.
I have indeed built a magnificent temple for you, a place for you to dwell forever.

Cast: **Narrator 1, Narrator 2, Solomon**

Solomon's Address to the People

1 Kings 8:14–21

Narrator   While the whole assembly of Israel was standing there, the king turned around and blessed them. Then he said:

Solomon   Praise be to the LORD, the God of Israel, who with his own hand has fulfilled what he promised with his own mouth to my father David. [For he said:]

The Lord
(voice only)   Since the day I brought my people Israel out of Egypt, I have not chosen a city in any tribe of Israel to have a temple built for my Name to be there, but I have chosen David to rule my people Israel.

Solomon   My father David had it in his heart to build a temple for the Name of the LORD, the God of Israel. But the LORD said to my father David:

The Lord
(voice)   Because it was in your heart to build a temple for my Name, you did well to have this in your heart. Nevertheless, you are not the one to build the temple, but your son, who is your own flesh and blood—he is the one who will build the temple for my Name.

Solomon   The LORD has kept the promise he made: I have succeeded David my father and now I sit on the throne of Israel, just as the LORD promised, and I have built the temple for the Name of the LORD, the God of Israel.

I have provided a place there for the ark, in which is the covenant of the Lord that he made with our fathers when he brought them out of Egypt.

Cast: **Narrator, Solomon, the Lord** (voice only)

The Final Prayer

1 Kings 8:54–66

Narrator When Solomon had finished all these prayers and supplications to the Lord, he rose from before the altar of the Lord, where he had been kneeling with his hands spread out toward heaven. He stood and blessed the whole assembly of Israel in a loud voice:

Solomon Praise be to the Lord, who has given rest to his people Israel just as he promised. Not one word has failed of all the good promises he gave through his servant Moses. May the Lord our God be with us as he was with our fathers; may he never leave us nor forsake us. May he turn our hearts to him, to walk in all his ways and to keep the commands, decrees and regulations he gave our fathers. And may these words of mine, which I have prayed before the Lord, be near to the Lord our God day and night, that he may uphold the cause of his servant and the cause of his people Israel according to each day's need, so that all the peoples of the earth may know that the Lord is God and that there is no other. But your hearts must be fully committed to the Lord our God, to live by his decrees and obey his commands, as at this time.

Narrator Then the king and all Israel with him offered sacrifices before the Lord. Solomon offered a sacrifice of fellowship offerings to the Lord: twenty-two thousand cattle and a hundred and twenty thousand sheep and goats. So the king and all the Israelites dedicated the temple of the Lord.

On that same day the king consecrated the middle part of the courtyard in front of the temple of the Lord, and there he offered burnt offerings, grain offerings and the fat of the fellowship offerings, because the bronze altar before the Lord was too small to hold the burnt offerings, the grain offerings and the fat of the fellowship offerings.

So Solomon observed the festival at that time, and all Israel with him—a vast assembly, people from Lebo Hamath to the Wadi of Egypt. They celebrated it before the Lord our God for seven days and seven days more, fourteen days in all. On the following day he sent the people away. They blessed the king and then went home, joyful and glad in heart for all the good things the Lord had done for his servant David and his people Israel.

Cast: **Narrator, Solomon**

The Lord Appears to Solomon

1 Kings 9:1–9

Narrator   When Solomon had finished building the temple of the LORD and the royal palace, and had achieved all he had desired to do, the LORD appeared to him a second time, as he had appeared to him at Gibeon. [The LORD said to him:]

The Lord
(voice only)   I have heard the prayer and plea you have made before me; I have consecrated this temple, which you have built, by putting my Name there forever. My eyes and my heart will always be there.

As for you, if you walk before me in integrity of heart and uprightness, as David your father did, and do all I command and observe my decrees and laws, I will establish your royal throne over Israel forever, as I promised David your father when I said, "You shall never fail to have a man on the throne of Israel."

But if you or your sons turn away from me and do not observe the commands and decrees I have given you and go off to serve other gods and worship them, then I will cut off Israel from the land I have given them and will reject this temple I have consecrated for my Name. Israel will then become a byword and an object of ridicule among all peoples. And though this temple is now imposing, all who pass by will be appalled and will scoff:

Person 1   Why has the LORD done such a thing to this land and to this temple?

[The Lord
(voice)   People will answer:]

Person 2   Because they have forsaken the LORD their God, who brought their fathers out of Egypt.

Person 3   And have embraced other gods, worshiping and serving them—

Person 1   That is why the LORD brought all this disaster on them.

Cast: **Narrator, the Lord** (voice only), **Person 1, Person 2, Person 3** (Persons 1–3 can be the same)

Solomon's Other Activities

1 Kings 9:10–13

Narrator   At the end of twenty years, during which Solomon built these two buildings—the temple of the LORD and the royal palace—King Solomon gave twenty towns in Galilee to Hiram king of Tyre, because Hiram had supplied him with all the cedar and pine and gold he wanted. But when

	Hiram went from Tyre to see the towns that Solomon had given him, he was not pleased with them.
Hiram	What kind of towns are these you have given me, my brother?
Narrator	And he called them the Land of Cabul, a name they have to this day.

Cast: **Narrator, Hiram**

The Queen of Sheba Visits Solomon

1 Kings 10:1–13

Narrator	When the queen of Sheba heard about the fame of Solomon and his relation to the name of the Lord, she came to test him with hard questions. Arriving at Jerusalem with a very great caravan—with camels carrying spices, large quantities of gold, and precious stones—she came to Solomon and talked with him about all that she had on her mind. Solomon answered all her questions; nothing was too hard for the king to explain to her. When the queen of Sheba saw all the wisdom of Solomon and the palace he had built, the food on his table, the seating of his officials, the attending servants in their robes, his cupbearers, and the burnt offerings he made at the temple of the Lord, she was overwhelmed. She said to the king:
Queen	The report I heard in my own country about your achievements and your wisdom is true. But I did not believe these things until I came and saw with my own eyes. Indeed, not even half was told me; in wisdom and wealth you have far exceeded the report I heard. How happy your men must be! How happy your officials, who continually stand before you and hear your wisdom! Praise be to the Lord your God, who has delighted in you and placed you on the throne of Israel. Because of the Lord's eternal love for Israel, he has made you king, to maintain justice and righteousness.
Narrator	And she gave the king 120 talents of gold, large quantities of spices, and precious stones. Never again were so many spices brought in as those the queen of Sheba gave to King Solomon.
Commentator	(Hiram's ships brought gold from Ophir; and from there they brought great cargoes of almugwood and precious stones. The king used the almugwood to make supports for the temple of the Lord and for the royal palace, and to make harps and lyres for the musicians. So much almugwood has never been imported or seen since that day.)
Narrator	King Solomon gave the queen of Sheba all she desired and asked for, besides what he had given her out of his royal bounty. Then she left and returned with her retinue to her own country.

Cast: **Narrator, Queen, Commentator** (can be the same as Narrator)

Solomon's Wives

1 Kings 11:1–13

Narrator King Solomon . . . loved many foreign women besides Pharaoh's daughter—Moabites, Ammonites, Edomites, Sidonians and Hittites. They were from nations about which the LORD had told the Israelites,

The Lord
(voice only) You must not intermarry with them, because they will surely turn your hearts after their gods.

Narrator Nevertheless, Solomon held fast to them in love. He had seven hundred wives of royal birth and three hundred concubines, and his wives led him astray. As Solomon grew old, his wives turned his heart after other gods, and his heart was not fully devoted to the LORD his God, as the heart of David his father had been. He followed Ashtoreth the goddess of the Sidonians, and Molech the detestable god of the Ammonites. So Solomon did evil in the eyes of the LORD; he did not follow the LORD completely, as David his father had done.

On a hill east of Jerusalem, Solomon built a high place for Chemosh the detestable god of Moab, and for Molech the detestable god of the Ammonites. He did the same for all his foreign wives, who burned incense and offered sacrifices to their gods.

The LORD became angry with Solomon because his heart had turned away from the LORD, the God of Israel, who had appeared to him twice. Although he had forbidden Solomon to follow other gods, Solomon did not keep the LORD's command. [So the LORD said to Solomon:]

The Lord
(voice) Since this is your attitude and you have not kept my covenant and my decrees, which I commanded you, I will most certainly tear the kingdom away from you and give it to one of your subordinates. Nevertheless, for the sake of David your father, I will not do it during your lifetime. I will tear it out of the hand of your son. Yet I will not tear the whole kingdom from him, but will give him one tribe for the sake of David my servant and for the sake of Jerusalem, which I have chosen.

Cast: **Narrator, the Lord** (voice only)

Solomon's Adversaries

1 Kings 11:14–25

Narrator The LORD raised up against Solomon an adversary, Hadad the Edomite, from the royal line of Edom.

Commentator Earlier when David was fighting with Edom, Joab the commander of the army, who had gone up to bury the dead, had struck down all the men in Edom. Joab and all the Israelites stayed there for six months, until they had destroyed all the men in Edom. But Hadad, still only a boy, fled to Egypt with some Edomite officials who had served his father. They set out from Midian and went to Paran. Then taking men from Paran with them, they went to Egypt, to Pharaoh king of Egypt, who gave Hadad a house and land and provided him with food.

Pharaoh was so pleased with Hadad that he gave him a sister of his own wife, Queen Tahpenes, in marriage. The sister of Tahpenes bore him a son named Genubath, whom Tahpenes brought up in the royal palace. There Genubath lived with Pharaoh's own children.

Narrator   While he was in Egypt, Hadad heard that David rested with his fathers and that Joab the commander of the army was also dead. Then Hadad said to Pharaoh:

Hadad   Let me go, that I may return to my own country.

[Narrator   [Pharaoh asked]:**]**

Pharaoh   What have you lacked here that you want to go back to your own country?

Hadad   Nothing, but do let me go!

Narrator   And God raised up against Solomon another adversary, Rezon son of Eliada, who had fled from his master, Hadadezer king of Zobah. He gathered men around him and became the leader of a band of rebels when David destroyed the forces ˌof Zobahˌ; the rebels went to Damascus, where they settled and took control. Rezon was Israel's adversary as long as Solomon lived, adding to the trouble caused by Hadad. So Rezon ruled in Aram and was hostile toward Israel.

Cast: **Narrator**, **Commentator** (can be the same as Narrator), **Hadad**, **Pharaoh**

Jeroboam Rebels against Solomon

From 1 Kings 11:26–43

Narrator   Also, Jeroboam son of Nebat rebelled against the king. He was one of Solomon's officials, an Ephraimite from Zeredah, and his mother was a widow named Zeruah.

Here is the account of how he rebelled against the king: Solomon had built the supporting terraces and had filled in the gap in the wall of the city of David his father. Now Jeroboam was a man of standing, and when Solomon saw how well the young man did his work, he put him in charge of the whole labor force of the house of Joseph.

About that time Jeroboam was going out of Jerusalem, and Ahijah the prophet of Shiloh met him on the way, wearing a new cloak. The two of them were alone out in the country, and Ahijah took hold of the new cloak he was wearing and tore it into twelve pieces. Then he said to Jeroboam:

Ahijah   Take ten pieces for yourself, for this is what the LORD, the God of Israel, says:

The Lord
(voice only)   See, I am going to tear the kingdom out of Solomon's hand and give you ten tribes. But for the sake of my servant David and the city of Jerusalem, which I have chosen out of all the tribes of Israel, he will have one tribe. I will do this because they have forsaken me and worshiped [foreign gods].

But I will not take the whole kingdom out of Solomon's hand; I have made him ruler all the days of his life for the sake of David my servant, whom I chose and who observed my commands and statutes. I will take the kingdom from his son's hands and give you ten tribes. I will give one tribe to his son so that David my servant may always have a lamp before me in Jerusalem, the city where I chose to put my Name. However, as for you, I will take you, and you will rule over all that your heart desires; you will be king over Israel. If you do whatever I command you and walk in my ways and do what is right in my eyes by keeping my statutes and commands, as David my servant did, I will be with you. I will build you a dynasty as enduring as the one I built for David and will give Israel to you. I will humble David's descendants because of this, but not forever.

Narrator   Solomon tried to kill Jeroboam, but Jeroboam fled to Egypt, to Shishak the king, and stayed there until Solomon's death.

As for the other events of Solomon's reign—all he did and the wisdom he displayed—are they not written in the book of the annals of Solomon? Solomon reigned in Jerusalem over all Israel forty years. Then he rested with his fathers and was buried in the city of David his father. And Rehoboam his son succeeded him as king.

Cast: **Narrator, Ahijah, the Lord** (voice only; or can be the same as Ahijah)

Israel Revolts against Rehoboam

1 Kings 12:1–24

Narrator   Rehoboam went to Shechem, for all the Israelites had gone there to make him king. When Jeroboam son of Nebat heard this (he was still in Egypt, where he had fled from King Solomon), he returned from Egypt. So they sent for Jeroboam, and he and the whole assembly of Israel went to Rehoboam [and said to him:]

Person 1   Your father put a heavy yoke on us.

Person 2   But now lighten the harsh labor and the heavy yoke he put on us, and we will serve you.

[Narrator	Rehoboam answered:]
Rehoboam	Go away for three days and then come back to me.
Narrator	So the people went away. (PAUSE) Then King Rehoboam consulted the elders who had served his father Solomon during his lifetime:
Rehoboam	How would you advise me to answer these people?
Elder 1	If today you will be a servant to these people—
Elder 2	and serve them and give them a favorable answer—
Elder 1	They will always be your servants.
Narrator	But Rehoboam rejected the advice the elders gave him and consulted the young men who had grown up with him and were serving him. [He asked them:]
Rehoboam	What is *your* advice? How should we answer these people who say to me, "Lighten the yoke your father put on us"?
Narrator	The young men who had grown up with him replied:
Young man 1	Tell these people who have said to you, "Your father put a heavy yoke on us, but make our yoke lighter"—tell them, "My little finger is thicker than my father's waist.
Young man 2	"My father laid on you a heavy yoke; I will make it even heavier.
Young man 1	"My father scourged you with whips; I will scourge you with scorpions." (PAUSE)
Narrator	Three days later Jeroboam and all the people returned to Rehoboam, as the king had said, "Come back to me in three days." The king answered the people harshly. Rejecting the advice given him by the elders, he followed the advice of the young men [and said:]
Rehoboam	My father made your yoke heavy; I will make it even heavier. My father scourged you with whips; I will scourge you with scorpions.
Narrator	So the king did not listen to the people, for this turn of events was from the LORD, to fulfill the word the LORD had spoken to Jeroboam son of Nebat through Ahijah the Shilonite.
	When all Israel saw that the king refused to listen to them, they answered the king:
Person 1	What share do we have in David.
Person 2	What part in Jesse's son?
Persons 1 and 2	To your tents, O Israel!
Person 2	Look after your own house, O David!

Narrator	So the Israelites went home. But as for the Israelites who were living in the towns of Judah, Rehoboam still ruled over them.
	King Rehoboam sent out Adoniram, who was in charge of forced labor, but all Israel stoned him to death. King Rehoboam, however, managed to get into his chariot and escape to Jerusalem. So Israel has been in rebellion against the house of David to this day.
	When all the Israelites heard that Jeroboam had returned, they sent and called him to the assembly and made him king over all Israel. Only the tribe of Judah remained loyal to the house of David.
	When Rehoboam arrived in Jerusalem, he mustered the whole house of Judah and the tribe of Benjamin—a hundred and eighty thousand fighting men—to make war against the house of Israel and to regain the kingdom for Rehoboam son of Solomon.
	But this word of God came to Shemaiah the man of God:
Shemaiah	Say to Rehoboam son of Solomon king of Judah, to the whole house of Judah and Benjamin, and to the rest of the people, "This is what the Lord says: Do not go up to fight against your brothers, the Israelites. Go home, every one of you, for this is my doing."
Narrator	So they obeyed the word of the Lord and went home again, as the Lord had ordered.

Cast: **Narrator, Person 1, Person 2, Rehoboam, Elder 1, Elder 2** (can be the same as Elder 1), **Young man 1, Young man 2, Shemaiah**

Golden Calves at Bethel and Dan

1 Kings 12:25–31

Narrator	Then Jeroboam fortified Shechem in the hill country of Ephraim and lived there. From there he went out and built up Peniel. Jeroboam thought to himself:
Jeroboam (to himself)	The kingdom will now likely revert to the house of David. If these people go up to offer sacrifices at the temple of the Lord in Jerusalem, they will again give their allegiance to their lord, Rehoboam king of Judah. They will kill me and return to King Rehoboam.
Narrator	After seeking advice, the king made two golden calves. He said to the people:
Jeroboam (to the people)	It is too much for you to go up to Jerusalem. Here are your gods, O Israel, who brought you up out of Egypt.

Narrator	One he set up in Bethel, and the other in Dan. And this thing became a sin; the people went even as far as Dan to worship the one there.
	Jeroboam built shrines on high places and appointed priests from all sorts of people, even though they were not Levites.

Cast: **Narrator, Jeroboam**

Worship at Bethel Is Condemned

1 Kings 12:32–13:10

Narrator	[Jeroboam] instituted a festival on the fifteenth day of the eighth month, like the festival held in Judah, and offered sacrifices on the altar. This he did in Bethel, sacrificing to the calves he had made. And at Bethel he also installed priests at the high places he had made. On the fifteenth day of the eighth month, a month of his own choosing, he offered sacrifices on the altar he had built at Bethel. So he instituted the festival for the Israelites and went up to the altar to make offerings.
	By the word of the Lord a man of God came from Judah to Bethel, as Jeroboam was standing by the altar to make an offering. He cried out against the altar by the word of the Lord:
Man of God	O altar, altar! This is what the Lord says: "A son named Josiah will be born to the house of David. On you he will sacrifice the priests of the high places who now make offerings here, and human bones will be burned on you."
[Narrator	That same day the man of God gave a sign:]
Man of God	This is the sign the Lord has declared: The altar will be split apart and the ashes on it will be poured out.
Narrator	When King Jeroboam heard what the man of God cried out against the altar at Bethel, he stretched out his hand from the altar:
Jeroboam	Seize him!
Narrator	But the hand he stretched out toward the man shriveled up, so that he could not pull it back. Also, the altar was split apart and its ashes poured out according to the sign given by the man of God by the word of the Lord. Then the king said to the man of God:
Jeroboam (to the Man of God)	Intercede with the Lord your God and pray for me that my hand may be restored.
Narrator	So the man of God interceded with the Lord, and the king's hand was restored and became as it was before. [The king said to the man of God:]

361

Jeroboam	Come home with me and have something to eat, and I will give you a gift.
Narrator	But the man of God answered the king:
Man of God	Even if you were to give me half your possessions, I would not go with you, nor would I eat bread or drink water here. For I was commanded by the word of the LORD: "You must not eat bread or drink water or return by the way you came."
Narrator	So he took another road and did not return by the way he had come to Bethel.

Cast: **Narrator, Man of God, Jeroboam**

The Old Prophet of Bethel

1 Kings 13:11–34

Narrator	Now there was a certain old prophet living in Bethel, whose sons came and told him all that the man of God had done there that day. They also told their father what he had said to the king. Their father asked them:
Old prophet	Which way did he go?
Narrator	And his sons showed him which road the man of God from Judah had taken. So he said to his sons:
Old prophet	Saddle the donkey for me.
Narrator	And when they had saddled the donkey for him, he mounted it and rode after the man of God. He found him sitting under an oak tree [and asked:]
Old prophet	Are you the man of God who came from Judah?
Man of God	I am.
[Narrator	So the prophet said to him:]
Old prophet	Come home with me and eat.
Narrator	The man of God said:
Man of God	I cannot turn back and go with you, nor can I eat bread or drink water with you in this place. I have been told by the word of the LORD: "You must not eat bread or drink water there or return by the way you came."
Old prophet	I too am a prophet, as you are. And an angel said to me by the word of the LORD: "Bring him back with you to your house so that he may eat bread and drink water."
Narrator	(But he was lying to him.) So the man of God returned with him and ate and drank in his house.

	While they were sitting at the table, the word of the LORD came to the old prophet who had brought him back. He cried out to the man of God who had come from Judah:
Old prophet	This is what the LORD says: "You have defied the word of the LORD and have not kept the command the LORD your God gave you. You came back and ate bread and drank water in the place where he told you not to eat or drink. Therefore your body will not be buried in the tomb of your fathers."
Narrator	When the man of God had finished eating and drinking, the prophet who had brought him back saddled his donkey for him. As he went on his way, a lion met him on the road and killed him, and his body was thrown down on the road, with both the donkey and the lion standing beside it. Some people who passed by saw the body thrown down there, with the lion standing beside the body, and they went and reported it in the city where the old prophet lived. (PAUSE) When the prophet who had brought him back from his journey heard of it, he said:
Old prophet	It is the man of God who defied the word of the LORD. The LORD has given him over to the lion, which has mauled him and killed him, as the word of the LORD had warned him.
Narrator	The prophet said to his sons:
Old prophet	Saddle the donkey for me.
Narrator	And they did so. Then he went out and found the body thrown down on the road, with the donkey and the lion standing beside it. The lion had neither eaten the body nor mauled the donkey. So the prophet picked up the body of the man of God, laid it on the donkey, and brought it back to his own city to mourn for him and bury him. Then he laid the body in his own tomb, and they mourned over him [and said:]
Old prophet	Oh, my brother!
Narrator	After burying him, he said to his sons:
Old prophet	When I die, bury me in the grave where the man of God is buried; lay my bones beside his bones. For the message he declared by the word of the LORD against the altar in Bethel and against all the shrines on the high places in the towns of Samaria will certainly come true.
Narrator	Even after this, Jeroboam did not change his evil ways, but once more appointed priests for the high places from all sorts of people. Anyone who wanted to become a priest he consecrated for the high places. This was the sin of the house of Jeroboam that led to its downfall and to its destruction from the face of the earth.

Cast: **Narrator, Old prophet, Man of God**

Ahijah's Prophecy against Jeroboam

From 1 Kings 14:1–18

Narrator Abijah son of Jeroboam became ill, and Jeroboam said to his wife:

Jeroboam Go, disguise yourself, so you won't be recognized as the wife of Jeroboam. Then go to Shiloh. Ahijah the prophet is there—the one who told me I would be king over this people. Take ten loaves of bread with you, some cakes and a jar of honey, and go to him. He will tell you what will happen to the boy.

Narrator So Jeroboam's wife did what he said and went to Ahijah's house in Shiloh.

Now Ahijah could not see; his sight was gone because of his age. But the LORD had told Ahijah:

The Lord
(voice only) Jeroboam's wife is coming to ask you about her son, for he is ill, and you are to give her such and such an answer. When she arrives, she will pretend to be someone else.

Narrator Ahijah heard the sound of her footsteps at the door.

Ahijah Come in, wife of Jeroboam. Why this pretense? I have been sent to you with bad news. Go, tell Jeroboam that this is what the LORD, the God of Israel, says:

The Lord
(voice) I raised you up from among the people and made you a leader over my people Israel. I tore the kingdom away from the house of David and gave it to you, but you have not been like my servant David, who kept my commands and followed me with all his heart, doing only what was right in my eyes. You have done more evil than all who lived before you. You have made for yourself other gods, idols made of metal; you have provoked me to anger and thrust me behind your back.

Because of this, I am going to bring disaster on the house of Jeroboam. I will cut off from Jeroboam every last male in Israel—slave or free. I will burn up the house of Jeroboam as one burns dung, until it is all gone. Dogs will eat those belonging to Jeroboam who die in the city, and the birds of the air will feed on those who die in the country. The LORD has spoken!

Ahijah As for you, go back home. When you set foot in your city, the boy will die. All Israel will mourn for him and bury him. He is the only one belonging to Jeroboam who will be buried, because he is the only one in the house of Jeroboam in whom the LORD, the God of Israel, has found anything good.

The LORD will raise up for himself a king over Israel who will cut off the family of Jeroboam. . . . And the LORD will strike Israel, so that it will be like a reed swaying in the water. He will uproot Israel from this good land that he gave to their forefathers and scatter them beyond the River, because they provoked the Lord to anger by making Asherah poles. And he will give Israel up because of the sins Jeroboam has committed and has caused Israel to commit.

Narrator Then Jeroboam's wife got up and left and went to Tirzah. As soon as she stepped over the threshold of the house, the boy died. They buried him, and all Israel mourned for him, as the Lord had said through his servant the prophet Ahijah.

Cast: **Narrator, Jeroboam, Ahijah, the Lord** (voice only)

Elijah Fed by Ravens

1 Kings 17:1–7

Narrator Elijah the Tishbite, from Tishbe in Gilead, said to Ahab:

Elijah As the Lord, the God of Israel, lives, whom I serve, there will be neither dew nor rain in the next few years except at my word.

Narrator Then the word of the Lord came to Elijah:

The Lord
(voice only) Leave here, turn eastward and hide in the Kerith Ravine, east of the Jordan. You will drink from the brook, and I have ordered the ravens to feed you there.

Narrator So he did what the Lord had told him. He went to the Kerith Ravine, east of the Jordan, and stayed there. The ravens brought him bread and meat in the morning and bread and meat in the evening, and he drank from the brook. (PAUSE) Some time later the brook dried up because there had been no rain in the land.

Cast: **Narrator, Elijah, the Lord** (voice only)

The Widow at Zarephath

1 Kings 17:8–16

Narrator The word of the Lord came to [Elijah]:

The Lord
(voice only) Go at once to Zarephath of Sidon and stay there. I have commanded a widow in that place to supply you with food.

Narrator So he went to Zarephath. When he came to the town gate, a widow was there gathering sticks. He called to her:

Elijah
(calling) Would you bring me a little water in a jar so I may have a drink?

Narrator	As she was going to get it, he called:
Elijah (calling)	And bring me, please, a piece of bread.
Widow	As surely as the LORD your God lives, I don't *have* any bread—only a handful of flour in a jar and a little oil in a jug. I am gathering a few sticks to take home and make a meal for myself and my son, that we may eat it—and die.
Elijah	Don't be afraid. Go home and do as you have said. But first make a small cake of bread for me from what you have and bring it to me, and then make something for yourself and your son. For this is what the LORD, the God of Israel, says:
The Lord (voice)	The jar of flour will not be used up and the jug of oil will not run dry until the day the LORD gives rain on the land.
Narrator	She went away and did as Elijah had told her. So there was food every day for Elijah and for the woman and her family. For the jar of flour was not used up and the jug of oil did not run dry, in keeping with the word of the LORD spoken by Elijah.

Cast: **Narrator, the Lord** (voice only), **Elijah, Widow**

The Widow's Son

1 Kings 17:17–24

Narrator	[Some time later] the son of the woman who owned the house [at Zarephath] became ill. He grew worse and worse, and finally stopped breathing. [She said to Elijah:]
Widow	What do you have against me, man of God? Did you come to remind me of my sin and kill my son?
Elijah	Give me your son.
Narrator	He took him from her arms, carried him to the upper room where he was staying, and laid him on his bed. Then he cried out to the LORD:
Elijah (praying)	O LORD my God, have you brought tragedy also upon this widow I am staying with, by causing her son to die?
Narrator	Then he stretched himself out on the boy three times and cried to the LORD:
Elijah (praying)	O LORD my God, let this boy's life return to him!

Narrator	The LORD heard Elijah's cry, and the boy's life returned to him, and he lived. Elijah picked up the child and carried him down from the room into the house. He gave him to his mother and said:
Elijah (to Widow)	Look, your son is alive!
Narrator	Then the woman said to Elijah:
Widow	Now I *know* that you are a man of God and that the word of the LORD from your mouth is the truth.

Cast: **Narrator, Widow, Elijah**

Elijah and Obadiah

1 Kings 18:1–19

Narrator	[After a long time, in the third year,] the word of the LORD came to Elijah:
The Lord (voice only)	Go and present yourself to Ahab, and I will send rain on the land.
Narrator	So Elijah went to present himself to Ahab. Now the famine was severe in Samaria, and Ahab had summoned Obadiah, who was in charge of his palace.
Commentator	(Obadiah was a devout believer in the LORD. While Jezebel was killing off the LORD's prophets, Obadiah had taken a hundred prophets and hidden them in two caves, fifty in each, and had supplied them with food and water.)
Narrator	Ahab had said to Obadiah:
Ahab	Go through the land to all the springs and valleys. Maybe we can find some grass to keep the horses and mules alive so we will not have to kill any of our animals.
Narrator	So they divided the land they were to cover, Ahab going in one direction and Obadiah in another. As Obadiah was walking along, Elijah met him. Obadiah recognized him [and] bowed down to the ground:
Obadiah	Is it really you, my lord Elijah?
Elijah	Yes. Go tell your master, "Elijah is here."
Obadiah	What have I done wrong, that you are handing your servant over to Ahab to be put to death? As surely as the LORD your God lives, there is not a nation or kingdom where my master has not sent someone to look for you. And whenever a nation or kingdom claimed you were not there, he

made them swear they could not find you. But now you tell me to go to my master and say, "Elijah is here."

I don't know where the Spirit of the LORD may carry you when I leave you. If I go and tell Ahab and he doesn't find you, he will kill me. Yet I your servant have worshiped the LORD since my youth. Haven't you heard, my lord, what I did while Jezebel was killing the prophets of the LORD? I hid a hundred of the LORD's prophets in two caves, fifty in each, and supplied them with food and water. And now you tell me to go to my master and say, "Elijah is here." He will kill me!

Elijah As the LORD Almighty lives, whom I serve, I will surely present myself to Ahab today.

Narrator So Obadiah went to meet Ahab and told him, and Ahab went to meet Elijah. When he saw Elijah, he said to him:

Ahab (calling) Is that you, you troubler of Israel?

Elijah (at a distance) I have not made trouble for Israel. But you and your father's family have. You have abandoned the LORD's commands and have followed the Baals. Now summon the people from all over Israel to meet me on Mount Carmel. And bring the four hundred and fifty prophets of Baal and the four hundred prophets of Asherah, who eat at Jezebel's table.

Cast: **Narrator**, **the Lord** (voice only), **Commentator** (can be the same as Narrator), **Ahab**, **Obadiah**, **Elijah**

Elijah on Mount Carmel

1 Kings 18:20–39

Narrator Ahab sent word throughout all Israel and assembled the prophets on Mount Carmel. Elijah went before the people [and said:]

Elijah (to the people) How long will you waver between two opinions? If the LORD is God, follow *him*; but if Baal is God, follow *him*.

Narrator But the people said nothing. (PAUSE) [Then Elijah said to them:]

Elijah I am the only one of the LORD's prophets left, but Baal has four hundred and fifty prophets. Get two bulls for us. Let them choose one for themselves, and let them cut it into pieces and put it on the wood but not set fire to it. I will prepare the other bull and put it on the wood but not set fire to it. Then you call on the name of your god, and I will call on the name of the LORD. The god who answers by fire—he is God.

[Narrator Then all the people said:]

Persons 1 and 2 What you say is good. (PAUSE)

Narrator	Elijah said to the prophets of Baal:
Elijah (to Prophets)	Choose one of the bulls and prepare it first, since there are so many of you. Call on the name of your god, but do not light the fire.
Narrator	So they took the bull given them and prepared it. (PAUSE) Then they called on the name of Baal from morning till noon. [They shouted:]
Prophets (shouting)	O Baal, answer us!
Narrator	But there was no response; no one answered. And they danced around the altar they had made. (PAUSE) At noon Elijah began to taunt them:
Elijah	Shout louder! Surely he *is* a god! Perhaps he is deep in thought, or busy, or traveling. Maybe he is sleeping and must be awakened.
Narrator	So they shouted louder and slashed themselves with swords and spears, as was their custom, until their blood flowed. Midday passed, and they continued their frantic prophesying until the time for the evening sacrifice. But there was no response, no one answered, no one paid attention. (PAUSE) [Then Elijah said to all the people:]
Elijah (to the people)	Come here to me.
Narrator	They came to him, and he repaired the altar of the LORD, which was in ruins. Elijah took twelve stones, one for each of the tribes descended from Jacob, to whom the word of the LORD had come, saying:
The Lord (voice only)	Your name shall be Israel.
Narrator	With the stones he built an altar in the name of the LORD, and he dug a trench around it large enough to hold two seahs of seed. He arranged the wood, cut the bull into pieces and laid it on the wood. [Then he said to them:]
Elijah	Fill four large jars with water and pour it on the offering and on the wood. (PAUSE)
Elijah (firmly)	Do it again.
Narrator	And they did it again. (PAUSE) [He ordered:]
Elijah	Do it a third time.
Narrator	And they did it the third time. The water ran down around the altar and even filled the trench. (PAUSE) At the time of sacrifice, the prophet Elijah stepped forward and prayed:

Elijah
(praying) O LORD, God of Abraham, Isaac and Israel, let it be known today that you are God in Israel and that I am your servant and have done all these things at your command. Answer me, O LORD, answer me, so these people will know that you, O LORD, are God, and that you are turning their hearts back again.

Narrator Then the fire of the LORD fell and burned up the sacrifice, the wood, the stones and the soil, and also licked up the water in the trench. (PAUSE) When all the people saw this, they fell prostrate [and cried:]

Person 1
(exclaiming) The LORD—he is God!

Person 2
(exclaiming) The LORD—he is God!

Cast: **Narrator, Elijah, Person 1, Person 2, Prophets** (2 or more)

The End of the Drought

1 Kings 18:41–46

Narrator Elijah said to Ahab:

Elijah Go, eat and drink, for there is the sound of a heavy rain.

Narrator So Ahab went off to eat and drink, but Elijah climbed to the top of Carmel, bent down to the ground and put his face between his knees.[He told his servant:]

Elijah Go and look toward the sea.

Narrator And he went up and looked: (PAUSE)

Servant There is nothing *there*.

Narrator Seven times Elijah said:

Elijah Go back.

Narrator The seventh time the servant reported:

Servant A cloud as small as a man's hand is rising from the sea.

[Narrator So Elijah said:]

Elijah Go and tell Ahab, "Hitch up your chariot and go down before the rain stops you."

Narrator Meanwhile, the sky grew black with clouds, the wind rose, a heavy rain came on and Ahab rode off to Jezreel. The power of the LORD came upon Elijah and, tucking his cloak into his belt, he ran ahead of Ahab all the way to Jezreel.

Cast: **Narrator, Elijah, Servant**

Elijah on Mount Sinai

1 Kings 19:1–18

Narrator   Ahab told Jezebel everything Elijah had done and how he had killed all the prophets with the sword. So Jezebel sent a messenger to Elijah:

Jezebel   May the gods deal with me, be it ever so severely, if by this time tomorrow I do not make your life like that of one of them.

Narrator   Elijah was afraid and ran for his life. When he came to Beersheba in Judah, he left his servant there, while he himself went a day's journey into the desert. He came to a broom tree, sat down under it and prayed that he might die.

Elijah   I have had enough, LORD. Take my life; I am no better than my ancestors.

Narrator   Then he lay down under the tree and fell asleep. (PAUSE) All at once an angel touched him [and said:]

Angel   Get up and eat.

Narrator   He looked around, and there by his head was a cake of bread baked over hot coals, and a jar of water. He ate and drank and then lay down again. (PAUSE) The angel of the LORD came back a second time and touched him [and said:]

Angel   Get up and eat, for the journey is too much for you.

Narrator   So he got up and ate and drank. Strengthened by that food, he traveled forty days and forty nights until he reached Horeb, the mountain of God. There he went into a cave and spent the night. (PAUSE) And the word of the LORD came to him:

The Lord
(voice only)   What are you doing here, Elijah?

Elijah   I have been very zealous for the LORD God Almighty. The Israelites have rejected your covenant, broken down your altars, and put your prophets to death with the sword. I am the only one left, and now they are trying to kill me too.

The Lord
(voice)   Go out and stand on the mountain in the presence of the LORD, for the LORD is about to pass by.

Narrator   Then a great and powerful wind tore the mountains apart and shattered the rocks before the LORD, but the LORD was not in the wind. After the wind there was an earthquake, but the LORD was not in the earthquake. After the earthquake came a fire, but the LORD was not in the fire. And after the fire came a gentle whisper. (PAUSE) When Elijah heard it, he pulled his cloak over his face and went out and stood at the mouth of the cave. [Then a voice said to him:]

The Lord (voice)	What are you doing here, Elijah?
Elijah	I have been very zealous for the LORD God Almighty. The Israelites have rejected your covenant, broken down your altars, and put your prophets to death with the sword. I am the only one left, and now they are trying to kill me too.
The Lord (voice)	Go back the way you came, and go to the Desert of Damascus. When you get there, anoint Hazael king over Aram. Also, anoint Jehu son of Nimshi king over Israel, and anoint Elisha son of Shaphat from Abel Meholah to succeed you as prophet. Jehu will put to death any who escape the sword of Hazael, and Elisha will put to death any who escape the sword of Jehu. Yet I reserve seven thousand in Israel—all whose knees have not bowed down to Baal and all whose mouths have not kissed him.

Cast: **Narrator, Jezebel, Elijah, Angel, the Lord** (voice only)

The Call of Elisha

1 Kings 19:19–21

Narrator	Elijah went from there and found Elisha son of Shaphat. He was plowing with twelve yoke of oxen, and he himself was driving the twelfth pair. Elijah went up to him and threw his cloak around him. Elisha then left his oxen and ran after Elijah.
Elisha	Let me kiss my father and mother good-by, and then I will come with you.
Elijah	Go back. What have I done to you?
Narrator	So Elisha left him and went back. He took his yoke of oxen and slaughtered them. He burned the plowing equipment to cook the meat and gave it to the people, and they ate. Then he set out to follow Elijah and became his attendant.

Cast: **Narrator, Elisha, Elijah**

Ben-Hadad Attacks Syria

1 Kings 20:1–22

Narrator	Ben-Hadad king of Aram mustered his entire army. Accompanied by thirty-two kings with their horses and chariots, he went up and besieged Samaria and attacked it. He sent messengers into the city to Ahab king of Israel, [saying:]

Messenger 1
(to Ahab)   This is what Ben-Hadad says: "Your silver and gold are mine—

Messenger 2   "And the best of your wives and children are mine."

Narrator   The king of Israel answered:

Ahab (to
Messengers
1 and 2)   Just as you say, my lord the king. I and all I have are yours.

Narrator   The messengers came *again* [and said:]

Messenger 1   This is what Ben-Hadad says: "I sent to demand your silver and gold, your wives and your children.

Messenger 2   "But about this time tomorrow I am going to send my officials to search your palace and the houses of your officials.

Messenger 1   "They will seize everything you value and carry it away."

Narrator   The king of Israel summoned all the elders of the land and said to them:

Ahab (to
Persons 1
and 2)   See how this man is looking for trouble! When he sent for my wives and my children, my silver and my gold, I did not refuse him.

Narrator   The elders and the people all answered:

Person 1   Don't listen to him—

Person 2   Or agree to his demands.

[Narrator   So he replied to Ben-Hadad's messengers:]

Ahab (to
Messengers
1 and 2)   Tell my lord the king, "Your servant will do all you demanded the first time, but this demand I cannot meet."

Narrator   They left and took the answer back to Ben-Hadad. (PAUSE) Then Ben-Hadad sent another message to Ahab:

Messenger 1   May the gods deal with me, be it ever so severely, if enough dust remains in Samaria to give each of my men a handful.

[Narrator   The king of Israel answered:]

Ahab   Tell him: "One who puts on his armor should not boast like one who takes it off."

Narrator   Ben-Hadad heard this message while he and the kings were drinking in their tents, and he ordered his men:

Ben-Hadad   Prepare to attack.

Narrator   So they prepared to attack the city. (PAUSE)

Meanwhile a prophet came to Ahab king of Israel and announced:

373

Prophet	This is what the LORD says: "Do you see this vast army? I will give it into your hand today, and then you will know that I am the LORD."
Ahab	But who will do this?
Prophet	This is what the LORD says: "The young officers of the provincial commanders will do it."
Ahab	And who will start the battle?
Prophet	*You* will.
Narrator	So Ahab summoned the young officers of the provincial commanders, 232 men. Then he assembled the rest of the Israelites, 7,000 in all. They set out at noon while Ben-Hadad and the 32 kings allied with him were in their tents getting drunk. The young officers of the provincial commanders went out first. (PAUSE) Now Ben-Hadad had dispatched scouts, who reported:
Scout	Men are advancing from Samaria.
Ben-Hadad	If they have come out for peace, take them alive; if they have come out for war, take them alive.
Narrator	The young officers of the provincial commanders marched out of the city with the army behind them and each one struck down his opponent. At that, the Arameans fled, with the Israelites in pursuit. But Ben-Hadad king of Aram escaped on horseback with some of his horsemen. The king of Israel advanced and overpowered the horses and chariots and inflicted heavy losses on the Arameans. (PAUSE) Afterward, the prophet came to the king of Israel [and said:]
Prophet	Strengthen your position and see what must be done, because next spring the king of Aram will attack you again.

Cast: **Narrator, Messenger 1, Messenger 2** (can be the same as Messenger 1), **Ahab, Person 1, Person 2** (can be the same as Person 1), **Ben-Hadad, Prophet, Scout** (can be the same as Messenger 2)

The Second Aramean Attack

1 Kings 20:23–34

Narrator	The officials of the king of Aram advised him:
Official 1	[The Israelites'] gods are gods of the hills. That is why they were too strong for us. But if we fight them on the plains, surely we will be stronger than they.
Official 2	Do this: Remove all the kings from their commands and replace them with other officers.
Official 1	You must also raise an army like the one you lost—horse for horse and chariot for chariot—so we can fight Israel on the plains.

Official 2	Then surely we will be stronger than they.
Narrator	He agreed with them and acted accordingly.
	The next spring Ben-Hadad mustered the Arameans and went up to Aphek to fight against Israel. When the Israelites were also mustered and given provisions, they marched out to meet them. The Israelites camped opposite them like two small flocks of goats, while the Arameans covered the countryside. The man of God came up and told the king of Israel:
Prophet	This is what the LORD says: "Because the Arameans think the LORD is a god of the hills and not a god of the valleys, I will deliver this vast army into your hands, and you will know that I am the LORD."
Narrator	For seven days they camped opposite each other, and on the seventh day the battle was joined. The Israelites inflicted a hundred thousand casualties on the Aramean foot soldiers in one day. The rest of them escaped to the city of Aphek, where the wall collapsed on twenty-seven thousand of them. (PAUSE) And Ben-Hadad fled to the city and hid in an inner room. His officials said to him:
Official 1	Look, we have heard that the kings of the house of Israel are merciful.
Official 2	Let us go to the king of Israel with sackcloth around our waists and ropes around our heads.
Official 1	Perhaps he will spare your life.
Narrator	Wearing sackcloth around their waists and ropes around their heads, they went to the king of Israel and said:
Official 1	Your servant Ben-Hadad says: "Please let me live."
[Narrator	The king answered:]
Ahab	Is he still alive? He is my brother.
Narrator	The men took this as a good sign and were quick to pick up his word.
Official 1	Yes, your brother Ben-Hadad!
Ahab	Go and get him.
Narrator	When Ben-Hadad came out, Ahab had him come up into his chariot. [[Ben-Hadad offered:]]
Ben-Hadad	I will return the cities my father took from your father. You may set up your own market areas in Damascus, as my father did in Samaria.
Ahab	On the basis of a treaty I will set you free.
Narrator	So he made a treaty with him, and let him go.

Cast: **Narrator**, **Official 1**, **Official 2** (can be the same as Official 1), **Prophet**, **Ahab**, **Ben-Hadad**

A Prophet Condemns Ahab

1 Kings 20:35–43

Narrator	By the word of the LORD one of the sons of the prophets said to his companion:
Prophet	Strike me with your weapon.
Narrator	But the man refused. So the prophet said:
Prophet	Because you have not obeyed the LORD, as soon as you leave me a lion will kill you.
Narrator	And after the man went away, a lion found him and killed him. (PAUSE) The prophet found another man and said:
Prophet	Strike me, please.
Narrator	So the man struck him and wounded him. Then the prophet went and stood by the road waiting for the king. He disguised himself with his headband down over his eyes. As the king passed by, the prophet called out to him:
Prophet (calling)	Your servant went into the thick of the battle, and someone came to me with a captive and said, "Guard this man. If he is missing, it will be your life for his life, or you must pay a talent of silver." While your servant was busy here and there, the man disappeared.
Narrator	[The king of Israel said:]
Ahab	That is your sentence. You have pronounced it yourself.
Narrator	Then the prophet quickly removed the headband from his eyes, and the king of Israel recognized him as one of the prophets. He said to the king:
Prophet (firmly)	This is what the LORD says: "You have set free a man I had determined should die. Therefore it is your life for his life, your people for his people."
Narrator	Sullen and angry, the king of Israel went to his palace in Samaria.

Cast: **Narrator, Prophet, Ahab**

Naboth's Vineyard

1 Kings 21:1–29

Narrator	Some time later there was an incident involving a vineyard belonging to Naboth the Jezreelite. The vineyard was in Jezreel, close to the palace of Ahab king of Samaria. Ahab said to Naboth:

Ahab	Let me have your vineyard to use for a vegetable garden, since it is close to my palace. In exchange I will give you a better vineyard or, if you prefer, I will pay you whatever it is worth.
[Narrator	But Naboth replied:]
Naboth	The LORD forbid that I should give you the inheritance of my fathers.
Narrator	So Ahab went home, sullen and angry because Naboth the Jezreelite had said, "I will not give you the inheritance of my fathers." He lay on his bed sulking and refused to eat. His wife Jezebel came in [and asked him:]
Jezebel	Why are you so sullen? Why won't you eat?
Ahab	Because I said to Naboth the Jezreelite, "Sell me your vineyard; or if you prefer, I will give you another vineyard in its place." But he said, "I will not give you my vineyard."
Jezebel	Is this how you act as king over Israel? Get up and eat! Cheer up. I'll get you the vineyard of Naboth the Jezreelite.
Narrator	So she wrote letters in Ahab's name, placed his seal on them, and sent them to the elders and nobles who lived in Naboth's city with him. [In those letters she wrote:]
Jezebel	Proclaim a day of fasting and seat Naboth in a prominent place among the people. But seat two scoundrels opposite him and have them testify that he has cursed both God and the king. Then take him out and stone him to death.
Narrator	So the elders and nobles who lived in Naboth's city did as Jezebel directed in the letters she had written to them. They proclaimed a fast and seated Naboth in a prominent place among the people. Then two scoundrels came and sat opposite him and brought charges against Naboth before the people:
Scoundrel	Naboth has cursed both God and the king.
Narrator	So they took him outside the city and stoned him to death. Then they sent word to Jezebel:
Elder	Naboth has been stoned and is dead.
Narrator	As soon as Jezebel heard that Naboth had been stoned to death, she said to Ahab:
Jezebel	Get up and take possession of the vineyard of Naboth the Jezreelite that he refused to sell you. He is no longer alive, but dead.
Narrator	When Ahab heard that Naboth was dead, he got up and went down to take possession of Naboth's vineyard. (PAUSE) Then the word of the LORD came to Elijah the Tishbite:
The Lord (voice only)	Go down to meet Ahab king of Israel, who rules in Samaria. He is now in Naboth's vineyard, where he has gone to take possession of it. Say to

377

him, "This is what the LORD says: Have you not murdered a man and seized his property?" Then say to him, "This is what the LORD says: In the place where dogs licked up Naboth's blood, dogs will lick up your blood—yes, yours!"

Narrator   Ahab said to Elijah:

Ahab (calling)   So you have found me, my enemy!

Elijah (at a
distance)   I have found you, because you have sold yourself to do evil in the eyes of the LORD. "I am going to bring disaster on you. I will consume your descendants and cut off from Ahab every last male in Israel—slave or free. I will make your house like that of Jeroboam son of Nebat and that of Baasha son of Ahijah, because you have provoked me to anger and have caused Israel to sin."

And also concerning Jezebel the LORD says: "Dogs will devour Jezebel by the wall of Jezreel."

Dogs will eat those belonging to Ahab who die in the city, and the birds of the air will feed on those who die in the country.

Commentator   (There was never a man like Ahab, who sold himself to do evil in the eyes of the LORD, urged on by Jezebel his wife. He behaved in the *vilest* manner by going after idols, like the Amorites the LORD drove out before Israel.)

Narrator   When Ahab heard these words, he tore his clothes, put on sackcloth and fasted. He lay in sackcloth and went around meekly.

Then the word of the LORD came to Elijah the Tishbite:

The Lord
(voice)   Have you noticed how Ahab has humbled himself before me? Because he has humbled himself, I will not bring this disaster in his day, but I will bring it on his house in the days of his son.

Cast: **Narrator, Ahab, Naboth, Jezebel, Scoundrel, Elder** (can be the same as Scoundrel), **the Lord** (voice only), **Elijah, Commentator** (can be the same as Narrator)

Micaiah Prophesies against Ahab

1 Kings 22:1–28

Narrator   For three years there was no war between Aram and Israel. But in the third year Jehoshaphat king of Judah went down to see the king of Israel. The king of Israel had said to his officials:

Ahab   Don't you know that Ramoth Gilead belongs to us and yet we are doing nothing to retake it from the king of Aram?

[Narrator   So he asked Jehoshaphat:]

Ahab (to Jehosha-phat)	Will you go with me to fight against Ramoth Gilead?
[Narrator	Jehoshaphat replied to the king of Israel:]
Jehoshaphat	I am as you are, my people as your people, my horses as your horses.
Narrator	But Jehoshaphat also said to the king of Israel:
Jehoshaphat	First seek the counsel of the LORD.
Narrator	So the king of Israel brought together the prophets—about four hundred men—[and asked them:]
Ahab	Shall I go to war against Ramoth Gilead, or shall I refrain?
Prophets 1 and 2	Go—
Prophet 2	For the Lord will give it into the king's hand.
[Narrator	But Jehoshaphat asked:]
Jehoshaphat	Is there not a prophet of the LORD here whom we can inquire of?
[Narrator	The king of Israel answered Jehoshaphat:]
Ahab	There is still one man through whom we can inquire of the LORD, but I *hate* him because he never prophesies anything *good* about me, but always bad. He is Micaiah son of Imlah.
[Narrator	Jehoshaphat replied:]
Jehoshaphat	The king should not say that.
Narrator	So the king of Israel called one of his officials and said:
Ahab	Bring Micaiah son of Imlah at once.
Narrator	Dressed in their royal robes, the king of Israel and Jehoshaphat king of Judah were sitting on their thrones at the threshing floor by the entrance of the gate of Samaria, with all the prophets prophesying before them. Now Zedekiah son of Kenaanah had made iron horns and he declared:
Prophet 1	This is what the LORD says: "With these you will gore the Arameans until they are destroyed."
Narrator	All the other prophets were prophesying the same thing.
Prophet 2	Attack Ramoth Gilead and be victorious, for the LORD will give it into the king's hand.
Narrator	The messenger who had gone to summon Micaiah said to him:
Official (firmly)	Look, as one man the other prophets are predicting success for the king. Let your word agree with theirs, and speak favorably.
[Narrator	But Micaiah said:]

Micaiah	As surely as the LORD lives, I can tell him only what the LORD tells me.
Narrator	When he arrived, the king asked him:
Ahab	Micaiah, shall we go to war against Ramoth Gilead, or shall I refrain?
Micaiah (casually)	Attack and be victorious, for the LORD will give it into the king's hand.
Ahab (frustrated)	How many times must I make you swear to tell me nothing but the truth in the name of the LORD?
Micaiah (sadly)	I saw all Israel scattered on the hills like sheep without a shepherd, and the LORD said:
The Lord (voice only)	These people have no master. Let each one go home in peace.
[Narrator	The king of Israel said to Jehoshaphat:]
Ahab (crossly, to Jehosha-phat)	Didn't I tell you that he never prophesies anything good about me, but only bad?
[Narrator	Micaiah continued:]
Micaiah	Therefore hear the word of the LORD: I saw the LORD sitting on his throne with all the host of heaven standing around him on his right and on his left. And the LORD said:
The Lord (voice)	Who will entice Ahab into attacking Ramoth Gilead and going to his death there?
Micaiah	One suggested this, and another that. Finally, a spirit came forward [and] stood before the LORD:
A spirit (voice)	*I* will entice him.
The Lord (voice)	By what means?
A spirit (voice)	I will go out and be a lying spirit in the mouths of all his prophets.
The Lord (voice)	You will succeed in enticing him. Go and do it.
Micaiah	So now the LORD has put a lying spirit in the mouths of all these prophets of yours. The LORD has decreed disaster for you.
Narrator	Then Zedekiah son of Kenaanah went up and slapped Micaiah in the face.

Zedekiah
(angrily) Which way did the spirit from the LORD go when he went from me to speak to you?

[Narrator Micaiah replied:]

Micaiah
(severely) You will find out on the day you go to hide in an inner room.

[Narrator The king of Israel then ordered:]

Ahab (to
Official) Take Micaiah and send him back to Amon the ruler of the city and to Joash the king's son and say, "This is what the king says: Put this fellow in prison and give him nothing but bread and water until I return safely."

Micaiah
(exclaiming If you ever return safely, the LORD has not spoken through me.
to all) Mark my words, all you people!

Cast: **Narrator, Ahab, Jehoshaphat, Prophet 1, Prophet 2, Official, Micaiah, the Lord** (voice only), **A spirit** (voice only), **Zedekiah**

Ahab Killed at Ramoth Gilead

1 Kings 22:29–40

Narrator The king of Israel and Jehoshaphat king of Judah went up to Ramoth Gilead. The king of Israel said to Jehoshaphat:

Ahab *I* will enter the battle in disguise, but *you* wear your royal robes.

Narrator So the king of Israel disguised himself and went into battle.

Now the king of Aram had ordered his thirty-two chariot commanders:

King of Aram Do not fight with anyone, small or great, except the king of Israel.

Narrator When the chariot commanders saw Jehoshaphat, they thought:

Commander
(thinking) Surely this is the king of Israel.

Narrator So they turned to attack him, but when Jehoshaphat cried out, the chariot commanders saw that he was not the king of Israel and stopped pursuing him.

But someone drew his bow at random and hit the king of Israel between the sections of his armor. The king told his chariot driver:

Ahab Wheel around and get me out of the fighting. I've been wounded.

Narrator All day long the battle raged, and the king was propped up in his chariot facing the Arameans. The blood from his wound ran onto the floor of the chariot, and that evening he died. (PAUSE) As the sun was setting, a cry spread through the army:

Soldier   Every man to his town; everyone to his land!

Narrator   So the king died and was brought to Samaria, and they buried him there. They washed the chariot at a pool in Samaria (where the prostitutes bathed), and the dogs licked up his blood, as the word of the LORD had declared.

As for the other events of Ahab's reign, including all he did, the palace he built and inlaid with ivory, and the cities he fortified, are they not written in the book of the annals of the kings of Israel? (PAUSE) Ahab rested with his fathers. And Ahaziah his son succeeded him as king.

Cast: **Narrator, Ahab, King of Aram, Commander, Soldier**

2 Kings

The Lord's Judgment on Ahaziah

2 Kings 1:1–18

Narrator	After Ahab's death, Moab rebelled against Israel. Now Ahaziah had fallen through the lattice of his upper room in Samaria and injured himself. So he sent messengers, saying to them:
King	Go and consult Baal-Zebub, the god of Ekron, to see if I will recover from this injury.
Narrator	But the angel of the LORD said to Elijah the Tishbite:
Angel (voice, to Elijah)	Go up and meet the messengers of the king of Samaria and ask them, "Is it because there is no God in Israel that you are going off to consult Baal-Zebub, the god of Ekron?" Therefore this is what the LORD says: "You will not leave the bed you are lying on. You will certainly die!"
Narrator	So Elijah went. (PAUSE) When the messengers returned to the king, he asked them:
King	Why have you come back?
Messenger 1	A man came to meet us. And he said to us, "Go back to the king who sent you and tell him, 'This is what the LORD says:
Messenger 2	"'Is it because there is no God in Israel that you are sending men to consult Baal-Zebub, the god of Ekron?
Messenger 3	"'Therefore you will not leave the bed you are lying on.
Messenger 1	"'You will certainly die!'"
[Narrator	The king asked them:]
King	What kind of man was it who came to meet you and told you this?
Messenger 2	He was a man with a garment of hair and with a leather belt around his waist.
King (exclaiming)	That was Elijah the Tishbite.
Narrator	Then he sent to Elijah a captain with his company of fifty men. The captain went up to Elijah, who was sitting on the top of a hill [and said to him:]
Messenger 1	Man of God, the king says, "Come down!"
[Narrator	Elijah answered the captain:]

Elijah	If I am a man of God, may fire come down from heaven and consume you and your fifty men!
Narrator	Then fire fell from heaven and consumed the captain and his men.
	At this the king sent to Elijah another captain with his fifty men. The captain said to him:
Messenger 2	Man of God, this is what the king says, "Come down at once!"
Elijah	If I am a man of God, may fire come down from heaven and consume you and your fifty men!
Narrator	Then the fire of God fell from heaven and consumed him and his fifty men.
	So the king sent a third captain with his fifty men. This third captain went up and fell on his knees before Elijah.
Messenger 3 (begging)	Man of God, please have respect for my life and the lives of these fifty men, your servants! See, fire has fallen from heaven and consumed the first two captains and all their men. But now have respect for my life!
Narrator	The angel of the LORD said to Elijah:
Angel (voice)	Go down with him; do not be afraid of him.
Narrator	So Elijah got up and went down with him to the king. He told the king:
Elijah	This is what the LORD says: Is it because there is no God in Israel for you to consult that you have sent messengers to consult Baal-Zebub, the god of Ekron? Because you have done this, you will never leave the bed you are lying on. You will certainly die!
Narrator	So he died, according to the word of the LORD that Elijah had spoken.
	Because Ahaziah had no son, Joram succeeded him as king in the second year of Jehoram son of Jehoshaphat king of Judah. As for all the other events of Ahaziah's reign, and what he did, are they not written in the book of the annals of the kings of Israel?

Cast: **Narrator, King, Angel** (voice only), **Messenger 1, Messenger 2, Messenger 3** (Messengers 1, 2, and 3 *cannot* be the same), **Elijah**

Elijah Taken Up to Heaven

2 Kings 2:1–15

Narrator	When the LORD was about to take Elijah up to heaven in a whirlwind, Elijah and Elisha were on their way from Gilgal. Elijah said to Elisha:
Elijah	Stay here; the LORD has sent me to Bethel.

[Narrator	But Elisha said:]
Elisha (to Elijah)	As surely as the Lord lives and as you live, I will not leave you.
Narrator	So they went down to Bethel. (PAUSE) The company of the prophets at Bethel came out to Elisha [and asked:]
Prophet 1	Do you know that the Lord is going to take your master from you today?
Elisha (to Prophets)	Yes, I know, but do not speak of it.
[Narrator	Then Elijah said to him:]
Elijah (to Elisha)	Stay here, Elisha; the Lord has sent me to Jericho.
Elisha (to Elijah)	As surely as the Lord lives and as you live, I will not leave you.
Narrator	So they went to Jericho. (PAUSE) The company of the prophets at Jericho went up to Elisha [and asked him:]
Prophet 2	Do you know that the Lord is going to take your master from you today?
Elisha (to Prophets)	Yes, I know, but do not speak of it.
Narrator	Then Elijah said to him:
Elijah (to Elisha)	Stay here; the Lord has sent me to the Jordan.
Elisha (to Elijah)	As surely as the Lord lives and as you live, I will not leave you.
Narrator	So the two of them walked on. Fifty men of the company of the prophets went and stood at a distance, facing the place where Elijah and Elisha had stopped at the Jordan. Elijah took his cloak, rolled it up and struck the water with it. The water divided to the right and to the left, and the two of them crossed over on dry ground. (PAUSE) [When they had crossed, Elijah said to Elisha:]
Elijah	Tell me, what can I do for you before I am taken from you?
Elisha	Let me inherit a double portion of your spirit.
Elijah	You have asked a difficult thing, yet if you see me when I am taken from you, it will be yours—otherwise not.
Narrator	As they were walking along and talking together, suddenly a chariot of fire and horses of fire appeared and separated the two of them, and Elijah went up to heaven in a whirlwind. Elisha saw this [and cried out:]
Elisha (crying out)	My father! My father! The chariots and horsemen of Israel!

385

Narrator	And Elisha saw him no more. (PAUSE) Then he took hold of his own clothes and tore them apart.
	He picked up the cloak that had fallen from Elijah and went back and stood on the bank of the Jordan. Then he took the cloak that had fallen from him and struck the water with it.
Elisha	Where now is the LORD, the God of Elijah?
Narrator	When he struck the water, it divided to the right and to the left, and he crossed over. The company of the prophets from Jericho . . . were watching.
Prophets 1 and 2	The spirit of Elijah is resting on Elisha.
Narrator	And they went to meet him and bowed to the ground before him.

Cast: **Narrator, Elijah, Elisha, Prophet 1, Prophet 2**

The Prophets Search for Elijah

2 Kings 2:15–18

Narrator	The company of the prophets from Jericho, who were watching . . . went to meet [Elisha] and bowed to the ground before him.
Prophet	Look, we your servants have fifty able men. Let them go and look for your master. Perhaps the Spirit of the LORD has picked him up and set him down on some mountain or in some valley.
Elisha	No, do not send them.
Narrator	But they persisted until he was too ashamed to refuse. [So he said:]
Elisha (reluctantly)	Send them.
Narrator	And they sent fifty men, who searched for three days but did not find him. (PAUSE) When they returned to Elisha, who was staying in Jericho, he said to them:
Elisha	Didn't I tell you not to go?

Cast: **Narrator, Prophet, Elisha**

Miracles of Elisha

2 Kings 2:19–25

Narrator	The men of the city said to Elisha:

Man 1	Look, our lord, this town is well situated, as you can see—
Man 2	But the water is bad and the land is unproductive.
Elisha	Bring me a new bowl, and put salt in it.
Narrator	So they brought it to him. (PAUSE) Then he went out to the spring and threw the salt into it [saying:]
Elisha	This is what the LORD says: "I have healed this water. Never again will it cause death or make the land unproductive."
Narrator	And the water has remained wholesome to this day, according to the word Elisha had spoken. (PAUSE)
	From there Elisha went up to Bethel. As he was walking along the road, some youths came out of the town and jeered at him.
Youths 1 and 2	Go on up, you baldhead!
Youth 2	Go on up, you baldhead!
Narrator	He turned around, looked at them and called down a curse on them in the name of the LORD. Then two bears came out of the woods and mauled forty-two of the youths. And he went on to Mount Carmel and from there returned to Samaria.

Cast: **Narrator, Man 1, Man 2** (can be the same as Man 1), **Elisha, Youth 1, Youth 2**

Moab Revolts

2 Kings 3:1–27

Narrator	Joram son of Ahab became king of Israel in Samaria in the eighteenth year of Jehoshaphat king of Judah, and he reigned twelve years. He did evil in the eyes of the LORD, but not as his father and mother had done. He got rid of the sacred stone of Baal that his father had made. Nevertheless he clung to the sins of Jeroboam son of Nebat, which he had caused Israel to commit; he did not turn away from them.
	Now Mesha king of Moab raised sheep, and he had to supply the king of Israel with a hundred thousand lambs and with the wool of a hundred thousand rams. But after Ahab died, the king of Moab rebelled against the king of Israel. So at that time King Joram set out from Samaria and mobilized all Israel. He also sent this message to Jehoshaphat king of Judah:
Joram	The king of Moab has rebelled against me. Will you go with me to fight against Moab?
Jehoshaphat	I will go with you. I am as you are, my people as your people, my horses as your horses.

387

Joram	By what route shall we attack?
Jehoshaphat	Through the Desert of Edom.
Narrator	So the king of Israel set out with the king of Judah and the king of Edom. After a roundabout march of seven days, the army had no more water for themselves or for the animals with them.
Joram (exclaiming)	What! Has the Lᴏʀᴅ called us three kings together only to hand us over to Moab?
Jehoshaphat	Is there no prophet of the Lᴏʀᴅ here, that we may inquire of the Lᴏʀᴅ through him?
Narrator	An officer of the king of Israel answered:
Officer	Elisha son of Shaphat is here. He used to pour water on the hands of Elijah.
Jehoshaphat	The word of the Lᴏʀᴅ is with him.
Narrator	So the king of Israel and Jehoshaphat and the king of Edom went down to him. (ᴘᴀᴜsᴇ)

Elisha said to the king of Israel: |
Elisha	What do we have to do with each other? Go to the prophets of your father and the prophets of your mother.
Joram	No, because it was the Lᴏʀᴅ who called us three kings together to hand us over to Moab.
Elisha	As surely as the Lᴏʀᴅ Almighty lives, whom I serve, if I did not have respect for the presence of Jehoshaphat king of Judah, I would not look at you or even notice you. But now bring me a harpist.
Narrator	While the harpist was playing, the hand of the Lᴏʀᴅ came upon Elisha and he said:
Elisha	This is what the Lᴏʀᴅ says: Make this valley full of ditches. For this is what the Lᴏʀᴅ says: You will see neither wind nor rain, yet this valley will be filled with water, and you, your cattle and your other animals will drink. This is an easy thing in the eyes of the Lᴏʀᴅ; he will also hand Moab over to you. You will overthrow every fortified city and every major town. You will cut down every good tree, stop up all the springs, and ruin every good field with stones.
Narrator	The next morning, about the time for offering the sacrifice, there it was—water flowing from the direction of Edom! And the land was filled with water.

Now all the Moabites had heard that the kings had come to fight against them; so every man, young and old, who could bear arms was called up and stationed on the border. When they got up early in the morning, the |

	sun was shining on the water. To the Moabites across the way, the water looked red—like blood.
Moabite 1	That's blood!
Moabite 2	Those kings must have fought and slaughtered each other.
Moabite 1	Now to the plunder, Moab!
Narrator	But when the Moabites came to the camp of Israel, the Israelites rose up and fought them until they fled. And the Israelites invaded the land and slaughtered the Moabites. They destroyed the towns, and each man threw a stone on every good field until it was covered. They stopped up all the springs and cut down every good tree. Only Kir Hareseth was left with its stones in place, but men armed with slings surrounded it and attacked it as well.
	When the king of Moab saw that the battle had gone against him, he took with him seven hundred swordsmen to break through to the king of Edom, but they failed. Then he took his firstborn son, who was to succeed him as king, and offered him as a sacrifice on the city wall. The fury against Israel was great; they withdrew and returned to their own land.

Cast: **Narrator, Joram, Jehoshaphat, Officer, Elisha, Moabite 1, Moabite 2** (can be the same as Moabite 1)

The Widow's Oil

2 Kings 4:1–7

Narrator	The wife of a man from the company of the prophets cried out to Elisha:
Widow	Your servant my husband is dead, and you know that he revered the LORD. But now his creditor is coming to take my two boys as his slaves.
Elisha	How can I help you? Tell me, what do you have in your house?
Widow	Your servant has nothing there at all, except a little oil.
Elisha	Go around and ask all your neighbors for empty jars. Don't ask for just a few. Then go inside and shut the door behind you and your sons. Pour oil into all the jars, and as each is filled, put it to one side.
Narrator	She left him and afterward shut the door behind her and her sons. They brought the jars to her and she kept pouring. When all the jars were full, she said to her son:
Widow	Bring me another one.
Son	There is not a jar left.
Narrator	Then the oil stopped flowing. (PAUSE) She went and told the man of God, and he said:

389

Elisha	Go, sell the oil and pay your debts. You and your sons can live on what is left.

Cast: **Narrator, Widow, Elisha, Son**

The Shunammite's Son Restored to Life

2 Kings 4:8–37

Narrator	One day Elisha went to Shunem. And a well-to-do woman was there, who urged him to stay for a meal. So whenever he came by, he stopped there to eat. She said to her husband:
Woman	I know that this man who often comes our way is a holy man of God. Let's make a small room on the roof and put in it a bed and a table, a chair and a lamp for him. Then he can stay there whenever he comes to us.
Narrator	One day when Elisha came, he went up to his room and lay down there. He said to his servant Gehazi:
Elisha	Call the Shunammite.
Narrator	So he called her, and she stood before him. Elisha said to him:
Elisha	Tell her, "You have gone to all this trouble for us. Now what can be done for you? Can we speak on your behalf to the king or the commander of the army?"
Woman	I have a home among my own people.
Elisha	What can be done for her?
[Narrator	Gehazi said:]
Gehazi	Well, she has no son and her husband is old.
Elisha	Call her.
Narrator	So he called her, and she stood in the doorway.
Elisha	About this time next year, you will hold a son in your arms.
Woman (exclaiming)	No, my lord. Don't mislead your servant, O man of God!
Narrator	But the woman became pregnant, and the next year about that same time she gave birth to a son, just as Elisha had told her. (PAUSE)
	The child grew, and one day he went out to his father, who was with the reapers. [He said to his father:]
Boy	My head! My head!
Narrator	His father told a servant:

Father	Carry him to his mother.
Narrator	After the servant had lifted him up and carried him to his mother, the boy sat on her lap until noon, and then he died. She went up and laid him on the bed of the man of God, then shut the door and went out. She called her husband and said:
Woman	Please send me one of the servants and a donkey so I can go to the man of God quickly and return.
Father	Why go to him today? It's not the New Moon or the Sabbath.
Woman	It's all right.
Narrator	She saddled the donkey and said to her servant:
Woman	Lead on; don't slow down for me unless I tell you.
Narrator	So she set out and came to the man of God at Mount Carmel. (PAUSE)
	When he saw her in the distance, the man of God said to his servant Gehazi:
Elisha	Look! There's the Shunammite! Run to meet her and ask her, "Are you all right? Is your husband all right? Is your child all right?"
Woman	Everything is all right.
Narrator	When she reached the man of God at the mountain, she took hold of his feet. Gehazi came over to push her away, [but the man of God said:]
Elisha (to Gehazi)	Leave her alone! She is in bitter distress, but the LORD has hidden it from me and has not told me why.
Woman (distressed)	Did I ask you for a son, my lord? Didn't I tell you, "Don't raise my hopes"?
Narrator	Elisha said to Gehazi:
Elisha (to Gehazi)	Tuck your cloak into your belt, take my staff in your hand and run. If you meet anyone, do not greet him, and if anyone greets you, do not answer. Lay my staff on the boy's face.
Narrator	But the child's mother said:
Woman (to Elisha)	As surely as the LORD lives and as you live, I will not leave you.
Narrator	So he got up and followed her.
	Gehazi went on ahead and laid the staff on the boy's face, but there was no sound or response. So Gehazi went back to meet Elisha [and told him:]
Gehazi	The boy has not awakened. (PAUSE)

Narrator	When Elisha reached the house, there was the boy lying dead on his couch. He went in, shut the door on the two of them and prayed to the LORD. Then he got on the bed and lay upon the boy, mouth to mouth, eyes to eyes, hands to hands. As he stretched himself out upon him, the boy's body grew warm. Elisha turned away and walked back and forth in the room and then got on the bed and stretched out upon him once more. The boy sneezed seven times and opened his eyes. (PAUSE) Elisha summoned Gehazi [and said:]
Elisha	Call the Shunammite.
Narrator	And he did. When she came, he said:
Elisha (to Woman)	Take your son.
Narrator	She came in, fell at his feet and bowed to the ground. (PAUSE) Then she took her son and went out.

Cast: **Narrator, Woman, Elisha, Gehazi, Boy, Father**

Two More Miracles of Elisha

2 Kings 4:38–44

Narrator	Elisha returned to Gilgal and there was a famine in that region. While the company of the prophets was meeting with him, he said to his servant:
Elisha	Put on the large pot and cook some stew for these men.
Narrator	One of them went out into the fields to gather herbs and found a wild vine. He gathered some of its gourds and filled the fold of his cloak. When he returned, he cut them up into the pot of stew, though no one knew what they were. The stew was poured out for the men, but as they began to eat it, they cried out:
Prophet	O man of God, there is death in the pot!
Narrator	And they could not eat it.
Elisha	Get some flour.
Narrator	He put it into the pot [and said:]
Elisha	Serve it to the people to eat.
Narrator	And there was nothing harmful in the pot. (PAUSE)
	A man came from Baal Shalishah, bringing the man of God twenty loaves of barley bread baked from the first ripe grain, along with some heads of new grain.
Elisha	Give it to the people to eat.

Man	How can I set this before a hundred men?
Elisha	Give it to the people to eat. For this is what the LORD says: "They will eat and have some left over."
Narrator	Then he set it before them, and they ate and had some left over, according to the word of the LORD.

Cast: **Narrator, Elisha, Prophet, Man**

Naaman Healed of Leprosy

2 Kings 5:1–14 [15]

Narrator	Naaman was commander of the army of the king of Aram. He was a great man in the sight of his master and highly regarded, because through him the LORD had given victory to Aram. He was a valiant soldier, but he had leprosy.
	Now bands from Aram had gone out and had taken captive a young girl from Israel, and she served Naaman's wife. [She said to her mistress:]
Girl	If only my master would see the prophet who is in Samaria! He would cure him of his leprosy.
Narrator	Naaman went to his master and told him what the girl from Israel had said.
King of Aram	By all means, go. (PAUSE) I will send a letter to the king of Israel.
Narrator	So Naaman left, taking with him ten talents of silver, six thousand shekels of gold and ten sets of clothing. The letter that he took to the king of Israel read:
King of Aram	With this letter I am sending my servant Naaman to you so that you may cure him of his leprosy.
Narrator	As soon as the king of Israel read the letter, he tore his robes:
King of Israel (exclaiming)	Am I God? Can I kill and bring back to life? Why does this fellow send someone to me to be cured of his leprosy? See how he is trying to pick a quarrel with me!
Narrator	When Elisha the man of God heard that the king of Israel had torn his robes, he sent him this message:
Elisha	Why have you torn your robes? Have the man come to me and he will know that there is a prophet in Israel.
Narrator	So Naaman went with his horses and chariots and stopped at the door of Elisha's house. Elisha sent a messenger to say to him:

Messenger	Go, wash yourself seven times in the Jordan, and your flesh will be restored and you will be cleansed.
Narrator	But Naaman went away angry:
Naaman (angrily)	I thought that he would surely come out to me and stand and call on the name of the LORD his God, wave his hand over the spot and cure me of my leprosy. Are not Abana and Pharpar, the rivers of Damascus, better than any of the waters of Israel? Couldn't I wash in them and be cleansed?
Narrator	So he turned and went off in a rage. (PAUSE) Naaman's servants went to him.
Servant 1	My father, if the prophet had told you to do some great thing, would you not have done it?
Servant 2	How much more, then, when he tells you, "Wash and be cleansed"!
Narrator	So he went down and dipped himself in the Jordan seven times, as the man of God had told him, and his flesh was restored and became clean like that of a young boy. [Then Naaman and all his attendants went back to the man of God. He stood before him [and said:]
Naaman	Now I know that there is no God in all the world except in Israel. Please accept now a gift from your servant.]

Cast: **Narrator, Girl, King of Aram, King of Israel, Elisha, Messenger, Naaman, Servant 1, Servant 2** (can be the same as Servant 1)

Naaman's Gift

2 Kings 5:15–27

Narrator	Naaman and all his attendants went back to the man of God. He stood before him [and said:]
Naaman	Now I know that there is no God in all the world except in Israel. Please accept now a gift from your servant.
[Narrator	The prophet answered:]
Elisha	As surely as the LORD lives, whom I serve, I will not accept a thing.
Narrator	And even though Naaman urged him, he refused.
Naaman	If you will not, please let me, your servant, be given as much earth as a pair of mules can carry, for your servant will never again make burnt offerings and sacrifices to any other god but the LORD. But may the LORD forgive your servant for this one thing: When my master enters the temple of Rimmon to bow down and he is leaning on my arm and I bow

	there also—when I bow down in the temple of Rimmon, may the LORD forgive your servant for this.
Elisha	Go in peace.
Narrator	After Naaman had traveled some distance, Gehazi, the servant of Elisha the man of God, said to himself:
Gehazi (musing)	My master was too easy on Naaman, this Aramean, by not accepting from him what he brought.
(determined)	As surely as the LORD lives, I will run after him and get something from him.
Narrator	So Gehazi hurried after Naaman. When Naaman saw him running toward him, he got down from the chariot to meet him.
Naaman	Is everything all right?
Gehazi	Everything is all right. My master sent me to say, "Two young men from the company of the prophets have just come to me from the hill country of Ephraim. Please give them a talent of silver and two sets of clothing."
Naaman	By all means, take *two* talents.
Narrator	He urged Gehazi to accept them, and then tied up the two talents of silver in two bags, with two sets of clothing. He gave them to two of his servants, and they carried them ahead of Gehazi. When Gehazi came to the hill, he took the things from the servants and put them away in the house. He sent the men away and they left. Then he went in and stood before his master Elisha.
Elisha	Where have you been, Gehazi?
Gehazi (hastily)	Your servant didn't go anywhere.
[Narrator	But Elisha said to him:]
Elisha	Was not my spirit with you when the man got down from his chariot to meet you? Is this the time to take money, or to accept clothes, olive groves, vineyards, flocks, herds, or menservants and maidservants? Naaman's leprosy will cling to you and to your descendants forever.
Narrator	Then Gehazi went from Elisha's presence and he was leprous, as white as snow.

Cast: **Narrator, Naaman, Elisha, Gehazi.** (This reading overlaps with the previous one.)

An Axhead Floats

2 Kings 6:1–7

Narrator	The company of the prophets said to Elisha:

Prophet 1	Look, the place where we meet with you is too small for us. Let us go to the Jordan, where each of us can get a pole; and let us build a place there for us to live.
[Narrator	And he said:]
Elisha	Go.
Narrator	Then one of them said:
Prophet 1	Won't you please come with your servants?
Elisha	I will.
Narrator	And he went with them.
	They went to the Jordan and began to cut down trees. As one of them was cutting down a tree, the iron axhead fell into the water.
Prophet 2 (exclaiming)	Oh, my lord, it was borrowed!
Narrator	The man of God asked:
Elisha	Where did it fall?
Narrator	When he showed him the place, Elisha cut a stick and threw it there, and made the iron float.
Elisha (firmly)	Lift it out.
Narrator	Then the man reached out his hand and took it.

Cast: **Narrator, Prophet 1, Elisha, Prophet 2**

Elisha Traps Blinded Arameans

2 Kings 6:8–23

Narrator	The king of Aram was at war with Israel. After conferring with his officers, he said:
King of Aram	I will set up my camp in such and such a place.
Narrator	The man of God sent word to the king of Israel:
Elisha	Beware of passing that place, because the Arameans are going down there.
Narrator	So the king of Israel checked on the place indicated by the man of God. Time and again Elisha warned the king, so that he was on his guard in such places.
	This enraged the king of Aram. He summoned his officers and demanded of them:

King of Aram	Will you not tell me which of us is on the side of the king of Israel?
Officer	None of us, my lord the king. But Elisha, the prophet who is in Israel, tells the king of Israel the very words you speak in your bedroom.
Narrator	[The king ordered:]
King of Aram	Go, find out where he is, so I can send men and capture him.
Narrator	The report came back:
Officer	He is in Dothan.
Narrator	Then he sent horses and chariots and a strong force there. They went by night and surrounded the city.
	When the servant of the man of God got up and went out early the next morning, an army with horses and chariots had surrounded the city.
Servant (exclaiming)	Oh, my lord, what shall we do?
Elisha	Don't be afraid. Those who are with us are more than those who are with them.
[Narrator	And Elisha prayed:**]**
Elisha (praying)	O Lord, open his eyes so he may see.
Narrator	Then the Lord opened the servant's eyes, and he looked and saw the hills full of horses and chariots of fire all around Elisha. (PAUSE)
	As the enemy came down toward him, Elisha prayed to the Lord:
Elisha	Strike these people with blindness.
Narrator	So he struck them with blindness, as Elisha had asked. Elisha told them:
Elisha (disguising his voice)	This is not the road and this is not the city. Follow me, and I will lead you to the man you are looking for.
Narrator	And he led them to Samaria. (PAUSE) After they entered the city, Elisha said:
Elisha	Lord, open the eyes of these men so they can see.
Narrator	Then the Lord opened their eyes and they looked, and there they were, inside Samaria. (PAUSE) When the king of Israel saw them, he asked Elisha:
King of Israel (excitedly)	Shall I kill them, my father? Shall I kill them?
Elisha	Do not kill them. Would you kill men you have captured with your own sword or bow? Set food and water before them so that they may eat and drink and then go back to their master.

| Narrator | So he prepared a great feast for them, and after they had finished eating and drinking, he sent them away, and they returned to their master. So the bands from Aram stopped raiding Israel's territory. |

Cast: **Narrator, King of Aram, Elisha, Officer, Servant, King of Israel**

Famine in Besieged Samaria

2 Kings 6:24–7:2

Narrator	Ben-Hadad king of Aram mobilized his entire army and marched up and laid siege to Samaria. There was a great famine in the city; the siege lasted so long that a donkey's head sold for eighty shekels of silver, and a quarter of a cab of seed pods for five shekels.
	As the king of Israel was passing by on the wall, a woman cried to him:
Woman	Help me, my lord the king!
Narrator	The king replied:
King of Israel	If the LORD does not help you, where can I get help for you? From the threshing floor? From the winepress? What's the matter?
Woman	This woman said to me, "Give up your son so we may eat him today, and tomorrow we'll eat my son." So we cooked my son and ate him. The next day I said to her, "Give up your son so we may eat him," but she had hidden him.
Narrator	When the king heard the woman's words, he tore his robes. As he went along the wall, the people looked, and there, underneath, he had sackcloth on his body. He said:
King of Israel (exclaiming)	May God deal with me, be it ever so severely, if the head of Elisha son of Shaphat remains on his shoulders today!
Narrator	Now Elisha was sitting in his house, and the elders were sitting with him. The king sent a messenger ahead, but before he arrived, Elisha said to the elders:
Elisha	Don't you see how this murderer is sending someone to cut off my head? Look, when the messenger comes, shut the door and hold it shut against him. Is not the sound of his master's footsteps behind him?
Narrator	While he was still talking to them, the messenger came down to him. And ⸢the king⸣ said:
King of Israel	This disaster is from the LORD. Why should I wait for the LORD any longer?
Elisha	Hear the word of the LORD. This is what the LORD says: About this time tomorrow, a seah of flour will sell for a shekel and two seahs of barley for a shekel at the gate of Samaria.

Narrator	The officer on whose arm the king was leaning said to the man of God:
Officer	Look, even if the LORD should open the floodgates of the heavens, could this happen? (PAUSE)
Elisha	You will see it with your own eyes, but you will not eat *any* of it!

Cast: **Narrator, Woman, King of Israel, Elisha, Officer**

The Siege Lifted

2 Kings 7:3–20

Narrator	There were four men with leprosy at the entrance of the city gate. [They said to each other:]
Man 1	Why stay here until we die?
Man 2	If we say, "We'll go into the city"—the famine is there, and we will die.
Man 1	And if we stay here, we will die.
Man 2	So let's go over to the camp of the Arameans and surrender.
Man 1	If they spare us, we live; if they kill us, then we die.
Narrator	At dusk they got up and went to the camp of the Arameans. When they reached the edge of the camp, not a man was there, for the Lord had caused the Arameans to hear the sound of chariots and horses and a great army, so that they said to one another:
Aramean	Look, the king of Israel has hired the Hittite and Egyptian kings to attack us!
Narrator	So they got up and fled in the dusk and abandoned their tents and their horses and donkeys. They left the camp as it was and ran for their lives. (PAUSE)
	The men who had leprosy reached the edge of the camp and entered one of the tents. They ate and drank, and carried away silver, gold and clothes, and went off and hid them. They returned and entered another tent and took some things from it and hid them also. [Then they said to each other:]
Man 1	We're not doing right.
Man 2	This is a day of good news and we are keeping it to ourselves.
Man 1	If we wait until daylight, punishment will overtake us.
Man 2	Let's go at once and report this to the royal palace.
Narrator	So they went and called out to the city gatekeepers:
Man 1 (calling)	We went into the Aramean camp and not a man was there—

Man 2	Not a sound of anyone—
Man 1	Only tethered horses and donkeys, and the tents left just as they were.
Narrator	The gatekeepers shouted the news, and it was reported within the palace. (PAUSE) The king got up in the night and said to his officers:
King	I will tell you what the Arameans have done to us. They know we are starving; so they have left the camp to hide in the countryside, thinking, "They will surely come out, and then we will take them alive and get into the city."
Narrator	One of his officers answered:
Officer	Have some men take five of the horses that are left in the city. Their plight will be like that of all the Israelites left here—yes, they will only be like all these Israelites who are doomed. So let us send them to find out what happened.
Narrator	So they selected two chariots with their horses, and the king sent them after the Aramean army. He commanded the drivers:
King	Go and find out what has happened.
Narrator	They followed them as far as the Jordan, and they found the whole road strewn with the clothing and equipment the Arameans had thrown away in their headlong flight. So the messengers returned and reported to the king. Then the people went out and plundered the camp of the Arameans. So a seah of flour sold for a shekel, and two seahs of barley sold for a shekel, as the LORD had said.

Now the king had put the officer on whose arm he leaned in charge of the gate, and the people trampled him in the gateway, and he died, just as the man of God had foretold when the king came down to his house. It happened as the man of God had said to the king: |
Voice of Elisha	About this time tomorrow, a seah of flour will sell for a shekel and two seahs of barley for a shekel at the gate of Samaria.
Narrator	The officer had said to the man of God:
Voice of Officer	Look, even if the LORD should open the floodgates of the heavens, could this happen?
Narrator	The man of God had replied:
Voice of Elisha	You will see it with your own eyes, but you will not eat any of it!
Narrator	And that is exactly what happened to him, for the people trampled him in the gateway, and he died.

Cast: **Narrator, Man 1, Man 2, Aramean, King, Officer, Voice of Elisha** (as if from a distance), **Voice of Officer** (as if from a distance—can be the same as Officer)

Hazael Murders Ben-Hadad

2 Kings 8:7–15

Narrator	Elisha went to Damascus, and Ben-Hadad king of Aram was ill. The king was told:
Messenger	The man of God has come all the way up here.
Narrator	He said to Hazael:
Ben-Hadad	Take a gift with you and go to meet the man of God. Consult the LORD through him; ask him, "Will I recover from this illness?"
Narrator	Hazael went to meet Elisha, taking with him as a gift forty camel-loads of all the finest wares of Damascus. He went in and stood before him, and said:
Hazael	Your son Ben-Hadad king of Aram has sent me to ask, "Will I recover from this illness?"
[Narrator	Elisha answered:]
Elisha	Go and say to him, "You will certainly recover"; but the LORD has revealed to me that he will in fact die.
Narrator	He stared at him with a fixed gaze until Hazael felt ashamed. Then the man of God began to weep.
Hazael	Why is my lord weeping?
Elisha	Because I know the harm you will do to the Israelites. You will set fire to their fortified places, kill their young men with the sword, dash their little children to the ground, and rip open their pregnant women.
Hazael	How could your servant, a mere dog, accomplish such a feat?
Elisha	The LORD has shown me that you will become king of Aram.
Narrator	Then Hazael left Elisha and returned to his master. Ben-Hadad asked:
Ben-Hadad	What did Elisha say to you?
Hazael	He told me that you would certainly recover.
Narrator	But the next day he took a thick cloth, soaked it in water and spread it over the king's face, so that he died. Then Hazael succeeded him as king.

Cast: **Narrator, Messenger, Ben-Hadad, Hazael, Elisha**

Jehu Anointed King of Israel

2 Kings 9:1–13

Narrator	The prophet Elisha summoned a man from the company of the prophets:

Elisha	Tuck your cloak into your belt, take this flask of oil with you and go to Ramoth Gilead. When you get there, look for Jehu son of Jehoshaphat, the son of Nimshi. Go to him, get him away from his companions and take him into an inner room. Then take the flask and pour the oil on his head and declare, "This is what the LORD says: I anoint you king over Israel." Then open the door and run; don't delay!
Narrator	So the young man, the prophet, went to Ramoth Gilead. When he arrived, he found the army officers sitting together.
Young prophet	I have a message for you, commander.
[Narrator	Jehu asked:]
Jehu	For which of us?
Young prophet	For you, commander.
Narrator	Jehu got up and went into the house. Then the prophet poured the oil on Jehu's head and declared:
Young prophet	This is what the LORD, the God of Israel, says:
[The Lord (voice only)]	I anoint you king over the LORD's people Israel. You are to destroy the house of Ahab your master, and I will avenge the blood of my servants the prophets and the blood of all the LORD's servants shed by Jezebel. The whole house of Ahab will perish. I will cut off from Ahab every last male in Israel—slave or free. I will make the house of Ahab like the house of Jeroboam son of Nebat and like the house of Baasha son of Ahijah. As for Jezebel, dogs will devour her on the plot of ground at Jezreel, and no one will bury her.
Narrator	Then he opened the door and ran.
	When Jehu went out to his fellow officers, one of them asked him:
Officer 1	Is everything all right? Why did this madman come to you?
Jehu	You know the man and the sort of things he says.
Officer 2	That's not true! Tell us.
Jehu	Here is what he told me: "This is what the LORD says: I anoint you king over Israel."
Narrator	They hurried and took their cloaks and spread them under him on the bare steps. Then they blew the trumpet and shouted:
Officers 1 and 2	Jehu is king!

Cast: **Narrator**, **Elisha**, **Young prophet**, **Jehu**, **[the Lord** (voice only)], **Officer 1**, **Officer 2**

Jehu Kills Joram and Ahaziah

2 Kings 9:14–26

Narrator	So Jehu son of Jehoshaphat, the son of Nimshi, conspired against Joram. (Now Joram and all Israel had been defending Ramoth Gilead against Hazael king of Aram, but King Joram had returned to Jezreel to recover from the wounds the Arameans had inflicted on him in the battle with Hazael king of Aram.) Jehu said.
Jehu	If this is the way you feel, don't let anyone step out of the city to go and tell the news to Jezreel.
Narrator	Then he got into his chariot and rode to Jezreel because Joram was resting there and Ahaziah king of Judah had gone down to see him.
	When the lookout standing on the tower in Jezreel saw Jehu's troops approaching, he called out:
Lookout (calling)	I see some troops coming.
Narrator	Joram ordered:
Joram	Get a horseman. Send him to meet them and ask, "Do you come in peace?"
Narrator	The horseman rode off to meet Jehu and said:
Horseman 1	This is what the king says: "Do you come in peace?"
[Narrator	[Jehu replied]:]
Jehu	What do you have to with peace? Fall in behind me.
Narrator	The lookout reported:
Lookout	The messenger has reached them, but he isn't coming back.
Narrator	So the king sent out a second horseman. [When he came to them he said:]
Horseman 2	This is what the king says: "Do you come in peace?"
[Narrator	Jehu replied:]
Jehu	What do you have to do with peace? Fall in behind me.
Narrator	The lookout reported:
Lookout	He has reached them, but he isn't coming back either. The driving is like that of Jehu son of Nimshi—he drives like a madman.
Narrator	[Joram ordered:]
Joram	Hitch up my chariot.
Narrator	When it was hitched up, Joram king of Israel and Ahaziah king of Judah rode out, each in his own chariot, to meet Jehu. They met him at the plot

of ground that had belonged to Naboth the Jezreelite. [When Joram saw Jehu he asked:]

Joram	Have you come in peace, Jehu?
[Narrator	[Jehu replied]:]
Jehu	How can there be peace, as long as all the idolatry and witchcraft of your mother Jezebel abound?
Narrator	Joram turned about and fled, calling out to Ahaziah:
Joram	Treachery, Ahaziah!
Narrator	Then Jehu drew his bow and shot Joram between the shoulders. The arrow pierced his heart and he slumped down in his chariot. Jehu said to Bidkar, his chariot officer:
Jehu	Pick him up and throw him on the field that belonged to Naboth the Jezreelite. Remember how you and I were riding together in chariots behind Ahab his father when the LORD made this prophecy about him:
[The Lord (voice only)]	Yesterday I saw the blood of Naboth and the blood of his sons . . . and I will surely make you pay for it on this plot of ground.
Jehu	Now then, pick him up and throw him on that plot, in accordance with the word of the LORD.

Cast: **Narrator, Jehu, Lookout, Joram, Horseman 1, Horseman 2,** [the Lord (voice only)]

Jezebel Killed

2 Kings 9:30–37

Narrator	Jehu went to Jezreel. When Jezebel heard about it, she painted her eyes, arranged her hair and looked out of a window. As Jehu entered the gate, she asked:
Jezebel (calling)	Have you come in peace, Zimri, you murderer of your master?
Narrator	He looked up at the window and called out:
Jehu (shouting)	Who is on my side? Who?
Narrator	Two or three eunuchs looked down at him.
Jehu	Throw her down!
Narrator	So they threw her down, and some of her blood spattered the wall and the horses as they trampled her underfoot.

	Jehu went in and ate and drank.
Jehu	Take care of that cursed woman, and bury her, for she was a king's daughter.
Narrator	But when they went out to bury her, they found nothing except her skull, her feet and her hands. They went back and told Jehu, who said:
Jehu	This is the word of the Lord that he spoke through his servant Elijah the Tishbite.
Voice of Elijah	On the plot of ground at Jezreel dogs will devour Jezebel's flesh. Jezebel's body will be like refuse on the ground in the plot at Jezreel, so that no one will be able to say, "This is Jezebel."

Cast: **Narrator, Jezebel, Jehu, Voice of Elijah**

Ahab's Family Killed

2 Kings 10:1–11

Narrator	There were in Samaria seventy sons of the house of Ahab. So Jehu wrote letters and sent them to Samaria: to the officials of Jezreel, to the elders and to the guardians of Ahab's children. [He said:]
Jehu	As soon as this letter reaches you, since your master's sons are with you and you have chariots and horses, a fortified city and weapons, choose the best and most worthy of your master's sons and set him on his father's throne. Then fight for your master's house.
Narrator	But they were terrified [and said:]
Official (terrified)	If two kings could not resist him, how can we?
Narrator	So the palace administrator, the city governor, the elders and the guardians sent this message to Jehu:
Elder	We are your servants and we will do anything you say. We will not appoint anyone as king; you do whatever you think best.
Narrator	Then Jehu wrote them a second letter, saying:
Jehu (writing)	If you are on my side and will obey me, take the heads of your master's sons and come to me in Jezreel by this time tomorrow.
Narrator	Now the royal princes, seventy of them, were with the leading men of the city, who were rearing them. When the letter arrived, these men took the princes and slaughtered all seventy of them. They put their heads in baskets and sent them to Jehu in Jezreel. When the messenger arrived, he told Jehu:

405

Messenger	They have brought the heads of the princes.
[Narrator	Then Jehu ordered:]
Jehu	Put them in two piles at the entrance of the city gate until morning.
Narrator	The next morning Jehu went out. He stood before all the people and said:
Jehu	You are innocent. It was I who conspired against my master and killed him, but who killed all these? Know then, that not a word the LORD has spoken against the house of Ahab will fail. The LORD has done what he promised through his servant Elijah.
Narrator	So Jehu killed everyone in Jezreel who remained of the house of Ahab, as well as all his chief men, his close friends and his priests, leaving him no survivor.

Cast: **Narrator, Jehu, Official, Elder, Messenger**

Relatives of King Ahaziah Killed

2 Kings 10:12–17

Narrator	Jehu set out and went toward Samaria. At Beth Eked of the Shepherds, he met some relatives of Ahaziah king of Judah [and asked:]
Jehu	Who are you?
[Narrator	They said:]
Relative 1	We are relatives of Ahaziah.
Relative 2	And we have come down to greet the families of the king and of the queen mother.
Jehu	Take them alive!
Narrator	So they took them alive and slaughtered them by the well of Beth Eked— forty-two men. He left no survivor. (PAUSE)
	After he left there, he came upon Jehonadab son of Recab, who was on his way to meet him. Jehu greeted him [and said:]
Jehu	Are you in accord with me, as I am with you?
Jehonadab	I am.
Jehu	If so, give me your hand.
Narrator	So he did, and Jehu helped him up into the chariot.
Jehu	Come with me and see my zeal for the LORD.
Narrator	Then he had him ride along in his chariot.

When Jehu came to Samaria, he killed all who were left there of Ahab's family; he destroyed them, according to the word of the LORD spoken to Elijah.

Cast: **Narrator, Jehu, Relative 1, Relative 2, Jehonadab**

Ministers of Baal Killed

2 Kings 10:18–29 [30–31]

Narrator Jehu brought all the people together and said to them:

Jehu Ahab served Baal a little; Jehu will serve him much. Now summon all the prophets of Baal, all his ministers and all his priests. See that no one is missing, because I am going to hold a great sacrifice for Baal. Anyone who fails to come will no longer live.

Narrator But Jehu was acting deceptively in order to destroy the ministers of Baal.

Jehu
(announ-
cing) Call an assembly in honor of Baal.

Narrator So they proclaimed it. Then he sent word throughout Israel, and all the ministers of Baal came; not one stayed away. They crowded into the temple of Baal until it was full from one end to the other. And Jehu said to the keeper of the wardrobe:

Jehu Bring robes for all the ministers of Baal.

Narrator So he brought out robes for them.

Then Jehu and Jehonadab son of Recab went into the temple of Baal. Jehu said to the ministers of Baal:

Jehu Look around and see that no servants of the LORD are here with you— only ministers of Baal.

Narrator So they went in to make sacrifices and burnt offerings. Now Jehu had posted eighty men outside with this warning:

Jehu
(quietly) If one of you lets any of the men I am placing in your hands escape, it will be your life for his life.

Narrator As soon as Jehu had finished making the burnt offering, he ordered the guards and officers:

Jehu Go in and kill them; let no one escape.

Narrator So they cut them down with the sword. The guards and officers threw the bodies out and then entered the inner shrine of the temple of Baal. (PAUSE) They brought the sacred stone out of the temple of Baal and burned it. They demolished the sacred stone of Baal and tore down the temple of Baal, and people have used it for a latrine to this day. (PAUSE)

So Jehu destroyed Baal worship in Israel. However, he did not turn away from the sins of Jeroboam son of Nebat, which he had caused Israel to commit—the worship of the golden calves at Bethel and Dan.

[The LORD said to Jehu:

The Lord
(voice only)   Because you have done well in accomplishing what is right in my eyes and have done to the house of Ahab all I had in mind to do, your descendants will sit on the throne of Israel to the fourth generation.

Narrator   Yet Jehu was not careful to keep the law of the LORD, the God of Israel, with all his heart. He did not turn away from the sins of Jeroboam, which he had caused Israel to commit.]

Cast: **Narrator, Jehu,** [**the Lord** (voice only)]

Athaliah and Joash

2 Kings 11:1–21

Narrator   When Athaliah the mother of Ahaziah saw that her son was dead, she proceeded to destroy the whole royal family. But Jehosheba, the daughter of King Jehoram and sister of Ahaziah, took Joash son of Ahaziah and stole him away from among the royal princes, who were about to be murdered. She put him and his nurse in a bedroom to hide him from Athaliah; so he was not killed. He remained hidden with his nurse at the temple of the LORD for six years while Athaliah ruled the land.

In the seventh year Jehoiada sent for the commanders of units of a hundred, the Carites and the guards and had them brought to him at the temple of the LORD. He made a covenant with them and put them under oath at the temple of the LORD. Then he showed them the king's son. He commanded them:

Jehoiada   This is what you are to do: You who are in the three companies that are going on duty on the Sabbath—a third of you guarding the royal palace, a third at the Sur Gate, and a third at the gate behind the guard, who take turns guarding the temple—and you who are in the other two companies that normally go off Sabbath duty are all to guard the temple for the king. Station yourselves around the king, each man with his weapon in his hand. Anyone who approaches your ranks must be put to death. Stay close to the king wherever he goes.

Narrator   The commanders of units of a hundred did just as Jehoiada the priest ordered. Each one took his men—those who were going on duty on the Sabbath and those who were going off duty—and came to Jehoiada the priest. Then he gave the commanders the spears and shields that had belonged to King David and that were in the temple of the LORD. The guards, each with his weapon in his hand, stationed themselves around the king—near the altar and the temple, from the south side to the north side of the temple.

Jehoiada brought out the king's son and put the crown on him; he presented him with a copy of the covenant and proclaimed him king. They anointed him [and the people clapped their hands and shouted:]

Persons 1 and 2 (clapping and shouting)   Long live the king!

Narrator   When Athaliah heard the noise made by the guards and the people, she went to the people at the temple of the LORD. She looked and there was the king, standing by the pillar, as the custom was. The officers and the trumpeters were beside the king, and all the people of the land were rejoicing and blowing trumpets. Then Athaliah tore her robes [and called out:]

Athaliah (calling out)   Treason! Treason!

Narrator   Jehoiada the priest ordered the commanders of units of a hundred, who were in charge of the troops:

Jehoiada   Bring her out between the ranks and put to the sword anyone who follows her.

Narrator   For the priest had said:

Priest   She must not be put to death in the temple of the LORD.

Narrator   So they seized her as she reached the place where the horses enter the palace grounds, and there she was put to death. (PAUSE)

Jehoiada then made a covenant between the LORD and the king and people that they would be the LORD's people. He also made a covenant between the king and the people. (PAUSE) All the people of the land went to the temple of Baal and tore it down. They smashed the altars and idols to pieces and killed Mattan the priest of Baal in front of the altars.

Then Jehoiada the priest posted guards at the temple of the LORD. He took with him the commanders of hundreds, the Carites, the guards and all the people of the land, and together they brought the king down from the temple of the LORD and went into the palace, entering by way of the gate of the guards. The king then took his place on the royal throne, and all the people of the land rejoiced. And the city was quiet, because Athaliah had been slain with the sword at the palace.

Joash was seven years old when he began to reign.

Cast: **Narrator, Jehoiada, Person 1, Person 2, Athaliah, Priest**

The Death of Elisha

2 Kings 13:14–20

Narrator	Elisha was suffering from the illness from which he died. Jehoash king of Israel went down to see him and wept over him.
Jehoash (weeping)	My father! My father! The chariots and horsemen of Israel!
[Narrator	Elisha said:]
Elisha	Get a bow and some arrows.
Narrator	And he did so. [Elisha said to the king of Israel:]
Elisha (with effort)	Take the bow in your hands.
Narrator	When he had taken it, Elisha put his hands on the king's hands.
Elisha	Open the east window. . . . Shoot!
Narrator	And he shot.
Elisha	The LORD's arrow of victory, the arrow of victory over Aram! You will completely destroy the Arameans at Aphek.
	Take the arrows.
Narrator	And the king took them. [Elisha told him:]
Elisha	Strike the ground.
Narrator	He struck it three times and stopped. The man of God was angry with him and said:
Elisha	You should have struck the ground five or six times; then you would have defeated Aram and completely destroyed it. But now you will defeat it only three times. (PAUSE)
Narrator	Elisha died and was buried.

Cast: **Narrator, Jehoash, Elisha**

Amaziah King of Judah

2 Kings 14:1–16

Narrator	In the second year of Jehoash son of Jehoahaz king of Israel, Amaziah son of Joash king of Judah began to reign. He was twenty-five years old when he became king, and he reigned in Jerusalem twenty-nine years. His mother's name was Jehoaddin; she was from Jerusalem. He did what was right in the eyes of the LORD, but not as his father David had done. In everything he followed the example of his father Joash. The high

410

places, however, were not removed; the people continued to offer sacrifices and burn incense there.

After the kingdom was firmly in his grasp, he executed the officials who had murdered his father the king. Yet he did not put the sons of the assassins to death, in accordance with what is written in the Book of the Law of Moses where the LORD commanded:

Lawyer   Fathers shall not be put to death for their children, nor children put to death for their fathers; each is to die for his own sins.

Narrator   He was the one who defeated ten thousand Edomites in the Valley of Salt and captured Sela in battle, calling it Joktheel, the name it has to this day.

Then Amaziah sent messengers to Jehoash son of Jehoahaz, the son of Jehu, king of Israel, with the challenge:

Amaziah   Come, meet me face to face.

Narrator   But Jehoash king of Israel replied to Amaziah king of Judah:

Jehoash   A thistle in Lebanon sent a message to a cedar in Lebanon, "Give your daughter to my son in marriage." Then a wild beast in Lebanon came along and trampled the thistle underfoot. You have indeed defeated Edom and now you are arrogant. Glory in your victory, but stay at home! Why ask for trouble and cause your own downfall and that of Judah also?

Narrator   Amaziah, however, would not listen, so Jehoash king of Israel attacked. He and Amaziah king of Judah faced each other at Beth Shemesh in Judah. Judah was routed by Israel, and every man fled to his home. Jehoash king of Israel captured Amaziah king of Judah, the son of Joash, the son of Ahaziah, at Beth Shemesh. Then Jehoash went to Jerusalem and broke down the wall of Jerusalem from the Ephraim Gate to the Corner Gate—a section about six hundred feet long. He took all the gold and silver and all the articles found in the temple of the LORD and in the treasuries of the royal palace. He also took hostages and returned to Samaria.

As for the other events of the reign of Jehoash, what he did and his achievements, including his war against Amaziah king of Judah, are they not written in the book of the annals of the kings of Israel? Jehoash rested with his fathers and was buried in Samaria with the kings of Israel. And Jeroboam his son succeeded him as king.

Cast: **Narrator**, **Lawyer**, **Amaziah**, **Jehoash**

Sennacherib Threatens Jerusalem

2 Kings 18:13–37

Narrator   In the fourteenth year of King Hezekiah's reign, Sennacherib king of Assyria attacked all the fortified cities of Judah and captured them. So Hezekiah king of Judah sent this message to the king of Assyria at Lachish:

Hezekiah	I have done wrong. Withdraw from me, and I will pay whatever you demand of me.
Narrator	The king of Assyria exacted from Hezekiah king of Judah three hundred talents of silver and thirty talents of gold. So Hezekiah gave him all the silver that was found in the temple of the LORD and in the treasuries of the royal palace.
	At this time Hezekiah king of Judah stripped off the gold with which he had covered the doors and doorposts of the temple of the LORD, and gave it to the king of Assyria.
	The king of Assyria sent his supreme commander, his chief officer and his field commander with a large army, from Lachish to King Hezekiah at Jerusalem. They came up to Jerusalem and stopped at the aqueduct of the Upper Pool, on the road to the Washerman's Field. They called for the king; and Eliakim son of Hilkiah the palace administrator, Shebna the secretary, and Joah son of Asaph the recorder went out to them. The field commander said to them:
Commander	Tell Hezekiah: "This is what the great king, the king of Assyria, says: On what are you basing this confidence of yours? You say you have strategy and military strength—but you speak only empty words. On whom are you depending, that you rebel against me? Look now, you are depending on Egypt, that splintered reed of a staff, which pierces a man's hand and wounds him if he leans on it! Such is Pharaoh king of Egypt to all who depend on him. And if you say to me, 'We are depending on the LORD our God'—isn't he the one whose high places and altars Hezekiah removed, saying to Judah and Jerusalem, 'You must worship before this altar in Jerusalem'?
	"Come now, make a bargain with my master, the king of Assyria: I will give you two thousand horses—if you can put riders on them! How can you repulse one officer of the least of my master's officials, even though you are depending on Egypt for chariots and horsemen? Furthermore, have I come to attack and destroy this place without word from the LORD? The LORD himself told me to march against this country and destroy it."
Narrator	Then Eliakim son of Hilkiah, and Shebna and Joah said to the field commander:
Eliakim	Please speak to your servants in Aramaic, since we understand it.
Shebna	Don't speak to us in Hebrew in the hearing of the people on the wall.
Narrator	But the commander replied:
Commander	Was it only to your master and you that my master sent me to say these things, and not to the men sitting on the wall—who, like you, will have to eat their own filth and drink their own urine?
Narrator	Then the commander stood and called out in Hebrew:

Commander	Hear the word of the great king, the king of Assyria! This is what the king says: Do not let Hezekiah deceive you. He cannot deliver you from my hand. Do not let Hezekiah persuade you to trust in the LORD when he says, "The LORD will surely deliver us; this city will not be given into the hand of the king of Assyria."
	Do not listen to Hezekiah. This is what the king of Assyria says: Make peace with me and come out to me. Then every one of you will eat from his own vine and fig tree and drink water from his own cistern, until I come and take you to a land like your own, a land of grain and new wine, a land of bread and vineyards, a land of olive trees and honey. Choose life and not death!
	Do not listen to Hezekiah, for he is misleading you when he says, "The LORD will deliver us." Has the god of any nation ever delivered his land from the hand of the king of Assyria? Where are the gods of Hamath and Arpad? Where are the gods of Sepharvaim, Hena and Ivvah? Have they rescued Samaria from my hand? Who of all the gods of these countries has been able to save his land from me? How then can the LORD deliver Jerusalem from my hand?
Narrator	But the people remained silent and said nothing in reply, because the king had commanded, "Do not answer him."
	Then Eliakim son of Hilkiah the palace administrator, Shebna the secretary and Joah son of Asaph the recorder went to Hezekiah, with their clothes torn, and told him what the field commander had said.

Cast: **Narrator, Hezekiah, Commander, Eliakim, Shebna** (can be the same as Eliakim)

Hezekiah Asks Isaiah's Advice

2 Kings 19:2–19

Narrator	[King Hezekiah] sent Eliakim the palace administrator, Shebna the secretary and the leading priests, all wearing sackcloth, to the prophet Isaiah son of Amoz. They told him, "This is what Hezekiah says":
Hezekiah	This day is a day of distress and rebuke and disgrace, as when children come to the point of birth and there is no strength to deliver them. It may be that the LORD your God will hear all the words of the field commander, whom his master, the king of Assyria, has sent to ridicule the living God, and that he will rebuke him for the words the LORD your God has heard. Therefore pray for the remnant that still survives.
Narrator	When King Hezekiah's officials came to Isaiah, Isaiah said to them:
Isaiah	Tell your master, "This is what the LORD says: Do not be afraid of what you have heard—those words with which the underlings of the king of Assyria have blasphemed me. Listen! I am going to put such a spirit in

413

him that when he hears a certain report, he will return to his own country, and there I will have him cut down with the sword."

Narrator   When the field commander heard that the king of Assyria had left Lachish, he withdrew and found the king fighting against Libnah.

Now Sennacherib received a report that Tirhakah, the Cushite king ⌐of Egypt⌐ was marching out to fight against him. So he again sent messengers to Hezekiah with this word:

Sennacherib   Say to Hezekiah king of Judah: Do not let the god you depend on deceive you when he says, "Jerusalem will not be handed over to the king of Assyria." Surely you have heard what the kings of Assyria have done to all the countries, destroying them completely. And will *you* be *delivered*? Did the gods of the nations that were destroyed by my forefathers deliver them: the gods of Gozan, Haran, Rezeph and the people of Eden who were in Tel Assar? Where is the king of Hamath, the king of Arpad, the king of the city of Sepharvaim, or of Hena or Ivvah?

Narrator   Hezekiah received the letter from the messengers and read it. Then he went up to the temple of the LORD and spread it out before the LORD. And Hezekiah prayed to the LORD:

Hezekiah
(praying)   O LORD, God of Israel, enthroned between the cherubim, you alone are God over all the kingdoms of the earth. You have made heaven and earth. Give ear, O LORD, and hear; open your eyes, O LORD, and see; listen to the words Sennacherib has sent to insult the living God.

It is true, O LORD, that the Assyrian kings have laid waste these nations and their lands. They have thrown their gods into the fire and destroyed them, for they were not gods but only wood and stone, fashioned by men's hands. Now, O LORD our God, deliver us from his hand, so that all kingdoms on earth may know that you alone, O LORD, are God.

Cast: **Narrator, Hezekiah, Isaiah, Sennacherib**

Isaiah Prophesies Sennacherib's Fall

2 Kings 19:20–37

Narrator   Isaiah son of Amoz sent a message to Hezekiah:

Isaiah   This is what the LORD, the God of Israel, says:

The Lord
(voice only)   I have heard your prayer concerning Sennacherib king of Assyria.

Isaiah   This is the word that the LORD has spoken against him:

The Lord
(voice)   The Virgin Daughter of Zion
     despises you and mocks you.

The Daughter of Jerusalem
   tosses her head as you flee.
Who is it you have insulted and blasphemed?
   Against whom have you raised your voice
and lifted your eyes in pride?
   Against the Holy One of Israel!
By your messengers
   you have heaped insults on the Lord.
And you have said,
   "With my many chariots
I have ascended the heights of the mountains,
   the utmost heights of Lebanon.
I have cut down its tallest cedars,
   the choicest of its pines.
I have reached its remotest parts,
   the finest of its forests.
I have dug wells in foreign lands
   and drunk the water there.
With the soles of my feet
   I have dried up all the streams of Egypt."

Have you not heard?
   Long ago I ordained it.
In days of old I planned it;
   now I have brought it to pass,
that you have turned fortified cities
   into piles of stone.
Their people, drained of power,
   are dismayed and put to shame.
They are like plants in the field,
   like tender green shoots,
like grass sprouting on the roof,
   scorched before it grows up.

But I know where you stay
   and when you come and go
   and how you rage against me.
Because you rage against me
   and your insolence has reached my ears,
I will put my hook in your nose
   and my bit in your mouth,
and I will make you return
   by the way you came.

Isaiah   This will be the sign for you, O Hezekiah:
This year you will eat what grows by itself,
   and the second year what springs from that.
But in the third year sow and reap,
   plant vineyards and eat their fruit.
Once more a remnant of the house of Judah

415

will take root below and bear fruit above.
For out of Jerusalem will come a remnant,
    and out of Mount Zion a band of survivors.

The zeal of the LORD Almighty will accomplish this.

Therefore this is what the LORD says concerning the king of Assyria:

The Lord
(voice)

He will not enter this city
    or shoot an arrow here.
He will not come before it with shield
    or build a siege ramp against it.
By the way that he came he will return;
    he will not enter this city. . . .
I will defend this city and save it,
    for my sake and for the sake of David my servant.

Narrator

That night the angel of the LORD went out and put to death a hundred and eighty-five thousand men in the Assyrian camp. When the people got up the next morning—there were all the dead bodies! So Sennacherib king of Assyria broke camp and withdrew. He returned to Nineveh and stayed there.

One day, while he was worshiping in the temple of his god Nisroch, his sons Adrammelech and Sharezer cut him down with the sword, and they escaped to the land of Ararat. And Esarhaddon his son succeeded him as king.

Cast: **Narrator, the Lord** (voice only), **Isaiah**

Hezekiah's Illness

2 Kings 20:1–11

Narrator

Hezekiah became ill and was at the point of death. The prophet Isaiah son of Amoz went to him and said:

Isaiah

This is what the LORD says:

The Lord
(voice only)

Put your house in order, because you are going to die; you will not recover.

Narrator

Hezekiah turned his face to the wall and prayed to the LORD:

Hezekiah
(praying)

Remember, O LORD, how I have walked before you faithfully and with wholehearted devotion and have done what is good in your eyes.

Narrator

And Hezekiah wept bitterly.

Before Isaiah had left the middle court, the word of the LORD came to him:

The Lord (voice, to Isaiah)	Go back and tell Hezekiah, the leader of my people, "This is what the LORD, the God of your father David, says: I have heard your prayer and seen your tears; I will heal you. On the third day from now you will go up to the temple of the LORD. I will add fifteen years to your life. And I will deliver you and this city from the hand of the king of Assyria. I will defend this city for my sake and for the sake of my servant David." (PAUSE)
Narrator	Then Isaiah said:
Isaiah	Prepare a poultice of figs.
Narrator	They did so and applied it to the boil, and he recovered. Hezekiah had asked Isaiah:
Hezekiah	What will be the sign that the LORD will heal me and that I will go up to the temple of the LORD on the third day from now?
Isaiah	This is the LORD's sign to you that the LORD will do what he has promised: Shall the shadow go forward ten steps, or shall it go back ten steps?
Hezekiah	It is a simple matter for the shadow to go forward ten steps. Rather, have it go back ten steps.
Narrator	Then the prophet Isaiah called upon the LORD, and the LORD made the shadow go back the ten steps it had gone down on the stairway of Ahaz.

Cast: **Narrator, Isaiah, the Lord** (voice only), **Hezekiah**

Envoys from Babylon

2 Kings 20:12–21

Narrator	At that time Merodach-Baladan son of Baladan king of Babylon sent Hezekiah letters and a gift, because he had heard of Hezekiah's illness. Hezekiah received the messengers and showed them all that was in his storehouses—the silver, the gold, the spices and the fine oil—his armory and everything found among his treasures. There was nothing in his palace or in all his kingdom that Hezekiah did not show them. Then Isaiah the prophet went to King Hezekiah and asked:
Isaiah	What did those men say, and where did they come from?
[Narrator	Hezekiah replied:]
Hezekiah (vaguely)	From a distant land. They came from Babylon.
Isaiah	What did they see in your palace?

Hezekiah
(proudly)   They saw *everything* in my palace. There is nothing among my treasures that I did not show them.

Narrator   Then Isaiah said to Hezekiah:

Isaiah
(firmly)   Hear the word of the LORD: The time will surely come when everything in your palace, and all that your fathers have stored up until this day, will be carried off to Babylon. Nothing will be left, says the LORD. And some of your descendants, your own flesh and blood, that will be born to you, will be taken away, and they will become eunuchs in the palace of the king of Babylon.

Hezekiah   The word of the LORD you have spoken is good. (PAUSE)

Narrator   For he thought:

Hezekiah   Will there not be peace and security in my lifetime?

Narrator   As for the other events of Hezekiah's reign, all his achievements and how he made the pool and the tunnel by which he brought water into the city, are they not written in the book of the annals of the kings of Judah? (PAUSE) Hezekiah rested with his fathers. And Manasseh his son succeeded him as king.

Cast: **Narrator, Isaiah, Hezekiah**

Manasseh King of Judah

2 Kings 21:1–18

Narrator   Manasseh was twelve years old when he became king, and he reigned in Jerusalem fifty-five years. His mother's name was Hephzibah. He did evil in the eyes of the LORD, following the detestable practices of the nations the LORD had driven out before the Israelites. He rebuilt the high places his father Hezekiah had destroyed; he also erected altars to Baal and made an Asherah pole, as Ahab king of Israel had done. He bowed down to all the starry hosts and worshiped them. He built altars in the temple of the LORD, of which the LORD had said:

The Lord
(voice only)   In Jerusalem I will put my Name.

Narrator   In both courts of the temple of the LORD, he built altars to all the starry hosts. He sacrificed his own son in the fire, practiced sorcery and divination, and consulted mediums and spiritists. He did much evil in the eyes of the LORD, provoking him to anger.

He took the carved Asherah pole he had made and put it in the temple, of which the LORD had said to David and to his son Solomon:

The Lord (voice)	In this temple and in Jerusalem, which I have chosen out of all the tribes of Israel, I will put my Name forever. I will not again make the feet of the Israelites wander from the land I gave their forefathers, if only they will be careful to do everything I commanded them and will keep the whole Law that my servant Moses gave them.
Narrator	But the people did not listen. Manasseh led them astray, so that they did more evil than the nations the LORD had destroyed before the Israelites. (PAUSE) The LORD said through his servants the prophets:
The Lord (voice)	Manasseh king of Judah has committed these detestable sins. He has done more evil than the Amorites who preceded him and has led Judah into sin with his idols. Therefore this is what the LORD, the God of Israel, says: I am going to bring such disaster on Jerusalem and Judah that the ears of everyone who hears of it will tingle. I will stretch out over Jerusalem the measuring line used against Samaria and the plumb line used against the house of Ahab. I will wipe out Jerusalem as one wipes a dish, wiping it and turning it upside down. I will forsake the remnant of my inheritance and hand them over to their enemies. They will be looted and plundered by all their foes, because they have done evil in my eyes and have provoked me to anger from the day their forefathers came out of Egypt until this day.
Narrator	Moreover, Manasseh also shed so much innocent blood that he filled Jerusalem from end to end—besides the sin that he had caused Judah to commit, so that they did evil in the eyes of the LORD. As for the other events of Manasseh's reign, and all he did, including the sin he committed, are they not written in the book of the annals of the kings of Judah? (PAUSE) Manasseh rested with his fathers and was buried in his palace garden, the garden of Uzza. And Amon his son succeeded him as king.

Cast: **Narrator, the Lord** (voice only)

The Book of the Law Found (i)

2 Kings 22:1–13

Narrator	Josiah was eight years old when he became king, and he reigned in Jerusalem thirty-one years. His mother's name was Jedidah daughter of Adaiah; she was from Bozkath. He did what was right in the eyes of the LORD and walked in all the ways of his father David, not turning aside to the right or to the left. In the eighteenth year of his reign, King Josiah sent the secretary, Shaphan son of Azaliah, the son of Meshullam, to the temple of the LORD. [He said:]

419

Josiah	Go up to Hilkiah the high priest and have him get ready the money that has been brought into the temple of the LORD, which the doorkeepers have collected from the people. Have them entrust it to the men appointed to supervise the work on the temple. And have these men pay the workers who repair the temple of the LORD—the carpenters, the builders and the masons. Also have them purchase timber and dressed stone to repair the temple. But they need not account for the money entrusted to them, because they are acting faithfully.
Narrator	Hilkiah the high priest said to Shaphan the secretary:
Hilkiah	I have found the Book of the Law in the temple of the LORD.
Narrator	He gave it to Shaphan, who read it. (PAUSE) Then Shaphan the secretary went to the king and reported to him:
Shaphan	Your officials have paid out the money that was in the temple of the LORD and have entrusted it to the workers and supervisors at the temple.
Narrator	Then Shaphan the secretary informed the king:
Shaphan (uncertainly)	Hilkiah the priest has given me a *book*.
Narrator	And Shaphan read from it in the presence of the king.
	When the king heard the words of the Book of the Law, he tore his robes. He gave these orders to Hilkiah the priest, Ahikam son of Shaphan, Acbor son of Micaiah, Shaphan the secretary and Asaiah the king's attendant:
Josiah	Go and inquire of the LORD for me and for the people and for all Judah about what is written in this book that has been found. Great is the LORD's anger that burns against us because our fathers have not obeyed the words of this book; they have not acted in accordance with all that is written there concerning us.

Cast: **Narrator, Josiah, Hilkiah, Shaphan**

The Book of the Law Found (ii)

2 Kings 22:14–20

Narrator	Hilkiah the priest, Ahikam, Acbor, Shaphan and Asaiah went to speak to the prophetess Huldah who was the wife of Shallum son of Tikvah, the son of Harhas, keeper of the wardrobe. She lived in Jerusalem, in the Second District. She said to them:
Huldah	This is what the LORD, the God of Israel, says: Tell the man who sent you to me, "This is what the LORD says":
The Lord (voice only)	I am going to bring disaster on this place and its people, according to everything written in the book the king of Judah has read. Because they

have forsaken me and burned incense to other gods and provoked me to anger by all the idols their hands have made, my anger will burn against this place and will not be quenched.

Huldah	Tell the king of Judah, who sent you to inquire of the Lord, "This is what the Lord, the God of Israel, says concerning the words you heard":
The Lord (voice)	Because your heart was responsive and you humbled yourself before the Lord when you heard what I have spoken against this place and its people, that they would become accursed and laid waste, and because you tore your robes and wept in my presence, I have heard you, declares the Lord. Therefore I will gather you to your fathers, and you will be buried in peace. Your eyes will not see all the disaster I am going to bring on this place.
Narrator	So they took her answer back to the king.

Cast: **Narrator, Huldah, the Lord** (voice only)

Josiah Renews the Covenant

2 Kings 23:1–12a [12b–15], 16–23

Narrator	The king called together all the elders of Judah and Jerusalem. He went up to the temple of the Lord with the men of Judah, the people of Jerusalem, the priests and the prophets—all the people from the least to the greatest. He read in their hearing all the words of the Book of the Covenant, which had been found in the temple of the Lord. The king stood by the pillar and renewed the covenant in the presence of the Lord—to follow the Lord and keep his commands, regulations and decrees with all his heart and all his soul—
Commentator	Thus confirming the words of the covenant written in this book.
Narrator	Then all the people pledged themselves to the covenant.
	The king ordered Hilkiah the high priest, the priests next in rank and the doorkeepers to remove from the temple of the Lord all the articles made for Baal and Asherah and all the starry hosts.
Commentator	He burned them outside Jerusalem in the fields of the Kidron Valley and took the ashes to Bethel.
Narrator	He did away with the pagan priests appointed by the kings of Judah to burn incense on the high places of the towns of Judah and on those around Jerusalem—

Commen- tator	Those who burned incense to Baal, to the sun and moon, to the constellations and to all the starry hosts.
Narrator	He took the Asherah pole from the temple of the LORD to the Kidron Valley outside Jerusalem and burned it there. He ground it to powder and scattered the dust over the graves of the common people. He also tore down the quarters of the male shrine prostitutes, which were in the temple of the LORD and where women did weaving for Asherah.
	Josiah brought all the priests from the towns of Judah and desecrated the high places, from Geba to Beersheba, where the priests had burned incense. He broke down the shrines at the gates—at the entrance to the Gate of Joshua, the city governor, which is on the left of the city gate.
Commen- tator	Although the priests of the high places did not serve at the altar of the LORD in Jerusalem, they ate unleavened bread with their fellow priests.
Narrator	He desecrated Topheth, which was in the Valley of Ben Hinnom, so no one could use it to sacrifice his son or daughter in the fire to Molech. He removed from the entrance to the temple of the LORD the horses that the kings of Judah had dedicated to the sun.
Commen- tator	They were in the court near the room of an official named Nathan-Melech.
Narrator	Josiah then burned the chariots dedicated to the sun.
	He pulled down the altars the kings of Judah had erected on the roof near the upper room of Ahaz, and the altars Manasseh had built in the two courts of the temple of the LORD. [He removed them from there, smashed them to pieces and threw the rubble into the Kidron Valley. The king also desecrated the high places that were east of Jerusalem. . . .
Commen- tator	The ones Solomon king of Israel had built for Ashtoreth the vile goddess of the Sidonians, for Chemosh the vile god of Moab, and for Molech the detestable god of the people of Ammon.
Narrator	Josiah smashed the sacred stones and cut down the Asherah poles and covered the sites with human bones.
Commen- tator	Even the altar at Bethel, the high place made by Jeroboam son of Nebat, who had caused Israel to sin—even that altar and high place he demolished.
Narrator	He burned the high place and ground it to powder, and burned the Asherah pole also.] Then Josiah looked around, and when he saw the tombs that were there on the hillside, he had the bones removed from them and burned on the altar to defile it, in accordance with the word

of the Lord proclaimed by the man of God who foretold these things. [The king asked:]

Josiah   What is that tombstone I see?

[Narrator   The men of the city said:]

Person 1   It marks the tomb of the man of God who came from Judah—

Person 2   And pronounced against the altar of Bethel the very things you have done to it.

Josiah   Leave it alone. Don't let anyone disturb his bones.

Narrator   So they spared his bones and those of the prophet who had come from Samaria.

Just as he had done at Bethel, Josiah removed and defiled all the shrines at the high places that the kings of Israel had built in the towns of Samaria that had provoked the Lord to anger. Josiah slaughtered all the priests of those high places on the altars and burned human bones on them. Then he went back to Jerusalem.

The king gave this order to all the people:

Josiah   Celebrate the Passover to the Lord your God, as it is written in this Book of the Covenant.

**Commen-
tator**   Not since the days of the judges who led Israel, nor throughout the days of the kings of Israel and the kings of Judah, had any such Passover been observed. But in the eighteenth year of King Josiah, this Passover was celebrated to the Lord in Jerusalem.

Cast: **Narrator, Commentator, Josiah, Person 1, Person 2**

Other Changes Made by Josiah

2 Kings 23:24–30

Narrator   Josiah got rid of the mediums and spiritists, the household gods, the idols and all the other detestable things seen in Judah and Jerusalem. This he did to fulfill the requirements of the law written in the book that Hilkiah the priest had discovered in the temple of the Lord. Neither before nor after Josiah was there a king like him who turned to the Lord as he did— with all his heart and with all his soul and with all his strength, in accordance with all the Law of Moses.

Nevertheless, the Lord did not turn away from the heat of his fierce anger, which burned against Judah because of all that Manasseh had done to provoke him to anger. So the Lord said:

The Lord
(voice only)   I will remove Judah also from my presence as I removed Israel, and I will reject Jerusalem, the city I chose, and this temple, about which I said, "There shall my Name be."

Narrator   As for the other events of Josiah's reign, and all he did, are they not written in the book of the annals of the kings of Judah?

While Josiah was king, Pharaoh Neco king of Egypt went up to the Euphrates River to help the king of Assyria. King Josiah marched out to meet him in battle, but Neco faced him and killed him at Megiddo. Josiah's servants brought his body in a chariot from Megiddo to Jerusalem and buried him in his own tomb. And the people of the land took Jehoahaz son of Josiah and anointed him and made him king in place of his father.

Cast: **Narrator, the Lord** (voice only)

Judah in Exile

2 Kings 25:22–30

Narrator 1   Nebuchadnezzar king of Babylon appointed Gedaliah son of Ahikam, the son of Shaphan, to be over the people he had left behind in Judah. When all the army officers and their men heard that the king of Babylon had appointed Gedaliah as governor, they came to Gedaliah at Mizpah—Ishmael son of Nethaniah, Johanan son of Kareah, Seraiah son of Tanhumeth the Netophathite, Jaazaniah the son of the Maacathite, and their men. Gedaliah took an oath to reassure them and their men.

Gedaliah   Do not be afraid of the Babylonian officials. Settle down in the land and serve the king of Babylon, and it will go well with you.

Narrator 1   In the seventh month, however, Ishmael son of Nethaniah, the son of Elishama, who was of royal blood, came with ten men and assassinated Gedaliah and also the men of Judah and the Babylonians who were with him at Mizpah. At this, all the people from the least to the greatest, together with the army officers, fled to Egypt for fear of the Babylonians.

Narrator 2   In the thirty-seventh year of the exile of Jehoiachin king of Judah, in the year Evil-Merodach became king of Babylon, he released Jehoiachin from prison on the twenty-seventh day of the twelfth month. He spoke kindly to him and gave him a seat of honor higher than those of the other kings who were with him in Babylon. So Jehoiachin put aside his prison clothes and for the rest of his life ate regularly at the king's table. Day by day the king gave Jehoiachin a regular allowance as long as he lived.

Cast: **Narrator 1, Gedaliah, Narrator 2**

1 Chronicles

David Becomes King over Israel

1 Chronicles 11:1–9

Chronicler   All Israel came together to David at Hebron [and said:]

Israelite 1   We are your own flesh and blood.

Israelite 2   In the past, even while Saul was king, you were the one who led Israel on their military campaigns.

Israelite 1   And the LORD your God said to you, "You will shepherd my people Israel, and you will become their ruler."

Chronicler   When all the elders of Israel had come to King David at Hebron, he made a compact with them at Hebron before the LORD, and they anointed David king over Israel, as the LORD had promised through Samuel.

David and all the Israelites marched to Jerusalem—

**Commen-
  tator**   (That is, Jebus)—

Chronicler   The Jebusites who lived there said to David:

Jebusite   You will not get in here.

Chronicler   Nevertheless, David captured the fortress of Zion, the City of David. David had said:

David   Whoever leads the attack on the Jebusites will become commander-in-chief.

Chronicler   Joab son of Zeruiah went up first, and so he received the command.

David then took up residence in the fortress.

**Commen-
  tator**   And so it was called the City of David.

Chronicler   He built up the city around it, from the supporting terraces to the surrounding wall, while Joab restored the rest of the city. And David became more and more powerful, because the LORD Almighty was with him.

Cast: **Chronicler, Israelite 1, Israelite 2** (can be the same as Israelite 1), **Commentator, Jebusite, David**

David Refuses to Drink

1 Chronicles 11:15–19

Chronicler   Three of the thirty chiefs came down to David to the rock at the cave of Adullam, while a band of Philistines was encamped in the Valley of Rephaim. At that time David was in the stronghold, and the Philistine garrison was at Bethlehem. David longed for water:

David   Oh, that someone would get me a drink of water from the well near the gate of Bethlehem!

Chronicler   So the Three broke through the Philistine lines, drew water from the well near the gate of Bethlehem and carried it back to David. But he refused to drink it; instead, he poured it out before the LORD.

David   God forbid that I should do this! Should I drink the blood of these men who went at the risk of their lives?

Chronicler   Because they risked their lives to bring it back, David would not drink it. (PAUSE)

Such were the exploits of the three mighty men.

Cast: **Chronicler, David**

Bringing Back the Ark

1 Chronicles 13:1–14

Chronicler   David conferred with each of his officers, the commanders of thousands and commanders of hundreds. He then said to the whole assembly of Israel:

David   If it seems good to you and if it is the will of the LORD our God, let us send word far and wide to the rest of our brothers throughout the territories of Israel, and also to the priests and Levites who are with them in their towns and pasturelands, to come and join us. Let us bring the ark of our God back to us, for we did not inquire of it during the reign of Saul.

Chronicler   The whole assembly agreed to do this, because it seemed right to all the people. (PAUSE)

So David assembled all the Israelites, from the Shihor River in Egypt to Lebo Hamath, to bring the ark of God from Kiriath Jearim. David and all the Israelites with him went to Baalah of Judah (Kiriath Jearim) to bring up from there the ark of God the LORD, who is enthroned between the cherubim—the ark that is called by the Name.

They moved the ark of God from Abinadab's house on a new cart, with Uzzah and Ahio guiding it. David and all the Israelites were celebrating with all their might before God, with songs and with harps, lyres, tambourines, cymbals and trumpets.

When they came to the threshing floor of Kidon, Uzzah reached out his hand to steady the ark, because the oxen stumbled. The LORD's anger burned against Uzzah, and he struck him down because he had put his hand on the ark. So he died there before God.

Then David was angry because the LORD's wrath had broken out against Uzzah, and to this day that place is called Perez Uzzah. David was afraid of God that day [and asked:]

David   How can I *ever* bring the ark of God to me?

Chronicler   He did not take the ark to be with him in the City of David. Instead, he took it aside to the house of Obed-Edom the Gittite. The ark of God remained with the family of Obed-Edom in his house for three months, and the LORD blessed his household and everything he had.

Cast: **Chronicler, David**

David Defeats the Philistines

1 Chronicles 14:8–17

Chronicler   When the Philistines heard that David had been anointed king over all Israel, they went up in full force to search for him, but David heard about it and went out to meet them. Now the Philistines had come and raided the Valley of Rephaim; so David inquired of God:

David   Shall I go and attack the Philistines? Will you hand them over to me?

Chronicler   The LORD answered him:

The Lord
(voice only)   Go, I will hand them over to you.

Chronicler   So David and his men went up to Baal Perazim, and there he defeated them. [He said:]

David   As waters break out, God has broken out against my enemies by my hand.

Chronicler   So that place was called Baal Perazim. The Philistines had abandoned their gods there, and David gave orders to burn them in the fire. (PAUSE)

Once more the Philistines raided the valley; so David inquired of God again [and God answered him:]

The Lord
(voice)   Do not go straight up, but circle around them and attack them in front of the balsam trees. As soon as you hear the sound of marching in the tops of the balsam trees, move out to battle, because that will mean God has gone out in front of you to strike the Philistine army.

Chronicler   So David did as God commanded him, and they struck down the Philistine army, all the way from Gibeon to Gezer.

So David's fame spread throughout every land, and the Lord made all the nations fear him.

Cast: **Chronicler, David, the Lord** (voice only)

David's Psalm of Thanks

1 Chronicles 16:8–36

Chronicler
(words
of David)   Give thanks to the Lord, call on his name;
    make known among the nations what he has done.
Sing to him, sing praise to him;
    tell of all his wonderful acts.
Glory in his holy name;
    let the hearts of those who seek the Lord rejoice.
Look to the Lord and his strength;
    seek his face always.
Remember the wonders he has done,
    his miracles, and the judgments he pronounced,
O descendants of Israel his servant,
    O sons of Jacob, his chosen ones.

He is the Lord our God;
    his judgments are in all the earth.
He remembers his covenant forever,
    the word he commanded, for a thousand generations,
the covenant he made with Abraham,
    the oath he swore to Isaac.
He confirmed it to Jacob as a decree,
    to Israel as an everlasting covenant:

The Lord
(voice only)   To you I will give the land of Canaan
    as the portion you will inherit.

Chronicler
(words
of David)   When they were but few in number,
    few indeed, and strangers in it,
they wandered from nation to nation,
    from one kingdom to another.
He allowed no man to oppress them;
    for their sake he rebuked kings:

The Lord
(voice)   Do not touch my anointed ones;
    do my prophets no harm.

Chronicler
(words
of David)   Sing to the Lord, all the earth;
      proclaim his salvation day after day.

      Declare his glory among the nations,
        his marvelous deeds among all peoples.
      For great is the Lord and most worthy of praise;
        he is to be feared above all gods.
      For all the gods of the nations are idols,
        but the Lord made the heavens.
      Splendor and majesty are before him;
        strength and joy in his dwelling place.
      Ascribe to the Lord, O families of nations,
        ascribe to the Lord glory and strength,
        ascribe to the Lord the glory due his name.
      Bring an offering and come before him;
        worship the Lord in the splendor of his holiness.
      Tremble before him, all the earth!
        The world is firmly established; it cannot be moved.
      Let the heavens rejoice, let the earth be glad;
        let them say among the nations, "The Lord reigns!"
      Let the sea resound, and all that is in it;
        let the fields be jubilant, and everything in them!
      Then the trees of the forest will sing,
        they will sing for joy before the Lord,
        for he comes to judge the earth.

      Give thanks to the Lord, for he is good;
        his love endures forever.
      Cry out,

Worshiper 1   Save us, O God our Savior;

Worshiper 2   Gather us—

Worshiper 1   And deliver us from the nations—

Worshiper 2   That we may give thanks to your holy name.

Worshiper 1   That we may glory in your praise.

Worshipers
1 and 2   Praise be to the Lord, the God of Israel,
      from everlasting to everlasting.

Chronicler   Then all the people said:

Worshipers
1 and 2   Amen! Praise the Lord.

Cast: **Chronicler, the Lord** (voice only), **Worshiper 1, Worshiper 2** (can be the same as Worshiper 1)

God's Promise to David

1 Chronicles 17:1–15

Chronicler   After David was settled in his palace, he said to Nathan the prophet:

David   Here I am, living in a palace of cedar, while the ark of the covenant of the LORD is under a tent.

Chronicler   Nathan replied to David:

Nathan   Whatever you have in mind, do it, for God is with you.

Chronicler   That night the word of God came to Nathan, saying:

The Lord
(voice only)   Go and tell my servant David, "This is what the LORD says: You are not the one to build me a house to dwell in. I have not dwelt in a house from the day I brought Israel up out of Egypt to this day. I have moved from one tent site to another, from one dwelling place to another. Wherever I have moved with all the Israelites, did I ever say to any of their leaders whom I commanded to shepherd my people, 'Why have you not built me a house of cedar?'"

Now then, tell my servant David, "This is what the LORD Almighty says: I took you from the pasture and from following the flock, to be ruler over my people Israel. I have been with you wherever you have gone, and I have cut off all your enemies from before you. Now I will make your name like the names of the greatest men of the earth. And I will provide a place for my people Israel and will plant them so that they can have a home of their own and no longer be disturbed. Wicked people will not oppress them anymore, as they did at the beginning and have done ever since the time I appointed leaders over my people Israel. I will also subdue all your enemies."

Nathan   I declare to you that the LORD will build a house for you:

The Lord
(voice)   When your days are over and you go to be with your fathers, I will raise up your offspring to succeed you, one of your own sons, and I will establish his kingdom. He is the one who will build a house for me, and I will establish his throne forever. I will be his father, and he will be my son. I will never take my love away from him, as I took it away from your predecessor. I will set him over my house and my kingdom forever; his throne will be established forever.

Chronicler   Nathan reported to David all the words of this entire revelation.

Cast: **Chronicler, David, Nathan, the Lord** (voice only)

David's Prayer

1 Chronicles 17:16–27

Chronicler   King David went in and sat before the LORD, and he said:

David   Who am I, O LORD God, and what is my family, that you have brought me this far? And as if this were not enough in your sight, O God, you have spoken about the future of the house of your servant. You have looked on me as though I were the most exalted of men, O LORD God.

What more can David say to you for honoring your servant? For you know your servant, O LORD. For the sake of your servant and according to your will, you have done this great thing and made known all these great promises.

There is no one like you, O LORD, and there is no God but you, as we have heard with our own ears. And who is like your people Israel—the one nation on earth whose God went out to redeem a people for himself, and to make a name for yourself, and to perform great and awesome wonders by driving out nations from before your people, whom you redeemed from Egypt? You made your people Israel your very own forever, and you, O LORD, have become their God.

And now, LORD, let the promise you have made concerning your servant and his house be established forever. Do as you promised, so that it will be established and that your name will be great forever. Then men will say:

Persons 1
and 2   The LORD Almighty, the God over Israel, is Israel's God!

David   And the house of your servant David will be established before you.

You, my God, have revealed to your servant that you will build a house for him. So your servant has found courage to pray to you. O LORD, you are God! You have promised these good things to your servant. Now you have been pleased to bless the house of your servant, that it may continue forever in your sight; for you, O LORD, have blessed it, and it will be blessed forever.

Cast: **Chronicler, David, Person 1, Person 2** (can be the same as Person 1)

The Battle against the Ammonites

1 Chronicles 19:1–15

Chronicler   Nahash king of the Ammonites died, and his son succeeded him as king. David thought:

David   I will show kindness to Hanun son of Nahash, because his father showed kindness to me.

431

Chronicler	So David sent a delegation to express his sympathy to Hanun concerning his father.
	When David's men came to Hanun in the land of the Ammonites to express sympathy to him, the Ammonite nobles said to Hanun:
Noble 1	Do you think David is honoring your father by sending men to you to express sympathy?
Noble 2	Haven't his men come to you to *explore* and *spy out the country* and overthrow it?
Chronicler	So Hanun seized David's men, shaved them, cut off their garments in the middle at the buttocks, and sent them away.
	When someone came and told David about the men, he sent messengers to meet them, for they were greatly humiliated. The king said:
David	Stay at Jericho till your beards have grown, and then come back.
Chronicler	When the Ammonites realized that they had become a stench in David's nostrils, Hanun and the Ammonites sent a thousand talents of silver to hire chariots and charioteers from Aram Naharaim, Aram Maacah and Zobah. They hired thirty-two thousand chariots and charioteers, as well as the king of Maacah with his troops, who came and camped near Medeba, while the Ammonites were mustered from their towns and moved out for battle.
	On hearing this, David sent Joab out with the entire army of fighting men. The Ammonites came out and drew up in battle formation at the entrance to their city, while the kings who had come were by themselves in the open country.
	Joab saw that there were battle lines in front of him and behind him; so he selected some of the best troops in Israel and deployed them against the Arameans. He put the rest of the men under the command of Abishai his brother, and they were deployed against the Ammonites. [Joab said:]
Joab	If the Arameans are too strong for me, then you are to rescue me; but if the Ammonites are too strong for you, then I will rescue you. Be strong and let us fight bravely for our people and the cities of our God. The LORD will do what is good in his sight.
Chronicler	Then Joab and the troops with him advanced to fight the Arameans, and they fled before him. When the Ammonites saw that the Arameans were fleeing, they too fled before his brother Abishai and went inside the city. So Joab went back to Jerusalem.

Cast: **Chronicler, David, Noble 1, Noble 2, Joab**

David Numbers the Fighting Men

1 Chronicles 21:1–13

Chronicler   Satan rose up against Israel and incited David to take a census of Israel. So David said to Joab and the commanders of the troops:

David   Go and count the Israelites from Beersheba to Dan. Then report back to me so that I may know how many there are.

[Chronicler   But Joab replied:]

Joab   May the Lord multiply his troops a hundred times over. My lord the king, are they not *all* my lord's subjects? Why does my lord want to do this? Why should he bring *guilt* on Israel?

Chronicler   The king's word, however, overruled Joab; so Joab left and went throughout Israel and then came back to Jerusalem. Joab reported the number of the fighting men to David: In all Israel there were one million one hundred thousand men who could handle a sword, including four hundred and seventy thousand in Judah.

But Joab did not include Levi and Benjamin in the numbering, because the king's command was repulsive to him. This command was also evil in the sight of God; so he punished Israel. [Then David said to God:]

David
(praying)   I have sinned greatly by doing this. Now, I beg you, take away the guilt of your servant. I have done a very foolish thing.

Chronicler   The Lord said to Gad, David's seer:

The Lord
(voice only)   Go and tell David, "This is what the Lord says: I am giving you three options. Choose one of them for me to carry out against you."

Chronicler   So Gad went to David and said to him:

Gad   This is what the Lord says: "Take your choice: three years of famine, three months of being swept away before your enemies, with their swords overtaking you, or three days of the sword of the Lord—days of plague in the land, with the angel of the Lord ravaging every part of Israel." Now then, decide how I should answer the one who sent me.

Chronicler   David said to Gad:

David   I am in deep distress. Let me fall into the hands of the Lord, for his mercy is very great; but do not let me fall into the hands of men.

Cast: **Chronicler, David, Joab, the Lord** (voice only), **Gad**

The Lord Answers David's Prayer

1 Chronicles 21:14–22:1

Chronicler   The LORD sent a plague on Israel, and seventy thousand men of Israel fell dead. And God sent an angel to destroy Jerusalem. But as the angel was doing so, the LORD saw it and was grieved because of the calamity and said to the angel who was destroying the people:

The Lord
(voice only)   Enough! Withdraw your hand.

Chronicler   The angel of the LORD was then standing at the threshing floor of Araunah the Jebusite.

David looked up and saw the angel of the LORD standing between heaven and earth, with a drawn sword in his hand extended over Jerusalem. Then David and the elders, clothed in sackcloth, fell facedown. David said to God:

David   Was it not *I* who ordered the fighting men to be counted? I am the one who has sinned and done wrong. These are but sheep. What have *they* done? O LORD my God, let your hand fall upon *me* and my family, but do not let this plague remain on your people.

Chronicler   Then the angel of the LORD ordered Gad to tell David to go up and build an altar to the LORD on the threshing floor of Araunah the Jebusite. So David went up in obedience to the word that Gad had spoken in the name of the LORD.

While Araunah was threshing wheat, he turned and saw the angel; his four sons who were with him hid themselves. Then David approached, and when Araunah looked and saw him, he left the threshing floor and bowed down before David with his face to the ground. David said to him:

David   Let me have the site of your threshing floor so I can build an altar to the LORD, that the plague on the people may be stopped. Sell it to me at the full price.

[Chronicler   Araunah said to David:]

Araunah   Take it! Let my lord the king do whatever pleases him. Look, I will give the oxen for the burnt offerings, the threshing sledges for the wood, and the wheat for the grain offering. I will give all this.

[Chronicler   But King David replied to Araunah:]

David   No, I insist on paying the full price. I will not take for the LORD what is yours, or sacrifice a burnt offering that costs me nothing.

Chronicler   So David paid Araunah six hundred shekels of gold for the site. David built an altar to the LORD there and sacrificed burnt offerings and fellowship offerings. He called on the LORD, and the LORD answered him with fire from heaven on the altar of burnt offering.

434

Then the LORD spoke to the angel, and he put his sword back into its sheath. At that time, when David saw that the LORD had answered him on the threshing floor of Araunah the Jebusite, he offered sacrifices there. (PAUSE) The tabernacle of the LORD, which Moses had made in the desert, and the altar of burnt offering were at that time on the high place at Gibeon. But David could not go before it to inquire of God, because he was afraid of the sword of the angel of the LORD. Then David said:

David The house of the LORD God is to be here, and also the altar of burnt offering for Israel.

Cast: **Chronicler, the Lord** (voice only), **David, Araunah**

Preparations for the Temple

From 1 Chronicles 22:2–23:1

Chronicler David gave orders to assemble the aliens living in Israel, and from among them he appointed stonecutters to prepare dressed stone for building the house of God. He provided a large amount of iron to make nails for the doors of the gateways and for the fittings, and more bronze than could be weighed. He also provided more cedar logs than could be counted, for the Sidonians and Tyrians had brought large numbers of them to David. David said:

David My son Solomon is young and inexperienced, and the house to be built for the LORD should be of great magnificence and fame and splendor in the sight of all the nations. Therefore I will make preparations for it.

Chronicler So David made extensive preparations before his death.

Then he called for his son Solomon and charged him to build a house for the LORD, the God of Israel. David said to Solomon:

David My son, I had it in my heart to build a house for the Name of the LORD my God. But this word of the LORD came to me:

The Lord
(voice only) You have shed much blood and have fought many wars. You are not to build a house for my Name, because you have shed much blood on the earth in my sight. But you will have a son who will be a man of peace and rest, and I will give him rest from all his enemies on every side. His name will be Solomon, and I will grant Israel peace and quiet during his reign. He is the one who will build a house for my Name. He will be my son, and I will be his father. And I will establish the throne of his kingdom over Israel forever.

David Now, my son, the LORD be with you, and may you have success and build the house of the LORD your God, as he said you would. May the LORD give you discretion and understanding when he puts you in command over Israel, so that you may keep the law of the LORD your God. Then you will

435

have success if you are careful to observe the decrees and laws that the LORD gave Moses for Israel. Be strong and courageous. Do not be afraid or discouraged. . . . Now begin the work, and the LORD be with you.

Chronicler   Then David ordered all the leaders of Israel to help his son Solomon.

David   Is not the LORD your God with you? And has he not granted you rest on every side? For he has handed the inhabitants of the land over to me, and the land is subject to the LORD and to his people. Now devote your heart and soul to seeking the LORD your God. Begin to build the sanctuary of the LORD God, so that you may bring the ark of the covenant of the LORD and the sacred articles belonging to God into the temple that will be built for the Name of the LORD.

Chronicler   When David was old and full of years, he made his son Solomon king over Israel.

Cast: **Chronicler, David, the Lord** (voice only)

David's Plans for the Temple

1 Chronicles 28:1–21

Chronicler   David summoned all the officials of Israel to assemble at Jerusalem: the officers over the tribes, the commanders of the divisions in the service of the king, the commanders of thousands and commanders of hundreds, and the officials in charge of all the property and livestock belonging to the king and his sons, together with the palace officials, the mighty men and all the brave warriors. King David rose to his feet.

David   Listen to me, my brothers and my people. I had it in my heart to build a house as a place of rest for the ark of the covenant of the LORD, for the footstool of our God, and I made plans to build it. But God said to me:

The Lord
(voice only)   You are not to build a house for my Name, because you are a warrior and have shed blood.

David   Yet the LORD, the God of Israel, chose me from my whole family to be king over Israel forever. He chose Judah as leader, and from the house of Judah he chose my family, and from my father's sons he was pleased to make me king over all Israel. Of all my sons—and the LORD has given me many—he has chosen my son Solomon to sit on the throne of the kingdom of the LORD over Israel. He said to me:

The Lord
(voice)   Solomon your son is the one who will build my house and my courts, for I have chosen him to be my son, and I will be his father. I will establish his kingdom forever if he is unswerving in carrying out my commands and laws, as is being done at this time.

David	So now I charge you in the sight of all Israel and of the assembly of the LORD, and in the hearing of our God: Be careful to follow all the commands of the LORD your God, that you may possess this good land and pass it on as an inheritance to your descendants forever.
(to Solomon)	And you, my son Solomon, acknowledge the God of your father, and serve him with wholehearted devotion and with a willing mind, for the LORD searches every heart and understands every motive behind the thoughts. If you seek him, he will be found by you; but if you forsake him, he will reject you forever. Consider now, for the LORD has chosen you to build a temple as a sanctuary. Be strong and do the work.
Chronicler	Then David gave his son Solomon the plans for the portico of the temple, its buildings, its storerooms, its upper parts, its inner rooms and the place of atonement. He gave him the plans of all that the Spirit had put in his mind for the courts of the temple of the LORD and all the surrounding rooms, for the treasuries of the temple of God and for the treasuries for the dedicated things. He gave him instructions for the divisions of the priests and Levites, and for all the work of serving in the temple of the LORD, as well as for all the articles to be used in its service. He designated the weight of gold for all the gold articles to be used in various kinds of service, and the weight of silver for all the silver articles to be used in various kinds of service: the weight of gold for the gold lampstands and their lamps, with the weight for each lampstand and its lamps; and the weight of silver for each silver lampstand and its lamps, according to the use of each lampstand; the weight of gold for each table for consecrated bread; the weight of silver for the silver tables; the weight of pure gold for the forks, sprinkling bowls and pitchers; the weight of gold for each gold dish; the weight of silver for each silver dish; and the weight of the refined gold for the altar of incense. He also gave him the plan for the chariot, that is, the cherubim of gold that spread their wings and shelter the ark of the covenant of the LORD. [David said:]
David	All this I have in writing from the hand of the LORD upon me, and he gave me understanding in all the details of the plan.
Chronicler	David also said to Solomon his son:
David (to Solomon)	Be strong and courageous, and do the work. Do not be afraid or discouraged, for the LORD God, my God, is with you. He will not fail you or forsake you until all the work for the service of the temple of the LORD is finished. The divisions of the priests and Levites are ready for all the work on the temple of God, and every willing man skilled in any craft will help you in all the work. The officials and all the people will obey your every command.

Cast: **Chronicler**, **David**, **the Lord** (voice only), **Solomon** (if desired, nonspeaking part)

Gifts for Building the Temple

1 Chronicles 29:1–9

Chronicler   King David said to the whole assembly:

David   My son Solomon, the one whom God has chosen, is young and inexperienced. The task is great, because this palatial structure is not for man
but for the LORD God. With all my resources I have provided for the temple of my God—gold for the gold work, silver for the silver, bronze for
the bronze, iron for the iron and wood for the wood, as well as onyx for
the settings, turquoise, stones of various colors, and all kinds of fine stone
and marble—all of these in large quantities. Besides, in my devotion to
the temple of my God I now give my personal treasures of gold and silver for the temple of my God, over and above everything I have provided
for this holy temple: three thousand talents of gold (gold of Ophir) and
seven thousand talents of refined silver, for the overlaying of the walls
of the buildings, for the gold work and the silver work, and for all the
work to be done by the craftsmen. Now, who is willing to consecrate himself today to the LORD?

Chronicler   Then the leaders of families, the officers of the tribes of Israel, the commanders of thousands and commanders of hundreds, and the officials
in charge of the king's work gave willingly. They gave toward the work
on the temple of God five thousand talents and ten thousand darics of
gold, ten thousand talents of silver, eighteen thousand talents of bronze
and a hundred thousand talents of iron. Any who had precious stones
gave them to the treasury of the temple of the LORD in the custody of
Jehiel the Gershonite. The people rejoiced at the willing response of their
leaders, for they had given freely and wholeheartedly to the LORD. David
the king also rejoiced greatly.

Cast: **Chronicler, David**

David Praises God

1 Chronicles 29:[9], 10–20

Chronicler   [*The people rejoiced at the willing response of their leaders, for they had
given freely and wholeheartedly to the LORD. David the king also rejoiced
greatly.]

David praised the LORD in the presence of the whole assembly:

David
(worship-
ing)   Praise be to you, O LORD,
God of our father Israel,
from everlasting to everlasting.

438

Yours, O Lord, is the greatness and the power
and the glory and the majesty and the splendor,
for everything in heaven and earth is yours.
Yours, O Lord, is the kingdom;
you are exalted as head over all.
Wealth and honor come from you;
you are the ruler of all things.
In your hands are strength and power
to exalt and give strength to all.
Now, our God, we give you thanks,
and praise your glorious name.

But who am I, and who are my people, that we should be able to give as generously as this? Everything comes from you, and we have given you only what comes from your hand. We are aliens and strangers in your sight, as were all our forefathers. Our days on earth are like a shadow, without hope. O Lord our God, as for all this abundance that we have provided for building you a temple for your Holy Name, it comes from your hand, and all of it belongs to you. I know, my God, that you test the heart and are pleased with integrity. All these things have I given willingly and with honest intent. And now I have seen with joy how willingly your people who are here have given to you. O Lord, God of our fathers Abraham, Isaac and Israel, keep this desire in the hearts of your people forever, and keep their hearts loyal to you. And give my son Solomon the wholehearted devotion to keep your commands, requirements and decrees and to do everything to build the palatial structure for which I have provided.

Chronicler	Then David said to the whole assembly:
David	Praise the Lord your God.
Chronicler	So they all praised the Lord, the God of their fathers; they bowed low and fell prostrate before the Lord and the king.

Cast: **Chronicler, David.** (*Please note: This section overlaps with the previous reading.)

2 Chronicles

Preparations for Building the Temple

2 Chronicles 2:1–16

Chronicler   Solomon gave orders to build a temple for the Name of the Lord and a royal palace for himself. He conscripted seventy thousand men as carriers and eighty thousand as stonecutters in the hills and thirty-six hundred as foremen over them.

Solomon sent this message to Hiram king of Tyre:

Solomon   Send me cedar logs as you did for my father David when you sent him cedar to build a palace to live in. Now I am about to build a temple for the Name of the Lord my God and to dedicate it to him for burning fragrant incense before him, for setting out the consecrated bread regularly, and for making burnt offerings every morning and evening and on Sabbaths and New Moons and at the appointed feasts of the Lord our God. This is a lasting ordinance for Israel.

The temple I am going to build will be great, because our God is greater than all other gods. But who is able to build a temple for him, since the heavens, even the highest heavens, cannot contain him? Who then am I to build a temple for him, except as a place to burn sacrifices before him?

Send me, therefore, a man skilled to work in gold and silver, bronze and iron, and in purple, crimson and blue yarn, and experienced in the art of engraving, to work in Judah and Jerusalem with my skilled craftsmen, whom my father David provided.

Send me also cedar, pine and algum logs from Lebanon, for I know that your men are skilled in cutting timber there. My men will work with yours to provide me with plenty of lumber, because the temple I build must be large and magnificent. I will give your servants, the woodsmen who cut the timber, twenty thousand cors of ground wheat, twenty thousand cors of barley, twenty thousand baths of wine and twenty thousand baths of olive oil.

Chronicler   Hiram king of Tyre replied by letter to Solomon:

Hiram   Because the Lord loves his people, he has made you their king.

Praise be to the Lord, the God of Israel, who made heaven and earth! He has given King David a wise son, endowed with intelligence and discernment, who will build a temple for the Lord and a palace for himself.

I am sending you Huram-Abi, a man of great skill, whose mother was from Dan and whose father was from Tyre. He is trained to work in gold and silver, bronze and iron, stone and wood, and with purple and blue and crimson yarn and fine linen. He is experienced in all kinds of engraving and can execute any design given to him. He will work with your craftsmen and with those of my lord, David your father.

Now let my lord send his servants the wheat and barley and the olive oil and wine he promised, and we will cut all the logs from Lebanon that you need and will float them in rafts by sea down to Joppa. You can then take them up to Jerusalem.

Cast: **Chronicler, Solomon, Hiram**

The Glory of the Lord

2 Chronicles 5:11–14

Chronicler   All the priests . . . had consecrated themselves, regardless of their divisions. All the Levites who were musicians—Asaph, Heman, Jeduthun and their sons and relatives—stood on the east side of the altar, dressed in fine linen and playing cymbals, harps and lyres. They were accompanied by 120 priests sounding trumpets. The trumpeters and singers joined in unison, as with one voice, to give praise and thanks to the LORD. Accompanied by trumpets, cymbals and other instruments, they raised their voices in praise to the LORD and sang:

Singer 1   He is good—

Singer 2   His love endures forever.

Chronicler   Then the temple of the LORD was filled with a cloud, and the priests could not perform their service because of the cloud, for the glory of the LORD filled the temple of God.

Cast: **Chronicler, Singer 1, Singer 2** (can be the same as Singer 1)

Solomon's Address to the People

2 Chronicles 6:1–11

Chronicler   Solomon said:

Solomon
(praying)   The LORD has said that he would dwell in a dark cloud; I have built a magnificent temple for you, a place for you to dwell forever.

Chronicler   While the whole assembly of Israel was standing there, the king turned around and blessed them. Then he said:

Solomon   Praise be to the LORD, the God of Israel, who with his hands has fulfilled what he promised with his mouth to my father David. [For he said:]

The Lord
(voice only)   Since the day I brought my people out of Egypt, I have not chosen a city in any tribe of Israel to have a temple built for my Name to be there, nor have I chosen anyone to be the leader over my people Israel. But now I have chosen Jerusalem for my Name to be there, and I have chosen David to rule my people Israel.

Solomon   My father David had it in his heart to build a temple for the Name of the LORD, the God of Israel. But the LORD said to my father David:

The Lord
(voice)   Because it was in your heart to build a temple for my Name, you did well to have this in your heart. Nevertheless, you are not the one to build the temple, but your son, who is your own flesh and blood—he is the one who will build the temple for my Name.

Solomon   The LORD has kept the promise he made. I have succeeded David my father and now I sit on the throne of Israel, just as the LORD promised, and I have built the temple for the Name of the LORD, the God of Israel. There I have placed the ark, in which is the covenant of the LORD that he made with the people of Israel.

Cast: **Chronicler, Solomon, the Lord** (voice only)

Solomon's Prayer of Dedication (i)

2 Chronicles 6:12–21

Chronicler   Solomon stood before the altar of the LORD in front of the whole assembly of Israel and spread out his hands. Now he had made a bronze platform, five cubits long, five cubits wide and three cubits high, and had placed it in the center of the outer court. He stood on the platform and then knelt down before the whole assembly of Israel and spread out his hands toward heaven.

Solomon   O LORD, God of Israel, there is no God like you in heaven or on earth— you who keep your covenant of love with your servants who continue wholeheartedly in your way. You have kept your promise to your servant David my father; with your mouth you have promised and with your hand you have fulfilled it—as it is today.

Now LORD, God of Israel, keep for your servant David my father the promises you made to him when you said, "You shall never fail to have a man to sit before me on the throne of Israel, if only your sons are careful in all they do to walk before me according to my law, as you have done." And now, O LORD, God of Israel, let your word that you promised your servant David come true.

But will God really dwell on earth with men? The heavens, even the highest heavens, cannot contain you. How much less this temple I have built! Yet give attention to your servant's prayer and his plea for mercy, O LORD my God. Hear the cry and the prayer that your servant is praying in your presence. May your eyes be open toward this temple day and night, this place of which you said you would put your Name there. May you hear the prayer your servant prays toward this place. Hear the supplications of your servant and of your people Israel when they pray toward this place. Hear from heaven, your dwelling place; and when you hear, forgive.

Cast: **Chronicler, Solomon**

Solomon's Prayer of Dedication (ii)

2 Chronicles 6:22–31

Voice 1   When a man wrongs his neighbor and is required to take an oath and he comes and swears the oath before your altar in this temple, then hear from heaven and act.

Voice 2   Judge between your servants, repaying the guilty by bringing down on his own head what he has done. Declare the innocent not guilty and so establish his innocence.

Voice 1   When your people Israel have been defeated by an enemy because they have sinned against you and when they turn back and confess your name, praying and making supplication before you in this temple—

Voice 2   Then hear from heaven and forgive the sin of your people Israel and bring them back to the land you gave to them and their fathers.

Voice 1   When the heavens are shut up and there is no rain because your people have sinned against you, and when they pray toward this place and confess your name and turn from their sin because you have afflicted them—

Voice 2   Then hear from heaven and forgive the sin of your servants, your people Israel. Teach them the right way to live, and send rain on the land you gave your people for an inheritance.

Voice 1   When famine or plague comes to the land, or blight or mildew, locusts or grasshoppers, or when enemies besiege them in any of their cities, whatever disaster or disease may come, and when a prayer or plea is made by any of your people Israel—each one aware of his afflictions and pains, and spreading out his hands toward this temple—

Voice 2   Then hear from heaven, your dwelling place. Forgive, and deal with each man according to all he does, since you know his heart (for you alone know the hearts of men), so that they will fear you and walk in your ways all the time they live in the land you gave our fathers.

Cast: **Voice 1, Voice 2**

Solomon's Prayer of Dedication (iii)

2 Chronicles 6:32–40

Voice 1　　As for the foreigner who does not belong to your people Israel but has come from a distant land because of your great name and your mighty hand and your outstretched arm—when he comes and prays toward this temple—

Voice 2　　Then hear from heaven, your dwelling place, and do whatever the foreigner asks of you, so that all the peoples of the earth may know your name and fear you, as do your own people Israel, and may know that this house I have built bears your Name.

Voice 1　　When your people go to war against their enemies, wherever you send them, and when they pray to you toward this city you have chosen and the temple I have built for your Name—

Voice 2　　Then hear from heaven their prayer and their plea, and uphold their cause.

Voice 1　　When they sin against you—for there is no one who does not sin—and you become angry with them and give them over to the enemy, who takes them captive to a land far away or near—

Voice 2　　And if they have a change of heart in the land where they are held captive, and repent and plead with you in the land of their captivity and say, "We have sinned, we have done wrong and acted wickedly"—

Voice 1　　And if they turn back to you with all their heart and soul in the land of their captivity where they were taken, and pray toward the land you gave their fathers, toward the city you have chosen and toward the temple I have built for your Name—

Voice 2　　Then from heaven, your dwelling place, hear their prayer and their pleas, and uphold their cause. And forgive your people, who have sinned against you.

Voices 1 and 2　　Now, my God, may your eyes be open and your ears attentive to the prayers offered in this place.

Cast: **Voice 1, Voice 2**

The Lord Appears to Solomon

2 Chronicles 7:11–22

Chronicler　　When Solomon had finished the temple of the Lord and the royal palace, and had succeeded in carrying out all he had in mind to do in the temple of the Lord and in his own palace, the Lord appeared to him at night [and said:]

444

The Lord
(voice only)   I have heard your prayer and have chosen this place for myself as a temple for sacrifices.

When I shut up the heavens so that there is no rain, or command locusts to devour the land or send a plague among my people, if my people, who are called by my name, will humble themselves and pray and seek my face and turn from their wicked ways, then will I hear from heaven and will forgive their sin and will heal their land. Now my eyes will be open and my ears attentive to the prayers offered in this place. I have chosen and consecrated this temple so that my Name may be there forever. My eyes and my heart will always be there.

As for you, if you walk before me as David your father did, and do all I command, and observe my decrees and laws, I will establish your royal throne, as I covenanted with David your father when I said, "You shall never fail to have a man to rule over Israel."

But if you turn away and forsake the decrees and commands I have given you and go off to serve other gods and worship them, then I will uproot Israel from my land, which I have given them, and will reject this temple I have consecrated for my Name. I will make it a byword and an object of ridicule among all peoples. (PAUSE) And though this temple is now so imposing, all who pass by will be appalled and say:

Person 1   Why has the LORD done such a thing to this land and to this temple?

The Lord
(voice)   People will answer:

Person 2   Because they have forsaken the LORD, the God of their fathers, who brought them out of Egypt—

Person 3   And have embraced *other* gods, worshiping and serving them.

Person 2   That is why he brought all this disaster on them.

Cast: **Chronicler, the Lord** (voice only), **Person 1, Person 2, Person 3** (can be the same as Person 2)

The Queen of Sheba Visits Solomon

2 Chronicles 9:1–12

Chronicler   When the queen of Sheba heard of Solomon's fame, she came to Jerusalem to test him with hard questions. Arriving with a very great caravan—with camels carrying spices, large quantities of gold, and precious stones—she came to Solomon and talked with him about all she had on her mind. Solomon answered all her questions; nothing was too hard for him to explain to her. When the queen of Sheba saw the wisdom of Solomon, as well as the palace he had built, the food on his table, the seating of his officials, the attending servants in their robes, the cupbearers in their robes and the burnt offerings he made at the temple of the Lord, she was overwhelmed.

Queen
(amazed)

The report I heard in my own country about your achievements and your wisdom is true. But I did not believe what they said until I came and saw with my own eyes. Indeed, not even half the greatness of your wisdom was told me; you have far exceeded the report I heard. How happy your men must be! How happy your officials, who continually stand before you and hear your wisdom! Praise be to the Lord your God, who has delighted in you and placed you on his throne as king to rule for the Lord your God. Because of the love of your God for Israel and his desire to uphold them forever, he has made you king over them, to maintain justice and righteousness.

Chronicler

Then she gave the king 120 talents of gold, large quantities of spices, and precious stones. There had never been such spices as those the queen of Sheba gave to King Solomon.

(The men of Hiram and the men of Solomon brought gold from Ophir; they also brought algumwood and precious stones. The king used the algumwood to make steps for the temple of the Lord and for the royal palace, and to make harps and lyres for the musicians. Nothing like them had ever been seen in Judah.)

King Solomon gave the queen of Sheba all she desired and asked for; he gave her more than she had brought to him. Then she left and returned with her retinue to her own country.

Cast: **Chronicler, Queen**

Israel Rebels against Rehoboam

From 2 Chronicles 10:1–19

Chronicler

Rehoboam went to Shechem, for all the Israelites had gone there to make him king. When Jeroboam son of Nebat heard this (he was in Egypt, where he had fled from King Solomon), he returned from Egypt. So they sent for Jeroboam, and he and all Israel went to Rehoboam and said to him:

Person 1

Your father put a heavy yoke on us—

Person 2

But now lighten the harsh labor and the heavy yoke he put on us, and we will serve you.

Chronicler

Rehoboam answered:

Rehoboam

Come back to me in three days.

Chronicler	So the people went away.
	Then King Rehoboam consulted the elders who had served his father Solomon during his lifetime.
Rehoboam	How would you advise me to answer these people?
Elder	If you will be kind to these people and please them and give them a favorable answer, they will always be your servants.
Chronicler	But Rehoboam rejected the advice the elders gave him and consulted the young men who had grown up with him and were serving him. He asked them:
Rehoboam	What is your advice? How should we answer these people who say to me, "Lighten the yoke your father put on us"?
Chronicler	The young men who had grown up with him replied:
Young man 1	Tell the people who have said to you, "Your father put a heavy yoke on us, but make our yoke lighter"—
Young man 2	Tell them, "My little *finger* is thicker than my father's waist.
Young man 1	"My father laid on you a heavy yoke; I will make it even heavier.
Young man 2	"My father scourged you with whips; I will scourge you with scorpions."
Chronicler	Three days later Jeroboam and all the people returned to Rehoboam, as the king had said, "Come back to me in three days." The king answered them harshly. Rejecting the advice of the elders, he followed the advice of the young men [and said:]
Rehoboam	My father made your yoke heavy; I will make it even heavier. My father scourged you with whips; I will scourge you with scorpions. . . .
Chronicler	When all Israel saw that the king refused to listen to them, they answered the king:
Person 1	What share do we have in David, what part in Jesse's son?
Person 2	To your tents, O Israel!
Person 1	Look after your own house, O David!
Chronicler	So all the Israelites went home. But as for the Israelites who were living in the towns of Judah, Rehoboam still ruled over them.
	King Rehoboam sent out Adoniram, who was in charge of forced labor, but the Israelites stoned him to death. King Rehoboam, however, managed to get into his chariot and escape to Jerusalem. So Israel has been in rebellion against the house of David to this day.

Cast: **Chronicler, Person 1, Person 2** (can be the same as Person 1), **Rehoboam, Elder, Young man 1, Young man 2** (can be the same as Young man 1)

Shishak Attacks Jerusalem

2 Chronicles 12:1–12

Chronicler   After Rehoboam's position as king was established and he had become strong, he and all Israel with him abandoned the law of the Lord. (PAUSE) Because they had been unfaithful to the Lord, Shishak king of Egypt attacked Jerusalem in the fifth year of King Rehoboam. With twelve hundred chariots and sixty thousand horsemen and the innumerable troops of Libyans, Sukkites and Cushites that came with him from Egypt, he captured the fortified cities of Judah and came as far as Jerusalem.

Then the prophet Shemaiah came to Rehoboam and to the leaders of Judah who had assembled in Jerusalem for fear of Shishak [and he said to them:]

Shemaiah   This is what the Lord says:

The Lord
(voice only)   You have abandoned *me*; therefore, I now abandon *you* to Shishak.

Chronicler   The leaders of Israel and the king humbled themselves and said:

Rehoboam   The Lord is just.

Chronicler   When the Lord saw that they humbled themselves, this word of the Lord came to Shemaiah:

The Lord
(voice)   Since they have humbled themselves, I will not destroy them but will soon give them deliverance. My wrath will not be poured out on Jerusalem through Shishak. They will, however, become subject to him, so that they may learn the difference between serving me and serving the kings of other lands.

Chronicler   When Shishak king of Egypt attacked Jerusalem, he carried off the treasures of the temple of the Lord and the treasures of the royal palace. He took everything, including the gold shields Solomon had made. So King Rehoboam made bronze shields to replace them and assigned these to the commanders of the guard on duty at the entrance to the royal palace. Whenever the king went to the Lord's temple, the guards went with him, bearing the shields, and afterward they returned them to the guardroom.

Because Rehoboam humbled himself, the Lord's anger turned from him, and he was not totally destroyed. Indeed, there was some good in Judah.

Cast: **Chronicler, Shemaiah, the Lord** (voice only), **Rehoboam**

Abijah King of Judah

2 Chronicles 13:1–17

Chronicler In the eighteenth year of the reign of Jeroboam, Abijah became king of Judah, and he reigned in Jerusalem three years. His mother's name was Maacah, a daughter of Uriel of Gibeah.

There was war between Abijah and Jeroboam. Abijah went into battle with a force of four hundred thousand able fighting men, and Jeroboam drew up a battle line against him with eight hundred thousand able troops.

Abijah stood on Mount Zemaraim, in the hill country of Ephraim [and said:]

Abijah Jeroboam and all Israel, listen to me! Don't you know that the LORD, the God of Israel, has given the kingship of Israel to David and his descendants forever by a covenant of salt? Yet Jeroboam son of Nebat, an official of Solomon son of David, rebelled against his master. Some worthless scoundrels gathered around him and opposed Rehoboam son of Solomon when he was young and indecisive and not strong enough to resist them.

And now you plan to resist the kingdom of the LORD, which is in the hands of David's descendants. You are indeed a vast army and have with you the golden calves that Jeroboam made to be your gods. (PAUSE) But didn't you drive out the priests of the LORD, the sons of Aaron, and the Levites, and make priests of your own as the peoples of other lands do? Whoever comes to consecrate himself with a young bull and seven rams may become a priest of what are not gods.

As for us, the LORD is our God, and we have not forsaken him. The priests who serve the LORD are sons of Aaron, and the Levites assist them. Every morning and evening they present burnt offerings and fragrant incense to the LORD. They set out the bread on the ceremonially clean table and light the lamps on the gold lampstand every evening. We are observing the requirements of the LORD our God. But you have forsaken him. God is with us; he is our leader. His priests with their trumpets will sound the battle cry against you. Men of Israel, do not fight against the LORD, the God of your fathers, for you will not succeed.

Chronicler Now Jeroboam had sent troops around to the rear, so that while he was in front of Judah the ambush was behind them. Judah turned and saw that they were being attacked at both front and rear. Then they cried out to the LORD. The priests blew their trumpets and the men of Judah raised the battle cry. At the sound of their battle cry, God routed Jeroboam and all Israel before Abijah and Judah. The Israelites fled before Judah, and God delivered them into their hands. Abijah and his men inflicted heavy losses on them, so that there were five hundred thousand casualties among Israel's able men.

Cast: **Chronicler, Abijah**

449

Asa King of Judah

2 Chronicles 14:1–13

Chronicler   Abijah rested with his fathers and was buried in the City of David. Asa his son succeeded him as king, and in his days the country was at peace for ten years.

Asa did what was good and right in the eyes of the LORD his God. He removed the foreign altars and the high places, smashed the sacred stones and cut down the Asherah poles. He commanded Judah to seek the LORD, the God of their fathers, and to obey his laws and commands. He removed the high places and incense altars in every town in Judah, and the kingdom was at peace under him. He built up the fortified cities of Judah, since the land was at peace. No one was at war with him during those years, for the LORD gave him rest. [Asa said to Judah:]

Asa   Let us build up these towns, and put walls around them, with towers, gates and bars. The land is still ours, because we have sought the LORD our God; we sought him and he has given us rest on every side.

Chronicler   So they built and prospered.

Asa had an army of three hundred thousand men from Judah, equipped with large shields and with spears, and two hundred and eighty thousand from Benjamin, armed with small shields and with bows. All these were brave fighting men.

Zerah the Cushite marched out against them with a vast army and three hundred chariots, and came as far as Mareshah. Asa went out to meet him, and they took up battle positions in the Valley of Zephathah near Mareshah. Then Asa called to the LORD his God:

Asa (praying)   LORD, there is no one like you to help the powerless against the mighty. Help us, O LORD our God, for we rely on you, and in your name we have come against this vast army. O LORD, you are our God; do not let man prevail against you.

Chronicler   The LORD struck down the Cushites before Asa and Judah. The Cushites fled, and Asa and his army pursued them as far as Gerar. Such a great number of Cushites fell that they could not recover; they were crushed before the LORD and his forces. The men of Judah carried off a large amount of plunder.

Cast: **Chronicler, Asa**

Asa's Reform

From 2 Chronicles 15:1–15

Chronicler   The Spirit of God came upon Azariah son of Oded. He went out to meet Asa and said to him:

Azariah	Listen to me, Asa and all Judah and Benjamin. The LORD is with you when you are with him. If you seek him, he will be found by you, but if you forsake him, he will forsake you. For a long time Israel was without the true God, without a priest to teach and without the law. But in their distress they turned to the LORD, the God of Israel, and sought him, and he was found by them. In those days it was not safe to travel about, for all the inhabitants of the lands were in great turmoil. One nation was being crushed by another and one city by another, because God was troubling them with every kind of distress. But as for you, be strong and do not give up, for your work will be rewarded.
Chronicler	When Asa heard these words and the prophecy of Azariah son of Oded the prophet, he took courage. He removed the detestable idols from the whole land of Judah and Benjamin and from the towns he had captured in the hills of Ephraim. He repaired the altar of the LORD that was in front of the portico of the LORD's temple. . . .
	They entered into a covenant to seek the LORD, the God of their fathers, with all their heart and soul. . . . They took an oath to the LORD with loud acclamation, with shouting and with trumpets and horns. All Judah rejoiced about the oath because they had sworn it wholeheartedly. They sought God eagerly, and he was found by them. So the LORD gave them rest on every side.

Cast: **Chronicler, Azariah**

Asa's Last Years

From 2 Chronicles 16:1–14

Chronicler	In the thirty-sixth year of Asa's reign Baasha king of Israel went up against Judah and fortified Ramah to prevent anyone from leaving or entering the territory of Asa king of Judah.
	Asa then took the silver and gold out of the treasuries of the LORD's temple and of his own palace and sent it to Ben-Hadad king of Aram, who was ruling in Damascus.
Asa	Let there be a treaty between me and you, as there was between my father and your father. See, I am sending you silver and gold. Now break your treaty with Baasha king of Israel so he will withdraw from me.
Chronicler	Ben-Hadad agreed with King Asa and sent the commanders of his forces against the towns of Israel. They conquered Ijon, Dan, Abel Maim and all the store cities of Naphtali. When Baasha heard this, he stopped building Ramah and abandoned his work. Then King Asa brought all the men of Judah, and they carried away from Ramah the stones and timber Baasha had been using. With them he built up Geba and Mizpah. (PAUSE)
	At that time Hanani the seer came to Asa king of Judah:

451

Hanani	Because you relied on the king of Aram and not on the LORD your God, the army of the king of Aram has escaped from your hand. Were not the Cushites and Libyans a mighty army with great numbers of chariots and horsemen? Yet when you relied on the LORD, he delivered them into your hand. For the eyes of the LORD range throughout the earth to strengthen those whose hearts are fully committed to him. You have done a foolish thing, and from now on you will be at war.
Chronicler	Asa was angry with the seer because of this; he was so enraged that he put him in prison. At the same time Asa brutally oppressed some of the people. . . . (PAUSE)
	In the thirty-ninth year of his reign Asa was afflicted with a disease in his feet. Though his disease was severe, even in his illness he did not seek help from the LORD, but only from the physicians. Then in the forty-first year of his reign Asa died and rested with his fathers. They buried him in the tomb that he had cut out for himself in the City of David. They laid him on a bier covered with spices and various blended perfumes, and they made a huge fire in his honor.

Cast: **Chronicler, Asa, Hanani**

Micaiah Prophesies against Ahab

2 Chronicles 18:1–27

Chronicler	Jehoshaphat had great wealth and honor, and he allied himself with Ahab by marriage. Some years later he went down to visit Ahab in Samaria. Ahab slaughtered many sheep and cattle for him and the people with him and urged him to attack Ramoth Gilead. Ahab king of Israel asked Jehoshaphat king of Judah:
Ahab	Will you go with me against Ramoth Gilead?
[Chronicler	Jehoshaphat replied:]
Jehoshaphat	I am as you are, and my people as your people; we will join you in the war.
[Chronicler	But Jehoshaphat also said to the king of Israel:]
Jehoshaphat	First seek the counsel of the LORD.
Chronicler	So the king of Israel brought together the prophets—four hundred men— and asked them:
Ahab	Shall we go to war against Ramoth Gilead, or shall I refrain?
Prophet 1	Go—
Prophet 2	For God will give it into the king's hand.
[Chronicler	But Jehoshaphat asked:]

452

Jehoshaphat	Is there not a prophet of the LORD here whom we can inquire of?
Ahab (petulantly)	There is still one man through whom we can inquire of the LORD, but I *hate* him because he never prophesies anything *good* about me, but always bad. He is Micaiah son of Imlah.
Jehoshaphat	The king should not say that.
Chronicler	So the king of Israel called one of his officials:
Ahab	Bring Micaiah son of Imlah at once.
Chronicler	Dressed in their royal robes, the king of Israel and Jehoshaphat king of Judah were sitting on their thrones at the threshing floor by the entrance to the gate of Samaria, with all the prophets prophesying before them. Now Zedekiah son of Kenaanah had made iron horns, and he declared:
Zedekiah	This is what the LORD says: "With these you will gore the Arameans until they are destroyed."
Chronicler	All the other prophets were prophesying the same thing.
Prophet 1	Attack Ramoth Gilead and be victorious.
Prophet 2	For the LORD will give it into the king's hand.
Chronicler	The messenger who had gone to summon Micaiah said to him:
Messenger (firmly)	Look, as one man the other prophets are predicting success for the king. Let your word agree with theirs, and speak favorably.
Micaiah	As surely as the LORD lives, I can tell him only what my God says.
Chronicler	When he arrived, the king asked him:
Ahab	Micaiah, shall we go to war against Ramoth Gilead, or shall I refrain?
Micaiah (casually)	Attack and be victorious, for they will be given into your hand.
Ahab (angrily)	How many times must I make you swear to tell me nothing but the truth in the name of the LORD?
Micaiah (sadly)	I saw all Israel scattered on the hills like sheep without a shepherd, and the LORD said:
The Lord (voice only)	These people have no master. Let each one go home in peace.
[Chronicler	The king of Israel said to Jehoshaphat:]
Ahab (sulkily, to Jehoshaphat)	Didn't I tell you that he never prophesies anything good about me, but only bad?

453

Micaiah	Therefore hear the word of the LORD: I saw the LORD sitting on his throne with all the host of heaven standing on his right and on his left.
The Lord (voice)	Who will entice Ahab king of Israel into attacking Ramoth Gilead and going to his death there?
Micaiah	One suggested this, and another that. Finally, a spirit came forward, stood before the LORD and said:
A spirit (voice only)	I will entice him.
The Lord (voice)	By what means?
A spirit (voice)	I will go and be a lying spirit in the mouths of all his prophets.
The Lord (voice)	You will succeed in enticing him. Go and do it.
Micaiah	So now the LORD has put a lying spirit in the mouths of these prophets of yours. The LORD has decreed disaster for you.
Chronicler	Then Zedekiah son of Kenaanah went up and slapped Micaiah in the face.
Zedekiah	Which way did the spirit from the LORD go when he went from me to speak to you?
Micaiah	You will find out on the day you go to hide in an inner room.
[Chronicler	The king of Israel then ordered:]
Ahab (angrily)	Take Micaiah and send him back to Amon the ruler of the city and to Joash the king's son, and say, "This is what the king says: Put this fellow in prison and give him nothing but bread and water until I return safely."
Micaiah (firmly, to Ahab)	If you ever return safely, the LORD has not spoken through me.
(to audience)	Mark my words, all you people!

Cast: **Chronicler, Ahab, Jehoshaphat, Prophet 1, Prophet 2** (can be the same as Prophet 1), **Zedekiah, Messenger, Micaiah, the Lord** (voice only), **A spirit** (voice only)

Ahab Killed at Ramoth Gilead

2 Chronicles 18:28–34

Chronicler	The king of Israel and Jehoshaphat king of Judah went up to Ramoth Gilead. The king of Israel said to Jehoshaphat:

Ahab	*I* will enter the battle in disguise, but *you* wear your royal robes.
Chronicler	So the king of Israel disguised himself and went into battle.
	Now the king of *Aram* had ordered his chariot commanders:
King of Aram	Do not fight with anyone, small or great, except the king of Israel.
Chronicler	When the chariot commanders saw Jehoshaphat, they thought:
Commander	This is the king of Israel.
Chronicler	So they turned to attack him, but Jehoshaphat cried out, and the Lord helped him. God drew them away from him, for when the chariot commanders saw that he was not the king of Israel, they stopped pursuing him.
	But someone drew his bow at random and hit the king of Israel between the sections of his armor. The king told the chariot driver:
Ahab (hurt)	Wheel around and get me out of the fighting. I've been wounded.
Chronicler	All day long the battle raged, and the king of Israel propped himself up in his chariot facing the Arameans until evening.
(slowly)	Then at sunset he died.

Cast: **Chronicler, Ahab, King of Aram, Commander**

A Prophet Reprimands Jehoshaphat

2 Chronicles 19:1–3

Chronicler	When Jehoshaphat king of Judah returned safely to his palace in Jerusalem, Jehu the seer, the son of Hanani, went out to meet him:
Jehu	Should you help the wicked and love those who hate the Lord? Because of this, the wrath of the Lord is upon you. There is, however, some good in you, for you have rid the land of the Asherah poles and have set your heart on seeking God.

Cast: **Chronicler, Jehu.** (This reading would normally be linked with the next.)

Jehoshaphat Appoints Judges

2 Chronicles 19:4–11

Chronicler	Jehoshaphat lived in Jerusalem, and he went out again among the people from Beersheba to the hill country of Ephraim and turned them back to the Lord, the God of their fathers. He appointed judges in the land, in each of the fortified cities of Judah.

Jehoshaphat   Consider carefully what you do, because you are not judging for man but for the LORD, who is with you whenever you give a verdict. Now let the fear of the LORD be upon you. Judge carefully, for with the LORD our God there is no injustice or partiality or bribery.

Chronicler   In Jerusalem also, Jehoshaphat appointed some of the Levites, priests and heads of Israelite families to administer the law of the LORD and to settle disputes. And they lived in Jerusalem. He gave them these orders:

Jehoshaphat   You must serve faithfully and wholeheartedly in the fear of the LORD. In every case that comes before you from your fellow countrymen who live in the cities—whether bloodshed or other concerns of the law, commands, decrees or ordinances—you are to warn them not to sin against the LORD; otherwise his wrath will come on you and your brothers. Do this, and you will not sin.

Amariah the chief priest will be over you in any matter concerning the LORD, and Zebadiah son of Ishmael, the leader of the tribe of Judah, will be over you in any matter concerning the king, and the Levites will serve as officials before you. Act with courage, and may the LORD be with those who do well.

Cast: **Chronicler, Jehoshaphat**

Jehoshaphat Defeats Moab and Ammon

From 2 Chronicles 20:1–30

Chronicler   The Moabites and Ammonites with some of the Meunites came to make war on Jehoshaphat. Some men came and told Jehoshaphat:

Messenger   A vast army is coming against you from Edom, from the other side of the Sea. It is already in Hazazon Tamar—

Chronicler   (That is, En Gedi.) Alarmed, Jehoshaphat resolved to inquire of the LORD, and he proclaimed a fast for all Judah. The people of Judah came together to seek help from the LORD; indeed, they came from every town in Judah to seek him.

Then Jehoshaphat stood up in the assembly of Judah and Jerusalem at the temple of the LORD in the front of the new courtyard [and said:]

Jehoshaphat
(praying)   O LORD, God of our fathers, are you not the God who is in heaven? You rule over all the kingdoms of the nations. Power and might are in your hand, and no one can withstand you. O our God, did you not drive out the inhabitants of this land before your people Israel and give it forever to the descendants of Abraham your friend? They have lived in it and have built in it a sanctuary for your Name, saying, "If calamity comes upon us, whether the sword of judgment, or plague or famine, we will

stand in your presence before this temple that bears your Name and will cry out to you in our distress, and you will hear us and save us."

But now here are men from Ammon, Moab and Mount Seir, whose territory you would not allow Israel to invade when they came from Egypt; so they turned away from them and did not destroy them. See how they are repaying us by coming to drive us out of the possession you gave us as an inheritance. O our God, will you not judge them? For we have no power to face this vast army that is attacking us. We do not know what to do, but our eyes are upon you.

Chronicler All the men of Judah, with their wives and children and little ones, stood there before the LORD.

Then the Spirit of the LORD came upon Jahaziel son of Zechariah, the son of Benaiah, the son of Jeiel, the son of Mattaniah, a Levite and descendant of Asaph, as he stood in the assembly.

Jahaziel Listen, King Jehoshaphat and all who live in Judah and Jerusalem! This is what the LORD says to you: "Do not be afraid or discouraged because of this vast army. For the battle is not yours, but God's. Tomorrow march down against them. They will be climbing up by the Pass of Ziz, and you will find them at the end of the gorge in the Desert of Jeruel. You will not have to fight this battle. Take up your positions; stand firm and see the deliverance the LORD will give you, O Judah and Jerusalem. Do not be afraid; do not be discouraged. Go out to face them tomorrow, and the LORD will be with you."

Chronicler Jehoshaphat bowed with his face to the ground, and all the people of Judah and Jerusalem fell down in worship before the LORD. Then some Levites from the Kohathites and Korahites stood up and praised the LORD, the God of Israel, with very loud voice.

Early in the morning they left for the Desert of Tekoa. As they set out, Jehoshaphat stood and said:

Jehoshaphat Listen to me, Judah and people of Jerusalem! Have faith in the LORD your God and you will be upheld; have faith in his prophets and you will be successful.

Chronicler After consulting the people, Jehoshaphat appointed men to sing to the LORD and to praise him for the splendor of his holiness as they went out at the head of the army:

Musician 1 Give thanks to the LORD—

Musician 2 For his love endures forever.

Chronicler As they began to sing and praise, the LORD set ambushes against the men of Ammon and Moab and Mount Seir who were invading Judah, and they were defeated. The men of Ammon and Moab rose up against the men from Mount Seir to destroy and annihilate them. After they finished slaughtering the men from Seir, they helped to destroy one another.

When the men of Judah came to the place that overlooks the desert and looked toward the vast army, they saw only dead bodies lying on the ground; no one had escaped. . . .

Then, led by Jehoshaphat, all the men of Judah and Jerusalem returned joyfully to Jerusalem, for the Lord had given them cause to rejoice over their enemies. They entered Jerusalem and went to the temple of the Lord with harps and lutes and trumpets.

The fear of God came upon all the kingdoms of the countries when they heard how the Lord had fought against the enemies of Israel. And the kingdom of Jehoshaphat was at peace, for his God had given him rest on every side.

Cast: **Chronicler, Messenger, Jehoshaphat, Jahaziel, Musician 1, Musician 2** (can be the same as Messenger; Musician 1 and Musician 2 can also be the same)

Athaliah and Joash

2 Chronicles 22:10–23:15

Chronicler 1 When Athaliah the mother of Ahaziah saw that her son was dead, she proceeded to destroy the whole royal family of the house of Judah. But Jehosheba, the daughter of King Jehoram, took Joash son of Ahaziah and stole him away from among the royal princes who were about to be murdered and put him and his nurse in a bedroom. Because Jehosheba, the daughter of King Jehoram and wife of the priest Jehoiada, was Ahaziah's sister, she hid the child from Athaliah so she could not kill him. He remained hidden with them at the temple of God for six years while Athaliah ruled the land.

Chronicler 2 In the seventh year Jehoiada showed his strength. He made a covenant with the commanders of units of a hundred: Azariah son of Jeroham, Ishmael son of Jehohanan, Azariah son of Obed, Maaseiah son of Adaiah, and Elishaphat son of Zicri. They went throughout Judah and gathered the Levites and the heads of Israelite families from all the towns. When they came to Jerusalem, the whole assembly made a covenant with the king at the temple of God. Jehoiada said to them:

Jehoiada The king's son shall reign, as the Lord promised concerning the descendants of David. Now this is what you are to do: A third of you priests and Levites who are going on duty on the Sabbath are to keep watch at the doors, a third of you at the royal palace and a third at the Foundation Gate, and all the other men are to be in the courtyards of the temple of the Lord. No one is to enter the temple of the Lord except the priests and Levites on duty; they may enter because they are consecrated, but all the other men are to guard what the Lord has assigned to them. The Levites are to station themselves around the king, each man with his weapons in his hand. Anyone who enters the temple must be put to death. Stay close to the king wherever he goes.

Chronicler 2 The Levites and all the men of Judah did just as Jehoiada the priest ordered. Each one took his men—those who were going on duty on the Sabbath and those who were going off duty—for Jehoiada the priest had not released any of the divisions. Then he gave the commanders of units of a hundred the spears and the large and small shields that had belonged to King David and that were in the temple of God. He stationed all the men, each with his weapon in his hand, around the king—near the altar and the temple, from the south side to the north side of the temple.

Jehoiada and his sons brought out the king's son and put the crown on him; they presented him with a copy of the covenant and proclaimed him king. They anointed him and shouted:

**Persons 1
and 2** Long live the king!

Chronicler 1 When Athaliah heard the noise of the people running and cheering the king, she went to them at the temple of the LORD. She looked, and there was the king, standing by his pillar at the entrance. The officers and the trumpeters were beside the king, and all the people of the land were rejoicing and blowing trumpets, and singers with musical instruments were leading the praises. Then Athaliah tore her robes and shouted:

Athaliah Treason! Treason!

Chronicler 2 Jehoiada the priest sent out the commanders of units of a hundred, who were in charge of the troops, and said to them:

Jehoiada Bring her out between the ranks and put to the sword anyone who follows her.

Chronicler 1 For the priest had said:

Jehoiada Do not put her to death at the temple of the LORD.

Chronicler 2 So they seized her as she reached the entrance of the Horse Gate on the palace grounds, and there they put her to death.

Cast: **Chronicler 1, Chronicler 2, Jehoiada, Person 1, Person 2, Athaliah**

Joash Repairs the Temple

2 Chronicles 24:1–14

Chronicler 1 Joash was seven years old when he became king, and he reigned in Jerusalem forty years. His mother's name was Zibiah; she was from Beersheba. Joash did what was right in the eyes of the LORD all the years of Jehoiada the priest. Jehoiada chose two wives for him, and he had sons and daughters.

Chronicler 2   Some time later Joash decided to restore the temple of the Lord. He called together the priests and Levites and said to them:

Joash   Go to the towns of Judah and collect the money due annually from all Israel, to repair the temple of your God. Do it now.

Chronicler 2   But the Levites did not act at once. Therefore the king summoned Jehoiada the chief priest:

Joash   Why haven't you required the Levites to bring in from Judah and Jerusalem the tax imposed by Moses the servant of the Lord and by the assembly of Israel for the Tent of the Testimony?

Commentator   Now the sons of that wicked woman Athaliah had broken into the temple of God and had used even its sacred objects for the Baals.

Chronicler 1   At the king's command, a chest was made and placed outside, at the gate of the temple of the Lord. A proclamation was then issued in Judah and Jerusalem that they should bring to the Lord the tax that Moses the servant of God had required of Israel in the desert. All the officials and all the people brought their contributions gladly, dropping them into the chest until it was full. Whenever the chest was brought in by the Levites to the king's officials and they saw that there was a large amount of money, the royal secretary and the officer of the chief priest would come and empty the chest and carry it back to its place. They did this regularly and collected a great amount of money.

Chronicler 2   The king and Jehoiada gave it to the men who carried out the work required for the temple of the Lord. They hired masons and carpenters to restore the Lord's temple, and also workers in iron and bronze to repair the temple.

The men in charge of the work were diligent, and the repairs progressed under them. They rebuilt the temple of God according to its original design and reinforced it. When they had finished, they brought the rest of the money to the king and Jehoiada, and with it were made articles for the Lord's temple: articles for the service and for the burnt offerings, and also dishes and other objects of gold and silver. As long as Jehoiada lived, burnt offerings were presented continually in the temple of the Lord.

Cast: **Chronicler 1, Chronicler 2, Joash, Commentator**

The Wickedness of Joash

2 Chronicles 24:14–22

Chronicler 1   When they had finished [repairing the temple], they brought the rest of the money to the king and Jehoiada, and with it were made articles for the Lord's temple: articles for the service and for the burnt offerings, and also dishes and other objects of gold and silver. As long as Jehoiada lived, burnt offerings were presented continually in the temple of the Lord.

Chronicler 2   Now Jehoiada was old and full of years, and he died at the age of a hundred and thirty. He was buried with the kings in the City of David, because of the good he had done in Israel for God and his temple.

After the death of Jehoiada, the officials of Judah came and paid homage to the king, and he listened to them. They abandoned the temple of the Lord, the God of their fathers, and worshiped Asherah poles and idols.

Chronicler 1   Because of their guilt, God's anger came upon Judah and Jerusalem. Although the Lord sent prophets to the people to bring them back to him, and though they testified against them, they would not listen.

Then the Spirit of God came upon Zechariah son of Jehoiada the priest. He stood before the people and said:

Zechariah   This is what God says: "Why do you disobey the Lord's commands? You will not prosper. Because you have forsaken the Lord, he has forsaken you."

Chronicler 2   But they plotted against him, and by order of the king they stoned him to death in the courtyard of the Lord's temple. King Joash did not remember the kindness Zechariah's father Jehoiada had shown him but killed his son, who said as he lay dying:

Zechariah   May the Lord see this and call you to account.

Cast: **Chronicler 1, Chronicler 2, Zechariah**

Amaziah King of Judah

2 Chronicles 25:1–4

Chronicler   Amaziah was twenty-five years old when he became king, and he reigned in Jerusalem twenty-nine years. His mother's name was Jehoaddin; she was from Jerusalem. He did what was right in the eyes of the Lord, but not wholeheartedly. After the kingdom was firmly in his control, he executed the officials who had murdered his father the king. Yet he did not put their sons to death, but acted in accordance with what is written in the Law, in the Book of Moses, where the Lord commanded:

The Lord
(voice only)   Fathers shall not be put to death for their children, nor children put to death for their fathers; each is to die for his own sins.

Cast: **Chronicler, the Lord** (voice only)

War against Edom

2 Chronicles 25:5–16

Chronicler   Amaziah called the people of Judah together and assigned them according to their families to commanders of thousands and commanders of hundreds for all Judah and Benjamin. He then mustered those twenty years old or more and found that there were three hundred thousand men ready for military service, able to handle the spear and shield. He also hired a hundred thousand fighting men from Israel for a hundred talents of silver. But a man of God came to him [and said:]

Prophet   O king, these troops from Israel must not march with you, for the LORD is not with Israel—not with any of the people of Ephraim. Even if you go and fight courageously in battle, God will overthrow you before the enemy, for God has the power to help or to overthrow.

Chronicler   Amaziah asked the man of God:

Amaziah   But what about the hundred talents I paid for these Israelite troops?

Prophet   The LORD can give you much more than that.

Chronicler   So Amaziah dismissed the troops who had come to him from Ephraim and sent them home. They were furious with Judah and left for home in a great rage. (PAUSE)

Amaziah then marshaled his strength and led his army to the Valley of Salt, where he killed ten thousand men of Seir. The army of Judah also captured ten thousand men alive, took them to the top of a cliff and threw them down so that all were dashed to pieces.

Meanwhile the troops that Amaziah had sent back and had not allowed to take part in the war raided Judean towns from Samaria to Beth Horon. They killed three thousand people and carried off great quantities of plunder.

When Amaziah returned from slaughtering the Edomites, he brought back the gods of the people of Seir. He set them up as his own gods, bowed down to them and burned sacrifices to them. The anger of the LORD burned against Amaziah, and he sent a prophet to him [who said:]

Prophet   Why do you consult this people's gods, which could not save their own people from your hand?

[Chronicler   While he was still speaking, the king said to him:]

Amaziah
(inter-
rupting)   Have we appointed you an adviser to the king? Stop! Why be struck down?

Chronicler   So the prophet stopped [but said:]

Prophet   I know that God has determined to destroy you, because you have done this and have not listened to my counsel.

Cast: **Chronicler, Prophet, Amaziah**

War against Israel

2 Chronicles 25:17–28

Chronicler   After Amaziah king of Judah consulted his advisers, he sent this challenge to Jehoash son of Jehoahaz, the son of Jehu, king of Israel:

Amaziah   Come, meet me face to face.

Chronicler   But Jehoash king of Israel replied to Amaziah king of Judah:

Jehoash   A thistle in Lebanon sent a message to a cedar in Lebanon, "Give your daughter to my son in marriage." Then a wild beast in Lebanon came along and trampled the thistle underfoot. You say to yourself that you have defeated Edom, and now you are arrogant and proud. But stay at home! Why ask for trouble and cause your own downfall and that of Judah also?

Chronicler   Amaziah, however, would not listen, for God so worked that he might hand them over to ⌞Jehoash⌟, because they sought the gods of Edom. So Jehoash king of Israel attacked. He and Amaziah king of Judah faced each other at Beth Shemesh in Judah. Judah was routed by Israel, and every man fled to his home. Jehoash king of Israel captured Amaziah king of Judah, the son of Joash, the son of Ahaziah, at Beth Shemesh. Then Jehoash brought him to Jerusalem and broke down the wall of Jerusalem from the Ephraim Gate to the Corner Gate—a section about six hundred feet long. He took all the gold and silver and all the articles found in the temple of God that had been in the care of Obed-Edom, together with the palace treasures and the hostages, and returned to Samaria.

Amaziah son of Joash king of Judah lived for fifteen years after the death of Jehoash son of Jehoahaz king of Israel.

Commentator   As for the other events of Amaziah's reign, from beginning to end, are they not written in the book of the kings of Judah and Israel? From the time that Amaziah turned away from following the LORD, they conspired against him in Jerusalem and he fled to Lachish, but they sent men after him to Lachish and killed him there. He was brought back by horse and was buried with his fathers in the City of Judah.

Cast: **Chronicler, Amaziah, Jehoash, Commentator**

Uzziah King of Judah

From 2 Chronicles 26:16–23

Chronicler After Uzziah became powerful, his pride led to his downfall. He was unfaithful to the LORD his God, and entered the temple of the LORD to burn incense on the altar of incense. Azariah the priest with eighty other courageous priests of the LORD followed him in. They confronted him:

Azariah It is not right for you, Uzziah, to burn incense to the LORD. That is for the priests, the descendants of Aaron, who have been consecrated to burn incense. Leave the sanctuary, for you have been unfaithful; and you will not be honored by the LORD God.

Chronicler Uzziah, who had a censer in his hand ready to burn incense, became angry. While he was raging at the priests in their presence before the incense altar in the LORD's temple, leprosy broke out on his forehead. When Azariah the chief priest and all the other priests looked at him, they saw that he had leprosy on his forehead, so they hurried him out. Indeed, he himself was eager to leave, because the LORD had afflicted him.

King Uzziah had leprosy until the day he died. He lived in a separate house—leprous, and excluded from the temple of the LORD. . . . Uzziah rested with his fathers and was buried near them in a field for burial that belonged to the kings, for people said:

Persons 1 and 2 (in awed tones) He had leprosy—

Person 1 Leprosy!

Cast: **Chronicler, Azariah, Person 1, Person 2** (can be the same as Person 1)

The Prophet Oded

2 Chronicles 28:8–15

Chronicler The Israelites took captive from their kinsmen two hundred thousand wives, sons and daughters. They also took a great deal of plunder, which they carried back to Samaria.

But a prophet of the LORD named Oded was there, and he went out to meet the army when it returned to Samaria. He said to them:

Oded Because the LORD, the God of your fathers, was angry with Judah, he gave them into your hand. But you have slaughtered them in a rage that reaches to heaven. And now you intend to make the men and women of Judah and Jerusalem your slaves. But aren't you also guilty of sins against the LORD your God? Now listen to me! Send back your fellow countrymen you have taken as prisoners, for the LORD's fierce anger rests on you.

Chronicler   Then some of the leaders in Ephraim—Azariah son of Jehohanan, Berekiah son of Meshillemoth, Jehizkiah son of Shallum, and Amasa son of Hadlai—confronted those who were arriving from the war:

Leader 1   You must not bring those prisoners here—

Leader 2   Or we will be guilty before the LORD.

Leader 3   Do you intend to add to our sin and guilt?

Leader 4   Our guilt is already great, and his fierce anger rests on Israel.

Chronicler   So the soldiers gave up the prisoners and plunder in the presence of the officials and all the assembly. The men designated by name took the prisoners, and from the plunder they clothed all who were naked. They provided them with clothes and sandals, food and drink, and healing balm. All those who were weak they put on donkeys. So they took them back to their fellow countrymen at Jericho, the City of Palms, and returned to Samaria.

Cast: **Chronicler**, **Oded**, **Leader 1**, **Leader 2**, **Leader 3** (can be the same as Leader 2), **Leader 4** (can be the same as Leader 2, or Leaders 1–4 can be the same)

Hezekiah Purifies the Temple

From 2 Chronicles 29:1–17

Chronicler   Hezekiah was twenty-five years old when he became king, and he reigned in Jerusalem twenty-nine years. His mother's name was Abijah daughter of Zechariah. He did what was right in the eyes of the LORD, just as his father David had done. (PAUSE)

In the first month of the first year of his reign, he opened the doors of the temple of the LORD and repaired them. He brought in the priests and the Levites [and] assembled them in the square on the east side:

Hezekiah   Listen to me, Levites! Consecrate yourselves now and consecrate the temple of the LORD, the God of your fathers. Remove all defilement from the sanctuary. Our fathers were unfaithful; they did evil in the eyes of the LORD our God and forsook him. They turned their faces away from the LORD's dwelling place and turned their backs on him. They also shut the doors of the portico and put out the lamps. They did not burn incense or present any burnt offerings at the sanctuary to the God of Israel. Therefore, the anger of the LORD has fallen on Judah and Jerusalem; he has made them an object of dread and horror and scorn, as you can see with your own eyes. This is why our fathers have fallen by the sword and why our sons and daughters and our wives are in captivity. Now I intend to make a covenant with the LORD, the God of Israel, so that his fierce anger will turn away from us. My sons, do not be negligent now, for the LORD

465

has chosen you to stand before him and serve him, to minister before him and to burn incense.

Chronicler   Then [the] Levites set to work. . . .

When they had assembled their brothers and consecrated themselves, they went in to purify the temple of the LORD, as the king had ordered, following the word of the LORD. The priests went into the sanctuary of the LORD to purify it. They brought out to the courtyard of the LORD's temple everything unclean that they found in the temple of the LORD. The Levites took it and carried it out to the Kidron Valley. They began the consecration on the first day of the first month, and by the eighth day of the month they reached the portico of the LORD. For eight more days they consecrated the temple of the LORD itself, finishing on the sixteenth day of the first month.

Cast: **Chronicler, Hezekiah**

The Temple Is Rededicated

From 2 Chronicles 29:18–36

Chronicler   [The Levites] went in to King Hezekiah and reported:

Levite 1   We have purified the entire temple of the LORD, the altar of burnt offering with all its utensils, and the table for setting out the consecrated bread, with all its articles.

Levite 2   We have prepared and consecrated all the articles that King Ahaz removed in his unfaithfulness while he was king.

Levite 1   They are now in front of the LORD's altar.

Chronicler   Early the next morning King Hezekiah gathered the city officials together and went up to the temple of the LORD. They brought seven bulls, seven rams, seven male lambs and seven male goats as a sin offering for the kingdom, for the sanctuary and for Judah. The king commanded the priests, the descendants of Aaron, to offer these on the altar of the LORD. So they slaughtered the bulls, and the priests took the blood and sprinkled it on the altar; next they slaughtered the rams and sprinkled their blood on the altar; then they slaughtered the lambs and sprinkled their blood on the altar. The goats for the sin offering were brought before the king and the assembly, and they laid their hands on them. The priests then slaughtered the goats and presented their blood on the altar for a sin offering to atone for all Israel, because the king had ordered the burnt offering and the sin offering for all Israel. . . .

The whole assembly bowed in worship, while the singers sang and the trumpeters played. All this continued until the sacrifice of the burnt offering was completed.

When the offerings were finished, the king and everyone present with him knelt down and worshiped. King Hezekiah and his officials ordered the Levites to praise the LORD with the words of David and of Asaph the seer. So they sang praises with gladness and bowed their heads and worshiped. . . . Hezekiah and all the people rejoiced at what God had brought about for his people, because it was done so quickly.

Cast: **Chronicler, Levite 1, Levite 2** (can be the same as Levite 1)

Preparations for Passover

2 Chronicles 30:1–12

Chronicler Hezekiah sent word to all Israel and Judah and also wrote letters to Ephraim and Manasseh, inviting them to come to the temple of the LORD in Jerusalem and celebrate the Passover to the LORD, the God of Israel. The king and his officials and the whole assembly in Jerusalem decided to celebrate the Passover in the second month. They had not been able to celebrate it at the regular time because not enough priests had consecrated themselves and the people had not assembled in Jerusalem. The plan seemed right both to the king and to the whole assembly. They decided to send a proclamation throughout Israel, from Beersheba to Dan, calling the people to come to Jerusalem and celebrate the Passover to the LORD, the God of Israel. It had not been celebrated in large numbers according to what was written.

At the king's command, couriers went throughout Israel and Judah with letters from the king and from his officials:

Courier 1 People of Israel, return to the LORD, the God of Abraham, Isaac and Israel, that he may return to you who are left, who have escaped from the hand of the kings of Assyria. Do not be like your fathers and brothers, who were unfaithful to the LORD, the God of their fathers, so that he made them an object of horror, as you see. Do not be stiff-necked, as your fathers were; submit to the LORD. Come to the sanctuary, which he has consecrated forever. Serve the LORD your God, so that his fierce anger will turn away from you.

Courier 2 If you return to the LORD, then your brothers and your children will be shown compassion by their captors and will come back to this land, for the LORD your God is gracious and compassionate. He will not turn his face from you if you return to him.

Chronicler The couriers went from town to town in Ephraim and Manasseh, as far as Zebulun, but the people scorned and ridiculed them. Nevertheless, some men of Asher, Manasseh and Zebulun humbled themselves and went to Jerusalem. Also in Judah the hand of God was on the people to give them unity of mind to carry out what the king and his officials had ordered, following the word of the LORD.

Cast: **Chronicler, Courier 1, Courier 2**

Hezekiah Celebrates the Passover

2 Chronicles 30:13–22

Chronicler   A very large crowd of people assembled in Jerusalem to celebrate the Feast of Unleavened Bread in the second month. They removed the altars in Jerusalem and cleared away the incense altars and threw them into the Kidron Valley.

They slaughtered the Passover lamb on the fourteenth day of the second month. The priests and the Levites were ashamed and consecrated themselves and brought burnt offerings to the temple of the LORD. Then they took up their regular positions as prescribed in the Law of Moses the man of God. The priests sprinkled the blood handed to them by the Levites. Since many in the crowd had not consecrated themselves, the Levites had to kill the Passover lambs for all those who were not ceremonially clean and could not consecrate ˻their lambs˼ to the LORD. Although most of the many people who came from Ephraim, Manasseh, Issachar and Zebulun had not purified themselves, yet they ate the Passover, contrary to what was written. But Hezekiah prayed for them:

Hezekiah
(praying)   May the LORD, who is good, pardon everyone who sets his heart on seeking God—the LORD, the God of his fathers—even if he is not clean according to the rules of the sanctuary.

Chronicler   And the LORD heard Hezekiah and healed the people.

The Israelites who were present in Jerusalem celebrated the Feast of Unleavened Bread for seven days with great rejoicing, while the Levites and priests sang to the LORD every day, accompanied by the LORD's instruments of praise.

Hezekiah spoke encouragingly to all the Levites, who showed good understanding of the service of the LORD. For the seven days they ate their assigned portion and offered fellowship offerings and praised the LORD, the God of their fathers.

Cast: **Chronicler, Hezekiah**

At the Feast of Unleavened Bread

From 2 Chronicles 30:24–31:21

Chronicler 1   Hezekiah king of Judah provided a thousand bulls and seven thousand sheep and goats for the assembly, and the officials provided them with a thousasnd bulls and ten thousand sheep and goats. A great number of priests consecrated themselves.

468

Chronicler 2   The entire assembly of Judah rejoiced, along with the priests and Levites and all who had assembled from Israel, including the aliens who had come from Israel and those who lived in Judah.

Chronicler 1   There was great joy in Jerusalem, for since the days of Solomon son of David king of Israel there had been nothing like this in Jerusalem. The priests and the Levites stood to bless the people, and God heard them, for their prayer reached heaven, his holy dwelling place.

Chronicler 2   When all this had ended, the Israelites who were there went out to the towns of Judah, smashed the sacred stones and cut down the Asherah poles. They destroyed the high places and the altars throughout Judah and Benjamin and in Ephraim and Manasseh. After they had destroyed all of them, the Israelites returned to their own towns and to their own property.

Chronicler 1   Hezekiah assigned the priests and Levites to divisions—each of them according to their duties as priests or Levites—to offer burnt offerings and fellowship offerings, to minister, to give thanks and to sing praises at the gates of the LORD's dwelling. The king contributed from his own possessions for the morning and evening burnt offerings and for the burnt offerings on the Sabbaths, New Moons and appointed feasts as written in the Law of the LORD. He ordered the people living in Jerusalem to give the portion due the priests and Levites so they could devote themselves to the Law of the LORD. As soon as the order went out, the Israelites generously gave the firstfruits of their grain, new wine, oil and honey and all that the fields produced. They brought a great amount, a tithe of everything. . . .

Chronicler 2   They began doing this in the third month and finished in the seventh month. When Hezekiah and his officials came and saw the heaps, they praised the LORD and blessed his people Israel.

Hezekiah asked the priests and Levites about the heaps; and Azariah the chief priest, from the family of Zadok, answered:

Azariah   Since the people began to bring their contributions to the temple of the LORD, we have had enough to eat and plenty to spare, because the LORD has blessed his people, and this great amount is left over.

Hezekiah gave orders to prepare storerooms in the temple of the LORD, and this was done. Then they faithfully brought in the contributions, tithes and dedicated gifts. . . .

Chronicler 1   This is what Hezekiah did throughout Judah, doing what was good and right and faithful before the LORD his God. In everything that he undertook in the service of God's temple and in obedience to the law and the commands, he sought his God and worked wholeheartedly. And so he prospered.

Cast: **Chronicler 1, Chronicler 2, Azariah.** (Please note: This reading overlaps with the next one.)

Sennacherib Threatens Jerusalem

From 2 Chronicles 31:[20–21]–32:23

Chronicler	[This is what Hezekiah did throughout Judah, doing what was good and right and faithful before the Lord his God. In everything that he undertook in the service of God's temple and in obedience to the law and the commands, he sought his God and worked wholeheartedly. And so he prospered.]

After all that Hezekiah had so faithfully done, Sennacherib king of Assyria came and invaded Judah. He laid siege to the fortified cities, thinking to conquer them for himself. When Hezekiah saw that Sennacherib had come and that he intended to make war on Jerusalem, he consulted with his officials and military staff about blocking off the water from the springs outside the city, and they helped him. A large force of men assembled, and they blocked all the springs and the stream that flowed through the land. "Why should the kings of Assyria come and find plenty of water?" they said. Then he worked hard repairing all the broken sections of the wall and building towers on it. He built another wall outside that one and reinforced the supporting terraces of the City of David. He also made large numbers of weapons and shields.

He appointed military officers over the people and assembled them before him in the square at the city gate and encouraged them [with these words:]

Hezekiah	Be strong and courageous. Do not be afraid or discouraged because of the king of Assyria and the vast army with him, for there is a greater power with us than with him. With him is only the arm of flesh, but with us is the Lord our God to help us and to fight our battles.
Chronicler	And the people gained confidence from what Hezekiah the king of Judah said.

Later, when Sennacherib king of Assyria and all his forces were laying siege to Lachish, he sent his officers to Jerusalem with this message for Hezekiah king of Judah and for all the people of Judah who were there:

Sennacherib	This is what Sennacherib king of Assyria says: On what are you basing your confidence, that you remain in Jerusalem under siege? When Hezekiah says, "The Lord our God will save us from the hand of the king of Assyria," he is misleading you, to let you die of hunger and thirst. Did not Hezekiah himself remove this god's high places and altars, saying to Judah and Jerusalem, "You must worship before one altar and burn sacrifices on it"?

Do you not know what I and my fathers have done to all the peoples of the other lands? Were the gods of those nations ever able to deliver their land from my hand? Who of all the gods of these nations that my fathers destroyed has been able to save his people from me? How then can your god deliver you from my hand? Now do not let Hezekiah deceive you and mislead you like this. Do not believe him, for no god of any nation or kingdom has been able to deliver his people from my hand or the hand of my fathers. How much less will your god deliver you from my hand! . . . Just as the gods of the peoples of the other lands did not rescue their people from my hand, so the god of Hezekiah will not rescue his people from my hand.

Chronicler   Then they called out in Hebrew to the people of Jerusalem who were on the wall, to terrify them and make them afraid in order to capture the city. They spoke about the God of Jerusalem as they did about the gods of the other peoples of the world—the work of men's hands.

King Hezekiah and the prophet Isaiah son of Amoz cried out in prayer to heaven about this. And the LORD sent an angel, who annihilated all the fighting men and the leaders and officers in the camp of the Assyrian king. So he withdrew to his own land in disgrace. And when he went into the temple of his god, some of his sons cut him down with the sword.

So the LORD saved Hezekiah and the people of Jerusalem from the hand of Sennacherib king of Assyria and from the hand of all others. He took care of them on every side. Many brought offerings to Jerusalem for the LORD and valuable gifts for Hezekiah king of Judah. From then on he was highly regarded by all the nations.

Cast: **Chronicler, Hezekiah, Sennacherib.** (Please note: This reading overlaps with the previous one.)

Manasseh King of Judah

2 Chronicles 33:1–13

Chronicler   Manasseh was twelve years old when he became king, and he reigned in Jerusalem fifty-five years. He did evil in the eyes of the LORD, following the detestable practices of the nations the LORD had driven out before the Israelites. He rebuilt the high places his father Hezekiah had demolished; he also erected altars to the Baals and made Asherah poles. He bowed down to all the starry hosts and worshiped them. He built altars in the temple of the LORD, of which the LORD had said:

The Lord
(voice only)   My Name will remain in Jerusalem forever.

Chronicler   In both courts of the temple of the LORD, he built altars to all the starry hosts. He sacrificed his sons in the fire in the Valley of Ben Hinnom, practiced sorcery, divination and witchcraft, and consulted mediums and spiritists. He did much evil in the eyes of the LORD, provoking him to anger.

He took the carved image he had made and put it in God's temple, of which God had said to David and to his son Solomon:

471

The Lord
(voice)

In this temple and in Jerusalem, which I have chosen out of all the tribes of Israel, I will put my Name forever. I will not again make the feet of the Israelites leave the land I assigned to your forefathers, if only they will be careful to do everything I commanded them concerning all the laws, decrees and ordinances given through Moses.

Chronicler

But Manasseh led Judah and the people of Jerusalem astray, so that they did more evil than the nations the Lord had destroyed before the Israelites.

The Lord spoke to Manasseh and his people, but they paid no attention. So the Lord brought against them the army commanders of the king of Assyria, who took Manasseh prisoner, put a hook in his nose, bound him with bronze shackles and took him to Babylon. In his distress he sought the favor of the Lord his God and humbled himself greatly before the God of his fathers. And when he prayed to him, the Lord was moved by his entreaty and listened to his plea; so he brought him back to Jerusalem and to his kingdom. Then Manasseh knew that the Lord is God.

Cast: **Chronicler, the Lord** (voice only)

The Book of the Law Found

From 2 Chronicles 34:1–21 [22–31]

Chronicler

Josiah was eight years old when he became king, and he reigned in Jerusalem thirty-one years. He did what was right in the eyes of the Lord and walked in the ways of his father David, not turning aside to the right or to the left. . . .

In the eighteenth year of Josiah's reign, to purify the land and the temple, he sent Shaphan son of Azaliah and Maaseiah the ruler of the city, with Joah son of Joahaz, the recorder, to repair the temple of the Lord his God.

They went to Hilkiah the high priest and gave him the money that had been brought into the temple of God, which the Levites who were the doorkeepers had collected from the people of Manasseh, Ephraim and the entire remnant of Israel and from all the people of Judah and Benjamin and the inhabitants of Jerusalem. Then they entrusted it to the men appointed to supervise the work on the Lord's temple. . . . They also gave money to the carpenters and builders to purchase dressed stone, and timber for joists and beams for the buildings that the kings of Judah had allowed to fall into ruin. . . .

While they were bringing out the money that had been taken into the temple of the Lord, Hilkiah the priest found the Book of the Law of the Lord that had been given through Moses. Hilkiah said to Shaphan the secretary:

Hilkiah (to Shaphan)	I have found the Book of the Law in the temple of the LORD.
Chronicler	He gave it to Shaphan. Then Shaphan took the book to the king [and reported to him:]
Shaphan	Your officials are doing everything that has been committed to them. They have paid out the money that was in the temple of the LORD and have entrusted it to the supervisors and workers. . . . (PAUSE) Hilkiah the priest has given me a book.
Chronicler	And Shaphan read from it in the presence of the king.
	When the king heard the words of the Law, he tore his robes. He gave these orders to Hilkiah, Ahikam son of Shaphan, Abdon son of Micah, Shaphan the secretary and Asaiah the king's attendant:
Josiah	Go and inquire of the LORD for me and for the remnant in Israel and Judah about what is written in this book that has been found. Great is the LORD's anger that is poured out on us because our fathers have not kept the word of the LORD; they have not acted in accordance with all that is written in this book.
[Chronicler	Hilkiah and those the king had sent with him went to speak to the prophetess Huldah, who was the wife of Shallum son of Tokhath, the son of Hasrah, keeper of the wardrobe. She lived in Jerusalem, in the Second District. She said to them:
Huldah	This is what the LORD, the God of Israel, says: Tell the man who sent you to me: "This is what the LORD says":
The Lord (voice only)	I am going to bring disaster on this place and its people—all the curses written in the book that has been read in the presence of the king of Judah. Because they have forsaken me and burned incense to other gods and provoked me to anger by all that their hands have made, my anger will be poured out on this place and will not be quenched.
Huldah	Tell the king of Judah, who sent you to inquire of the LORD: "This is what the LORD, the God of Israel, says concerning the words you heard":
The Lord (voice)	Because your heart was responsive and you humbled yourself before God when you heard what he spoke against this place and its people, and because you humbled yourself before me and tore your robes and wept in my presence, I have heard you. . . . Now I will gather you to your fathers, and you will be buried in peace. Your eyes will not see all the disaster I am going to bring on this place and on those who live here.
Chronicler	So they took her answer back to the king. (PAUSE)
	Then the king called together all the elders of Judah and Jerusalem. He went up to the temple of the LORD with the men of Judah, the people of Jerusalem, the priests and the Levites—all the people from the least to

the greatest. He read in their hearing all the words of the Book of the Covenant, which had been found in the temple of the LORD. The king stood by his pillar and renewed the covenant in the presence of the LORD—to follow the LORD and keep his commands, regulations and decrees with all his heart and all his soul, and to obey the words of the covenant written in this book.]

Cast: **Chronicler, Hilkiah, Shaphan, Josiah, Huldah, the Lord** (voice only)

The Death of Josiah

2 Chronicles 35:20–27

Chronicler   When Josiah had set the temple in order, Neco king of Egypt went up to fight at Carchemish on the Euphrates, and Josiah marched out to meet him in battle. But Neco sent messengers to him, saying:

Neco   What quarrel is there between you and me, O king of Judah? It is not you I am attacking at this time, but the house with which I am at war. God has told me to hurry; so stop opposing God, who is with me, or he will destroy you.

Chronicler   Josiah, however, would not turn away from him, but disguised himself to engage him in battle. He would not listen to what Neco had said at God's command but went to fight him on the plain of Megiddo. (PAUSE)

Archers shot King Josiah, and he told his officers:

Josiah   Take me away; I am badly wounded.

Chronicler   So they took him out of his chariot, put him in the other chariot he had and brought him to Jerusalem, where he died. He was buried in the tombs of his fathers, and all Judah and Jerusalem mourned for him.

Commentator   Jeremiah composed laments for Josiah, and to this day all the men and women singers commemorate Josiah in the laments. These became a tradition in Israel and are written in the Laments.

The other events of Josiah's reign and his acts of devotion, according to what is written in the Law of the LORD—all the events, from beginning to end, are written in the book of the kings of Israel and Judah.

Cast: **Chronicler, Neco, Josiah, Commentator** (can be the same as Chronicler)

Ezra

Cyrus Helps the Exiles to Return

Ezra 1:1–11

Narrator 1   In the first year of Cyrus king of Persia, in order to fulfill the word of the LORD spoken by Jeremiah, the LORD moved the heart of Cyrus king of Persia to make a proclamation throughout his realm and to put it in writing. This is what Cyrus king of Persia says:

Cyrus   The LORD, the God of heaven, has given me all the kingdoms of the earth and he has appointed me to build a temple for him at Jerusalem in Judah. Anyone of his people among you—may his God be with him, and let him go up to Jerusalem in Judah and build the temple of the LORD, the God of Israel, the God who is in Jerusalem. And the people of any place where survivors may now be living are to provide him with silver and gold, with goods and livestock, and with freewill offerings for the temple of God in Jerusalem.

Narrator 2   Then the family heads of Judah and Benjamin, and the priests and Levites—everyone whose heart God had moved—prepared to go up and build the house of the LORD in Jerusalem. All their neighbors assisted them with articles of silver and gold, with goods and livestock, and with valuable gifts, in addition to all the freewill offerings. Moreover, King Cyrus brought out the articles belonging to the temple of the LORD, which Nebuchadnezzar had carried away from Jerusalem and had placed in the temple of his god.

Narrator 1   Cyrus king of Persia had them brought by Mithredath the treasurer, who counted them out to Sheshbazzar the prince of Judah.

This was the inventory:

gold dishes—

Narrator 2   30

Narrator 1   silver dishes—

Narrator 2   1,000

Narrator 1   silver pans—

Narrator 2   29

Narrator 1   gold bowls—

Narrator 2   30

Narrator 1   matching silver bowls—

Narrator 2   410

Narrator 1	other articles—
Narrator 2	1,000.

In all, there were 5,400 articles of gold and of silver. Sheshbazzar brought all these along when the exiles came up from Babylon to Jerusalem.

Cast: **Narrator 1, Cyrus, Narrator 2** (with pen and paper)

Rebuilding the Temple

Ezra 3:7–13

Narrator 1	[Jeshua son of Jozadak and his fellow priests and Zerubbabel son of Shealtiel and his associates] gave money to the masons and carpenters, and gave food and drink and oil to the people of Sidon and Tyre, so that they would bring cedar logs by sea from Lebanon to Joppa, as authorized by Cyrus king of Persia.
Narrator 2	In the second month of the second year after their arrival at the house of God in Jerusalem, Zerubbabel son of Shealtiel, Jeshua son of Jozadak and the rest of their brothers—
Commentator	(The priests and the Levites and all who had returned from the captivity to Jerusalem)—
Narrator 2	Began the work, appointing Levites twenty years of age and older to supervise the building of the house of the LORD.
Narrator 1	Jeshua and his sons and brothers and Kadmiel and his sons—
Commentator	(Descendants of Hodaviah)—
Narrator 1	And the sons of Henadad and their sons and brothers—all Levites—joined together in supervising those working on the house of God.
Narrator 2	When the builders laid the foundation of the temple of the LORD, the priests in their vestments and with trumpets, and the Levites—
Commentator	(The sons of Asaph)—
Narrator 2	With cymbals, took their places to praise the LORD, as prescribed by David king of Israel. With praise and thanksgiving they sang to the LORD:
Singers 1 and 2	He is good.
Singer 1	His love to Israel endures forever.
Narrator 1	And all the people gave a great shout of praise to the LORD, because the foundation of the house of the LORD was laid.

476

Narrator 2	But many of the older priests and Levites and family heads, who had seen the former temple, wept aloud when they saw the foundation of this temple being laid—
Narrator 1	While many others shouted for joy.
Narrator 2	No one could distinguish the sound of the shouts of joy from the sound of weeping, because the people made so much noise. And the sound was heard far away.

Cast: **Narrator 1, Narrator 2, Commentator, Singer 1, Singer 2** (can be the same as Commentator)

Opposition to the Rebuilding of the Temple

Ezra 4:1–5

Narrator	When the enemies of Judah and Benjamin heard that the exiles were building a temple for the LORD, the God of Israel, they came to Zerubbabel and to the heads of the families:
Enemy 1	Let us help you build.
Enemy 2	Like you, we seek your God and have been sacrificing to him since the time of Esarhaddon king of Assyria, who brought us here.
Narrator	But Zerubbabel, Jeshua and the rest of the heads of the families of Israel answered:
Zerubbabel	You have no part with us in building a temple to our God.
Jeshua	We alone will build it for the LORD, the God of Israel, as King Cyrus, the king of Persia, commanded us.
Narrator	Then the peoples around them set out to discourage the people of Judah and make them afraid to go on building. They hired counselors to work against them and frustrate their plans during the entire reign of Cyrus king of Persia and down to the reign of Darius king of Persia.

Cast: **Narrator, Enemy 1, Enemy 2** (can be the same as Enemy 1), **Zerubbabel, Jeshua** (can be the same as Zerubbabel)

Opposition to the Rebuilding of Jerusalem

From Ezra 4:6–23

Narrator	At the beginning of the reign of Xerxes, [the peoples around them] lodged an accusation against the people of Judah and Jerusalem. . . .
	Rehum the commanding officer and Shimshai the secretary wrote a letter against Jerusalem to Artaxerxes the king as follows: . . .

Shimshai	To King Artaxerxes,
	From your servants, the men of Trans-Euphrates:
Rehum	The king should know that the Jews who came up to us from you have gone to Jerusalem and are rebuilding that rebellious and wicked city.
Shimshai	They are restoring the walls and repairing the foundations.
Rehum	Furthermore, the king should know that if this city is built and its walls are restored, no more taxes, tribute or duty will be paid, and the royal revenues will suffer. . . .
Shimshai	In these records you will find that this city is a rebellious city, troublesome to kings and provinces, a place of rebellion from ancient times. That is why this city was destroyed.
Rehum	We inform the king that if this city is built and its walls are restored, you will be left with nothing in Trans-Euphrates.
Narrator	The king sent this reply: . . .
King	I issued an order and a search was made, and it was found that this city has a long history of revolt against kings and has been a place of rebellion and sedition. Jerusalem has had powerful kings ruling over the whole of Trans-Euphrates, and taxes, tribute and duty were paid to them. Now issue an order to these men to stop work, so that this city will not be rebuilt until I so order. Be careful not to neglect this matter. Why let this threat grow, to the detriment of the royal interests?
Narrator	As soon as the copy of the letter of King Artaxerxes was read to Rehum and Shimshai the secretary and their associates, they went immediately to the Jews in Jerusalem and compelled them by force to stop.

Cast: **Narrator, Shimshai, Rehum, King**

Tattenai's Letter to Darius

Ezra 4:24–5:17

Narrator	The work on the house of God in Jerusalem came to a standstill until the second year of the reign of Darius king of Persia.
	Now Haggai the prophet and Zechariah the prophet, a descendant of Iddo, prophesied to the Jews in Judah and Jerusalem in the name of the God of Israel, who was over them. Then Zerubbabel son of Shealtiel and Jeshua son of Jozadak set to work to rebuild the house of God in Jerusalem. And the prophets of God were with them, helping them.
	At that time Tattenai, governor of Trans-Euphrates, and Shethar-Bozenai and their associates went to them and asked:
Tattenai	Who authorized you to rebuild this temple and restore this structure?

Shethar-Bozenai	What are the names of the men constructing this building?
Narrator	But the eye of their God was watching over the elders of the Jews, and they were not stopped until a report could go to Darius and his written reply be received.
	This is a copy of the letter that Tattenai, governor of Trans-Euphrates, and Shethar-Bozenai and their associates, the officials of Trans-Euphrates, sent to King Darius. The report they sent him read as follows:
Tattenai	To King Darius:
	Cordial greetings.
	The king should know that we went to the district of Judah, to the temple of the great God. The people are building it with large stones and placing the timbers in the walls. The work is being carried on with diligence and is making rapid progress under their direction. We questioned the elders:
Shethar-Bozenai	Who authorized you to rebuild this temple and restore this structure?
Tattenai	We also asked them their names, so that we could write down the names of their leaders for your information.
Shethar-Bozenai	This is the answer they gave us:
Elder 1	We are the servants of the God of heaven and earth, and we are rebuilding the temple that was built many years ago, one that a great king of Israel built and finished.
Elder 2	But because our fathers angered the God of heaven, he handed them over to Nebuchadnezzar the Chaldean, king of Babylon, who destroyed this temple and deported the people to Babylon.
Elder 1	However, in the first year of Cyrus king of Babylon, King Cyrus issued a decree to rebuild this house of God.
Elder 2	He even removed from the temple of Babylon the gold and silver articles of the house of God, which Nebuchadnezzar had taken from the temple in Jerusalem and brought to the temple in Babylon.
Elder 1	Then King Cyrus gave them to a man named Sheshbazzar, whom he had appointed governor, and he told him:
Cyrus	Take these articles and go and deposit them in the temple in Jerusalem. And rebuild the house of God on its site.
Elder 1	So this Sheshbazzar came and laid the foundations of the house of God in Jerusalem.
Elder 2	From that day to the present it has been under construction but is not yet finished.

Tattenai	Now if it pleases the king, let a search be made in the royal archives of Babylon to see if King Cyrus did in fact issue a decree to rebuild this house of God in Jerusalem.
Shethar-Bozenai	Then let the king send us his decision in this matter.

Cast: **Narrator, Tattenai, Shethar-Bozenai, Elder 1, Elder 2** (can be the same as Elder 1), **Cyrus**

The Decree of Darius

Ezra 6:1–12

Narrator	King Darius then issued an order, and they searched in the archives stored in the treasury at Babylon. A scroll was found in the citadel of Ecbatana in the province of Media, and this was written on it:
Reader	Memorandum: In the first year of King Cyrus, the king issued a decree concerning the temple of God in Jerusalem:
	Let the temple be rebuilt as a place to present sacrifices, and let its foundations be laid. It is to be ninety feet high and ninety feet wide, with three courses of large stones and one of timbers. The costs are to be paid by the royal treasury. Also, the gold and silver articles of the house of God, which Nebuchadnezzar took from the temple in Jerusalem and brought to Babylon, are to be returned to their places in the temple in Jerusalem; they are to be deposited in the house of God.
[Narrator	Then Darius sent the following reply:]
Darius	Now then, Tattenai, governor of Trans-Euphrates, and Shethar-Bozenai and you, their fellow officials of that province, stay away from there. Do not interfere with the work on this temple of God. Let the governor of the Jews and the Jewish elders rebuild this house of God on its site.
	Moreover, I hereby decree what you are to do for these elders of the Jews in the construction of this house of God:
	The expenses of these men are to be fully paid out of the royal treasury, from the revenues of Trans-Euphrates, so that the work will not stop. Whatever is needed—young bulls, rams, male lambs for burnt offerings to the God of heaven, and wheat, salt, wine and oil, as requested by the priests in Jerusalem—must be given them daily without fail, so that they may offer sacrifices pleasing to the God of heaven and pray for the well-being of the king and his sons.
	Furthermore, I decree that if anyone changes this edict, a beam is to be pulled from his house and he is to be lifted up and impaled on it. And for this crime his house is to be made a pile of rubble. May God, who has

caused his Name to dwell there, overthrow any king or people who lifts a hand to change this decree or to destroy this temple in Jerusalem.

I Darius have decreed it. Let it be carried out with diligence.

Cast: **Narrator, Reader, Darius**

King Artaxerxes' Letter to Ezra

From Ezra 7:11–28

Narrator   This is a copy of the letter King Artaxerxes had given to Ezra the priest and teacher, a man learned in matters concerning the commands and decrees of the LORD for Israel:

Artaxerxes   [From] Artaxerxes, king of kings,

To Ezra the priest, a teacher of the Law of the God of heaven:

Greetings.

Now I decree that any of the Israelites in my kingdom, including priests and Levites, who wish to go to Jerusalem with you, may go. You are sent by the king and his seven advisers to inquire about Judah and Jerusalem with regard to the Law of your God, which is in your hand. Moreover, you are to take with you the silver and gold that the king and his advisers have freely given to the God of Israel, whose dwelling is in Jerusalem, together with all the silver and gold you may obtain from the province of Babylon, as well as the freewill offerings of the people and priests for the temple of their God in Jerusalem. With this money be sure to buy bulls, rams and male lambs, together with their grain offerings and drink offerings, and sacrifice them on the altar of the temple of your God in Jerusalem.

You and your brother Jews may then do whatever seems best with the rest of the silver and gold, in accordance with the will of your God. Deliver to the God of Jerusalem all the articles entrusted to you for worship in the temple of your God. And anything else needed for the temple of your God that you may have occasion to supply, you may provide from the royal treasury.

Now I, King Artaxerxes, order all the treasurers of Trans-Euphrates to provide with diligence whatever Ezra the priest, a teacher of the Law of the God of heaven, may ask of you. . . . Why should there be wrath against the realm of the king and of his sons? . . .

And you, Ezra, in accordance with the wisdom of your God, which you possess, appoint magistrates and judges to administer justice to all the people of Trans-Euphrates—all who know the laws of your God. And you are to teach any who do not know them. Whoever does not obey the law of your God and the law of the king must surely be punished by death, banishment, confiscation of property, or imprisonment.

Ezra
(praying)   Praise be to the LORD, the God of our fathers, who has put it into the king's heart to bring honor to the house of the LORD in Jerusalem in this way and who has extended his good favor to me before the king and his advisers and all the king's powerful officials.

(to audience) Because the hand of the LORD my God was on me, I took courage and gathered leading men from Israel to go up with me.

Cast: **Narrator, Artaxerxes, Ezra**

Ezra's Prayer about Intermarriage

From Ezra 9:1–15

Ezra   [Some of] the leaders came to me [and said:]

Leader 1   The people of Israel, including the priests and the Levites, have not kept themselves separate from the neighboring peoples with their detestable practices. . . .

Leader 2   They have taken some of their daughters as wives for themselves and their sons, and have mingled the holy race with the peoples around them. And the leaders and officials have led the way in this unfaithfulness.

Ezra   When I heard this, I tore my tunic and cloak, pulled hair from my head and beard and sat down appalled. Then everyone who trembled at the words of the God of Israel gathered around me because of this unfaithfulness of the exiles. And I sat there appalled until the evening sacrifice.

Then, at the evening sacrifice, I rose from my self-abasement, with my tunic and cloak torn, and fell on my knees with my hands spread out to the LORD my God [and prayed:]

Younger Ezra
(praying)   O my God, I am too ashamed and disgraced to lift up my face to you, my God, because our sins are higher than our heads and our guilt has reached to the heavens. From the days of our forefathers until now, our guilt has been great. Because of our sins, we and our kings and our priests have been subjected to the sword and captivity, to pillage and humiliation at the hand of foreign kings, as it is today.

But now, for a brief moment, the LORD our God has been gracious in leaving us a remnant and giving us a firm place in his sanctuary, and so our God gives light to our eyes and a little relief in our bondage. Though we are slaves, our God has not deserted us in our bondage. He has shown us kindness in the sight of the kings of Persia: He has granted us new life to

482

rebuild the house of our God and repair its ruins, and he has given us a wall of protection in Judah and Jerusalem.

But now, O our God, what can we say after this? For we have disregarded the commands you gave through your servants the prophets [when you said:

The Lord
(voice only) The land you are entering to possess is a land polluted by the corruption of its peoples. By their detestable practices they have filled it with their impurity from one end to the other. Therefore, do not give your daughters in marriage to their sons or take their daughters for your sons. Do not seek a treaty of friendship with them at any time, that you may be strong and eat the good things of the land and leave it to your children as an everlasting inheritance.

Younger Ezra What has happened to us is a result of our evil deeds and our great guilt, and yet, our God, you have punished us less than our sins have deserved and have given us a remnant like this.] . . . O LORD, God of Israel, you are righteous! We are left this day as a remnant. Here we are before you in our guilt, though because of it not one of us can stand in your presence.

Cast: **Ezra, Leader 1, Leader 2, Younger Ezra, the Lord** (voice only)

The People's Confession of Sin

Ezra 10:1–17

Narrator While Ezra was praying and confessing, weeping and throwing himself down before the house of God, a large crowd of Israelites—men, women and children—gathered around him. They too wept bitterly. Then Shecaniah son of Jehiel, one of the descendants of Elam, said to Ezra:

Shecaniah We have been unfaithful to our God by marrying foreign women from the peoples around us. But in spite of this, there is still hope for Israel. Now let us make a covenant before our God to send away all these women and their children, in accordance with the counsel of my lord and of those who fear the commands of our God. Let it be done according to the Law. Rise up; this matter is in your hands. We will support you, so take courage and do it.

Narrator So Ezra rose up and put the leading priests and Levites and all Israel under oath to do what had been suggested. And they took the oath. Then Ezra withdrew from before the house of God and went to the room of Jehohanan son of Eliashib. While he was there, he ate no food and drank no water, because he continued to mourn over the unfaithfulness of the exiles.

A proclamation was then issued throughout Judah and Jerusalem for all the exiles to assemble in Jerusalem. Anyone who failed to appear within three days would forfeit all his property, in accordance with the decision of the officials and elders, and would himself be expelled from the assembly of the exiles.

Within the three days, all the men of Judah and Benjamin had gathered in Jerusalem. And on the twentieth day of the ninth month, all the people were sitting in the square before the house of God, greatly distressed by the occasion and because of the rain. Then Ezra the priest stood up and said to them:

Ezra　　You have been unfaithful; you have married foreign women, adding to Israel's guilt. Now make confession to the Lord, the God of your fathers, and do his will. Separate yourselves from the peoples around you and from your foreign wives.

Narrator　　The whole assembly responded with a loud voice:

Persons 1　　You are right!

Person 2　　We must do as you say.

Person 1　　But there are many people here and it is the rainy season; so we cannot stand outside.

Person 2　　Besides, this matter cannot be taken care of in a day or two, because we have sinned greatly in this thing.

Person 1　　Let our officials act for the whole assembly.

Person 2　　Then let everyone in our towns who has married a foreign woman come at a set time, along with the elders and judges of each town—

Person 1　　Until the fierce anger of our God in this matter is turned away from us.

Narrator　　Only Jonathan son of Asahel and Jahzeiah son of Tikvah, supported by Meshullam and Shabbethai the Levite, opposed this.

So the exiles did as was proposed. Ezra the priest selected men who were family heads, one from each family division, and all of them designated by name. On the first day of the tenth month they sat down to investigate the cases, and by the first day of the first month they finished dealing with all the men who had married foreign women.

Cast: **Narrator, Shecaniah, Ezra, Person 1, Person 2** (can be the same as Person 1)

Nehemiah

Nehemiah's Prayer

Nehemiah 1:1–11

**Old
Nehemiah**   In the month of Kislev in the twentieth year, while I was in the citadel of Susa, Hanani, one of my brothers, came from Judah with some other men, and I questioned them about the Jewish remnant that survived the exile, and also about Jerusalem. They said to me:

Man 1   Those who survived the exile and are back in the province are in great trouble and disgrace.

Man 2   The wall of Jerusalem is broken down, and its gates have been burned with fire.

**Old
Nehemiah**   When I heard these things, I sat down and wept. (PAUSE) For some days I mourned and fasted and prayed before the God of heaven. Then I said:

**Young
Nehemiah**
(praying)   O LORD, God of heaven, the great and awesome God, who keeps his covenant of love with those who love him and obey his commands, let your ear be attentive and your eyes open to hear the prayer your servant is praying before you day and night for your servants, the people of Israel. I confess the sins we Israelites, including myself and my father's house, have committed against you. We have acted very wickedly toward you. We have not obeyed the commands, decrees and laws you gave your servant Moses. Remember the instruction you gave your servant Moses [saying:]

The Lord
(voice only)   If you are unfaithful, I will scatter you among the nations, but if you return to me and obey my commands, then even if your exiled people are at the farthest horizon, I will gather them from there and bring them to the place I have chosen as a dwelling for my Name.

**Young
Nehemiah**
(praying)   They are your servants and your people, whom you redeemed by your great strength and your mighty hand. O Lord, let your ear be attentive to the prayer of this your servant and to the prayer of your servants who delight in revering your name. Give your servant success today by granting him favor in the presence of this man.

**Old
Nehemiah**   I was cupbearer to the king.

Cast: **Old Nehemiah, Man 1, Man 2, Young Nehemiah, the Lord** (voice only; or can be the same as Young Nehemiah)

Artaxerxes Sends Nehemiah to Jerusalem

Nehemiah 2:1–8

Old Nehemiah In the month of Nisan in the twentieth year of King Artaxerxes, when wine was brought for him, I took the wine and gave it to the king. I had not been sad in his presence before [so the king asked me:]

King Why does your face look so sad—when you are not ill? This can be nothing but sadness of heart.

Old Nehemiah I was very much afraid [but I said to the king:]

Young Nehemiah May the king live forever! Why should my face not look sad when the city where my fathers are buried lies in ruins, and its gates have been destroyed by fire?

King What is it you want?

Old Nehemiah Then I prayed to the God of heaven, and I answered the king:

Young Nehemiah If it pleases the king and if your servant has found favor in his sight, let him send me to the city in Judah where my fathers are buried so that I can rebuild it.

Old Nehemiah Then the king, with the queen sitting beside him, asked me:

King How long will your journey take, and when will you get back?

Old Nehemiah It pleased the king to send me; so I set a time. (PAUSE) [I also said to him:]

Young Nehemiah If it pleases the king, may I have letters to the governors of Trans-Euphrates, so that they will provide me safe-conduct until I arrive in Judah? And may I have a letter to Asaph, keeper of the king's forest, so he will give me timber to make beams for the gates of the citadel by the temple and for the city wall and for the residence I will occupy?

Old Nehemiah And because the gracious hand of my God was upon me, the king granted my requests.

Cast: **Old Nehemiah, King, Young Nehemiah**

Nehemiah Inspects Jerusalem's Walls

Nehemiah 2:9–20

Old Nehemiah I went to the governors of Trans-Euphrates and gave them the king's letters. The king had also sent army officers and cavalry with me.

When Sanballat the Horonite and Tobiah the Ammonite official heard about this, they were very much disturbed that someone had come to promote the welfare of the Israelites.

I went to Jerusalem, and after staying there three days I set out during the night with a few men. I had not told anyone what my God had put in my heart to do for Jerusalem. There were no mounts with me except the one I was riding on.

By night I went out through the Valley Gate toward the Jackal Well and the Dung Gate, examining the walls of Jerusalem, which had been broken down, and its gates, which had been destroyed by fire. Then I moved on toward the Fountain Gate and the King's Pool, but there was not enough room for my mount to get through; so I went up the valley by night, examining the wall. Finally, I turned back and reentered through the Valley Gate. The officials did not know where I had gone or what I was doing, because as yet I had said nothing to the Jews or the priests or nobles or officials or any others who would be doing the work. Then I said to them:

Young Nehemiah You see the trouble we are in: Jerusalem lies in ruins, and its gates have been burned with fire. Come, let us rebuild the wall of Jerusalem, and we will no longer be in disgrace.

Old Nehemiah I also told them about the gracious hand of my God upon me and what the king had said to me. They replied:

Persons 1 and 2 Let us start rebuilding.

Old Nehemiah So they began this good work. (PAUSE)

But when Sanballat the Horonite, Tobiah the Ammonite official and Geshem the Arab heard about it, they mocked and ridiculed us.

Sanballat What is this you are doing?

Tobiah Are you rebelling against the king?

Old Nehemiah I answered them:

Young Nehemiah The God of heaven will give us success. We his servants will start rebuilding, but as for you, you have no share in Jerusalem or any claim or historic right to it.

Cast: **Old Nehemiah, Young Nehemiah, Person 1, Person 2** (can be the same as Person 1), **Sanballat, Tobiah** (can be the same as Sanballat)

487

Opposition to the Rebuilding

Nehemiah 4:1–23

**Old
Nehemiah** When Sanballat heard that we were rebuilding the wall, he became angry and was greatly incensed. He ridiculed the Jews . . . in the presence of his associates and the army of Samaria:

Sanballat What are those feeble Jews doing? Will they restore their wall? Will they offer sacrifices? Will they finish in a day? Can they bring the stones back to life from those heaps of rubble—burned as they are?

**Old
Nehemiah** Tobiah the Ammonite . . . was at his side:

Tobiah What they are building—if even a fox climbed up on it, he would break down their wall of stones!

**Young
Nehemiah
(praying)** Hear us, O our God, for we are despised. Turn their insults back on their own heads. Give them over as plunder in a land of captivity. Do not cover up their guilt or blot out their sins from your sight, for they have thrown insults in the face of the builders.

**Old
Nehemiah** So we rebuilt the wall till all of it reached half its height, for the people worked with all their heart. (PAUSE)

But when Sanballat, Tobiah, the Arabs, the Ammonites and the men of Ashdod heard that the repairs to Jerusalem's walls had gone ahead and that the gaps were being closed, they were very angry. They all plotted together to come and fight against Jerusalem and stir up trouble against it. But we prayed to our God and posted a guard day and night to meet this threat.

Meanwhile, the people in Judah said:

Person 1 The strength of the laborers is giving out—

Person 2 And there is so much rubble that we cannot rebuild the wall.

**Old
Nehemiah** Also our enemies said:

Sanballat Before they know it or see us, we will be right there among them and will kill them—

Tobiah And put an end to the work.

**Old
Nehemiah** Then the Jews who lived near them came and told us ten times over:

Person 1 Wherever you turn, they will attack us.

[Person 2 Wherever you turn, they will attack us.]

Old
Nehemiah   Therefore I stationed some of the people behind the lowest points of the wall at the exposed places, posting them by families, with their swords, spears and bows. (PAUSE) After I looked things over, I stood up and said to the nobles, the officials and the rest of the people:

Young
Nehemiah   Don't be afraid of them. Remember the Lord, who is great and awesome, and fight for your brothers, your sons and your daughters, your wives and your homes.

Old
Nehemiah   When our enemies heard that we were aware of their plot and that God had frustrated it, we all returned to the wall, each to his own work. (PAUSE)

From that day on, half of my men did the work, while the other half were equipped with spears, shields, bows and armor. The officers posted themselves behind all the people of Judah who were building the wall. Those who carried materials did their work with one hand and held a weapon in the other, and each of the builders wore his sword at his side as he worked. But the man who sounded the trumpet stayed with me. Then I said to the nobles, the officials and the rest of the people:

Young
Nehemiah   The work is extensive and spread out, and we are widely separated from each other along the wall. Wherever you hear the sound of the trumpet, join us there. Our God will fight for us!

Old
Nehemiah   So we continued the work with half the men holding spears, from the first light of dawn till the stars came out. (PAUSE) At that time I also said to the people:

Young
Nehemiah   Have every man and his helper stay inside Jerusalem at night, so they can serve us as guards by night and workmen by day.

Old
Nehemiah   Neither I nor my brothers nor my men nor the guards with me took off our clothes; each had his weapon, even when he went for water.

Cast: **Old Nehemiah, Sanballat, Tobiah, Young Nehemiah, Person 1, Person 2** (can be the same as Person 1)

Nehemiah Helps the Poor

Nehemiah 5:1–13

Old
Nehemiah   The men and their wives raised a great outcry against their Jewish brothers.

Woman 1
(com-
plaining)   We and our sons and daughters are numerous; in order for us to eat and stay alive, we must get grain.

Man 1
(angry)   We are mortgaging our fields, our vineyards and our homes to get grain during the famine.

Man 2
(pleading)   We have had to borrow money to pay the king's tax on our fields and vineyards.

Woman 2
(resentful)   Although we are of the same flesh and blood as our countrymen and though our sons are as good as theirs, yet we have to subject our sons and daughters to slavery.

Man 1
(sad)   Some of our daughters have already been enslaved.

Woman 1
(despairing)   But we are powerless, because our fields and our vineyards belong to others.

**Old
Nehemiah**   When I heard their outcry and these charges, I was very angry. I pondered them in my mind and then accused the nobles and officials. I told them:

**Young
Nehemiah**
(angry)   You are exacting usury from your own countrymen!

**Old
Nehemiah**   So I called together a large meeting to deal with them and said:

**Young
Nehemiah**   As far as possible, we have bought back our Jewish brothers who were sold to the Gentiles. Now you are selling your brothers, only for them to be sold back to us!

**Old
Nehemiah**   They kept quiet, because they could find nothing to say. So I continued:

**Young
Nehemiah**   What you are doing is not right. Shouldn't you walk in the fear of our God to avoid the reproach of our Gentile enemies? I and my brothers and my men are also lending the people money and grain. But let the exacting of usury stop! Give back to them immediately their fields, vineyards, olive groves and houses, and also the usury you are charging them—the hundredth part of the money, grain, new wine and oil.

Noble 1   We will give it back.

Noble 2   And we will not demand anything more from them. We will do as you say.

**Old
Nehemiah**   Then I summoned the priests and made the nobles and officials take an oath to do what they had promised. I also shook out the folds of my robe and said:

**Young
Nehemiah**   In this way may God shake out of his house and possessions every man who does not keep this promise. So may such a man be shaken out and emptied!

**Old
Nehemiah**   At this the whole assembly said:

**Women 1
and 2,
Men 1
and 2,
Nobles 1
and 2**   Amen!

**Old
Nehemiah**   And [they] praised the LORD. And the people did as they had promised.

Cast: **Old Nehemiah, Woman 1, Man 1, Man 2** (can be the same as Man 1), **Woman 2** (can be the same as Woman 1), **Young Nehemiah, Noble 1, Noble 2** (can be the same as Noble 1)

Further Opposition to the Rebuilding

Nehemiah 6:1–16

**Old
Nehemiah**   When word came to Sanballat, Tobiah, Geshem the Arab and the rest of our enemies that I had rebuilt the wall and not a gap was left in it—though up to that time I had not set the doors in the gates—Sanballat and Geshem sent me this message:

Sanballat   Come, let us meet together in one of the villages on the plain of Ono.

**Old
Nehemiah**   But they were scheming to harm me; so I sent messengers to them [with this reply:]

**Young
Nehemiah**   I am carrying on a great project and cannot go down. Why should the work stop while I leave it and go down to you?

**Old
Nehemiah**   Four times they sent me the same message, and each time I gave them the same answer.

Then, the fifth time, Sanballat sent his aide to me with the same message, and in his hand was an unsealed letter in which was written:

Sanballat   It is reported among the nations—and Geshem says it is true—that you and the Jews are plotting to revolt, and therefore you are building the

	wall. Moreover, according to these reports you are about to become their king and have even appointed prophets to make this proclamation about you in Jerusalem: "There is a *king* in Judah!" Now this report will get back to the king; so come, let us confer together.
Old Nehemiah	I sent him this reply:
Young Nehemiah	Nothing like what you are saying is happening; you are just making it up out of your head.
Old Nehemiah	They were all trying to frighten us [thinking]:
Sanballat (thinking aloud)	Their hands will get too weak for the work, and it will not be completed.
Old Nehemiah	⌊But I prayed:⌋
Young Nehemiah (praying)	Now strengthen my hands.
Old Nehemiah	One day I went to the house of Shemaiah son of Delaiah, the son of Mehetabel, who was shut in at his home. He said:
Shemaiah	Let us meet in the house of God, inside the temple, and let us close the temple doors, because men are coming to kill you—by night they are coming to kill you.
Young Nehemiah	Should a man like me run away? Or should one like me go into the temple to save his life? I will not go!
Old Nehemiah	I realized that God had not sent him, but that he had prophesied against me because Tobiah and Sanballat had hired him. He had been hired to intimidate me so that I would commit a sin by doing this, and then they would give me a bad name to discredit me.
Young Nehemiah	Remember Tobiah and Sanballat, O my God, because of what they have done; remember also the prophetess Noadiah and the rest of the prophets who have been trying to intimidate me.
Old Nehemiah	So the wall was completed on the twenty-fifth of Elul, in fifty-two days. When all our enemies heard about this, all the surrounding nations were afraid and lost their self-confidence, because they realized that this work had been done with the help of our God.

Cast: **Old Nehemiah, Sanballat, Young Nehemiah, Shemaiah**

Ezra Reads the Law

Nehemiah 8:1–12 (Version A: with lists of names)

Narrator   All the people assembled as one man in the square before the Water Gate. They told Ezra the scribe to bring out the Book of the Law of Moses, which the LORD had commanded for Israel.

So on the first day of the seventh month Ezra the priest brought the Law before the assembly, which was made up of men and women and all who were able to understand. He read it aloud from daybreak till noon as he faced the square before the Water Gate in the presence of the men, women and others who could understand. And all the people listened attentively to the Book of the Law.

Ezra the scribe stood on a high wooden platform built for the occasion. Beside him on his right stood:

Secretary   Mattithiah, Shema, Anaiah, Uriah, Hilkiah and Maaseiah.

Narrator   And on his left were:

Secretary   Pedaiah, Mishael, Malkijah, Hashum, Hashbaddanah, Zechariah and Meshullam.

Narrator   Ezra opened the book. All the people could see him because he was standing above them; and as he opened it, the people all stood up. Ezra praised the LORD, the great God; and all the people lifted their hands and responded:

People   Amen! Amen!

Narrator   Then they bowed down and worshiped the LORD with their faces to the ground. The Levites—

Secretary   Jeshua, Bani, Sherebiah, Jamin, Akkub, Shabbethai, Hodiah, Maaseiah, Kelita, Azariah, Jozabad, Hanan and Pelaiah—

Narrator   Instructed the people in the Law while the people were standing there. They read from the Book of the Law of God, making it clear and giving the meaning so that the people could understand what was being read. (PAUSE)

Then Nehemiah the governor, Ezra the priest and scribe, and the Levites who were instructing the people said to them all:

Ezra   This day is sacred to the LORD your God. Do not mourn or weep.

Narrator   For all the people had been weeping as they listened to the words of the Law. [Nehemiah said:]

Nehemiah   Go and enjoy choice food and sweet drinks, and send some to those who have nothing prepared. This day is sacred to our Lord. Do not grieve, for the joy of the LORD is your strength.

493

Narrator	The Levites calmed all the people:
Levite	Be still, for this is a sacred day. Do not grieve.
Narrator	Then all the people went away to eat and drink, to send portions of food and to celebrate with great joy, because they now understood the words that had been made known to them.

Cast: **Narrator, Secretary, People** (two or more), **Ezra, Nehemiah, Levite.** (The inclusion of the names adds a humorous element, provided the casting is right.)

Ezra Reads the Law

Nehemiah 8:1–12 (Version B: omitting lists of names)

Narrator	All the people assembled as one man in the square before the Water Gate. They told Ezra the scribe to bring out the Book of the Law of Moses, which the LORD had commanded for Israel.
	So on the first day of the seventh month Ezra the priest brought the Law before the assembly, which was made up of men and women and all who were able to understand. He read it aloud from daybreak till noon as he faced the square before the Water Gate in the presence of the men, women and others who could understand. And all the people listened attentively to the Book of the Law.
	Ezra the scribe stood on a high wooden platform built for the occasion. Beside him on his right stood [six men, and seven stood on his left.]
	Ezra opened the book. All the people could see him because he was standing above them; and as he opened it, the people all stood up. Ezra praised the LORD, the great God; and all the people lifted their hands and responded:
People	Amen! Amen!
Narrator	Then they bowed down and worshiped the LORD with their faces to the ground. The Levites . . . instructed the people in the Law while the people were standing there. They read from the Book of the Law of God, making it clear and giving the meaning so that the people could understand what was being read. (PAUSE)
	Then Nehemiah the governor, Ezra the priest and scribe, and the Levites who were instructing the people said to them all:
Ezra	This day is sacred to the LORD your God. Do not mourn or weep.
Narrator	For all the people had been weeping as they listened to the words of the Law. [Nehemiah said:]
Nehemiah	Go and enjoy choice food and sweet drinks, and send some to those who have nothing prepared. This day is sacred to our Lord. Do not grieve, for the joy of the LORD is your strength.

494

Narrator	The Levites calmed all the people:
Levite	Be still, for this is a sacred day. Do not grieve.
Narrator	Then all the people went away to eat and drink, to send portions of food and to celebrate with great joy, because they now understood the words that had been made known to them.

Cast: **Narrator, People** (two or more), **Ezra, Nehemiah, Levite**

The Festival of Tabernacles

Nehemiah 8:13–18

Nehemiah	The heads of all the families, along with the priests and the Levites, gathered around Ezra the scribe to give attention to the words of the Law. They found written in the Law, which the Lord had commanded through Moses, that the Israelites were to live in booths during the feast of the seventh month and that they should proclaim this word and spread it throughout their towns and in Jerusalem:
Leader 1	"Go out into the hill country and bring back branches—
Leader 2	"From olive and wild olive trees, and from myrtles, palms and shade trees, to make booths"—as it is written.
Nehemiah	So the people went out and brought back branches and built themselves booths on their own roofs, in their courtyards, in the courts of the house of God and in the square by the Water Gate and the one by the Gate of Ephraim. The whole company that had returned from exile built booths and lived in them. From the days of Joshua son of Nun until that day, the Israelites had not celebrated it like this. And their joy was very great.
	Day after day, from the first day to the last, Ezra read from the Book of the Law of God. They celebrated the feast for seven days, and on the eighth day, in accordance with the regulation, there was an assembly.

Cast: **Nehemiah, Leader 1, Leader 2** (can be the same as Leader 1)

Nehemiah's Final Reforms (i)

Nehemiah 13:15–22

Old Nehemiah	In those days I saw men in Judah treading winepresses on the Sabbath and bringing in grain and loading it on donkeys, together with wine, grapes, figs and all other kinds of loads. And they were bringing all this into Jerusalem on the Sabbath. Therefore I warned them against selling food on that day. Men from Tyre who lived in Jerusalem were bringing

495

in fish and all kinds of merchandise and selling them in Jerusalem on the Sabbath to the people of Judah. I rebuked the nobles of Judah:

Young
Nehemiah   What is this wicked thing you are doing—desecrating the Sabbath day? Didn't your forefathers do the same things, so that our God brought all this calamity upon us and upon this city? Now you are stirring up more wrath against Israel by desecrating the Sabbath.

Old
Nehemiah   When evening shadows fell on the gates of Jerusalem before the Sabbath, I ordered the doors to be shut and not opened until the Sabbath was over. I stationed some of my own men at the gates so that no load could be brought in on the Sabbath day. Once or twice the merchants and sellers of all kinds of goods spent the night outside Jerusalem. But I warned them:

Young
Nehemiah   Why do you spend the night by the wall? If you do this again, I will lay hands on you.

Old
Nehemiah   From that time on they no longer came on the Sabbath. Then I commanded the Levites to purify themselves and go and guard the gates in order to keep the Sabbath day holy.

(praying)   Remember me for this also, O my God, and show mercy to me according to your great love.

Cast: **Old Nehemiah, Young Nehemiah**

Nehemiah's Final Reforms (ii)

Nehemiah 13:23–31

Old
Nehemiah   [In those days] I saw men of Judah who had married women from Ashdod, Ammon and Moab. Half of their children spoke the language of Ashdod or the language of one of the other peoples, and did not know how to speak the language of Judah. I rebuked them and called curses down on them. I beat some of the men and pulled out their hair. I made them take an oath in God's name:

Young
Nehemiah   You are not to give your daughters in marriage to their sons, nor are you to take their daughters in marriage for your sons or for yourselves. Was it not because of marriages like these that Solomon king of Israel sinned? Among the many nations there was no king like him. He was loved by his God, and God made him king over all Israel, but even he was led into sin by foreign women. Must we hear now that you too are doing all this

terrible wickedness and are being unfaithful to our God by marrying foreign women?

Old
Nehemiah   One of the sons of Joiada son of Eliashib the high priest was son-in-law to Sanballat the Horonite. And I drove him away from me.

(praying)   Remember them, O my God, because they defiled the priestly office and the covenant of the priesthood and of the Levites.

(to audience) So I purified the priests and the Levites of everything foreign, and assigned them duties, each to his own task. I also made provision for contributions of wood at designated times, and for the firstfruits.

(praying)   Remember me with favor, O my God.

Cast: **Old Nehemiah, Young Nehemiah**

Esther

Queen Vashti Deposed

From Esther 1:1–22

Narrator 1	This is what happened during the time of Xerxes, the Xerxes who ruled over 127 provinces stretching from India to Cush.
Narrator 2	At that time King Xerxes reigned from his royal throne in the citadel of Susa, and in the third year of his reign he gave a banquet for all his nobles and officials. The military leaders of Persia and Media, the princes, and the nobles of the provinces were present.
Narrator 1	For a full 180 days he displayed the vast wealth of his kingdom and the splendor and glory of his majesty. When these days were over, the king gave a banquet, lasting seven days, in the enclosed garden of the king's palace, for all the people from the least to the greatest, who were in the citadel of Susa. The garden had hangings of white and blue linen, fastened with cords of white linen and purple material to silver rings on marble pillars. There were couches of gold and silver on a mosaic pavement of porphyry, marble, mother-of-pearl and other costly stones. Wine was served in goblets of gold, each one different from the other, and the royal wine was abundant, in keeping with the king's liberality. By the king's command each guest was allowed to drink in his own way, for the king instructed all the wine stewards to serve each man what he wished.
Narrator 2	Queen Vashti also gave a banquet for the women in the royal palace of King Xerxes.
Narrator 1	On the seventh day, when King Xerxes was in high spirits from wine, he commanded the seven eunuchs who served him—Mehuman, Biztha, Harbona, Bigtha, Abagtha, Zethar and Carcas—to bring before him Queen Vashti, wearing her royal crown, in order to display her beauty to the people and nobles, for she was lovely to look at. But when the attendants delivered the king's command, Queen Vashti refused to come.
Narrators 1 and 2	Then the king became furious and burned with anger.
Narrator 2	Since it was customary for the king to consult experts in matters of law and justice, he spoke with the wise men who understood the times and were closest to the king. . . .
King	According to law, what must be done to Queen Vashti? She has not obeyed the command of King Xerxes that the eunuchs have taken to her.
Narrator 1	Then Memucan replied in the presence of the king and the nobles:
Memucan	Queen Vashti has done wrong, not only against the king but also against all the nobles and the peoples of all the provinces of King Xerxes. For the

queen's conduct will become known to all the women, and so they will despise their husbands and say:

Woman 1 King Xerxes commanded Queen Vashti to be brought before him—

Women 1 and 2 But she would not come.

Memucan This very day the Persian and Median women of the nobility who have heard about the queen's conduct will respond to all the king's nobles in the same way. There will be no end of disrespect and discord.

Therefore, if it pleases the king, let him issue a royal decree and let it be written in the laws of Persia and Media, which cannot be repealed, that Vashti is never again to enter the presence of King Xerxes. Also let the king give her royal position to someone else who is better than she. Then when the king's edict is proclaimed throughout all his vast realm, all the women will respect their husbands, from the least to the greatest.

Narrator 1 The king and his nobles were pleased with this advice, so the king did as Memucan proposed.

Narrator 2 He sent dispatches to all parts of the kingdom, to each province in its own script and to each people in its own language, proclaiming in each people's tongue that every man should be ruler over his own household.

Cast: **Narrator 1, Narrator 2, King, Memucan, Woman 1, Woman 2** (can be the same as Woman 1)

Esther Wins Favor

Esther 2:1–9

Narrator Later when the anger of King Xerxes had subsided, he remembered Vashti and what she had done and what he had decreed about her. Then the king's personal attendants proposed:

Attendant 1 Let a search be made for beautiful young virgins for the king.

Attendant 2 Let the king appoint commissioners in every province of his realm to bring all these beautiful girls into the harem at the citadel of Susa.

Attendant 1 Let them be placed under the care of Hegai, the king's eunuch, who is in charge of the women; and let beauty treatments be given to them. Then let the girl who pleases the king be queen instead of Vashti.

Narrator This advice appealed to the king, and he followed it.

Now there was in the citadel of Susa a Jew of the tribe of Benjamin, named Mordecai son of Jair, the son of Shimei, the son of Kish, who had been carried into exile from Jerusalem by Nebuchadnezzar king of Babylon, among those taken captive with Jehoiachin king of Judah. Mordecai had a cousin named Hadassah, whom he had brought up because she had neither father nor mother. This girl, who was also known as Esther, was lovely in form and features, and Mordecai had taken her as his own daughter when her father and mother died.

When the king's order and edict had been proclaimed, many girls were brought to the citadel of Susa and put under the care of Hegai. Esther also was taken to the king's palace and entrusted to Hegai, who had charge of the harem. The girl pleased him and won his favor.

Cast: **Narrator, Attendant 1, Attendant 2** (can be the same as Attendant 1)

Esther Becomes Queen, and Mordecai Uncovers a Conspiracy

Esther 2:15–23

Narrator 1   When the turn came for Esther to go to the king—

Narrator 2   (The girl Mordecai had adopted, the daughter of his uncle Abihail)—

Narrator 3   She asked for nothing other than what Hegai, the king's eunuch who was in charge of the harem, suggested.

Narrator 1   And Esther won the favor of everyone who saw her.

Narrator 2   She was taken to King Xerxes in the royal residence in the tenth month, the month of Tebeth, in the seventh year of his reign.

Narrator 3   Now the king was attracted to Esther more than to any of the other women, and she won his favor and approval more than any of the other virgins.

Narrator 1   So he set a royal crown on her head and made her queen instead of Vashti.

Narrator 2   And the king gave a great banquet, Esther's banquet, for all his nobles and officials. He proclaimed a holiday throughout the provinces and distributed gifts with royal liberality. (PAUSE)

Narrator 3   When the virgins were assembled a second time, Mordecai was sitting at the king's gate.

Narrator 1   But Esther had kept secret her family background and nationality just as Mordecai had told her to do—

Narrator 2   For she continued to follow Mordecai's instructions as she had done when he was bringing her up.

Narrator 3   During the time Mordecai was sitting at the king's gate, Bigthana and Teresh, two of the king's officers who guarded the doorway, became angry and conspired to assassinate King Xerxes.

Narrator 1   But Mordecai found out about the plot and told Queen Esther, who in turn reported it to the king, giving credit to Mordecai.

Narrator 2   And when the report was investigated and found to be true, the two officials were hanged on a gallows. (PAUSE)

Narrator 3   All this was recorded in the book of the annals in the presence of the king.

Cast: **Narrator 1, Narrator 2, Narrator 3**

Haman's Plot to Destroy the Jews

From Esther 3:1–15

Narrator 1   King Xerxes honored Haman son of Hammedatha, the Agagite, elevating him and giving him a seat of honor higher than that of all the other nobles. All the royal officials at the king's gate knelt down and paid honor to Haman, for the king had commanded this concerning him.

Narrator 2   But Mordecai would not kneel down or pay him honor. Then the royal officials at the king's gate asked Mordecai:

Official   Why do you disobey the king's command?

Narrator 2   Day after day they spoke to him but he refused to comply. Therefore they told Haman about it to see whether Mordecai's behavior would be tolerated, for he had told them:

Mordecai   [I am] a Jew.

Narrator 2   When Haman saw that Mordecai would not kneel down or pay him honor, he was enraged.

Narrator 1   Yet having learned who Mordecai's people were, he scorned the idea of killing only Mordecai. Instead Haman looked for a way to destroy all Mordecai's people, the Jews, throughout the whole kingdom of Xerxes. . . .

Haman
(to King)   There is a certain people dispersed and scattered among the peoples in all the provinces of your kingdom whose customs are different from those of all other people and who do not obey the king's laws; it is not in the king's best interest to tolerate them. If it pleases the king, let a decree be issued to destroy them, and I will put ten thousand talents of silver into the royal treasury for the men who carry out this business.

Narrator 1   So the king took his signet ring from his finger and gave it to Haman son of Hammedatha, the Agagite, the enemy of the Jews.

King   Keep the money, and do with the people as you please.

Narrator 1   Then on the thirteenth day of the first month the royal secretaries were summoned. They wrote out in the script of each province and in the language of each people all Haman's orders to the king's satraps, the governors of the various provinces and the nobles of the various peoples.

Narrator 2	These were written in the name of King Xerxes himself and sealed with his own ring.
Narrator 1	Dispatches were sent by couriers to all the king's provinces with the order to destroy, kill and annihilate all the Jews—young and old, women and little children—on a single day, the thirteenth day of the twelfth month, the month of Adar, and to plunder their goods.
Narrator 2	A copy of the text of the edict was to be issued as law in every province and made known to the people of every nationality so they would be ready for that day.
Narrator 1	Spurred on by the king's command, the couriers went out, and the edict was issued in the citadel of Susa.
Narrator 2	The king and Haman sat down to drink, but the city of Susa was bewildered.

Cast: **Narrator 1**, **Narrator 2** (can be the same as Narrator 1), **Official**, **Mordecai**, **Haman**, **King**

Mordecai Persuades Esther to Help

Esther 4:1–17

Narrator 1	When Mordecai learned of all that had been done, he tore his clothes, put on sackcloth and ashes, and went out into the city, wailing loudly and bitterly. But he went only as far as the king's gate, because no one clothed in sackcloth was allowed to enter it. In every province to which the edict and order of the king came, there was great mourning among the Jews, with fasting, weeping and wailing. Many lay in sackcloth and ashes.
Narrator 2	When Esther's maids and eunuchs came and told her about Mordecai, she was in great distress. She sent clothes for him to put on instead of his sackcloth, but he would not accept them. Then Esther summoned Hathach, one of the king's eunuchs assigned to attend her, and ordered him to find out what was troubling Mordecai and why.
Narrator 1	So Hathach went out to Mordecai in the open square of the city in front of the king's gate. Mordecai told him everything that had happened to him, including the exact amount of money Haman had promised to pay into the royal treasury for the destruction of the Jews. He also gave him a copy of the text of the edict for their annihilation, which had been published in Susa, to show to Esther and explain it to her, and he told him to urge her to go into the king's presence to beg for mercy and plead with him for her people.
Narrator 2	Hathach went back and reported to Esther what Mordecai had said. Then she instructed him to say to Mordecai:
Esther	All the king's officials and the people of the royal provinces know that for any man or woman who approaches the king in the inner court with-

502

out being summoned the king has but one law: that he be put to death. The only exception to this is for the king to extend the gold scepter to him and spare his life. But thirty days have passed since I was called to go to the king.

Narrator 1   When Esther's words were reported to Mordecai, he sent back this answer:

Mordecai   Do not think that because you are in the king's house you alone of all the Jews will escape. For if you remain silent at this time, relief and deliverance for the Jews will arise from another place, but you and your father's family will perish. And who knows but that you have come to royal position for such a time as this?

Narrator 2   Then Esther sent this reply to Mordecai:

Esther   Go, gather together all the Jews who are in Susa, and fast for me. Do not eat or drink for three days, night or day. I and my maids will fast as you do. When this is done, I will go to the king, even though it is against the law. And if I perish, I perish.

Narrator 1   So Mordecai went away and carried out all of Esther's instructions.

Cast: **Narrator 1, Narrator 2, Esther, Mordecai**

Esther's Request to the King

Esther 5:1–8

Narrator   Esther put on her royal robes and stood in the inner court of the palace, in front of the king's hall. The king was sitting on his royal throne in the hall, facing the entrance. When he saw Queen Esther standing in the court, he was pleased with her and held out to her the gold scepter that was in his hand. So Esther approached and touched the tip of the scepter.

[Then the king asked:]

King   What is it, Queen Esther? What is your request? Even up to half the kingdom, it will be given you.

Esther   If it pleases the king, let the king, together with Haman, come today to a banquet I have prepared for him.

King   Bring Haman at once, so that we may do what Esther asks.

Narrator   So the king and Haman went to the banquet Esther had prepared. As they were drinking wine, the king again asked Esther:

King   Now what is your petition? It will be given you. And what is your request? Even up to half the kingdom, it will be granted.

Esther   My petition and my request is this: If the king regards me with favor and if it pleases the king to grant my petition and fulfill my request, let the king and Haman come tomorrow to the banquet I will prepare for them. Then I will answer the king's question.

Haman's Rage against Mordecai

Esther 5:9–14

Narrator Haman went out that day happy and in high spirits. But when he saw Mordecai at the king's gate and observed that he neither rose nor showed fear in his presence, he was filled with rage against Mordecai. Nevertheless, Haman restrained himself and went home.

Calling together his friends and Zeresh, his wife, Haman boasted to them about his vast wealth, his many sons, and all the ways the king had honored him and how he had elevated him above the other nobles and officials.

Haman And that's not all. I'm the only person Queen Esther invited to accompany the king to the banquet she gave. And she has invited me along with the king tomorrow. But all this gives me no satisfaction as long as I see that Jew Mordecai sitting at the king's gate.

Narrator His wife Zeresh and all his friends said to him:

Wife Have a gallows built, seventy-five feet high, and ask the king in the morning to have Mordecai hanged on it. Then go with the king to the dinner and be happy.

Narrator This suggestion delighted Haman, and he had the gallows built.

Mordecai Honored

Esther 6:1–13

Narrator The king could not sleep; so he ordered the book of the chronicles, the record of his reign, to be brought in and read to him. It was found recorded there that Mordecai had exposed Bigthana and Teresh, two of the king's officers who guarded the doorway, who had conspired to assassinate King Xerxes. [[The king asked:]]

King What honor and recognition has Mordecai received for this?

[Narrator [His attendants answered:]]

Servant Nothing has been done for him.

504

King	Who is in the court?
Narrator	Now Haman had just entered the outer court of the palace to speak to the king about hanging Mordecai on the gallows he had erected for him. [His attendants answered:]
Servant	Haman is standing in the court.
King	Bring him in.
Narrator	[When] Haman entered [the king asked him:]
King	What should be done for the man the king delights to honor?
[Narrator	Now Haman thought to himself:]
Haman (to himself)	Who is there that the king would rather honor than me?
[Narrator	So he answered the king:]
Haman (to King)	For the man the king delights to honor, have them bring a royal robe the king has worn and a horse the king has ridden, one with a royal crest placed on its head. Then let the robe and horse be entrusted to one of the king's most noble princes. Let them robe the man the king delights to honor, and lead him on the horse through the city streets, proclaiming before him:
Prince	This is what is done for the man the king delights to honor!
King (urgently)	Go at once. Get the robe and the horse and do just as you have suggested for Mordecai the Jew, who sits at the king's gate. Do not neglect anything you have recommended.
Narrator	So Haman got the robe and the horse. He robed Mordecai, and led him on horseback through the city streets, proclaiming before him:
Haman (miserably)	This is what is done for the man the king delights to honor!
Narrator	Afterward Mordecai returned to the king's gate. But Haman rushed home, with his head covered in grief, and told Zeresh his wife and all his friends everything that had happened to him. [His advisers and his wife Zeresh said to him:]
Adviser	Since Mordecai, before whom your downfall has started, is of Jewish origin, you cannot stand against him—
Wife	You will surely come to ruin!

Cast: **Narrator, King, Servant, Haman, Prince, Adviser, Wife**

Haman Hanged

Esther 6:14–7:10

Narrator   While they were still talking with him, the king's eunuchs arrived and hurried Haman away to the banquet Esther had prepared.

So the king and Haman went to dine with Queen Esther, and as they were drinking wine on that second day, the king again asked:

King   Queen Esther, what is your petition? It will be given you. What is your request? Even up to half the kingdom, it will be granted.

[Narrator   Then Queen Esther answered:]

Esther   If I have found favor with you, O king, and if it pleases your majesty, grant me my life—this is my petition. And spare my people—this is my request. For I and my people have been sold for destruction and slaughter and annihilation. If we had merely been sold as male and female slaves, I would have kept quiet, because no such distress would justify disturbing the king.

[Narrator   King Xerxes asked Queen Esther:]

King   Who is he? Where is the man who has dared to do such a thing?

Esther
(slowly)   The adversary and enemy is this vile Haman.

Narrator   Then Haman was terrified before the king and queen. The king got up in a rage, left his wine and went out into the palace garden. But Haman, realizing that the king had already decided his fate, stayed behind to beg Queen Esther for his life.

Just as the king returned from the palace garden to the banquet hall, Haman was falling on the couch where Esther was reclining. [The king exclaimed:]

King
(exclaiming)   Will he even molest the queen while she is with me in the house?

Narrator   As soon as the word left the king's mouth, they covered Haman's face. Then Harbona, one of the eunuchs attending the king, said:

Harbona   A gallows seventy-five feet high stands by Haman's house. He had it made for Mordecai, who spoke up to help the king.

King   Hang him on it!

Narrator   So they hanged Haman on the gallows he had prepared for Mordecai. Then the king's fury subsided.

Cast: **Narrator, King, Esther, Harbona**

The King's Edict in Behalf of the Jews

From Esther 8:[1–2], 3–17

[Narrator 1   King Xerxes gave Queen Esther the estate of Haman, the enemy of the Jews. And Mordecai came into the presence of the king, for Esther had told how he was related to her.

Narrator 2   The king took off his signet ring, which he had reclaimed from Haman, and presented it to Mordecai. And Esther appointed him over Haman's estate.]

Narrator 1   Esther again pleaded with the king, falling at his feet and weeping. She begged him to put an end to the evil plan of Haman the Agagite, which he had devised against the Jews. Then the king extended the gold scepter to Esther and she arose and stood before him.

Esther   If it pleases the king, and if he regards me with favor and thinks it the right thing to do, and if he is pleased with me, let an order be written overruling the dispatches that Haman son of Hammedatha, the Agagite, devised and wrote to destroy the Jews in all the king's provinces. For how can I bear to see disaster fall on my people? How can I bear to see the destruction of my family?

Narrator 1   King Xerxes replied to Queen Esther and to Mordecai the Jew:

King   Because Haman attacked the Jews, I have given his estate to Esther, and they have hanged him on the gallows. Now write another decree in the king's name in behalf of the Jews as seems best to you, and seal it with the king's signet ring—for no document written in the king's name and sealed with his ring can be revoked.

Narrator 1   At once the royal secretaries were summoned—on the twenty-third day of the third month, the month of Sivan.

Narrator 2   They wrote out all Mordecai's orders to the Jews, and to the satraps, governors and nobles of the 127 provinces stretching from India to Cush. These orders were written in the script of each province and the language of each people and also to the Jews in their own script and language.

Narrator 1   Mordecai wrote in the name of King Xerxes, sealed the dispatches with the king's signet ring, and sent them by mounted couriers, who rode fast horses especially bred for the king.

Narrator 2   The king's edict granted the Jews in every city the right to assemble and protect themselves; to destroy, kill and annihilate any armed force of any nationality or province that might attack them and their women and children; and to plunder the property of their enemies. . . .

The couriers, riding the royal horses, raced out, spurred on by the king's command.

Narrator 1   And the edict was also issued in the citadel of Susa.

507

Narrator 2   Mordecai left the king's presence wearing royal garments of blue and white, a large crown of gold and a purple robe of fine linen. And the city of Susa held a joyous celebration. For the Jews it was a time of happiness and joy, gladness and honor.

Narrator 1   In every province and in every city, wherever the edict of the king went, there was joy and gladness among the Jews, with feasting and celebrating.

Cast: **Narrator 1, Narrator 2** (can be the same as Narrator 1), **Esther, King**

Subject Index

Scripture Index

515